The Brave New World

 W9-BRQ-524

The Brave New World

A HISTORY OF EARLY AMERICA

Second Edition

PETER CHARLES HOFFER

THE JOHNS HOPKINS UNIVERSITY PRESS   Baltimore

© 2000, 2006 Charles Peter Hoffer

All rights reserved. Published 2006

Printed in the United States of America on acid-free paper

First edition published in 2000 by Houghton Mifflin Company

9 8 7 6 5 4 3 2 1

The Johns Hopkins University Press

2715 North Charles Street

Baltimore, Maryland 21218-4363

www.press.jhu.edu

Library of Congress Cataloging-in-Publication Data

Hoffer, Peter Charles, 1944–

   The brave new world : a history of early America / Peter Charles

Hoffer—2nd ed.

     p. cm.

   Includes bibliographical references and index.

   ISBN 0-8018-8483-7 (pbk. : alk. paper)

   1. United States—History—Colonial period, ca. 1600–1775.

2. Indians of North America—History. 3. America—Discovery and

exploration. I. Title.

   E188.H74 2006

   973.2—dc22   2006005648

A catalog record for this book is available from

the British Library.

Contents

Preface

In 1994, a blue ribbon panel of historians, teachers, and community leaders presented to K–12 school boards across the nation the *National History Standards*. The standards were inclusive of all peoples who made America, their achievements and their conflicts. In short, it pulled no punches. One would have thought the seven-year effort would be widely welcomed. Not so. In the so-called culture wars of the day, the teaching of history had become a political issue. Every proposal was scanned for its supposed biases. Was it too critical of Americans? Was it too celebratory?

Early Americanist Gary Nash, the lead author of the *National History Standards*, had made his own position on them clear at the outset: "The view that history is with the people is not only more fitting for a democratic society, in which it is assumed that an active citizenry is essential to the maintenance of liberty, it is more accurate." Nash gave this social history / many voices approach a pedigree: "The peculiar disjunction of fabricating an elitist history for a democratic society has been challenged for at least a century by a long but thin line of historians connecting the contemporary scene with past generations."

Nash had correctly depicted the weight of opinion among the experts, but he had badly misguessed how more conservative observers would regard the whole project and the proposed standards. Lynne Cheney, who as director of the National Endowment for the Humanities had sponsored the collaboration of scholars and school-teachers at the project's outset, condemned the final product. She found that the *National History Standards* "reflected the gloomy, politically driven revisionism" that had become "all too familiar on college campuses." From its pages the heroes were all gone, according to Cheney, replaced by minor figures. Enduring values were gone too; only oppression remained. Speaker of the House Newt Gingrich agreed. Gingrich took aim at the professional historians: "The fiasco over the American and Western history standards is a reflection of what has happened to the world of academic history. The profession and the American Historical Association are now dominated by younger historians with a familiar agenda: Take the West down a peg, romanticize 'the Other' (non-whites), treat all cultures as equal, refrain from criticizing non-white cultures." The U.S. Senate resolved its disapproval of the *Standards* ninety-nine to one.

Plainly, historians and teachers needed to take a long and sober look at the state of what we wanted students to learn. The very term *colonial history* was contested, for it seemed to suggest that the proper approach to our early history was from the east to west, traveling with Columbus and his crew of European mariners. Colonial history would then be the spread of European values, peoples, and technologies across what the Puritans had called "a howling wilderness." What if, instead of following this relentless progress of civilization (as nineteenth-century American historians described our history) we shifted our perspective? What if, like Daniel Richter, we first tried an "east-facing" perspective: seeing our early history from "Indian country"? Then we might look south, to the world that the Indians and the Spanish newcomers made in the Caribbean and along the rim of the Gulf of Mexico. Then turn our eyes north, as the tendrils of French- and English-speaking societies planted themselves among the native peoples.

So one could move across the continent, seeing the terrain and the people with the eyes of those who lived our early history. It is a vast project, for the land was vast: two continents, girdled by two oceans. No one who lived on the continents—not even the Carib Indians who fished the inland sea that would, when they were gone, gain their name—knew the full expanse of the waters or the land. Groping their way along the coastlines in their caravels, Europeans only gradually grasped the size of the domain they claimed for their respective monarchs. In a world where mapping is now done by Landsat from satellites, we may not credit the achievement of the Dutch and Portuguese mapmakers. They turned bits and pieces of often unverified observations into charts of a Brave New World.

Could such a diverse history have any unifying theme? It appeared to me that research findings in the field supported two quite distinct, in fact contradictory, points of view. One could say that over the long span of human occupation of the North American continent, there had been a spasmodic and uneven but undeniable improvement in the material standard of living and the degree of personal liberty. An old world of tradition, privilege, and rank gave way to a new society based on individual talent and desire. "Overall," Richard D. Brown, the leading exponent of the modernization thesis, judged, "American realities in economics, politics, religion, and social relationships delivered shattering blows to basic traditional structures." Jon Butler's *Becoming America* found in our founding period "rapid economic transformation . . . energetic provincial and local politics . . . evolving secular and material culture . . . rapidly expanding pluralistic religions . . . vigorous subsocieties within the larger culture; and a widespread drive for authority to shape individual and collective destinies." As Jack P. Greene concluded in *Pursuits of Happiness*, "In this situation, the achievement of peaceful enjoyment of personal independence, the objective that had initially drawn so many of both the first settlers and later immigrants to the colonies, continued to be the most visible and powerful imperative in the emerging American culture, the principal aspiration and animating drive in the lives of colonists of all regions."

At the same time, one could find overwhelming evidence that some people did not advance in this way, indeed, that their labor and sacrifice paid the price for others' success, and that entire peoples and cultures were subordinated or forced to assimilate to other peoples. Under relentless pressure from the expansion of European populations, and weakened by epidemics of European diseases, Native Americans lost control of their ancestral territory. As Richard White movingly writes, by the end of the colonial era, the world of the eastern woodlands Indians had become a "dreamscape" of remembered forests and animals. Africans forcibly removed to the Americas as slaves struggled to maintain their dignity and regional identity against a brutal regime that homogenized all Africans as "black" and presumed that bondage fitted all blacks.

Perhaps this stark contrast in expectations and experiences is the unifying theme of early American history. For all their losses, Native Americans creatively built new confederations from the fragments of old tribes, adopted European tools and technologies, and learned how to combine European languages and customs with native traditions. Individual slaves bargained successfully for personal space, and African Americans found ways to incorporate and acculturalize newly arrived Africans, surmount old African tribal animosities, fashion effective hybrids of family and community, and even attain freedom.

In the end, then, the story is not of simple progress or relentless oppression, but one of irony, contradiction, and contingency that continuously reconfigured the spacing among individuals, groups, and polities. There were winners and losers, but people had agency to affect their everyday lives. And while broad categories like race, gender, and class seemed to mark the outlines of success and failure, these categories were not then, any more than they are now, universalistic or fixed. Instead, they are products of human choices, social and cultural constructions that people in the past deployed to make sense of their world.

I concluded that one must set the two themes in simultaneous motion, following the complex and sometimes ironic way in which they interact. That interaction brings together all the stories in early American history.

I have learned that no work of the scope of *The Brave New World* can be completed without the labor of many people. James Miller encouraged me to go forward with the project. My thanks for the first edition go to Jean Woy, who kept faith with the project through its early stages, and to Leah Straus, editor of that edition. Sally Constable, Jean's successor, commissioned further reviews and allowed me to reuse them. John Crowley, Brian Levack, Sharon Salinger, and Michael Winship allowed me to see and use unpublished materials for the first edition, for which I am endlessly grateful. Their work is now published and cited in the bibliography. Robert J. Brugger and the Johns Hopkins University Press made possible a second edition.

I would like to thank the reviewers who offered suggestions and made corrections on successive drafts and portions of the first edition manuscript: Jonathan M. Chu, Charles L. Cohen, Christine Daniels, Gregory Dowd, Richard Godbeer, Cynthia A. Kierner, Gloria Main, Gregory Nobles, Herbert Sloan, Thomas Whigham, and Karin

Wulf. Thomas Altherr, Williamjames Hoffer, Frank Lambert, Russell M. Lawson, Daniel Mandell, Paul Otto, Bill Pencak, Thomas M. Ray, Sheila L. Skemp, Michael Winship, and Marianne S. Woceck improved the Johns Hopkins University Press edition. These individuals bear no responsibility for any remaining errors of fact or interpretation.

Worlds in Motion

I

Though inspired by reports of the shipwreck of an English vessel, the *Sea Adventurer*, on the island of Bermuda in 1609, Shakespeare's comedy *The Tempest* is set on an imaginary island in the Mediterranean. There Miranda, the ingénue, utters her famous lines, but audiences and author knew that it was the "brave new world" across the Atlantic that mattered in England's mortal struggle against its European rivals. When the play opened at the Globe Theatre in 1611, all London eagerly awaited news of the beleaguered outpost on a little peninsula in the James River. Founded in 1607, the Virginia colony was barely clinging to existence four years later.

Shakespeare invented characters for his imaginary island and concocted involuted plots and counterplots, mirroring the wonder and danger of Europe's thrust into the worlds beyond itself. Indeed, this first English settlement in the New World was a microcosm of all that had gone before and was to come in early American history: a mixed multitude of peoples experiencing poverty and riches, violence and compassion, enslavement and liberty, whole worlds in motion, now coming together.

Imagine ourselves spectators at that moment, able to see all the worlds in motion that came together in Shakespeare's imagination. Whirling above the Atlantic on the eve of Columbus's epic voyage, on a Landsat photographic mission, North America fills our widest lens, and the diversity of the landscape awes us. From a great distance, in daylight, using a wide-angle view, we might conclude that the lands were uninhabited. Only by night would the sparkling cooking fires of the hundreds of towns and thousands of villages of the American natives alert us that two to three million people live below in the grandeur of the mountains, forests, and prairies. The next day, refocusing our camera to capture details of the landscape would reveal rock-walled apartment complexes in the Southwest and wooden-palisaded trading centers along the Mississippi and its tributaries. These signs of cultivation and commerce would pale beside our dis-

O Wonder!
How many goodly
* creatures are there*
* here!*
How beautious mankind
* is! O brave new*
* world, That has such*
* people in't.*
—Miranda in The
Tempest, *Act 5, Scene 1*

covery of the cities of Nahuatl-speaking peoples of the Mexican plateau. The pyramidal temples of the Aztec at Tenochtitlán would seem to touch the clouds.

Our aerial view of Europe would disclose a different scene. Even in the lowest resolution of the lens, we would discern old cultivated fields and weatherworn castle towns. Because, unlike Indians, Europeans use wheels, roads would crisscross the land. As well, Europeans sail in large ships, and thus populous port cities would dot the coast of the Mediterranean, Atlantic, and North Sea. We would become aware of the extent to which Europeans had constructed machines to harness the wind and grind wheat. From the sky we would see the shadows of windmills and gristmills. The Europeans' hand was as heavy on the land as the Indians' was light.

Our overhead shots of West Africa would uncover a landscape as diverse as North America's and as densely populated as Europe's. The coast gives way to the Sahara desert, a highway for the Berbers and other seminomadic, Arabic-speaking peoples, and then three horizontal zones of vegetation: the Sahel, or shore, between the desert and the belt of savanna or grasslands, and finally the forests. The people speak dozens of languages and hundreds of dialects. Most are fishermen, farmers, or herdsmen and live in small villages, but cities of stone and mud-brick, homes to powerful kings and wealthy merchants, control the trade in salt, textiles, copper, gold, ironwork, kola nuts, and grains. Skilled craftsmen contribute elegant clay statuary and intricately carved woodwork to the stream of commerce.

Our eye-in-the-sky would expose the outward signs of the faiths of these peoples. The North Americans are pantheists, finding powerful spirits in the earth and the skies. It did not matter that different tribes call the chief god in their pantheon by different names, or give that god different features and attributes. All the Indians worship the landscape, regarding its natural features as a map of the homes of spirits and demigods. Places have power because they shelter primal forces or were the settings of events in the story of creation.

For the Indians of the Southwest, the Grand Canyon is the opening through which the corn daughters had climbed from their homes underground to the surface of the earth. The Navajo hold that Tsah Dzil (Mount Taylor) in New Mexico is one of the four pillars of the sky. In Ohio, Georgia, Missouri, and Nebraska, Indians contour the land in the shape of horned snakes to control the power of the underworld. In April, the end of the dry season, the Aztec kings of central Mexico make a pilgrimage to the temple at the top of Mount Tlaloc to call forth rain. On cliff sides and rock outcroppings throughout the continent, Indians carve petroglyphs and terraglyphs of animals, people, and religious symbols to remind themselves that the sacred is everywhere.

By contrast, Christian Europe believes in one God (monotheism), and the gothic spires of its cathedrals pierce the skies. Rituals of prayer divide the day into parts, and in the marketplace and on the roads, pilgrims and passersby mark time according to the church bells. Courts, schools, and governments set their calendars according to the cycle of festivals and fast days. Churchmen hold court, to punish those who sinned against God's ordinances. The church sanctifies the burial of kings and commoners, and its priests can be found at every important domestic event from baptism to burial.

Christianity in western Europe speaks in the voice of the Roman Catholic Church, a faith that has evolved much in the nearly fifteen hundred years since its founding. In theory, the church is a hierarchy at whose top sits Saint Peter's legate in Rome, the pope, though by the 1400s, the choice of popes, cardinals, and bishops is riven with political intrigue, and princes lobby for local autonomy in matters of religion. The officials of the church face charges of political manipulation and corruption, and the clergy, pledged to poverty and celibacy, finds itself under fire from time to time for neglecting those vows and failing to minister to their flocks. Reform movements have periodically spawned new monastic orders like the mendicant Franciscans and Dominicans. For all that, the average European is still intensely and devoutly Christian, accepting the divinity of Jesus Christ, the mysteries of the Trinity, the holiness of the Bible, and the saving power of the seven sacraments.

Still, alongside the sacraments and discipline of the "Holy Mother Church" lives another religious tradition, older and still attractive to many. In rural areas, far from centers of learning, ordinary people worship pre-Christian deities and cling to folk beliefs in magic, demons, witches, and healing spirits. Through persuasion, reeducation, and the threat of excommunication or denial of Christian burial, the Holy Office of the Inquisition tries to root out these folk religions, along with heretics who preach false doctrine, and converts who backslide into their old ways. When these mild solutions fail, or heretics openly flout the authority of the church and confute its teachings, the Inquisition turns to the civil authorities and seeks sterner punishments.

West African religious beliefs combine elements similar to European Christianity and North American animism. North Africa and parts of West Africa had welcomed Muslim traders from the beginning of the millennium, and by the fourteenth century mud-brick and wood Islamic mosques grace the trading centers of West Africa. Like Christianity, Islam is a crusading religion, and missionaries teach it to converts in Mali, Ghana, Songhay, and the Hausa States of West Africa. There Muslims read the Koran and practice the five precepts: to submit to the will of the one god, Allah, whose prophet was Muhammad; to pray five times a day; to give generously to charity; to keep the fast of Ramadan; and to make at least one trip to the holy city of Mecca.

Islam has a strong oral tradition and incorporates myths and legends as teaching tools. The supernatural world retains its place in West African worship. Muslim priests permit families to enjoy pre-Islamic naming ceremonies, divination, rites for planting and harvesting, and burial rituals. Islam proscribes fetishes and idols, but cannot suppress magic (particularly when used to counteract the spells of witches and sorcerers) and secret societies. Thus Islam thrives side by side with older forms of ancestor worship and pantheistic animism, particularly among poorer, rural populations and women.

In all three regions, religion consoles and uplifts people's spirits and helps them to make sense of their world. Worship unifies diverse peoples and renders them equal before their gods.

But were we to refocus our camera once more, this time to pinpoint details of daily life, we would see a more disturbing picture, one filled with invidious distinctions and open discrimination. In river valleys of North America, a caste of warrior priests subjugate their neighbors and intimidate surrounding peoples into providing tribute. Aztec priests rip out the hearts of prisoners taken in endless rounds of warfare. In Europe, a nobility extorts service and taxes from a mass of peasants and laborers in return for protection. Cities are pestholes for the poor. In West Africa, lines of men and women bound in chains shuffle along, herded by armed guards. These are the slaves taken in the many wars among the kingdoms of the region, to be bought and sold like cattle.

As we imagine ourselves spinning through the heavens above these continents more than five hundred years ago, we see everywhere the contradictory evidence of our thesis and antithesis: of improvement and suffering, of faith and malignity. Historians are taught not to ask questions that have no answers, not to make moral judgments, and not to speculate. But we cannot help asking ourselves how these disparities of human fortune arose and what they meant to the peoples of North America, Europe, and West Africa on the eve of contact.

———

All of early American history revolves about the topic of the contact between different peoples. We might describe that contact as an invasion followed by a conquest. Certainly Europeans came to the New World armed to the teeth, displaced native peoples, employed in their place African slaves, and ruled as imperial masters. But "invasion" and "conquest" paint a two-dimensional picture, without background or depth. Better is the term "encounter." An encounter involves more than one person or group, and as used here requires us to re-create the Native American and African points of view as well as the Europeans'.

In our minds, all of us have a store of everyday judgments, views, and experiences that make up our common sense of the world around us. Our culture scripts these frameworks; that is, it not only teaches us how to see and hear but how to make sense of what we see and hear. No one's mind is isolated or objective in contact with the world. When we confront others, thus, we see them as through a window latticework of preconceived notions and expectations.

And when we confront people who are very different from us for the first time, the differences we see can threaten our mental equilibrium. Ordinarily, we desire that all our perceptions fit together, and we try to relieve the dissonance caused by novelty in a number of ways. We reinforce our existing beliefs by denying any differences between what we see and what we already know, or by categorizing the "other" as something we've heard about, but not yet met. We might dismiss or denigrate the newcomer as something inferior, thereby denying him or her the power to shake our preconceptions, or reconfigure what we see, literally changing its shape to make it less dangerous. In their encounters with one another in early America, Europeans, Indians, and Africans assayed all of these techniques.

It would be wonderful to have reliable records of Indian and African perceptions, in their own words, to complement the evidence we have of Europeans' views. Unfortunately, we have to rely on the Europeans' contemporary reports, archaeological and linguistic evidence, and much later native and African American folk recollections. But we do have enough to lay out an outline of the first encounters.

We know that little in their culture prepared the Indians to explain or manage their encounter with the Europeans. Indian culture depended upon memory and recitation, methods that perpetuated the essential conservatism of Indian culture. Insofar as newcomers and novelties of life could be fit into traditional categories, oral traditions helped Indians to embrace the unexpected. But so bizarre did Indians find European conduct, they could find no categories for it in their vocabulary.

When Indians met Europeans face to face, the Indians did not abandon the teachings of their own cultures—quite the contrary. The novelty of the actual encounter caused them to cling to their preconceptions all the more strongly. As rumors of the appearance and conduct of the Europeans circulated in advance of their actual appearance, the Indians searched through dreams and prophecies, omens and older stories for some way to assess the newcomers. There is some evidence that the Indians at first regarded the Europeans as gods—not as Europeans conceived the deity, but as powerful spirits who commanded the forces of nature, in other words, like the gods in Indian pantheism.

Thus some Indians greeted European mariners enthusiastically—touching, rubbing, and fondling the newcomers. The Indians then seated the travelers in places of honor, and feted them. Dances and songs of welcome were part of ceremonies not only fit for gods (or the emissaries of gods) but to make the newcomers into friends and allies. Finally, the Indians gave gifts, for gift exchange was the foundation of all Indian hospitality. Other Indians, however, would not allow the Europeans to land on the shore or ran away from the newcomers, fearing that they were evil spirits who meant no good.

All this the Europeans understood not in the Indians' terms, but in light of European customs. If the Indians brought gifts, it was because they recognized the superiority of the Europeans' technology, morals, and faith. In any case, Europeans believed that great men did not give, they took. Conquest meant possession. Even the European rituals of proprietorship of foreign lands, like reading a legal document that claimed the land for one's monarch, erecting a cross, or building a fort, declared ownership. If the Indians fought or fled, it was because they were less than human, and could not undertake the common diplomatic courtesies that Europeans expected of one another.

Using their own highly developed legal codes and theories of warfare as their authority, Europeans concluded that Indians could not own land, for they did not "improve" it with permanent homes. Later, when Europeans learned about the Aztec cities in Mexico, they revised their argument to say that the Indians' practices of human sacrifice, cannibalism, and overt sexuality proved that Indians had no true morality—a second excuse to occupy the Indians' cities and seize their belongings.

But little in the Europeans' mental framework prepared them for the vastness of space, the harshness of conditions, or the differences between their ways and the ways of the people whose fate was now intertwined with theirs in America. Some Europeans were terrified at what they saw and rebelled in their eagerness to return home. Others died because they gave up the desire to live, or succumbed to the heat, humidity, and parasites of the islands. Still others dealt with the dissonance by dumping their old views and going native, or by reconceptualizing the natives as childlike innocents, and recasting themselves as the Indians' tutors and protectors.

The result of the first encounters was profound mutual misperception, which slid, inexorably, into violence. When relations took their inevitable turn for the worse, Indians resisted by fleeing or fighting. Nomadic Indian peoples waged the fiercest resistance, sometimes engaging in guerrilla warfare. More sedentary peoples, with farms to defend or cities to protect, tried harder to propitiate the newcomers, or grudgingly submitted.

But why, if both sides were equally perplexed by the other, and both failed to understand the other, did the Europeans impose so much of their ways upon the natives? After all, the Indians outnumbered the Europeans a thousandfold. At the time, the Europeans boasted that God was on their side. In later years, European scholarship concluded that European technologies of war and weaponry, including firearms, war horses, and armor, awed the natives and outweighed their numerical superiority. In fact, native warriors soon took the measure of European technologies and either adopted them—for example, becoming expert marksmen with firearms and learning to ride horses themselves—or developing countertactics and weapons.

Ultimate European victory lay not in human actions or beliefs, but in the array of microbes, pollens, insects, and domesticated animals Europeans brought with them, which decimated Indian populations, ousted native flora and fauna, and destroyed local ecologies. Indians had no natural or acquired immunities to diseases like mumps, measles, and chicken pox. Smallpox, an epidemic killer of Europeans, was even more destructive among the Indians because they had not learned to quarantine the victims. Instead, Indian curing rituals involved laying on hands, fasting, cold baths, and visits from friends and family. Family visits only served to spread disease, so that a single case would result in the devastation of an entire village. In some areas, nearly 90 percent of the native populations died as the result of such visitations.

European grazing animals like horses, cows, and sheep contested the meadow and grasslands with the deer and buffalo, animals on which the Indians depended for food and clothing. European pigs rooted up Indian gardens, and European rats and cockroaches ran rampant through Indian storehouses. Opportunistic European weeds took advantage of the destruction of Indian fields and gardens and spread across the Caribbean and North America.

But the Indians coped. They pulled together new tribes out of the fragments of old ones; selectively adapted European technologies to hunt, cook, dress, and deal with European military forces; and played one European power off against another to protect native interests. Over the course of two centuries, the Indian population began to recover its losses from European diseases (although there were periodic outbreaks of new epidemics, particularly among those Indians who lived in the interior of the North American continent and had not yet been exposed to the European pathogens). And in time, out of the wreckage of initial conflict came new, hybridized Euro-Indian communities and concessions on both sides.

The natives were not the only people to pay the price of the Europeans' foothold on the American continent, however. When Indian populations declined, Europeans introduced African slaves to the New World. In their advertisements for their wares, slave traders boasted that one hardy African slave could do the work of four Indians. In fact, slavery in the New World was a sentence of brutal exploitation and early death for almost all of the Africans. Colonial officials, settlers, and merchants knew that they would have to replace one-fourth of all imported slaves each year just to maintain the same size labor force, but the profits of European plantations and mines were worth it—to some.

Looking at the European presence in North America at the beginning of the seventeenth century, one finds a vast but unevenly populated Spanish colonial system (some 243,000 *peninsulares* came during the "Spanish century," most from the southern third of Spain and most destined for Hispaniola, Mexico, or Peru) and a handful of tiny Dutch, English, French, and Portuguese enclaves. European germs, pollen, cattle, horses, and pigs had done far more to change the New World landscape than had the Europeans.

By the first decades of the eighteenth century, this picture had changed so drastically as to be unrecognizable. The Spanish had advanced on the New Mexico and Florida frontiers, and were creeping into a land the Indians called Tejos. The outposts of empire had become little Europes—homes away from home for entire families. Indeed, the flow of women to the Spanish colonies had increased from a trickle to over one-fourth of the total. The home government underwrote the emigration of poor people, shipped over fifty thousand soldiers to the Americas, and admitted foreigners to the Spanish overseas lands. By the second decade of the eighteenth century, more than fifty thousand French had migrated to America, and the French Empire stretched from the mouth of the Saint Lawrence River in the north to the Great Lakes in the west, south to the Gulf of Mexico, and into the Caribbean.

But the Britons (English, Welsh, Scots, and Scots-Irish) and the Africans made the most striking impression on North American and Caribbean life. Almost four hundred thousand Britons (English, Welsh, Scots, and Scots from Northern Ireland) departed the home country for the Caribbean and North American mainland colonies from 1600 to 1700. Most were English. The Scots contributed about seven thousand (the major Scottish and Scots-Irish migration took place in the next century). Three to four thousand Irish settlers and servants inhabited islands in the British Caribbean in 1678, and by one estimate about one thousand Irish immigrants journeyed to the British colonies each year in the later seventeenth century. Over one hundred thousand Africans joined them, bound in the holds of slave ships. With a relative handful of Dutch emigrants (perhaps no more than ten thousand altogether) and Swedes, the Britons and Africans moved the line of settlements from the coast to the edge of the Appalachian spine; built villages, towns, and cities; and produced more wealth than Spain's and France's colonies combined.

In addition to the lure of abundance, a sense of adventure and an antipathy toward England's enemies in the colonization enterprise, like France and Spain, energized the colonizers. Religious conflict combined push and pull factors. Religious dissent and persecution were a part of British life. Under the settlement of 1558, Roman Catholics were forbidden to worship in public but still held private services, and Catholic nobles retained power in politics. Within English Protestantism, sects of "hot blooded perfectionists" called "Puritans" began to criticize both the government and the established church. After years of debate and growing fears of persecution, some of these critics began to see migration as the only way to save their ideals of Christianity from corruption. Ministers and their congregations together fled to the New World.

But the British colonists did not emigrate because they wanted to abandon their old ways, nor did they welcome innovation for its own sake. The wilderness conditions and the expanse of cheap land in the New World never stripped the habits of the Old World from the minds and hearts of the newcomers, nor did their new environs lead them to experiment with democracy and individualism as we know them. The majority of settlers tried to reconstruct the world they had left. The better born expected in the New World the deference that they had received in England, and ordinary people generally conceded privileges to persons of rank and status.

Even in their homes and clothing, the British colonists manifested their attachment to old ways. The first houses of the settlers of New England resembled the shanties of poor English cottagers. Later, they rebuilt with strong oaken timbers and plastered with wattle and dab, just as they would have done in England. The emigrants to Virginia wore the clothing of the old country even when the heat and humidity of their new home dictated more comfortable dress, and they ached for the beer and cider they had left behind. Local variations in English speech like the nasal twang of eastern England and the drawl of southern England also survived the crossing and influenced the speech patterns of New England and the Chesapeake colonies, respectively.

The ingrained conservatism of the colonists reminds us to contextualize their story properly. We tend to see the English-speaking colonies as precursors of the first United States and treat the founding of the colonies as the introductory chapter in our nation's history. But viewed in historical perspective, the colonists' actions and beliefs were a continuation and extension of European history, and the colonies were the far-western edge of a transatlantic community. Thus the two political upheavals that profoundly changed English politics in the seventeenth century—the period of civil wars and parliamentary rule (1642–1660) and the so-called Glorious Revolution of 1688–1689—are vital parts of the story.

In the life of every community, there are moments of particular stress, crises that force men and women to reassess their goals and values. A series of such crises swept across the North American colonies from 1675 to 1700, interrupting and redirecting the development of politics and society. The crisis heightened conflict between colonists and their Indian neighbors over land, livestock, and crops; intensified disputes between home country and colonial merchants over customs duties; and led to efforts of royal officials to regulate and centralize power. In turn, these led to war, rebellion, and disorder in the colonies and threatened to destroy the fragile bonds of empire.

CHRONOLOGY— PART ONE

30,000–10,000 B.P.	Paleolithic era
10,000–8000 B.P.	Extinction of the North American megafauna
10,000–2500 B.P.	Archaic era
7,000–5000 B.P.	Introduction of Indian horticulture
3500 B.P.	First mound cultures in North America
2500 B.P.–A.D. 800	Adena and Hopewell cultures in the Midwest
2000 B.P.	Corn comes to the Southwest
A.D. 800–1450	Expansion of Islam into West Africa
900–1250	Anasazi flourish in the Four Corners region
900–1600	Rise of West African empires
1000	Corn culture begins in the Northeast
1000–1250	Cahokia dominates the Mississippian culture
1000–1300s	Vikings in Greenland and Vineland
1100	Tobacco cultivation spreads in North America
1200s	Iroquois League (Confederacy) founded

1250–1300s	Drought afflicts Anasazi and other Indians
1300–1450	Period of war and migration in North America
1342–1493	Portuguese and Spanish conquest of Canary Islands
1347	Bubonic plague comes to Europe
1350–1500s	Renaissance in Europe
1440s	Portuguese African slave trade begins
1452	Invention of plate printing
1460s–1490s	Portuguese exploration of Atlantic and Indian oceans
1469	Isabel of Castile weds Ferdinand of Aragon
1485	End of the Wars of the Roses and rise of Tudors in England
1492	Reconquest of Spain is completed
1492–1504	Columbus's four voyages to America
1494	Treaty of Tordesillas
1494–1512	Spanish conquest of the Antilles
1497–1498	Cabot's voyages to Newfoundland
1513	Spanish conquest of Florida begins
1517	Martin Luther's protests open the Reformation
1519–1521	Cortés defeats the Aztecs in Mexico
1523–1524	Verrazano explores the North American coast
1533	King Henry VIII of England breaks with Rome
1534–1542	Cartier explores the Saint Lawrence River
1536	Calvin's *Institutes of the Christian Religion*
1539–1542	De Soto invades the Southeast
1540s	English Reformation begins
1540–1542	Coronado explores the Southwest
1558	Elizabeth I crowned
1565	Spanish establish Saint Augustine, Florida
1579–1583	Irish rebellion against England
1584–1587	Roanoke colony
1585–1602	Harriot and the Hakluyts write about America
1588	Defeat of the Spanish Armada
1598	Spanish return to New Mexico
1602	English begin exploration of Maine
1603	Stuart era in England begins with James I
1603–1608	Champlain founds settlements in Canada
1607	Virginia Colony reestablished at Jamestown
1607–1608	Sagadahoc fiasco in Maine
1609	Santa Fe becomes capital of New Mexico
1609–1664	Dutch colony of New Netherland
1610s	Africans in Virginia

1611	First Virginia tobacco exports
1614	John Smith names New England
1619	First session of Virginia House of Burgesses
1620	Pilgrims begin the Plymouth colony
1622	Powhatan Indians attack Virginia settlements
1624	English begin colonies in Antilles
1624–1629	Puritans settle along the coast of New England
1630	Founding of the Massachusetts Bay Colony
1634	First settlements in Maryland Colony
1635–1636	Roger Williams banished from Massachusetts and begins Rhode Island Colony
1636	First English settlements in Connecticut
1637	Pequot War in Connecticut and Rhode Island
1637–1638	Ann Hutchinson tried and banished
1640s	Sugar cultivation begins in Barbados
1642–1649	Civil wars in England, execution of Charles I
1649–1658	Interregnum in England; Cromwell named Lord Protector
1651–1774	Navigation Acts
1655	English conquer Jamaica
1660s	Virginia makes slavery an inheritable status
1660s	Settlements in North Carolina
1660	Restoration of Stuarts; Charles II returns to England
1661	Barbados slave code
1663	Carolina proprietary granted
1664	Duke of York conquers New Netherland; New York and New Jersey colonies established
1670s	Settlements in South Carolina
1670s	East and West Jersey become separate colonies
1675	Slave uprising in Barbados
1675–1676	King Philip's War in New England
1676	Bacon's Rebellion in Virginia
1678–1681	Exclusion crisis in England
1680s	French explorations along the Mississippi
1680–1692	Pueblo uprising in New Mexico
1681	Pennsylvania Colony established
1685	James II crowned
1686–1689	Dominion of New England
1688–1689	Glorious Revolution in England
1689–1691	Leisler's Rebellion in New York
1689–1697	King William's War

1692–1693	Salem witchcraft trials
1701	Jerseys reunited as royal colony
1702	Delaware becomes separate colony
1729	Proprietors surrender North and South Carolina to the crown

Note: Before the present 3000 B.P. = 1000 B.C.

1

The First Americans

The descendants of the first Americans have a treasure trove of origin tales. Modern scholars treat these tales as myths and legends, and in truth their authors mixed the fantastic and the plausible. But the purpose of the origin tales goes beyond amusement. The storytellers blended the sacred and the profane to make a point about the value of harmony. For example, the Mohawks, who guarded the "eastern door" to the Iroquois League, in what is now upstate New York, tell of how the daughter of first man and first woman was thrown from the heavens by her husband in a fit of rage, and how the animals cushioned her fall and helped her make the earth. From her body came the twins, good and evil. In their struggle over how to treat their new world came the beginnings of Iroquois society.

The Hopi people who live on three mesas in northern Arizona tell a different story of the origins of the world. It began not in the sky but in the bowels of the earth, where two girls were born. To each of the girls Thought Woman gave a basket filled with pollen and seeds to plant and clay models of all the animals of the earth. One of the plants grew so tall that it pushed a hole through the earth and came out above ground. The sisters climbed it, and from the seeds they carried grew the corn to feed the people. But the people were arrogant and fractious and made war on one another.

The lessons of these stories are plain and capture a facet of Native American history that repeated itself throughout early American experience. In the stories, the gods give the land, its fruits, and the animals to the Indians in trust for their safekeeping, but the Indians betray the trust. The gods expect humans to multiply and improve their lot but warn against disharmony and avarice. The warning goes unheeded.

Captivated by the timeless quality of these tales, we are tempted to regard their lessons as a morality play in a distant, static "then." By so doing, we ignore the dynamic forces in Indian life over the many centuries of their sole habitation of the Americas. In fact, the first Americans traveled far, changed much, and built durable communi-

Pleasant it looked; this newly created world. Along the entire length and breadth of the earth, our grandmother extended the green reflection of her covering and the escaping odors were pleasant to inhale.
—Winnebago song

Clear the way in a sacred manner. I come, the earth is mine.
—Lakota war chant

ties in the face of difficult obstacles. Although lost to us, powerful individuals and social and political events affected their lives. In short, they had a history.

We do know that small groups of migrants from Asia and the Pacific came to America in waves going back thirty thousand years. They came to improve their lives, and some did. Indians settled, farmed, multiplied, and diversified their diet, dress, and personal belongings. Simple dwellings of saplings and dirt gave way to stone and mud-brick apartment houses. Hand-to-mouth subsistence hunting and gathering became complex economies, featuring thousand-mile-long trade networks and the production of sufficient food surpluses to support urban populations.

Ritual human sacrifice, war, and cannibalism accompanied the progress of Indian civilization. In urban complexes along the Mississippi River, archaeologists have found burial chambers for the rich filled with the skeletons of servants. When a rich person died, his or her family sacrificed the dead person's retainers to serve in the next world. In the most elegant and prosperous of Mexican Indian cities, priests ripped the hearts from bound prisoners of war and constructed blocks of the victims' skulls taller than a one-story house. History confirms what the origin tales decry.

PALEOLITHIC AMERICA

The earliest era of American history is called the Paleolithic, or Old Stone Age, named for the tools the first Americans made and used. It lasted from the arrival of the first humans to about 10,000 B.P. (years before present). The most recent findings of archaeologists suggest that human beings lived in North America as long ago as 16,000 B.P., when glaciers covered the continent as far south as Indiana and New Jersey. More conservative readings of the evidence from the earliest sites suggest that settlement began about 13,000 B.P., after the glaciers had begun their long retreat northward.

As America warmed and dried, some species of wildlife and plant life prospered while others disappeared. The Paleolithic hunter-gatherers spread over the land. By the end of the Paleolithic era, the Indians had developed more sedentary lifestyles, and the population had grown denser. Different native groups came into closer contact, and the potential for conflict grew.

The First Peopling

Today it is the Bering Strait, a waterway between the eastern edge of Siberia and the western reaches of Alaska named after the eighteenth-century Danish-born mariner Vitus Bering. However, thirty thousand years ago, during the last Ice Age, Beringia was a vast grassy plain more than eight hundred miles across, stretching from Siberia to Alaska. The land, at its highest point hundreds of feet above sea level, rose out of the sea when the glaciers, some more than a mile high, trapped the waters of the oceans.

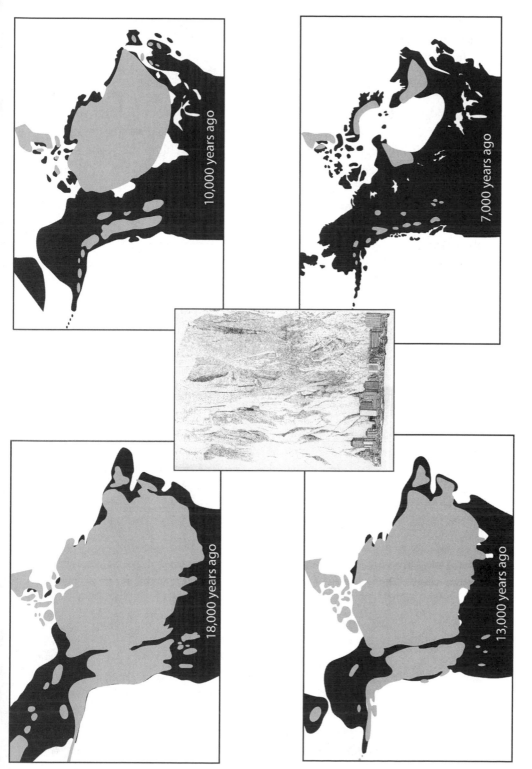

18,000 years ago

13,000 years ago

10,000 years ago

7,000 years ago

The Ice Age Recedes

The northern parts of this subcontinent were frozen hard in winter, like the tundra above the sixty-fifth parallel in modern Canada and Alaska. But in summer, the northern reaches of the Beringian subcontinent defrosted to a depth of two to three feet. Water sat on top of permafrost, creating a frigid, marshlike surface. For a brief time, flowering plants and grasses exploded in growth, feeding swarming insects, birds, and a few hearty grazing herbivores. Climate in southern Beringia was more hospitable and the landscape more varied, home to herds of hairy bison, caribou, and woolly mammoths. Under scattered clumps of dwarf birch, alder, cottonwood, wormwood, and aspen trees lurked cats twice the size of leopards and packs of gray wolves.

But the most dangerous predators on the Beringian landmass were small bands of Asian men and women who followed the game herds out of the Asian steppe. Their life in Beringia was grueling. We have no archaeological evidence of their presence because the subcontinent is now under water, but arctic hunter-gatherers in historical times had a life expectancy of less than forty years. The perils of starvation, death from exposure and accident, and the attacks of wolves and bears must have been even greater thirty thousand years ago.

In all likelihood, the Beringians traveled by boat as well as on foot. Animal hides cured and stretched across wooden frames sealed by tree gum carried them into the bitterly cold waters off the southern coast of Beringia, where fish like the Alaskan grayling still gather. The remains of such boats have been uncovered on Alaskan shores.

Facing the long subarctic winter, the people became inured to darkness. Smoky and dimly lit, rancid with the smell of human sweat and rotting animal fat, the Beringians' tents were also filled with the warmth of companionship and the comfort of parental ministrations. Perhaps men and women spent much of their time apart—separate social functions dictating separate spheres of life. But in the tents families reunited. There the Beringians relieved the drabness of subarctic life with song, story, dance, and decoration of their bodies and their clothing.

The people had to hunt and travel in small family groups, typically numbering about two dozen individuals. Hunter-gatherer bands could not be large, for they could not carry with them or store surpluses of food, even when good fortune favored them with additional supplies. Thus feasting times and starving times followed the change of the seasons. Because they could not save in times of abundance, they developed the habit of sharing. The highest-status individuals were those who gave away the most food, rather than those who accumulated the most.

Over thousands of years, the Beringians established a way of life, and then climatic changes forced them to alter their ways or die. When and how they entered North America proper are now the subject of much debate. From glacial lake basins we have fragments of human artifacts, but we do not know if they were deposited in the lakes or came from elsewhere. The dating remains difficult even with the most modern techniques, for the total number of immigrants must have been small compared with the vastness of the land.

According to the account commonly accepted a decade ago, when the earth warmed and the glaciers receded, the seas rose, and water flooded back across the Bering Strait 15,000 B.P., and the Beringians had to become Americans. The first reliable evidence for human habitation in the far north can be found in the Bluefish Cave region of Alaska and is dated at about 14,000 B.P.

The Beringian subcontinent was one highway into the North American landmass, but recent redating of old sites of habitation and a growing body of new finds suggest that immigrants traveled many routes to the New World. For example, the discovery of a woman's bones on Santa Rosa Island off the coast of California proves that southeastern Asians used the sea to reach America at about the same time that the Beringians were moving into Alaska. Sites in eastern Virginia, New Mexico, and Wisconsin hold tools and bones older than those in Alaska.

The most telling evidence of multiple entry comes not from North America but from South America. Incontrovertible evidence places Paleo-Indians in Monte Verde, Chile, ten thousand miles from Alaska, over fourteen thousand years ago. The Monte Verde site, on the sandy banks of a creek not far from the Pacific shore, was the home of a hunter-gatherer band of perhaps thirty individuals. Hides, lodgepoles notched to fit together in a frame, and thatched roofs housed these first Chileans. The residents were toolmakers and left behind the detritus of their labors: grinding slabs, digging sticks, and projectile points litter the peat bog that filled in the creek. The bog also yielded seeds and nuts. Indigenous potatoes, mushrooms, grasses, and berries grow nearby and could have been harvested in season. But the major food source was animal protein—the bones of a large mammal were scattered about the site. A child's footprint in the soft clay of the bank, hardened with time, allows us to imagine the young one watching the elders performing their chores.

The Land

The newcomers to North America found a rich and varied landscape. As the two great ice fields, the Cordilleran (reaching deep into the Rockies) and the Laurentide (covering much of the mid-Atlantic states and the Midwest), receded after 15,000 B.P., they changed the face of North America. The retreating glaciers gouged out lakebeds and waterways, such as Puget Sound and the Great Lakes, and filled them with melted ice. The tundra drew back as well, replaced by opportunistic boreal forests of fir and spruce and great bogs of peat moss. The evergreen trees could not sink their roots deep (the spodosol, or gray soil, is rich on top from decomposing evergreen needles, but rocky beneath), so they ran roots everywhere along the ground. The descendants of these forests still thrive as far south as Minnesota and western New York State.

To the south and east, from the Mississippi to the Atlantic coast, forests of mixed broadleaf and evergreen covered the land. The earth ran from the brown soil of the northeastern and mid-Atlantic regions to the thinner yellow soil of the coastal plains and the red clay of the upper South. The richer the soil, the greater the diversity of flora. Fire and windstorms downed trees, opening spaces in the canopy for smaller trees and brush to rush in, creating varied patterns of growth. On the sandy edge of the Atlantic coast, pines thrived, along with the adventurous red maple. In the great hardwood forests of the Appalachian spine, oak and hickory wove the canopy of climax (undisturbed) forest, but a single cove of woods might have as many as twenty-five different species of trees. In marshes, hemlock and basswood coexisted. The eastern woodlands were temperate in climate, but the variation in wetness and temperature from north to south was distinct. Northern seasons were far more sharply defined than southern ones, with bright yellow, red, and orange foliage in the fall.

To the west of the midline of the continent, rolling grasslands reigned, broken by a series of north-south mountain ranges. Wind and rain determined the ground cover. The mountains prevented the Pacific rainfalls from reaching the grassy plains, and the wind blowing across the grassland evaporated whatever rainfall came. Lightning fires prevented forest growth over much of the land, but the grasses started earlier in the year and grew faster than the fires.

As the eastern forests exhibited many species of trees, so the land between the great river and the high mountains offered many species of grasses. From the Mississippi River to ninety-eight degrees longitude in the West, long grasses grew, in summer standing six feet high. The long-grass prairie faded into mixed prairie in the Dakotas, central Nebraska, Kansas, Oklahoma, and north Texas. In the foothills of the Rockies, the short grasses hugged the land. These were the Great Plains, or the "high plains." It was drier on the plains than on the prairies, and sometimes the rainfall on the high plains was no more than ten inches a year. But able to adapt to the aridity of the land, the short grasses survived.

To the south of the prairies and the plains, the land was even drier and hotter—a landscape of high mesas, deep canyons, rolling desert, and snow-covered mountains. Where rivers ran there were floodplains, but even the broadest of rivers were seasonal visitors in their old courses, and high summer left the watercourses wind-blown dust chutes. Along the valleys and the watercourses of the Rio Grande and the Colorado, midget piñon and juniper trees dotted the land, some of the latter a thousand years old. On the sides of the mountains, some reaching up twelve thousand feet, ponderosa pine proliferated. Thousands of years ago these southwestern lands were cooler and wetter than they are today. Pollen samples from the canyons show that great forests once thrust as far south as southern New Mexico. As that forest receded, the plants of the South came north.

From the spine of the Rockies to the Pacific coast, the land was wrinkled and cold. The mountain ridges cut off the rain in summer, but glacial lakes and fast-running streams carried the winter snow down the hillsides in spring. Short grasses and hardy pines like the ponderosa flourished and sustained herds of deer, antelope, elk, and buffalo. The mountains, many of them former volcanoes, must have seemed to the Indians the pillars of the heavens.

The coast itself, unlike the sandy, marshy Atlantic shore, was rocky. From east to west, the Cascade and Coast ranges and the Olympic Mountains obstructed the Pacific storms, and the western slopes of the Olympics were like rain forests. Giant spruce and hemlock towered over moss and fern. Plant fossils reveal that the flora was once even more varied, including species now found only in Central and South American rain forests. The northwest plateau from the coast to the Cascade Mountains was cut through by one of America's largest waterways, the Columbia River. Its tributaries were a haven for salmon and other food fish.

Migrations

When they arrived, the first Americans moved over the land in relatively small bands of probably no more than twenty to thirty individuals, knit by kinship bonds. These clans spurted out from existing hunting territories into new areas. Their forays into unknown parts were hesitant and spasmodic, driven by a sudden increase in the population of the band or the appearance of other hunters nearby. The migrations traced river courses, lake edges, or coastlines, for fish and fowl lived in such places, and browsing animals had to drink. In general, these migrations passed north to south or west to east, following the drainage courses of the rivers.

Archaeologists have found evidence of hunter-gatherer sites along five natural highways. The first was the northwest-to-southeast corridor that leads from the central provinces of Canada, under the Hudson Bay region (the Canadian Shield) to the basin of the Saint Lawrence River, then down the Atlantic coast as far as the Chesapeake Bay. Algonquian peoples traveled this route, and their descendants, including the Micmacs and Abenakis of Maine and Nova Scotia, the Mahicans of the lower Hudson River, the Leni-Lenapes (or Delawares) of Pennsylvania and New Jersey, and the Powhatans of the James River in Virginia, were among the first Indians to greet the English and French in the sixteenth and seventeenth centuries.

The second great corridor was the Pacific Ocean rim from Alaska to Oregon and down the coast of California. The Indians of the Northwest and California are the distant descendants of these emigrants. The mountains fragmented the migration, dividing larger bands into smaller ones, until the peoples of the region developed microcultures in isolation from one another.

The third highway was the river system irrigating the Great Plains and the Southwest. The northernmost of the migrants on this trail became the Great Plains tribes of Siouan speakers that followed the buffalo herds. To the south, along the floodplains of the Rio Grande and other watercourses, the Pueblo people (Spanish *pueblo*, "village") settled. They included the ancestors of modern Hopis, Zunis, Tewas, Tiwas, Towas, and Keresan speakers of New Mexico and Arizona. Some of the ancient migrants traveled farther south, into Mexico, as well as Central and South America.

A fourth corridor radiated out from the Mississippi to the Tennessee, Cumberland, Chattahoochie, and Ohio rivers. Along this route Native American settlers left the great monuments of woodlands life, the burial mounds of the Adena and Hopewell peoples (2500 B.P. to A.D. 800) and the temple mounds of Cahokia and other cities along the Mississippi basin (ca. A.D. 1000). Farther along this corridor, the Indians followed the river courses up the Ohio River to the north and east, and south to Alabama and Georgia. Among the descendants of that migration are the Muskegon-speaking Creeks of Alabama and Georgia, and the Iroquoian-speaking Cherokees of the southeastern Piedmont, as well as the five Iroquois tribes of New York—the Senecas, Oneidas, Onondagas, Cayugas, and Mohawks.

The fifth pathway was the Gulf of Mexico, from the Meso-American settlements to Florida and the Caribbean. The Antilles Islands (the largest of which are Cuba, Hispaniola, Jamaica, and Puerto Rico) may have been the last frontier of the natives, settled by boat people from South or Central America about 5000 B.P.

Survival

There was no guarantee that the newcomers would survive, much less prosper, in North America. Far larger and more imposing animals became extinct shortly after people spread over the continent. The mammoth, giant bison and beaver, huge sloths, hairy oxen, horses, and camels vanished between 10,000 and 8000 B.P., along with some of the most fearsome of their predators. The extinction overtook only those animals that had been in North America for hundreds of thousands of years. Newer, more adaptive arrivals such as deer, bison, and rabbits actually multiplied their numbers.

Scientists debate whether human predation, climatic change, or some catastrophe hurried the departure of the megafauna. One group of scientists accuses the hunters of wanton slaughter of the animals. Certainly Paleolithic hunters' favored method of driving whole herds of browsing animals off cliffs depleted animal populations. But the sheer numbers and extent of geographical distribution of the largest animals so dwarfed the human population that there simply were not enough hunters to support this thesis. Nor does the overkill theory explain the extinction of the giant predators.

Proponents of a climatic explanation for the extinction of the largest mammals reason that as the cold, steppelike northern plains turned into grassy prairie in the great warming of 13,000–12,000 B.P., animals that spent too much time rearing too few offspring were outproduced and outbrowsed by more prolific, smaller, faster, nimbler rivals. Thus deer, elk, sheep, and rabbits filled the ecological niche that the larger browsers had previously occupied. But the climatic theory does not explain why the large animals survived all the severe climatic changes prior to 13,000 B.P.

The same warming trends that aided the smaller animals made survival easier for people. The woodlands and prairies that replaced the receding glaciers provided fuel, clothing, and game for the newcomers. Cold is the worst enemy of primitive human beings. Evidence from cave sites from Utah to Pennsylvania indicates that Paleolithic wanderers returned to these shelters year after year to take refuge from the chill of ancient winter nights. But as winter became a season rather than a way of life, humans did not have to devote so much of their time and energy to staying warm. The altered climate provided a greater variety of clothing materials as well. Paleolithic peoples of the north added fibers of bark and grass, and other products of the forests and grasslands, to the animal skins of their wardrobe.

Warming climate made hunting and gathering food safer. The staple in the diet of these hunters was animal suet. Bone marrow mixed with pounded meat and berries, known today as pemmican, sustained hunters on the trail; lightly cooked or raw meat sustained the band. To hunt the deer and other herd animals of the grasslands and forests, the hunters adapted the methods they used to trap the megafauna, such as digging pits next to waterholes and driving herds over cliffs. The Indian camp doubled as a slaughterhouse, and archaeologists know that they have uncovered an ancient Indian campsite when they find piles of bones scraped clean of meat.

In their search for food, Paleolithic Americans had an advantage over all the other predators on the continent. Humans made tools. Indeed, the Stone Age gets its name from the stone piercing, scraping, slicing, and bludgeoning tools the first Americans employed. Stone possessed desirable qualities of endurance and weight; stone tools also cracked, flaked, and broke. From the Bluefish Cave sites in Alaska to the Monte Verde settlement in Chile, craftspeople left piles of discarded chips, microliths (tiny stone blades), and wedge-shaped stone cores for working hides.

In making projectile points, craftspeople apparently used sandstone, granite, or quartzite to knap the target stones of flint, obsidian (a volcanic glass), and chert (a quartzite) into the rough shape of the spear point or the knife. Shorter sharp blows chipped off flakes to produce an edge. For fine work the toolmaker used deer or elk antler to shape points to perfection. The center of the projectile could then be hollowed out, or small notches chipped from either side of its base, to fasten it to a shaft with animal sinews.

The Paleolithic hunter carried all manner of weapons, including clubs, knives, and thrusting spears, but the preferred long-distance killer was the javelin, with a stone-tipped or fire-hardened wood point. Sometime after 12,000 B.P., hunters extended the range, force, and accuracy of the javelin with the throwing stick, or (to use the later Aztec term) atlatl. The atlatl is a narrow wooden shaft on which the javelin rests, its end pressed against the raised butt of the atlatl. Over the years, the atlatl was improved by making it longer and jointed in the middle, its whipping motion imparting even greater velocity to the projectile.

Until the 1990s, the oldest type of North American spear point was thought to be the lancelike shape named after Clovis, New Mexico, where it was discovered. Examples of it in North American sites range from 13,000 B.P. to well into the first millennium. More recent finds suggest that Paleolithic craftspeople turned out spear points thousands of years before the Clovis points appeared. When the bow and arrow replaced the lance and spear as weapons of choice, stone workers adapted older spear-point shapes to produce arrowheads.

Gatherings

The Paleo-Indians were not just wanderers with weapons. They were adaptive and provident gatherers of grasses, roots, tubers, berries, and oily seeds. Nut-bearing trees offered a seasonal buffet. Piñons in the Southwest and acorns, walnuts, hickory nuts, and chestnuts in the eastern forests provided high-fat or high-carbohydrate staples. The nuts were cracked and boiled, the shells falling to the bottom of the rock cistern and the nut meats floating. Wild onion grew everywhere. Winter was hard, and natives had to make do on the harvest cached in pit storage areas, but in the spring, tubers and greens reappeared. Sunflower, marsh elder, goosefoot, and maygrass provided starchy greens. Eaten with wild berries, they made a reasonable diet, if supplemented with proteins, the latter supplied by fish, fowl, eggs, and small animals. The Indians' toolkit included implements for preparing the foods they gathered—for example, grass baskets to carry nuts and berries, and baskets coated with clay to heat water for nut mush.

A second kind of gathering was equally vital to Native American life. Although the density of population of North America in these times rarely exceeded one person per sixty square miles, few people lived in such isolation. Instead, as many as five hundred members of a loosely related clan ranged through the clan's hunting grounds. Some meetings of clan members would be accidental, but many assemblies had specific social purposes. For example, all Indian peoples had taboos against procreation with close relatives. Partners would have to be found in nearby groups. Hunting bands came together to create domestic unions.

Natives also enjoyed the give and take of barter and appreciated fine craftsmanship. Some sites, particularly at river fords, served as trade marts. Archaeologists have found incontrovertible evidence of long-distance commerce in rare metals, such as Great Lakes copper, and in semiprecious stones, such as New Mexican turquoise. In fact, copper and turquoise jewelry was so prized that its owners insisted on wearing it in the next world, and some burial sites are treasure troves of finely crafted necklaces, bracelets, and pendants. To facilitate trade, diverse Indian groups had to develop rudimentary political, legal, and cultural institutions, including a way to resolve disputes over personal injuries.

Over time, communal trade sites were perhaps the first semipermanent settlements. One such site (albeit from a much later time period) was found in northeast Louisiana, at Watson Brake. The site lies above the floodplain of the Ouachita River. Middens (trash heaps) indicate that the Indians who came to trade feasted on animals and fish as well as wild grasses. The traders built an earthen wall three feet high to connect ten mounds, the tallest of which rose twenty-five feet above the flood-plain. The circular shape of the mounds-and-earthworks complex suggests that as festive as these meetings might have been, the hosts were ready to defend the compound.

Words for Work and Words for Prayer

At the Watson Brake site, different groups of hunter-gatherers communicated with one another, probably using both signs and gestures. No doubt, in the course of the trading, the two sides conversed in signs, the common language of traders. Some signs were simply visual, pointing to an item, holding it up, smiling, frowning. Such signs could be matters of life and death, however. The most obvious sign was the laying down of weapons in sight of the other party. For this we have evidence from the contact period, when Europeans first met Native Americans.

When in 1620 Miles Standish and his party of English Pilgrims wished to parley with approaching Indians of unknown intention, the Pilgrims laid down their muskets and signaled to the Indians to lay down their bows. One group of coastal Carolina Indians, desperate to identify themselves as friends of the English in 1587, begged "that there might be some token or badge given them of us, whereby we might know them to be our friends, when we met them anywhere out of [their] town or island." When the Narragansetts wanted the Pilgrims of Plymouth to leave, in 1621, they sent a snakeskin full of arrows. The meaning of the arrows was plain. Snakes were powerful animistic figures, able to move in and out of the ground, to hide, and to attack from ambush. The Pilgrims got the message, but had no intention of leaving. They sent the snakeskin back, filled with lead musket balls. The Narragansetts apparently understood the reply, and kept the peace with Plymouth. Indians were practiced in "reading" such signs as belts of wampum, hatchets, and the way in which body parts or weapons were held.

Signs were only a poor substitute for words, however. Peoples who traded with one another developed what are called today "pidgin" languages, which simplified and combined the vocabulary and grammar of their home tongues.

Perhaps the most remarkable physical trait of humans is the ability to create languages from a wide variety of sounds. Some physical anthropologists claim that the ability to develop intelligible speech was more important in the evolution of humans than the use of tools.

One of the most basic uses of language among the first Americans must have been in naming people and places. Individuals' names recalled some incident of their early lives, a physical characteristic or trait, or an omen at their birth. Naming customs—for example, the assignment of secret clan and totem names—allowed mothers and fathers to link themselves to their offspring and enabled native peoples to create social structures. The bands gave themselves names. As Tall Oak, a Narra-

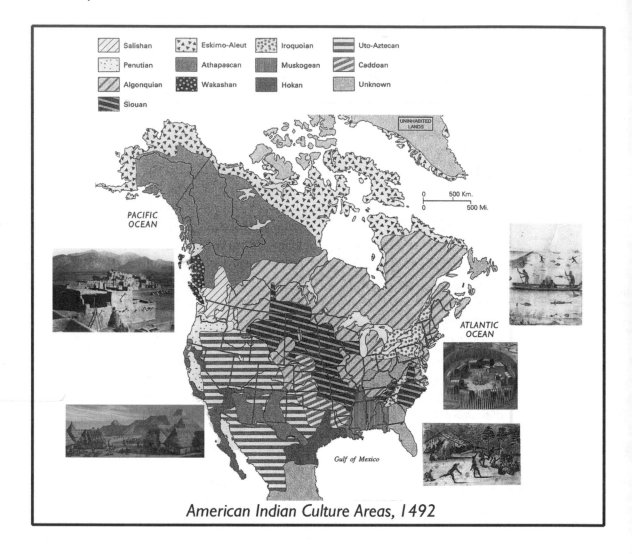

Salishan	Eskimo-Aleut	Iroquoian	Uto-Aztecan
Penutian	Athapascan	Muskogean	Caddoan
Algonquian	Wakashan	Hokan	Unknown
Siouan			

UNINHABITED LANDS

PACIFIC OCEAN

0   500 Km.

0   500 Mi.

ATLANTIC OCEAN

Gulf of Mexico

American Indian Culture Areas, 1492

gansett Indian, explained in a recent interview, "When you translate the word that [every single tribe] had for [itself], without knowledge of each other, it was always something that translated to basically the same thing. In our language it's *ninuog*, or 'the people,' 'the human beings.'" Such names defined those who belonged within the group and those who were outside it.

As migration brought hunting bands into new terrains, evolving vocabularies allowed people to identify natural phenomena and physical places like caves, trails, meadows, rivers, lakes, and favored hunting sites. Sometimes the name was representative of some feature of the landscape or recalled an event. Knowing names of the places in one's territory not only allowed one to describe a route or depict a spot without going there, it also gave one a sense of power over what were otherwise vast and forbidding spaces.

Linguists dispute whether all the migrants shared a language that diverged as different streams of travelers went their own ways, or whether different groups of migrants brought their own languages. One school of thought divides Indian languages into three major groups, each associated with a distinct migration. The first group, called the Amerinds, had a single language, and the major North American language groups we know as Siouan, Algonquian, Penutian (including Muskegon), and the original languages of the Utes and the Aztecs are all related. A second and later-arriving group of speakers shared the Na-Dene tongues (including the Athabaskan peoples now called Apache and Navajo). The last group of migrants spoke some dialect of Eskimo-Aleut.

It is impossible for scientists to determine the extent to which Indians in the prehistoric period could understand one another's dialects. Sixteenth- and seventeenth-century European visitors consistently remarked on the mutual unintelligibility of Indian tongues, likening it to the biblical story of the Tower of Babel. Even within major language groups like the Algonquian in New England, neighboring tribes professed not to comprehend one another's speech. Linguists have estimated over three hundred major dialects within the parent languages. Much of the divergence within the latter came not in syntax but in vocabulary and pronunciation—variations resulting from the dispersing of people over the land.

The travelers did not have writing or an alphabet, but the absence of writing did not mean Paleolithic bands had no aids to memory. In addition to stories and songs passed from one generation to the next, memory beads; necklaces of stone, bone, and wooden objects; pictographs on birchbark or garments; and other forms of decoration helped individuals remember tribal history and allowed people to record the great events of their own lives. Petroglyphs (rock carvings), like those in the Flint Hills of central Kansas or on the cliffs just to the west of present-day Albuquerque, or rings of large stones, like those in Rhode Island or the ones recently uncovered in Miami, Florida, combined sacred messages with practical information (such as the location of a water source or an astronomical calendar). Hunters and foragers drew maps on animal skins. Shamans (native priests) fashioned stories and practiced rites to ensure that the appropriate rituals accompanied the celebration of births, the initiation of young into adulthood, the seasons of the hunt, the conduct of war, and the interment of the dead.

The importance of the shamans among the Indians reveals the crucial link between language and religion. Religious beliefs tied the natural world to the human one. The rhythms of the seasons and features of climate such as wind, rain, lightning, and the sun contained supernatural power that ritual could channel. Sacred places housed demigods who had to be propitiated. Many of the objects found in early North American hunter-gatherer sites are totemic relics of these demigods. In Utah, archaeologists have found eight-thousand-year-old clay figurines that Indians probably carried in small "medicine bags" or pouches.

These images fit into a system of "sympathetic magic" in which Indian hunters used song, dance, and other forms of incantation to entice their prey. Although Indians had no abstract conception of "nature," they recognized that natural forces tied the hunter and the prey together. Eastern woodlands Indians apologized to the animals they killed and scattered the bones of their prey back in the forest to ensure another good season of hunting. In the stories that accompanied these rituals, animals gained anthropomorphic powers, such as the ability to speak, reason, and play tricks on one another. Coyote and rabbit excelled as tricksters. Beaver was smart but quarrelsome. Bear's strength matched his unpredictability.

Evidences of religion from modern Indian groups suggest that as Indian societies became more complex, secret societies or specially chosen individuals took charge of religious rites. Perhaps these tasks passed down from father to son, or from uncle to nephew. Women performed special roles, and some gods were female. Masks and dances were important parts of seasonal religious festivals. Archaeological evidence confirms that native priests wore special costumes, often depicting themselves as animals or birds of prey. Worshippers purified themselves—for example, by ritual sweat baths or herbal hallucinogens. Dreams and hallucinatory experiences put the worshipper in touch with powerful spirit forces.

ARCHAIC WAYS

Archaeologists have found that a distinct shift in Indian lifestyles swept over the continent between 10,000 and 2500 B.P. The changes did not appear everywhere at once, nor did native peoples entirely abandon migratory hunting and gathering, but more and more among them shifted from nomadic to semisedentary lives. The term *Archaic* best denotes the new way of life, although technically it refers only to eastern Indian cultures. In the Archaic period, part-year residence in fixed settlements and the harvesting of crops fostered population growth, improved diets, and introduced more creature comforts, but it also forced Indians to grapple with novel problems.

Homes, Tools, Pots, and Animals

Paleolithic peoples constructed easily movable huts with wooden frames and animal skin or grass coverings. Archaic builders introduced "pit houses" by erecting frameworks of branches, mud, and grasses over an excavated circle in the ground. In the Southwest, timber was easier to find then than it is now (recall that the climate was cooler and wetter), but never plentiful, so wood was only used for support beams and roof cross-members. By the end of the Archaic period, southwestern home builders adopted dried mud-bricks or masoned stone to create substantial structures. Dwellings clustered in semicircles around storage areas and refuse dumps. Some of the buildings had a religious purpose. The sacred space, or kiva, in these ceremonial rooms served both public worship and meetings of secret religious societies. Eastern woodlands Indians constructed circular wigwams of branches, bark, reeds bundled as thatch, and walls of mixed mud and straw. By the end of the Archaic period, builders had progressed from small ovular houses to larger circular huts many yards in diameter or long, rectangular houses with curved roofs.

The tools and utensils of the Indians offer a second evidence of the shift from Paleolithic to Archaic culture. The sedentary way of life, and with it the growth of specialization of labor, allowed native craftspeople to increase the variety and durability of their tools and utensils. Artisans worked obsidian, mica, and shells into breastplates, combs, and other items for personal adornment. Fishing equipment became more complex, with hooks and nets of greater variety and efficiency. East Coast Indians developed the weir—a fence of brush and netting that could be strung below the surface of tidal rivers. Fish could swim upstream at high tide but were caught in the weir when the tide went out.

Even more important, Archaic peoples discovered that local clays could be soaked to remove impurities; molded by hand (the American potter did not have the wheel) into jugs, jars, bowls, and cauldrons; and then fired in ovens or over hearths to make hard pottery. The first North American pottery, found it at Stallings Island, Georgia, dates to 3500 B.P. Potters introduced glazes to seal porous clays and decorate pots, jugs, and storage vats. In the Four Corners region of Arizona, Colorado, New Mexico, and Utah, craftspeople painted on or pressed patterns into the pottery in the shape of ropelike coils or geometric figures.

Pottery vessels surpassed wood, woven, and stone containers in a variety of ways. Unlike the baskets and stoneware they replaced as cooking utensils, clay pots maintain water temperature, which allows cooks to simmer and boil foods. Archaic cooks could thus leave their cooking unattended while they did other tasks. Slow cooking turned dried grains into porridge. Pottery, properly sealed, preserved foods, cooked or uncooked. Using clay cooking utensils in sedentary camps, cooks began to experiment with recipes—adding a variety of ingredients at different times in the cooking process.

In Archaic North American settlements, dogs were the only domesticated working animal, and turkeys the only herd animal. Human hunters must have found wolf pups and adopted the most sociable and docile. Thousands of years of breeding resulted in the first North American dogs. They resembled the spitz dog family of more recent times—heavily muscled, short eared, curly tailed, and thick furred.

But why domesticate only dogs? Middle Eastern goatherds and shepherds in the time of the Hebrew Bible were contemporaries of late-Archaic Americans and had already domesticated cattle, chickens, sheep, pigs, and goats, and rode horses and camels. Perhaps the animals of America were not amenable to domestication. Or it may be that the Americans did not need to domesticate animals—why feed and care for herds when wild animals could be taken in their natural haunts? In addition, North American natives' symbiotic relationship with the animals may have precluded domestication. To tame such beasts would have been unnatural and perhaps even unthinkable.

One salubrious byproduct of their failure to domesticate a wide variety of animals was that the Americans escaped the diseases that animals like rats and mice, horses, sheep, pigs, poultry, and cattle carry. Cattle incubate measles, tuberculosis, and smallpox. Pigs are hosts to influenza and whooping cough, and sheep are notorious for the wide array of microbes they bear. Overall, humans share fifty different diseases with cattle, forty-six with sheep, forty-two with pigs, thirty-five with horses, thirty-two with rats and house mice, and twenty-six with poultry.

Old World herdsmen and farmers literally lived with their animals (and the animal feces) and died from animal-borne plagues. The first Americans suffered from dietary diseases like rickets, a form of tuberculosis, and perhaps even the ancestor of the Hanta Virus, but the dispersion of native population prevented outbreaks of disease from becoming plagues. Unfortunately, when Europeans brought all these diseases to the Americas in the sixteenth and seventeenth centuries, the natives had no resistance to them, and the resulting "virgin-ground" epidemics sometimes carried off 80 to 90 percent of the native population who came in contact with the germs.

Villages

The social and cultural life of the Archaic settlement differed from life in the Paleolithic hunting camp. Increasing density of population required complex adjustments in social and economic arrangements. Sedentary peoples must have surpluses of food, and archaeologists have found Archaic food caches and storage areas. The litter of shellfish fragments (mussel and clam shells, for example) on the Atlantic and Pacific coasts prove that Archaic sites were occupied time and again for long periods by substantial numbers of foragers. But forage and storage required more complex social organization than hunting and gathering. Some individuals and families within the group emerged as leaders. These men and women probably exercised a good deal of influence, although Archaic native chiefs did not have the kind of absolute formal power that European monarchs and princes exercised.

Increasing population also spurred more organized religious practices. Four thousand years ago, the "red ochre" Indians of Labrador, Newfoundland, and northeastern Maine fashioned large cemeteries and conducted elaborate burials. Mourners broke and laid copper, greenstone, and chert objects in the graves. At Poverty Point, Louisiana, archaeologists have found evidence of a series of Archaic Indian ridges in the shape of a circle, each ridge over twenty feet in height. This amphitheater of burial mounds was topped by houses or campsites. At ceremonial sites like the Adena burial grounds in Newark and Chillicothe, in south-central Ohio, priests and villagers remade the landscape itself to honor the dead. At either end of a road stood two enclosures, one round and the other polygonal, lined with logs and bark. The road itself, parts of which are still visible from the air, was raised above ground and pounded smooth.

The increasing population density of the sedentary way of life brought with it a political crisis. Given that the maximum human carrying load of any ecological region—the largest population that it can support—depends on what it can produce on a "bad day," the Archaic settlement had to command its surrounding territory in a way that hunter-gatherers did not. That is, a band of hunters can share a territory with other bands if the game is abundant because the two bands are small in population and because neither band can store up its take. A more densely populated society—even one that shifts its living quarters seasonally—does not have the luxury of sharing in this way: it must have surpluses.

But specialization of labor enabled villages with growing populations to turn size into a competitive advantage. Archaic settlements established castes or societies of warriors whose job included raiding enemy settlements and keeping the peace at home. The larger Archaic settlements could prey on weaker neighbors. Bands had always raided one another, but "tribute" in the form of gifts of food was the invention of Archaic Indians. Tribute allowed a densely populated group to force more ecologically balanced but smaller groups to share their wealth. Captives could be taken to replace members of the victorious band lost to accidents, disease, or warfare. Some Archaic peoples developed the system of dual leadership, a war chief and a civil or domestic leader, to manage external and internal affairs, respectively.

The Horticulture Age Begins

Seven thousand years ago, on the Mexican Plateau, Indians who regularly harvested the wild grass teosinte for its small, coblike seedpods began to plant the seeds. The growers evidently experimented with different varieties of the plant, selecting and cultivating the variants with the largest cobs. Maize (corn) was not the first crop the Indians planted, but its cultivation spread out of the Mexican Plateau north and east as migrating farmers carried its seeds. Northern farmers did not adopt corn because they immediately saw its superiority in energy yield to earlier food sources, but because they could fit its cultivation into already established harvesting cycles of wild grasses.

When people can become horticulturalists (students of Indian life prefer to call Indian food production of this era horticulture rather than agriculture because it was closer to gardening than working fields) and grow food crops instead of just pursuing or gathering their food, they can profoundly change the way they live. Horticulture fosters even greater population density than Archaic living styles because people are assured of a surplus to tide them over in starving times. Long before anyone practiced horticulture, Indians harvested crops of wild grasses and fruits, but corn culture changed every facet of Native American life.

Corn loves a moist, moderate climate, but just as the Meso-American farmers had bred larger and hardier varieties for themselves, so the farmers of the Southwest experimented with hybrids that could thrive with less water. By 2000 B.P., corn was a mainstay for the Pueblo peoples of the Southwest. By A.D. 800, corn had reached the farmers of the Mississippi River valley. It was not until a variant of the crop, "midwestern twelve row" as it is now called (the reason is obvious if one looks at an ear of it), came to the Ohio Valley and the northeast, that corn took root there. The new hybrid was resistant to frost and matured a little sooner than its southern cousins. Corn made its way into the everyday diets of southeastern and northeastern Indians by A.D. 1000, joining already domesticated varieties of beans and squash.

Corn cultivation sustained another burst of population growth in farming communities along fertile river valleys and floodplains. The introduction of corn planting led to a vast increase in the amount of acreage under the hoe. As more and more land was cleared for corn cultivation, the carrying capacity of the land increased— in turn allowing greater concentrations of population. Corn is an excellent source of complex carbohydrates; added to other crops as well as seasonal hunting and fishing, the new culture produced the first truly "balanced diet" in American history. Corn can be ground and stored, allowing a family some security against bad years. In corn-consuming regions, life expectancy must have taken another leap beyond that which marked the shift from the Paleolithic to Archaic period.

In corn-growing regions, farm families of ten to twenty individuals remained the norm, but the visible signs of a new prosperity appeared everywhere. Aboveground corncribs, larger houses with conical roofs and wickerwork paneling, and, by the beginning of the eleventh century, the appearance of towns and cities marked the rise of corn culture. The largest of these "mound cities" north of the Rio Grande would have populations in excess of forty thousand people.

But if the swiftness of the transformation of lifestyles in the new population centers changed the face of the land and the customs of the people, there were costs as well. The level and frequency of violence increased. The appearance of walled towns—for example, in Ohio River and Illinois River Hopewell settlements in the middle farming age (2500 B.P.–A.D. 500)—implied that the people outside the walls wanted something that the people inside had.

Like the Adena who preceded them, the Hopewell erected huge conical burial mounds for their leaders, part of geometrically shaped ceremonial centers featuring massive mounds and ditches. Mounds were filled with rare and precious jewelry and weapons, suggesting that the leaders' role was military. During the same period, town dwellers dug new kinds of deeper storage pits, insulated with grass or hides. But abundance had its built-in irony—the walls around the towns.

The corn culture in the settlements also introduced new distinctions based on gender. Women and men have distinct roles in hunting societies, but men's roles are dominant. Men are the primary protein providers. Women gather grains, prepare hides, cook food, and take care of the young and old. In corn culture, this balance of status shifted. Women are the planters, tenders, and harvesters of the grain. In corn-era native mythologies, corn mothers, associated with the fertility of the land, became major figures, equal to and sometimes eclipsing male spirits and heroes.

NATIVE AMERICA IN THE MIDDLE PERIOD

Spurred by the increasing efficiency of corn culture, Native American life went through a remarkable series of transformations between A.D. 1000 and 1450, an era we may call (for want of a better term) the middle period of Native American history. Despite the great dispersion of peoples, civilizations began to emerge in some areas that might, in the fullness of time, have come to rival those already established in other areas of the world. In other regions of North America, time had not moved so swiftly, and older ways still predominated.

The Southwest

In the middle period, the world of the southwestern farmers grew remarkably sophisticated. The Chaco Canyon of the Anasazi peoples (Anasazi means "ancient enemies" in the Navajo tongue, perhaps an unfortunate choice for modern scholars to adopt, for the descendants of the Anasazi are the Hopis, not the Navajos) in northwestern New Mexico offers one example of this complexity. From a central site in the canyon, where some six hundred family dwellings stood, workers built roads in all directions. Along these roads and at their ends were hamlets and satellite towns. In the canyon settlements, ceremonial centers fifty feet in diameter were covered with hundreds of roof timbers. The timbers were a huge investment in public use, for the ponderosa pines needed had to be carried down from the mountainsides.

To the south, in the Mogollon country that straddled the border between New Mexico and Mexico, walled towns similar to those of the ancient Mayan cities of Yucatan appeared. In the Mogollon centers, archaeologists have found large, rectangular enclosures for ball games, facial jewelry (for example, nose plugs and ear rings), copper bells, and musical instruments that came from as far south as the central plateau of Mexico. There were no real boundaries between Mexico and the American Southwest then—it was a single cultural region.

Throughout the territory of the Hohokam, in southern Arizona, people preferred to live in widely spaced villages rather than in densely populated towns, but farmers dug deep catchpools for rainwater and laid out over three hundred miles of irrigation ditches to tap the waters of the Gila River. When the ditches proved too shallow to prevent evaporation, the Hohokam dug canals. When the first Europeans came, in the 1540s, they found a sea of grass growing where the Hohokam had irrigated the land.

In middle-period southwestern villages, dress and the rituals of dress became more elaborate. Different styles of body adornment and hair became vital markers of tribal identity. Hairstyles were the most visible feature of adornment, for they could be seen from a distance by friend and foe. Hairstyles conveyed other information—for example, maidens wore their hair differently from matrons.

Within limitations of clan identity and availability of materials, individual dress was a matter of individual choice. Jewelry, for example, was part a matter of tribal custom and part personal—what one liked, and what one could afford. Women sported many-stranded necklaces with beads and shell ornaments. Variations in pottery design and decoration also illustrated the elaboration of distinct southwestern cultures.

Pottery demonstrated a similar individualism. Particular districts of potters shifted from organic to mineral paint as decoration sometime in the eleventh century. Anasazi potters chose gray with black paint and covered the entire surface of their work with complex geometric designs. At first, the Mogollon preferred brown ware, but by A.D. 900 potters there adopted white slip or glaze as a contrast color and later painted black-on-white designs. The Hohokam potters went further, decorating their buff-colored pottery with stylized pipe-players and dancers.

The profusion of cheap pottery meant that even the poorest southwestern native groups could decorate their dwellings and vary their diet. Of course, corn remained the staple, but it could be baked on the cob as a between-meals snack, or ground and mixed with salt and water and baked on an oiled flat rock. Finely ground corn could be dropped into boiling salted water, stirred, and then removed. The paste could then be kneaded, rolled out in between corn husks, and then boiled again. The result was a tamale.

Sophisticated corn culture enabled southwestern village peoples to improve their diets, experiment with personal adornment, and engage in trade. The development of exchange networks and communications among these settlements, like the Chaco Canyon road system, tied cities to the countryside in a mutually beneficial manner.

But in the twelfth and thirteenth centuries, the old Pueblo way of life crumbled. Athabaskan newcomers from the north and west drove homesteaders off their small farms and cut the supply lines to the city. Refugees from the frontiers fell back upon more settled areas. Increasing density in the towns led to crime, alienation, and anger as accommodating the rural immigrants, sharing existing food supplies, and watching for raiders made life more and more stressful. Perhaps the Anasazi regional centers themselves became more aggressive and waged war on one another. For whatever reason, Anasazi peoples left their mesa-top and canyon-bottom homes and rebuilt in more easily guarded cliff sides. In the twelfth century, great urban centers like the Chaco Canyon complex that had thrived for hundreds of years fell silent.

Then another blow fell. In the thirteenth century, the prevailing wet, cool weather turned dry and hot. Years of drought put new pressure on all southwestern Indians to leave their upland sites and journey once again, this time south to lands along the Rio Grande. Modern Hopi and Zuni clans claim to be descended from the old mesa and cliff dwellers, but the settlements the Spanish found (and called "pueblos") in the 1540s were nothing like the grand cities of four centuries earlier.

Eastern Woodlands

Planting corn in the eastern woodlands required that land be cleared. Native horticulturalists transformed forest into field by girdling or slashing the trees, and when they died, pulling out the roots. Fires turned underbrush into a carpet of nutrients. The basic farming tool was the hoe, and to plant their crops Indians used little models of their burial mounds. They made a small hill of soil and pressed corn seed into it. Around the corn they planted beans in vines and squash. The cornstalks held up the vines. When the soil lost its fertility in a dozen years or so, the Indians moved on, slashing and burning new fields. The old field returned to a parklike landscape of native grasses and brush, perfect for browsing animals like deer. Indeed, parkland drew the deer in mating season (and the Indian hunter arrived at the same time).

Diet among the sedentary farmers of the woodlands revolved around corn. The Apalachees of western Florida, for example, cultivated three varieties of corn, including a soft white "bread corn." With this, they mixed chestnuts, beans, or sweet potatoes and baked the bread on flat stones. Oil from hickory nuts mixed with the white corn went into nut breads. With the corn they cooked stews whose ingredients included meat, fish, and roots.

But evidence from precontact burial sites suggests that in the same years as the Anasazi were fleeing their cities, the diet of southeastern Indians was declining in quality and quantity. Conflict over land and food overtook the woodlands communities. Perhaps increasing population density had decreased the space between tribes and increased the pressure within groups of people for food and fuel.

Some Eastern woodlands Indian peoples found a solution to competition for resources and territory in confederations of villages. For example, in the 1300s or 1400s five major groups of Iroquois in New York—the Senecas, Oneidas, Onondagas, Cayugas, and Mohawks—arranged a league of friendship to end years of friction and raiding. They modeled their confederation upon the way that families who lived together in longhouses and village councils resolved disputes.

The longhouse, sometimes two hundred feet long and fifty feet wide, was home to families related by blood and marriage. As population density increased in Iroquois lands, more and more farming families moved into fortified towns, and the size of individual longhouses grew. Residents of the longhouses turned to the village council when trouble erupted. The village council, an assembly of local leaders more or less in continuous session, talked out the problem. In the village council, men and women respected for their wisdom and their moderation used the arts of persuasion to defuse enmities and quarrels.

Iroquois leaders replicated this pattern and these skills in yearly meetings of the League. At the Onondaga principal town, the leaders of the five peoples met in council and exchanged gifts, worked out disputes, and reaffirmed their mutual interests. The confederation council had no formal power over the individual tribes, just as the village elders could not order the villagers around, but the League survived because the Iroquois as a whole wanted it to survive. The alternative was a renewal of the internecine warfare that the League had quieted.

Another method to resolve conflicts over land and food in the middle-period woodlands was the creation of city-empires. The most powerful of these appeared in the broad floodplain of the American Bottom that surrounds the Mississippi River at Saint Louis. From 900 to 1250, the city-empire of Cahokia ruled satellite towns and villages for hundreds of miles around. A mound city whose central pyramid-shaped temple was hundreds of feet high, Cahokia's kings and priests exacted tribute in corn and captives. The copper gorgets and headpieces its rulers wore, representing falcons and other birds of prey, gave visual testimony to the rapaciousness of the great mound cities. Smaller versions of Cahokia materialized along the Ohio, Tennessee, Arkansas, and other eastern river bottoms. All were connected to networks of outlying villages, extracted tribute from neighboring peoples, and warred with rivals.

The rise of ceremonial and commercial centers in the river valleys of the East marked a flowering of native culture. But something happened to bring down Cahokia and its clones within two hundred years of their founding, leaving the walls to topple and the mounds to wash away. The corn supply may simply have fallen off as the land around the cities lost its fertility. Larger settlements also meant the increased use of woodlands, for wood was a source of building material, tools, weapons, and, most important, fuel. Perhaps Cahokia faced a fuel crisis as timber supplies gave out. It may be that raiders from nearby lands caused the city's rulers to invest so much of their energy and wealth in defense that the city could not survive. There is archaeological evidence to support all of these possibilities.

But some mound centers survived well into the sixteenth century, particularly in the Southeast. On the lower Mississippi and the river bottoms of Alabama and Georgia, paramount chiefs living in walled towns still ruled over scattered villages. In these mound centers one would find slaves, Indians taken in war by other Indians and incorporated within the victors' clans. Such slaves were sometimes mistreated, but never denied their humanity.

Hunter-Gatherers on the Margins of Native Life

Not all Native Americans in the middle period adopted farming. All Indians supplemented their diets with seasonal hunting, and in some regions the shift from hunter-gatherer to farmer was late in coming or never came at all. California's mild climate and natural resources supported a vast population of Indians in the middle period, but this abundance—and the mountains that crisscrossed the region—retarded development of cities and confederations of peoples. Instead, small kin groups speaking mutually unintelligible dialects scattered over the land. There is no evidence of corn cultivation.

Along the Pacific Northwest coast, the Indians, relative newcomers to America, developed a unique culture with a complex social system. Although the northwestern Indians did not practice agriculture, they were superb fishermen. They harvested salmon from the rivers and shellfish from the shore. In their fifty-man oceangoing canoes, they took cod and halibut from the seas. Skilled craftspeople took advantage of the proximity of extensive forests to build large wooden homes, totem poles, and decorative wooden tableware and furniture. Trade in wooden goods, foodstuffs, animal fiber clothing, and slaves (usually prisoners captured in war) linked villages together, although each village had its own government.

The newest of the newcomers, the Aleut peoples of Alaska, like the northern Algonquians on the Canadian plains and on the upper Northeast coast, remained hunter-gatherers. Indeed, many of the northern Algonquians were still largely hunter-gatherers in postcontact times, trading furs with the French and later the English, just as they traded the commodities of the northern hunt with Great Lakes and southern New England Indian farmers before the Europeans came.

On the prairies and the plains in the center of the continent, villages of mixed hunter-gatherers speaking dialects of Siouan and Caddoan dominated the landscape. For them, the herds of bison provided food, clothing, and housing materials. The wave of raiders who struck the Anasazi and other Pueblo peoples in the thirteenth century were the ancestors of the Apaches and Navajos. In time, the Navajos gradually adopted many Pueblo customs, including farming; the Apaches did not. When these Indian groups did not war, they traded. The Apache and Navajo dog sleds brought dressed buffalo meat and hides to the Hopis in Arizona and Zunis and Tewas in New Mexico in return for corn, textiles, and pottery vessels.

NATIVE AMERICA ON THE EVE OF CONTACT

Offering a generalized portrait of Indian culture on the eve of contact with the European explorers is artificial to this extent: The year A.D. 1492 on the Christian calendar had no special significance in native historical development. Its importance derives solely from an event over which Indians had no control, and the vast majority of Indians had no contact with Europeans until long after Columbus arrived. Yet in the fullness of time, contact did alter the lives of all Indians.

Historical demographers cannot agree on North American native population on the eve of contact. Plain guessing; multiplying known numbers (such as warriors who arrived at a conference and were counted) by some fixed ratio to produce overall population; working backward from postcontact figures to prehistoric numbers; and inflating early counts because they missed Indians who were hiding leads to figures ranging from five hundred thousand to eighteen million. Perhaps a prudent count would put twelve million people in North and South America, with the Mexican Plateau and central America the most heavily populated region. In the area of the modern United States, perhaps two million people made their homes on the eve of contact.

Mobility and Conflict

Precontact Indians traveled. The many roadways emanating from Chaco Canyon echoed with the greetings of farmers and tradespeople. Footpaths through the Appalachians were sometimes two or three feet deep and many paces wide, so often did hunters, raiders, and messengers traverse them. The "great warrior's path" led from the Iroquois lands in central New York, south through Pennsylvania, and into the Cherokee country of the Carolinas. The various smaller paths that fed this highway were marked with blazes on trees. Paths led to sacred sites and council areas as well as to major centers of population. Sometimes Indians got lost in the woods, and even when Indians traveled well-worn roads, they were aware that the woods were filled with powerful spirits that must not be disturbed.

Entire peoples were on the move in the century before contact. In the Southwest, drought set villagers and seminomads on collision courses. In the Northeast, the Iroquois moved out of Ohio and into New York. The folklore of the Creek peoples of Alabama recalls how the warriors migrated east and south along the river courses looking for suitable hunting grounds. Some followed the "red path" of war, others chose the "white path" of peace, until they fashioned a policy of peaceful incorporation of other peoples into their confederation.

In general, warfare among these people was endemic but limited. For the surviving Mississippian peoples, it might begin when a chief died and rival claimants for the position fought. Some groups—for example, the Iroquois and their neighbors—engaged in seasonal warfare. For the most part, Indian combat consisted of small-scale raids. As the English naturalist Thomas Harriot reported of the first Indians the English met, at the end of the sixteenth century, "Their manner of wars amongst themselves is either by sudden surprising one another most commonly about the dawning of the day, or moonlight, or else by ambushes, or some subtle devices. Set battles are rare." Villagers in the Great Lakes regions took turns raiding one another, as did the Choctaw and Chickasaw peoples in the Southwest.

The purpose of these confrontations was more to demonstrate one's qualities as a warrior than to control territory. As Samuel de Champlain, a French fur trader, recalled of one such Huron raid on the Mohawks at the beginning of the seventeenth century: "The [Hurons] sent two canoes . . . to learn from their enemies whether they wished to fight. . . . They said that as soon as the sun should rise, they would attack us, and to this our Indians agreed. Meanwhile, the whole night was spent in dances and songs on both sides, with many insults and other remarks." Until the Europeans arrived, rarely did such battles result in masses of casualties. Eastern Indians wore wooden armor and learned to duck or hide when their enemies launched flights of arrows. Pitched battles between western tribes like the Shoshones and Blackfeet might continue from dawn to nightfall without inflicting a dozen casualties.

But in the years between the collapse of the major Mississippian centers and the arrival of the Europeans, warfare among eastern Indian groups may have worsened. Certainly, the Mississippi region itself became a cockpit of conflict—with the ancestors of the Choctaws, Chickasaws, Creeks, and Natchez peoples engaging in an endless round of raids and retaliation. Groups of villages sought protection from one set of enemies by forming temporary military alliances and trading partnerships with neighbors, and the most successful of these became confederations, or as Europeans later called them, tribes.

In cultural terms, war was the extension of the hunt, and as in Indian hunting, the point was not to kill all the game, but to prove oneself against it. Thus guile and surprise predominated Indian tactics in raids, and manifest courage marked warriors in battle. Taking a captive or two proved a man's mettle, and when captives were taken, the victors retired from the scene. On some occasions, the victors tortured or killed and ate captives at the site of battle. More often, the winning side carried its captives home to be displayed. Some who met tests of courage and comeliness gained membership in their captors' clans. Between the raids, Indians engaged in almost continuous diplomacy with one another. At tribal councils, famous orators spoke for hours at a time, and were as highly esteemed as noted warriors. Exchanges of gifts, long speeches followed by feasting and dancing, and temporary alliances or truces were as common as warfare.

By the 1400s, Indian horticulture had reached a high level of sophistication. Their mound-and-hoe method of cultivation was kind to the land and highly productive. In addition to varieties of corn, beans, and squash, Indians bred a wide variety of melons. Seasonal crops such as berries, apples, and maple sugar added variety to the Indian diet. Tobacco, another crop almost universally cultivated by eastern woodlands Indians, from the Hurons in the North to the Apalachees in the South, provided its smokers with a mild narcotic.

Indians had learned the medicinal properties of many plants and used them to aid digestion, reduce pain and inflammation, and relieve the symptoms of breathing disorders. They also had herbal cures for snake and insect bites and dressed burns and wounds with balms and potions. Indian curing rituals had potent psychological power, for the idea was not to cure disease so much as to enable people to live in harmony with nature. "The parties that are sick or lame being brought before them," William Wood reported of New England Indians at the start of the seventeenth century, "the powwow [shaman] sitting down, the rest of the Indians giving attentive audience to his imprecations and invocations, and after the violent expression . . . of hideous bellowing and groaning, he makes a stop, and then all the auditors with one voice utter a short canto." On and on they went, the shaman bellowing and writhing, the Indians replying in chorus. Healing was a communally visible and auditory process—group primal therapy, for want of a better description.

Some Indian groups lived in communal housing, others dwelt in wigwams or wickiups that amounted to single-family homes. Few Indians opted to live outside of the village, however, for social life was vital. Indeed, for the Indians, the only truly human life was communal. Exile was the punishment Indians most dreaded. One's identity was given by kin (family) and clan or totem affiliations. Some groups might pass names through the mother's line, others through the father's line, but life was always lived in close proximity to relatives.

Indians did not write down their laws, but law speakers recited the people's customs each year at festivals and at solemn councils like those of the Iroquois. Elders met to settle disputes and to make decisions. Indians cooperated in the hunt and shared its product. Farming was also communal, the fields belonging to the entire village. Women planted, weeded, and harvested the crops, though men helped in clearing the land. Everyone shared the harvest. When there was abundance, Indians gorged themselves; in times of scarcity, everyone went hungry.

Indian religion reinforced other social activity. Clan totems and animal spirits shared the religious and social realms of Indian life, for there was no set boundary between the everyday and the otherworldly. Thus, when adventurer John Smith was taken before the chief of the Powhatan confederation, the Englishman was treated to a communal performance of the Indians' cosmology. Dancers and singers, he recalled, were "painted ugly as the devil, howling" as they laid down rows of corn and bunches of sticks, then drank and feasted. It was the relationship between the visible and the hidden powers in nature that mattered to the shamans, and their dancing and singing tied the story to the past and the future, to nature and the people.

But the pressures of the last two centuries before contact gave rise to new religious cults. In the Southwest, for example, the kachina cult swept through the pueblos. The kachinas were nature spirits of immense power who acted as intermediaries between the people and the seven principal deities, including the gods of life, death, and the sun. Men, boys, and girls, dressed in costumes and masks, impersonated the kachinas during ceremonial dances and parades at various times of the year.

In the mound societies of the Mississippi, Tennessee, and Arkansas valleys, another cult appeared, perhaps influenced (like the mound culture itself) by Mexican Indian belief systems. In this so-called southern cult, priest-kings ruled over well-defined social hierarchies and presided over temples serviced by large numbers of attendants. New religious motifs, including the human eye, flying wings, crosses, and sunbursts, appeared on decorative pieces as well as on war axes and maces. The new cult, strongly resembling certain portions of Aztec worship, focused on the trophies of war (including severed heads) and death.

Gendered roles marked every aspect of Indian community. Men hunted, and women gardened. When the men were away, the women had charge of the village. Men's songs were those of the hunt; women sang and danced to the corn gods. In all Indian societies, women reared the children. Fathers were not disciplinarians; correction, usually gentle and persistent, was generally left to mothers, aunts, and grandmothers. Women were also in charge of childbirth, sometimes going off by themselves to bear the child, more often sharing the travail with women kinfolk. Some Indian groups, notably the Cherokee and the Iroquois, gave political power to women. Others, like the Creek confederation, tended to be less likely to give women positions of authority.

———————

This, then, was the Indians' world on the eve of contact. The pace of change had accelerated, and as population in some regions began to approach the carrying capacity of the land, there were scarcities and conflicts for essential resources. Powerful post-Mississippian confederacies emerged to control trade routes and food supplies. Weaker neighbors submitted themselves to the yoke of the powerful or risked ruinous war. Indian elders must have wondered what the world was coming to, now that aggression replaced honored traditions of reciprocity.

Yet for Indian culture as a whole, the long course of adaptation to the deep rhythms of nature still gave life its strength and shape. The landscape itself reminded Indians of their obligations to the old ways. The sacred places that Indians chose as their shrines—for example, the four sacred mountains that Navajos believed held up the sky—embodied the qualities of resiliency and permanence. The sacred shapes that Indians carved on cliff sides and rock outcroppings taught messages of harmony and fidelity to old usages. The purpose of communal worship services like the snake dance was mastery of the forces of change. The esteem that Indians accorded their elders reinforced this preference for tradition over novelty.

When opportunity beckoned, like arrival of the corn plant, Indians made room in their cosmology for new demigods and in their fields for new crops, but the Native Americans rarely innovated for the sake of innovation, and nothing in their culture prompted them to abstract theorizing or radical experimentation.

Thus when war erupted between villages or peoples, tradition and religious beliefs controlled the use of violence. The aggressiveness of some peoples might restructure power relationships in large regions, and the raids of other groups might force settlements to uproot themselves and seek shelter, but the winners preferred to subjugate the losers, and the losers put themselves under the protection of the winners. Custom and wise counsel limited the damage that the winners inflicted on the losers.

One may say, then, that tradition and traditionalism in Indian life kept a balance between aggressiveness and aggrandizement, on the one hand, and reciprocity and hospitality, on the other. This balance, along with the traditions sustaining it, would be destroyed when Europeans arrived. To understand how and why, we must turn to the powerful historical currents transforming Europe on the eve of its contact with America.

2

Europe in the Age of Discovery, 1400–1500

In the cabin boy's ditty calling the ship's officers to their meal, one can hear all the sirens that lured fifteenth-century Europeans to seek adventure, wealth, and salvation in far-off places. Appetite, patriotism, technology, pride, and faith in God beckoned the mariners to sea, beguiled the merchants into underwriting the voyages, and bedazzled the ruling houses of Europe with dreams of foreign treasures. But the fact that Europeans reached out to explore the far corners of the globe at the end of the fifteenth century does not mean that they had intended such bold steps at the beginning of the century, or that they had at hand a ready rationale for their daring. In fact, they hadn't.

At the start of the century, Europeans were self-satisfied—one might even say smug—in their belief in the superiority of the Christian faith, the authority of "classical" Greek and Roman philosophy, and the inferiority of all other peoples. From the aristocrats at the top of European society to the peasants at the bottom, everyone agreed that God had created a "great chain of being," a living pyramid with Europe's nobility at the apex and the mass of common toilers at the base. Contemporary men of learning, surrounded by their libraries of religious and classical works and insulated from novelty by their conservative educational traditions, never suspected that two great continents lay to the west of Europe, or that European encyclopedias of animals and plants and histories of the "known world" were woefully incomplete. Thus one must be careful not to regard the momentous events and ideas that unfold in this chapter as though they were the "prelude" to, or the "preconditions" of, the era of colonization that followed.

Yet a series of closely linked transformations in European economic, intellectual, military, and political life was paving the way for the explorations. A revolution in tastes and the patterns of consumption led merchants to seek cheaper sources of goods. A rebirth of interest in humane studies and technological innovation enabled Euro-

Table, table, sir captain and master and good company, table ready; meat ready. . . . Long Live the King of Castile by land and sea! Who say to him war; off with his head; who won't say amen, gets nothing to drink. Table is set, who don't come wont eat.
—Chant of a Spanish ship's boy, calling the officers to dinner (ca. 1490)

peans to map out exploration of foreign lands. At the same time, the flow of information pouring into Europe from other places upset the Europeans' neat and logical scheme of ideas. Novelties of diet, dress, and customs from Asia and Africa sparked widespread interest. As hard as European thinkers and leaders worked to tailor these discoveries to fit into classical or Christian intellectual jackets, the sheer volume of the new facts challenged time-honored concepts and threatened to burst old views of the world at the seams. The growing scale and depersonalization of war and the accompanying rise of the nation-state to pay for the new kind of war provided the organization and skills for overseas adventures. And the mariners of two of these nations, Portugal and Spain, carried out the initial reconnaissances.

Europe's turn to the west benefited kings, merchants, men of letters, scientists, investors, and consumers. However, the Age of Discovery, as this era of European history is often termed, had its victims as well as its beneficiaries. The mariners and pilots who simply vanished from the seas, the men and women who lost all in overseas scams and get-rich-quick speculations, and the Africans who provided involuntary labor for Europe's gain all represent the other side of the equation of Europe's triumphant expansion.

THE REVOLUTION IN TASTE

Today the word *taste* has two meanings: (1) the reaction of the glands in the palate to food or any soluble substance, and (2) a measure of aesthetic or artistic discernment. In the Age of Discovery, Europeans' tastes changed in both senses of the word. First, gustatory perception changed markedly, and food and food preparation gained new importance. Pepper and other spices from islands in the Indian Ocean camouflaged the taste of aging meat. Refined sugar crystals from sugarcane turned sour breads into sweet cakes. Wealthy Europeans demanded the condiments necessary for the new menu and willingly spent whatever it cost to put spices and sweets on the table. With the growing sophistication of the palate arrived a revolutionary new concept of "good taste," focusing the attention of the upper classes, and then the middle classes, on worldly possessions, humanistic studies, artistic embellishment, and technological improvement.

Appetite

At first, the word *appetite* had nothing to do with the palate. Instead, it denoted one's inclinations or predispositions. In the Christian West, such inclinations revolved around piety and self-denial. But in the fifteenth century, appetite gained a new, more worldly meaning that stuck: hunger for food. In the Middle Ages (1000–1400), the consumption of food had religious implications. Charity often consisted of giving away or sharing food. Fasting—that is, denying oneself food—emptied the body of vile matter and made space for true faith. Gluttony could cost one the kingdom of heaven and was believed to lead to other sins, like sexual excess.

But after the Crusades that the Christian princes waged against the Muslims for control of Jerusalem (1095–1291) reopened the Mediterranean trade routes, Europeans developed a taste for fine foods. Feasting had long occupied an important place in the cultural life of the wealthy; now it became more elaborate. In some aristocratic houses, on feast days, meals stretched through twelve and thirteen courses. Servants laid out banquets on boards stretched across trestles in the great hall of the house. Favorite recipes featured spices like pepper, cinnamon, cloves, nutmeg, ginger, and saffron, all of which had to be imported, but sugar became the essential ingredient in almost all recipes. Sugarcane, an Asian plant whose sap could be boiled and then cooled into crystals, became a staple of every course, and was celebrated in poetry and song as a little bit of heaven on earth.

Inspired by the new dishes, Europeans rethought the meaning of taste. The upper classes set the pace. With the emphasis on food tasting good came the requirement that food look good and be served elegantly. Thus individual place settings and eating utensils replaced shared bowls and spoons, and the bench gave way to individual chairs. The trestle boards table became a dinner table, and food service moved from the drafty, dark central hall of the house to a dining room. Elegant dining required new styles of architecture, with larger windows. Dining rooms thus had an open, airy, clean appearance.

The table itself had to be "dressed" with a clean, smooth white cloth. Civility required that one should not eat in a fashion that annoyed others at the table. Hosts who set a "good table" frowned on gluttony, objected to diners spitting food on the table, and banished servants and children to another room to eat. Books of manners warned gentlemen not to wipe their hands on the bread. Good cooking became an art form, and people began to train as master chefs.

The revolution in the procurement and consumption of sugar, spices, and other condiments went hand in hand with the growth of other consumer industries and dictated a far-reaching shift in commercial priorities. The cultivation of the culinary arts was only one part of an awakening to fine clothing and decorative furniture. Wealthy Europeans fell in love with carpets and sofas, damask tablecloths, and velvet draperies. The clothing chest, once a simple, heavy wooden container, became as elegant as the garb it now housed, with polished inlays of rare woods and enameled tiles.

Cooking with spices, like decorating with fine fabrics and displaying expensive furniture, was conspicuous consumption, meant to show one's wealth. The aroma of imported spices, like the sheen of imported silks, betokened high social station— or at least the aspiration for high station.

But the brute fact remained that sugar, spices, and other creature comforts were expensive. All were Asian or Middle Eastern in origin, and the European consumer had to pay a middleman to deliver the goods. The middlemen had high overhead costs as well: storage prices and loss of cargoes from storms at sea, bandits on land, and spoilage. Nevertheless, importers and merchants made enough profit to build mansions and endow libraries, as well as to pay for a boom in fine art, higher learning, and city beautification. This investment of the profits of the spice trade led to the enrichment of cities and the growth of a service cadre of merchants, bankers, lawyers, accountants, and artisans—a "middle class" between the nobility and the peasants.

The Middle Classes and the City

The small but growing and aggressive coterie of lawyers, bankers, merchants, accountants, and successful master craftspeople of all types envied the luxuries that the nobility enjoyed and, gaining wealth from the rise of commerce, began to afford the luxuries of tablecloths and clothing chests. In law, this middle class was part of an omnibus "third estate" (the first two estates were the nobility and the clergy), but in fact the wealthy commoners had broken away from the mass of rural peasants and urban laborers. Self-conscious about its status and calculating in its outlook and daily pursuits, the new middle class exerted more influence than its sheer size would suggest. It provided the skills and human capital behind the growth of European economic activity.

The middle class gathered in towns and cities and demanded from princes the privileges governing the city, holding councils and courts, and passing local ordinances on wages, prices, and taxation. Over time, the city changed from the home of these merchants and professionals to their pride and joy. Indeed, the names finally given to the rising middle class, *burghers* and *bourgeoisie*, mean "city dwellers."

Transformed by the profits of the merchants, bankers, and their peers, rustic castle towns became busy market centers, and port cities evolved into the nodes of an international network of commerce. Cities were still small by modern standards. The largest city in Europe in 1500 was probably Naples, with 200,000 people. Venice had 100,000, as did Milan. Florence had 70,000; London, 60,000; Paris, 150,000. Cologne, on the Rhine, had 40,000. In Spain, the cities of Burgos, Toledo, and Seville each contained 50,000 people; Salamanca had 100,000 and Lisbon, 40,000. In the Low Countries (modern Belgium, the Netherlands, and Luxembourg), Leiden, Amsterdam, and Haarlem barely exceeded 10,000, though they were growing swiftly.

Most market activities, whether in the city or at a market fair, still involved barter (the exchange of goods and services for other goods and services), but in the course of the fifteenth century a new kind of economy gained preeminence. In ports in the Low Countries, along the North Sea coast, and at the heads of the Adriatic and Aegean seas, businesspeople needed credit to carry on overseas trade and money to pay their debts.

Banks, usually family run or partnerships, provided credit. But banks not only lent to merchants, they took the merchants' repayment (with its interest) and loaned money to other businesses. Credit also required written evidence of indebtedness— that is, some tangible proof of promise to pay. Banks sponsored a monetary economy that flourished alongside traditional bartered exchanges. The loans and investments created a new kind of paper wealth, the forerunner of the modern bank check and stocks and bonds. Commercial paper was based not on land or its products, but on the promise to pay debts and the faith that the economy would grow.

Behind the network of credit and debt was the lenders' and the borrowers' furious business activity—visible personal evidence that loans would be repaid and investments would bear fruit. The more time businesspeople gave to their businesses, the more moral value they assigned to the attributes of success in business. In the end, merchants and bankers not only came to believe that greater investment of effort, time, and efficiency would improve their competitive place in the market, but that the drive for profits constituted a moral good in itself. This was the message of a new ideology that modern scholars call capitalism.

Capitalism is an economic system, a way of conceiving and explaining economic activity, and a comprehensive faith. As a system, it requires private ownership of property, a network of financial institutions to provide credit—the "capital" for investment—and a commitment to reinvest substantial amounts of profit back into the business. Fifteenth-century commerce exhibited these traits.

Counting

Until the fifteenth century, most of Europe's businesspeople kept their books in sloppy fashion. No one needed mathematics. Rarely did assets and debits exactly balance in the ledgers. Qualities of goods were specified, but measurements of price, distance, and weight were approximated. But at the same time as the clock began to render the hours of the day into precise, unchanging units of time, merchants began to organize their businesses differently. The double-entry system of bookkeeping, developed in the mid-1300s in Italy, listed assets and liabilities on different pages or opposite sides of ruled columns, and enabled merchants to calculate the profit and loss precisely.

The account book and double-entry bookkeeping spurred a surge in mathematical literacy. Mathematics was an old subject in 1400, but most people, including businesspeople, had little use for it. However, European mathematicians had already obtained from the Arabs a numbering system that facilitated computation, with zero as a place keeper. Numbers and numbering became objects of fascination in themselves as Europeans began to study mathematics as well as apply it. Some innovations came slowly—the first European text reference to the plus, minus, and equal signs occurred in 1485, in Germany, and the decimal point was first used in 1585. Trigonometry was first proposed in the early seventeenth century, and probability theory arrived a few years later. Still, even the application of simple mathematics transformed business practices.

Businesspeople were not the only beneficiaries of the rise in mathematical skills. The next most obvious application of the new mathematics was in navigation, a fact that maritime powers like the Italian city-states immediately recognized. The first chair of mathematics, created in Venice, had as its stated purpose the advancement of navigation. Mathematics soon went everywhere, from the study of the smallest motions of objects to the recomputation of the size of the solar system; from new notational systems that made musical tempo uniform and precise to exact calculation of architectural proportions.

Abstraction and Worldliness

The intellectual curiosity behind the rage for measurement went hand in hand with renewed interest in philosophical inquiry. By 1400, Europeans had recovered many works of classical Greek and Roman thinkers long lost to the West. These humane works on politics, medicine, and history opened a world of liberal learning to European scholars and their students. As teacher Pier Paolo Vergerio of Padua wrote in 1403: "In [the classics] we see unfolded before us vast stores of knowledge, for our delight, it may be, or for our inspiration. In them are contained the records of the great achievements of men; the wonders of nature; the works of providence in the past, the key to her secrets of the future."

Classical studies became a mainstay of university curriculum. Rhetoric, in particular, taught students how to flatter, insinuate, inspire, and command the support of others. (Law, it may be noted, was a subcategory of rhetoric.) If most humanistic education still relied on rote memorization of a handful of texts, and if even the best humanistic scholars lacked all the tools needed to penetrate the veil of antiquity, humanism still focused the student's attention on human deeds and motives.

Humanism contributed to a rebirth, or Renaissance, of high culture—including architecture, literature, painting, and music—that took hold in the fifteenth-century cities of Italy and eventually spread to the rest of Europe. Renaissance humanism's stress on the importance of human action made the secular and material sphere as important as the spiritual and divine world. Ornate urban mansions took their place alongside cathedrals as objects of civic pride. Heroic romances featuring chases and rescues joined religious devotionals on the shelves of the educated person's library. Musicians experimented with the *ars nova* (new art) style of composition, featuring chords and integration of music and lyrics. Religious motifs and themes remained important in the new style, but its practitioners and audience spilled out from the church into the concert hall.

Secular concerns and material values permeated this new worldview. In northern Europe, wealthy merchants commissioned portraits of themselves and their families that featured everyday objects such as coins, account books, and expensive art pieces.

In Italy, the flat, intensely pious Christian painting of the late Middle Ages became more worldly, and at times downright voluptuous. In the new art, the human form was not only prominently and accurately displayed, it was celebrated even in sacred works such as Michelangelo Buonarroti's depiction of Creation on the ceiling of the Sistine Chapel in the Palace of the Vatican in Rome. The nude reemerged as a popular subject, and artists used the nude form to introduce themes of sensuality into their work. Whether portrayed in classical poses or contemporary dress, women became objects of beauty.

In similar fashion, the Renaissance reformatted courtly behavior. The self-effacing medieval knight gave way to the gaudy, arrogant courtier in books of advice and manuals of conduct, such as the *Book of the Courtier*, by the Italian diplomat Count Balthazar Castiglione. Counseled by Castiglione, the would-be courtier flattered the prince and anticipated his every whim. By subterfuge and dissimulation, the most cunning would rise to the top. Nothing could have been more worldly, indeed, cynical, than Castiglione's message, but Castiglione was less a cynic than a realist. He merely reported what he believed worked.

Technology

The calculating, individualistic, materialistic angle of vision that characterized much of Renaissance thinking gave new prominence to technology and science. During the Middle Ages, Europe had been a relative backwater in technology, but an invention in the middle of the fifteenth century enabled Europeans to end their inferiority. Johann Gutenberg's introduction of movable type led to the development of plate printing in the 1450s. Printing allowed faster, broader, and more accurate dissemination of information than had hand-copying manuscripts. Within two decades, printing had spread to cities from London in the West to Budapest in the East.

The new technology created a demand for more books. In Valencia, Spain, between 1500 and 1550 the average doctor's library grew from twenty-six to sixty-two books; the lawyer's from twenty-five to fifty-five; and the merchant's from four to ten. Similar growth in book ownership occurred in England and France. Books elevated the importance of accurate depiction and forced authors to think about logic, evidence, and precision. Printers pioneered new kinds of illustrations such as the cutaway view, the cross section, and the see-through view to show what words alone could never fully describe.

Although the most popular sellers remained religious tracts and meditations, another standard-bearer of the printing trade was the how-to book. These manuals diffused new ideas about everything from turning coal into coke and smelting metals to mastering the new arithmetic. Utilizing the technology depicted in these books, manufacturers were able to provide consumers with everything from more efficient plows to better and cheaper nails. The technical literature also included tracts on architecture and engineering—the practical sciences. Engineers could thus share information on hydraulic pumps (making the dikes of the Low Countries much more secure), canals (facilitating commerce between rivers and from cities to the sea), and textile production (permitting manufacturers to multiply their productivity). The machine age had begun.

Beginning in the late fifteenth century, Europe surged ahead of the rest of the world in the practical application of science and technology. One must use the latter terms with care, because Renaissance experimenters did not draw a clear distinction between alchemy and chemistry, or between astrology and astronomy. Men like Leonardo da Vinci of Florence were as interested in the occult as in science. What is more, invention and discovery came piecemeal, conception running far ahead of practical realization. For all the inventions that da Vinci, for example, drew in his notebooks, including submarines, airplanes, and war machines, not one saw the light of day for hundreds of years. Still, da Vinci's drawings illustrate not only the genius and foresight of one man, but the boldness of spirit that accompanied this age of technological advance. If the ideal of scientific objectivity was not yet enthroned—that would come hundreds of years later—the revived interest in science and technology bade Europeans dare to know more.

But western European humanism, the Renaissance passion for learning, and technological advances had a hard-edged arrogance that would impose a heavy cost on non-Europeans. Schooled Europeans traveling in the non-European world assumed that Renaissance humanistic culture was inherently superior to all local, native cultures. If natives could not read and write their own language (much less Latin, Greek, and contemporary European languages that the educated Renaissance courtier-explorer had mastered), the native must be inferior to the European.

Humanists divided into two schools over the question of how to handle the supposed inferiority of nonliterate native populations. One school of thought was that nature or God had permanently handicapped the ignorant locals. In other words, they were less than human. Thus they must be displaced and their land given to nature's and God's favorites—the Europeans. The other school assumed that human nature was everywhere the same, and that God wanted the Europeans to "civilize" the natives. Civilizing meant replacing native culture with European religion, language, and custom. The natives could then retain their lands under the tutelage of benevolent European "fathers." Either way, European humanism lent itself to intolerance and condescension.

A NEW KIND OF WAR LEADS TO THE RISE OF THE NATION-STATE

Europe may have been united by the revolution in taste and the rise of Renaissance humanism and its mechanistic handmaidens, but it was a profound change in the nature of warfare between 1400 and 1500 that actually started Europe on its program of overseas conquest. This is not surprising, for in the Middle Ages, European society was organized along military lines. A warrior mentality dictated the main themes of European culture, and in some deeper sense, war enabled men-at-arms to see beyond local identities and take pride in something called "Europe."

The essence of the feudal system that replaced Roman imperial institutions between 500 and 1000 was homage. Every warrior was someone else's vassal, loyal in peacetime and ready to serve in war. Society resembled an army, and personal allegiance and duty held communities together. The senior officers became the nobility. Mounted knights and foot soldiers obeyed their lords, and nobles rewarded vassals with land. Paying money for service was dishonorable, and in any event money was scarce. Over the course of the Middle Ages, time encrusted essentially military arrangements with a patina of civility, and knights gained courtly duties. A code of chivalry curbed the conduct of violent men in a violent age and dictated relations between men and women.

Because of the militarization of European society under feudalism, women had a lower status in medieval Europe than they had attained in the Roman Empire. With a few notable exceptions like France's Joan of Arc, women did not lead troops into battle or fight as soldiers or sailors. Christian teachings opened the kingdom of heaven to women, and notable women led noble families, directed religious orders, and became saints. But men directed almost all secular and religious institutions. In marriage, the wife was the subordinate partner.

A New Kind of War

Warfare in the Middle Ages involved relatively small formations of troops and often turned on the combat of a relatively small number of highly skilled mounted warriors against one another. But by the 1400s, warfare had profoundly changed. The chief cause of the shift was the widespread introduction of gunpowder-powered firearms and cannons. Individual skill, with its accompanying expressions of chivalric honor, became less important than the ability to maneuver large numbers of men into a position where they could deliver gunfire and artillery fire most effectively. One's family lineage and former achievements in tournaments or on the field of battle no longer mattered, not when any peasant could be trained to shoot down the most distinguished knight. Indeed, even accuracy was not necessary if a sufficiently large number of men fired at the target simultaneously.

In the smoke and noise of the new kind of warfare, chivalry did not die; it simply no longer applied to the professional fighting man. Some princes and cities developed a contract system for their armed forces, replacing the feudal knights and men at arms with mercenary troops who fought for a living. Under their influence, fighting became a deadly but lucrative business.

An armaments race spurred the development of new tactics. More and more wealth was invested in armaments industries. The weight and range of projectiles grew, and the caliber of weapons increased apace. Iron ordnance replaced stone balls. Gunpowder was improved as well. Most warfare on land revolved around sieges of heavily fortified positions. The better the siege gun, the faster the siege, commanders realized. Military designers responded by building walls within walls and developing fortifications that exposed attacking forces to artillery crossfire.

Cannon mounted on ships made naval warfare even more sanguinary than land combat, and ships were redesigned to utilize the cannons and small arms carried on board. Gun ports were cut above the waterline and sealed with waterproof doors. Decks were rearranged to facilitate the running out and pulling back of the cannons, and "castles" were built fore and aft to shelter sharpshooters firing down upon the enemy's decks.

On land, large-scale infantry combat was less common than sieges, but new military formations of harquebusiers (a heavy early firearm), and later musketeers, protected by infantry with pikes (spears on poles), replaced archers and heavy cavalry in the field. The Spanish mastered these new tactics, making the Spanish army the most formidable in Europe. What was more, the Spanish formations outnumbered their enemies—a vital advantage in the new tactics. By the middle of the sixteenth century, Spanish armies in the field numbered over 150,000 men, unheard of figures but fifty years earlier.

However, no military innovation went without a countermeasure for long. Late in the century, the Dutch under Prince Maurice of Nassau introduced even greater regimentation to infantry tactics. Maurice's soldiers drilled every day in marching and countermarching and in loading and firing their weapons on command. Christian and Muslim combatants made the Mediterranean the scene of ferocious sea battles.

A Continuous State of War

The new style of war, with its larger and more ferocious armies, ravaged the countryside of Europe. Borders became little more than no-man's lands through which armies moved to attack one another. Powerful kings, such as Henry V of England at the beginning of the fifteenth century and Charles VIII of France at the end of the fifteenth century, had no hesitation about claiming rights to cities or territories in foreign lands and backing up those claims with masses of troops. The Italian city-states of Milan, Venice, and Florence carried on a three-cornered war. The Swiss fought vicious battles against the forces of Bourgogne (a semiautonomous region in what is now France), then joined in the wars raging in Italy. The Swedes and the Danes fought a running war for control of the Swedish throne. Everyone in Europe sent troops to fight in the war against the Turks.

When not attacking neighbors, Europeans rose in civil insurrections against their rulers. In England, the Wars of the Roses (1455–1485) pitted two aristocratic houses, York and Lancaster, against one another. The struggle ended when Henry Tudor defeated the last of the Yorkist kings, Richard III, at the battle of Bosworth Field in 1485. In 1457, a civil war in Sweden removed Charles VIII from the throne. In 1462, the Austrians engaged in a civil conflict that divided loyalties between rival claimants to the office of Holy Roman Emperor, and interrupted Austria's long-running war against the Turks. The city-states of Italy were hotbeds of intrigue and faction. On one notorious occasion, dissidents assassinated the rulers of Florence while they attended mass in a cathedral.

Diplomats hastened all over Europe, not to prevent war but to ensure its favorable outcome through duplicity and betrayal. For example, Charles VIII of France protected his flanks by entering into treaties with Emperor Maximilian of Germany and the monarchs of Spain and England before France invaded Italy in 1494. The next year, seeing how well the French had progressed, Maximilian and the rulers of Spain simply switched sides and entered into a league against the French. In these days of well-practiced perfidy, the surest guarantee of amity was not a treaty but a bribe. Thus Charles VIII bribed Henry VII of England to stay out of French affairs while Charles was off campaigning in Italy.

The Cost of Warfare and the Rise of Nation-States

Constant warfare of the new sort was appallingly expensive. For example, before the new era, the cost of keeping an English soldier in the field had rarely exceeded two shillings a day, but between 1382 and 1388 the English spent £1,800 just for the purchase of eighty-seven siege guns.

As the cost of warfare skyrocketed, rulers found it difficult to foot the bill. The most efficient way to raise money was to tax one's subjects, and rulers introduced all manner of novelties to finance their campaigns. They allowed former vassals to buy their way out of military service, taxed hearths and herds of sheep, levied customs duties and sales taxes, demanded "free gifts" from their nobles, and charged fees for city councils to hold court and for merchants to mount fairs. The English crown invented the "subsidy," a precursor to the income tax. When revenues from the subsidy fell short of needs, the kings taxed the property of churches. French kings sold titles of nobility to wealthy commoners to raise money. Other princes "farmed out" the right to collect taxes to private individuals who prepaid a portion of the tax, then used whatever methods necessary to collect the rest of the tax for themselves. The danger of relying on taxation as a source of income was the restiveness of the taxpayers. Henry VIII of England's misnamed "Amicable Grant" so raised the hackles of cloth workers and London merchants that they protested directly to him. He ended the collections.

Princes also borrowed money to pay for their wars. The moneylenders could make a good profit on these loans, for they were exempt from the legal ban on usury (lending money at high interest rates). But princes had greater financial needs than individual lenders could satisfy and had to turn to banks. Repaying the loans was not easy, and rulers found themselves mired in debt.

The Emergence of the Central State

Falling deeper and deeper into debt, rulers of kingdoms such as England, France, and Spain looked to a more comprehensive answer to the ever-increasing costs of waging war. They began to consolidate and centralize their governments. No longer entirely dependent upon the military services the knights and their men-at-arms provided, princes consolidated their own power at the expense of the nobility.

King Henry VII of England, for example, forbade nobles to go about the countryside with armed bands dressed "in livery"—the colors and coats of arms of their houses. In France, Francis I kept the nobles busy fighting in wars, and when they died without heirs, he took their lands and made them part of his domain. The same centralizing tendencies marked government in smaller dukedoms and city-states, such as Florence and Venice in Italy and Geneva in Switzerland. In such states, hereditary or elective chief magistrates cooperated with leading families and wealthy citizens, periodically assembled in parliaments or councils, to raise funds for armies and navies.

To aid in this effort to raise funds, leaders expanded the administrative apparatus of the state. The clerks and judges of the Middle Ages had been clerics or nobles. In the fifteenth-century state, however, the bureaucrats (the word is French and came into fashion in the seventeenth century) sometimes came from the ranks of the educated clergy, but just as often from the lesser nobility, merchants, and others with middle-class backgrounds. Academics, doctors, merchants' sons, and, above all, lawyers became the backbone of the new officialdom. They were the king's tax collectors and accountants, his legal pleaders and his judges, his advisers and his lawmakers.

The Idea of the State

The consolidation of the state to enable it to wage war effectively, collect taxes, and administer the law posed an old problem in new guise: what right had kings to assume so much power over their subjects? Throughout the fifteenth century, spokesmen for the monarchs had to develop a more powerful justification for royal authority than military ability, for kings were doing more with that authority. The justification the kings' lawyers and judges formulated rested upon the doctrine of the divine right of kings, under which kings ruled not because they were the ablest leaders in war, but because God had selected them. In turn, they were responsible only to God. Resistance to kings was always wrong.

The most thoroughgoing explication of the evolving doctrine came after the consolidation of royal power. In 1576, French jurist Jean Bodin published a carefully reasoned case for placing absolute power in the hands of the king. His *Six livres de la république* (*Six Books of the Commonwealth*) argued that only an all-powerful monarch could suppress localism, end religious and civil warfare, and improve the lot of the people.

As princes claimed more power, opponents constructed a variety of theories that justified opposition to unjust rulers. Most of these ideas were not new, but pieced together older notions of liberty and self-government. The most articulate version of this defense of liberty appeared in Italian city-states such as Florence. There, at the beginning of the fifteenth century, men like the lawyer and civil administrator Caluccio Salutati argued that a truly healthy polity must rest upon liberty instead of coercion. Talent rather than lineage, and civic virtue rather than might, would ensure the longevity of the state.

The Florentine Republic was unusual, even in Italy, where most of the cities had princes, but even when the republic toppled, its intellectuals, such as the former magistrate Niccolò Machiavelli, defended liberty. In 1517, Machiavelli composed a treatise called Il principe (The Prince), in which he described how princes could acquire and maintain political power. His motives in so doing were so obscure that many of his readers thought he was pandering to the ruling class, when in fact he was drawing upon older republican ideas to promote disinterested and virtuous self-restraint in government.

Another theory that justified resistance to the tyranny of princes in this era came from religious writers. They developed the notion that rulers should not be able to coerce their subjects in matters of conscience, particularly when the king or prince was in conflict with the church.

Thomas More, a London lawyer who served King Henry VIII of England in a series of high-ranking posts, explored many of these themes in his essay Utopia (1516). More opposed war and the dispossession of poor people from their lands by the rich. Literally meaning "nowhere," Utopia was the ideal state, where no poverty and misery existed. The key to human happiness there lay in strict morality, full employment, and enlightened magistrates.

In later years, theologians like the Spanish Jesuit Francisco Suárez preached that men were equal before God and that kings' authority came not from God, but from the consent of men. Suárez was not naive—he admitted that kingdoms rose and even prospered through tyranny—but in such cases "the ruler cannot be said to possess any genuine legislative authority." In such situations, it was lawful "for the community to make use of its natural power to defend itself."

Whether praised or denounced, the new armies and the new state left their impress everywhere. The devastation of the princes' wars and the burden of their debts victimized both the highborn and the lowly peasant. Scarcity and disease marked the battle zones. The new bureaucracy might resolve disputes and collect taxes more efficiently, but justice and fairness were not the goal.

Only in Portugal and Spain, the former isolated from European dynastic wars and the latter finally unified by a dynastic marriage, did princes make full use of their new powers to attempt a solution to the endless cycle of conflict and indebtedness. Sadly, their efforts only widened the sphere of suffering.

THE AGE OF DISCOVERY

The transformation of war and politics was a general phenomenon in Europe, but the initial exploration and colonization of the Americas was the work of a small number of western European states, two of which, Portugal and Spain, led the way. These maritime powers' geographical proximity to the Atlantic Ocean afforded an initial advantage in pursuing seaborne trade. The maritime states were already home to large fishing fleets, whose sailors provided a skilled labor pool for maritime ventures. In cities like Lisbon and Seville, merchant communities financed the venture, but the monarchs saw political and religious advantage as well as riches in voyages of discovery.

Portugal and Spain

At the beginning of the Age of Discovery, Portugal was a small kingdom on the Atlantic edge of the Iberian Peninsula. In 1383, the peasants had risen against their overlords, the townspeople joined the rebellion, and quiet did not come until the Parliament named John of Avis as King John I. With his reign began a remarkable Portuguese thrust into the Atlantic. The port cities of Lisbon and Oporto practiced a policy of toleration of religious differences, which attracted Jews and Muslims, joining Celts, Iberians, and Italians—a rich pool of talent and enterprise.

John's sons, Peter and Henry, worked with their father to further Portugal's commercial interest. Peter founded a school for navigators, but Henry "the Navigator" has rightly received the lion's share of credit for the Atlantic enterprise. Portugal had long coveted the gold mines of West Africa, and Henry's campaigns in North Africa convinced him that the sea route to the Gold Coast would bring riches to Portugal. He and his father and brother commissioned mapmakers, ship designers, and expeditions to the West African shore in the first half of the fifteenth century. For the rest of the century, Alfonso V and his son, John II, continued the enterprise. When the rulers of China shut down the land route to the spices in 1453, Alfonso pushed his pilots even harder to find a waterway to the Spice Islands.

Spain was Portugal's rival on the Iberian Peninsula, but Spain was disunited in 1400. Of the regions of the Iberian Peninsula in the fifteenth century, which included Aragon, Castile, Granada, Navarre, and Portugal, Castile was the largest, with five million people, but its economy was backward, its attitude provincial, and its ways doggedly conservative. The model Castilian—an uncompromising and ferocious Christian warrior—was drawn from the long war that Castile had waged to recapture the peninsula from the North African Moors. Navarre, in the Pyrenees, was sparsely populated. Granada, in the South, was rich in resources but remained in the clutches of the Moors. The Aragonese, in a union with the Catalans on the northern Mediterranean coast, had built an international trading empire with Barcelona as its heart, but disease and depression at the start of the fifteenth century had led to civil wars.

At the beginning of the fifteenth century, Castile's prospects brightened. Its wool industry flourished, and the Atlantic fishing fleet, based in Santander and Corunna, expanded. Castilian nobles conspired against one another and refused to obey their royal overlords, but Isabel, heir to the throne of her half brother, Henry IV, was a young woman of steely determination and vision. Rather than allow herself to become the pawn of Portugal's Alfonso V, in 1469 she married the heir to Aragon, young Ferdinand. He helped Isabel to quell the dissidents in her own land, and together they planned to finish the reconquest of Spain from the Moors, then to invade North Africa to promote Christianity there.

Wherever the Portuguese mariners went, the Spanish were soon to follow. The competition the two nations waged on the peninsula spilled out into the Atlantic. In 1452, from Pope Nicholas V, the kingdom of Portugal gained the right to occupy islands the Portuguese discovered along the coast of Africa. But no papal decree could keep the Spanish from raiding Portuguese settlements. And what Portugal could obtain from one pope, Spain could and did have reversed by a successor in the Vatican.

Finally, the two nations agreed to a limited form of cooperation. At the request of Spain, the pope in 1493 gave to Ferdinand and Isabel the legal right to conquer all non-Christian lands about three hundred miles west of the Azores; the inshore territories belonged to Portugal. In 1494, the Spanish and Portuguese concluded the Treaty of Tordesillas, shifting the line to twelve hundred miles west of the Azores and granting to Portugal the right to conquer all non-Christian peoples east of the line.

Maps, Ships, and Winds

When the Iberian navigators turned the prows of their ships south and west into the Atlantic, they drew upon two thousand years of Mediterranean and coastal Atlantic seamanship. Along the way, they disproved legends of sea monsters, scholarly misconceptions about the size of the world, and long-held maxims that in the Torrid Zone around the equator the sea would be boiling hot.

The Mediterranean is an inland sea that Europeans had traversed for two thousand years before Columbus, but they had always clung to its shorelines. The Homeric epic the *Odyssey* cautioned all Mediterranean sailors not to stray from coastlines, lest they wander, like him, for ten years. Coasting required a thorough knowledge of landmarks, and the earliest maps were charts of coastal features.

The development of the compass in the twelfth century allowed pilots to leave the shore and follow straight-line directional readings across bodies of open sea. Maps based on the new compass, called *portolans*, featured straight lines ("rhombs") radiating from the center of a circle in the principal directions. Eventually, these maps displayed eight primary and sixteen "quarter" winds.

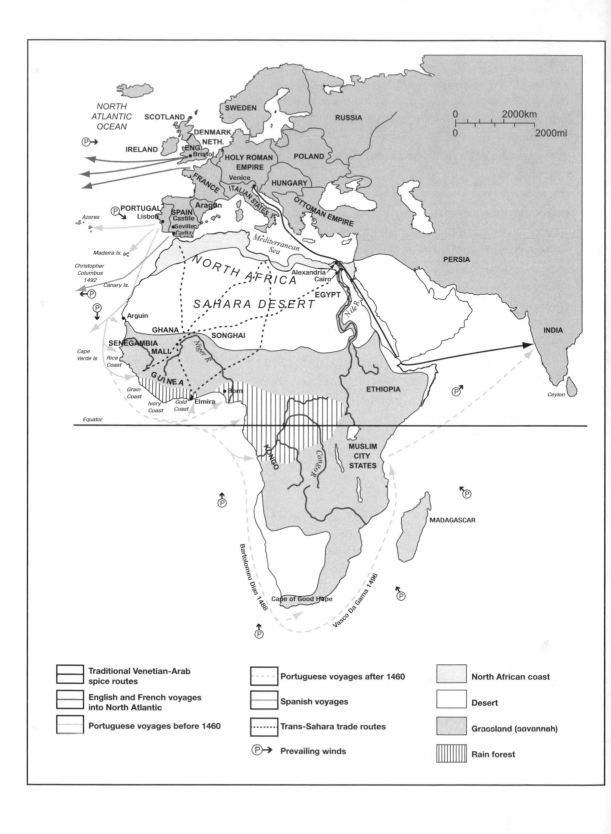

NORTH
ATLANTIC
OCEAN

SCOTLAND

SWEDEN

RUSSIA

DENMARK
NETH.

IRELAND

ENG.
Bristol

HOLY ROMAN
EMPIRE

POLAND

FRANCE

Venice

HUNGARY

ITALIAN STATES

OTTOMAN EMPIRE

PERSIA

PORTUGAL
Lisbon

Aragon

SPAIN
Castile
Sevilla
Cadiz

Azores

Mediterranean
Sea

Madeira Is.

Christopher
Columbus
1492

Canary Is.

NORTH AFRICA

Alexandria
Cairo

EGYPT

SAHARA DESERT

Nile R.

INDIA

Arguin

GHANA

SONGHAI

Cape
Verde Is

SENEGAMBIA

MALI

Niger R.

Rice
Coast

GUINEA

Grain
Coast

Ivory
Coast

Gold
Coast

Elmira

Born

ETHIOPIA

Ceylon

Equator

KONGO

Congo River

MUSLIM
CITY
STATES

MADAGASCAR

Bartolomeu Dias 1488

Cape of Good Hope

Vasco Da Gama 1496

Traditional Venetian-Arab spice routes

English and French voyages into North Atlantic

Portuguese voyages before 1460

Portuguese voyages after 1460

Spanish voyages

Trans-Sahara trade routes

(P)→ **Prevailing winds**

North African coast

Desert

Grassland (savannah)

Rain forest

In turn, mapmakers incorporated pilots' reports into new and more accurate charts. Though the empty spaces of the maps still featured fabulous creatures, the mapmakers gradually abandoned the older Christological formulae that placed Jerusalem at the top center of every map and adopted a more accurate ordering of geography.

Early in the 1400s, Renaissance humanism weighed in with its own spectacular contribution to Europeans' growing knowledge of geography. In the second century A.D., the Alexandrine Greek astronomer Ptolemy had demonstrated that Earth must be a sphere. His *Geography* was a classic in its time, but like so many ancient works, it was lost to Western audiences all through the Middle Ages. Renaissance humanists recovered it, and sometime before 1450 Jacobo d'Angelo, a humanist scholar, translated Ptolemy's Hellenistic Greek into Latin. The new book of maps became a best seller, wedding the humanist's passion for all things ancient, the bookmaker's art, and the mapmaker's new precision.

Merchants celebrated the publication of new maps, for they meant that seaborne goods would be delivered on time and at lower cost. One Renaissance merchant, the Florentine Goro Dati, waxed rhapsodic about the maps:

> With maps that layout like a frieze
> The winds, the ports, the seven seas,
> Pirates and Merchants sail the main,
> Hunting for plunder or for gain.
> A single day, from dawn to dusk,
> Can bring them either boo[m] or bust:
> No other trade, no other way
> Of life thus makes men fortune's prey.

Compass headings in the *portolan* and maps like those in Ptolemy's *Geography* helped mariners cross bodies of water whose boundaries were known, for the lines were like roads from place to place. But what about the great oceans? What lay beyond sight and off the edges of the maps? In particular, was there a way south to the Indies around the African landmass?

That feat required the introduction of another simple machine—the astrolabe. The crude astrolabe (like the compass, an Arabian invention) and the more sophisticated quadrant worked in the same way. Both were little more than semicircular metal-and-wood instruments with degrees marked off on the outside of the semicircle. At noon (or thereabouts), the pilot aligned the base of the instrument with the horizon (zero degrees) and "shot" the sun—that is, found how many degrees it was above the horizon. The same could be done at night with the North Star in the Northern Hemisphere or another fixed point in the heavens. The pilot referred to printed tables that gave the angles of the sun or the star at different latitudes at different days of the year. The latitude was then entered in the ship's sea log. The same log contained the distances traveled each day—measured by dumping a float overboard and calculating how fast the ship passed the knots placed at regular intervals on the rope tied to the float. Finally, the pilot recorded landfalls, the color of the sea, and, most important, wind directions (according to his compass).

Many mariners, including some pilots, were illiterate, and thus not able to make full use of the new technologies, but the Portuguese trained their captains well, and their logs circulated within the guild of navigators. These became the raw material for more comprehensive navigational charts. Using the astrolabe, Portuguese mariners inched their way south and west along the African coast. By 1460, they had reached ten degrees north latitude. By 1485, they had crossed the equator. There, according to the ancient authorities, one would find boiling seas and skies. The Portuguese saw nothing like this and quietly put aside what had been, in the medieval European mind, a major obstacle to exploration.

The Portuguese sailed in an adapted Arabian ship design. By the 1300s, they had learned from watching and testing single-masted Arabian *caravos* that a sail need not be fastened squarely across the mast. Arabian mariners mounted the so-called lateen sails diagonally to the mast. The lateen sail moved through 270 degrees, allowing the *caravos* to tack, in effect going back and forth across a head-wind to make crab-like progress. The Portuguese caravel added to the square-rigged European cargo ship a lateen sail. Later, larger versions of the caravel featured multiple masts, the forward ones rigged with square sails, the rearmost mast, or mizzenmast, rigged with a lateen sail. The size of caravels varied from as little as fifteen or twenty tons to eighty, ninety, and even greater tonnage, but the average caravel was a ship of fifty tons that carried a crew of twenty.

The caravel allowed the pilot to tack across the trade winds, but only experience would teach him how the prevailing winds blew. The trade winds of the Northern Hemisphere blow clockwise over the oceans; but in the Southern Hemisphere, the motion is reversed. Ten degrees north and south of the equator the winds billow away from the equator, then truckle back under the influence of the heat of the sun. Along the equator itself lie the doldrums, where a sailing ship can be becalmed for weeks, until its fresh water and food give out and its sailors go mad.

Nothing in the Mediterranean or along the northwestern edge of the African coast taught Portuguese navigators these winds, or how to return to Europe from the equator. In 1487, Bartolomé Dias discovered the answer to this problem. Pushing his ship and crew past the mouth of the Congo River south of the equator, he found he could no longer beat south and turned, perhaps by instinct, to the southwest. He ran with the wind into the South Atlantic, then north, across the equator. There he found the friendly northerlies that took him back to Portugal.

A decade later, Vasco da Gama tried the same tack but started on it much farther south and so caught the South Atlantic trades and was carried in a great counterclockwise circle back to the southern tip of Africa, around it, and thence to the Indian Ocean. A century of daring had rewarded the Portuguese with a way to the East that bypassed the Arabian middlemen. Da Gama and his fleet toured the east coast of Africa, where his cannons impressed the rulers of its chiefdoms. He reached India in short order, but coming back he took ninety-five days and during the trip lost much of his ships' complement.

Da Gama had learned three facts that he shared with John III. First, European military technology surpassed that of the Asians. Second, the merchants of Asia were not interested in European trade goods. Third, the riches of Asia—silks, spices, and jewels—were worth the sacrifice of ships and men. King John appreciated these lessons and decided that if Asian rulers did not want to trade with the Portuguese, his mariners would take what they wanted by force. He also changed the name of the southernmost point of Africa from the Cape of Storms to the Cape of Good Hope. The king believed that the power to name was the power to subdue, a power that later European explorers would exploit.

The Portuguese had mastered the winds and could ride them to foreign lands— but how would they treat the people they met? Would the Portuguese and the Spanish try to fit in, respecting the mores of the locals, as had Marco Polo, the Venetian merchant and traveler who visited the court of Mongol emperor Kublai Khan in the 1290s and became a minor bureaucrat in the great khan's administration? Or would they fire their cannons to intimidate the natives, as da Gama's sailors did in Madagascar?

The Fortunate Isles

In the 1340s, the Portuguese stumbled upon islands in the Atlantic that they called the Fortunate Isles—the Azores, Madeira, and the Canary Islands archipelago. The subsequent history of this chance discovery presaged the conduct and thinking of the European voyagers to the west. The Azores were barren rocks in the mid-Atlantic, but a welcome stopover for ships trying to tack their way back to Portugal from Africa. Madeira was covered with forest until a brushfire set there by accident burned for seven years and laid down a carpet of potash perfect for the planting of grapevines. Madeira wine became a staple of the European diet. The Canaries, seven volcanic outcroppings sixty to a hundred miles off the Moroccan coast, were occupied by a North African people, the Guanches, and promised even greater riches to the men who could subdue the natives.

The Portuguese asserted that the islands were theirs, and Prince Henry sent two expeditions to conquer them in 1425 and 1427. However, the Guanches proved unwilling to cede sovereignty over their land to the Portuguese or to the Spanish, who announced their own claim to the islands. In 1493, the desperate defenders of the largest island, Tenerife, finally surrendered to a Spanish army of eleven hundred men, replete with steel armor, horses, and cannons. In 1497, Portugal conceded sovereignty of the islands to Spain. They remain Spanish possessions.

Spanish horses and guns were not as decisive weapons in the war with the natives as the microbes, pollens, and animals the Europeans brought with them. The Guanches had no inherited resistance to European diseases, and measles, mumps, chickenpox, and smallpox, not to mention bubonic plague and tuberculosis, ran through the native population like wildfire.

While tiny microorganisms assaulted the people, nonnative grass and flower pollen attacked the land. We call such invaders weeds though they are in fact wildflowers. Weeds love to insinuate themselves in ground that has been disturbed, and the war-torn Canaries offered near perfect terrain. The weeds ousted the native flora, a process that would be repeated in every temperate climatic zone that Europeans colonized. The animals the Europeans brought acted like weeds—they bred out of control. Wild asses, rabbits, and dogs soon overran the islands.

Why did the Europeans persist in their invasion of the Canaries when all around them they left carnage? Were they indifferent to the charitable tenets of Christianity and to the sufferings of another people? The answer they gave to these questions were fourfold, based on legal doctrines, European perceptions of other peoples, prior European experience with epidemic diseases, and economics.

During the Crusades, Europeans developed two legal concepts to justify waging war against non-Europeans. The pope or another high church official could declare a "holy war" on the infidel or the pagan in the name of Christ. The enemy had put itself outside the protection of Christianity by committing sacrileges or refusing to accept the teachings of the church. A head of state could declare a "just war" under the same rationale. In 1452, Pope Nicholas V gave the Portuguese permission to attack Muslims in Africa under this doctrine, and it sanctioned the 1493 papal division of the pagan world between Spain and Portugal. Thus the Europeans could attack the Guanches without violating the precepts of Christianity or law.

Another part of the answer is that the Europeans did not see the Guanches as "people." Europeans were ethnocentric. Take, for example, the Vikings' treatment of the native peoples of Greenland. The Vikings came from the kingdoms of Norway, Sweden, and Denmark. A warrior tradition, combined with scarcity of arable land, made the Vikings into feared raiders throughout the northern coasts of Europe in the eighth through eleventh centuries. Vikings established kingdoms in Iceland, in the British Isles, on the coasts of Europe, and even in the Mediterranean.

In the tenth century, the Vikings sailed their longboats west from Iceland searching for arable land. Navigating by the sun and the North Star, they brought their longships to the coast of Greenland and then passed beyond it to a land they called Vinland, probably modern Newfoundland. The North Atlantic was warmer then, warm enough to allow the newcomers to transship livestock and household furnishings. Even the names Greenland and Vinland (either "land of wine" or "land of meadows," depending on how one translates the Old Norse) recalled the comparatively moderate winters of those years.

In Greenland and Vinland, the Vikings laid out homes, fields, and pastures that looked like Scandinavian and Icelandic farmsteads. When the native peoples arrived in boats to take the measure of the newcomers, tempers turned sour, and both sides rushed for their weapons. The Vikings drove the natives off. But before that, they recorded their view of the *skraelings:* "small ill favored men, [who] had ugly hair on their heads." The Vikings' virtues were those of the warrior—few words, brave deeds, and no sympathy (much less empathy) for their enemies. That particularly applied to men who "had ugly hair on their heads." In the fourteenth century, colder weather did what the natives could not—drive the Vikings from their western abodes. Historians speculate that the Vikings might have been able to withstand the change in climate if they had adopted some of the native hunting techniques, clothing, and housing, but the Vikings refused to change their ways to conform to people with "ugly hair on their heads," creatures the Vikings disdained.

Another example of the same general phenomenon comes from Spain. In January 1492, Ferdinand and Isabel drove the last of the Muslim Moors from their realm. This Reconquista had lasted over seven hundred years, but in the reign of Ferdinand and Isabel its pace had accelerated. Isabel, heir to the militant energy and fierce piety of the ancient kingdom of Castile, regarded the expulsion of the Moors as a crusade. Muslims were not a national enemy to be fought with statecraft, but an abomination to God.

Thus when the armies of the last Moorish prince had departed in 1492, Isabel began a campaign to purge the land of practicing Muslims and Jews (although some had served with honor and ability in the Spanish government under her). There were precedents for the persecution of minorities in Castile. Riots, purges, and inquisitions preceded Isabel's decree. After one riot, in 1449, in Toledo, a *limpieza de sangre* (purity of blood) decree banned all persons of Jewish descent, including those *conversos* who had abandoned the faith of their ancestors in favor of Christianity, from holding public office.

Isabel drew upon this rich vein of anti-Semitism in applying to Rome for a commission of the Inquisition to ferret out backsliding among the *conversos.* In 1483, the commission began its investigations, under her direct control. Fearing the outcome, thousands of *conversos* fled. The expulsion decree of 1492 was the natural sequel to the Inquisition. Jewish and Moorish children kidnapped and raised as Catholics were not returned to their non-Catholic parents. In subsequent years, royal proclamations even barred converted Moors and Jews from wearing their old apparel. Visible differences were as objectionable to Isabel as they were to the Vikings in Vinland—and to the invaders of the Canaries.

The next part of the explanation of the Europeans' treatment of the Guanches comes from the European experience with epidemic disease. From 1347 to 1353, a catastrophic epidemic had inured Europeans to the sights and smells of mass death. In 1347, the so-called Black Plague came to Genoa on ships from India, Constantinople, and the Muslim Mediterranean ports. The epidemic had already carried off two-thirds of China's population and had devastated India and the Middle East.

The plague, an infection of the bacterium *Pasteurella pestis*, took two forms. The first, bubonic plague, named for the large dark lymph node (buboes) swellings in the armpits and groin, caused high fevers and hemorrhages and usually resulted in death within two weeks. A more virulent form, pneumonic plague, in which the bacteria took root in the lungs, caused death in a matter of days. Bubonic plague was incubated in black rats and other rodents and spread to people through the bites of fleas. Pneumonic plague was airborne, traveling on droplets of moisture from the lungs of infected people.

The epidemic overwhelmed the Continent. Authorities tried to quarantine the sick, and those who could fled from highly infected regions, but so swift and virulent were the outbreaks that in some towns and villages the dead and dying littered roads, fields, and homes. Wheat rotted in the fields, and urban food distribution systems ceased to function. The population of Venice sank from over one hundred thousand to fifty thousand people in the first three years of the plague. Milan suffered even more, losing 60 percent of its inhabitants. The port cities of southern France suffered similar mortality. Fleeing men and women and migratory rodents carried the plague north to Normandy and the Paris region, where one-third of the population perished in 1349. By 1350, the pestilence had arrived in Scandinavia and spread through Germany and England.

No one was safe, not even those who had pledged their lives to the service of God. In England, 50 percent of the clergy died, many, no doubt, from exposure to sick parishioners. By 1351, plague had killed off one-third of Europe. Charnel houses, where the bodies of the plague dead came to rest, cast the fetid odor of burning flesh over cities day and night. Outbreaks of plague continued for the next three hundred years.

The plague fostered a culture preoccupied with sudden and unpredictable death. Religious revivals failed to halt its progress. Wealth, fame, and nobility could not parry its thrust. Survivors donated large sums to religious charities, made pilgrimages to shrines, and wondered why God had so afflicted his people. But scapegoats were easy to find. In 1350, a Parisian scholar named Jean de Venette informed the pope that "the Jews were suddenly and violently charged with infecting the wells and water, and corrupting the air."

In light of these pieces of evidence, who would expect kindness for the Guanches from the Europeans, when the Guanches were not a Christian people and looked, sounded, and acted differently from the Europeans? When so many Europeans had died from plague, who would lament the passing of the Guanches?

SUGAR AND SLAVES

There is a fourth part of the answer to the European treatment of the Guanches that involves no speculation about legal doctrines or cultural attitudes. As Prince Henry the Navigator's biographer put it, who would "want to go to a place where he did not stand to make money?" The demise of the Guanches hardly weighted the scales against the potential profits of the conquest—that is, from sugar cultivation in the Canaries.

Sugarcane was an Asian plant whose refined crystals had become a vital part of the European diet, but importing it from the East meant paying all the middlemen whom the Portuguese and their European rivals were trying to bypass. Cyprus and Sicily, Europe's first sugar islands, belonged to the Genoese and the Venetians. The Spanish and Portuguese coveted the Canaries because their climate, soil, and long growing season so well suited sugarcane cultivation.

With the rapid demise of the Guanches, however, the Iberians needed some other labor force to work the sugar plantations. They found that labor source not far away—in West African slavery. One should bear in mind that slavery was a common institution throughout the Mediterranean world, in Europe and in Africa, for thousands of years before the Spanish and Portuguese came to the Canaries. But changes in Mediterranean geopolitics in the fifteenth century (principally the rise of the Ottoman Empire) closed the eastern Mediterranean slave trade to Western customers and opened the West African coastal slave market to the Portuguese and the Spanish.

Slavery in West Africa

In the fifteenth century, West African politics and society were in flux. In the wake of Islamic forces moving south in the previous centuries, powerful trade kingdoms rose from the Senegalese coast in the west to the Sudanese deserts in the east. These kingdoms' wealth included slaves taken in the wars by which these states came to power. Islam, the religion of many of the victors in these wars, forbade the enslavement of those who accepted the faith and encouraged masters to treat their slaves with kindness and free them when possible, but not every slave trader obeyed the Koran in this matter. And non-Muslims were fair game.

Nor were Muslims the only slave traders. The displacement of peoples from the Sahel to the grasslands, and from the grasslands to the forests, created new supplies of slaves in non-Muslim areas. Unscrupulous slavers there not only sold prisoners of war, they raided peaceful villages and stole children for the slave market. By the middle of the fifteenth century, slaves constituted both a major source of personal wealth and a medium of exchange, like stocks or bonds.

The new African states sponsored trade, in which slavery again played a vital part. For the most part, the trade involved not money, but goods. For example, the Akan-speaking peoples of Ghana traded gold, and the Yoruba peoples of the Kingdom of Benin on the lower Niger River contributed kola nuts and palm oil to the stream of commerce in return for textiles, salt, copper ingots (to be melted down into coins), and grain from the savanna. Slaves flowed through these same channels of trade.

Market cities grew rich from the trade in slaves. Merchants and kings employed some slaves in positions of honor and trust, and these slaves kept accounts of business using Arabic numbers and arithmetic and wrote letters in Arabic. Other slave day-laborers built and maintained the bustling capital cities and the heavily walled palaces. Most slaves did not achieve such high rank, however, and labored in harsh conditions.

If the economics of West African slavery seemed to be based on concepts of supply and demand similar to those characterizing the capitalism of Europe, African slavery's social and cultural side was not entirely driven by market forces. The arrival of armies and the establishment of large-scale chiefdoms absorbed and expanded older ways of servitude, such as self-enslavement (for example, to pay off family debts). And although it was true that slaves were outsiders, and thus never more than marginal members of the community, they were never merely chattel (movable personal property like jewelry or furniture).

African slaves could not claim the protection of kin against an abusive master; they lacked the power to inherit, the ability to marry, and the mobility of free persons; and to be or to have been a slave was an indelible mark of dishonor. Nevertheless, slaves were still persons and could claim rights to sustenance and property of their own. In the Hausa states of what is now eastern Nigeria, slaves even owned slaves. Slaves sold to a family farm were treated as dependent members of the families. The children of slaves might gain the status of free persons within the village, city, or clan.

The Invention of "Race"

To the Portuguese and Spanish engaged in the slave trade in the second half of the fifteenth century, the African slave was never a human being with rights. Slaves were objects, not persons. In 1441, Portuguese raiders stole twelve Africans off the coast of Mauritania and carried them into bondage. By the late 1440s, Italian and Spanish kidnappers were working the coast alongside the Portuguese. In 1448, the Portuguese purchased their first load of Guinean slaves and brought them back to Lisbon. The thirty men and women were sold into bondage in Portugal. The demand for slaves in Spain was even greater. In 1452, as part of Christianity's continuing struggle against Islam, Pope Nicholas V gave formal approval to the Portuguese to enslave "moors, heathens, and other enemies of Christ" in West Africa, a belated dispensation for the raids. By 1482, the Portuguese had built forts on the coast of Guinea to process the commerce with local African slave traders. In the towns that grew up around the Portuguese forts, Europeans and Africans developed a pidgin tongue based on a combination of Portuguese and African words and grammars to facilitate the slave trade.

Initially, race and color had nothing to do with the slave trade, for Europeans had enslaved Europeans and Africans had enslaved Africans for thousands of years. But the Iberians soon developed a justification for slavery that Europeans would use in one form or another until European nations finally renounced slavery in the nineteenth century. The Spanish and Portuguese became color conscious.

There was already a prejudice against dark colors in many European languages and literatures. Blackness connoted inferiority, immorality, and death. In later years, the Spanish invented terms like *Negro retinto*, meaning "double-dyed," and *amulatados* for lighter-skinned individuals. The lighter the color, the better opinion the Spanish had of the Africans, though many Spanish thought all Africans naturally evil, a "vicious people" who had to be controlled by an institution like slavery. Thus color itself became a badge of inhumanity and paganism and wrapped the economic incentives for the slave trade in convenient moral rationalization.

The Europeans who traded in slaves also based the invidious distinction of dark color on a passage in the Bible. There was slavery in the Bible, but it was not based on color. Still, European apologists for African slavery cited the curse of Ham in the book of Genesis. For exposing his nakedness, Noah cursed his "dark-skinned son Ham" to be a servant and the founder of a nation of servants. Plainly the Genesis passage supported servitude of some kind, perhaps connected to ethnic discrimination, but not "race."

Although the Iberians could now justify the trade in African slaves, the demand for slaves on the Iberian Peninsula in the second half of the fifteenth century was limited. The Portuguese could not dump more than a few thousand on the market every year. The slave market in Italy and France had disappeared.

But the opening of the Canaries to sugar cultivation gave the Portuguese slave trade its reason for being. The sugar plantations the Spanish introduced on the Canary Islands gobbled up slaves as fast as they climbed down from the ships. The islands were deadly pestholes, and Africans exposed to European diseases died as quickly as the Guanches. The planters could not wait for natural increase through the birth of slave children to fill the gap, so they relied on importation—a cycle of demand and supply that made slave trading lucrative.

Looking back on the century of European history that preceded and propelled European New World adventures, one can see the complex counterpoint of enrichment and impoverishment. The standard of living and life expectancy of the middle classes crept ahead; technology and business formed a lasting partnership; science and education labored against old prejudices; and the first buds of artistic and political individualism showed themselves. Yet wars for plunder, religious and intellectual arrogance, and the merchants' reinvestment of their gains back into their businesses instead of into social improvement prevented the full benefits of change from flowing down to the lowest ranks of society. Peasants and city poor lived much as they had in previous centuries. Perhaps the exploration of new lands would better the lot of the masses, although if one regarded the fate of the African slaves as a portent, one could only expect colonization to make the rich richer and the mighty more confident of their right to rule.

3

The Spanish Century, 1492–1588

In 1486, Queen Isabel rejected a proposal from a Genoese-born, Portuguese-trained mariner named Christopher Columbus to reach the East Indies by sailing west from Spain. There were many Genoese like him in Portugal and Spain, and they promoted all manner of schemes like his. In 1491, with victory over the Moors assured, Isabel changed her mind. She gave him three ships and allowed him to recruit crews and soldiers. He left in August 1492, with her blessing "on some business that touches the service of God and the expansion of the Catholic faith, and our own benefit and utility."

For nearly a century, from Columbus's landing in the Bahamas in 1492 to the defeat of its great armada (fleet) in 1588, Spain ruled the western Atlantic. The motives of Spain's explorers, colonizers, and monarchs combined all of the elements reviewed in chapter 2. Columbus saw the Indians as gentle primitives, ready for conversion to the true faith, but he also craved their gold and demanded they reveal its source to him. Hernan Cortés, who conquered Mexico's Aztec Empire in 1521, respected the Aztecs' civilization but did not hesitate to destroy their cities if they opposed his dreams of domination.

Intense religiosity, combative and ethnocentric patriotism, a hunger for riches, and confidence in technology gave Spain's conquistadors a sense of purpose. They would bring to the New World their martial ardor, leave behind secure military bases, and return home with gold. Ferdinand and Isabel and their successors had equally complex motives. Upon the riches of the Indies trade they would build a centralized, hierarchical, well-disciplined empire to milk the New World of its wealth to carry on their crusade against the infidel.

With the brutal Spanish expulsion of the Moors as a backdrop, the Spanish crown's religious fanaticism as a recurrent theme, and Spanish missionaries' revelations of their countrymen's misdeeds in the Americas as evidence, sixteenth- and seventeenth-century English writers published gruesome accounts of Spanish injustices in America. This often-repeated "black legend" of Spanish inhumanity suited English propagandists because by the end of the sixteenth century,

Many men came, and many women, each one with something, giving thanks to God; throwing themselves on the ground; and they raised their hands to heaven, and afterward they called to us in loud voices to come ashore.
—Christopher Columbus's journal entry for October 14, 1492

Cortés then spoke [to the Indians of Cozumel off the Yucatan peninsula, in Mexico] through his interpreter and told them that he had not come to do them harm but to instruct them and bring them to the knowledge of our Holy Catholic Faith, so that they might become Your Majesties' vassals and serve and obey you, as do all the other Indians in these parts which are inhabited by Spaniards.
—Hernan Cortés to Emperor Charles V of Spain, 1519

England was Spain's rival in America. But the term itself, *la leyenda negra*, with its glaringly prejudicial association of blackness with evil, is not a translation of an English phrase. Spanish writers introduced the wording.

In truth, the conduct of the Spanish and the response of the Indians and the Africans were not a one-way or uniform process of oppression, but another example of the complex relationship between the drive for wealth and fame, on the one hand, and the struggle of subordinate groups to gain some measure of autonomy, on the other. On Hispaniola, Cuba, and the other islands of the Antilles, adventurers like Juan Ponce de León boasted of walking across the dead and dying Indians. But Spanish missionaries like the Dominican Bartolomé de las Casas just as strenuously defended the Indians' rights. In areas under Spanish control, Indians and Spanish immigrants created multiracial, multicultural societies, though these societies never promoted equality. And in rural areas of Florida, Mexico, the north coast of South America (the "Spanish Main"), and the southwestern borderlands, Indians retained their autonomy.

The governance of the Spanish colonies demonstrates a similarly complicated dialectic of compassion and depredation. The crown did not leave the Indians to the mercies of the conquistadors. Ferdinand and Isabel created a Council of the Indies to oversee the conduct of the conquistadors. Influenced by reports of atrocities, the council in 1512–1513 promulgated the Laws of Burgos, admonishing the conquistadors to treat the Indians with kindness. When Spanish subjects in America ignored the instructions of 1512–1513, in 1542 the council drafted the "New Laws," which abrogated many of the rights the heirs of the conquistadors claimed and ended Indian slavery (except for crimes or insurrection). In 1581, the council codified the laws of the Indies, reminding the Spanish officials to protect the Indians.

But laws could not stop the Spanish in America from abusing their trust as protectors of the Indians. Missionaries, mine owners, sugar planters, and textile manufacturers might not be able to enslave the Indians, but they could and did work the *mesaguales* (the Mexican term for Indian commoners) as though they were serfs. And when Indian populations fell from fifteen million to less than one and a half million people, the Spanish adapted the Canary Islands' precedent of slavery.

In 1501, the Spanish governor of Hispaniola formally requested African slaves. In 1518, a direct trade opened between Africa and the Spanish Caribbean possessions, as the missionaries applauded the importation of African slaves to relieve the burden on their Indian converts. In general, the Spanish arranged to purchase already enslaved Africans and transport them to the New World rather than kidnapping slaves, although Spanish and Portuguese ships continued raiding for slaves when the opportunity presented itself.

INITIAL ENCOUNTERS

Columbus recorded the details of his first crossing in a journal he would deliver to his royal patrons. On the first page, he commended himself and his men to God, for he knew that every ocean voyage had its own dangers. Southern Atlantic storms ripped the masts out of the bowels of ships. Uncharted reefs tore the caravels' keels and punctured the ships' bottoms. Some vessels simply vanished. Over the course of the crossing, from August 3 to October 12, 1492, he quelled two near mutinies, lied to his crew about the distance they had traveled from home, and rehearsed what he would say to the potentates of the East when he arrived, for he was certain then that he had found the way to the Indies (and went to his grave in 1506 still certain in his belief). Columbus made four crossings between 1492 and 1504, explored much of the Caribbean and some of the coast of Central and South America, and changed forever the course of European, Native American, and West African history.

The Vision of Columbus

Before they saw the land, Columbus and his mariners watched for its signs. When the color of the sea changed from blue to green and seabirds that nested on nearby islands swooped over the ships, the crew joined in chants of praise to God. They then smelled the vegetation. For seamen accustomed to the brown, treeless shores of Europe, the brilliant white sand and deep green forest of the Caribbean islands seemed unreal and amazingly beautiful.

Though landfall beckoned, caution tempered the joy of arrival. Columbus scanned the shoreline for a good harbor. He knew that sandbars and rocky shoals lurked beneath the placid surface, so he sent men aloft to look for underwater obstacles and ordered soundings of the depth. The *Santa Maria* and Columbus's other two ships tiptoed into the shallows. Though he had badly underestimated the distance to the Indies (he placed Japan where modern Orlando, Florida, is), he was lucky that the outbound voyage was swift and the weather clear, and his skill in the use of compass and sails brought the fleet to safe harbor in the Bahamas.

Columbus recalled his first meeting with the natives as cordial. They beckoned him ashore and treated him with kindness, and he reciprocated. He envisioned their participation in the empire as loyal subjects and good Christians. But he assumed that the focal point of that empire would be Spain, and with no thought to ascertaining the Indian names for places, he gave every significant feature of the landscape a Spanish name.

For Columbus as for King John II, the power of naming was magical. On maps, it established legal claims. On the land itself, it made the unfamiliar familiar. Some of the names Columbus gave invoked the power of the saints, like San Salvador for the island on which he landed. Other names were secular, like Hispaniola, linking a spot in the New World to a place in the Old World.

Columbus not only assumed that he could take control of the land by christening it with Spanish names, he wrote as if he could understand what the natives said. Repeatedly he entered in his journal that "the Indian told the Admiral" something, when in fact neither understood the other's tongue.

Soon enough, however, Columbus's men and the Indians would develop a pidgin tongue. No one is certain of the origin of the word *pidgin*, but one of the first historically documented pidgins was the language that the European Crusaders spoke with the peoples of the Middle East. Because so many Crusaders were French, the pidgin was called "lingua franca," and that term for a universal language has passed into common usage. It is also the origin of the word *lingo*, meaning dialect. In the fifteenth century, Portuguese words like *saber* (to know) and *pequeño* (small) became part of pidgins along the coast of Africa, where Portuguese sailors and traders did business with African merchants and slavers. Pidgin is no one's first language, but wherever speakers need to communicate across language barriers, they develop pidgins. French, Spanish, and other European merchants followed the Portuguese example by creating their own pidgins on the West African coast. For example, in Cameroon, the African-English pidgin is called Kamtok.

On his first voyage, Columbus kidnapped a number of younger Taíno Indians from the Caribbean islands to take back to Spain, where they learned enough Spanish to communicate with their captors. Once their language skills were adequate and their loyalty to Spain certain, they were returned to their homes by Columbus to act as his interpreters.

Columbus recorded that there were no trees, birds, or flowers in Spain resembling those he found on the islands. As much as he wanted to compare his discoveries with the plants and animals of the Old World, he had to admit that the islands were different. But by accepting the fact of difference, he opened a door to a controversy that would continue for the next two hundred years among European scientists, theologians, and philosophers on the relationship between nature in the New World and the Old World. If the trees were higher, the food more plentiful, and the land richer, was the New World some kind of Eden that the Europeans had lost? Or did the relative impoverishment of the natives of this Eden prove that they were the children of the Fall—forever mired in Adam's sin?

The Taíno

The natives Columbus met in the Bahamas were part of a vast island culture about one thousand years old. Columbus happened upon on the northwestern edge of Taíno settlement, in effect, the Taíno frontier. The core of Taíno settlement lay to the south, in the Antilles chain of volcanic islands that form an arc from the southeast to the northwest. The southern tip of the arc lies sixty-five miles away from the Guiana coast of Latin America. The northwestern tip approaches the west coast of Florida. The Lesser Antilles, stretching to the southeast, are two chains of small, tropical volcanic islands. The Greater Antilles include the mountainous, richly soiled islands of Cuba, Hispaniola, Jamaica, and Puerto Rico. The Antilles are the eastern barrier islands of a vast sea—later called the Caribbean after the warlike Caribs who inhabited the southernmost of the islands.

As many as one and a half million Taínos occupied Cuba, Hispaniola, Puerto Rico, Jamaica, and the smaller islands in 1492. They lived in villages of circular grass-roofed huts surrounding the larger polygonal houses of their elected chiefs. The is-lands offered an abundance of fruit and fish. The soil was also suitable for tuber (root) crops like casaba and sweet potato, which the Taíno pressed into three-foot-high conical mounds of soil arranged in rows. The Taíno also used slash-and-burn techniques to clear land for corn planting. They grew tobacco and pineapples, along with squash, beans, peppers, and peanuts. These, with fish, provided a balanced diet. There were no domesticated animals; indeed, because the Antilles were oceanic islands and were never part of the mainland, they had no large indigenous mammals. The Spanish would bring the first of large mammals, rats, when they came in 1492.

Columbus reported that the Taíno loved body paint, necklaces, and belts. Their religious beliefs were recorded in some detail by Father Ramón Pané, on Columbus's orders. There were two central gods—the lord of the casaba and the sea, and his mother, the goddess of fertility. The people of the towns on Hispaniola kept the household god figurines in niches or on tables. So important were they that they were hidden in caves when invaders came. Shamans who performed both curing rituals and led festival worship employed special idols for the task.

When his storm-tossed return voyage was successfully concluded at the Por-tuguese port of Lisbon in 1493, Columbus traveled overland to meet Ferdinand and Isabel in Castile, presenting to them his journal, samples of island flora and fauna, and the young Taínos he had kidnapped to be tutored in Spanish and Catholicism. They named him admiral of the ocean sea and governor of the islands, and promised him a share of all the riches he found. This grant of power was never unconditional, and in fact the crown revoked it in 1500, but the system of conferring wide discre-tionary powers on private individuals characterized the governance of the Spanish Empire for the next two hundred years.

Hispaniola

In 1493, Columbus hired fifteen hundred men and assembled a fleet of seventeen ships to return to Hispaniola, which he had already visited. He intended to make it a permanent colony like the Canaries. The ships left the port of Cadiz, Spain, on Sep-tember 23, filled with the same kinds of European germs, pollens, and animals that had transformed the Canary Islands into a little Spain. A month later, Columbus ar-rived in the Antilles. After some exploration, during which he found evidence of the cannibalism of the island Caribs, he pressed on to Hispaniola.

At the fort he had called La Navidad, the site of his previous stay in Hispaniola, he found that the men he had left to occupy the site had vanished, but he took no action against the natives. As a mariner, he was without peer, but Columbus had neither the mediating skills of a good colonial governor nor the rapacious single-mindedness of a bad colonial governor. Perhaps the men had fought among themselves; after all, they were riffraff from Columbus's *Santa Maria* crew.

In any case, he founded a new town, called Isabella (to honor Queen Isabel). His choice was flawed—a swamp bordered the site for the town, and mud slithered everywhere underfoot—but he pushed his men to begin building the walls of what would look like a medieval castle town, unloaded his livestock, and settled in. Columbus's virtue of determination at sea had on land become the vice of stubbornness.

The pigs soon ran wild, uprooting Indian gardens. Worse, the swine brought with them influenza, to which the Indians had no natural immunities. The Spanish recovered from the flu; the Indians did not. As a later Spanish explorer recorded, the Indians' countermeasures consisted of laying hands on the sick and blowing into their mouths. Instead of curing the ill, these folk rituals only spread the disease.

In 1518, the first smallpox cases reached the Caribbean. Within a year, the population of Hispaniola dropped by one-third. Measles arrived in 1519 and killed more people than smallpox. From a population of perhaps one million in 1491, the Taíno of Hispaniola had declined to a few thousand by 1540. Epidemics flowed in waves from the Old World to the New World. The only passenger on the return trip was syphilis, an American disease that became epidemic in Europe after 1493.

Historians have called this deadly traffic in microbes a part of the "Columbian Exchange." Europeans brought with them viruses and bacterial pathogens to which Indians had no native immunities. Infectious diseases spread through native populations wherever Indians came in contact with Europeans, sometimes wiping out the entire Indian population.

But not all of the Columbian Exchange was harmful. To the east went turkeys, peanuts, pineapples, corn, potatoes, tomatoes, and cacao (the bean source of chocolate). To the west went cattle, chickens, horses, goats, wheat, rice, sugarcane, coffee, bananas, oats, and the honeybee. Nothing in the history of the world matched the trade in food technologies. The food crops Europeans brought back from the Americas enabled Europe's population to grow dramatically and bettered life expectancy. The crops the Europeans brought to the New World would become the basis for the wealthiest colonies the world had ever seen.

Columbus had not recruited men with the skills he needed to build, farm, and drain the land. Instead, fearing European rivals and Indian raids, he had brought soldiers, and they soon began to succumb to the heat, humidity, and native infirmities. Everyone ran fevers, developed skin diseases, and sickened from diarrhea. They refused to lay aside their heavy steel armor or adapt their style of living to the place and its ways—insisting, for example, on the high-fat meat and dairy fare of Europe.

The dream of great wealth drove the Spanish on. No sooner did Columbus build a temporary camp on the coast than he led his men inland, through fetid tropical forests, to seek the gold mines of the city of "El Dorado" that he imagined lay somewhere just ahead. Every gold trinket local Indians wore bewitched the Spanish, though all of it was placer gold panned in streams. There was no mother lode.

In the meantime, the Indians had grown tired of their visitors, who showed no inclination to leave, and began raiding Columbus's settlement. In response, the Spanish adopted a policy of divide and conquer to keep the Indians at bay. They played one chief against another. Indian allies scouted and fought for the Spanish on punitive expeditions against other Indians, whom the Spanish carried off in chains. Columbus, who still had no interest in running a colony, arranged for a substitute to govern in his place and sailed for Spain. His vision for the colony had failed. Though he reappeared twice more to explore the whole of the Antilles island chain and reassert his royal license to govern, his dream of civilization had become a nightmare of conquest.

ENTRADAS

Columbus's successors in the Caribbean twisted his commission to their own purposes. In 1499, the crown "commended" (*encomienda*) to Columbus the service of the Indians in lands he explored. In turn, he was obliged to instruct these new, involuntary servants of the Spanish crown in the true faith. The *encomienda* system was debased by Columbus's successors, becoming an excuse to demand tribute and later to enslave the Indians. The crown explicitly ordered the Spanish *encomenderos* not to treat Christian Indians as slaves, or to mistreat them, but the conquerors of Cuba, Puerto Rico, and the other islands ignored this royal order.

Colonial lands were soon partitioned into private estates, some large enough to be small kingdoms. The first sugarcane mill came to Hispaniola in 1516. By 1548, there were thirty-five of them. Although planters exported refined sugar from Hispaniola, Cuba, and Puerto Rico after 1520, sugar did not dominate the islands' economies until a century later. Spanish gentleman planters preferred to raise horses and cattle.

The Spanish encounter with the island natives had turned into an *entrada* (invasion). Pánfilo de Narvaez, the sacker of Jamaica, later wrote that he did not remember how much blood they spilled in terrorizing the natives. In 1508, Juan Ponce de León led the troops into Puerto Rico, slaughtering the Taínos. Cuba fell in 1511, as did Jamaica, the conquistadors' violence so appalling that Dominican missionaries began to complain in earnest to the royal authorities about their countrymen's barbarism.

The Aztecs and Cortés in Mexico

Even the most powerful of Indian peoples did not know what to do with the Europeans when they persisted in what appeared to be senseless violence. Rarely did the Spanish record what Indians had to say in these early years of contact, but the Aztecs of central Mexico were so numerous and their culture so literate that their response to the Spanish *entrada* has survived. An imperial power themselves, they exacted tribute from other Nahua peoples throughout Mexico.

When Hernan Cortés and several hundred Spanish soldiers and sailors landed on the east coast of Mexico in 1519 and defeated Tlaxcala, a coastal city-state that had defied the Aztecs, their king, Moctezuma, a veteran soldier himself, took notice. For Moctezuma and his councilors, the Spanish presented a dilemma. The discipline Cortés's men showed against the far more numerous Tlaxcalan force impressed the Aztecs. The Spanish fought in tight formations of infantry and used firearms and a cannon to break the Tlaxcalan charges. What is more, the Mexican peoples had no experience fighting against the Spanish cavalry.

Long after the Spanish had defeated the Aztecs, the Aztecs would invent the story that Moctezuma feared that Cortés was the embodiment of the pale-skinned god Quetzalcoatl, returning to Mexico to claim his land. In fact, Moctezuma was confident that he and his army could handle Cortés. But what of the unknown multitudes that Cortés had announced his advance guard represented? Far better to greet the Spanish with diplomatic courtesy and wait to see what would happen. So Moctezuma invited Cortés to see the glories and the might of Tenochtitlán.

The Aztecs had occupied the "floating city" of Tenochtitlán for a hundred years before Cortés approached its eastern causeway. In 1519, the city, a massive grid of stone streets and buildings laid over an island at the northern edge of Lake Texcoco, contained nearly two hundred thousand Aztecs, who inhabited its four quadrants according to their trades and their ranks. Satellite villages, farms, quarries, and ceremonial centers dotted the lakeshore.

The military caste, with a priest-king at its top, dominated Aztec society, and strict rules of privilege dictated everyone's place. The army, composed of conscripts from Aztec and nearby city-states, ensured that tribute arrived from outlying provinces in the Aztec Empire. Although the armies of these city-states were huge, even by Spanish standards, battle among their armies devolved into individual combats, much as medieval knights had faced one another. The victors carried off the vanquished alive. Taking prisoners was far more honorable than slaying the enemy. At festival times in the city, the Aztecs and other Nahua peoples sacrificed prisoners of war on the steps of their temples.

Cortés wrote home that the island capital of the Aztec Empire was without comparison in Spain. But Cortés, despite his prolonged stay in the city, had no interest in learning about Aztec life. He wanted to give the city (and its riches) to his Spanish master.

When diplomacy failed and Cortés turned to war, the Indians learned that Cortés and his lieutenants observed none of the Aztecs' rules. The Spaniards fought at night, when no sane Aztec would wage war (for the night was filled with ghosts and demons). Cortés and his men refused to engage in face-to-face combat, butchered Aztec priests in their own temple sanctuary, and fled like cowards when they were outnumbered. They spread fearsome diseases and turned the Aztecs' allies against their masters (although the former exceeded the Spanish in their animosity against the Aztecs). In the final battle, in May 1521, Cortés's army destroyed the city that was the heart and soul of the Aztecs' world. The Aztecs fought bravely but lost, wailing, "We have torn our hair in our grief; the houses are roofless now, and their walls are red with blood."

Cortés's treatment of the Aztecs may have been incomprehensible to them, but from the first he had a plan. He had violated direct orders from his nominal superior, the governor of Cuba, in remaining in Mexico; he had fought a war against a people at peace with Spain; he had violated the Laws of Burgos mandating humane treatment of the Indians; and he had made himself titular head of a conquered land without permission from his overlord, Charles V of Spain. But all would be forgiven, Cortés hoped, if he could categorize his conduct as a "just war."

Thus Cortés prepared and sent four long letters to Charles V detailing why the Indians deserved punishment. He cited the Aztec custom of ritual sacrifice, which he described in one of his letters: "whenever they wish something from their idols . . . they take children, girls and boys alike, and even men and women of mature age, and in the presence of those idols, they take them—still living!—and they cut their chests open, and, out of them, they rip out their hearts and entrails." The dismembered corpses were then apportioned among families who had housed the captives. Cortés cited the Aztecs' cannibalism as another "abominable sin." In other words, Cortés sought to rearrange his war against the Aztecs to fit a European category—the just war against the enemies of Christ—that would both exculpate his actions and allow him to claim his own right to the land. In the end, Cortés convinced his imperial master to make him the first governor of the province of New Spain.

Yet Cortés understood that an integrated Indian and European society must emerge from the conquest, if the colony of New Spain was to survive. The first requirement was an interpreter. Columbus had kidnapped young Taínos for this task. Cortés's own interpreter was a young slave woman given him and his troops after he defeated the Tabascans on the east coast of Mexico. Dona Marina, as she was baptized, became Cortés's constant and invaluable companion.

But interpreting was only the beginning of his uses for Indians. Cortés foresaw an alliance of native and newcomer, at least on the aristocratic level. He had at hand for this purpose one of the daughters of Moctezuma, the seventeen-year-old Tecuichpotzin. He arranged for her instruction and conversion to Christianity, and she was baptized Dona Isabel; he then granted her as an *encomienda* the lands (and the labor of the Indians) in the town of Tacuba (formerly Tlacopan), thus fusing the Aztec tradition of tribute and the Spanish legal formula for a trusteeship. Finally, he arranged her marriage to one of his senior officers. Dona Isabel's sons and daughters by her Spanish husbands gained lands and titles, and begat a mixed-ancestry aristocracy. By accommodating the Spanish through assimilation of Spanish customs and creeds, they protected the Nahua culture of the Aztecs from the fate of the Taíno.

The Borderlands of Florida, the Southeast, and New Mexico

In 1521, while Cortés watched Tenochtitlán burn, Ponce de León, under a license from the crown, entered "La Florida." Eight years earlier, he had touched the east coast of the Florida peninsula, seeking gold, slaves, and, the story went, the rejuvenating waters of a mysterious fountain of youth. The Ais Indians drove him off with their arrows. They had already met the Spanish brigands who, like the Portuguese on the west coast of Africa, raided the Atlantic shoreline looking for slaves. Ponce de León rounded the Florida Keys and sailed up the west coast of the peninsula, where the Caloosas greeted him just as the Ais had. They, too, knew about Spanish aims. When he returned to the Caloosa territory in 1521 and tried to build a fort, the Indians attacked in force and wounded him. He died three days later, in Cuba.

In the meantime, El Dorado—the fantasy of untold wealth—still beckoned the Spanish. In 1527, Narvaez, the despoiler of Cuba, returned from Spain with royal permission to claim the land that Ponce de León had coveted. Narvaez entered west Florida coastal wasters with five ships. One went aground, and three, driven off by storms, lost sight of Narvaez and his men. Instead of turning back, Narvaez pressed on, avoiding the Caloosas by going north of their villages, but finding the Caloosas' neighbors, the Timucuas, just as unwelcoming.

The Timucuas hit upon an ingenious scheme to rid themselves of the Spanish. They foisted the newcomers upon the Timucuas' northern enemies, the Apalachees. The Apalachees were the southernmost people whose lifestyle was close to the Mississippian manner as described in chapter 1. Unlike the Caloosas and Timucuas, who lived in widely dispersed, small farming communities, the Apalachees had large towns, surrounded by extensive cornfields, and the paramount chiefs kept granaries to distribute surplus food to their client villages in times of famine. With a ferocity that would make them a legend among the Spanish, they decimated Narvaez's troops.

The treasurer of the expedition, Álavar Núñez Cabeza de Vaca, pleaded for a return to the ships, but Narvaez's refusal to retreat cost Narvaez his life and that of all but four of the three hundred adventurers he had brought ashore. The survivors, Cabeza de Vaca, along with two other Spaniards and the Moorish slave Esteban, wandered for eight years among the native peoples of the Gulf of Mexico. They saw extremes of wealth and poverty. Some natives had great stores of meat and corn—others lived on shellfish and buffalo hides in lean seasons. When the refugees turned up in Mexico, they were greeted as heroes by the Spanish colonizers.

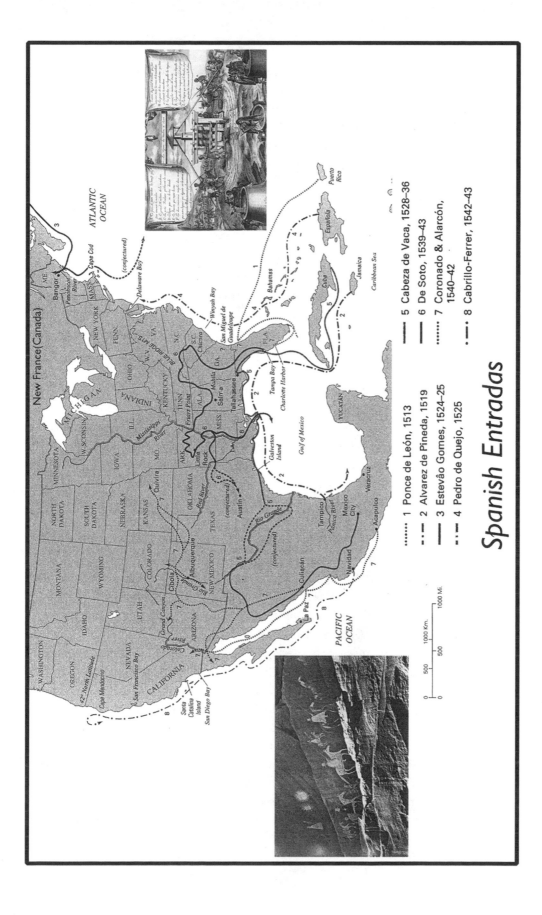

Spanish Entradas

.... 1 Ponce de León, 1513
—·—· 2 Alvarez de Pineda, 1519
——— 3 Estevão Gomes, 1524–25
—··— 4 Pedro de Quejo, 1525

——— 5 Cabeza de Vaca, 1528–36
——— 6 De Soto, 1539–43
.... 7 Coronado & Alarcón, 1540–42
—·—· 8 Cabrillo-Ferrer, 1542–43

Cabeza de Vaca's narrative did not convince the conquistadors to avoid the borderlands. In May 1539, Hernando de Soto followed the path of Ponce de León and Narvaez to west Florida. De Soto had brought nearly six hundred fighting men, including 270 cavalry and their mounts, along with slaves, native guides, and supplies. De Soto had already seen service in Central America and Peru, where his reputation for single-minded ferocity was unsurpassed. And he hoped that he would become as wealthy as the conquerors of the Incas.

De Soto pressed on into the interior of the Southeast, from 1539 to 1542 traveling over two thousand miles through Florida, Georgia, the Carolinas, Tennessee, Alabama, Mississippi, and Arkansas. He crossed the tail of the Appalachians and was the first European to see the Mississippi. His progress through the South devastated the native population. Not only did he wage war on anyone who resisted him, the diseases his men carried became a plague among the Indians he met. Most of them lived in towns of some size, carried on trade, and thus came into contact with one another frequently. They were thus perfect targets for a "virgin ground" epidemic. De Soto also let loose his herd of pigs upon the crops he did not seize for himself. To carry his baggage he took more slaves, and when they ran away, he and his officers hunted the runaways on horseback for sport.

Some Indian peoples, such as the Coosas of North Georgia and the Chickasaws of Mississippi, assaulted him, cutting his force in half. Others courted him with diplomacy. A relief fleet waited in the Gulf of Mexico, but de Soto, still beguiled by the dream of a city of gold, turned north, away from rescue. At last, sick, he reached the Mississippi River and marched south to safety, but his illness overcame him, and he died in May 1542. A year later, the remnant of his forces reached a Spanish settlement.

While de Soto ravaged the Southeast, Francisco Vásquez de Coronado embarked upon an even longer trek across the deserts and mountains of the Southwest looking for the rumored "Cibola" and other cities of gold. In their two-year trek, Coronado and his men, some three hundred Spanish soldiers of fortune and over a thousand Mexican Indian allies, explored the Grand Canyon, lower California, the upper Rio Grande, and the Great Plains.

His expedition proved that the Spanish could treat the Mexican Indians with respect and honor. The Indians who accompanied him were not slave baggage handlers but warriors who fought alongside the Spanish. Indeed, mindful of the instructions of the first viceroy (literally "substitute king") of Mexico, Antonio de Mendoza, to treat all natives with kindness and liberality, Coronado tried to keep peace with the Indians he met.

The rumor of great wealth in the Rio Grande valley was mistaken, unless one counted the extensive stores of corn and beans of the Pueblo village complexes of northwestern New Mexico. When in May 1540 Coronado reached Hawikuh pueblo, the westernmost of a confederation of six villages on a plain above the Zuni River, and found no gold, he could not hide his anguish. But his troops must be fed. In exchange for food, Coronado offered to take the Indians under the protection of the Spanish crown. The Indians answered with insults and arrows. Coronado ordered an attack. With their battle cry "for Saint James and Spain" ringing in the air, the Spanish force pursued the fleeing Indians into their village. Unable to slow the Spanish, the Indians carried off their wounded and dead fifteen miles to a sacred (and impregnable) mesa refuge, Dowa Yalanne, the corn mountain. The Spanish looted the abandoned houses and storage wells.

From Hawikuh pueblo, Coronado sent his captains in all directions to convince the Indians of Spanish goodwill, but his forces soon wore out their welcome. Coronado despaired, and his army fell into backbiting and mischief. By the winter of 1540–1541, with supplies running out, he abandoned all pretense of cooperation with the natives and began to assault those pueblos that resisted.

Only Coronado's retreat the next year prevented full-scale warfare, leaving behind a mixed legacy. The diseases the Spanish and their Mexican allies brought with them continued to ravage the natives, but the cattle, horses, and sheep abandoned in the retreat transformed native economies. The peoples of the Southwest mounted themselves on runaway Spanish horses and added mutton to their diets and wool and leather to their wardrobes.

SPANISH PLAN FOR EMPIRE

By the 1540s, the Spanish in America had progressed from sporadic explorations and expeditions in search of gold, to the founding of a chain of loosely connected colonies, to the establishment of an integrated, centrally directed empire. The vast distance between the monarchs in Madrid and the Spanish in the New World, and the headstrong arrogance of the conquistadors, diluted the force of the monarch's instructions. Even so, the Spanish colonizers expected to end their days wealthy and honored in Spain and thus ultimately had to obey imperial commands.

Although the conquistadors seemed to have little regard for law, whether their own or their hosts', the Spanish did not come to the New World without a plan of conquest. Indeed, on the eve of the first *entrada* of the Spanish into the Americas, Spain was the most legalistic of all the European powers. It was also the most aggressively Christian. Thus the conquistadors' instructions concerned law and religion as well as government.

Law on the Frontier

Law became the first pillar supporting the Spanish Empire abroad. The Council of the Indies in Spain prepared for all the explorers detailed instructions on everything from the size and geographical orientation of new towns to drills for the soldiers in the garrisons. The Spanish New World pueblo was to resemble a Roman provincial city: the streets laid out in a grid, the major thoroughfares aligned with the principal directions of the compass. At the center of the town stood the church and the presidio—a fortresslike structure whose thick walls would house the government and a garrison. The natives were to be gathered up in villages near the Spanish settlements, taught Spanish and Latin, instructed in the true faith, and put to work in the fields and mines.

Intended as a reform to protect the natives, the benevolent language of the laws caused the conquistadors "much amusement." Typical of the Spanish conquistadors' deliberate misreading of the intent of the royal plan was their treatment of the *requerimiento* (notification), a portion of the 1512 law that the Spanish conquistadors were to read to the Indians when they met. Its text was simple: if the natives acknowledged the sovereignty of the Spanish crown and accepted the Catholic religion, they would be treated well and remain free. Those who did not might be preyed upon with merciless savagery. But American Indians neither understood it nor envisioned the savagery with which its provisions would be carried out. One Spanish missionary in sympathy with the plight of the Indians recorded that when he saw the way the *requerimiento* worked, he did not know whether to laugh or to weep.

The conquistadors' treatment or mistreatment of the natives should not be viewed with twentieth-century sentiments. Native peoples routinely warred on one another. The Taíno greatly feared the neighboring Caribs, apparently for good reason. The Carib were ferocious warriors and often carried off Taíno captives. The Aztecs and their neighbors made war into a form of celebration, and ritually executed the defeated. The various peoples of the Southwest carried out raids for slaves and booty against one another. So important were warfare and slaving in the culture of the region that ritual recollections of both became part of the folklore of the Indians and remain so to this day.

The Fate of Indian Souls

As law was the first pillar of the empire, religion was the second. While the conquistadors read the *requerimiento* to bewildered natives, Spanish scholars, priests, and royal lawyers debated the moral basis for empire. At issue for these thinkers was whether the natives were by nature only fit for slavery or could become loyal, productive, and pious subjects of the king of Spain—in effect, whether the Indians had souls.

Reports from the New World like Amerigo Vespucci's accounts of the cannibals of the West Indies and the voluminous *General and Natural History of the Indies* (1537) by the former colonial administrator Gonzalo Fernández de Oviedo y Valdés bolstered the self-serving and Eurocentric view that the natives were semihuman. Vespucci depicted the natives as animals. They were not, in Oviedo's opinion, "men like us." Indeed, instead of heads, they had "hard and thick helmets . . . and just as their heads were hard, so their understanding was bestial and evilly inclined."

Yet saddened and conscience stricken by evidence of the barbarity of Spaniards in the New World, teachers like the Dominican monk Francisco de Vitoria and his students at the university in Salamanca argued that the Indians had all the natural rights of men and women—they were not by nature inferior. Not so, replied Juan Gines de Sepúlveda. Vitoria and his allies, Sepúlveda argued, were misled by their theological temperament. Sepúlveda was a canon lawyer and professor of law. For him, a correct reading of the law, aided by an understanding of Aristotle and the other classical authorities, proved that the Indians' animal nature suited them to slavery. Although he conceded that individual Indians might have mechanical ability and personal skills, their practice of human sacrifice and cannibalism was incontrovertible proof of their barbarism.

Although Sepúlveda relied upon the authority of old textbooks and treatises, his argument was forward looking in an ironic way. It fit the economic needs of the expanding Spanish Empire. To concede the humanity of the Indians might lead to a reexamination of the practices by which the Spanish Empire enriched the Spanish economy. It was hardly coincidence that the importation of hides and skins, raw silk, and, most important, silver from the New World dramatically boosted what had been a stagnant Spanish economy.

The last word was not Sepúlveda's, however, for a former slaveholder turned monk and reformer, Dominican Bartolomé de Las Casas, had seen with his own eyes what others mistook from far away. Unlike Sepúlveda and Vitoria, Las Casas had lived for a time in the Spanish Caribbean. Indeed, the force of his observations derived from the credibility of an eyewitness. As he wrote late in life, "I am the oldest of those who went over to the Indies, and in the many years that I have been there and in which I have seen with my eyes, I have not read [others'] histories which could be lies, but instead I have experienced."

In a series of exposés in direct refutation of Sepúlveda, Las Casas insisted that in many ways the Indians were the moral superiors of those who had subjugated them in the name of Christ. "I know by certain infallible signs that the wars waged by the Indians against the Christians have been justifiable wars and that all the wars waged by the Christians against the Indians have been unjust wars, more diabolical than any wars ever waged anywhere in the world," he wrote. Las Casas concluded that the Indians had "the facts and the law natural, divine and human" on their side. Greatly moved by his testimony, in 1551 King Philip II replaced the reading of the *requerimiento* with specific instructions to treat the Indians with gentleness.

In the Spanish provinces, missionaries directed worship and instructed the natives in the sacraments. The mendicant orders (Franciscans and Dominicans in the lead) went barefooted and unarmed among the Indians, though soldiers were never far away. The friars set up schools as well as churches. Imbued with utopian ideals, some of them saw the New World as a prototype for a return to simple worship, communal ownership of property, and the representative government associated with the first Christian churches.

The enthusiasm and self-sacrifice of the friars reached to the northern frontiers of the empire. There, the friars warned the Spanish that they must act the part of good Christians or the Indians would never get the idea. Unfortunately, the friars' zeal sometimes overleaped its purpose. The sexual taboos of European society, given greater intensity by the friars' own vows of celibacy, ill fit the Indians' concept of the naturalness of sexual display and intercourse. Overt sexuality was not sinful among the Pueblo peoples of New Mexico, for example, for even their demigods enjoyed sex. Indian songs delighted in sexual puns, and Indian names of landmarks included references to genital parts. Appalled by this frankness, missionaries destroyed native fetish objects and barred dances and songs with sexual content.

The missionaries' attack on what they saw as native immorality and their attempts to replace it with Christian precepts undermined the place of women in native societies. Indian women might not share political power with Indian men, but Indian ways honored women's sexuality. Among the Aztecs, for example, female gods had obvious sexual attributes, and Aztec women were proud of their sexual prowess. Pueblo women, according to missionaries among them, "went half naked." When the missionaries blasted female nudity and open female sexuality by treating it as prostitution, and ridiculed "harlots" as "rotten fruit," they condemned women's traditional roles. The only acceptable alternative, the chaste virgin and modest wife, denied women the wide variety of social roles they filled in Indian cultures.

The State

The third pillar supporting the Spanish empire in America was the state. Unlike the private rights of the *encomenderos* and the sacerdotal powers of the priests, the state operated publicly, through appointment, review, visitation, and revolution in office. Unfortunately, from the top, the viceroy, in charge of a territory, to the bottom, the local alcaldes, equivalent to a combination of mayor and local judge, the public sphere was riddled with corruption. Indeed, corruption was the rule, honesty the exception. Royal appointees sought these posts to get rich, and the only way to get rich on the frontiers of the empire was to extort bribes, expropriate public funds, and pillage the locals.

But corruption had its counterweight in the operation of collective and special overseers. Watching the viceroys were the *audiencias*—a mixture of judicial body and administrative arm of the crown—sitting in the cities where the viceroys had their offices. Inferior *audiencias* met in provincial towns. The *audiencias* acted as appeals courts in cases of felony and heard petitions against the local officials. At the end of an official's term, he faced a *residencia*, or hearing, on his conduct. Judges and other officials conducted these hearings, and no one could leave office without one. The crown also sent *visitadores* to the colonies to provide a check on the whole system, report on particular problems, and simply keep everyone on their toes.

AFRICAN SLAVERY IN THE FIRST NEW WORLD COLONIES

No sooner did the Spanish relieve most Indians of the weight of slavery than the Spanish and Portuguese hoisted it upon the shoulders of transported Africans. The ironies in this transfer of burdens abound. Although the missionaries lobbied for the end of Indian slavery, they acquiesced in the importation of African bondmen and women. That the Spanish and Portuguese, so concerned with racial purity, would import into their colonies over twelve million people of what the Spanish proclaimed to be an inferior race seems equally contradictory on its face. The need for laborers outweighed all ironies and contradictions, however.

The Transatlantic Slave Trade

In the fifteenth and sixteenth centuries, the Atlantic slave trade was overwhelmingly a Portuguese business, driven by the Portuguese and Spanish commitment to New World colonization. In the seventeenth century, French, Dutch, and English companies would muscle into the trade, fighting for the royal *asiento* (literally, permission) to sell slaves to the Spanish colonies, as well as supplying their own colonies' needs.

The demand for slave labor in the New World turned what had been European participation in an essentially African slave trade into an entirely different kind of enterprise, where profit lay not in the carrying trade but in the profit of selling human cargoes. The rise of the transatlantic slave trade dramatically changed the complexion of slavery in Africa. The insatiable demands of the New World market caused African leaders to increase their efforts to obtain new slaves, promoting war in Africa.

The importation of slaves to the New World began as a trickle in the 1510s, but with the opening of gold mining in Mexico, Peru, and Brazil, and later with the introduction of large-scale sugar production in Brazil, Mexico, and the Antilles after 1516, the flow of slaves became a torrent.

The drain on African peoples and resources to service the new demand varied over time and from place to place. In the sixteenth century, Senegambia, on the far western coast of Africa, and Guinea supplied almost 40 percent of the initial demand for slaves. Then their contribution tapered off. The slack was taken up in later years by the "gold coast" of what is now Ghana and the "slave coast" of what is now Benin, the Ivory Coast, and Nigeria. An even larger supplier was the Congo River basin. By the middle of the seventeenth century, 75 percent of the slaves came from Angola and the Congo.

The cold figures are frightening: in the first decades of the trade, from 1500 to 1550, an average of two thousand Africans a year were carried from their homes to the New World. By the second half of the century, the yearly average had risen to four thousand men, women, and children. By the first half of the 1600s, the number had

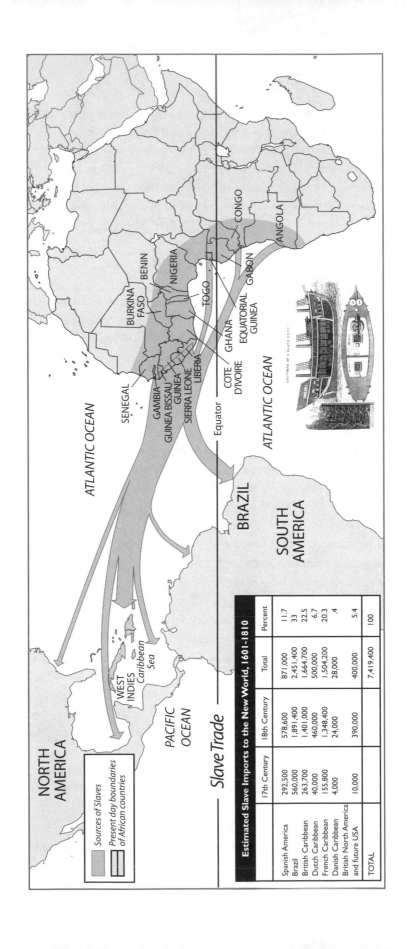

Slave Trade

NORTH AMERICA

ATLANTIC OCEAN

PACIFIC OCEAN

WEST INDIES

Caribbean Sea

SOUTH AMERICA

BRAZIL

ATLANTIC OCEAN

Equator

SENEGAL
GAMBIA
GUINEA BISSAU
GUINEA
SIERRA LEONE
LIBERIA
COTE D'IVOIRE
GHANA
TOGO
BENIN
BURKINA FASO
NIGERIA
EQUATORIAL GUINEA
GABON
CONGO
ANGOLA

Sources of Slaves

Present day boundaries of African countries

Estimated Slave Imports to the New World, 1601-1810				
	17th Century	18th Century	Total	Percent
Spanish America	292,500	578,600	871,000	11.7
Brazil	560,000	1,891,400	2,451,400	33
British Caribbean	263,700	1,401,000	1,664,700	22.5
Dutch Caribbean	40,000	460,000	500,000	6.7
French Caribbean	155,800	1,348,400	1,504,200	20.3
Danish Caribbean	4,000	24,000	28,000	.4
British North America and future USA	10,000	390,000	400,000	5.4
TOTAL			7,419,400	100

again risen to seventy-three hundred each year, a figure that almost doubled between 1650 and 1675. In the last quarter of the seventeenth century, twenty-three thousand slaves each year were bound in chains and borne across the Atlantic to European plantations in America. In other terms, before 1580 slaves were less than one-fourth of all transatlantic passengers. After 1580, they were over 60 percent of migrants going west. Plainly, slaves were the laborers on whose backs the European empires were built.

Although the Portuguese introduced the Western slave trade, competitors appeared by the end of the sixteenth century. The Dutch were the most efficient and ruthless of these, though the English and the French not only carried slaves from Africa to the Spanish colonies, they (along with the Dutch) also preyed on the Portuguese slavers. In fact, at any one time one might find any of these seagoing powers kidnapping people from African coastal villages, raiding one another's ports of call and stealing slaves, forcing slave cargoes on unwilling purchasers (by threatening to destroy the colonial settlement if its planters did not buy the cargo), and cutting into one another's territories to put together slave cargoes for distant ports. Slave traders were also one of the early modern world's first efficiency experts, always looking for ways to improve profits, package their wares, and reduce turnaround time. Transporting slaves was almost as big a business as putting slave labor to work.

Initially, Hispaniola received the bulk of the Portuguese slave shipments. By the middle of the sixteenth century, Brazil became the most lucrative port of call for the slavers, and its sugar plantations remained steady customers. But by the end of the sixteenth century and well into the seventeenth, Mexico rivaled Brazil in demand for slaves. From 1600 to 1622, Mexican buyers absorbed from 40 to 80 percent of yearly slave imports. With demand skyrocketing, prices rose as well, and some Mexican purchasers nearly bankrupted themselves to obtain slaves for their silver mines, sugar plantations, and textile works.

Behind these figures lies an even more terrifying fact: the Spanish and Portuguese colonies of the New World were graveyards for slaves. In the seventeenth century, sugar island importations of slaves averaged between one thousand and two thousand persons per year, an indicator of the number of slaves who had to be replaced. Slave populations there actually declined despite high regular infusions of imported slaves. As King Ferdinand admonished the governor of Hispaniola, "I do not understand how so many Negroes have died; take much care of them." But care cost money, and until it became cheaper to "take much care of them" than to buy replacements, high mortality rates would be the rule.

What justification did the transatlantic slave traders give for their efforts, knowing as they did the fate that awaited most of their cargoes? The racial motifs that the Portuguese and Spanish introduced in defense of the Canary Island slave trade did double duty in support of the transportation of Africans to the Caribbean, based on the idea that similarity in climate, natural disposition, and "blood" made Africans better suited to labor in the subtropics and tropics of the Americas than Europeans. There was some truth in the common claim that the Africans could better withstand the climate of the tropics than European workers—but it was only a relative truth. European servants and laborers died in the tropics at ten times the rate of mortality for their age group in temperate zones. Africans carried to the New World died at rates only twice as high as the same age groups in Africa.

Apologists for the trade employed legalistic arguments as well. When priests like Brazil's Father Sandoval questioned the way in which Africans were brought to the New World, the Portuguese Jesuit Luis Brandaon, ministering to the Portuguese slave "factory" in Angola, replied: "Since the traders who bring these Negroes [to Brazil] bring them in good faith, those inhabitants [of the Portuguese plantations in Brazil] can very well buy them from such traders without any scruple, and the latter on their part can sell them, for it is a generally accepted opinion that the owner who owns anything in good faith can sell it and that it can be bought. . . . Besides, I found it true indeed, that no Negro will ever say he has been captured legally." The standard bill of sale for slaves born in Africa and auctioned in Mexico included the phrase "captured in just war," which reduced Brandaon's argument to its essentials. But no buyer at the auctions knew or cared how the individual slave was obtained. More important information on the bill of sale included the price, the work skills, and any distinguishing marks on the slave (so that runaway slaves could be returned to their "rightful" owners).

Europeans also argued that exposure to Christianity was a boon to the slaves in itself, for their souls would now be saved. As Brandaon wrote, "to lose so many souls as sail from here [Angola] out of whom many are saved [when purchased by a Christian master] does not seem to be doing much service to God." But masters in the Spanish colonies of the New World decided the slaves would not be freed even if they became Christians, undercutting the logic of this rationale.

None of these justifications or rationalizations could conceal the fact that the slave trade had its roots in a market strategy in the age of nascent capitalism. Part and parcel of Europe's embrace of the values of commerce and accumulation in the age of exploration was the acceptance of ruthless business practices and calculation of material self-interest. Had the price of slave labor on the West African coast not been low enough, or the costs of carrying slaves to the New World been too high, the slave traders would not have undertaken the enterprise. Demand in the colonies itself would not have induced the slavers to engage in an unprofitable business. But the cost was low, for war in Africa had created an oversupply of captives, and the Portuguese had plenty of space in their cargo ships.

The same calculus of profit and loss dictated the treatment of slaves on the infamous "middle passage" from Africa to America. At first, the slavers tried to keep the costs of transporting the slaves low and packed the ships with little concern for the physical or mental health of the slaves. Models for the "ideal" packing of slaves in the holds and on the decks of these ships resemble the packaging of sardines in a tin. The losses of captives to disease and starvation soon mounted to almost 20 percent of the average cargo, and economic considerations dictated more humane treatment in the middle passage across the Atlantic.

Who was taken in this slave trade? As Gwendolyn Midlo Hall and other historians have recently documented, a wide variety of African peoples came to America in the slavers' ships' holds. The fact that the Europeans purchased the slaves at a relatively small number of coastal marts tends to obscure the origins and diversity of the captives' ways. Some slaves came from the Senegambian north, a land where kings had long ruled well-organized states. Muslim herdsmen, townspeople, and soldiers occupied the region. The peoples of the Guinean coast, to the south, were more tied to their small villages. Fishermen and farmers, they were preyed upon by nearby warrior kingdoms. Farther south, Angolans spoke different tongues and governed themselves by different customs. Enslaved African peoples were of many different colors, looked and sounded different from one another, and prayed to different gods.

The World the Slaveholders Made

Historians distinguish between slave societies and slaveholding societies in the early Americas. In the latter, slavery is only one form of labor, and slaves are not the majority of the population. Initially, the Spanish and Portuguese colonies fit this description. In slaveholding societies, slaves have some degree of personal independence, controlling their time, space, and social and domestic relations. Individual slaves negotiate the terms of their labor, bring complaints against abusive masters, choose a marriage partner, and even negotiate to change owners. They can, with luck and perseverance, even become free. Among the early colonies, a small group of such slaves acted as interpreters and brokers for European merchants. Though subject to reenslavement for the slightest infraction, their language skills and knowledge of both cultures gave them bargaining power, and some used it to amass wealth of their own.

In the slave society, slavery is the predominant labor system, and all social institutions bend to protect the absolute power of the master over the slave. Within a relatively short time—the space of one generation—the Spanish and Portuguese possessions in the Antilles and Brazil became slave societies. Where the demands of production and profit dictated and sufficient capital or credit for purchases of slaves could be found, slaveholding societies devolved into slave societies.

Slave owners valued slaves for their labor. Thus masters sought to acquire slaves at their peak production years. For this reason, masters purchased few children or older males. Owners preferred men to women, but women lived longer once they were on the plantation, so the sex ratios on the plantations tended to even out. The more economically successful the master, the better pick he had of the slaves available, and the more healthy and able his slave workforce would be. Unsuccessful planters could not afford the best workers and had to make do with a reject or unruly slave labor force.

Planters soon worked out a rough index of the desirability of slaves from different regions. They preferred Congolese craftspeople because they were believed to be healthier than other Africans. The masters selected Fulani as herdsmen, because of their experience with cattle in Africa. The Hausa of eastern Nigeria were the most trusted *suciers*—men who oversaw the last stages of transformation of sugarcane juice into sugar crystals, a task that required long hours standing over giant boiling vats.

Patterns of slave work varied according to the size of the plantation or the mine. In general, the larger the plantation or mine, the more stable the workforce and the more reliable the work routines. But wielding the hoe to cut holes in the ground to plant the cane "cuttings" each spring was backbreaking. Fertilizing the fields with animal manure, shellfish, lime, and cane trash was scarcely less onerous. Less physically demanding but far more dangerous was the pressing and the boiling of the cut cane in great vats. Although sugar cultivation was backbreaking, working in the silver mines was more physically dangerous for slaves. Small planters and mine owners asked individual slaves to perform a greater variety of tasks. Large plantations and mines had large craft shops and offered slaves a greater chance to learn and practice different crafts than did smaller plantations.

The worst job assignment for the slave worker, on whatever size plantation, was the labor "gang." The Portuguese colony in Brazil, the first of the great New World centers of sugar production, set the pattern for large-scale slave gangs. The gang was a group of slave workers organized by gender, age, and ability. Planters drove slave gangs from sunup to sundown. The incapacitated or ill, the very young and the very old, and women bearing children worked shorter hours on the second or third gangs.

When the crops fell in market value, and the value of the slaves correspondingly rose, masters might switch to the "task system." In the task system, slaves performed a given task and then enjoyed free time. Slave craftspeople, herdsmen, and house servants labored under the task system. Tasking afforded slaves more time for themselves, and thereby extended their lives. It also made slaves happier workers. Slave herdsmen on cattle ranches in Mexico and Hispaniola were able to use the extra time to visit with relatives. Slave gold miners in Colombia could employ off-task time to pan enough gold to buy their own freedom. The reverse of this coin was that owners often expected slaves to use their spare time to find food and shelter for themselves.

Although women were less often imported than men (the ratio was three men for each woman), and some women were able to obtain domestic employment in or around the homes of the masters, the vast majority of women (and a larger proportion of them than men) worked in the fields at repetitive and filthy tasks. The fatality rates among such women and their young children were very high, even by sixteenth- and seventeenth-century standards. Although masters suspected their slave mothers of practicing infanticide, the death rate of newborns and infants was more often due to poor prenatal and postnatal care, disease, and accidents than to infanticide.

Individual members of the owning classes and individual slaves could and did develop relations of mutual trust and even affection. Slave codes in the Spanish colonies followed the *Siete Partidas*, the slave code of medieval Spain. This in turn was modeled upon Roman slave law. Roman law gave to the master all but absolute power over the slave, and if the master wished to mitigate the institution or to free the slave, the state would not stand in the way. Some masters permitted slaves to celebrate holidays, march in parades, join religious mutual-aid societies, attend church, and learn to read and write. In America, the Spanish and Portuguese laws abetted the existence of a class of free persons of color and made manumission relatively easy.

But the demography and the internal dynamics of the slave society militated against humane treatment. If slave populations had remained stable over time, the natural bonds of affection might have overcome or mitigated the severities of the system, but disease and consequent mortality in the slave quarters continually undercut the development of long-term personal ties. The danger of disease also drove masters to leave their families in the home country. Thus slave children did not grow up knowing free children, one way in which the barbarity of slavery might have been lessened. Above all, the resistance of some slaves made all masters uneasy about the loyalty of any slave. The result was a psychology among the master classes that the slaves had to be made to stand in fear or they would rise up, run away, or simply refuse to labor. As one European observer warned of slaves, "however they may disguise it, they hate their masters and wish them destroyed."

Thus there appeared in the slave colonies the instruments of routine, almost casual oppression—the leg irons, collars, chains, and whipping stocks. Mexican masters favored *pringar*, dropping burning wax or animal fat on the slave's skin. Insolent slaves were branded and runaways mutilated. On Hispaniola, slaves were not to bang drums or blow horns, lest the sound signal a revolt. Merely offering a gesture of violence to a white person was grounds for a severe whipping. The parental language that the masters used when "correcting" a slave concealed quick tempers and brutal punishments. The power that slave masters exercised over their bondmen and women corrupted the master class.

Some masters forced intercourse upon female slaves, the worst corruption of the institution of slavery, and these sexual unions produced a welter of children of mixed parentage. In 1570, the first Mexican census recorded that one in eleven slaves was a mulatto. Over time, that number increased steadily. By the middle of the seventeenth century in cities like Mexico City, one out of every eight slaves was a mulatto.

Although such men and women enjoyed a far higher rate of manumission than children of slave parents—in Mexico, over 90 percent of slaves freed by their masters were mulattos—freed men and women remained at risk of reenslavement because of their color.

Ironically, despite the submersion of a handful of Europeans in a sea of Africans in these slave societies and the appearance of large numbers of slaves and free persons of mixed ancestry, the master classes clung tightly to preexisting legal and cultural notions of color. Rather than surrender entrenched ideas of purity of blood to the reality of racial mixing, the Spanish invented a complex system of classifying everyone according to their parentage. Mulattos were the result of European and African unions. Mestizos were children of European and Indian parentage. Sambos were products of African and Indian parents.

The World the Slaves Made

Beyond the anguish of enslavement itself, the middle passage and the initial years of slavery bewildered and challenged the bondmen and women. Most of the slaves came from isolated rural areas and had little experience of other African cultures. For them, the loss of familiar scenes and family ties, added to the babble of unfamiliar voices, was a psychological as well as a physical trial, which the everyday task of communicating with their new comrades had to overcome.

Conversations in gestures and loan words began on the ships lying at anchor off the coast of West Africa, continued below and above decks on the voyage, and intensified in the slave quarters. Slaves developed pidgin speech to communicate with other slaves and with masters. Later, if they survived, slaves turned pidgin into "creoles," stable compound languages that blended African and locally spoken European languages. Slaves also created fictional kinship networks based on West African models, featuring "uncles" and "aunts" who were not blood kin but performed the nurturing and socializing roles of biological parents.

Hybrid customs pieced together from memory and necessity allowed slaves to build communities. Although African peoples retained their distinct regional heritages as well, in matters as minute as the marks, or scarifications, that they wore to denote different group affiliations, in the slave quarters of rural plantations men and women fabricated a composite of African building styles and cultures. They also recreated the cooking utensils and approximated the recipes (of course, substituting some new ingredients) for foods they had enjoyed in Africa.

Slaves who had survived the first years of bondage next faced the problem of finding a suitable partner. Wherever slaves worked, the greatest obstacle was the unbalanced sex ratio of men to women. A handful of slaves married free persons of color. In the cities, slaves had a wider range of choice than on the plantations or in the mines.

Sometimes Spanish and Portuguese owners encouraged marriages, arranging with priests to perform a mass for slaves who had converted to Roman Catholicism, making the marriage into a festive event. Slaves also married in secret, according to African rites. But these adaptations and achievements ran against the tide, for African communities in the New World were always impermanent and imperiled.

Stable communities are collections of families, in which parents pass their values on to their children. But slaves often did not have the time to create families and rear children. Like the Indians whose death from disease led to the Atlantic slave trade, the Africans were vulnerable to a wide spectrum of European maladies. The infirmities and infections the masters and white indentured servants brought with them included killers like influenza, bubonic plague, and smallpox. Chickenpox and measles were not usually fatal to Europeans, but they were to the Africans, who had no resistance. So, too, were the tropical parasites the newcomers found on the islands and the Spanish Main. Waiting in the tropics—a perfect breeding ground for parasites, viruses, and bacteria—were native maladies like yellow fever. Slaves also carried illnesses from West Africa, including elephantiasis and sleeping sickness.

There were a few Europeans who practiced medicine, bleeding the sick with leeches or inducing vomiting and diarrhea with emetics, most of which made the sickness worse. Masters applied emetics and other "heroic remedies" not only to cure disease but to assert their control over the slaves' bodies as well. The Africans preferred their own medicine, although providers of folk remedies faced new diseases and had to adapt to new flora and fauna.

On some occasions, slaves may have taken out some of their animosity on surrounding native peoples. Spanish and Portuguese officials passed laws to prevent violence between the Africans and the Indians. In one case, recorded in 1538 in Mexico, "a Negro belonging to a judge forcibly took an Indian, tied him to the tail of his horse, mounted the horse and dragged the Indian along until he died." Pueblo Indians complained constantly about gangs of African slaves pillaging houses and stealing food. When the two groups worked alongside one another, there was constant friction. In the end, the authorities laid out strict partitions between occupations for Indians and Africans. For example, Africans were forbidden to sell chilies—that was to be an Indian monopoly.

Slave Resistance

Although the masters and their overseers aimed at a docile labor force, the slaves did not comply. The least serious forms of slave resistance—breaking tools, slowing down on the job, vanishing for a time, and refusing to perform a task—occurred commonly. More serious resistance included assaulting masters or overseers, running away, and rebellion.

The first African slaves in the Americas, Christianized slaves from Spain brought to the Antilles to replace Indian laborers, no sooner alit from the ships than they fled into the bush. These were the first *cimarrons* (later called "maroons" in English)—

African men and women who liberated themselves and established communities in the jungles of Guiana and Panama and the mountains of Mexico, Jamaica, and Hispaniola.

Most maroon communities were heavily male and predominantly immigrant rather than second-generation and family based in composition. Maroons had to steal much of what they consumed and thus could never stray far from the plantations whose constraints they had rejected. Maroons were, from the first, formidable military opponents for the settler militia, but the maroons' purpose was more often to remain at liberty than to take vengeance on the slaveholders.

In 1574, the Spanish ordered death for anyone who induced a slave to run away, but by the middle of the sixteenth century there were seven times as many maroons on Hispaniola as there were Spanish colonists. Despite rebel slaves' difficulties in coordinating their uprisings, a major slave revolt rocked Spanish Hispaniola in 1522, and another erupted in Puerto Rico in 1527. Revolts in Cuba in 1538 and in Honduras in 1548 nearly succeeded. Most often a slave either gave away the plot inadvertently or wished to prevent violence to a particular master or mistress and so revealed the details of the plot. Some slaves gained their freedom from informing.

Authorities tried and executed the ringleaders of these rebellions, sometimes after torturing them to learn the identities of conspirators. The tribunals were rarely concerned with precise degrees of culpability, and reluctant rebels were hanged alongside committed incendiaries. Sometimes their heads were stuck on spikes at crossroads to deter other potential rebels.

THE END OF THE SPANISH CENTURY

By 1587, the Spanish had established a remarkable record of exploration, conquest, and settlement in America, but the extent of Spanish success had drawn rivals. Enviously, two northern European sea powers, England and France, probed Spanish settlements in the Caribbean and the shores of North America looking for weak points. In the second half of the sixteenth century, French corsairs burned and pillaged Spanish settlements in Cuba and Hispaniola. At the same time, English sea dogs—skilled and bold mariners from the southern and western ports of England—harried the Spanish treasure fleets and raided Spanish settlements in the Caribbean and on the Spanish Main. Spain's diplomatic entreaties brought no relief, but Philip II of Spain had formulated a plan to resolve the problem: he would invade England.

King Philip's Armada

By the early 1580s, Philip had convinced himself that Elizabeth I of England, his sister-in-law, was behind all his troubles. Elizabeth promised the Spanish she would punish the sea dogs but gave them titles and honors instead. More was at stake for

Philip and Spain than the loss of the treasure cargoes, for the gold and silver the English took from the Spanish paid for England's naval building program.

Perhaps even more important to Philip, whoever controlled the wealth of the empire could dictate the outcome of the wars that Spain waged in Europe. Spain claimed the Low Countries as part of its European empire, but the Dutch had risen in rebellion. Spain's new commander in the Low Countries, the brilliant and bold Duke of Parma, had little trouble subduing the rebellious South (now Belgium), but English mercenaries and English conscripts joined with Dutch fighters to hold off the Spanish veterans in the North. English aid to the Dutch had to be stopped, and the best way to do this was to attack England.

Philip knew he had little time to crush the Dutch and the English. He had reached the age of sixty, outliving four wives and many of his children. All the paperwork of the empire still flowed into his small, cell-like office and through his arthritic hands, but he had lost his fabled patience. In the spring of 1587, he demanded from his advisers a plan for the seaborne invasion of England. He was told he needed five hundred ships and seventy thousand men—a ruinous estimate for a king already in great debt, but he plowed ahead anyway.

While Philip planned his strike at England, the English struck at Cadiz, Spain's largest port. Francis Drake, one of the boldest of the sea dogs, sailed in with thirty ships, and for two days, at the end of April and the beginning of May 1587, destroyed every vessel sent against him and all the ships at anchor in the port. Then he escaped. Furious, Philip ordered the armada assembled.

The English fleet, now nearly one hundred ships strong, gathered as well. Elizabeth's commanders, notably John Hawkins and Drake, had rebuilt her navy, adding wider, faster ships and arming them with the long guns called ship killers. The English planned a new kind of battle—intending to sink the enemy at a distance with cannon fire instead of coming in to close quarters and boarding.

The armada sailed against England in early May 1588. It comprised 130 ships, 20 of them war galleons, supported by armed merchant men and troop ships to pick up the Duke of Parma's army and carry it across the English Channel to invade England. The English did not wait for the armada to arrive off their coast. The queen's navy was fully manned, supplied, and at sea by the end of April. The commander of the fleet, Charles Howard, Lord Effingham, had agreed with his subordinates to attack the Spanish at sea. He led 90 ships, some of them as big as, and most of them faster than, the Spanish warships.

The two fleets came into sight of one another late on July 30, 1588. The English formed a simple line astern. The Spanish sailed into a U-shaped formation. The leading vessels raised their battle ensigns, almost as though they were engaging in a knightly salute; then the killing began. The battle raged for nearly two weeks. With great courage and discipline, the Spanish ships of the line tried to bring the English to close battle, but the English held off, and their long guns played havoc with the Spanish. Finally, Lord Effingham's ships ran out of shot and powder, and the Spanish escaped.

But the wind would not let the Spanish return as they had come, through the English Channel, and they set off to the northwest, hoping to sail home by rounding the northern coast of Scotland, passing the western shore of Ireland, and slipping down into Iberian waters. A series of unusually violent storms again scattered the surviving ships, however, and the trip around Ireland cost the fleet more vessels. The Spanish sailors who reached the shore alive were executed on the spot or hunted down and slaughtered by English forces in Ireland.

Forty-four ships returned to Iberian waters, only half of which would ever sail again; thousands of men had died, and millions of ducats in gold had been spent to no good purpose for Spain. Though Philip still had a formidable naval force and even tried to assemble another armada, England was now master of the North Atlantic. The wrecks of the galleons that had once convoyed the treasure ships littered the ocean floor along the track of the armada's flight. The Spanish century, and Spain's monopoly on the New World, was over.

————

Though the Spanish did not plan on it, diversity had become the hallmark of the early Iberian empires in the Caribbean and North America. Peoples of three continents lived and worked in close proximity with one another and in time fashioned a multicultural society. Mixed parentage created classes of mestizos and mulattos, whose function and status in society further complicated social relationships and blunted the sharp edge of oppression.

Yet all this said, the riches of the mines, the plantations, and the ranches did not go to those who labored to produce them. Instead, a class of owners and officials siphoned off the wealth. Spanish American society in these early years may have been multiracial and multicultural, but it was never equitable.

4

Rivals for the Northland
England and France in America

Visitors at the court of Ferdinand and Isabel spread the news of Columbus's discovery all over western Europe soon after Columbus returned to Spain in the winter of 1493. As exaggerated as some of these accounts might have been, the prospect of wealth was real, and other European powers soon felt the consequences of Spanish exploitation of the Americas. American gold and silver flowing into Spanish coffers paid for its military adventures in Europe and the growth of the largest fleet in the world.

The English and the French envied the Spanish their success, but until the defeat of the Spanish armada in 1588, neither England nor France could outduel the Spanish in the Caribbean or the borderlands of the Spanish Empire in North America. Still, Spain had not established any outposts above the thirty-fifth parallel. Just as the Spanish sought El Dorado in the jungles and the deserts of the semitropics, so sixteenth-century English and French navigators and princes searched for a passage to the East Indies north of the Spanish New World possessions.

When their initial reconnaissances ended in failure and further probes were interrupted by unforeseen crises at home, the northern European powers rethought their enterprise. They decided to establish fortified trading posts along the coast from Newfoundland to the Carolinas. From these, they could deny the North to the Spanish conquistadors and friars and make a profit in the process. In the course of a century of lost ships and inept explorations, the French and English uncovered a marketable commodity in the North—fur—and the Indians happily traded it for European goods. The northern lands became the fur frontier.

The Indians and the Europeans had radically different conceptions of the meaning and use of trade, but for a time, perceived mutual advantage convinced them to put those differences aside. The pelts the Indians trapped and traded employed European craftspeople and

Whilst we followed on our course, there came from the land odors incomparable for sweetness, brought with a warm wind so abundantly that all the Orient parts could not produce greater abundance. We did stretch out our hands as it were to take them, so palpable were they, which I have admired a thousand times since.
—Marc Lescarbot, *off the coast of French Canada, 1606*

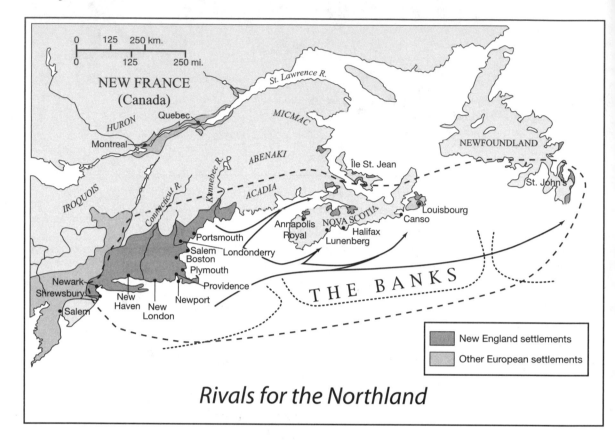

Rivals for the Northland

gave a much needed lift to European commerce. The finished goods the Europeans brought to America elevated the Indians' standard of living.

ENGLAND AND FRANCE EYE THE NORTHLAND

Because the Europeans did not populate the land or seek to conquer its native peoples, these first northern ventures of the French and English lacked some of the oppressive features of the Spanish and Portuguese empires. In addition, the French and English did not buy or bring to their trading posts African slaves. Thus the coming together of peoples in the North might have provided historical examples of that rarest of situations in history—an encounter among different peoples that benefited all of them.

But the Europeans did not regard one another's advantage with equanimity. They raided one another's camps, hijacked one another's ships, and set their Indian allies against one another. By competing in such a manner, they turned Indians' intertribal suspicion and rivalry into all-out wars for access to European weapons, alcohol, and control of the supply of game. Europe's first northern American explorations became a cold war.

Initial English and French Explorations

In the wake of the Spanish explorers' reports, European geographers busied themselves redefining the Atlantic world, and mapmakers could not assimilate new information fast enough. When Fernando Magellan skirted the southern tip of South America (Cape Horn) on his way to Asia in the winter of 1519–1520, he proved that the East Indies could be reached by sailing west and south from Europe. According to ancient Greek theory, the world must be symmetrical, and the classical ideal of the globe still gripped the Europeans' imagination. Hence geographers theorized that just as the Western Hemisphere had a southern terminus, it also must have a northern terminus. Whoever could find that "Northwest Passage" to the Pacific would reap the wealth of Asia.

Geography placed England nearest the hoped-for Northwest Passage and made it Spain's natural rival in the North Atlantic. Henry VII of England immediately saw the dangers of Spanish domination of the Atlantic Ocean after Columbus's voyage. Like Ferdinand and Isabel, Henry had well-schooled Italian pilots among his subjects. Indeed, in 1496, just such a man petitioned the king to exceed Columbus's feat. In 1495, John Cabot, a Genoese pilot, had moved to England with his family. The next year he resettled in Bristol, a prosperous fishing port on the Severn River, and approached Henry VII with a plan to find a Northwest Passage.

Always parsimonious, Henry provided Cabot with only one ship, the fifty-ton caravel *Matthew,* and a commission to explore the northern coast of the New World. Cabot sailed across the North Atlantic to what he called the "new found land" (Newfoundland) and returned to England. His journey was swift and without incident. Indeed, his return took but fifteen days. The king was pleased and outfitted Cabot with four ships the next year. If it did not match Columbus's fleet of seventeen ships, Henry's was nonetheless a commitment of some scope. Unfortunately for Cabot and for England, Cabot and his four ships vanished in the North Atlantic.

In 1501, Henry VII chartered a mixed company of English and Portuguese merchants to explore Newfoundland and find a Northwest Passage. They made two trips, but nothing substantial came of their efforts. Nor was John Cabot's son, Sebastian, any more successful, though his 1509 crossing duplicated his father's feat. Henry VII's son, Henry VIII, inaugurated a massive program of shipbuilding to protect England's commerce and fishing, but his interests in European affairs dwarfed his commitment to western exploration, and his half-hearted efforts to explore the North Atlantic led nowhere. Henry VIII's son, Edward VI, died young, and Henry's older daughter, Mary I, married Philip of Spain. Neither Mary nor Philip saw any reason why England should compete with Spain in the New World.

Problems at home and wars abroad delayed France's entry into the race for empire until the 1520s, though a few French explorers, on their own, made the Atlantic crossing. Still, France was Spain's great rival on the continent of Europe, a power struggle that dictated France and Spain would also become rivals for New World empire. Francis I determined that France would find the Northwest Passage and deny Spain (and England) the riches of the Pacific.

Francis's plan for empire faced a series of obstacles, including the chronic indebtedness of the monarchy, but he forged ahead nonetheless. In 1523, he gave to Giovanni da Verrazano, a seasoned Atlantic mariner, a royal commission to find the elusive Northwest Passage. Verrazano commanded four ships, but storms crippled two of the vessels, and in the end only Verrazano's ship, the *Dauphin*, crossed the Atlantic, in April 1524.

Verrazano sailed up the Atlantic shore from South Carolina to Newfoundland. He dropped anchor in what is now New York Harbor and traded with the Indians, recording how pleased they seemed to accommodate him. He was also impressed by the dignity of the Wampanoags of Cape Cod. He dismissed the Abenakis of Maine as mere savages because "we found no courtesy in them, and when we had nothing more to exchange and left them, the men made all the signs of scorn and shame that any brute creature would make."

Though he looked in vain for a Northwest Passage, Verrazano still believed in its existence and included in his journal the Indians' report of a fabulous city they called Norumbega, at the mouth of a great "in-drawing sea." Whoever found this city, he believed, would also find the entrance to the Northwest Passage. More important, he concluded that North America was not the tip of Asia but a continent in itself.

All this he reported to King Francis, but the king was too busy in 1525 waging war with the Spanish in Italy to do anything with his navigator's information. When the Spanish defeated the French at the Battle of Pavia in February of that year, they delayed France's imperial enterprise for a decade. Still, Francis was not finished with America.

By the 1530s, the Normandy and Brittany coasts had become a center of the North Atlantic fishing industry. The ships left European ports in late spring, joining the Portuguese and English fleets bound for the codfish banks of Nova Scotia and Newfoundland. The French and Portuguese had plentiful supplies of salt, and packed newly caught cod wet and salted in barrels. When the ships were filled, the mariners returned to Europe to sell their catches, then returned to the banks for a second helping.

After concluding with his archrival Spain what both sides knew was a fragile peace, King Francis traveled to Le Mont-Saint-Michel on the coast of Brittany in 1532. There he met Jacques Cartier, an experienced Atlantic mariner. The king listened to Cartier's plans to find a Northwest Passage, remembered Verrazano's report, surmised that any French presence in North America would discomfit the Spanish, and gave his royal consent to the enterprise. The king even persuaded the pope to allow the French to explore the new lands, despite the 1493 papal division of the New World into Spanish and Portuguese spheres of interest.

Like Verrazano, Cartier was a superb navigator and shipmaster. He got around the problem of paying for the voyage by recruiting his kinsmen for the trip. In three voyages to what is now Newfoundland, Labrador, and the Saint Lawrence River of Canada between 1534 and 1542, Cartier lost neither ship nor sailor—save to disease and hunger while his crew was on land.

In twenty days in April and May 1534, he led his first two ships and 122 men across the North Atlantic and circumnavigated Newfoundland. When he could, he landed longboats, and his men explored. Soon the Micmacs, an Algonquian people of the far northern coast, signaled their willingness to trade by holding up fur pelts on sticks and gesturing the French ashore. On June 12, 1534, the French and the Indians met, smoked, danced, ate, and eyed each other warily.

Cartier wrote that the Indians seemed healthy and muscular and had good posture. In this, the French were only repeating what many Europeans said about the physical comeliness and athleticism of Indian men. In fact, the life expectancy of the Indians was actually less than that of the Europeans. A fifty-year-old Indian was a rarity.

Cartier continued that they seemed to him "untamed and savage" in their dress of pelts and their body paint. For their own part, the Indians thought facial hair was ugly and stupid and looked down upon people with curly hair. The French sailors, many of whom had curly beards, must have seemed a sorry lot.

On July 2, Cartier dallied just long enough to erect a giant cross on the shore of what is now Gaspé Harbor and greet another Indian arrival. The Indian leader, Donnaconna, a Laurentian, recognized that the ceremony was a serious religious moment for his guests and respected it, but he objected to the erection of the cross. This was his territory. The French distributed gifts (thinking that they were bribing the Indians), but the Indians assumed that the French were behaving properly, giving gifts to show their goodwill. To cement an alliance based on mutual misunderstanding, Donnaconna allowed two of his sons to join the French on the trip back to their homeland. Cartier sailed for France on July 25, 1534.

The next year Cartier and the boys returned. Cartier had been listening to their tales of the wealth of "Saguenay." Supposedly it lay up the great river that flowed into the bay Cartier had explored the year before. With three ships and a crew of relatives, friends, and gentlemen eager for the adventure, Cartier entered the mouth of the river he named Saint Lawrence for the saint's day on which he first saw it, then sailed upriver to Donnaconna's palisaded town, Stadaconé, today Quebec City. There the chief feted the Frenchman but warned him not to go farther up the river. Cartier went anyway.

Upriver lay Hochelaga. From the hill above the Indian town, which Cartier called Mont Royal (later Montreal), he could see the falls of the Saint Lawrence River and the end of his dream of a Northwest Passage to the East Indies. The riches of Saguenay were not rare and precious metals (*caignetdaze* to the natives, Canada to Cartier) but the land itself. Had Cartier not been a man of the sea, he might have appreciated the possibilities of a colony based on farming rather than trade. Again the Indians warned him against going on—for beyond Hochelaga ranged war parties of Iroquois. The Hochelaga villagers called them *magua*—eaters of human flesh.

Cartier called the people of Hochelaga Hurons. Historians now dispute whether they, or Donnaconna's band, for that matter, were actually Hurons, a branch of the Iroquoian peoples whose language they shared, or a distinct people who paid tribute to the Hurons to the west and the Iroquois to the south. The Hurons (from the French *hure*, meaning "a tousled head," "a boar's head," or, in derogatory terms, "a savage") called themselves the Wendat, meaning "the people of the islands." The name survives as the Wyandot peoples of Canada. Their homes were in southern Ontario, clustered around the lakes and rivers of the region, but they traveled in search of seasonal game and fish like all the Indians of the North.

At the time of contact, there were perhaps as many as forty thousand Hurons living in four large clans (based on lineages represented by animal or nature totems) in very close and evidently peaceful proximity to each other. Like their southern cousins the Iroquois, the Hurons lived in fortified communities, some as large as two thousand people. Relatives shared longhouses.

Of all of the northern Indians, the Hurons were the best farmers. Their corn, beans, and squash fields were well tended, and they bartered surpluses of these crops for fish and game with their Algonquian-speaking neighbors. Men cleared the land and were responsible for the hunt and warfare. Women tended the crops and gathered seasonal fruits and nuts. Nearly 90 percent of the daily intake of food came from the labor of women. Women were also potters, and the importance of pottery storage and cooking ware further enhanced the status of women in the community.

The French had little to say about Huron women, for women had little to do with matters of state, war, and diplomacy. The Hurons practiced strict segregation of the sexes. Little boys and girls dressed differently from one another, girls always wearing aprons, while boys went about naked in summer until puberty. Women obeyed, and men enforced this modesty. For example, women stayed away from strangers except when certain polite customs required the appearance of women. Thus, when the Hurons danced for Cartier, he noted that the women and children made their circle some distance from the French.

When the river was free of ice, Cartier returned home, laden with ten additional passengers—Donnaconna, two of his sons, and seven other natives, all kidnapped during a farewell ceremony. The Indians were a gift to the French king, and Cartier no doubt hoped that some among them would learn French, convert to Catholicism, and help later expeditions establish themselves in Saguenay. In fact, none of them would see their homeland again.

Five years later, in May 1541, Cartier returned, this time as captain general of a fleet of five ships. But Cartier was no longer his own master. A nobleman, the Sieur

(Lord) de Roberval, was to be the governor of the new colony. Nothing Cartier found repaid the cost of the expedition, however, and he and Roberval soon departed. The first French settlement in the North ended with a whimper.

Hochelaga and Stadaconé vanished soon after the French left. Indian legends that French missionaries recorded told of a massive Iroquois assault on the towns. Another possibility is that Indians to the west, wishing to avail themselves of trade with Europeans on the coast, simply drove off or absorbed the Laurentian peoples—a pattern of conduct that would repeat itself throughout the history of native-European trade relations. A third scenario might have been the decimation of the Indians from diseases the French left behind.

The English Try Again to Find the Northwest Passage

In the years after Cabot disappeared, English mariners had not forgotten Cabot's dream, and English geographers and pilots still believed that the Northern and Southern hemispheres were divided into more or less equal parts of land and water. In 1595, English mariner John Davis opined that if the two hemispheres were symmetrical, there had to be a northern passage to the Pacific. Davis's countryman, geographer and mathematician John Dee, proposed that one of the river mouths north of forty-five degrees north latitude must be the "in-drawing sea."

In support of their theory, the geographers pointed to Verrazano's story of Norumbega. Sixteenth-century cartographers placed Norumbega in various latitudes, from the north coast of Long Island Sound all the way to the Acadian Peninsula. Though there never was such a city, the name itself had a magic for the English and French, the equal of El Dorado to the Spanish conquistadors.

In 1576, Sir Martin Frobisher outfitted the first of three voyages to discover if the passage lay north of the fiftieth parallel, but found only the perils of the ice pack. In a sudden gale, "the ice came upon us so fast, we were in great danger, looking every hour for death." The mariners pushed at the ice floes with oars and staves and chipped ice from the rigging and the spars. Still, Frobisher's crew marveled at the sights: "and thus we layoff and on we came by a marvelous huge mountain of ice, which surpassed all the rest that we saw . . . being there nine score fathoms deepe, and of compasse about half a mile." In 1577 and 1578, Frobisher tried again, but there was no reward for all his crew's exertions—only another dead end.

THE PROTESTANT REFORMATION SPURS
FURTHER NORTHERN EXPLORATION

Why had France abandoned the Canadian project, and what explained the episodic and unfocused nature of the English explorations of the Americas? The answer lay not in America but in Europe, with the explosion of the Reformation. In what is surely another great irony of history, the Renaissance's emphasis on close reading of texts brought about the destruction of the unity and harmony of Christianity in Europe.

By the end of the 1400s, leading Christian humanists like the Dutch scholar Erasmus claimed that key concepts in Roman Catholic worship, such as "doing penance" for sins, were based upon corrupted Latin texts of the Hebrew Bible. The correct translation, Erasmus asserted, was to "repent." Erasmus and others then went on to hint that repentance was an individual and internal process, as opposed to the external good works that the church required of the penitent sinner. The Reformation had begun.

Lutheranism and Calvinism

In 1517, the German monk and teacher Martin Luther expanded the distinction between internal repentance and external penance. Outraged by what he concluded were corruptions in the way the Roman Catholic Church supervised the doing of penance, he posted ninety-five grievances on the door of the Wittenberg Castle Church.

There had been protests against real and imagined abuses long before Luther voiced his concerns. Luther, however, objected to the worldliness and political meddling of German bishops and their agents. In particular, he decried the methods churchmen used to raise money for the church.

His protest created an immediate sensation, and he was called to account for his opinions by officers of the Roman Catholic Church. When he refused to recant, he was excommunicated, but he found political allies and sanctuary among German princes whose politics were opposed to those of Rome. A theological debate thus fed into political rivalries within the Holy Roman Empire.

Luther did not anticipate that his own protests would lead to a lasting schism among Christians, nor did the authorities in Germany or in Rome. But with his public protest, the Protestant Reformation began in earnest. The leaders of this movement envisioned a very different role for the church, the priest, and the believer than existed in Roman Catholicism. Like Luther, they saw salvation as God's gift to the truly faithful. Mere conformity would not save a sinner, nor would good works alone.

Almost all of the new Protestant sects retained portions of the old liturgy and the sacraments, including baptism and the Lord's Supper (communion), though some Protestants believed in the essential goodness of people, while others emphasized that only God's grace could save the sinner from the abyss of hell. The essential relationship in the reform churches was between God and the worshipper. Because all baptized Christians were equal—the fellowship of believers—the importance of sacraments at which ordained priests officiated, such as private confession, declined.

Luther and those who came after claimed that his was the correct reading of scripture and that the Roman Catholic Church was at best an imposition and at worst an impostor. In Luther's teaching and the worship services of his followers, the Bible became the most important part of everyday religious study. Luther translated the Bible from Latin into German, and Lutheran families gathered to read and study the Bible daily.

Luther had attacked the idea of priestly celibacy, and he married and had, with his wife, Katherine von Bora, six children. Following Luther, all of the Protestant sects encouraged their ministers to marry. Ministers and theologians regarded women as helpmeets but did not argue for their equality at home or in the public arena. Instead, women in Protestantism gained at best a second-class equality. Yet the fact that some women could now choose which faith to adopt gave them a kind of power they did not have previously.

In the meantime, accusations of heresy flew thick and fast, and entire communities divided over religion. There was no concept of freedom of worship as it is understood today, nor was there a willingness on the part of the contending religious factions or government to allow people to choose their own faiths. Instead, the end of uniformity led to revolts within princedoms and war between them over religious doctrine.

The contagion of religious dissent spread across Europe. In the 1530s, John Calvin, a French-born lawyer who had fled his native land to live in the Swiss city-state of Geneva, pushed Protestant doctrine even farther away from Roman Catholicism than Luther had. Calvin stressed the importance of God's grace and the idea of predestination (the doctrine that, from creation, God has chosen those who will be saved and those who are damned). Although he did not pioneer the latter notion, he made it central to his teachings.

Calvinism thus raised the psychological stakes for the Protestant who wanted to be saved. Perfect faith was still a true proof of salvation, but perfect faith was hard to prove to oneself and others. Instead, the elect (those whom God had chosen for salvation) had to live as though they were truly justified in their faith, search their souls for evidence of grace, and agonize over their sinfulness.

Calvin's Protestantism emphasized self-discipline, public virtue, and the purity of the community of believers. Calvinists were militant reformers of personal conduct rather than radical rethinkers of doctrine. They regarded churches as a necessary place of gathering for the elect and the sinner, but ministers taught, guided, inspired, and counseled, rather than interceded with God for the congregant.

Calvin's reforms were not the last word in the Reformation story. A variety of religious radicals lumped by critics under the rubric Anabaptists challenged Calvin's retention of infant baptism. They argued it should be reserved for those who could make a conscious profession of faith. Some Anabaptists also departed from Luther's and Calvin's conservative political and social message to argue for the redistribution of wealth among the poor and other economic reforms.

The Roman Catholic Church launched the Counterreformation, enhancing many social and community programs, on the one hand, while redoubling the efforts of the Inquisition, on the other. Spain became a center of Counterreformation efforts, and in 1534 one of its soldiers, Ignatius de Loyola, organized a militant religious order to reinvigorate the faith. The Society of Jesus trained its members rigorously, and by the 1550s they were among the leading educators in Europe and the New World.

Religion and Politics

The princes of Europe feared that religious upheaval would lead to political unrest in their lands, and it did. France succumbed to an explosion of religious divisions followed by civil insurrection that crippled its overseas program. Lutheranism had made its way into France before Cartier returned from Stadaconé, but Catholics Francis I and his son, Henry II, used their patronage to dampen religious controversy. Henry II even commissioned Protestants to prey upon the Spanish treasure ships—so long as the privateers gave the crown its share of the loot. The arrival of Calvinism upset this balance, for Calvinists not only demanded moral purity from true believers, they objected to the state-sponsored church itself.

The first rounds of religious warfare on the Continent ended under the terms of the Peace of Augsburg of 1555. The new rule was that faith of the prince was to be the official religion of the state, but that declaration did not settle domestic religious contentions in France. What was more, the creation of state churches meant that rulers had to find ways to prevent vying religious factions within the church from becoming political factions in the government.

In the late 1550s and early 1560s, the Guise family, dominant at court, tried to stamp out the Calvinists, and for the next thirty years open rebellion and pitched battles among the nobility, massacres of Protestants in Paris and other cities, and the spectacle of Henry III besieging his own capital city of Paris wracked the realm. Only the succession of Henry of Navarre, crowned Henry IV of France in 1594, ended the wars. Henry IV was a Calvinist, but to unify the nation he converted to the Roman Catholic faith. When his old allies threatened to renew the civil wars, he proclaimed the Edict of Nantes (1598), officially granting toleration to the French Protestants, by now called Huguenots.

In England, Henry VIII faced an even more complicated scenario than the French kings. By all accounts a brilliant and accomplished young man, Henry wed Catherine, a Spanish princess, and with the marriage seemed to cement an alliance with Spain. Thus Henry had every reason to reject Lutheran heresies. In 1521, his religious views were so orthodox and his attacks on Luther so fierce that the pope conferred on Henry the title of "defender of the faith."

But Henry had a problem that titles could not solve. He needed a male heir. No one had to tell an English king how easily the uncertainty of succession could lead to devastating civil war. Henry's wife bore him a daughter, Mary, but no son survived. He fell in love with Anne Boleyn, a young noblewoman, and made her pregnant, then appealed to the pope for an annulment of the marriage to Catherine so he could marry Anne and legitimate her offspring. Unfortunately for Henry's plan, Pope Clement VII was a pawn of the Spanish interest and thus disinclined to allow the insult to Catherine. Henry then acted decisively. He made himself the head of the new "Church of England," married Anne, and confiscated the property of Roman churches and monasteries in England. Parliament ratified the king's moves.

Henry never adopted Protestant doctrine, but when he died in 1547, advisers to his son, Edward, moved the Church of England into the Protestant fold. Edward, who ruled from 1547 to 1553, was born in 1537 to Henry and Jane Seymour. Archbishop Thomas Cranmer led the Reformation party, and his work, including the *Book of Common Prayer* (1549), set England on a Protestant course. But Edward was succeeded by Henry VIII's and Catherine's daughter, Mary.

Mary was a devout Roman Catholic and with her husband, Philip II of Spain, steered England back in a pro–Roman Catholic direction. Those who did not change course with her were burned at the stake or forced to flee.

When Mary I died in 1558, childless, her successor and half sister, Elizabeth I, daughter of Henry VIII and Anne Boleyn, faced a dilemma. Elizabeth had seen enough of the terror of religious persecution to fear it, and thus when she returned England to the Protestant standard, she balanced the concessions to the radical Protestant party with others to former Catholics. Above all, she understood that she must steer a middle course for the sake of peace in the country.

Elizabethan Explorations

Ever mindful of the dangers of Reformation and Counterreformation intrigue, Elizabeth viewed the exploration of North America as part of the larger religious contest between England and its Catholic enemies. Increasingly, she perceived that her brother-in-law, King Philip II of Spain, was behind every conspiracy against her and English Protestantism.

At hand to "singe the king's beard" waited courtiers like Sir Humphrey Gilbert and Sir Walter Ralegh and merchants' sons like John Hawkins and Francis Drake. These sea dogs happily plundered the Spanish posts in the Antilles, Mexico, Panama, and the Spanish Main, infuriating King Philip.

Hawkins led the way. His Plymouth friends and family helped him to outfit a small fleet of three ships to scour the Canaries, the coast of West Africa, and the Caribbean for profits. Part raider, part trader, he stole Africans from villages on the shore of Senegal and sold them to Spanish planters in the Caribbean. If the Spanish resisted, he bombarded them into compliance. As he wrote during one such episode, "By the Spanish desire of Negroes . . . we obtained a secret trade, whereupon the Spaniards resorted to us by might, and bought of us to the number of 200 Negroes." He made four of these voyages from 1562 to 1568, when, during the last, a pitched battle with Spanish troops and ships off the coast of Yucatan ended his career.

Not fazed by Hawkins's fate, Francis Drake pestered Elizabeth to let him outdo Hawkins's feats. Elizabeth unleashed Drake in 1577. With six ships, he set out to terrorize the Spanish settlements on the coast of South America. In his flagship, the *Golden Hind*, a vessel of eighty tons, he coasted down to Cape Horn, following Magellan's course, then up the west coast of South America. The Spanish silver ships were like chickens caught in a henhouse by a fox. On his way north along the Pacific coast of South America, he attacked Valparaiso, Chile, and Lima, Peru, and the western ports of Central America; then, to avoid the Spanish ships no doubt awaiting his return south, he went as far north as thirty-eight degrees north latitude (modern San Francisco Bay). He thought seriously about leaving a colony in Nova Albion, as he called it, and parleyed and partied with the Indians before he decided to return to England.

From California, Drake pressed on to the Philippines, where he harassed the Spanish settlements, then traveled to the Moluccas (the Spice Islands) to fill what was left of his cargo space with spices. Finally, he sailed into the East Indian Ocean, around the Cape of Good Hope, out into the Atlantic again, and home. He had lost only seventeen men at sea and brought his ship back intact.

The sea dogs' achievement, though much storied in the realm, hardly repaid its cost. If the raids kept the English appetite for New World adventures whetted, the truth of the matter was that the English navy was ill-prepared for anything more than spasmodic activity. In 1582, when Elizabeth was already contemplating the possibility that she would have to go to war with Spain, England's merchant marine had only 250 ships of more than eighty tons and but 20 over two hundred tons. The ships were sluggish, slow, and often leaked. The masts and spars were sometimes too big for the ships, and the anchors were too light to hold in a gale. The sailors complained, with good reason. On long voyages, they subsisted on hard bread, salted meat, and whatever fish they could catch. Only the beer and cider, to which was later added rum, kept their spirits up.

Recognizing these weaknesses, Gilbert proposed a different way to strike at Spain. Instead of hit-and-run raids, he proposed to establish a series of fortified posts—a kind of picket line—to deter Spanish expansion north. The strategic benefit to the crown was obvious, and Gilbert added that he and his agents would convert the Indians to the Protestant faith. His return would be whatever treasure he could find in the New World.

Crown lawyers drafted a patent, or contract, with Gilbert combining the Spanish imperial model with medieval English ideas of the border march. First, like the grants Spanish rulers gave to the *adelantados* (literally, "entrepreneurs") going to America, Gilbert's charter promised him control of "all the soyle of all such lands, countries, and territories so to be discovered or possessed as aforesaid, and of all Cities, Castles, Townes, and Villages, and palaces in the same." There were no castles or palaces where Gilbert was going; not even in the mythical Norumbega—the lawyers were thinking of the Spanish conquest of Mexico.

The English crown lawyers also filled the charter with the language of feudal land tenures already outdated in England. Gilbert was to hold and defend the land for the crown, in return for which he gained tenure "in fee simple" (a freehold, or absolute ownership—not subject to other feudal encumbrances). Like the medieval vassals of the English crown on the border marches with Wales and Scotland, Gilbert swore to defend Protestant England's front lines against Catholic Spain and France.

Elizabeth did not pay for Gilbert's venture (thereby setting a long-standing precedent that the colonies should cost the crown as little as possible), but the patent helped him raise money among his West Country relatives and friends, one of whom was Ralegh. Gilbert chartered ships and signed on crew, but his first efforts went for naught. Despite repeated attempts to sail, his small and ill-equipped fleets returned to English ports without ever reaching the New World. Finally, in 1583, he managed to get himself and two other small ships to Newfoundland. In Saint John's (named, like Cartier's Saint Lawrence, for the saint's day on which Gilbert arrived), he claimed the land for Elizabeth. Then he vanished at sea.

THE ROANOKE COLONY

Ralegh secured for himself Gilbert's patent, and with it planned a colony. He had a precedent in mind for this project, a place where he had come of age as a soldier and had seen firsthand how determined and well-organized Englishmen could carve homes for themselves out of hostile territory. Although England had long regarded its immediate neighbors—Wales and Scotland—as parts of a "Great Britain," the model for American colonies was Ireland.

The Irish Precedent

The English entered Ireland in the middle of the twelfth century. The first English invaders amalgamated with the native population, forming an Anglo-Irish aristocracy. These "Old English" maintained close relations with the English crown. In the 1540s, they arranged a deal between the crown and many of the leading Irish families, by which the latter gave up any claims they might have to independence in return for English guarantees to their lands and local authority. But when the English chose Protestantism as their state religion, rabid Protestants found the Old English adoption of Irish ways objectionable, and a wave of new English immigrants pronounced the Old English leaders' policy of outward conformity or silence on Protestantism unacceptable.

In an attempt to wrest power from the Old English and turn Ireland into a province under direct English rule, the newcomers launched a propaganda offensive. All Irish-men were allegedly "degenerated from all manhood and humanity." English writers echoed the insults of the Anglo-Irish Protestants—Ireland was that "dark corner" and "rude parte" of English dominions, inhabited by "the wild Irish." Analogies be-tween the Irish and the Native Americans became fashionable—both dressed in skins, or went about half naked, exulted in knavery, and perfected torture and am-bush of their enemies.

Furious at the English immigrants' provocations, some of the Irish families rose in rebellion. By the end of the 1570s, the uprising had spread from Ulster in the North to Munster in the South. The level of violence, pitting neighbor against neighbor, far exceeded that of "the troubles" that would erupt in Northern Ireland in the 1960s. By the 1570s, all the Old English leaders were caught in the trap. Some followed Ger-ald Fitzgerald, the Earl of Desmond, into rebellion. Others protested their continued loyalty but pleaded against repression of the Irish.

But matters worsened when, in 1580, a papal army raised in Europe arrived in Ire-land. An English army under the Lord Grey de Wilton followed, and for three years, from 1580 to 1583, when Desmond was captured and executed, the English and the papal armies attacked each other mercilessly. When a village or fort refused to sur-render immediately, its population—men, women, and children—were put to the sword.

The English subjugation of Ireland proceeded according to a well-developed plan. First, the English established armed camps. Sometimes, these were old fortified cities, which the English repopulated after the native inhabitants fled. Sometimes these were new settlements. The natives were given the choice of acting as dutiful subjects or being violently dispossessed. In the latter case, the land would be offered to English settlers—in reality often the very soldiers who had despoiled Ireland.

In justification of these policies, the English argued that God wanted the Protes-tants to have the land. It was the duty of the civilized English to uplift and reeducate the Irish. Missionaries, trained in the Irish tongue, would be sent among them to preach the word and explain the Bible. A second justification revolved around the use of the land. Ireland was rich in natural resources, but the Irish did not develop these, forfeiting their right to the land. Both these arguments could and would be used to justify the conquest of the Native Americans.

Ralegh took part in the Irish campaign of 1580 as a captain in Lord Grey's army. At the June 1580 capitulation of the papal forces at Smerwich, Ralegh and his men hanged a dozen women, some of them pregnant, and killed hundreds of prisoners of war. Denied a grant of land in Ireland for his zealous service, he still gained prefer-ment at Queen Elizabeth's court, including Gilbert's patent. Ralegh remembered the methods and justifications of the reduction of Ireland, and planned to introduce them in his American colony.

The First Voyage, 1584

Ralegh intended to go to the New World himself, but first he had to entice backers for the venture, lease ships, find pilots, and hire mariners. In the latter effort Ralegh proved most fortunate. His crew included Thomas Harriot, a young Oxford-trained mathematician and scientist; John White, an artist of merit and imagination whose depictions of the Indians would make him and them famous; Philip Amadas, a Bristol pilot; and Arthur Barlowe, an experienced ship master and a loyal friend.

In April 1584, these men and their shipmates sailed two small barks across the Atlantic to Puerto Rico, thence to the Carolina coast. Barlowe, Amadas, and their crews followed Verrazzano's course up the barrier reefs, looking for a way through the sandbars. The shallows posed obvious dangers, and the mariners undoubtedly "gunkholed," taking depth soundings to find a safe passage into the roads between the Pamlico and the Albemarle Sound. At the confluence of the two bays lies Roanoke Island, and opposite it, on the land, Barlowe's men decided to pause.

The littoral of the Carolinas is sandy wetland. The sand gives way to brush and palmettos, and then forests of pine, red oak, and hickory. The Spanish moss that overhangs the trees gives the forest a gloomy aspect. For the English, used to open fields and rocky coasts, the dunes and forest must have seemed as mysterious as the Antilles had appeared to Columbus.

The Indians watched Barlowe's small boat approach the mainland warily, for the Spanish had already been there, and the stories of natives taken and never brought back were widely shared by natives. Finally, a Roanoke *werowance*, or headman, approached the English. Bit by bit, trade began, then common dining and attempts at communication. The chief, Granganimeo, allowed the English to visit his village, and warned them, just as Donnaconna had warned Cartier, not to tarry among his enemies on Roanoke Island.

The English, like Cartier, did the opposite, meeting the chief of the Roanoke people, Wingina, and sharing his hospitality. Two of his youths offered to travel back to England with the ships. Within a month's time, the English departed. The four young men, Harriot, White, Manteo, and Wanchese, grew fond of one another, as they learned one another's language and customs. Soon all four would return with an even larger number of English adventurers the next year.

The English did not know that these relatively small and scattered settlements in the Albemarle and Pamlico sounds were backwaters in the development of native society, in effect the far eastern fringe of the Mississippian world. None of these chiefs commanded the allegiance of more than a few villages.

The Roanokes lived simply—in some ways closer to the woodlands cultures of a thousand years earlier than to the more sophisticated, densely populated, and hierarchically organized population centers of the Mississippian period. Even dress was minimal by Indian standards—loincloth in summer and deerskin cloak in winter.

The smaller villages did not even have palisades. In them were gathered no more than thirty rectangular thatched huts, compared to the eighty to one hundred dwellings in the Mississippian towns that de Soto visited forty years earlier. Cornfields ringed the village, but corn culture had come late to these shores, and the gardens devoted to corn were barely large enough to supply the natives through the winter. In times of scarcity, the Indians starved.

The Indians of Roanoke were lucky in some respects. The germs Hernando de Soto and his men spewed out had depopulated a large area of the Southeast. But the region was so large and so sparsely populated that the Roanokes had been spared. The Roanoke villagers were not so fortunate when it came to their immediate northern neighbors. These were the aggressive and numerous Powhatans of the lower Chesapeake. A young and able Powhatan *werowance* named Wahunsonacock extorted tribute from twelve thousand Indians in the area between the James and the York rivers.

But chiefs like Wingina had ambitions of their own, and the English might be persuaded to help further these goals. The Indians assumed that the English would be willing allies in war just as they had become friendly trading partners. With such powerful friends, the Roanokes might defend themselves—or even extend their sway—north into the Chesapeake.

Plans for a Permanent Colony

Ralegh delighted in the safe return of his ships and crews. In their absence, he arranged for Harriot and Richard Hakluyt the younger, a scholar turned writer and promoter of western exploration, to prepare a "Discourse of Western Planting," laying out for the queen and her advisers the reasons for a more extensive investment in North America. They were the same as the rationalizations the English Protestants had given for the reduction of Ireland. True religion demanded that the Indians be converted to the English version of Christianity. The potential of trade (and wealth to the realm) beckoned the English. The land was fruitful and in proper hands would bring a fortune. And expansion of the Spanish dominions in North America must be prevented at all costs. Still hoping for royal support, he named the colony "Virginia" after the "Virgin Queen," Elizabeth.

Plainly, Ralegh dreamed of a genuine colony like the English enclaves in Ireland. His plans resembled de Soto's—eight hundred men with horses and livestock, the building of a major fort, a tin mine, glass blowing and other crafts, and a "high treasurer" to count the gold and silver.

But the queen would not let Ralegh go, and Sir Richard Grenville led the new expedition. He set off with a squadron of five ships, stopping first in the Spanish Antilles, looking for loot. During the campaign, his flotilla scattered. By the time it reconvened, some men had been lost, and many of the supplies intended for their stay at Roanoke were ruined. In the end, instead of planting a colony of eight hundred men, Grenville could spare but one hundred men under one of his infantry captains, Ralph Lane.

On July 11, 1585, the expedition hove to outside Pamlico Sound. Grenville landed Lane and his men on Roanoke Island. Lane, an experienced infantry officer and something of a martinet, determined to intimidate the natives with a show of force. He ordered construction of a small fort, with a ditch, rampart, walls, and mounts for small swivel cannons. Following Ralegh's instructions, Lane ordered construction of craft shops, but with no customers, that part of the project folded. Too, there was no gold or silver for a treasurer to count.

White and Harriot filled journals and sketchbooks with accounts of native ways and drawings of the region's animals and flowers. Indians from all over the coastal area visited the English camp, just as curious about the English as the English were about the natives. White and Harriot praised the natives as masters of a poor environment, using seasonal gathering and planting to sustain themselves. "In respect of us," White later wrote, "they are a people poor, and for want of skill and judgment in the knowledge and use of our things, do esteem our trifles . . . things of greater value. Notwithstanding . . . they seem very ingenious. For although they have no such tools . . . yet in those things they do, they show excellency of wit."

The two young Indians taken to England had proven themselves good students and impressed learned observers with their inquiring minds, though in later years, when the English needed a reason to dispossess the Indians, White's and Harriot's candid assessments fell out of favor. Then, English writers recast the natives as awkward and inferior in body and mind to the Europeans.

Isolated and concerned with the defense of the tiny colony, Lane began to worry that Wingina plotted against the English. Wingina's Indian rivals inflamed Lane's fears. For his own part, Wingina had changed his name to Pemisapan, meaning watchful or wary—a good idea around the aggressive and unpredictable English. In the winter of 1585–1586, relations with the Indians grew critical as Lane and his men exhausted their food supply and needed to get at the small stores that Wingina had set aside for his villages.

By the spring of 1586, Lane had worn out his welcome among the Roanokes, and chose to strike first rather than to become a target. In his defense, he might have cited lawyer Richard Hakluyt the elder's logic of divide and conquer: "Where there be many petie kings . . . planted on the rivers . . . wee may join with this king heere, or that king there, at our pleasure, and may so with a few men be revenged of any wrong offered by any of them."

On the morning of June 1, 1586, Lane burst into Pemisapan's village and murdered the chief. In his report to Ralegh, Lane explained that no sooner had he appeared, than "the cry arose, for in truth they, privie to their owne villanous purposes against us, held as good espial upon us, both day and night, as we did upon them.

The alarum given, they took themselves to their bowes and we to our armes." Francis Drake arrived off the coast later that month and carried Lane, White, Harriot, and the others back to England.

A supply fleet Ralegh sent to the colony just missed the departure of the colonists. Grenville, at the head of the supply fleet, left a few volunteers behind to seek out the whereabouts of the colonists. When White returned in the spring of 1587, he found the old fort abandoned and destroyed. Apparently, the Roanokes' vengeance against Lane had fallen on Grenville's volunteers.

The Men, Women, and Children of Virginia

In early 1587, indifferent to the dangers the aroused natives posed to further colonization, Ralegh and White continued to recruit investors and enroll settlers for a permanent settlement. Backers could purchase shares, to be repaid from the profits of the colony. To potential emigrants, Ralegh offered membership in the "Bodye Politique and Corporate," making them into citizens as well as landowners. In a last touch of ego, Ralegh named the new settlement "The City of Ralegh in the Colony of Virginia" and commissioned a coat of arms for it.

White gathered his little troop, about 150 men, along with an unknown number of their wives, servants, and children, in April 1587 and set sail. On Roanoke Island he found old friends, including Manteo, one of the young men who went to England, but the political situation was far from stable. Lane had upset a delicate balance.

Still, the settlers were willing to take their chances, and the first English child born in Virginia, appropriately named Virginia Dare, was christened on August 24, 1587. The settlers built posthole houses by driving logs vertically into the ground, pounded the earthen floors, thatched the roofs with straw, and again laid out a fort. Food remained the great problem, as it would for every newly laid English settlement, for there was neither time nor space to plant English grain crops, and the weather had turned dry. The settlers begged White to return to England and bring back supplies.

White left, and the rest of the story of the Roanoke colony remains a mystery. He could not return to Carolina until 1590—the armada delayed him—by which time the settlers were gone, perhaps to Croatoan, fifty miles southwest, as three letters carved in a tree truck suggested, or perhaps dispersed among the many Indian peoples of the region. Perhaps the local Indians dealt with the men and women as they had with Grenville's volunteers.

We know that terrible drought came to the region in the years immediately after 1587—parching Indian corn and forcing the natives to exhaust their reserves. Surely the natives realized, with the arrival of English women, that the newcomers intended to stay, and would thus become permanent rivals for scarce food supplies. The only certainty is that these men, women, and children became a lost colony.

The Principal Navigations

The battle between the English fleet and the armada was the greatest sea battle of its time, and its outcome allowed the English to roam freely on the Atlantic. Thus one might expect the English victory to prompt England to expand its interests all over the western Atlantic. But the assembly and supply of its fleet had exhausted the queen's treasury. In addition, with the defeat of the armada, one of the major reasons for the English thrust into American waters had disappeared. Ralegh turned his attention south, and led an expedition up the Orinoco River in modern Venezuela to find gold, but came back empty-handed. White resumed his artistic career.

While England's North American venture stuttered, the Hakluyt cousins, Richard the elder and Richard the younger, turned the tales of the voyages into a plea for further colonization. The elder Hakluyt cousin was a lawyer by training but a book collector and amateur geographer by avocation, and the author of *Inducements Toward the Liking of the Voyage Intended Towards Virginia* (1585), a promotional pamphlet. Hakluyt the elder offered thirty-one reasons for undertaking the expedition, and summarized them: to "plant the Christian religion," "to trafficke" (trade), and "to conquer."

The elder Hakluyt tutored his younger cousin, whose early intention to become a clergyman lost out to his passion for the new worlds. The younger Hakluyt used his Oxford training in languages to republish Cartier's and others' accounts in *Diverse Voyages Touching the Discovery of America* (1582) and help Ralegh promote his colony with the *Discourse of Western Planting* (1584). In between, at the urging of the crown, the younger Hakluyt visited France, learning there the extent of French interest in the New World and reporting back to Queen Elizabeth's ministers. The *Discourse* thus had a slightly different perspective from the *Diverse Voyages*, emphasizing England's rivalry with its European competitors for empire.

In 1589, the younger Hakluyt readied the first draft of a seven-hundred-page volume, *The Principall Navigations, Voiages and Discoveries of the English Nation*. By 1600, he had two more volumes in print. The heroes of the work, Hawkins, Drake, and Ralegh, among others, were also the heroes of the English defeat of the Spanish armada, linking the North American adventure to the patriotic victory over Spain. The volumes also included the text of the grants and charters that Elizabeth had given to her explorers, laying the foundation for her claims to the New World. The volumes not only celebrated England's achievements and gave the color of law to conquest, they appealed to English readers' love of adventure.

TRADE AND THE REVIVAL OF THE NORTHERN ENTERPRISE

The Reformation had discouraged and dislocated the colonization efforts of France and England, the failure of the Cartier and Ralegh colonies dampened enthusiasm for additional "plantings," the lure of finding a Northwest Passage to the Indies flagged, and the defeat of the armada removed the immediate threat from Spain. The contest between England and France for colonies had little bite, for neither had gained a march on the other in America. The revival of English and French colonization efforts at the beginning of the seventeenth century was a response to an economic, not a military, crisis.

Slowly but inexorably throughout the second half of the sixteenth century, the price of basic commodities in Europe had risen. The increase in European population strained the more or less fixed supply of food, fuel, and clothing available on the Continent. Inflation amounted to no more than 1 percent a year, on average, but rising costs of necessities hurt peasants and nobles alike. Old systems of price control faltered. Fixed rents that farmers paid their landlords in crops and livestock declined in value.

By the late sixteenth century, authorities had noticed the rising prices and ascribed them to the venality and immorality of the merchants. An untoward love of luxury and corruption lay behind inflation, learned men warned. Other observers argued that the demand for costly consumer goods like spices, sugar, silks and brocades, and books drove the inflationary spiral. Conspiratorial thinkers blamed the moneylenders for charging high rates of interest and buying up food supplies until they could pass on high prices to the poor.

The case of England is both instructive and typical. In the year of Elizabeth's coronation, 1558, England staggered on the brink of economic chaos. The harvests had been poor, and the bulk of the population lived on short rations, such as "poor John" (dried codfish), cheese, and bread. Inflation drove up the price of everything. Already in short supply because England's forests were consumed by charcoal makers, glassblowers, and brewers, and because a new fad in housing for the well-to-do that we call the "Tudor style" featured heavy-timbered, two-story homes, wood was 150 percent more costly in 1590 than it was in 1540. Remaining forests that common folks had scrounged for fallen timber to heat their cottages became game preserves for the wealthy. Taking firewood from the preserves was a hanging offense. Many towns and cities suffered a decline in per capita wealth, as their resources were strained to meet the new burdens. London grew in size and activity, but crime outpaced all other enterprises in it, and fire, disease, and unemployment made the capital the graveyard of the realm.

Trading Partners

A few men saw as the answer to the economic crisis a different kind of colony. Instead of importing gold, silver, and pearls that inflated prices, they argued, extract from the New World raw materials for the Old World. Importing staple Native American food crops like corn and potatoes, raw materials like furs and pelts for craftspeople, wood products, and consumer items like tobacco would provide work and nourishment for European workers and wealth for European businessmen. Instead of oppressing the Indians, make them into trading partners.

The first step in the deployment of this model of imperial enterprise was creation of Venetian-style joint stock companies. In these, investors bought stock, and the directors of the company used the capital to engage in trade. Some of these companies did their business at home, but others reached out to buy timber and furs from North Sea merchants, spices from traders in the Mediterranean, and fish from Atlantic fishermen. Ralegh's Virginia Company was organized on this model. The only obstacle in the path of increasing commercial development of this sort was the uncertain political situation, but Elizabeth in England and Henry of Navarre in France sufficiently stabilized domestic politics for the overseas enterprises to proceed.

There remained the problem of establishing the colonial side of this commercial enterprise. The Europeans and the Indians had different conceptions of the purposes of trade. The Indians had long traded among themselves for necessities and luxury items, but for Indians, trade was not just a bargained-for exchange, it was part of a larger social and cultural process. Trade among villages and peoples created amity and paved the way for broader alliances. Ceremonies of trade, including feasting, reciprocal gift giving, and speeches of welcome and farewell, transformed the traffic in goods into occasions of social bonding. Thus when Indians paddled out to trade with crews of European ships, they bore with them a long social tradition of trading.

By contrast, Europeans conceived of trade in terms of profit and loss—that is, as a calculated economic transaction rather than a spontaneous social event. Europeans in North America traded not just to obtain goods they wanted for their own use, but to improve their employer's material position, in other words, to accumulate wealth for someone else. European traders on the North Atlantic coast were the agents of a far-flung trading network. Distant companies controlled the prices the traders set, the goods they exchanged, and the competition among them for territory. As the Indians would soon discover, the European traders were not free to act on their own.

Despite the differences between the European employee-conducted, commodity-based idea of commerce and the native custom of social exchange–based trading, by the last decades of the sixteenth century the French and the English (shortly thereafter followed by the Dutch) committed themselves to a policy of trading with the Indians rather than following the Spanish model of imperial conquest. But what to trade for? Cartier had reported on an Indian "plant, of which a large supply is collected in summer for the winter's consumption. They hold it in high esteem. . . . After drying it in the sun, they carry it about their necks in a small skin pouch . . . then at frequent intervals they crumble this plant into powder, which they place in one of the openings of the hollow instrument, and laying a live coal on top . . . they fill their bodies so full of smoke, that it streams out of their mouths and nostrils as from a chimney." But neither Cartier nor his French masters, nor the first English explorers thought this plant—tobacco—would sell in Europe. Instead, they sought the pelts of a large American rodent—the beaver.

The Importance of Beaver Skins

Although they had spread over the whole of North America, beaver preferred the northern climate and watercourses. They built their houses on water and reared their young in the tangle of sticks and branches that coincidentally dammed up the streams. The resulting dam created an "edge culture," where forest, marsh, and pond water met. There deer could drink, fish could spawn, and hunters could come to find their prey. Inadvertently, the beaver made themselves into a vital ecological force in the northern environment.

The Indians of the North hunted the beaver for its warm, insulating fur and for its fatty meat, but the Indians also respected the spiritual power of the beaver. It was often one of the Indians' clan totems, along with the wolf and the bear. Indian leaders wore beaver skins as badges of high office, for Indians revered the beaver's cunning. The Micmacs thought that the beaver was smart enough to talk, but refused to do so out of sheer orneriness. The Ojibwas who lived in the Great Lakes area believed that long ago beavers were people.

The beaver, with its cousins the otter and the marten, was a symbol of an entirely different kind to the European—the mark of high fashion and elevated economic status. Dressed sable and ermine were part of aristocratic European costume, and fur robes, collars, and muffs graced men's and women's fashionable clothing. As native European fur supplies dwindled, Europeans looked elsewhere for pelts. Cartier reported the extensive fur supplies of the Northeast; Gilbert confirmed the fact, and the rush was on.

Beaver hats became the choice of elegant fops and sober merchants. The hat took on all manner of shapes, from the floppy-brimmed, ostrich feather–plumed hat for the cavalier to the softer beribboned hat for gentlewomen. The Dutch favored a "cocked" beaver hat with both sides drawn up, much like the modern cowboy's Stetson. The French preferred a conical beaver hat with a round brim.

Under the inducement of European traders' demand for pelts, Indians began to hunt the beaver to extinction. Hunting became a commercial exercise instead of a quasi-religious act. It may be that some Indians blamed the beaver for the epidemic diseases the Europeans in fact had introduced, but this argument fails to explain why most Indians continued to regard the beaver with respect.

A different explanation for the change in Indian hunting ways is that Indians simply wanted European trade goods. Although Europeans thought that Indians virtually gave away valuable pelts for less expensive goods, Indians became enamored with European trade goods like firearms and ammunition for a variety of reasons, not the least of which was the Indians' own ability to adapt European technologies to Indian ends. For example, firearms and ammunition gave Indian buyers the advantage over traditional enemies who did not have firearms. Indeed, with practice, Indians became far better shots with European firearms than were the Europeans.

In return for the pelts, Indians also obtained European textiles, cooking utensils, and tools. These were put to use in Indian fashion. For example, Indians wanted European long shirts, but not pants, for most Indians did not wear pants, but shirts could be worn over Indian leggings. Iron cooking pots and tools lasted longer and retained heat better than Indian pottery and wooden ware. Iron pots could also be reworked into other useful tools. Indians accepted beads, mirrors, and other fashion items in trade because Indians, like Europeans, expressed their individuality through jewelry and other decorative baubles.

Another vital part of the trade for both Indians and Europeans was distilled spirits. Indians grew so fond of liquor that traders could ensure a steady supply of pelts only so long as they could offer Indian trappers distilled beverages. Indians soon demanded liquor not only in trade but as an inducement to come to the trading post in the first place. But the image of the drunken and dangerous Indian is misplaced. Indians rarely drank as heavily or as often as the Europeans with whom the Indians traded. Equally rare, though much publicized, was the occasion when drinking led to violence. Even then, it was the inebriated European who was as likely to start the fracas as the Indian.

Still, there was a cruel irony to the introduction of alcohol into the trade, for it was so much in demand among the Indians that they willingly impoverished themselves to obtain it. Recognizing the demand among their own people, some Indians set themselves up as middlemen in the trade, reselling alcohol to villages deeper in the interior, where the traders did not go. Indian shamans and European missionaries inveighed against the alcohol trade, and over the years Europeans passed laws banning liquor sales to Indians, with little effect.

The French Return to Canada

By the final decades of the 1500s, the French had fully grasped the implications of the idea of a trading empire. French fishing fleets, numbering from three hundred to four hundred vessels each year, traded regularly with Indians at the mouth of the Saint Lawrence and all along the Newfoundland coast. The mariners and the natives exchanged knives, axes, pots, and clothing for furs. Indian groups so prized these trade goods that they began to battle one another for control of the coast. As well, European fishermen competed for access to the Indian trade goods. Some of the fishermen established seasonal camps on the islands at the mouth of the river and spent more time trading than fishing.

If these sedentary arrangements could be made permanent, the French could monopolize the trade, or so went the thinking of a French soldier, traveler, and merchant adventurer named Samuel de Champlain. Champlain was born to the sea, in a coastal town south of the Brittany peninsula. He served in the French army that drove the Spanish from France and was decorated for bravery. With his uncle, he then traveled to the Caribbean, spending three years in Cuba, Mexico, Panama, and ports of call on the Spanish Main. In 1603, he signed on the fleet that sailed to Canada to found a trading colony with the Indians of the Saint Lawrence, traveled up the river, and renamed the abandoned Indian town of Stadaconé, "Kebec."

These were not good years for France's commerce, which makes the Canadian mission all the more remarkable. Crop failures and inflation, abetted by continuing debt and the economic strain of warfare abroad, crippled the national economy. But under Pierre du Guast, the Sieur De Monts, the French Canadian fur-trading enterprise took off. De Monts found credit for a year-round trading post. He organized three ships, 120 men (Champlain among them), and two clerics (one a Catholic priest, the other a Huguenot minister) and arrived in the New World in May 1604.

The clammy weather and the swarms of black flies and mosquitoes did not deter Champlain from carefully charting the coast. He even went looking for the fabled city of Norumbega, but found nothing that resembled a castle city. Another myth, like the boiling waters of the equator, was put to rest.

From 1604 to 1608, Champlain continued to search for a defensible, livable center for the French trading venture. The first site, on the island of Saint Croix in the middle of the Saint Johns River, was defensible but not livable. The fresh water exhausted, the soil unable to support vegetable gardens, the timber soon gone, the French barely survived the winter. The next three years, Champlain explored the coasts of Maine and Massachusetts, looking for a better site. Cape Cod appeared suitable, until the Nauset Indians objected to his presence.

In 1607, the French selected the coast of Nova Scotia for their first permanent settlement. "Port Royal" would become a vital French bastion. But Champlain still had to find a supply of pelts to make the whole enterprise worthwhile. In 1608, he steered up the Saint Lawrence for Kebec (now called Quebec) and there ordered his men to build a "habitation." Quebec would become the hub of the French fur trade.

Champlain realized that the fate of the French in Canada could not depend upon their own strength. French Canada had to be a joint European-Indian project. When his fur-trading partners among the Huron and their Algonquin allies went south to raid the Iroquois, Champlain joined the war party. At a battle against a Mohawk band, Champlain and his men introduced the Indians to firearms. The Mohawks fled. Champlain had proven the power of European technology and forever changed the rules of Indian war.

Quebec, later joined by Montreal, linked a French chain of trading posts reaching from Port Royal on the coast to the Great Lakes. In the coming years, the French would penetrate to the heart of the continent in search of furs. Without the aid of the Indians, the fur trade would have been impossible, so the French continued Champlain's wise policy of conciliation and alliance.

The English North of the Fortieth Parallel

Unlike the French, whose numbers of migrants never exceeded five figures, in time Britain would send hundreds of thousands of its daughters and sons to the New

World. Behind the mass migration from the British Isles lay two simple ideas. First, colonies could be warehouses for surplus population. The idea itself was hardly novel. Ancient Greek colonies took this form. As early as 1584, the younger Hakluyt had argued that the colonies could profitably absorb the excess of "numbers of idle men" who might otherwise employ themselves as vagabonds, beggars, or wastrels. Although the seventeenth-century colonies did become a dumping ground of sorts for debtor prisons and city slums, it was the voluntary migration of young people and families that transformed the American settlements, in the words of contemporary English writers, from a "wilderness" into a "garden."

The second idea was that the colonies could become homelands for the immigrants. Some historical geographers have argued that the very act of deciding to emigrate changes people's ways of thinking, inducing them to think not as sojourners but as lifetime residents. The question remains why would people willingly give up familiar places and family ties to venture out on the dangerous ocean and make their homes in America? Scholars have concluded that a combination of push and pull factors motivated the first immigrants.

Among the push factors was a growing shortage of fuel and food in Europe, part of the cause of the inflationary spiral that had led at the end of the sixteenth century to the reconceptualization of the colonies. The years 1590 to 1630 featured long winters and short growing seasons, reducing yields of food grains. To top off the crisis, rich farmers (many of whom were the squires of the county and therefore doubled as the local legal officials) were "enclosing" the wastelands poor people used for their livestock and their own wood supply. The enclosed land was devoted to grazing sheep, whose wool went to the European cloth markets. The same wealthy owners bought up grain crops and sold them for a profit abroad. This "forestalling and engrossing" fell so heavily upon the poor that in some localities they rioted. As hunger and the fear of famine stalked the land, women led "bread riots" to force the engrossers of grain to disgorge their stocks.

Crushing burdens of debt impoverished tradespeople, craftspeople, and middling farmers. Driven off their small parcels by the enclosure movement, men and women flowed down rural lanes to the market towns and the port cities. In London, Bristol, Exeter, and elsewhere, city councils watched the flood of unemployed young people approach and grew fearful. Men in power hoped that colonization would skim off the excess of these dangerous multitudes.

At the same time, reports of vast stores of timber, game, and fields ready for the plow pulled immigrants to the Americas. English promoters of colonization often exaggerated the ease of life in the colonies, depicting them as a new Eden. Even when the author of a promotional tract poked fun at competitors' unwarranted enthusiasm, the essential message was "go." As Christopher Levett wryly remarked in 1627, "I will not do therein as some have done, to my knowledge speak more than is true; I will not tell you that you may smell the corne-fields before you see the land, nor will the Deare come when they are called. . . . But certainly there is fowle, Deare, and fish enough for the taking . . . of each great plenty."

In 1602, the vanguard of this great migration came to North America. The Britons' initial voyages to Maine and Massachusetts were private ventures, undertaken willy-nilly by men of little vision. Unlike De Monts and Champlain, who conceived a far-flung, centrally directed French trading empire, Bartholomew Gosnold, Gabriel Archer, and Bartholomew Gilbert simply stocked a ship, the *Concord*, and traveled to America to seek their fortunes. They looked for furs and found few, cut sassafras and cedar, got into arguments with Indians, and worked their way south and west along the coast making enemies of the natives as they went. When the weather cooled, Gosnold and company returned to England, no richer and no wiser than when they had left.

The next year, at the behest of a Bristol trading company, Martin Pring arrived on Cape Cod to trade with the Indians, but he, too, soon wore out his welcome. The Nausets were particularly displeased when the English threatened them with two giant mastiffs (appropriately named Fool and Gallant). A war party of 140 Nausets set fire to the English encampment, but the English escaped without injury. Pring came back twice more in later years, his only mark on history the Cape Cod Indians' enmity for Europeans.

As in Ireland, and unlike their French rivals, the English refused to treat the natives with kindness or to conform to native notions of good manners. Though Harriot and White had come to know and respect individual Indians and praised Indian customs, men like Pring, Gosnold, and their successors demeaned the natives. In a reversal of prejudicial stereotyping, they depicted the Indians as Irishmen.

Undeterred by their failures, the English persisted in looking for furs. George Weymouth's trip to Maine in 1605 originated as a trading mission and ended as a crime. When the Abenakis, who preferred to deal with the French, used unmistakable signs to order the English to leave, Weymouth coaxed the Indians to change their minds. He gave guided tours of his ship, and otherwise seemed to act as a polite visitor. He shared what he had and gave gifts—behavior the Indians thought they understood. Then Weymouth's men seized five natives by the hair and dragged them off as captives.

Two years later, three of the five Abenaki captives returned with a new and more substantial English expedition. Behind it stood Sir John Popham, chief justice of England. In 1606, Sir John had sent Martin Pring back to Maine to find a site for a permanent trading post, and Pring selected the mouth of the Kennebec River, which he called the Sagadahoc.

Popham turned the prospective colony into a family affair in 1607. Sir Francis Popham, the chief justice's oldest son, arranged financing for three ships, to be commanded by George Popham and Ralegh Gilbert. Sir Fernando Gorges, another West

Country squire, added his influence and capital to the venture. He would remain one of the mainstays of Maine colonization for the next thirty years.

George Popham and Gilbert recruited a motley crew for the venture, and the expedition reached the river mouth on August 17, 1607. By October 8, they threw together a fort on Sabino Head, a promontory jutting out into the western channel of the lower Kennebec. The elevated semicircular site was protected on the east by the bend of the river and from the land by its elevation. Gilbert later drew and circulated a diagram of the fort that bears an uncanny resemblance to an Irish fortified town, with castlelike gates, high walls, and many lodgings. The diagram was pure fantasy. Atkins Point, the only flat place on Sabino Head, is about one hundred paces in diameter—hardly one-fifth the space needed for the barracks, church, storehouses, and other buildings the map featured.

Relations with the Indians soon degenerated. The three Abenakis Weymouth had kidnapped and Gilbert brought back to Maine promised to help the English but vanished as soon as they could. The fort was a provocation, for the English neglected to get permission to occupy the land from the local chief, Sabenoa. When he admonished the English for their lack of manners, they agreed to a meeting but gave no gifts to pave the way. A violent, midriver confrontation ended without casualties, but violence simmered beneath the surface. The newcomers regarded the natives as shifty thieves; the natives saw the newcomers as rude boors.

The winter was not especially cold by Maine standards, but the colonists suffered from malnutrition and fatigue. Popham died in February 1608. By the end of the first winter, the disorganized little colony had achieved only one unquestioned success. The colonists had built a seaworthy craft of thirty tons. It was one of the vessels the survivors later used to transport themselves home, in the summer of 1608. Only 65 of the original 120 colonists scrambled aboard for the return to Plymouth.

Across the mouth of the Gulf of Saint Lawrence, Elizabeth's successor to the English throne, James I, gave to his friend Sir William Alexander the first "proprietorship." The king, claiming the land was his to bestow, simply transferred title to the land to Alexander. Like Humphrey Gilbert and Walter Ralegh, Alexander's duty was to keep it safe for his royal overlord. In return, Alexander could govern it as he saw fit and profit from it if he could. In 1621, the royal seals were placed on the grant, to be known as Nova Scotia (New Scotland), in honor of Alexander's (and the king's) place of birth. Alexander saw himself as a true lord of his new manor, but all his efforts to people his new lands with servants failed.

In the meantime, John Mason joined with Fernando Gorges to gain a patent to "The Province of Maine." After a number of short-lived attempts to set up trading posts and fishing ports along the coast, Mason agreed to a partition of the grant. From 1629, the southern portion, to be known as New Hampshire, belonged to Mason. At a relatively flat place near the mouth of the Piscataqua River, named

Portsmouth, fishermen and traders gathered. The village became a town. Opposite it, in the Maine grant, the smaller farming settlement of Kittery appeared. Kittery became the first of a series of fishing and farming villages stretching up the coast, including York, Wells, and Saco.

The English had never given up the idea of trading with the Canadian Indians, and interlopers like the four Scottish Kirke brothers were able to skip in and out of territory the French had claimed. In 1628, the English and the French engaged in a short war, which permitted the Kirkes to organize a trading company for Canada and then rush across the Atlantic to capture Quebec. Basques among the French settlers there had no love for Champlain and readily switched sides, leading the English to the French settlements in 1629. Champlain and his men were already in dire straits because of the terrible winter of 1628–1629 and surrendered to the English without firing a shot.

The garrison (less the Basque turncoats, who stayed on to do business with the Kirkes) returned to France while the British company occupied Quebec and resumed the fur trade. In 1632, a treaty of peace between England and France restored Canada to the French, and the Kirkes lost the fruits of their aggression. But David Kirke received the governorship of Newfoundland, which was not returned to France, and one of the Kirkes' men, William Berkeley, went on to be governor of Virginia in 1641.

————

The northland outposts of English and French trade remained small, and most of the time ended in the bankruptcy of the organizers and the abandonment of the settlement. Until then, the traders huddled in hastily constructed shanties by jury-rigged wharves, waiting in vain for trade to make them rich. Those among them not bedridden with disease looked anxiously out to sea lest some European rival catch them unawares. Fear of their enemies and rumors of war caused the English and the French to select sites that were defensible against seaborne raiders but unhealthy and uninhabitable over long periods of time, a pattern repeated throughout the next century.

In their wake, men like the Kirke brothers left havoc. French and English parties struck at one another without warning, and the once- or twice-a-year set-piece battles between the Hurons and the Iroquois had became constant war, as both sides vied for European trade goods. Coastal Indians, forced to choose between French and English allies, divided in loyalties and warred on one another. Indeed, it seemed to one English observer that the rivals in the North were engaged in "a war of each against all." But a migration had begun that would soon change the scattered dots of abandoned trading posts into a vast coastal empire.

5

The Planter Colonies

From their first settlement to the end of the seventeenth century, the American colonies of the English Empire south of the fortieth parallel (in later years, a survey of the boundary between Maryland and Pennsylvania slightly south of the fortieth parallel gave the name Mason-Dixon to this dividing line) possessed certain basic configurations that differed from English colonies to the north. The planter colonies of Virginia, Maryland, the sugar islands of the Caribbean, and the Carolinas fulfilled the first commandment of empire—they produced wealth for the home country—in a way that the northern colonies could not duplicate.

The staple crops the southern planters and laborers grew enabled England to attain first rank among the nations of Europe. For a few of the colonists, great wealth and status were the rewards of risk and toil. Some did not achieve either but bettered themselves nonetheless. Others died young—from malaria, yellow fever, typhoid, dysentery, and a host of other diseases—or returned to England empty-handed. A growing number came not from the British Isles but from Africa. Slaves, they labored for others' profit.

In general, the southern colonizers saw trade with the natives as a secondary objective. A few merchants developed a lucrative deerskin trade, transforming southeastern Indian life just as the beaver trade in the North altered Native American values there, but the returns from trade paled beside the potential profits of the cultivation of staple export crops like tobacco, sugar, and rice. Most colonists regarded the Indians as obstacles to the expansion of the plantation system rather than as trading partners.

There are no more striking examples in the seventeenth century of the bifurcation of the American experience into disparate streams of success story and declension narrative than the planter colonies. By the end of the century, a small cadre of landowners were lords of all they surveyed. Their estates spread over the coast and bit deeply into the hinterland. The richest of them could afford three-story mansions and import fine furniture and raiment from Europe. A larger group of

You brave heroique minds, Worthy your countries name, That honour still pursue, Goe, and subdue, Whilst loy'tring hinds Lurke here at home, with shame.
—Michael Drayton, "To the Virginian Voyage" (1606)

freeholders longed to join the elite. But a mass of poorer laborers, including slaves, produced the staple crops that made the entire system flourish. Although the Indians, servants, and slaves were not automata—they, too, had cultural values and social yearnings that shaped the planter colonies—their prospects were far less savory than the planters'.

THE CHESAPEAKE

Over the whole course of the seventeenth century, 120,000 men and women left the British Isles to people the Chesapeake Bay area—many, though not all, single young men and women. Of these immigrants, 70 to 80 percent were "unfree"—bound by contracts called indentures to labor for three, four, or seven years to pay the costs of their passage. More than three-fourths of them were nineteen years old or younger and fled from abject poverty. Other immigrants were of the "middling sort"—men and women with some property who hoped to set up farms. A few immigrants were the younger sons of merchant families or noble houses. They came for adventure or to make their fortunes.

No one was prepared for what they found in America. The muggy summers shocked the immigrants, accustomed as they were to England's temperate summer weather. Habituated to workdays of four to five hours, they found they had to labor from sunup to sundown clearing and planting land and erecting housing. There were no markets at which to buy food. When supplies transported from England ran out, the colonists either had to trade with the Indians for food or catch, kill, and cook their meals, although few colonists had any experience as hunters or trappers. Even when the colonists planted garden crops and imported livestock, these had to be guarded day and night, for unlike England, the Chesapeake was home to panthers, bears, and wolves. Finally, the Chesapeake was a pesthole. Fewer than half of these migrants would survive long enough to see their children grow to adulthood.

The Lay of the Land

Chesapeake Bay runs a course of 125 miles from its northern terminus at the mouth of the Susquehanna River south to Cape Henry, on the Atlantic. Cut on its western banks by the Patapsco, Severn, Saint Mary's, Potomac, Rappahannock, York, and James rivers, and on its eastern shore by the Chester, Choptank, and Nanticoke rivers, in addition to innumerable sounds, bays, streams, and inlets, it fostered a diffuseness of settlement quite unlike prior European colonization sites. Waterways rather than roads connected the islands and peninsulas, and water travel dictated the flow of commerce. The marshy low-lying shore of the Chesapeake, unlike the sandy banks of the Carolinas around Roanoke, is immensely fertile, and farmers could grow a wide variety of crops, but the sluggish, shallow-bottomed streams and the brackish swamps provided homes for malaria-bearing mosquitoes, typhoid fever, dysentery, and other dangerous diseases.

The Chesapeake supported as many as fifty thousand Algonquians in the first years of the seventeenth century, but the broken landscape denied any single clan's ability to control the others. Although from 1570 until the early 1620s the Powhatan confederacy claimed preeminence from the Potomac River to the James River on the western coast of the bay, the Powhatans never established a city-state on the Mississippian model. Instead, they congregated in small villages, usually on streams or riverbanks. The Powhatans produced a sufficient surplus to sustain the hierarchy of local *werowances* and a paramount chief, however. Tribute passed up the chain of command and paid for priests, feasts, and war.

White had told Ralegh that the Powhatans might have slaughtered the remnant of the Roanoke settlers. If so, the Indians' actions had a precedent. In the early 1570s, the Powhatans had murdered a group of Spanish Jesuits at their newly founded mission. But Ralegh no longer led the Virginia Company. Imprisoned in the Tower of London for plotting to depose King James I, Ralegh passed the time writing a history of the world and dreaming of a city of gold somewhere on the Spanish Main. Others, no less bold but far less able than he, planned the second English colony in Virginia.

The Virginia Company of London and the Jamestown Settlement

Bartholomew Gosnold was the prime mover of the renewed effort to colonize Virginia. His misadventures in Maine had done nothing to diminish his influence in English overseas enterprise. Gosnold had learned the importance of sufficient financing from the sorry state of the nearly bankrupt Plymouth Company, his former employer. In 1606, he found a sponsor, Sir Thomas Smyth, whose family ties and political connections gained him access to other powerful patrons. Gosnold also brought a cousin, Edward Wingfield, into the new venture.

The promoters hired Christopher Newport as commander of the expedition. Newport was an experienced West Indian privateer who had served with distinction against the armada. Newport was to deliver the settlers, see that they were safely entered into their business, then carry back to England the fruits of their trading and mining. The settlers were to elect a president from among the councilors named in a document to be opened once the colony was secure.

The company charter of 1606 resembled Ralegh's. Crown lawyers adapted elements of the borough franchises that the monarchy granted to cities and towns to facilitate their self-government. James I endowed the company with "all liberties, franchises, and immunities, within any of our other dominions, to all intents and purposes, as if they had been abiding and born, within this our realm of England, or any other of our said dominions." This included the right to hold a council to make local ordinances, a provision that led to the first colonial legislatures. At the same time, the drafters of the charter required that the laws the merchant adventurers made in their own settlements must be "neere as conveniently may [be] to the forme of the laws and policy of England."

The king's lawyers finished drafting the charter for the new Virginia Company in November 1606, and within a month the investors had hired three ships, the 120-ton *Susan Constant*, the 40-ton *Godspeed*, and the 20-ton pinnace *Discovery*. The smallest ship was intended as an exploratory vessel. The ships would carry a total of 105 settlers: gentlemen, laborers, craftspeople, and four boys. Gosnold would go, along with George Percy, a gentleman and director of the company; George Kendall; and John Ratcliff. Finally, Gosnold recruited John Smith, an experienced mercenary soldier, to join the expedition.

Short in stature but muscular and sharp witted, Smith combined a realistic, worldly outlook on life with a lust for adventure that was typical of the late Renaissance soldier of fortune. He had served with English forces in European wars and had distinguished himself in battle. After his Virginia adventure ended, he proved himself a master of self-promotion. Indeed, his accounts of the first two years of the Virginia colony of Jamestown remain one of the foremost sources for scholars, although each version he penned was more elaborate and fanciful than its predecessor.

On April 26, 1607, Newport brought his little fleet safely to Cape Henry, then spent the next three weeks exploring the banks of the James River looking for a suitable site for the settlement. The directors had instructed him to find a place on the river at a point narrow enough for the colonists to hit enemy ships in midstream with cannon fire and deep enough to permit ships to dock directly at the settlement's edge. His masters wanted him to be able to protect himself against a seaborne Spanish attack, but he was to allow no Indian villages between the settlement and the river. (It was assumed that the Roanoke settlers were wiped out by an Indian assault.)

Newport chose a potato-shaped peninsula of marsh, woods, and grass connected to the mainland by a narrow isthmus. He called it James Island, and on May 14 the colonists and sailors stepped onto the northwestern edge of it. There they began to build the shelters of Jamestown.

James Island is a natural wetlands crossed by two sluggish streams. Its eight hundred acres are highly fertile but mosquito ridden. Moreover, the land is flat, offering no vantage point to see downriver or inland. Worst of all, it is situated at the confluence of the freshwater and the saltwater on the James, causing the groundwater on the island to retain just about all the waste that the colonists produced. In no time at all, they would be drinking and washing in their refuse. In all, Jamestown was about the poorest choice that Newport could have made.

John Smith's Colony

Newport's movements concerned the Indians nearby. The Paspahegh, part of the Powhatan confederation, had decided that these strange visitors intended to stay. James Island belonged to the Paspaheghs, but the English did not ask the Paspaheghs' permission, or present them with gifts, or in any way placate them. The natives watched with growing irritation as the sailors and settlers constructed a half-moon-shaped fort of brush and then proceeded to unload stores and wander off farther into Paspahegh territory. They saw Newport and Smith assemble twenty men and journey up the James while Bartholomew Gosnold took another twenty men to annoy the Indians inland. They no doubt heard that the Newport party was warmly greeted by the Weanocs, no friend to the Paspaheghs.

Rebuffed in their one attempt to open diplomatic relations through an exchange of gifts, the Paspaheghs assaulted the little settlement. The defenders fought off the attack, and a fragile truce followed the Indian withdrawal, but neither side expected the peace to last for long. The colonists built a much more substantial triangular fortress around the hutches and warehouse. Satisfied that he had done his job, Newport sailed off with the *Susan Constant* and the *Godspeed.*

As the threat of Indian attack abated, three more insidious enemies appeared within the settlement itself. The first was illness, the second sloth, and the third political wrangling. Worse than the Indians' surprise attack, disease crippled the little colony. Dysentery and typhoid from fouled waters spread through the camp. Every day one or two of the men were buried, and the survivors grew weaker. Gosnold died after a lingering illness, but some of the company passed away in a matter of days. By the end of August, there were but five or six healthy Englishmen left within the walls. Some of the English left the encampment and lived for a time with the Indians.

Starvation abetted the spread of disease. The ships had brought with them a supply of food, but some had spoiled en route, and the ships' crews hid some for their return voyage. Everyone was too busy looking for gold or fighting off disease to lay in garden crops or plant English grains. The Indian women were fine gardeners, and in time the English would learn to copy Indian techniques, but for now the newcomers only bickered about the remaining stores, plotted ways to barter for or steal Indian corn, or lay about hoping that Newport would return with provisions.

The quarrels over food were echoed in a struggle over who would make rules for the settlement. Smith thought the other councilors incompetent, venal, and weak willed, and eventually he earned command of the colony. In the meantime, with Smith away in search of food, some of the councilors plotted to abandon the colony entirely, using the *Discovery* to escape. One of the conspirators, the enigmatic George Kendall, had a different purpose. A Catholic, he was a spy in the pay of Spain and intended to hijack the boat and sail it to the nearest Spanish possession. His plan revealed, he was tried for treason and shot.

Smith thwarted the plotters, but there was still the Powhatan paramount chief

Wahunsonacock to placate or overawe, fame to be won, and Tidewater Virginia to be mapped and surveyed. Smith set out to explore the tributaries of the James River and fell into the hands of yet another Indian band, the Pamunkeys. The Indians ambushed and killed his companions, but they spared Smith because he was the chief of the English and the Indians respected chiefs.

Some historians, relying on Smith's later account, have judged that the local *werowance*, Opechancanough, Wahunsonacock's half brother, was awed by Smith's eloquence and bravery or beguiled by a demonstration of his compass, but more than likely Opechancanough simply appreciated Smith's performance. Smith had proved to possess both spiritual power and the ability to speak with authority in public. Indians appreciated both kinds of skill. Opechancanough reciprocated with a speech of his own, proving that he, too, could claim the high station of an orator. And Wahunsonacock had undoubtedly spread the word that Smith was not to be killed— at least not yet and not by a subordinate chief.

After exhibiting him to all the allied villages in a tour that was part carnival and part test of his manhood, the Indians put on their own ceremony for Smith. For three days running, seven shamans dressed in all their finery danced about a fire and spread cornmeal in ritual patterns. The shamans were laying out on the ground a two-dimensional cosmology of the world. The fire at the center and the inner ring of cornmeal represented the Indians' homeland. A pile of sticks inside an outer ring of cornmeal was Smith's home, placed by the Indians near the edge of their known world.

Smith may not have grasped the meaning of the pile of sticks, but Wahunsonacock understood perfectly. When Smith was brought before him, the paramount chief wanted to know about England and its enemies, particularly the Spanish, whether Newport would return, and what the English plans were for Virginia. The Powhatan leader, like Moctezuma facing Cortés, was more concerned about long-term relations with the powerful nation Smith described than about the immediate danger Smith and his men posed.

In later versions of his story, Smith avowed that young "Pocahontas," the old chief's daughter, rushed to Smith's side and saved him from death. His version missed much—for example, the name Pocahontas simply meant "playful one," and her family called her Matoaka. In later days she would be kidnapped by the English, held as a hostage, convert to Christianity, and marry an English settler named John Rolfe. Together they would travel to England and become celebrities, and she would die of the English pox. In reality, Pocahontas's role in saving Smith, if any, was part of a ritual, and Wahunsonacock had simply decided to wait and see who else sailed up the James before he did away with Smith.

In the meantime, Newport was running his shuttle service back and forth. Smith's self-important account denied Newport the credit he deserves. He never failed the colony, transporting a steady stream of supplies across the pirate-infested ocean. In

September 1608, Newport reappeared with seventy new settlers and the first two women to reside in the colony. He also had orders to make good the company's expenses by loading the ships with timber and other cargo.

Smith was incensed. Winter was coming, and the fort and housing had to be repaired, food stockpiled, and natives kept at arm's length. The survival of the colony still balanced on a knife point. Only one-fourth of the original settlers were still alive, and but half of the 120 who came with Newport's first resupply. All told, the colony numbered barely two hundred souls. Most of the seventy newcomers were gentlemen layabouts and exotic craftspeople instead of the farmers and fishermen that Smith knew the settlement needed. But the company was thinking about quick profits, this time from pitch and tar, soap, and glass making, as well as clapboard and other wood products. Meanwhile, the settlers were trading all their tools to the sailors for the food on the ships, and the sailors were trading the tools to the Indians for furs.

Tobacco Transforms Virginia

Obviously neither Smith's efforts nor Newport's shuttle service could sustain the colony without further assistance from the company. To the rescue came a reorganized Virginia Company of London (the first to actually bear that formal title). In early 1609, the new organization determined that the follies of the past two years would end. Armed with a revised charter written by Sir Edwin Sandys that read like a military order, the new company sent seven hundred soldiers and a seven-ship fleet to the colony, under the command of Thomas West, Lord De la Warr. The new governor-general, Thomas Gates, had the powers of a dictator. Gates shipwrecked on Bermuda and did not get to Virginia for almost a year, but four of the ships arrived in August 1609, and two more straggled in later.

In the coming years over five thousand English servants, planters, mariners, and others would stop over on the island of Bermuda. Few stayed for long. Some blamed it on the rats that the first arrivals had brought, grown to huge size and rapacious in attitude, others, more sensibly, on the declining price they got for their crops. By midcentury, the island had a few well-to-do planters, but was inhabited primarily by fishermen, farmers, and transients. As a port, a whaling station, a place where ships might be repaired, and an outpost against the Spanish and French, the island retained its utility. It became a royal colony in 1684, by which time the white population of slightly over five thousand had acquired over three thousand slaves.

Smith, seriously burned in an accident shortly after the relief party arrived, left for England, never to return to the colony. In his wake, the colony again lost more than half of its number and nearly starved before the winter was over and Gates arrived. Smith wanted to come back, but the company, listening to the complaints of his rivals, would not permit it. The irony is that his iron rule was flexible and just compared to the laws laid down by De la Warr; his deputy, Sir Thomas Dale, governor from 1610 to 1611; and Gates, governor from 1611 to 1614. Indeed, in Virginia martial law became the order of the day, much as it was in the parts of Ireland that England occupied.

Under the new government, the colonists began to spread themselves up and down the river, setting up fortified hamlets and laying in fields of corn, peas, and barley. Virginia became the testing ground for the theory that the colonies could drain off England's surplus population. At first, young men dominated the immigrant pool, a characteristic of most frontier settlements. Throughout the first half century of the colony, men outnumbered the women by a ratio of three or four to one. Only at the end of the century did the sex ratio approach one to one.

But the sternness of the new regime and the additional resources the company poured into the colony would not have helped had the colonists and the company not agreed upon a new focus for their activities—growing tobacco. Recognizing the increasing demand in England and on the Continent and wishing to overcome the Spanish Caribbean planters' head start on the production and shipment of the weed, the company sought its own monopoly on the importation of the Virginia crop.

In 1611, one of the settlers, John Rolfe, replaced the native variety with a Caribbean type of tobacco. He also discovered that air drying the leaves preserved their full flavor. Rolfe exported his first harvest in 1614. In 1615, the colony sent home two thousand pounds; by 1629 that figure had risen to one and a half million pounds. Everyone from governors to servants devoted themselves to the new crop.

So great was the need for labor and so promising the returns on the new export that the planters bought African slaves from Dutch raiders (who captured them from Portuguese slavers, who in turn had purchased them from warring chieftains at the Congo slave port of Luanda). Recent research indicates that at least fifty-four Congolese labored in the colony in 1619. In the coming years, their numbers would grow slowly at first, to four hundred in 1650, then skyrocket at the end of the century. Their new masters knew all about slavery, but there was no legal basis in the charter or the laws of England for chattel slavery, so the planters treated some of the Africans as indentured servants and allowed others to buy their freedom.

A few of the latter, like Antonio, took on an English name (he became Anthony Johnson) and took up farming. Most Africans never escaped slavery but nevertheless found ways to participate in a wide variety of economic and social activities. They moved about freely, often (with the permission of their owners) selling their labor or skills, hoping to buy freedom, like Johnson. Others acted the role of go-betweens or interpreters, gaining a measure of independence and sometimes their freedom by brokering slave trading.

As the numbers of Africans increased and the labor shortage became more acute in the 1650s and 1660s, the masters wrote laws to perpetuate the servitude of Africans into the next generation. For example, runaway black servants faced enslavement if they were caught (while Europeans would only have their term of service lengthened), and Virginians replaced the English common law rule that one's father's status determined the child's status with a rule that the child of a slave mother shared her status. Additional laws announced that slaves could not gain their freedom by adopting Christianity.

Without question, English racial prejudice played a part in the progressive debasement of Africans, but if one bears in mind that the drafters of these laws were also the Africans' masters, one can see an economic incentive behind the laws. Not only were slaves essential as laborers, they represented an increasing portion of the planters' capital.

From Company to Colony

Meanwhile, in England, the Virginia Company sold stock and held auctions and lotteries to raise money for its colony. In 1616, to attract settlers, the company abandoned the idea of common stores and introduced private ownership of land plots, in effect changing a trading company into a land development firm. For an investment of £12.10s one could purchase fifty acres. The company also gave to its patrons and agents fifty acres (called headrights) for every person they transported or brought with them to the new colony. Finally, the directors of the company granted huge tracts of land to its major investors, a form of land distribution that would become common in the other colonies. The new manor lords of the Americas were supposed to bring their own servants and work the land, though in fact they often sold off or leased out parcels of their grants.

In 1618, the company conceded that it had to change the manner of local government to conform to the altered purpose of the settlement. In the instructions for 1618–1619, the directors gave to the settlers who were freeholders of the company the privilege (not the right—a privilege is a gift that can always be revoked) to hold an assembly among themselves. The new elective House of Burgesses sat with two members from each of the towns or precincts. The resolutions of this assembly had the force of a city council's ordinances and had to be acceptable to the governor-general in the colony. The burgesses got rid of martial law, reduced the authority of the governor-general over crimes and punishments, and petitioned the company for more laborers. The company also authorized the creation of monthly inferior courts for the "hundreds" (minisettlements) on the fringes of the colony. These would become county courts in 1634.

The survival of Virginia was not only a victory for the idea of staple-producing colonies, it was a military achievement. Virginia anchored the southern flank of the English empire against the Spanish. Spanish governors in Florida and ministers of state in Madrid recognized the military importance of Virginia but did not attempt to attack the colony. The Spanish had done this against French incursions into Florida, destroying the French colony and killing all but a few of the colonists in 1568. In 1608, the Spanish merely complained at James I's court that Virginia belonged to Spain. Perhaps the cost of mounting an expedition motivated the Spanish to desist, and the fate of the armada remained fresh in their minds.

The Spanish threat was hardly illusory, but a more dangerous one lay closer at hand. Confident in their armor and firearms, the settlers dismissed their Indian neighbors as savages. English sneers and rudeness pained the natives, and English atrocities drove the Indians past endurance. In 1618, Opechancanough, succeeding to his brother's paramount chiefdomship, began planning to oust the English from Powhatan lands. In the winter of 1622, after the English had murdered one of the village chiefs and the company had refused to pay compensation, he and his allies decided to strike at the settlements.

Opechancanough wanted the attack on the English to be an event that any surviving colonists would never forget. But to succeed, the attack had to be stealthy. Indian numbers and power were too weak for anything else, not to say that Indian warriors were not masters of ambush. The *werowance* knew that the English had grown careless. He set the plan to begin in the early morning of March 22, 1622.

At breakfast time, his people would enter the homes of the unsuspecting Virginians carrying no weapons but those concealed on their person, engage in friendly conversation over the first meal, then use the English people's tools to murder their hosts, according to Smith, "not sparing either age or sex, man woman or child . . . neither did these beasts spare those amongst the rest well known unto them, from whom they had daily received many benefits."

To enforce the message of the Indians' fury on the minds of the settlers, victims would be mutilated and then displayed and body parts eaten. For example, Nathaniel Powell and his entire family were decapitated and hanged in plain sight. Some of the gruesome details in John Smith's account of the massacre resulted from hysterical reports; some were propaganda, but the decapitation of enemies was a common Indian and European tactic to heighten the terror of the warfare. Torture of the captives served the same purpose. Indian cannibalism simultaneously humiliated the enemy and stole his inner spirit. He could never gain revenge from the other world, and his strength passed to those who consumed him. Practiced in the sight of survivors, it was never forgotten.

Friendly Indians warned the people of Jamestown of the approaching carnage, and they were able to defend themselves, but 347 Virginians, a fourth of the total number of settlers, died in the massacre. The rest would never forget what they had seen and heard. Opechancanough's sneak attack worked too well, however, for the English response to the "massacre of 1622" was total warfare of the European variety. The English systematically burned Indian villages and gardens. With the Indians driven away from the Tidewater, their patchwork of common woods, paths, and native villages gave way to an English-style checkerboard of fenced-in, privately owned farms and plantations.

Opechancanough sued for peace, at least until 1644. Then, nearly one hundred years old, he tried one more time to rout the colonists. After two years of war and nearly five hundred dead among the colonists, Opechancanough was captured and shot. Not all Algonquians followed Opechancanough, and Indians remained in the region after his final uprising was suppressed. Even the Powhatan confederation survived, though a shadow of its former power. In 1645, its leaders conceded that they held their lands at the pleasure of the crown. By the 1650s, under Cockacoeske, queen of the Pamunkey Indians, the Powhatans proved to be the most reliable of all the Indian allies of the English. For her loyalty, the English gave her a medal, though she had asked for the return of her people's lands.

The colony survived the massacre of 1622, but the company had gone bankrupt, and its directors were discredited. In 1624, the crown stepped in to take over the colony. Henceforth, the governor would be a crown appointee. The first of these, Sir Francis Wyatt, set the precedent of consulting the burgesses on matters of policy, even though, under the law, his power was almost untrammeled. In fact, as the directors of the company had already discovered, no one could rule the colony without the consent of its leading planters.

The governor, under instructions from the crown, chose a small group of these men to advise him. They became the council—in effect, the upper house of the legislature. They doubled as the high court of appeals for the colony. The county court system functioned much as in England. Justices of the peace holding commissions from the crown sat as individual magistrates and came together once a month (though no one attended every session) to hear civil suits and presentments by the grand jurors, hold trials, and keep the administrative records of the county. Invariably, the gentlemen justices of the county were its leading planters. Thus the judges, administrators, and legislators were one and the same men. What is more, the men who controlled public life dominated private life as well—loaning money, renting land, giving out jobs, and running the vestry of the churches.

Not every royal governor got along with the local magnates. In 1635, the burgesses condemned and the council arrested the royal governor, John Harvey, and stowed him, along with a petition of grievances against his conduct, on board a ship for England. The legislators' action, in effect the first American impeachment, underlined the message: an effective governor could not ignore the leading planters' wishes. Subsequent governors learned to draw a cadre of planters to their side by patronage and flattery. William Berkeley, governor from 1641 to 1652, and from 1661 to 1677, was so successful at this process in his second term that the ruling clique was nicknamed the Green Spring faction after his plantation home.

Maryland

Maryland was the second of the great proprietary colonies after Nova Scotia, a grant from Charles I to George Calvert. William Alexander did little to populate Nova Scotia, but Calvert (after 1625, Lord Baltimore) had visited the Chesapeake himself and expected to join his colonists there. He died in 1632, before he could execute his plan, but his son Cecil would keep watch over the colony from England, and a younger son, Leonard, would come to America as the first lieutenant governor of Maryland.

Behind the settlement of the colony was Lord Baltimore's commitment to provide a refuge for persecuted English Catholics. The elder Calvert was born a Protestant, but as a young man he moved into the company of well-born Catholics. A supporter of Charles I and his French Catholic wife, Henrietta Maria, Calvert sought a haven for in-laws and friends. In 1632, he was successful—the king's Privy Council agreed to the grant of land on the eastern shore of the bay. George suddenly died, at fifty-two, but Charles I kept his promise, enlarging the grant to include lands on the western side of the Chesapeake as well, up to the fortieth parallel. The Virginia settlers protested, to no avail.

Cecil Calvert now began to recruit settlers. He could not offer a haven to the Catholics openly, for they could not take the required oaths of allegiance to the Church of England, but to the 128 Protestants who boarded the Dove and the Ark in November 1633 to travel to the new colony, Calvert secretly added as many Catholics. The ships arrived in February 1634, and the settlers laid out their capital in Saint Mary's.

Calvert ordered the land to be distributed as though it were the fiefdoms of a feudal barony, but the proprietor had not counted on the siren's song of tobacco, to which the immigrants soon succumbed. By the 1640s, the Maryland coast was dotted with tobacco farms. A fair hand could tend five thousand to six thousand plants a year. With experience and crop rotation, that figure could be doubled. The door was thus open to middling families (called "ordinary" planters in the records) to try their luck.

Nor was politics in the colony as harmonious as the Calverts wished. Indeed, because the root of political contests in Maryland was intractable religious differences, the partisans preferred to fight rather than compromise. One must recall that fear and hatred of Roman Catholics were staples of English Protestant thought. And with civil strife looming in England over very similar religious issues, religiously motivated antiproprietary leaders in Maryland could find potent allies in the home country.

As King Charles I and Archbishop of Canterbury William Laud in the 1630s began making life easier for the Catholics and harder for the radical religious dissenters like the Puritans, the Puritans began arriving in Maryland. Although far more numerous in the New England colonies (and for that reason more fully discussed in the next chapter), Puritan emigrants to Maryland like Richard Ingle were numerous enough to foment political unrest. From 1644 to 1646, Ingle led a mini–civil war in Maryland that ended only when Lieutenant Governor Leonard Calvert raised armed forces to chase Ingle back to England. But Ingle's plundering time was only the prologue to the troubles in Maryland, for Ingle and his allies now had powerful friends in England.

The English Civil Wars and the Interregnum

To understand who Ingle's English allies were, one must return to English politics, and the civil wars between 1642 and 1649 and the interregnum (kingless period) that followed. To some extent, the crisis began as a quarrel within the ruling elite over the conduct of the king. Charles ruled without calling a Parliament from 1628 to 1639, taxing his subjects without their consent and using his prerogative courts, such as the Star Chamber, to throttle dissent. Most of the nobility sided with the king, but others joined with the majority in the House of Commons to object to the king raising funds without the consent of Parliament.

Both the king and the Parliament precipitated the onset of the first civil war (1642–1646). Needing more money to press a war against the Scots, Charles called and then dissolved a Parliament in 1640. In November of that year, a council of lords called for the election of another Parliament (in later years called the Long Parliament, for it was to sit in one form or another until 1660). In the first sessions of this reform Parliament, the Commons abolished the hated Star Chamber court and decreed that henceforth Parliament would be elected every three years. More radical reformers, led by Puritans like John Pym, demanded punishment of Catholics and the creation of a Presbyterian national church to replace the Episcopal system.

The king tried to arrest Pym and failed, and war erupted in August 1642. The war dragged on until 1646, when parliamentary forces, led by self-taught and highly disciplined Puritan generals like Oliver Cromwell, defeated the king's forces in battle. London remained solidly pro-Parliament, and this tipped the scales in favor of the Puritans.

Parliament dismantled the state church but did not replace establishment with toleration. Instead, religion was to be regulated by national conferences and local associations of ministers. But within Parliament, many Independents attacked this new Presbyterian system, demanding instead that each congregation be free to pursue its own way. When the Presbyterian faction in Parliament tried to disband the army without paying it, the army, led by Independents like Cromwell, revolted and took Parliament captive. In the meantime, in the army and in the city of London, even more radical reformers were appearing. The "Levelers" demanded a democratic republic. The "Diggers" wanted a more equal distribution of wealth. In 1648, the army purged Parliament of moderates, and the new Parliament resumed the war against King Charles. This minority of a minority in Parliament executed the king in 1649.

During the Commonwealth period (1649–1653), an even smaller portion of the Parliament (derisively termed "the rump") itself fell to factional squabbling. Its most radical members demanded dismantling the state church completely. The remaining moderates turned to Cromwell and his Council of Officers to take charge of the nation. Parliament still met, but from 1653 to his death in 1658, Cromwell, supported by the army, ruled as Lord Protector.

In some ways, Cromwell remained a reformer—for example, seeking to purify the law of its feudal remnants and arguing in favor of toleration of Baptists, Jews, and other sects' right to conscience. In other ways, his rule was as high-handed as the king's, and more dangerous, for the king had Parliament to fear, and Cromwell only feared God.

When Cromwell died in 1658, and his son proved incompetent, the generals of his army argued among themselves about who would rule and finally allowed a free election of Parliament. Parliament restored Charles I's son, Charles II, to the throne. The acts of Parliament from 1642 and the instructions of Cromwell's council of state were annulled. With his younger brother James, his wife, and his entourage, Charles left Holland and returned to England and there began the restoration of the English monarchy.

Maryland's Travails

The proprietors could not prosecute Ingle's followers in Maryland so long as Ingle's friends ruled England. Maryland politics did not quiet until the Restoration. In 1648, Cecil Calvert chose a Protestant, William Stone, to govern the colony, but Stone could not prevent more civil strife, for the next year Parliament ordered the end of toleration of Catholicism in Maryland. In 1649, the Maryland Assembly, run by a set of Puritan commissioners, decreed that Catholics could not hold office in Maryland. In England, Lord Baltimore barely retained his patent. Only the timely arrival in the colony of another of Lord Baltimore's brothers, Philip, prevented a civil war in 1661.

The antiproprietary sentiments of many of the planters never abated. In 1676, a mutiny against the proprietary government ended with the hanging of two planters, William Davyes and John Pate. In 1681, former governor Josias Fendall, who had fomented a 1660 uprising against the proprietor, reappeared to lead a crusade against all Catholics in government. He was captured, tried, fined forty thousand pounds of tobacco, and banished from the colony.

By this time the focus of dissent had shifted from religion to high taxation, the proprietors' supposed favoritism in giving out patronage, and absentee government. The proprietors had also to contend with Virginia claims to Maryland land, Dutch interlopers seeking to trade with Maryland's Indian clients, and, after 1683, a new neighbor, William Penn (on whom see chapter 7).

In the vacuum where Calvert's official policy of toleration once stood, a tacit, fragile sufferance of religious diversity persisted. Catholic priests held masses and tried to convert the Indians. Puritans worshiped in private. A few "Quakers," the derisive name given a radical Protestant sect, arrived and held meetings.

Members of the Society of Friends were Protestants who believed that every person was a vessel of the inner light and so could be saved. Following the preacher

George Fox, they rejected priests and ordained ministers; were unorthodox in their view of the Trinity, the Bible, and the prayer book; and encouraged adults at their meetings to testify to their own spiritual state. For their objections to the state church and their refusal to swear oaths and remove their hats in court, as well as their resistance in some cases to military service and paying taxes, they were persecuted in England. In Maryland, the Quakers made only a handful of converts.

Chesapeake Farms and Plantations

Plantations (the word derived from the English farms in Ireland and did not yet connote the great holdings of wealthy landholders) in the Chesapeake ranged in size from a few acres to thousands of acres. Land was cheap and plentiful, but labor was scarce. The average size of households—parents, children, servants—working the land was seven people. It took about a year to clear and plant an acre. Thus large portions of all homesteads remained wooded or marshy. A few great plantations, worked by servants, appeared early in the seventeenth century in Virginia, and the first Maryland manors grants were extensive, but they were parceled out among renters. The typical living style in the 1650s in both colonies was the family farm.

Like the Spanish in the Caribbean, the English brought to Virginia a host of animals, insects, and germs. The malarial parasite, the plague of the Chesapeake, was introduced to the region by the English. Local mosquitoes then did the rest. The newcomers also carried with them their domesticated animals. Cattle and horses were most prized. Dogs, cats, pigs, sheep, chickens, and goats completed the family circle. Whether allowed to range freely (and so bedevil Indian gardens) or kept close to home by fences, yards, and stiles, well-kept animals evidenced a well-ordered household. Prized animals had names and were encouraged to breed. In fact, a family's wealth was more accurately measured by the size of livestock herds than by cultivated acreage.

Tobacco farms and plantations spread along the inlets and coves of the Chesapeake Bay and its many tributaries. The cured leaves were packed in giant heavy barrels called hogsheads, which weighed from two hundred to a thousand pounds and could not be moved easily overland. Thus every farm needed to touch a waterway or have access to a jetty at the water's edge.

The tobacco fields surrounded the planter's dwelling, generally little more than a one-room wooden shack with a fireplace at one end. Few homes exceeded sixteen by twenty feet in area, and most had a hard-packed dirt floor. Furniture was sparse— the family and the servants ate squatting against the walls or sitting on trunks of clothing. Benches and chairs were luxuries, as were individual plates and cups. Men and women ate and drank from common containers passed from hand to hand. Nightfall ended all communal activity. Candles were prohibitively expensive. The only light came from the dying embers of the fire in the fireplace.

The poorest families lived in little more than huts. Even the better sort slept three and four to a bed or wrapped in blankets on the floor. No one bathed. All but the wealthiest households lacked chamber pots and outhouses. To relieve themselves, the residents stepped outside (and from the archaeological evidence, not too far from the door). By the 1670s, successful planters would construct houses that had two rooms, then homes that had two stories. They would buy or build furniture, plank their floors, and plaster their walls. The poor would still occupy one-room cabins.

The lot of the indentured servants was even harder than the poor yeoman farmer. The law gave them the right to protest against their master's brutality, but nothing helped when the master was indifferent or the conditions simply prohibited kindly treatment. As Richard Frethorne piteously informed his parents in 1623: "The nature of this country is such that it causeth much sickness, as the scurvy and bloody flux and divers other diseases, which maketh the body very poor, and weak, and when we are sick there is nothing to comfort us; for since I came out of the ship, I never ate any thing but peas and loblollie (porridge). . . . We must work both early and late for a mess of water gruel, and a mouthful of bread." Frethorne wanted to go home, but even those who stayed, waiting for their freedom and the forty acres and tools that came with it, lived in rude shanties and ate meager rations.

Servant women suffered more than the men, for not only did they have to labor, they faced ingrained legal disabilities and had to fend off the unwelcome advances of fellow servants and planters. Even when those invitations were solicited, a servant woman who became pregnant and denounced the father to the courts faced punishment along with the father of the child, making the serving woman a victim twice over. Masters shifted the expense of servants' misconduct, such as bearing a child out of wedlock or running away, onto the servants by elongating their years of service. In theory, the additional term of service given women for bearing a bastard child compensated the master for her lost time when pregnant and caring for her child, but surely the imposition of longer terms was meant to serve as a deterrent—and thus as a punishment—as well.

The dream of the early immigrants was to duplicate the success of men like Thomas Cole. Cole's farm on Saint Clement's Bay, Maryland, brought in an average gross income of £38 per year, and the value of his holdings increased from an initial investment of £54 in 1652 to £360 in 1673. Two-thirds of his income came from the tobacco crop, but the increase in value of the estate came from the land he cleared and farmed and his livestock herd. It had grown fourfold in the twenty years from 1652 to 1672.

Much of what Cole produced he and his family and workers consumed, but export earnings were 36.2 percent of his yearly income. He and his family spent over 55 percent of that income on imported manufactured goods such as clothing, shoes, spices, and tools. Little went for purchase of household items, indicating that his preferences, rather than his wife Rebecca's, dictated the shopping list. In the next century this would change, as the well-to-do became major customers for imported fabrics, dishware, and luxury items. Then, women's preferences would be as important as men's.

There was no need to purchase the basics of food—abundant meat from the herds of cattle and pigs, dairy products from the cattle and goats, corn and garden vegetables, fruits and fruit ciders, all supplemented by hunting, provided a diet heavy in calories and fats. Shellfish from the bay provided variety. The Coles ate far better in Maryland than comparable families did in England.

Chesapeake Gatherings

No doubt the Coles missed the communal life they left behind in England, centered around church and town green. Throughout the Chesapeake, communal spaces like market villages, church grounds, and courthouses only belatedly followed the clearing of farmlands. The landscape itself, with its swamps and watercourses, the distances between farms, and the absence of roads, made communal activities difficult.

Planters found private amusements to compensate for the paucity of public gatherings. The wealthy entertained one another and offered hospitality to visitors. A man's reputation depended in part upon his graciousness, and reputation meant a great deal to the planters. With increasing density of population in the 1670s and after, the number of occasions for visiting increased. Planters' wives and daughters especially benefited from this, as the difficulty and danger of travel in previous years had prevented extensive visiting. Visiting the sick and comforting mourners were also occasions when women traveled.

The Sabbath brought together people from all ranks and classes to worship, because the churches in the Tidewater, like the English country churches, served all who resided in the area. Virginia law made no provision for practice of any other rites than the Church of England's, though many people worshipped in the privacy of their homes. Still, the founders of the Chesapeake colonies intended that public worship services foster a sense of community. The largest building in Jamestown was Lord De la Warr's chapel. Its bells called the settlers to worship. Dale's laws provided sanguinary punishments for anyone who robbed this chapel, and those who did not attend services lost one day of their food allowance. In later years, nonattendance remained a misdemeanor punished by fines.

So insistent were the demands of tobacco cultivation, so high spirited were the young men who came to Virginia, and so dispersed were their farmsteads that religiosity had a low priority in the early settlements. The chapel in Jamestown was in constant disrepair, and the vestrymen for Jamestown and other churches seemed disinclined to spend money or time on religious matters. The first ministers to arrive were enthusiastic preachers, but by the middle of the century, one-third of the parishes still had no ministers, and those ministers who came in midcentury included, according to their parishioners, "black cotted raskolls" and drunks who "babble in a pulpet [and] roare in a tavern." These depictions are not fair to many of the ministers, but even those who combined piety and learning had no overt impact upon the life of the colony.

Court day, when the county court sat, was both a solemn legal occasion and a festive social rite for all (except for the defendants in criminal prosecutions). County courts performed a vital integrative function in the otherwise dispersed and often disorderly Chesapeake world. With the gentlemen justices of the county court presiding, grand juries, composed of men from all walks of life, presented accusations of misconduct. The most common offenses were swearing, fighting, failure to attend church, public drunkenness, and slander. The accused might profess their innocence, but most confessed their error. The court then arranged for two other people to put up a surety or bond that the confessor would not repeat the offense. In this fashion the court served as an agency to bind people in the community together in the interests of social harmony and good conduct.

The courts also heard civil suits over damage to property (for example, taking down one's neighbor's fences for one's own use or letting one's pigs root out a neighbor's garden), disputed wills, and agreements that were not honored. Sometimes these suits ran on for session after session as various parties failed to appear, paperwork bounced from one party to another, and the parties negotiated settlements. The majority of suits were resolved within two sessions of the court, however.

But some lawsuits stretched the fabric of social harmony to its limit. Slander occupied much of the courts' time, although the number of cases filed represent a small percentage of the times that people abused one another verbally or besmirched one another's reputations to third parties. For women, the most important component of reputation was sexual continence. Hence the most telling accusation (or, from the other side, the most hurtful slander) alleged sexual misconduct. Men sued one another for slander as well, but for them credit and reputation depended on other virtues—honorable dealings, telling the truth, and upright fiscal conduct. Thus to defame another man, one called him a rogue, knave, or liar.

Courts also sat to hear serious cases of criminal conduct. The most common involved offenses against property such as petty theft and grand larceny, robbery (taking from another by force), and burglary (entering a building at night with intent to commit a crime). These were violent communities, and serious cases of assault and battery, affray (mob attacks), and wounding occurred in almost every county every year. Sexual abuse was less often reported, but not uncommon. Felonies like rape and murder were investigated in the county and sent to Jamestown, Virginia, or Saint Mary's, Maryland, the colonial capitals, for trial. Felonies (capital crimes) of both types were comparatively rare. With no police forces to patrol or pursue criminals, courts asked settlers to "watch and warn" of criminal activity. If a crime occurred, neighbors raised "hue and cry" and chased the suspect. Such a *posse comitatus* could easily become a mob, and often did.

While the courts served as an aegis to moderate and resolve disputes for every free person, one's economic and social position mattered in court. The judges came from the upper ranks of society. Qualification for jury duty included owning land. Most (but not all, by any means) of the people the grand jurors presented for personal misconduct came from the lower orders of society, but the men who put up the sureties for others' good conduct came from the upper class, obligating the defendants to their betters. At the other end of the social scale, slaves could not testify on oath, nor could they compel the production of evidence or the testimony of others. Women, Indians, and Africans never served on the bench or in the jury box. In these ways, process and outcomes in the courts reminded everyone of their place in the society.

Life and Death in the Chesapeake Family

Against the efforts of the Chesapeake's farmers to build families and communities stood the stark demographic fact that without periodic infusions of newcomers, the total number of English and other Europeans in the Tidewater would have declined throughout the century. "Natural increase" through births did not offset deaths until the end of the century. Because of the prevalence of disease in the low-lying and swampy areas favored by the planters, most marriages were short-lived. Those adults who did survive usually married again. Although childbirth was inherently dangerous for women, women were more likely to survive marriage than their husbands, which meant that women were more likely than men to be married two or three times. Marriage could not be based upon family ties or negotiations between families, as it often was in England, and parents did not have the same control over their children that they had in England. The result was a tangled web of partial families, step- and half-siblings, and adopted children.

The children who survived disease faced another emotionally and economically devastating hurdle. Parents were almost as likely to die before their children had reached their teens as the children were to die before they reached maturity. In Middlesex County, Virginia, a child was likely to lose a parent before the child reached the age of five. More than 30 percent of the time, a child lost both parents before the child reached maturity. Young people put out as servants because they had no parents shared the fate of all other poor unless a relative could take them in. Even then most were treated as servants, having to work for their keep.

One unintended byproduct of the demographic uncertainty may have been that women and young people gained more power and status than they would have had in a settled system like England's. Historians still debate this issue, but it is a fact that women acted as executors of estates in a larger percentage of cases in seventeenth-century Chesapeake than in England because male children in the colonies were either too young to administer the estate or had predeceased the father. Women also came into court as "attorneys" representing themselves or others, or held from their husbands "power of attorney" to act for the family. These appearances in court did not demonstrate the liberation of women in the law, so much as the necessary discretion that men had to confer on women in order to safeguard family property. Widows also received a larger portion of the deceased husband's estate than the law required he give them.

At the same time, widows did not receive the land in "fee simple"—that is, outright. Instead, their husbands willed them a "life estate," with the land reverting to his kin when the wife died or wed another. Husbands, expecting that widows would remarry, did not want the land to become part of another man's estate, for under English law, the remarried widow lost control of her property to her new husband. For example, Mathias Marriott of Surry County provided in his will, "My wife Alice to have and enjoy the land I live on for her widowhood. After her death or remarriage the Land is to return to my son Wm. Marriott."

In the founding years, the relative scarcity of women had also given them power to select among different suitors. In the process, definitions of the proper roles of women firmly established in England came into question in the early Chesapeake. The law still made women second-class citizens, merging their legal identity with that of their husbands, but in reality early Chesapeake women had great influence upon husbands, sons, and lovers who were members of the governing elite. As one testator wrote in his will, "My Sons Michael, Rupert, and Matthew are to obey their mother, follow her orders, or they are not to get their land."

Whether or not the prevalence of early death and the frailty of marriage opened the door to more sexual freedom among the young people is another matter of controversy among historians. There was certainly a good deal of premarital pregnancy, although nothing like the epidemic of sexual incontinence that swept through the colonies in the next century. Perhaps the relaxation of traditional controls upon courting and marriage allowed Chesapeake couples to express affection before marriage. Magistrates and ministers condemned the lascivious behavior of young people but rarely punished it except when it produced a child.

Facing all these troubles, it may seem remarkable that families expected to improve their lot in life, but they did. Householders in the region tried to recruit family and friends. As John Hammond optimistically portrayed the region in 1656: "As I affirm the country to be wholesome, healthy and fruitful, and a model on which industry may as much improve itself in, as in any habitable part of the world. . . . Seldom if ever any that hath continued in Virginia any time, will or do desire to live in England, but post back with what expedition they can, although many are landed men in England, and have good estates here, and divers ways of preferments propounded to them to entice and persuade their continuance."

Heads of households like Hammond invested in new lands, purchased refinements for the home from England, and laid out towns, roads, and churches. They wanted a "civilized" world, which to them meant the accouterments of upper-crust English country life. Cole had achieved the first step in this direction, but at death, the average farmer had little to offer children beyond a small plot of land, some tools, and a personal estate worth less than £35. Plainly, the road to wealth was hard to travel.

The Crisis of the Labor Supply

The stagnation of tobacco prices in Europe after 1662 meant that further income growth (as opposed to growth of the capital value of the land and herds) for planters like Thomas Cole depended on a shift away from family farming toward some other, larger-scale means of production. The problem with this program was the continuing scarcity of labor.

For example, Cole worked with his family and a few servants. Others had a few slaves. "Natural increase" did not solve the problem, because so few children lived to adulthood. With improved living conditions in England in the second half of the seventeenth century, the supply of indentured servants began to decline. During the civil wars, the English government shipped prisoners of war to the colonies, but after 1660 this source vanished. Recruiters found Irish and Scottish poor people driven from their land by English landlords (principally to make way for sheep and cattle herds), but these young people preferred to start farms of their own rather than work for others in the Chesapeake. And the indentured servant was always a potential rival to the planter, for servants who survived would become tobacco farmers themselves.

Planters found an answer to the labor crisis of the 1660s in the adoption of the Caribbean labor system. As already noted, African slaves lived and worked in the Chesapeake from the 1610s, and the number imported had grown modestly thereafter. In the 1680s, Maryland and Virginia planters began to import slaves avidly. In 1680, Maryland white servants outnumbered slaves by four to one. By 1710, there were five slaves for every servant in the colony. Over the entire course of the years 1680 to 1740, the ratio of African immigrants to English immigrants was three to one.

The demographic shape of entire communities changed with the decision to invest in slave labor. By Virginia law, planters had to report "tithables," a category of dependents that included slaves in their households, to the county court and be assessed taxes thereon. The county court records reveal that the slave population of the Tidewater counties outraced the free population. Richmond County, Virginia, on the neck of land between the Rappahannock and the Potomac, was in the 1690s largely free of slaves. Indentured laborers, tenants, and poor farmers lived in a more or less homogeneous English-speaking society. By 1710, slaves were almost half of the workforce.

The decision to import large numbers of slaves meant that slave communities would be, at least for a time, heavily African, which posed a new set of problems.

Africans were more likely to commit acts of rebellion, run away, or resist discipline than African Americans or slaves "seasoned" in the West Indies before they were carried to the Chesapeake. African Americans looked down on the Africans, and Africans bullied and laughed at the African Americans, but over time the two groups learned to cooperate, the African Americans teaching the newcomers how to work the system, the Africans reminding the African Americans of the traditions of homelands they had never seen. When, from natural increase, the sex ratios approached one to one and African and African American men did not have to compete for lovers and wives, much of the friction vanished.

To maximize the labor of the newcomers, the planters imported the gang system from the Caribbean. Slaves were kept busy year round with tobacco and corn cultivation. But the newcomers generally worked in small gangs surrounded by a largely free, white, English population. Thus they learned the language of their masters and even found companionship among the white servants.

In embracing slavery, the whites of the planter colonies had gained a kind of freedom. Henceforth, even the meanest among them were potential masters. But if the plantation masters had the freedom to buy and sell others, still they were not masters of their own fates. The widespread importation of African slaves surrounded the masters with new and vexing dilemmas of how to police those who had no stake in society.

Theft on the plantation became commonplace as slaves augmented their food allotments and the produce of their garden plots with the master's stocks. Even more troubling was the question of interracial intercourse. In 1661, when slaves and free persons had sexual congress, Virginia law provided for double fines. By 1691, the legislators explicitly condemned interracial sexual unions as "abominable mixtures" and ordained that free persons marrying a slave be banished from the colony.

The number of cases was small, with only twenty-six recorded cases among slaves and white servant women from 1660 to 1729, but their significance belied their numbers. A single case would resonate for years because its social implications—that Virginia could be truly multicultural—challenged the ongoing ordering of society in the opposite direction. Moreover, even as the laws and prosecution against interracial sex between slaves and servants tightened, the penalties against fornication and adultery were never enforced against the masters or the masters' children having sex with slaves. For some in the master class, the temptation to commit an act (or more likely a series of acts) with one's bondwomen that was decried by one's neighbors and detested by the laws made every day an agonizing battle between conscience and desire. Thus slavery to some degree enslaved the masters.

The Sugar Islands

In time, the English sugar plantations in the Caribbean produced more wealth for the empire than the tobacco colonies, but the English first came to the Caribbean not

THE PLANTER COLONIES **145**

to plant but to plunder other Europeans' settlements. When the English found the Lesser Antilles uninhabited by their European rivals, however, the opportunity to settle beckoned. Under the leadership of a variety of joint-stock companies, and later the home government, the English swarmed unto the islands of Saint Christopher (in 1624), Barbados (1627), Nevis (1628), Montserrat and Antigua (1632), and finally Jamaica (1655).

Nearly two hundred thousand English, Scottish, and Irish young people made their way to these West Indian islands in the seventeenth century. The bulk of the immigrants were servants or laborers. Some came of their own free will. Others were prisoners of war and rebels from Scotland and Ireland whom the English "Barbadoed." Transported convicts filled out the roster of emigrants. Some would return to the British Isles, homesick or ill, penniless and disillusioned, or because relatives or political events called them back. Many more died far from friends and familiar places. Some made lives miserable for their masters, as Barbados's governor Daniel Searle complained in 1657: "Several of the . . . freemen and women, who have no certain place of residence, and as vagabonds refuse to labor, or put themselves into any service, but contriving in a dissolute, leud, and slothful kinds of life, put themselves to evil practices." If the servants and laborers found solace in dissolution, even the planters rarely cared for island life and happily escaped it when their fortunes seemed secure.

Barbados

Until the conquest of Jamaica in 1655, Barbados was the center of English interest in the Caribbean. It differed in important respects from the other islands in the Antilles. Hundreds of miles to the south and east of its neighbors, Barbados has no volcanic history. Instead, it is a limestone block of 166 square miles of gentle slopes and terraces. Heavily wooded, it was uninhabited when the English arrived.

William Courteen (an Anglo-Dutchman who changed his name from Willem Coerten) sent settlers to Barbados between 1627 and 1629. Courteen intended to copy the Virginia plan—to plant and export tobacco. However, before the Courteen Company could wrangle a royal patent to govern the island, more powerful interests, led by James Carlisle, intervened, and the island became the object of intense rivalry.

On the island, representatives of the two companies battled with one another. The result was that throughout most of the 1640s and into the 1650s, Barbados was as close to self-governing (or rather, ungoverned) as an English possession could get. This was not altogether a blessing, for the island was swept into the English civil wars, the first Dutch War of 1652–1654, and the continuing Anglo-Spanish Caribbean conflict. Only the restoration of the Stuarts in England, in 1660, and the imposition of a royal government for the colony quieted domestic discord and rendered the planters relatively secure.

Just as the price of tobacco was falling, the planters, with Dutch help, shifted to sugarcane production. (The Dutch were not acting out of generosity. Sugarcane required intensive labor, and the Dutch provided the slave laborers.) Although the Caribbean offered many ways to make a living—raiding someone else's slaves, fishing, ranching, and cultivating cotton, tobacco, ginger, and cacao (cocoa)—sugar cultivation outperformed them all.

English sugar production on Barbados was the seventeenth-century version of big business, with large-scale production, sophisticated (for the time) marketing, and lobbyists in England to ensure that parliamentary regulation favored the planters. Although the average plantation was about three hundred acres, a few exceeded a thousand acres. The largest seventeenth-century plantations employed hundreds of slaves and cut eighty tons of cane a year.

Like tobacco cultivation, the process of sugarcane production was onerous. One had to put individual cuttings from old cane stalks into new holes each year, weed and manure the stalks, and then hope that sixteen months later one would be able to harvest the eight-foot-tall plants. Slaves dug the holes or trenches, weeded and fertilized, chased or burned out the rats that infested the fields, and then cut the fully developed plants by hand. Then they removed the outer leaves and toted the stalks to the mill—where the real production of sugar began.

For example, Henry Drax planted 705 acres, supported 332 workers, had two mills to extract the juice from the cane, and kept a boiling house going constantly to clarify the crystals, a curing house to dry the sugar and drain out the molasses, and a distillery to convert the molasses into rum. He exported £5,000 worth of sugar, molasses, and rum in 1680.

But even a planter as successful as Drax could not prevent the hurricanes from leveling the crops, control the price or demand in Europe, or prevent war from interfering with his cargoes. Sugar cultivation was always risky. Less able, lucky, and well-backed planters came to the island seeking riches and left bankrupt. Still, Drax and his counterparts shipped nearly twenty thousand tons of sugar to England in 1683. Three hundred ships a year came from North America and England to carry off the sugar, molasses, and rum.

The Cauldron of Slavery

Given the potential for riches and the need for labor, it was inevitable that the planters would follow the Spanish example and import masses of slaves. By the 1660s, slave importation had zoomed, and gang labor had become the rule. In Barbados alone, the slave population rose from twenty thousand out of forty-five thousand total inhabitants in 1655 to over forty-five thousand slaves against slightly less than twenty thousand free persons in 1684. Local landlords gradually abandoned the island and left the duties of overseeing planting to younger relatives or hired managers, called overseers.

Just as their peers had in the Spanish sugar islands, the Barbadian slaves created

Creole societies and coped. But the average life span was little more than a year for newcomers, and thus a continuous influx of slaves was needed. The slave auction became a regular feature of the island's life. As the cargo ships docked, shipmasters brought up their weary and sickened captives from the holds and tried to make them look better, sometimes by rubbing lampblack over bruises and lesions.

Worried about the same kinds of slave resistance that had bedeviled the Spanish master class, the Barbadian Assembly fashioned the slave code of 1661. Without any precedent in English law and indifferent to the myriad small ways in which Spanish law and the Catholic Church mitigated the severities of slavery in the Spanish and Portuguese colonies, the Barbadian planters denied to their African laborers all personal, civil, and political identity.

Under the code, slaves could not choose a marriage partner; direct the upbringing of a child; hold, sell, or buy property; or enter into contracts for services. They could not take part in civil government, sit on juries, take or give oaths, or serve in the military. Slaves could leave the plantation only with the master's permission and had to have a pass to walk the roads or fish on the shore. They could not practice medicine, gather in groups, or move about at night. Accused of crimes, slaves were tried by a court of their master's friends and neighbors, without any right to call their own witnesses, cross-examine their accusers, or present their case to a jury. Any free person had the right, indeed the duty, to use whatever force necessary to "correct" unruly slaves or punish slaves' "insolence." Soon after 1661, Jamaican and Leeward Island slaveholders adopted slave codes of their own, modeled upon the Barbadian. The English mainland colonies followed suit, starting in the 1680s.

In reality, slaves violated all of the code's impositions. They visited other plantations at night, without passes, practiced folk healing, and contemplated freeing themselves. Some masters quietly allowed slaves to "own" animals and tools, domestic goods, and clothing and to control much of the space in the slave quarters. Slave rebellions, much feared by the masters, passed by Barbados until 1675, and maroonage was almost nonexistent.

Little Europes

Its forests cut down for fuel to boil the sugarcane and its population far too large to feed from its own resources, Barbados became dependent on imports for most of its food and fuel. But that did not deter the planters. As in the tobacco mania in the Chesapeake, the power of avarice was all consuming in the sugar islands. Thus the planters burned out themselves, their families, and their white and black laborers in an unrelenting heat to produce crystallized cane and rum. Had the English sought an island paradise for ease and leisure, they could hardly have done better (hurricanes and disease aside) than Barbados. But they did not desire Eden—they wanted El Dorado.

Successful in creating a West Indian sugar lobby to protect their interests in English politics, the planters exercised a degree of political, legal, economic, and social autonomy on the islands that exceeded that of any of the other elites on the mainland. They were as close to absolute rulers as might be imagined, exercising an effectual veto over all royal instructions. Again and again throughout the seventeenth and eighteenth centuries, they proved that the crown had to negotiate with the planters rather than dictate policy.

A similar pattern of development transformed Spanish Jamaica into English Jamaica. Far larger than Barbados, Jamaica was a bastion of Spanish power until English forces seized it in 1655. The weather, disease, and continued warfare killed off many of the English, but the value of the colony outweighed the perils for the planters, and servants and slaves had no say in the matter. By the end of the century its planters outdid the Barbadians in sugar production and the importation of slaves.

Maroonage soon made its appearance. Over 140 miles from east to west and fully 50 miles at its widest point, much of the island's center was high mountain and mist-shrouded vale. In these "cockpits," whole settlements of runaways could hide themselves.

Despite the substantial autonomy of the world they had made for themselves, the planters, merchants, and their servants longed for the Old World. In Bridgetown, the port on the southwestern edge of Barbados, and Kingstown, on the southern coast of Jamaica, English and Scottish businessmen built counting houses, warehouses, and churches. And in ramshackle, low-ceilinged taverns rank with sweat and alive with insects of every description, Englishmen drank, gambled, swore, and pined for home.

THE CAROLINAS

While the planters and laborers of the Chesapeake struggled to make ends meet, and the colonizers of the sugar islands labored to profit from sugarcane, men in England dreamed of vast American fiefdoms between Virginia and the Spanish settlements in Florida. In 1629, Charles I granted the lands to the south of Virginia from the thirty-first parallel to the thirty-sixth parallel to Robert Heath. He called the territory New Carolana (from the Latin for Charles). Heath then invited a number of individuals to develop the grant, but the first settlement of any magnitude came not from England but from Virginia. In 1653, the Virginia Assembly, having no title to the land, nevertheless authorized Francis and Argall Yeardly to begin peopling the lands around the Albemarle Sound, just north of the old Roanoke Colony. The Commonwealth Parliament made no objection to the burgesses' plan.

With the Restoration, Virginia's plans for Carolana were superseded by those of Charles II. In the early years of the Restoration, Charles surprised both his friends and his father's former enemies by pursuing a policy of conciliation. He offered high office to moderates of both parliamentary and royalist parties. The "regicides" were executed for presiding over the trial and death of the king in 1649, but others in the previous government gained royal pardon. Former parliamentary leaders were even taken into the government.

Charles tried to reestablish the state church on a similarly broad-based foundation, but the Anglican interests refused to compromise, and the die-hard Puritans refused to accept the posts that were offered them. In the end, the Restoration religious settlement was far crueler to dissenters than Cromwell had been. But Charles still looked after the interests of the Roman Catholics, for his brother was now Catholic.

Proprietary Precedents

Charles II resumed his royal predecessors' policy of granting huge territories in America to private proprietors. His policy served two purposes. First, it reminded supporters of the late parliamentary regime, including those who had fled to America, that the colonies belonged to the king. Second, it was a cheap way to repay Charles's political debts. Both of these purposes made eminent sense in terms of English politics, but proprietorship was at best an ineffective method to develop colonies.

A long string of precedents should have taught this lesson to Charles and his advisers. The Spanish had developed the prototype of proprietorship in the fifteenth century, when the princes of Castile and Aragon gave baronies to *adelantados* who undertook to recapture those lands from the Moors. The *adelantado* spent his own money in the quest, but if he was successful, the crown confirmed him and his descendants as the legal rulers of the newly recaptured territory. Spain extended the practice in the conquest of the Caribbean, Mexico, and South America and found it almost impossible to prevent corruption and neglect. In the second half of the sixteenth century, King Philip again granted proprietorships to military chieftains Juan de Oñate in New Mexico and Pedro Menendez de Avilés in Florida, but the two colonies did not flourish, and their governors impoverished themselves trying to make a profit from the grants.

James I and Charles I had presented huge tracts of land to friends and family, but neither the crown nor the grantees gained much from the grants. Nor did the resulting colonies prosper. Nova Scotia remained poor throughout the seventeenth century. The Maryland Colony did better, but the division of settlers into pro- and antiproprietary camps slowed its development and caused the Calvert family endless grief. In 1649, Charles II, in exile, granted five million acres between the Rappahannock and the Potomac rivers in Virginia to Lord Hopson (which, through a complex process of sale and inheritance ended up the property of Thomas Fairfax), but the grant became the subject of hundreds of lawsuits still under adjudication when the American Revolution erupted.

In part the problem with the proprietary colonies rested on the fact that they were not simple gifts of land but complex transfers of political authority. The proprietors were the governors, but they rarely came to America. Instead, they sent agents (lieutenant governors) to rule in their stead. Thus dissidents could always try to appeal over the head of the lieutenant governor to the proprietor in England. A lot could happen in the three months it took for information and messengers to cross and re-cross the Atlantic with petitions to the proprietors and instructions to the colonial government. As a result, the proprietary colonies boiled with political turmoil.

The Carolina Proprietors

These unhappy precedents notwithstanding, in 1663 Charles II rescinded the 1629 grant of Carolana and gave the land to eight noblemen who lobbied for it. The actual patents did not go into much detail, but it was understood that the proprietors had the right to make and enforce laws with "the advice, assent, and approbation of the freemen"; transport and remove settlers; collect quitrents (a form of land tax); as well as sell off any pieces of the land they wished within the colony. Two years later, Charles enlarged the grant to include all of northern Florida, infuriating the Spanish and forcing the new proprietors to accept an enlarged military obligation. (The Spanish later negotiated a boundary somewhere south of Charleston—but no one ever surveyed it, and the dispute between the two empires raged on until 1763.)

Although from time to time they commissioned detailed plans for the governance of their colonies, the first great proprietors treated the grants more as commercial property to be traded, sold, parceled out and divided up, or given away than as polities. With a few (as it turned out disastrous) exceptions, the Carolina proprietors did not travel to the New World, but sent their agents to govern in their stead.

As a group, in 1663 the Carolina proprietors were old men even by our standards and had survived upheavals in government, civil wars, and finally the Restoration. Some had proved their loyalty to the royalist cause during the interregnum. For example, when Governor William Berkeley of Virginia learned that Parliament had executed Charles I, he tried to hold the colony for Charles II (thus gaining it the sobriquet "my old dominion" from a grateful sovereign). Virginia became a haven for royalists fleeing England. In 1662, Berkeley, reappointed governor, journeyed to England to lobby for further rewards and gained a share of Carolina. Sir John Colleton, a planter and politician in Barbados, had kept faith with the king, serving first in his army in England, then retiring to the West Indies in 1650. He got a piece of the Carolina grant, as did the Earl of Clarendon, the king's closest adviser. They joined Lord John Berkeley; George Monck, the Duke of Albemarle, the general who paved the way for the Restoration; William Craven, made Earl Craven for his services; and Sir George Carteret.

The eighth proprietor, Anthony Ashley Cooper, Lord Shaftesbury, was the chancellor (the king's secretary) of England. He had served Cromwell, then switched in

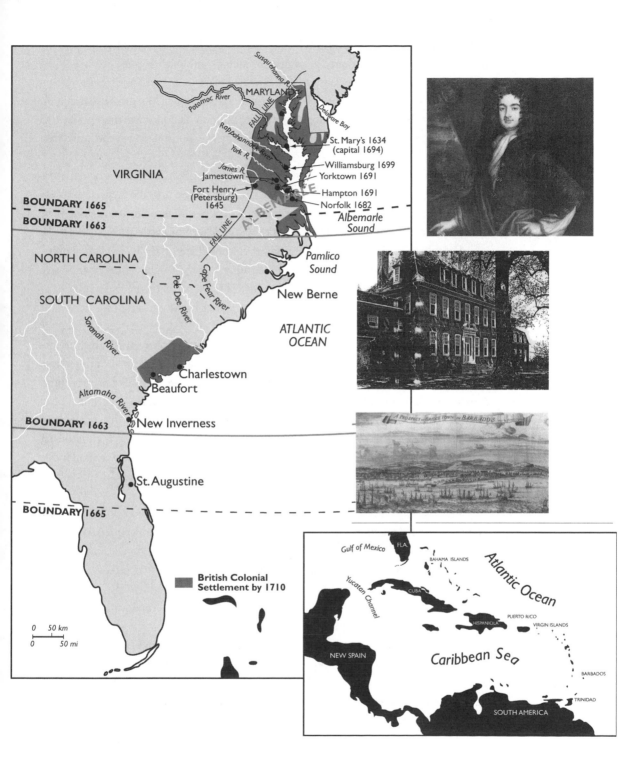

Susquehanna R.

MARYLAND

Potomac River

FALL LINE

Delaware Bay

St. Mary's 1634
(capital 1694)

Rappahannock River

York R.

VIRGINIA

James R.

Williamsburg 1699

Jamestown

Yorktown 1691

Fort Henry
(Petersburg)
1645

Hampton 1691

Norfolk 1682

BOUNDARY 1665

*Albemarle
Sound*

BOUNDARY 1663

ALBEMARLE

FALL LINE

*Pamlico
Sound*

NORTH CAROLINA

Cape Fear River

SOUTH CAROLINA

Pee Dee River

New Berne

Savannah River

ATLANTIC
OCEAN

Altamaha River

Charlestown

Beaufort

BOUNDARY 1663

New Inverness

St. Augustine

BOUNDARY 1665

British Colonial
Settlement by 1710

0   50 km

0   50 mi

Gulf of Mexico   FLA.

Atlantic Ocean

BAHAMA ISLANDS

Yucatan Channel

CUBA

PUERTO RICO

HISPANIOLA

VIRGIN ISLANDS

NEW SPAIN

Caribbean Sea

BARBADOS

TRINIDAD

SOUTH AMERICA

time to support the Restoration. With his townhouse in London and his circle of intellectual friends, particularly a young physician and philosopher from Oxford
named John Locke, Ashley Cooper was a powerhouse of ideas and patronage. On his
own, Locke would become one of the English-speaking world's greatest thinkers,
making contributions in psychology, education, religion, and political theory. Shaftesbury would turn to Locke for help when the colony was floundering at the end of the
decade.

While the proprietors explored ways to exploit the grant, land-hungry squatters
targeted the area between the south side of the James River and the Spanish possessions in Florida for themselves. For example, a group of Massachusetts settlers had
arrived in Carolina in 1663, complete with a small herd of cattle, but did not stay.
Word of the grant also reached the Barbados colony (through Colleton), and a number of its planters formed a development company of their own, but Barbados settlement in the Cape Fear area was doomed from the start. Storms, the madness of
one of the ship captains, and Indian opposition undermined the small settlement. It
was abandoned in 1667.

In 1665, William Berkeley, having resumed his post as governor of Virginia, organized settlements in the northern part of the grant, on Albemarle Sound. He was
moderately successful until an uprising in Virginia required his full attention (and
nearly cost him his life). The other proprietors shared Berkeley's ill luck. Lord
Clarendon had offended his royal master and had gone into exile. Albemarle soon
died, as did Craven and Colleton. The interests of these men passed to their children
(for proprietorships, like any feudal grant, were hereditary), but the heirs had made
no plans for the colony. John Berkeley was in his seventies and not inclined to waste
his last years worrying about far-off Carolina.

To reverse the slide into chaos, Shaftesbury in March 1669 asked Locke to write
"Fundamental Constitutions" for the colony, and Locke complied. At the top of
Locke's proposed pyramid of settlement stood the proprietors; beneath them were
landgraves, caciques, manor lords, and finally freeholders—an idealized version of
feudal vassalage.

At the same time, Locke included guarantees of religious freedom and the right
to hold representative assemblies, a reflection of his and his patron's forward-looking views and the ideas that the reformers of the 1650s had published. They assumed
that wide distribution of land ownership would encourage domestic tranquility and
loyalty to the proprietary regime. No matter: the assembly that the Fundamental Orders created never acceded to the document. By the end of the 1690s, despite periodic efforts of the proprietors to revive them, the orders were a dead letter.

Factions and Fracases in the Carolinas

The proprietors simply could not govern their colony. Fitful development and endemic factionalism resulted, with a proprietary faction battling an antiproprietary

faction. One tempest in a teapot was Culpepper's Rebellion. In 1672, the Albemarle settlement persuaded Lieutenant Governor Peter Carteret to return to England to seek greater proprietary investment in the venture. Carteret appointed John Jenkins, a settler, as stand-in. Jenkins, reflecting the wishes of his neighbors, refused to collect the customs duties required by the royal Navigation Acts (about which more in chapters 9 and 13), nor would he ensure, as he was bound to do under the acts, that certain trade goods only go to English ports. The proprietors could not let this affront to their dignity (and the revenues of the crown) pass in silence and sent a new lieutenant governor, Thomas Miller, to collect the duties.

Antiproprietary elements in the assembly quickly tumbled to Miller's program, and he had to call out the militia to act as his bodyguard. When he dissolved the assembly—a power he legally possessed but used unwisely on this occasion—he was forced to rule through martial law. Under it, Miller jailed those who opposed his action. A group of men, led by John Culpepper, a proprietary official who became a leader of the antiproprietary faction, armed themselves and set out to oust Miller. Culpepper's band threw the lieutenant governor into jail, summoned a new assembly, and tried Miller for treason. Miller broke out of jail and fled to England to fill the proprietors' ears with accusations, and Culpepper, chosen to explain all this in England, found himself facing charges of sedition.

A second series of tussles arose in the southern part of the colony. Settlers there engaged in trade with Indians, selling European goods for deerskins and slaves. The proprietors explicitly forbade the latter portion of the exchange, not wishing to antagonize any of the Indians (particularly those whose villages were raided to gain the captives). The planters simply ignored the proprietors' instructions. The bloody results would explode in the next century.

The pattern of local unrest and episodic political upheaval against the proprietors repeated itself throughout the rest of the 1600s and into the first three decades of the 1700s. In the 1680s, the colonists in the south of the colony proved so averse to obeying the proprietors that Lieutenant Governor Joseph Morton dissolved the assembly. In 1689, the leaders of the northern settlements ousted Governor Seth Southel, even though he had purchased Colleton's interest in the colony. Southel went south and claimed to be governor there, causing such unrest that his fellow proprietors brought charges against him in England.

The northern and southern settlements became separate colonies in 1691, and after 1712 North Carolina gained its own governor, but the new provisions did not resolve the quarrel with the proprietors (or increase compliance with England's laws). After repeated attempts to cajole or coerce the colonial assemblies into a cooperative stance, the proprietors surrendered their charters to the crown in 1729. South and North Carolina became royal colonies.

South Carolina

South Carolina has far less variation in its seasons than Virginia or North Carolina, and its coast, broken by low-lying islands, is far moister and warmer. The extensive saltwater marshes there provided feed for cattle, and the lowland climate was perfect for cultivation of semitropical crops like rice. The settlers placed their plantations on either side of a series of four short, slow-moving rivers that flowed into the ocean. They also laid out Charles Town, named in honor of the king, at the mouth of the Ashley and Cooper rivers (somewhat redundant tributes to Anthony Ashley Cooper, Lord Shaftesbury).

West Indian slaveholders and expatriate French Huguenots joined a small colony that Shaftesbury dispatched in 1670, largely Londoners fleeing another outbreak of the plague. From their plantations on the sugar islands the West Indian planters brought slaves, but at first they did not transplant a slave society. Instead, the Africans occupied themselves as "pioneers," clearing land and watching over herds of cattle. Slaves running cattle reproduced African-style cattle enclosures, hunted for their food, and lived isolated lives. Soon cow pens were as common as settlers' houses or slave huts. The meat and dairy products, along with pork from the pigs the settlers allowed to forage, went back to the West Indies.

The colony did not prosper until the introduction of more advanced forms of rice culture and varieties of rice seed. Earlier, Carolina planters grew rice in upland plots, depending upon rainfall to irrigate the crops. In the 1690s, African slaves from Senegambia, experienced rice growers in their homeland, aided their masters in transforming the coastal areas into rice plantations. While historians debate how important the African contribution was, no one can doubt that African labor made the rice enterprise into a success.

Relying on British merchants and purchasing agents, the rice planters surmounted the problems of fluctuating demand and price for rice on the Continent. Profits skyrocketed for the planters and the London, Bristol, and other middlemen. Newly rich planters haggled over sales and prices, complained constantly about the weather, and willy-nilly turned lowland South Carolina into a slave society.

Lowland rice cultivation was labor-intensive. To avoid contamination of the crops by saltwater, planters needed to dig and maintain ponds and ditches and build sluice gates for freshwater irrigation. From the 1660s to the 1690s, when rice emerged as the staple crop, blacks were no more than one in four South Carolinians. By the 1720s, blacks outnumbered whites.

The shift from a slaveholding society to a slave society, and the increasing proportion of slaves imported directly from Africa, made bondage for all slaves more onerous. With a larger proportion of resources dedicated to rice cultivation, the variety of employment opportunities for individual slaves declined. As in the Chesapeake in the same period, the newcomers fought with more acclimatized slaves. Although the newcomers fashioned the Gullah Creole, a mixture of English with African loan words, low-country slaves did not master English as quickly or as well as bondmen and women in the Chesapeake because, unlike Chesapeake slaves, who worked in integrated settings, low-country slaves worked in segregated surroundings. The unbalanced sex ratio (caused by importation of more men than women) meant that slaves wishing to begin families of their own had to wait. Finally, instead of the healthy life of herdsmen away from the coastal marshes, the slaves now worked in the malarial wetlands, and disease took its toll. For some slaves, immunities acquired in Africa, such as the sickle cell, prevented the malarial parasite from doing its worst work, but many Africans perished.

Faced with a steadily increasing black majority, the planters imported the brutal administrative apparatus of the Caribbean slave society. The colony's legislature mandated mounted patrols to monitor slave movements in the hinterlands and organized a watch in the city. If many poor whites refused to serve in the patrols and the watch, and often the patrols and watch performed their duties haphazardly, the men in both of these paramilitary organizations exercised almost untrammeled discretion in meting out corporal punishment to suspected black offenders. The slave codes of the sugar islands became Carolina law.

North Carolina

Unlike the southern portion of Carolina, the northern settlements grew slowly. Widely dispersed farms and farming villages predominated. Ninety-five percent of the people were subsistence farmers. John Lawson, who traveled the country in the early 1700s as surveyor general, noted that the soil was rich, but the farms unkempt and primitive. William Byrd II, a Virginia gentleman traveling through the northern tier of the colony, concurred: "We could see no other tokens of husbandry or improvement [but a few corn fields] . . . both cattle and hogs ramble in the neighborhood marshes and swamps, where they maintain themselves the whole winter long. . . . Thus these indolent wretches [the North Carolina farm folk] lose the advantage of the milk of their cattle, as well as their dung, and many of the poor creatures perish in the mire, into the bargain, by this ill management."

Byrd's contempt was not quite fair. Freely ranging hogs and cattle were common in all American farming communities. But in fact North Carolina farms were not as well kept or productive as those of its neighbors. As Byrd noticed, there was no crop rotation or manuring in rural North Carolina. Iron plows were in short supply, and many farmers made do with wooden implements well into the eighteenth century. The assembly even put a bounty on vermin, so prevalent were pests in the fields. There were few roads, bridges were ill-kept, and bargemen were ill-mannered.

Tobacco and corn ruled the land, the former for export, the latter for porridge, for bread, and to feed the hogs and chickens. The cattle and swine foraged for themselves. In the waning years of the colonial period, farmers began to plant wheat and rice, but these had to be policed against the omnipresent danger of wild hogs. The only truly profitable products were naval stores (tar, turpentine, and the like) and lumber, and the production of these stripped the land. The assembly was aware of these problems and duly passed admonitory legislation on how to farm, which everyone ignored.

A few wealthy planters' mansions with their slave quarters occupied the coasts and the waterways, but these could not compete in size and wealth with the tobacco magnates to the north or the rice nabobs to the south. Inventories of the North Carolina planters' estates show few luxury goods. The leaders of society were less likely to send their children to England to find marriage partners or to get an education than were the great families of the Tidewater.

————

The achievement of the elite tobacco, sugar, and rice planters of the seventeenth-century English colonies was in one obvious way remarkable. They had "improved" economically underdeveloped land, turning coastal marsh and inland forest into the richest staple-producing areas in the world. Their success fueled the rise of the British Empire and proved that the "plantation complex" style of agriculture could be highly profitable. But the cost in human life was appalling, and the treatment of natives and slaves repulsive. Such stark contrasts were common in the planter colonies.

6

A New England

We habitually associate the founding of New England with Puritanism. If this identification is far too simplistic, it nevertheless contains a large element of truth. The founders of New England shared a profound religious sensibility. There would have been New England colonies without religious dissension and persecution in England. Promoters urged settlement long before the first religiously motivated immigrants arrived, and many seventeenth-century New Englanders preferred taverns to churches on the Sabbath. But the tenor of life and the course of government of the first New England colonies owed themselves to a powerful movement of religious self-examination among the English. Late-sixteenth-century scoffers dismissed these intensely pious men and women as narrow-minded busybodies and "hot-blooded perfectionists." In 1605, one of the latter, William Bradshaw, adopted the word *puritan* to depict the objective of the movement. That term stuck.

Chapter 5 revealed that the improvement of the planter colonies came at a terrible cost in human life. Even among the survivors, chasms of inequity separated the free and the enslaved, planters and tenants, men and women. The New England colonies were not only healthier than the planter colonies (life expectancy in seventeenth-century New England exceeded all known contemporary societies), New England never evinced the extremes of poverty and riches or the general maldistribution of wealth of the planter colonies.

But New Englanders fashioned another kind of discrimination that drew bright lines of power and powerlessness. The Puritan refugees from England's High Church orthodoxy and royal high-handedness never embraced political freedom, religious toleration, or social diversity. Convinced of the righteousness of their views, their leaders persecuted men and women who challenged, flouted, or threatened the laws and doctrines of the colonial church and state. The result was an almost unbearable tension between the ideal of sanctity and a real world filled with contention, competition, and self-interest.

Thus this poore people populate this howling Desart, marching manfully on (the Lord Assisting) through the greatest difficulties and sorest labours that ever any with such weak means have done.
—Edward Johnson, Wonder-Working Providence of Sions Savior in New England (1654)

ENGLISH DISSENTERS AND THEIR BELIEFS

Queen Elizabeth was a reluctant partisan in the religious controversies in her realm. She did not permit resistance to her leadership of the state church but was not doctrinaire in her views. Thus she offered some concessions to the clamor of the radical Protestants that the Church of England be purged of all Roman Catholic rituals. In 1563, a convocation of churchmen approved thirty-nine articles ensuring that the Church of England remain Protestant in form and rite, rejecting basic Catholic doctrines such as transubstantiation and adopting basic Protestant doctrines such as absolute predestination.

But concessions never satisfied this first generation of Puritans. An anonymous pamphlet, entitled *The Admonition to Parliament* (1572), spelled out their grievances. The authors decried the vestiges of popery and the lax discipline in the churches, barely skirting the obvious conclusion that the Church of England was not a proper church at all. Robert Brown, a college graduate and lay preacher, went further, urging his followers to separate themselves from the impure state church. Following him, some Brownists—or Separatists, as they were called—would eventually transport themselves out of England and journey to a place they called Plymouth. Later scholars refer to this group as the Pilgrims. But the majority of the Puritans did not adopt the logical extremity of their own arguments. They remained a dissenting cadre within the English church, skirting the edge of separatism.

A Congregation of the Faithful Called and Gathered

Historians debate the extent and social basis of English Puritanism. Although it flourished in the environs of London and East Anglia, there were pockets of Puritanism throughout the country. One can document a strong connection between Puritanism and the rising middle class, particularly in the woolens industry, but an equally strong argument can be made for the importance of charismatic Puritan ministers reaching out to men and women from all walks of life. Puritans also gathered in conventicles, groups that met outside of church to fast, pray, and study. Together, the mixture of the intense piety of the Puritan laity and the intense preaching of the Puritan ministers culled out Puritans from the mass of Protestants and brought them into touch with one another in a network of dissenters.

At the core of this network was the Puritans' commitment to a gathered, or "called," church. The congregation would choose its own ministers and teachers and decide for itself who would belong and who would not. A few Puritan thinkers also called for presbyteries, assemblies of congregational leaders, to set policy. However organized, this order of gathered churches violated the basic precepts of the Church of England. The Puritans objected to the hierarchy of bishops in the state church, and by giving to the congregation the power to name its own minister and control its own membership, the Puritans undermined the system of state-supported "livings," by which local nobles selected ministers.

In the meantime, Puritans tried to set a moral example for their neighbors by keeping the Sabbath, studying, and observing high standards of personal morality, all the while continuing their attack upon the lax conformist and the "vulgar sort" who thought the sacraments, good works, and unreflecting faith were enough to save a soul. Puritans engaged in this private exercise of "practical divinity"—seeking the godly in themselves and decrying the sinfulness in others—and still spoke of a loving society whose members mutually assisted one another in moral improvement and refrained from "all discord or revenging by wordes or actions."

But the Puritans themselves divided over the way to ensure the spread of godliness within the realm. Some moderates espoused compromise in order to convert the whole nation to true Christianity. Moderates argued the necessity of maintaining a united front against Catholicism, particularly in view of the efforts the papacy was making to sneak priests into England (649 actually came, despite laws forbidding their preaching on pain of death; some 125 were executed before 1603). Radical Puritans wanted no compromises and accepted the possibility that only a portion of the English people could be brought within the fold of true godliness. Such disagreements opened schisms within the ranks of the schismatics.

The debate between the moderates and the radicals reflected the fact that Puritanism was much more a movement within the larger community of English Protestantism than a distinct theological position. Within the movement coexisted elements of apocalyptic millenarianism and longing for ancient biblical simplicity, a commitment to logical exegesis of texts alongside a passion for mystical godliness, and a utopian ideal of the good society warring with a tendency to self-denying militancy.

When James I of Scotland succeeded Elizabeth in 1603, he politely listened to the Puritans' case for restructuring of the church. Indeed, at the Hampton Court conference of 1604, he sponsored a debate between the bishops and the leading Puritan ministers. In a concession to the latter, he agreed to a new translation of the Bible and some modification of the *Book of Common Prayer*. He refused to accede to the Puritans' wishes to dismantle the English episcopal hierarchy, but did appoint a number of Puritans to bishoprics, diffusing their animosity toward the system. When he died in 1625, the great debate within English Protestantism seemed to have ebbed.

THE PLYMOUTH COLONY

While the Puritans labored to gain a voice in the English church, the Brownists made plans to found their own separate, sacred community. They found an unlikely ally in John Smith. Unable to gain employment from the Virginia Company of London, in

1614 he signed on as captain of a small whaling fleet sent to the coast of what he later called New England. There Smith busied himself surveying and drawing maps, including one of the Accomac and the Patuxet promontories on the southern coast of Massachusetts. He pondered the prospects for settlement of the interior and remarked that the bay between the Accomac and Patuxet would be a good place for a settlement.

Smith's *A Description of New England* (1617) envisioned a "New England planted with gardens and corn fields, and so well inhabited with a goodly, strong and well proportioned people [the Indians] besides the greatness of the timber growing on them, the greatness of the fish and the moderate temper of the year (for of twenty five [men with him] not any was sick . . .). Who can but approve this a most excellent place, both for health and fertility? And of all the foure parts of the world that I have yet seene not inhabited, could I have but meanes to transport a colonie, I would rather live here than any where."

The *Description* became a guidebook for future settlers, including the Pilgrims. William Brewster, of the English manor of Scrooby in Lincolnshire, obtained a copy of Smith's *Description* and read it avidly. So did his neighbor, William Bradford. The site between the Accomac and the Patuxet that Smith described would become their American home.

Both Brewster and Bradford were Pilgrims and with their cobelievers fled England for Amsterdam, and then Leiden, in the Netherlands. There they found freedom to worship as they chose, but also hard times and the danger that they would become lax in their worship. To forestall the latter danger, they asked John Robinson, a university-trained minister, to serve them, and he agreed. Still, from 1609 to 1620 the English Separatist exiles in Leiden dreamed of a home where they would be masters of their own fate.

Coming Over

The opportunity came in 1620. For the previous three years, the Pilgrims had negotiated with the Dutch for a place in the New Netherland Colony but then decided to sign on with the Virginia Company of Plymouth. Agreeing to pool their lands and goods once they arrived in the New World, and to give a portion of the profits of their trade with the Indians to the company, the Pilgrims prepared to sail to America. John Robinson remained in Leiden with the bulk of the English exiles but continued to exhort his former congregants and periodically sent over more settlers.

On November 11, 1620, the *Mayflower* dropped anchor in what is now Provincetown Harbor, on the northwestern tip of Cape Cod. Planning to continue on to the Hudson River, but turned back by foul weather, the Pilgrims decided to settle where they were. Although the voyage had been relatively safe and quick, the Pilgrims already suffered from scurvy. Miles Standish and sixteen men volunteered to go ashore and seek food. The Indians, remembering past visits from strangers like these, fled, and the Pilgrims expropriated bushels of Indian corn, leaving nothing in return. God had provided for them, they reasoned, just as God had chosen them to seek salvation an ocean away from the impurities of English state religion.

Subsequent exploration of Cape Cod revealed no satisfactory site for settlement, however, and the *Mayflower* weighed anchor and crossed the bay to deliver the settlers to a steeply sloping, rock-strewn landing in the place John Smith had described in his *Discovery*. The Pilgrims named it Plymouth.

Bradford, whose journal remains historians' primary source for the first forty years of the colony, saw God's hand in the Pilgrims' safe landing. The Patuxet Indians, who had lived there for hundreds of years and whose clearings the Pilgrims now occupied, had been annihilated by diseases that earlier English visitors—perhaps Smith and his crew—brought. Bradford recalled that some of the victims' bones "were found in many places, lying still above the ground, where their houses and dwellings had been; a very sad spectacle to behold."

For much of the winter of 1620–1621, the Pilgrims remained aboard ship in Plymouth Harbor. Bradford confided to his journal that the "strangers"—people not affiliated with the Leiden community—seemed "not well affected to unity and concord, but gave *some* appearance of faction." In a secular version of the way the Leiden congregation (and all Separatist or Puritan congregations ideally) formed, Bradford and the other Pilgrim leaders "thought good there should be an association and agreement, that we should combine together in one body, and to submit to such government and governors as we should by common consent agree to make and choose." All free men who wished to be part of this commonwealth signed the document. Plymouth Colony henceforth rested upon a contract, "for our better ordering and preservation . . . and by virtue hereof to enact, constitute, and frame such just and equal laws . . . as shall be thought most meet and convenient for the general good of the Colony."

Without the benefit of the king's lawyers, the Pilgrims thus drafted the Mayflower Compact. The rights and duties of the signatories and the limitations and obligations they placed upon their government had force because the signatories and their successors honored their commitments. Their ideal of government by the consent of the governed, founded on a written agreement, would become a fundamental tenet of American constitutionalism. Over the years, this basic frame of government was amended to change it from a direct democracy of the male heads of households to a representative legislative assembly, but the innovation of the document in its time—that government was the right and the burden of the common people—withstood the dispersion of the settlers, the arrival of newcomers, and the Pilgrim leaders' decision to drop the communal property scheme and adopt private ownership of land.

William Bradford's Colony

Bradford became the guiding spirit of the colony when John Carver, the first elected governor, died in the spring of 1621. Half of the settlers had preceded him. Scurvy, in its last stages a hideously disfiguring disease, had carried off the largest number. (Tragically, cranberry bogs lay a short distance away from the settlement, and cranberry is high in vitamin C—a cure for scurvy.) The pious and the scoffer suffered the same travail. The discontented cried that God had deserted them. The survivors turned to Bradford, who retained the office until he died in 1657.

In religious matters, this fiercely pious sectarian proved himself prudent and flexible. Despite the potential for backbiting and self-righteousness that the English perfectionists demonstrated at home, the coercive power of the church in Plymouth was limited. Except for the brief tenure of John Lyford, a nondissenting minister who stirred up factions as soon as he arrived, no ordained minister served Plymouth until 1629. Nor did the law require church attendance. Though he complained about his fellow colonists' backsliding, Bradford nevertheless refused to impose absolute religious harmony. The only religious group severely punished during his tenure were the Quakers, in large measure because they loudly and publicly attacked the established churches. Yet Bradford refused to sanction the kind of brutal suppression of the Quakers that English authorities often practiced.

Bradford took the same patient tack with his native neighbors. Relations with the Indians were peaceful, for they were few, relatively powerless, and led by Massasoit, a Wampanoag sachem who thought that he might borrow some of the Pilgrims' spiritual power to improve his own status among his people. He allowed English settlement of lands made vacant by the Indians' loss of population. Samoset, an Abenaki who knew some English, came into the settlement in 1620 and acted as an interpreter. When he left, his place was taken by Squanto, a Patuxet taken to England sometime before 1620 and later returned to Plymouth. He stayed with the Pilgrims on a small plot of his own until his death in 1622. So long as Massasoit and Bradford lived, contacts were generally friendly.

But Bradford could not prevent Plymouth from changing from a single community to a dispersed confederation of distinct towns. As more Pilgrims arrived, the newcomers soon established Taunton, Duxbury, Scituate, Yarmouth, and Sandwich and moved onto Cape Cod. Bradford and his council treated the newcomers as though they had been original settlers. Land grants to the settlers of the new towns were still relatively equal in size, following the original Plymouth pattern. And after 1638, the new towns could send representatives to the meeting of the General Court (the assembly), ensuring that the residents would enjoy the same privileges as the founders.

The New England Way

In the towns and farmsteads of Plymouth, the Pilgrims assumed that they were maintaining familiar English customs, but necessity and opportunity dictated otherwise. What emerged, without their realization, was a New England way of life that would extend out from Plymouth to later New England colonies.

Housing was the first priority for the settlers, and at first houses in Plymouth looked like English cottages: one-room wooden-frame shacks covered by clay daub and animal manure (and plaster, if one could afford it), with roofs of bundled reeds. Later the Pilgrims replaced the reeds with shingles, for reeds easily caught fire. The first chimneys of clay-lined wood gave way to stone ones, again to prevent sparks from igniting the timbers or the shingles.

Over time, the settlers turned the one-room cottage of the first generation into a toolshed or an animal shelter and built clapboard two-story houses (really a story and a half, because the upstairs rooms had low roofs). Some of these homes had steeper roofs on one side than the other (to shed snow), giving them the famous New England saltbox design. Larger houses had second floors that overhung the first floor. The best homes had gables—extended window boxes pushing out from the steeply sloped roofs. The Pilgrims had learned that winter in the new land was far harsher than winter in England, and beside every house stood a woodpile.

Inside this second generation of houses, the entry opened onto a stairway to the two bedrooms above. Behind the stairway was a central fireplace that heated all the first-floor rooms. In time, the well-to-do could afford a more elaborate floor plan, with chimneys at either end of the house. Their downstairs consisted of four or more separate rooms: a sitting room (sometimes called "the best room") and a living room in front of the house, and in back a kitchen/dining room and a storage room or a small bedroom. Whatever the floor plan, all the rooms were dark, for even when the occupants could afford glass for the windows, the windows were small and the panes of glass expensive.

Damp, smoky, and chilly in winter and hot in summer, the house nevertheless brought the family together. The basic living unit in New England was the household, a combination of nuclear family members (parents and children), servants, boarders, and sometimes near relatives. Rarely did more than two generations of any family occupy the same household. The composition of individual households changed over time as the owners grew older and children moved out, but often one child stayed (sometimes with his or her own family) to take care of the parents in their old age.

Much of the time the household gathered in the kitchen area. In the morning, the mistress of the house or a servant raked the embers of the old fire to begin a new one, boiled water carried from the well, and began cooking. As the rest of the household awoke to its chores, the kitchen filled with noise and movement. A bowl and ewer served for personal hygiene. A servant or a child emptied the night jars outside, by the outhouse.

Much of the daily business of the homemaker revolved about food preparation, for it was hard to preserve fresh foods for more than a few days, and foods that were easily preserved, like dried cereal grains or cheeses, required a good deal of preparation before they were edible. Baking, boiling, and stewing were favored food preparations among New Englanders. Baking took place in miniature caverns in the kitchen fireplace wall. Beans, breads, pies, and puddings (meat and fat concoctions) baked for hours, sometimes overnight. Menus varied with the seasons, but bread, porridge, cheese, and stews were staples. Salt and pepper made everything palatable; other prized spices included sugar and cinnamon. Salting, pickling, drying, and smoking preserved foods, but most food was consumed within a few days of its preparation. The large wrought-iron kettles and pots were always steaming with something—if not food, then clothing or soap.

Every home had the same basic kitchen furniture—a long table with benches, a chair for the head of the family placed at one end of the table (hence the term to sit "at the head of the table"), wooden bowls, and flatware (though the well-to-do would use pewter and, later, porcelain dishes and serving pieces). Linens were a luxury, as were individual utensils other than the ubiquitous spoon. Kitchen conveniences in addition to pots and pans included trivets, butter churns, kettles, skillets, roasting spits and dripping pans, and rudimentary toasters (wrought-iron racks that could be swung in and out of the fire).

Family

When the men and boys left the table to work in the fields, the women and girls took care of the chickens and other barnyard livestock, put out the washing, and began the daily rounds of household chores. The house was not only a home, it was a little factory in which women made and mended clothing. In storage rooms (or sometimes the corner of the kitchen), the family kept its wheels for spinning wool and flax into fabric.

Housecleaning as practiced today was impossible, for houses were always dusty, mold and mildew ridden, and soot filled. The furniture required little upkeep; it was solid, almost immobile, and packed with clothing and personal effects. Every bedroom had its sea chests. In better homes, one might also find a treasured clothing bureau or a mirror. Beds were wooden frames with a web of ropes upon which lay a mattress filled with straw or feathers. The nighttime wish "sleep tight" referred to the latticework of ropes that supported the mattress. Many beds were hinged, so that they could be put up during the day.

In the domestic or household economy that characterized these farmsteads, women played a vital role that might be overlooked if one were to focus on monetary rewards. Women not only cooked and took care of children, they were nurses, food preservation specialists, makers and repairers of clothing, and stores of lore and wisdom that other, younger women could tap.

The exchange of labor and goods in a form of ongoing barter was far more common than the payment of money for goods or services. Employers offered room and board to servants instead of a salary. When one wanted to buy something—for example, an imported item—one might barter for it or promise to pay in the future. The debt was then written down in the "book" of the seller. Women often kept these books and carried debts like these without interest for years until the farmer or fisherman or shepherd got a little ahead and had the money (or a debt from someone else that could be transferred) to remit what was owed.

If families in New England did not have all the Old World social ranks, some families were able to build for themselves or their children larger houses than those of their neighbors and to furnish them with more expensive goods. Dutch eatingware (called Delft after the city of its origin); individual chairs and place settings at the table; larger pieces of furniture, particularly cabinets; and other marks of socioeconomic status demonstrated that a few men and women stood above the rest. Glass in windows and ownership of a horse were sure signs that a family ranked near the top of society, but a quicker measure was counting the number of pewter serving pieces and plates in the kitchen.

Clothing also marked the differentiation of classes. In contrast to Tudor-Stuart England (and later, Massachusetts), there were no sumptuary laws regulating what people could wear in Plymouth. Clothing was not drab—the Pilgrims loved color— but they had a sense of propriety and natural conservatism that controlled the impulse to display or perform in public. Orange, brown, red, blue, purple, yellow—soft tones, then called "sadd" colors—appealed to them. Most of the clothing was heavy. Wool and linen fabrics predominated. Cotton was too expensive to be common. Women's clothing was literally in pieces—a skirt, a vest/blouse, and sleeves, all sewn or tied together. Clothing was layered, the overclothing worn above underskirts and bodices, and these over smocks. In summer, women omitted some of the layers; in winter, they added heavy cloaks and robes. Stockings, heavy leather or wooden shoes, and linen caps (a requirement for modest women) completed the attire.

With rare exceptions, women's clothing did not vary enough to become a marker of status, but men's "good cloths" were a telltale sign of wealth and rank. The middling sort of men donned shirts, breeches, and vests of wool, though leather and even canvas might be used for overgarments. Underneath was a linen shirt. Men wore boots and shoes of leather or canvas. Caps were common, including the heavy woolen steeple hat with its solid buckle, but not required by any social convention, as hats were for modest women. But the leaders of the society sported finer clothing of cotton, fur, and imported items of quality manufacture such as gloves, muffs, silk stockings, and beaver hats.

Children wore smaller, looser versions of adult clothing, reflecting the fact that children were regarded as miniature adults, prey to all manner of temptations but lacking understanding of their inherent sinfulness. The concept that children lacked the capacity to make decisions for themselves, or were responsible for their actions (in short, the notion of "age of consent"), did not become part of New England law or social customs until the next century.

New England parents loved and paid attention to their children but insisted that children learn the dangers of disobedience to their elders. The first reading lesson of the young began, "In Adam's fall we sinned all," for even the youngest child had to be mindful that life could be short and painful and that everyone must be prepared, at all times, for death and judgment.

The Passing of Pilgrim Uniqueness

As the Pilgrims dug their roots into the land, the Virginia Company of Plymouth that sent the Pilgrims to Plymouth collapsed. Ironically, one of the reasons for the company's failure was the Pilgrims' inability to pay what they owed on time. The settlers had brought land under cultivation, built houses and a fort, and spread out, but they were still farmers and fishermen and had little left over for trade. The beaver was soon gone. For a time, the Plymouth farmers sold their corn and meat to later-arriving English settlers, but when the number of newcomers leveled off in the late 1640s, this market disappeared. Land speculation still thrived, but its profits were confined to a few entrepreneurs. In the end, the Pilgrims remitted most of their debt, but they never did make their venture commercially profitable.

Bradford watched Pilgrims become New Englanders, more concerned about land and cattle than about the communal, pietistic ideals of the founders of Plymouth. Just before he passed away, he wrote: "I have been happy, in my first times, to see, and with much comforte to injoye, the blessed fruits of sweet communion, but it is now a parte of my miserie in old age, to find and feele the decay and wante thereof (in a great measure), and with greefe and sorrow of hart to lamente and bewaile the same." Plymouth continued as a separate colony until 1686, when it was absorbed into the Dominion of New England. In 1691, Plymouth became part of the Massachusetts Bay Colony.

MASSACHUSETTS

While the Pilgrims settled into Plymouth, relations between the Puritans and the Church of England hierarchy took a turn for the worse. Charles I named William Laud bishop of Wells in 1626 and archbishop of Canterbury in 1633. With Laud came a party of clerics who leaned toward Catholic rituals and away from the intense self-examination that the Puritans favored. Charles also allowed the Catholics to resurface at his court, which frightened the Puritans.

Laud and Charles did not tolerate Puritan criticism and began to drive Puritan ministers from their pulpits. Those who would not be silent faced jail terms as well. With the Laudians in power in the church and the Catholics making a comeback in politics, the Puritans began to plan a two-front war—first against the crown and second against the church. The Puritans also secured a line of retreat in case of need—a refuge in America.

A Great Migration

The fact that English authorities did not permit unlicensed emigration to the king's American domain, as the Pilgrims had already discovered, presented a challenge to Puritan ingenuity, but the Puritans decided that they were not bound by laws made by such ungodly authorities. New England was already inhabited by Pilgrims, and soon, quietly, a number of Puritans joined them. In 1624, the first Puritans, at the urging of John White, a well-connected Puritan minister from Dorchester, moved up and down the northern coast setting up fishing villages. The only one that lasted was at Naumkeag, in a sheltered harbor about fifty-five miles south of the settlement at Portsmouth. By 1628, White had found backers to support a larger-scale effort. Under their aegis, White's New England Company became the Massachusetts Bay Company in 1629, and William Fiennes, Viscount Saye and Sele, a Puritan who sat on the Privy Council, rushed the new company through the legal chartering process.

In the meantime, John Endecott, who had arrived in Naumkeag in September 1628, renamed the town Salem and created with his fellow settlers the first Puritan congregational church in the New World. The congregational form was not without precedent in England, as we have seen, but Plymouth had a congregational system, and it became Salem's model.

The members of the church gathered, and, as one of the congregants wrote to Governor Bradford, "every fit member [recall that this was a "gathered church" in which only those fit for membership could belong] wrote, in a note, his name whom the Lord moved him to think was fit for a pastor." Salem's settlers elected the minister and teacher of the church, as well as the lay elders. Indeed, the entire ceremony fused the religious and the political: "We Covenant with the Lord, and one with another and do bynd ourselves in the presence of God to walke together in all his waies." The covenant, a contract among the congregants, not only created their church, it laid the basis for their polity.

While Endecott labored to keep the Salem project going, other Massachusetts Bay Company leaders were meeting in the English university town of Cambridge. On August 12, 1629, twelve of the directors bound themselves to go to Massachusetts and to take the charter of the company with them. Their contract was far more than a business deal; it was a public confirmation and secular mirror of the Puritan covenant with God. Among them, John Winthrop, an able lawyer, knew that the removal of the charter was illegal, and urged his cosignatories to win over the other directors, which was done. Elected governor of the company by the directors, Winthrop started planning for a fleet of immigrants to join Endecott.

A worldly and ambitious youth, Winthrop attained faith—the key to Puritan sanctity—through a long-term, hard-fought education of his moral sensibilities. Winthrop came from the lesser nobility of Suffolk, the heartland of English Puritanism, and inherited a small manor and the status that went with it. He loved his first wife and by her had six children. But she died in 1615, when he was twenty-seven. He married again, and one year later his second wife passed away. What God had given, he took away. Winthrop married Margaret Tyndal in 1618, and that union lasted well into his middle age, by which time he had learned not to love life too well and to be conscious of his failings.

In the meantime, he studied law, gained a commission from the king as a justice of the peace, and later served as a crown attorney in the Court of Wards in London. There he saw sin and learned to examine himself for signs of his own state of salvation. He practiced good works, not believing that they would save him but wishing to conduct himself in a more righteous manner. Acting in a godly fashion opened the soul to examination, through which came self-knowledge and, finally, understanding of God's design.

Winthrop and his fellow directors hired eleven ships for the migration, and other Puritans chartered six more, making this and the subsequent removals (between 1629 and 1643 almost two hundred ships made the crossing) a great migration. With reason, the Puritans later compared their flight from England to the Israelites' flight from Egypt. On board the *Arabella*, as it sailed to New England in the late spring of 1630, Winthrop preached a lay sermon. Its message was one of hope and love: "We must be knit together in this work as one man, we must entertain each other in brotherly affection, we must be willing to abridge ourselves of our superfluities, for the supply of others' necessities, we must uphold a familiar Commerce together in all meekness, gentleness, patience, and liberality for . . . we shall be as a City upon a Hill, the eyes of all people are upon us."

In England, other claimants to New England lands watched this semicovert exodus with alarm. In particular, Fernando Gorges, whose lands in Maine would soon come under Puritan control, protested to the crown. His suit in the king's courts against the Massachusetts Bay Company began in 1635 and dragged on for two years, when he won a Pyrrhic victory. The Court of King's Bench ordered the Massachusetts Bay Company directors who had not gone to New England to produce the charter. As Winthrop and others had planned, however, the charter was now safely across an ocean from the royal judges. Gorges even leased a ship to carry him and the judgment to Massachusetts, but the vessel sprang a leak, and the venture aborted. The king did not intervene because he was beset by criticism at home—much of it from Puritans.

Between 1629 and the early 1640s, nearly nine thousand men and women, a combination of family groups and single young men and women, traveled from England to New England. For most of the participants in the great migration, the leave-

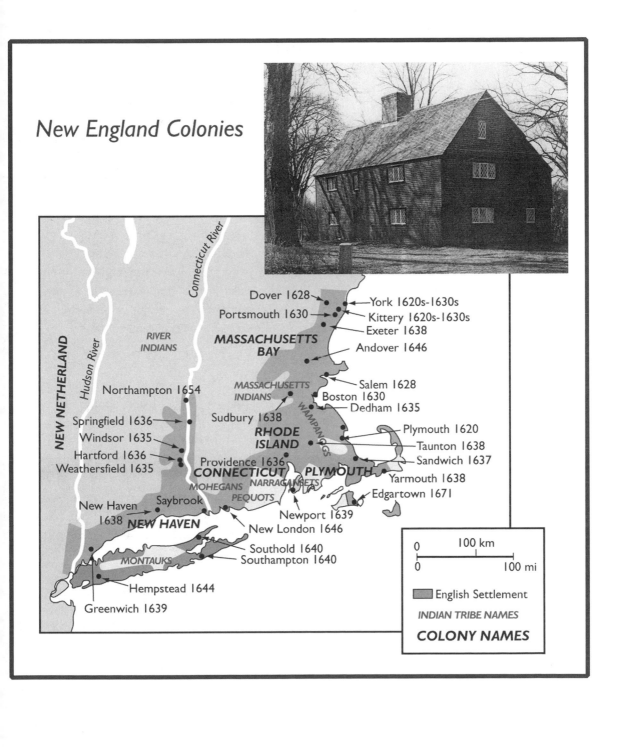

New England Colonies

NEW NETHERLAND

Hudson River

Connecticut River

RIVER INDIANS

MASSACHUSETTS BAY

Dover 1628
Portsmouth 1630
York 1620s-1630s
Kittery 1620s-1630s
Exeter 1638
Andover 1646

Northampton 1654

MASSACHUSETTS INDIANS

Salem 1628
Boston 1630
Dedham 1635

Springfield 1636
Windsor 1635
Hartford 1636
Weathersfield 1635

Sudbury 1638

RHODE ISLAND

WAMPANOAGS

Plymouth 1620
Taunton 1638
Sandwich 1637

Providence 1636
CONNECTICUT **PLYMOUTH**

Yarmouth 1638

MOHEGANS *NARRAGANSETS*
PEQUOTS

New Haven 1638 Saybrook
NEW HAVEN

Newport 1639
New London 1646

Edgartown 1671

Southold 1640
Southampton 1640

MONTAUKS

Hempstead 1644

Greenwich 1639

| 0 | 100 km |
| 0 | 100 mi |

◼ English Settlement

INDIAN TRIBE NAMES

COLONY NAMES

taking was fraught with emotion. Even though they never cut their ties with family and friends, they had to wind up their affairs and arrange for the family members who stayed behind. Often there were legal matters to resolve.

The travelers who came from rural areas had to make two transitions in a very short time. They had to take their leave of their country way of life and journey to crowded, noisy, busy port cities such as London, Bristol, and Plymouth. There, in shabby seaside inns, they waited for their ships to be supplied, their papers to be checked, and the boarding to be completed. Sharpies and thieves introduced the sojourners to the underside of the city. Often, contrary winds kept a ship in port for weeks or chased an outbound vessel back to its berth.

The overseas trip begun, country folk and city folk had to sleep, eat, and pray alongside one another for six weeks in the close confines of a thirty- or forty-ton vessel. Crossing the ocean was a searing experience for all of these emigrants. The bad food and almost nonexistent hygiene on the ship, the unnerving motion of wind and waves, and the rude manners of the sailors hardened the immigrants. The vastness of the ocean raised anxieties, which storms and fear of enemy ships did nothing to relieve. After the voyage, landfall truly seemed like divine deliverance.

Motivations

Religious motives predominated among the Puritan migrants, but flight from persecution blended into other, more secular goals. In their letters home and their diaries, Puritans revealed this diversity of motives. Many came because they feared that England itself was becoming unregenerate or because they had seen firsthand evidence of the persecution of their religious cohorts. The letters also demonstrate the attractive force of economic prospects—land for farming and livestock herds, for example—in the New World. Psychological reasons were just as potent as the economic ones. Some migrated because they wanted to build a pure Christian community in America. Others fled from disappointment and sadness in their English experiences.

The Puritans were never a majority of Massachusetts immigrants. Servants, laborers, ship's crews, soldiers, and craftspeople, some of whom had little religious commitment, constituted the majority of the newcomers. They fled indebtedness (which might mean imprisonment in England) or came to seek their fortunes. In the coming years, New England towns would "warn out" many rootless or penniless individuals, but they kept coming anyway. Others were seduced by the depiction of easy pickings in the promotional literature that the Massachusetts Bay Company circulated.

Finally, some immigrants were carried to New England to labor. For example, ironworkers, a rowdy lot in England, arrived in the Bay Colony "distempered" and undisciplined. A few master colliers prospered, but the majority remained in the lower third of the economic scale. Skilled and unskilled laborers at the bog iron de-

posits in Saugus and Braintree, Massachusetts, created rough-and-tumble little societies of their own, which the larger rules of Puritan culture did little to temper.

Neither saints nor sinners cut their ties to England. Over one-sixth would eventually return permanently, and many others visited home for long periods of time.
They continued to hold and dispose of property in England, fought off creditors and
collected debts there, ran businesses long distance, reported on events in the colony,
and arranged for family matters. The New England settlements remained part of a
transatlantic community.

A Less Than Charitable Model of Government

When Winthrop's fleet arrived in Salem in June 1630, he found not a "City upon
a Hill," but a collection of hovels. Half of the settlers that Endecott had brought were
dead or dying. The council members decided to look for a better site for the permanent settlement. Winthrop and Thomas Dudley, the deputy governor, disagreed
about the best alternative, but the season was getting late, and the newcomers feared
the harshness of New England winters. In addition, rumors circulated of an imma-
nent French attack. In the end, instead of congregating in a single place, the Puritans fanned out in all directions. They laid out towns on the coast, like Boston; beside rivers, like Watertown and Cambridge on the Charles River; and inland, like
Newtown, Dedham, and Reading.

Winthrop settled in Boston and with other councilors gathered a church. At first
it had only a few covenanting members, but the number soon rose. By 1635, of the
roughly six hundred people in Boston, fully one-third were full members of the
church. But the organization of churches was not enough to maintain secular order,
as Winthrop soon discovered. In Boston and the other new towns, settlers began to
grab off pieces of choice land. Townspeople took for themselves the powers of local
government. The directors were still squabbling. Winthrop, who loved order almost
as much as he loved God, saw that something must be done or the focus—both religious and secular—of the entire enterprise would be lost.

Soon after he arrived, Winthrop called the directors together, and they reconsti-
tuted themselves as the government of a colony. Although he had spoken of mutual
love and equality when he gave his lay sermon on the *Arabella*, Winthrop's plan of
government was a tight little circle of trustworthy men. The directors of the company
restyled themselves the assistants, a conciliar executive/legislature/supreme court.
Heads of households from the towns who could come to Boston and there prove that
they were, or were about to be, members in good standing of churches could vote as
freemen. The assistants also assumed the powers of English justices of the peace,
an office Winthrop held in England, with the magisterial power to keep order.

They carried to the New World the attitudes toward power and order of most men
of property in England. English government was theoretically representative, but the
elected House of Commons actually represented few Englishmen. The right to vote

(the "franchise") was limited to Protestant men of property who could take the oath of supremacy and the oath of allegiance, the two oaths promising loyalty to the monarch and to the established church. What is more, the various electoral districts were hardly representative of the distribution of the population. Some districts, created hundreds of years earlier by the crown, had only a handful of eligible voters, while the teeming metropolis of London had only a few members in the House of Commons. There simply was no precedent for a broader distribution of political power—save in neighboring Plymouth, and the assistants eschewed the Plymouth model.

For a year Winthrop and the assistants, sitting with the regular meetings of the freemen, ruled the colony, but the freemen were becoming restless. Reluctantly, under pressure from the freemen, Winthrop and the other assistants made concessions. Towns gained the privilege of choosing their own officers, distributing their own lands, and finally having the power to send delegates (called deputies) to the meetings of the government. In effect, the latter compromise created a lower house of the legislature (the assistants, sitting with the governor, were the upper house), although the two houses did not begin to meet and vote separately until 1644. Over the course of years, the franchise expanded from full members of the churches to most of the adult male residents.

At first, the deputies had conceded much discretion to the assistants. By the middle 1630s, however, the deputies were unwilling to make such open-ended grants. They demanded a written code of law—a demand that the Puritans in England were making at the same time—to define and limit the power of government. Given the first definition of freemanship—membership in the churches—and the continuing presence of ministers in the councils of power, it was not surprising that the assistants turned to John Cotton, a learned and revered Boston minister, to prepare a draft. But Massachusetts was not a theocracy (the ministers did not hold political office), and Cotton's "Moses his Judicials," despite its many citations of Old Testament law, relied more on English precepts and precedents than on biblical precedent.

Still, the deputies, aided by some of the assistants, thought that the draft gave too much power to the assistants, and Nathaniel Ward, a minister (and formerly a lawyer), tried his hand. The resulting Body of Liberties of 1641 became law. In 1645, the colony again began revision of its laws, and these, the Laws and Liberties of 1648, lasted until the charter of the colony was dissolved in 1684. The Laws and Liberties, a landmark legal document, combined biblical injunctions against immorality with what may be seen as the outline of a modern bill of rights. The code featured concepts like due process of law and the right to a jury trial, defined the duties of officials and times of election, and spelled out crimes and punishments.

The Towns

The town was the heart and soul of New England, and the town-based system of settlement distinguished New England from the planter colonies. New England towns originated in grants of land the General Court made to groups of families. The founders of the town then distributed the land within the township, either by lot or in some other fashion. Originally, most towns laid out plots along a central road or two crossing roads. The idea was that house lots, which ranged from two to four acres, would form a central village area. There the founders built a church, which often doubled as a town meetinghouse. The "green" or "commons" opposite the church was open to any resident to graze cattle.

Although all heads of households received lots scattered throughout the township, the first generation always reserved large areas for future development. In general, there were no giant grants to families, and thus no manors or plantations, but the grants were never quite equal. Higher-status families received more land or better-quality parcels. Moreover, as the towns granted more of their reserved land, wealthier families bought up large parcels, and some towns soon featured large farms of six hundred to one thousand acres. Sometimes these large holdings fell into the hands of powerful figures in colonial politics who did not live in the town. They would subdivide and rent or lease the lands, creating a class of tenants. By the middle of the century, land speculation was rife, and land speculators used the colonial government to further their private aims.

Heads of households in the town elected selectmen who met regularly and reported to the town meeting. The town as a corporate body had the duty of redividing unused land and admitting new persons to town privileges. Freeholders spoke and voted at the town meeting, but these were hardly miniature democracies. Although in most towns the franchise was broad, the freemen usually deferred to a well-established elite. The members of the church elected its deacons and selected its teacher and pastor (if it could afford both). The rates the town set paid for the churchmen.

Within towns, the selectmen or town meeting, the elders of the church, and, if necessary, the local justices of the peace settled disputes by arbitration, shaming, and threats of force. When these failed, litigants could bring civil actions in court. If settlers did not like their town's government, they were free to leave. Entire clans sometimes petitioned the General Court for a new town grant precisely for this reason. If they did not like the minister, they could agitate against him and, this failing, were free to find another church in which to pray, if the other church would admit them.

Our picture of the typical New England town is a generalization. In fact, there were as many variations as there were similarities. Some towns were agricultural villages; others were dairying or livestock centers; some became thriving port cities; others languished in the doldrums. Some, like Salem, fostered the creation of other towns, and some, like Deerfield, were frontier bastions. In Dedham, there was little commercial activity and even less out-migration. The families that came reproduced themselves, and their offspring remained through four generations. In other towns, like Newbury, there was a constant flow of people in and out and a steady hum of land speculation and sales.

The English experience of the founders of a town determined its initial shape and government. Some towns, like Sudbury, Salem, and Boston, owed their settlement to men and women from all over the east and south of England, but most towns were organized by families from distinct regions of England. Towns whose founders came from the north of England, where open field tillage and manorial governance were the rule, laid out the town lands in strips and made sharp distinctions between men of worth and lesser men in the distribution of land. Settlers from Suffolk and Essex, just north of London, brought with them to Ipswich and Watertown their canny acquisitive instincts. Already familiar with the rapid turnover of land in London's exurbs, they brought an almost manic attachment to land speculation with them to the New World.

English-speaking people were not the only town dwellers in New England. The Algonquian Indians of eastern and southern New England lived in towns. Indeed, their loyalty to their town exceeded their loyalty to any larger political unit. Depopulation following contact with Europeans led to the abandonment of many of these towns, but by the 1640s communal life among the natives had made a comeback.

To these towns in the 1640s came John Eliot, a Puritan missionary. Many Indians scoffed that the English did not practice what they preached, but the Massachusetts sachem Waban found Eliot's message attractive, and with his aid, Eliot's audiences grew in size and receptivity. For them, Eliot translated the Bible into the Natick dialect of Algonquian so that the Indians could understand the Word in their own language.

Eliot's sponsorship gained Waban and his Christian followers a two-thousand-acre tract for a "praying Indian town" from the General Court. Named Natick, it became a model for other Christian Indian towns. By the 1660s, there were seven of these towns, two with churches. There the new God brought a spiritual message worth loyalty, but even the most fervent converts did not abandon all Indian ways. They accepted monogamy for example, and came to church, but they retained their clan and kin ties. Some Puritan ministers never trusted the converts, and most Indians never trusted the English.

Women and Men Together

In work and social activity, women and men occupied separate spheres of time and space that overlapped within the structure of family life but did not coincide precisely. In some spheres of activity, the division of the sexes was almost complete. Men and women sat in separate pews in the church and entered and left by different doors. Male heads of households were enjoined to "govern" the home, provide for their families, and lead prayers. Unmarried men were to find a family with whom to live and subject themselves to the head of that household.

Just as men occupied the public offices, so were they to police the domestic sphere, taking responsibility for the good conduct of their children, servants, apprentices, and wives. Ironically, the power to govern inferiors conferred on heads of households almost untrammeled discretion to "correct" wives, children, and servants, which sometimes led to verbal or physical abuse.

But there were times and places when women took the lead. Widows could sue and be sued in their own name and discipline their children and servants with the same discretion as a male head of the household. Midwives tended to the sick and to pregnant women. Women helped other women perform the daily tasks of running households and rearing children, forming a circle of support and comfort. Although the boundaries of most married women's worlds focused on home and garden, visiting and charity stretched those bounds.

In groups of women, the elderly had a special role. Women over the age of fifty comprised but 2 percent of the population, but they were sources of experience and comfort. They knew folk remedies, took care of children, taught younger women how to weave and spin, and gave spiritual advice. Anne Bradstreet's epitaph for her mother, Dorothy Dudley, lined out the ideal chronology of Puritan womanhood: "A worthy matron of unspotted life, A loving mother and obedient wife, A friendly neighbor, pitiful [showing pity] to poor, Whom oft she fed, and clothed in store. . . . A true instructor of her family. . . . Religious in all her words and ways, Preparing still for death, till end of days."

Teenaged servants occupied yet another segment of this circle of women, for it was part of the life cycle of most young New Englanders to serve in others' households. In their early twenties, these servants would go on to marry and have families of their own.

In some areas men and women came together. Marriage was the most important of these overlapping areas. In the seventeenth century, over 75 percent of New Englanders married. Widows and widowers were encouraged to find a new mate. In marriage, women occupied the subordinate place. Just as John Winthrop saw the magistrates as divinely anointed heads of state, so most Puritans regarded the heads of households as biblical patriarchs—as father/masters. Despite such patriarchal distinctions in the law of families, wives and husbands were enjoined to be loving helpmeets and pious couples, and apparently, most were.

Social subordination mirrored legal debility. Under the rules of "baron and femme," a married woman took her husband's name and bowed to his will. Their property was his to use. She could not buy or sell their land without his permission. Nor could she be held to the terms of a contract she had made without his consent. One scholar has calculated that in 80 percent of suits brought or defended by married women, husbands represented their wives or accompanied them. In law, a wife's murder of a husband was a "petty treason," far more serious than a husband's murder of a wife (though both were capital offenses). If a married woman had sex with a man not her husband, she committed adultery, a capital offense (though there is only one documented case of the courts carrying out that penalty). If a married man had sex with a woman not his wife, he was guilty of fornication, punishable by fines and corporal punishment.

Sex was not a taboo subject, though the Puritans insisted that it take place within the marriage contract. Parents often arranged marriages, but they could not force young people to wed. On average, women married at age twenty-three, men later, at age twenty-six, which suggests that men delayed marrying until they could support a family. Parents often gave couples small gifts of land and goods to get them started but prevented married people from moving too far away by withholding a portion of the inheritance until the father had passed away. Thus the young people often remained within a day's journey of their parents' abode.

Families were large by modern standards—almost six live births for each "completed marriage" (that is, the parents were alive when the children were old enough to leave home). Mortality among these children was far lower than anywhere else in the British Empire and the home country. Nine-tenths of all children lived to be twenty years old, and if they made it to that age, they were likely to live well into their sixties.

Young people—whether servants or scions—were not coddled in New England towns. Orphans and poor children were bound to labor as apprentices or placed in households as servants. Teenagers who wandered into a town were asked to leave if they had no job. Even the children of the best families faced private correction and public shaming when they strayed in their conduct.

Parental control over children was an economic necessity. Parents of future husbands expected the wife-to-be's family to provide a dowry. Her family weighed the prospective groom's financial future. Children were also vital contributors to the local labor supply. The towns were farming communities, but they were chronically short of farm labor. No lucrative staple crop like tobacco underwrote the importation of indentured labor. There were few profits to spend on slaves, and the growing season was so short that buying field hands made no sense even for the wealthy farmer. The farmers' helpers were their own boys and girls. Without their labor, New England farms would have gone fallow.

Speculators and Businessmen

Despite the shortage of field hands, a favored New England economic activity was land speculation. The Chesapeake region, with its staple-crop economies and its heavy capital investments, may have been the more capitalistic of the two regions, but New England had its entrepreneurs.

Some founders of towns, like William Pynchon of Springfield, had dreams of wealth in mind when they came. The Pynchons built a little empire on the lower Connecticut River based on land speculation, trade with the Indians, and lumber and grist mills. Another New England leader, John Winthrop Jr., the son of the founding governor of Massachusetts and later governor of Connecticut, was a successful land speculator in the Nipmuck region of Rhode Island and Connecticut. Wealthy Puritans Joseph Dudley, Simon Bradstreet, and William Stoughton joined in the enterprise.

As the elite land speculators demonstrated, there was plenty of room in the Puritan way for profit. True, usury or other evidences of naked avarice by a merchant earned universal opprobrium. For price gouging during a time of terrible inflation and crop failure in 1639, merchant Robert Keayne faced public censure. He apologized. His avarice violated the balanced approach ministers like John Cotton advocated. Cotton found no sin in taking "all opportunities to be doing something, early and late, and loseth no opportunity [to] go any way and bestir himself for profit" so long as the profit did not tempt one to forget one's duty to others and to God.

Cotton applied one of the central tenets of Puritanism—that one must "improve the time," not waste or "kill time." Heads of family as well as young people who lacked jobs or neglected their work were shamed, fined, whipped, and subject to incarceration. The result was a culture of industriousness. Work was godly. Not everyone accepted this discipline, as the records of the criminal courts document, but the connection between the ethic of stewardship and the ethos of business promoted enterprise in New England.

It was no surprise, then, that a merchant community developed in the towns of New England. English merchants had been part of the original Puritan movement and had underwritten the costs of the Massachusetts Bay Company. Family, religious, and fraternal ties between New England and English merchants continued to benefit both groups. The first arena for commercial activity was the fur trade, soon joined by the grain market. In fact, Puritan grain merchants like Keayne began to engage in some of the same unpopular tactics that had led to bread riots in England. They engrossed corn and wheat, held off selling until the price had risen, then gouged their fellow Puritans.

Credit necessary for the merchants' original purchases came from England, again proving that the Puritan community was transatlantic. Merchants set themselves up importing English goods for sale to the New Englanders. Ties to the old country and ingrained conservative tastes still dictated buying habits. Predictably, some farmers overextended their indebtedness, and some merchants went bankrupt. Both groups turned to the General Court for relief.

John Winthrop Jr., among others, assayed one solution to the credit problem— instead of buying manufactured goods from England, he argued that New Englanders should develop local industries. In 1644, he organized the ironworks at Saugus. Other New England businessmen entered the logging and lumber industry. The ironworks were successful, but the market for the finished products was not sufficient to pay off the debts the projects had incurred. The foundries failed.

The lumber project was successful. Timber products, like barrel hoops and staves, as well as tar and pitch, profitably sold at home and overseas. Shipbuilding did even better. Whole towns joined with merchants to invest in the industry, and builders placed orders with sawmills and hired young men to work in the shipyards. The fishing industry benefited immediately, as New England ships with New England crews developed both coastal and deep-sea fishing industries. New England cod soon fed the home country and the West Indies, and New England ships entered the coastal trade.

Another answer to the credit crisis lay in the development of overseas trade. If Massachusetts ships and sailors, merchant companies, and suppliers could become middlemen in the growing trade between England, Europe, West Africa, and the Caribbean, they could make enough profits to pay for New Englanders' consumption of imports. By the 1660s, New England ships were the regular suppliers of West Indian planters. From these ports, the New Englanders returned home with refined sugar, molasses, and rum. In the 1680s, New Englanders used the profits to join in the slave trade out of West Africa and the wine trade from Portugal.

The pattern of trade, sometimes depicted as a triangle, was actually many sided. Some New England ships simply went back and forth to the West Indies, or between the West Indies and West Africa, or between England and New England. Others made a series of stops along the coast of North America. Merchants who had family in the various ports or connections to English merchant houses did best, for they had the best credit opportunities, and everything depended upon credit.

THE TRIBULATIONS OF THE SAINTS

Winthrop insisted from the start that the Puritans live in good order and obey the commands of the government. That was the point of the oath of allegiance required of all freemen. But, ironically, the very attractiveness of Massachusetts as a refuge for Puritan opponents of King Charles drew to it men and women who rejected the authority of the state in matters of faith.

Nothing Winthrop said could curb the tongues of those who were sure they were saved but doubted their ministers' or magistrates' state of grace. In sermons, lessons, tracts, and synods (gatherings of ministers), Puritan religious leaders called for harmony, but if each church was autonomous, there was no way for the ministers to suppress a disgruntled minister or congregation, save through the intervention of the state.

Roger Williams's Exile

Roger Williams was the most important individual to challenge the power of the state over conformity of worship. Williams was born in England in 1603 to a merchant family and studied at Pembroke College, Cambridge, in the late 1620s. By then, he regarded himself as a Puritan and with his considerable charm, comeliness, and ability could have become a power in Massachusetts ministerial circles after he emigrated to Boston. But he was steeled in his determination to sever all ties to the Church of England. Shortly after he arrived in the colony in 1631, he refused the Boston congregation's invitation to serve it, because, although it was a true gathering of saints, it would not formally distance itself from what Williams saw as the corruptions of the English state church.

Winthrop liked Williams but was appalled at Williams's views—prudence dictated that formal separatism would cost the colony its support among nonseparating Puritans in England. Winthrop's intervention cost Williams an offer from the Salem congregation, and Williams moved to Plymouth, where for the next two years he expressed his opinions openly. Controversy followed. Williams left for Salem in 1633, where he added agitation against the king to criticism of the English church. There he ignored his fellow ministers' pleas that he conform.

Hailed before the assistants in October 1635 to give an account of himself, Williams was a study in meekness and contrition, but no sooner was he back in Salem than he expressed his opposition to all law issued by a corrupt and unregenerate king—including the Massachusetts Bay charter.

When John Cotton and other ministers could not persuade him to recant, and a second round of testimony before the assistants ended in acrimony, the General Court pressed the Salem congregation to dismiss Williams. Williams took this to be a renunciation of the principle of congregational independence and demanded that Salem's church, in effect, separate from Massachusetts. Even his Salem followers thought he had gone too far, and turned against him. Warned by Winthrop, still his friend, that the government was sending troops to arrest him and ship him back to England, Williams fled to the Narragansett Bay in January 1636.

In his travail, he reached the conclusion that if no church could be truly pure in its membership or free of corruption, then churches must be open to all who wished to enter and worship. In so arguing, he decided that magistrates had no business enforcing religious conformity, an argument even more dangerous to the Massachusetts orthodoxy than his separatist views. John Cotton wrote Williams a stern admonition to relinquish his position, but Williams replied that he was right and that Cotton's views were "bloody to the souls of all men forced to the . . . invented worships . . . [and] slaughtering each other for their several respective religions . . . which every civil state . . . compels all subjects to in a dissembled uniformity."

The Silencing of the Free Grace Party

In the middle of the controversy over Williams's challenge, Henry Vane, a nobly born Puritan, arrived in the colony. In his early twenties, well educated, and charismatic, he won the governorship in May 1636 with the help of the Boston freemen. Among these were William Hutchinson and his wife, Anne Marbury Hutchinson, who had arrived in 1634. Both Hutchinsons belonged to the Boston church and supported Vane's application for membership.

With him and others in the congregation, they cheered on minister John Cotton's views of the preparation a true Puritan needed for salvation. Cotton taught the Boston congregants that those who doubted the sincerity of their faith must wait for some sign of divine approval before seeking membership in the church. Without the spirit of Christ active within the worshipper, Cotton averred, the soul was dead. Grace was God's free gift. It could not be earned; it was never sure from externals; and only the seal of the spirit brought safety.

Most of the other ministers, led by Cambridge's Thomas Shepard, disagreed: the biblical promise of salvation for the regenerate and the practice of "holy duties" sufficed for a start. One might thus prepare for salvation. A small difference, perhaps, but for men and women who searched scripture, their neighbors' conduct, and their own souls for signs that they belonged to the invisible church of saints, small differences loomed large.

In weekly meetings with other women to discuss Cotton's sermons, Anne Hutchinson argued that the covenant of works had never really been banished from some (as yet unnamed) Massachusetts ministers' teachings. Too many of them, she implied, still clung to a kind of partial covenant of works, wherein outward piety sufficed for godliness. Those who believed in the sufficiency of outward signs were only "legal Christians" at best, and hypocrites at worst, even if they did not realize their own duplicity. The implication of this lesson was that such ministers should not be allowed to preach—a revolutionary thought in a colony built upon respect for the ministry.

Hutchinson was never the leader of this "free grace" party—that role went to Vane; her brother-in-law John Wheelwright, himself an ordained minister; and ultimately to Cotton himself. But she became the focus of the controversy when Wheelwright was banished and Cotton compromised with his critics in the synod of 1637.

Hutchinson came from educated, well-to-do Puritan stock. She was born in 1591, the daughter of a clergyman, married well in England, and had a large family. She adopted the view that the covenant of grace, the covenant that God made with the few elect and for which Christ died on the cross, could only be known through a series of searing stages.

First, the smug Christian who merely acted the righteous part must see that no human act or desire could ever change God's edict, nor should visible sanctity ever be taken as a guarantee that one was saved. Salvation was not deserved or merited, it was absolutely God's choice. The true Christian recognized how innately sinful people were, and only then, perhaps, might a moment of true conversion occur. Then and only then would the penitent heart receive evidence of grace and assurance, the faith that one was saved. This reading of Calvinism sailed close to the heresy of antinomianism, for it hinted that those who knew of their salvation need not obey their clerical or civil authorities. They were a church and a nation unto themselves. But Hutchinson never went this far.

Once Vane left the colony and Cotton concluded a tense peace with Shepard, Hutchinson's increasingly vocal insistence that ministers who did not have the seal should not hold pulpits, and that those were saved could tell who was fit to preach and who not, made her a target. What had begun as a technical doctrinal dispute within the ministerial fellowship had became a political crisis because the Boston congregation, the most important in the colony, was talking schism.

Winthrop, her neighbor and a member of Cotton's congregation, wanted her to curb her words. Her intransigence set the colony afire. But Winthrop was politically savvy, and managed to move the elections for 1637 out of Boston, the hotbed of support for Vane and Hutchinson, to Cambridge. There he regained the governorship. When Winthrop and his allies convened the General Court in November 1637, they refused to seat pro-Wheelwright delegates from Boston and Wheelwright, convicted of sedition in March, was expelled. Winthrop held punishment in abeyance in the hope that Wheelwright would recant, but Wheelwright only retreated from the extremity of his position, asserting that the unregenerate knew who they were. Wheelwright moved to New Hampshire and with a few of his Massachusetts loyalists and some locals established the town of Exeter.

Pressed by Thomas Shepard, Winthrop and Dudley insisted that Hutchinson face trial in the General Court. Winthrop still hesitated to press her as hard as he might have. We would love to know more than the few records that survive about the case. Some of them, written after the trial was over, he designed to explain and defend his own actions.

Still, her case allows scholars to lift the veil that surrounds so much of women's roles in early America, and some historians have uncovered antifeminist themes in her prosecution. Though Hutchinson's views were a throwback to much older Puritan attacks on Protestants who did not practice their Christianity rigorously enough, her attackers agreed with minister Hugh Peter that Hutchinson had renounced the proper role for a woman and become a "husband, magistrate, and minister"—all roles reserved for men—instead. The irony of this situation was that Puritanism's insistence that one not sit back and simply conform, and that anyone might be a saint, theoretically empowered women to take an active role in the governance of congregations, but men forbid women to assume roles of public leadership.

Anne Hutchinson was tried in the General Court in November 1637 for defamation of the ministries, traducing their authority, and causing civil disorder. Trading biblical exegesis with her accusers, she held up her end of the discourse admirably, but the court, stacked with her adversaries, concluded that she had "disparaged all our ministers" and ordered her expelled from the colony.

In March 1638, pregnant and noticeably weaker, she faced a trial before her own ministers and congregation in Boston. Thomas Shepard could now come out of the shadows, for this was a religious rather than a secular hearing. Cotton, ineffectually, and for the last time, tried to shield her, but Shepard led a relentless attack. On March

22, 1638, she admitted to some errors in her views but would not concede that congregants could never criticize the ministry. Shepard then brilliantly and cruelly charged that not only were her views wrong (grounds for expelling her from the congregation), but she was a liar and thus could never be readmitted to membership, even if she accepted the ministers' corrections.

Hutchinson and her family left the colony in May 1638 and traveled to join Williams on Narragansett Bay. After some controversial years there, she removed once again to a Puritan community in Pelham, the Bronx, New York, where she and members of her family were killed in an Indian raid in 1643.

Williams, Wheelwright, and Hutchinson were not the only dissidents exiled. Samuel Gorton, who proclaimed himself a "professor of the mysteries of Christ," fled Massachusetts for Williams's settlement. Pynchon, who occasionally spent the Sabbath as a lay preacher, wrote and published a tract on the meaning of Christ's sacrifice that the General Court found blasphemous and publicly burned. Forced to leave the colony, he continued his religious agitation in England.

Baptists in Massachusetts and Plymouth who began to preach against infant baptism and called for a return to the precepts of the first New Testament churches were driven from Massachusetts. These groups found a home in Newport, Rhode Island, in 1644. By 1656, a handful of Quakers—some of them, such as Mary Dyer, former followers of Wheelwright and Hutchinson—attacked the very basis of an established church. Banished, they too found sanctuary in Rhode Island.

Governor John Endecott saw Dyer and her fellow schismatics not only as religious fanatics, but threats to the government: "open and capital blasphemers, open seducers from the glorious trinity . . . and . . . open enemies to the government itself." Blasphemy was a capital offense under Massachusetts law. The Quaker challenge to the authority of government to enforce religious conformity, more than Quaker doctrine itself, underlay tragic events in 1660. Ignoring warnings that she would be executed if she returned and did not recant, Dyer led three Quakers back into Boston, where according to a supporter, "she spake the words that the Lord spake in her." Unmoved by her witness, the General Court convicted and hanged her.

American Puritans and the English Civil Wars

The irony of Massachusetts's suppression of religious dissent within its borders was that the dissidents' challenge to the authority of the magistrates and ministers in Massachusetts echoed a parallel struggle Puritans waged against the crown and the established church in England in the 1630s. When the civil wars erupted and later, during the interregnum, Puritans played a vital role in Parliament. Throughout all these events, Puritans in England called to their brethren in New England to return. Some, like the Reverend Hugh Peter, did, but the vast majority remained in their new homes.

The founders of New England had committed themselves to the reform of the English church, a purpose the next generation of American Puritans had to reformulate in order to justify their decision not to return to the home country in its travail. The rationale recast the very essence of their original mission. They no longer portrayed themselves as models for others to follow but as those chosen to build the new Jerusalem. Still part of the transatlantic Puritan community, they were no longer a people motivated by the example of the flight of the Jews from Egypt, but the reincarnation of those refugees. The Atlantic became the Red Sea, and Charles I a new pharaoh.

Having decided to stay, the Puritans faced new and unanticipated doctrinal problems. The most vexing of these was the problem of church membership for their children and grandchildren. The founders of New England had chosen to cross the sea. Whether they were saints or not, they were volunteers. To reinforce the notion, they had added to their church rules a new codicil. Those who came after them would have to recite, before the minister and the congregation, some experience of grace to become full members of a church, in effect, become "visible saints." Full members could take communion and baptize their children.

But would congregations allow the baptism of children of those adults who could not or had not been able to narrate an experience of grace? Without baptism, the children would be exposed to the devil and hell. Without the assurance of baptism of their children, those who were not in full membership would bolt the church. In a synod that led to the Cambridge Platform of 1648, the ministers confronted the problem of making a uniform policy on church membership. They agreed that they had the duty and the authority to announce such a policy—a step away from the control of individual churches by their congregants—then failed to come up with a formula. A majority of the ministers would have conceded to a more liberal policy of baptism, but powerful members of their churches objected to such liberality, and worse, to a synod of ministers telling the members of a congregation who could join their fellowship.

When the ministers met in 1657, they again tried to frame a policy for the baptism of nonmembers' children and this time proposed that children of members, after they turned sixteen, had to bring their own offspring to church for baptism. Thus the second generation could be halfway members and able to gain baptism for the third generation, their children, but not able to vote for ministers or take communion until they could fulfill the confessional requirement for full membership. The new proposal hung fire until another synod, in 1662, authorized the "halfway covenant" by a simple majority vote. No synod's output ever gained universal approval, however, and some ministers and congregations never did buy into the idea of a halfway covenant.

HIVING OUT

While the ministers were fretting and their congregants battling over doctrine, New Englanders spread into the interior and along the coasts of New England, "hiving out" like a colony of bees. The town system of government proved itself an adaptable framework for expansion. Massachusetts authorities tried to retain control of all the new towns, with some success. Massachusetts annexed Portsmouth, on the coast of New Hampshire, in 1643, and Kittery and York, on the southern coast of Maine, in 1651. (New Hampshire became a royal colony in 1680; Maine remained a province of Massachusetts until 1820.) But the distances of some of the towns from Boston stretched too far for the General Court to oversee them, and the founders of some of the new towns were antagonistic to the ruling party in Boston. Towns in Connecticut and Rhode Island gained independence from Massachusetts in the late 1630s.

Connecticut

In a wholesale removal beginning in 1635, many of the townspeople of Newtown (now Cambridge), Massachusetts, led by minister Thomas Hooker, relocated to the broad, grassy meadows of the upper Connecticut River and called their town Hartford. Much respected in Massachusetts, Hooker's notions of salvation and preparation for grace, including the qualifications for full church membership, did not quite square with the ideas of other ministers. Hartford also had much more grazing land than Newtown. Residents of Dorchester, Roxbury, and Watertown shortly thereafter left Massachusetts and founded the towns of Wethersfield, slightly south of Hartford, and Windsor, slightly north of Hartford.

None of the settlers had any legal claim to the land beyond permission of the General Court to relocate, but they convinced the Dutch and the Plymouth inhabitants of the area to leave or accept incorporation into the new towns. But the migration brought the English into the heartland of a powerful and jealous rival—the Pequots.

The Pequots had dominated southeastern Connecticut for a century. To ensure their power, they built forts along the Thames and Mystic rivers and traded with the Dutch for firearms until a series of wanton murders on both sides soured the relationship. Hoping to find another source for European weapons, they turned to Massachusetts. Governor Winthrop encouraged the trade until the Narragansetts and the Mohegans, the Pequots' chief rivals, spread rumors that the Pequots intended to attack the Connecticut settlements.

The English wanted Pequot land, not trade, and undoubtedly many among the English also saw the Pequots as agents of Satan. Thus when war began the English offered no quarter. On May 26, 1637, with the aid of Narragansett and Mohegan allies, English forces from Massachusetts burned the central Pequot town on the Mystic, killing warriors, women, and children indiscriminately. From Plymouth, Bradford reported: "Those that escaped the flame were slain with the sword, some hewed to pieces, others run through with the [soldiers'] rapiers. . . . It was a fearful sight to see them thus frying in the fire and the streams of blood quenching the same, and horrible was the stink and scent thereof; but the victory seemed a sweet sacrifice, and [the soldiers] gave the praise thereof to God, who had wrought so wonderfully for them."

The Narragansett paramount sachem, Miantonomo, objected to the butchery, but the Mohegan leader, Uncas, saw a chance to further his own and his people's interest at the expense of the Pequots. The surviving Pequots became Mohegan slaves until one Pequot spokesman, Cassasinamon, petitioned the Connecticut authorities for relief. For his people he gained 214 acres of "reservation" land ten miles to the west of the Thames River, a small percentage of the tribe's original holdings but enough for a fort and fields for cattle. The precedent of reserving enclaves for dispossessed or defeated Indians would eventually become a staple of the United States' Indian policy. The reservation is now the site of the Mashantucket Pequot Museum and Research Center.

Disenchanted with the English, Miantonomo tried to rally a confederation of Indians to protect their lands. Uncas assassinated the Narragansett chief while the latter was in Uncas's custody. In 1676, Pequot warriors would join the English against the Narragansetts, paying the Narragansetts back in kind for the battle of Mystic. Such was the deadly revolving door of New England's Indian diplomacy.

The Connecticut River settlers faced a threat of a different kind from a company of English land speculators. In 1635, John Winthrop Jr. had arrived in Boston with a commission as the governor of a settlement at the mouth of the Connecticut River. Wealthy English Puritans had funded the commission. The Massachusetts General Court had no intention of allowing these settlers to form their own colony but could hardly offend such important English patrons. As a temporizing measure, the General Court created a commission of Connecticut settlers in 1636 to keep order in the colony. The commission government gave way to a general court that the freeholders of the Connecticut towns elected.

A final challenge came from New Haven, begun as a separate colony in 1638 at the mouth of the Quinnipiac River. Theophilus Eaton and John Davenport, the latter a Puritan minister, and the founders agreed to a biblical polity, and the courts of the town met without juries. The result, for a time, was a regime much less concerned with traditional men's and women's legal roles and more with fair dealing and pious living. Indeed, the relaxation of the common law rules gave women a voice in the courts of New Haven that they lacked in other colonies. New Haven retained its distinctive character even after it was formally absorbed into Connecticut in 1664.

In January 1639, the towns of Connecticut, with the exception of New Haven, came together to adopt Fundamental Orders for the colony. Under the Fundamental Orders, town government rested largely in the hands of well-known local elites, and town offices passed from generation to generation within these families. The measure for voting in town elections became an inhabitant's "honest conversation"—in other words, upright personal conduct, qualifying most adult males as town voters. Each town certified those of its number who might vote for the general assembly, council, and governor. The freemen so named had to be twenty-one years old and hold at least a small piece of property—easy to do with so much land so easily had.

The Fundamental Orders had no standing in English law, nor was there a formal charter for the colony until Connecticut governor John Winthrop Jr. went to England in 1661 and persuaded the government there to issue a charter. Connecticut recognized Charles as the legitimate king in that year, and Charles granted the charter in 1662. He consented in part because Winthrop convinced him that Connecticut's moderation and loyalty would offset Massachusetts's stiff-necked reluctance to acknowledge Charles's return. Charles would remember the insult, though Massachusetts acknowledged his rule over the colonies three months after Connecticut.

Connecticut remained throughout the seventeenth century a relatively tranquil landscape of villages and family farms. Visitors noted with disapproval that Connecticut farms seemed poorly run. Livestock, particularly hogs and sheep, wandered about. Nevertheless, there was enough of a surplus for Connecticut farmers to send to market biscuits, flour, barreled beef, and salted pork. The goods went from the farms to warehouses in New London, New Haven, Norwalk, and other Long Island Sound towns, and from there primarily to the West Indies.

Rhode Island

Unlike the settlers of Connecticut, who sought the permission of the Massachusetts General Court to remove themselves, the inhabitants of Rhode Island were, as we have seen, largely a collection of exiles and malcontents fleeing Massachusetts's authority. At the head of the Narragansett Bay, by the Pawtuxet River, Williams found refuge among the Narragansett Indians. He was never a lover of Indian ways but came to respect many of the Indians, eventually preparing a lexicon of their Algonquian dialect. Over the years he would win their trust and support their claims to land and livelihood.

In 1638, William Coddington, a former Boston magistrate who had supported Wheelwright and Hutchinson, brought eighty of his followers to join her and Williams. With Williams's help, they were able to establish themselves on the island of Aquidneck, in Narragansett Bay. At first they settled the northeastern portion of the island, on former Indian fields, and called their new town Portsmouth. Contentions erupted among these contentious refugees, however, and Coddington and his closest friends removed themselves once again, this time to the southwestern edge of the island. They named the settlement Newport.

Portsmouth was next visited by Gorton, lively, spiteful, generous, nasty, and impossible to ignore. Still moved by the immediate presence of the divine spirit, he was a sect unto himself and soon wore out his welcome among the Portsmouth founders. He bought land from the Indians and called the new town Warwick. The Indians found Gorton as difficult to swallow as the Puritans of Massachusetts Bay had, however, and there soon was strife. The Massachusetts government used this controversy as an excuse to send a troop of militia to arrest Gorton. Taken to Boston to be tried by the General Court, he huffed and puffed and got himself sent back to England, then returned to Rhode Island to finish his days as a biblical patriarch on his own land.

Williams's own town grew slowly, reaching up the north bank of the Pawtuxet. He called it Providence, for he believed his mission was guided by a divine hand. From Providence, over the years, Williams carried on his quarrel with Massachusetts, firing off sermons like broadsides. His opposition to a state church opened Rhode Island to people of other religious persuasions—as he wrote, to "Papists, Protestants, Jews, and Turks."

In a twist of events, Williams, driven from Massachusetts for resisting the power of the magistrates, became the leading magistrate in Rhode Island. It was he who journeyed twice to England to get a charter for the colony, once in the 1640s from Parliament, and again in 1662 from King Charles II. He drafted the Acts and Orders of 1647 creating the government of the colony.

The assembly under the Acts and Orders united the four towns of Providence, Newport, Portsmouth, and Warwick, giving almost universal voting rights to male inhabitants and guaranteeing freedom of conscience. A general court, inferior courts, and town courts dispensed justice, and Williams was named chief judge of the general court, a member of the council, and, for a time, governor.

In the coming years, Rhode Island would have to fight hard to protect its lands and its charter from encroachment by other colonies. Still a magnet for troublemakers from these colonies, its internal politics remained raucous. But its economic situation improved when merchants in Newport and Providence became leading patrons of the Atlantic slave trade.

————

By the end of the century, New England villages were among the most healthy and orderly communities in the world. In work and family settings, meetings of local freemen, church life, and even the governance of the colonies, there was a commonality of purpose, vision, and expectation. Neighbors relied upon local institutions like county courts and accepted, by and large, the authority of judges. Delegates to local and colonywide representative bodies spoke with a good deal more freedom than anywhere else in the world. By comparison with other colonies and homelands, the New England settlements were indeed peaceable kingdoms.

But there was no real security in New England, even in the summer quiet of the lush meadows along the Connecticut River or on the sun-dappled islands that guarded the mouth of the Narragansett Bay. The natural beauty of New England hid the demons of war, civil discord, and debt.

Shunted to the edges of their old lands, Pequots, Narragansetts, and Wampanoags harbored real grievances that sometimes burst out in violence, which the English reciprocated in kind. The trader in his canoe, the farmer in the field, and the nursing mother in her village never knew a moment's true peace.

Among themselves, the English vied for the best lands, argued about the true faith, and undermined local government by appealing to neighboring colonies and English officialdom. There were always debts to pay: to the town for taxes, to the land speculators for mortgages, and to the merchants for the one nice piece of silk, the new chair, or the imported tableware.

Strains pulled towns apart. Those who had moved to the outskirts of the township, away from the town center, wanted their own churches and roads, then demanded to become new towns. Outliers were unhappy to pay taxes that went for improvements to buildings, roads, and churches that were miles away, in the center of the town. In newly established towns, speculators and investors were able to grab large and favorable plots for themselves. They then resold or leased for profit the lots, changing towns from communities to mere geopolitical entities. Titles to land in the new towns, resting on purchase and sale instead of family use, created an explosion of litigation and the accompanying bad feeling.

New England had come a long way from Winthrop's vision of a "City upon a Hill." He and his generation had planned to congregate in a city of God, but necessity mandated that they spread themselves widely and thinly over the land. They had expected their churches to be gathering places of saints, but they edged inexorably toward the very open-door policies of English local churches that they decried. They had demanded that the regenerate and the unregenerate make their way together in meekness and fellowship, but they faced crisis after crisis in which some of their number claimed to be holier than the rest, then read the ironic outcome of their plans as God's judgment.

7

The Middle Colonies

Samuel Maverick was just what his name implied—a difficult and complex individual. Over the course of many years, he had made himself unwelcome in Puritan Massachusetts by demanding greater religious and political liberty. Exiled, he insinuated himself into the most unlikely of places—the circle of courtiers around James Stuart, the Duke of York and younger brother of the king of England, Charles II. On March 22, 1664, anticipating (or rather, in the course of precipitating) the outbreak of a second war with the Dutch, Charles gave his younger brother all of the Dutch colony of New Netherland (including modern New York, New Jersey, northern Delaware), as well as western and coastal Connecticut and Maine. As much to be rid of Maverick as to reward him, James appointed him a commissioner in the government of New York.

On August 29, 1664, Maverick arrived in the duke's new province accompanying the small fleet and army sent to conquer the Dutch there. He had no use for the stiff-necked Puritans who had made their homes on Long Island (perversely regarding it as a part of Connecticut), but he reveled in what he perceived to be the relative lenience of the duke's regime in New York. He had seen the future—the colony offered the potential for the liberty he had sought in vain in New England.

The development of politics, economics, and society in early New York, New Jersey, Delaware, and Pennsylvania—the Middle Atlantic colonies, or "middle colonies"—is of a piece. All were proprietorships, like Maryland and the Carolinas, and in some ways, similar. The majority of the settlers were white Protestant farmers, farm laborers, or tenants, and their families, living in households with parents or children. They were conservative in their social views and pious after a fashion, and they accepted the authority of their betters. But a string of simple contingencies surrounding the founding and peopling of the middle colonies opened the door to greater liberty than existed in any of the other European settlements.

These colonies, chartered as the personal domains of powerful po-

Ecclesiastical liberties are, 1, Liberty of conscience to all, provided they raise not fundamentalls in religion, nor disturbe the publique peace. 2, Ceremonies may be used or omitted. 3, the Booke of Common Prayer may be made use of or not. Civil liberties are,—All freeholders, not scandalous in theire lives & conversations, are capable to vote att the election of officers, military and civill, in theire several towneshipps.
—Samuel Maverick on the laws of New York, 1669

litical figures in England, became the homes of religious sectaries, cunning entrepreneurs, factious brawlers, and wide-eyed idealists. None of these individuals
planned to make the proprietaries a new Eden, but they knew that they did not want
to be ordered about by highborn men in fine lace an ocean away. The middle
colonies' ethnic and religious diversity fostered toleration and popular government.
Maverick was right.

Yet these colonies had an "underclass" as well: tenants, servants, and slaves who
might be free to worship as they chose but bore other burdens. So, too, women might
have status in these colonies exceeding what their sisters could claim to the north
and south, but middle-colony women remained a subordinate group. Liberty did not
mean equality.

NEW YORK

Before the English came, the Dutch had ruled the lands around the mouth of the
Hudson and built forts upriver to tap the beaver trade. And before the Dutch arrived,
the Iroquois had spread their towns and longhouses from the Hudson River in the
East to Lake Erie in the West. The power of their confederation of thousands of warriors brought fear to all their neighbors. But the Iroquois were afraid, too, for the
Hurons and Ottawas had gained a powerful ally in the French, and the Iroquois had
to find a counterweight. Thus they welcomed the Dutch—and Dutch guns.

A New Netherland

In 1566, the Dutch nobles (the word *Dutch* is an English version of the word
Deutsche, and comes from the dialect of German spoken in the north of the Low Countries) revolted against Spain, the ruler of the Low Countries. The Spanish had tightened their control of the region, imposed higher taxes, and abused Protestant dissenters. The Dutch withstood sieges and even flooded their own land to deny it to
the Spanish. Finally, in 1579, at Utrecht, the seven northernmost provinces of the
Low Countries formed a defensive alliance against Spain. These so-called United
Provinces delegated control of foreign affairs and war to an Estates-General in which
each of the provinces cast one vote. Domestic affairs remained the concern of the
provincial governments. In each of the provinces, particularly the largest and southernmost, Holland, commercial centers dominated local policy making. Powerful
merchants and landholding families ruled these centers and perpetuated themselves
in power.

Dutch influence in the North Sea and Baltic trade antedated the formation of the
Dutch Republic, but blossomed at the end of the sixteenth century. Dutch shipping
accounted for three-fourths of the total carrying trade of the Baltic, ferrying timber
from the north and Portuguese wine and salt from the south. The Dutch specialized

in carrying other nations' goods, and the Estates-General fostered the carrying trade by lifting all customs duties and tariffs and trading with all contestants in time of war. Internal manufacturing was similarly unencumbered by restrictions, except for the government-run herring fishery.

Capable of narrow-minded, spiteful, and pompous moralism, the Dutch people were also clear-sighted and tough-minded. Although the United Provinces were staunchly Protestant, the local nobles and city merchants who ran the government allowed Jews and other minorities to emigrate to the Netherlands. Thus Amsterdam, from a mere ten thousand people in 1500, grew to over one hundred thousand by 1625. The wealth of the city rose even faster. Unlike other regions, where enmity between the city and the surrounding countryside hampered growth, Amsterdam sellers and rural producers worked in close accord. Cooperation between private citizens and government also turned the Netherlands' greatest natural enemy—the sea—into a friend. Using dikes to hold out the North Sea and cutting canals to drain the marshes, the Dutch made the sea their partner. River mouths at the seacoast became ports, and canals became highways.

The North Sea and the canals were gateways to the northern European market, but the Dutch had more ambitious ideas. The lucrative spice trade of the Moluccas and other East Indian islands beckoned, and in 1602 the Estates-General organized the East India Company. Heavy timbered and broad beamed, the Dutch East Indian carricks were armed like battleships, for the East Indies trade required Dutch ships to raid Spanish and Portuguese sea-lanes. Every cargo the Dutch brought home was one denied to the Spanish and Portuguese enemy.

The Dutch East Indian merchants thought little of converting the natives to Protestantism, and did little to establish colonies for permanent Dutch settlers. No need—native labor was cheap and plentiful. The Dutch extended the same basic campaign plan to trading posts in Africa, Indonesia, and the Western Hemisphere in the 1610s and 1620s, planting settlements in the Guianas, in Brazil, and on the island of Curaçao off the coast of Venezuela.

In the course of its expansion all over the world, the East India Company offered a cash prize to any mariner who could find a western route to the East Indies. Henry Hudson, an English pilot previously employed in the North Sea by an English company, offered his services. In January 1609, he contracted with the Dutch East India Company to find the Northwest Passage. The company leased the *Half Moon*, hired a crew of Dutch and English sailors, and ordered Hudson on his way. Hudson, a stubborn but able mariner, fussed with the company over his route and provisions, a harbinger of the traits that would make him famous and then get him killed.

North Atlantic storms endangered the ship on its outward voyage, but by July Hudson had reached the French fishing fleet off Newfoundland, and he stopped off the banks to do some cod fishing for himself. He then traveled south to Maine, explored Penobscot Bay, and stayed around long enough for a visit from a canoe full of natives. They addressed the delighted crew in halting but understandable French, ate herring with the sailors, and accepted gifts of beads and blankets.

After some misunderstandings, the Indians returned with furs to trade. They expected that the Dutch wanted what the French had wanted, but Hudson was no Champlain. He was a blue-water pilot who dreamed of faraway places and dramatic vistas. He reembarked and sailed south to Virginia, then turned north and on September 10, 1609, dropped anchor in the mouth of the river that was later named after him.

Convinced that the Hudson must be the mouth of the "in-drawing river" that led to the Northwest Passage, he sailed up as far as modern Albany. He found a number of likely sites for a trading post, but his hopes for a Northwest Passage were dashed by his discovery that the river sharply narrowed. More important, trading with the Indians ended abruptly when a fracas broke out between Hudson's men and an enterprising Indian sneak thief. The result was a hasty withdrawal by the Dutch with the Indians in pursuit.

Hudson returned to England and sent his report on to the East India Company. Word soon reached King James I that the English captain had sailed for the Dutch company. Hudson was arrested instead of honored for his achievement. The Dutch tried to bail him out of trouble and failed, but English investors eager to find a way around the French fur-trading posts on the Saint Lawrence thought that Hudson might be their answer. While the Dutch found other pilots to take the *Half Moon* back to the New World, Hudson signed on to explore the northern end of Labrador and found the great bay that would be named after him.

There the ship and its English crew spent the winter of 1610–1611, wedged in the grip of winter ice. The unrelieved vista of tundra, uncertainty about their future, and Hudson's arrogance led the crew to mutiny when the ship was finally able to clear the ice, in June 1611. They threw Hudson, his young son, and a handful of other men into the ship's boat, without provisions, and the mutineers sailed back to England. A rescue mission the next year found no sign of Hudson or his men. Fifty-eight years later, the English established the Hudson's Bay Company to tap the fur trade and began to reap the profits of Hudson's daring.

In the meantime, the Dutch returned to Hudson's river; built a fort on the island that lies next to Albany, calling it Fort Orange, after Holland's leading noble family; and began trade with the Indians. Fort Orange was part of a plan to build fort trading posts on the mouth of the Delaware, up the Hudson, and on the tip of the Indian island of Manahatta (now called Manhattan), following the model of the East India Company's settlements in Indonesia and the Spice Islands. The Dutch called the colony itself—stretching from the tip of Long Island and the Connecticut coast to Cape Henlopen on the Delaware shore—New Netherland.

In 1621, the merchants of Amsterdam created a new company to handle trade for the Western Hemisphere and the Atlantic. The company did not confine its efforts to the Hudson River region. It sponsored a Dutch invasion of Portuguese Brazil and underwrote the Dutch West African slave trade. But the company did not neglect New Netherland. In 1623, the company's ships carried emigrants, many of them refugees from Europe's religious wars, to the tip of Manhattan. By 1625, a fort and a windmill, protected by a wall across the tip of the island, marked the town of New Amsterdam. A year later, the first governor of the New Netherland colony, Peter Minuit, "bought" the tip of the island from a local Indian clan for trade goods worth sixty guilders.

The first artist's view of New Amsterdam shows a string of houses along a shore. The most prominent feature, from a distance, was the fort, but as one approached the shoreline, perhaps in one of the single-masted Dutch cargo scows, one could see that the houses looked remarkably like those of Amsterdam. They were heavy-timbered structures with triangular fronts and steep gable roofs. Although there was plenty of room to build, the houses were constructed next to each other, often with common retaining walls, as if the owners could not bear to live any distance from one another.

At the urging of its Dutch backers, the company gave to prominent investors large tracts on Manhattan, on neighboring Long Island, and up the shores of the Hudson, conveying with the land the right to govern it as a little polity. Only three of these first "patroonships" (manors) were settled, and only one, Renssalaerswyck, survived through the colonial period.

Kiliaen Van Renssalaer, the proprietor of this little fiefdom, expected it to produce windfall profits and to run like a medieval manor. He selected a young Dutch lawyer, Adriaen Van der Donck, to be his steward in America. Van der Donck, liberally educated, broad minded, and independent in his ways, came to the patroons' lands up the Hudson (around modern Albany) but did not stay. He lingered long enough to learn local Indian dialects, explore the woodlands, and decide that his fortunes lay in New Amsterdam. He became part of the popular party there, opposed to the absolute rule of the company's governors and in favor of trade, tolerance, and good living. Granted his own lands and the title of Jonker, in later years the town of Yonkers would honor his name.

Company officers also began a full-time trade with the Montauk Indians of Long Island, the Mahicans on the Hudson, and the more powerful Mohawks on the river named after them. The latter two tribes were already rivals, and the competition for Dutch arms and ammunition set them at one another's throats. In 1643, Governor Willem Kieft tried to oust all the Indians from Dutch territory, starting a war, and after two years the Indians had driven just about all of the Dutch from the upper Hudson and had ravaged the Dutch and English settlements on Long Island. The Mohawks stepped in to broker a peace, and used it to remove the Mahican middlemen from the beaver trade with the Dutch.

As more English settlers arrived in the lands the Dutch company governed, contacts between the English and the Dutch grew factious. The English ousted the Dutch from Connecticut and settled Long Island. Although the English cooperated with the Dutch during Kieft's War, the Dutch could not establish authority over the Connecticut-spawned towns on the eastern end of Long Island.

At the same time, wary of the Maryland Colony on the southern flank of their lands, the Dutch set a fort on the northern tip of Cape Henlopen, Delaware. Angry at the uninvited Dutch intrusion, the Leni-Lenapes, Delaware's first inhabitants, sacked the Dutch town of Lewes in 1631. A Swedish group established itself near the site of today's Wilmington, Delaware, in 1638, but the Dutch, under Kieft's replacement as governor-general of New Netherland, Peter Stuyvesant, besieged the Swedes in 1655, and they surrendered.

The Dutch had established a very loosely governed colony, making little effort to dislodge the Puritans from Long Island or discourage the refugees who wandered into the colony. In 1647 this changed, under the influence of two men. One was Stuyvesant, named governor of the colony by the West India Company in 1646. A soldier who formerly governed the Dutch Caribbean island of Curaçao like an autocrat, he preferred fiat and threat to consultation and consensus. When the company required him to choose a council, he named his friends but only listened to them when they agreed with him. Nevertheless, his vigorous campaign of fort construction and militia drills roused the colony from its slumber.

Just the sort of governor that Van der Donck detested, Stuyvesant could be cunning and uncompromising by turns. He wanted military order and profit for the company, found men who would do his bidding, and played politics when brute force did not work. He imprisoned Van der Donck for his insolence and opposition, then let him go to the Netherlands to plead his case. When Van der Donck had finished, the Netherlands Estates-General demanded that Stuyvesant appear in person to explain his high-handed ways. Fortunately for Stuyvesant, the first Anglo-Dutch war erupted, and his presence in the colony became essential. There he held the far-flung pieces of New Netherland together—up the Hudson, along the Connecticut coast, down the Jersey Shore, into Delaware.

The other dominant figure was the senior Dutch Reformed minister Dominie (Reverend) Johannes Megapolensis. Born and reared a Roman Catholic in the Netherlands, he converted to the Dutch Reformed faith as a young man. In New Amsterdam, he imposed his will upon the churches. He was a thoroughgoing bigot, despising the Indians and disparaging other Christian faiths than his own. For example, when a small number of Jews arrived at the port in 1654, fleeing the collapse of the Dutch colony in Brazil, Megapolensis, with Stuyvesant's full support, wanted to turn the refugees away. They would "infect and trouble the colony," the minister warned. Fortunately for the newcomers, the directors of the Dutch company insisted that the doors be open to Jews, for they were important members of the Dutch overseas merchant community.

Stuyvesant's hand was heavy in regulation of the economy. The price and ingredients of every loaf of bread were specified. Megapolensis redoubled his efforts to control local Dutch Reformed worship. But there were limits to what the new governor and the minister could do. The outlying English settlements on Long Island resisted, as did the powerful families beginning to gather lands on the east bank of the Hudson River.

To be fair, one must remember that the Dutch authorities had only a few soldiers and the colonial militia to protect the colony. The English on Long Island contributed little to the general defense, except when Indian attacks fell on both Dutch and English communities. The Dutch finally learned what the French already knew: the little colony must have Indian friends. From Fort Orange, the Dutch supplied firearms and ammunition to the Mohawks. In turn, the Mohawks defended Dutch interests. Indeed, they continued to call the governor of the colony "Corlear" (after Dutch trader Arendt van Curler) long after the Dutch had lost the colony to the English.

The Dutch had another weapon in their contest for possession of the land: their mapmakers. Maps were not only guides to mariners and settlers, they were semilegal documents claiming territory and setting boundaries. As far back as the end of the fifteenth century, European maps of the New World used empty spaces and name labels to make political statements. For example, leaving empty space on a map implied that the land was uninhabited and thus open to colonization (even if the mapmaker knew that Indians occupied the land). Following Columbus's example, mapmakers gave classical and European names to features of land, ignoring Indian names, even when the latter were known. (John Smith's maps of New England were exceptions to this rule because he had learned how important it was for colonists to know which Indians claimed which parcels of land.)

To support Dutch title to the full extent of New Netherland, the company commissioned new maps. When presented with the evidence of the maps, the English sneered that the Dutch had "baptized" the land with Dutch names. Indeed they had, but more important, Dutch geographers and Dutch engravers had beaten the English to the punch. Dutch maps of the Hudson River mouth had appeared as early as 1614, but the triumph of Dutch mapmaking of the New World came in Joannes Jansson's and Nicholas Visscher's detailed and strikingly accurate maps of New Netherland in the 1650s.

Iroquois Diplomacy

As the Iroquois' relations with the Dutch indicate, the leaders of the Iroquois League were astute diplomats. By the middle of the seventeenth century, however, harmony among the so-called five nations of the Iroquois confederation was fraying at the edges. Voluntary ties, burnished each year at council meetings held on the Onondagas' land in the middle of the Iroquois territory, held the confederation together. But by the 1640s, the Senecas, the "guardians of the western gate," slid toward alliance with the French while the Mohawks, at the eastern gate, remained steadfast in their loyalty to the Dutch.

At the root of growing internal dissent was the need for arms and ammunition to fight the enemies of the League, but the Iroquois were caught in a trap of their own making. The price of Dutch weapons was beaver pelts, but the Iroquois had hunted the beaver in their territory to extinction. The League made the decision to steal beaver from the Great Lakes Indians—the Ottawas, Hurons, and Eries—leading to twenty years of war from the 1620s to the 1640s. The beaver wars enabled the Iroquois to purchase weapons, but cost the five nations many warriors. Again the League made the choice to replace the losses by directly attacking the villages of the Hurons and the Eries (both of whom spoke Iroquoian dialects) and incorporating the most worthy and comely of the captives into the Iroquois people.

Women played a vital role in these latter "mourning wars," for they had the power to accept or reject the captives. Those rejected were tortured and killed. Those accepted took their place in the village as full members of the family and clan of the dead warrior they replaced. The assimilated captives were never really happy in their new situation, a fact the Iroquois appreciated. The newcomers were carefully watched.

As warfare wracked the Iroquois, they also felt the full brunt of European diseases. Smallpox and other epidemics ravaged the villages of the Iroquois nearest the Dutch. There was no way for the Iroquois to avoid the pestilence, and the death of so many made the mourning wars even more important. Every captive taken was a potential addition to the Iroquois strength—but every captive taken stiffened the resolve of the Iroquois' many enemies. Iroquois dependence on European trade goods had imprisoned them in a vicious circle.

The Onondagas stepped into the breach to make the peace and save the League. The Onondagas, the "People of the Mountain," saw themselves as the diplomatic corps of the League, especially of the four western tribes. In 1654, Garacontié, a young sachem, journeyed with his band to Montreal, to "console" with traditional gestures the French for their losses against the Iroquois. The French and the Iroquois were still in a state of war, but the French greeted the mission with formal courtesy, for the French had a favor to ask of the Onondagas.

The Oneidas, another member of the League, had captured a French surgeon, and the French asked Garacontié to arrange his rescue. Garacontié pledged his own life that French captives among the Iroquois would be returned unharmed, and he was as good as his word. The surgeon was saved in the nick of time, and eighty-eight other French captives would owe their lives to the Onondaga diplomat in the coming years. In return, the French allowed Garacontié to persuade Hurons who had taken refuge in Montreal to join the Onondagas and sent artisans, missionaries, and soldiers to guard the Onondaga towns.

The Mohawks were furious that Garacontié and the Onondagas, ostensibly allies, had acted unilaterally. They, too, hurried to Montreal to make peace. In the meantime, the Onondagas had tied themselves to the French, or so it seemed. And if the French alliance lasted, the western Iroquois would no longer depend on the Mohawk-Dutch connection for arms and ammunition. But Iroquois diplomacy was never so simple. The Mohawks pressured the Onondagas to abandon the French, and the Oneidas and the Senecas followed suit. Garacontié switched sides repeatedly, rushing to Montreal to assuage the French then dashing off to councils with the Dutch. He invited Jesuit missionaries to his villages, then used them as hostages and go-betweens with the French. The League survived, and Garacontié, duplicitous, cunning, and brilliant, became its spokesman.

The Mohawks, never fully reconciled to the Onondaga strategy, and still resentful of having to follow the Onondagas' lead, reported all this to the Dutch, warning that the French would fall upon the Dutch once again. In the meantime, the League stepped up its campaign against the Mahicans, the Susquehannocks of Maryland, and the Indian peoples of Ohio.

The Duke of York's Province

While Charles II had mastered moderation at a French court known for royal excess and demonstrated it in generous treatment of his father's parliamentary enemies, James, Duke of York, had learned other, less commendable lessons. He could be vengeful and narrow-minded, though in religion he was tolerant, for he was a Roman Catholic in a land formally committed to Protestantism. He had other concerns as well. As Lord Admiral of England, he wished to see the power of the navy expand. As the head of a number of merchant companies (notably the Royal Africa Company that made its money in the slave trade), he encouraged plans for expansion of trade. Both his naval and his commercial interests inclined him to wage war against England's great naval and commercial rival—the Netherlands. That war led to the English occupation of New Netherland in 1664.

When it came to ruling his new lands (including the colony named New York in his honor), he let his agents and representatives work out a series of comparatively mild compromises with the Dutch in New Amsterdam (renamed New York City in his honor) and Beverwyck (renamed Albany, another of the duke's hereditary titles), the Puritans on Long Island, and the polyglot population of the rest of the colony. Indeed, one can say that the Duke's Province, as it was called, was never really his (though in the late 1670s and the 1680s, he did take a more active interest in the day-to-day administration of his colony). From 1664, in crucial ways New York belonged to its inhabitants.

The long train of accommodations began on August 29, 1664, as Stuyvesant watched the Duke of York's fleet arrive off the tip of Manahatta Island. Stuyvesant had tried to muster his garrison, but the Dutch refused to fight. The English on Long Island celebrated cautiously, for they wanted nothing more than to be reunited with Puritan Connecticut, and the Duke of York was hardly a Puritan. For his part, the duke's deputy governor, Richard Nicolls, an experienced soldier whose family had come to England from Scotland with James I, and whose loyalty to the Stuart cause had led to years of exile with Charles II and James in France, gave the Dutch every opportunity to surrender, which they did on September 7.

One reason why the overwhelmingly Dutch population of the colony accepted the English overlords was Nicolls's policy of accommodation with the Dutch. The government officers were renamed—for example, the Dutch *burgomaster* became the English mayor. Nicolls confiscated the property of the West India Company, but confirmed individual Dutch property rights and allowed the Dutch to govern their own local affairs. On his own authority, Nicolls made them "denizens," in effect giving them citizenship status within the empire. When the Dutch complained that they could not get supplies from England, Nicolls arranged for continued trade with the Netherlands. Nicolls himself paid for basic supplies when they were scarce, expecting to be repaid by the duke.

In 1665, Nicolls proclaimed the "Duke's Laws," though it was a misnomer on two counts. First, Nicolls wrote the laws in the duke's name, and second, they were more directed to the Puritan settlers on Long Island than to the Dutch. In them, Nicolls guaranteed religious toleration, but did not define any kind of colony-wide political rights, nor did he set up a legislature. The Dutch, accustomed to rule by the governor and his council, accepted the situation, but the Long Islanders insisted upon a representative lawmaking body. Nicolls placated them by giving their town governments great autonomy.

Peace between the two nations came in 1667, but it turned out to be only a respite between wars. Fighting resumed in 1672, and a Dutch fleet retook the province in 1673. Colonel Francis Lovelace, Nicolls's successor in 1668, surrendered with scarcely more resistance than Stuyvesant had offered in 1664. The Dutch in New York City and up the Hudson welcomed the Dutch forces as liberators, but did not turn on the English in their midst. It was a prudent decision, for the fleet soon departed.

Predictably, the Long Island English refused to take oaths to the Dutch and reattached themselves to Connecticut. The Dutch contented themselves with changing all their offices' names back to Dutch and trying to reestablish trade with the Netherlands. Unfortunately for the Dutch, the Treaty of Westminster (1674) that ended the Anglo-Dutch wars ceded the colony back to the English.

Politics without Politicians

Nicolls had governed wisely and well, and Lovelace followed Nicolls's precepts in dealing with the Puritans of Long Island and the Dutch. In 1674, the duke sent Edmund Andros to rule his province, and Andros, unlike Nicolls and Lovelace, courted no one's favor but the duke's. Indeed, one of his first official acts was to confiscate Lovelace's estate.

Andros brought with him a new, hard-edged policy of heightened proprietary supervision. A soldier who had seen service in Europe and Barbados, Andros's mission was to centralize and rationalize the defense of the colony. First the northern frontier with Canada must be secured. He traveled to Albany to confer with the leaders of the Iroquois confederation and came away with a "covenant chain" alliance against the French. For their part, the eastern Iroquois called Andros Corlear, their true friend and older brother, and with his support they turned with renewed fury against their traditional enemies, the Susquehannocks of Maryland (with consequences traced in chapter 8).

But Andros had other, more mercenary, goals as well. The deputy governorship was a patronage plum, and like Lovelace before him, Andros joined in business ventures with rich Dutch colonists such as Frederick Philipse and Stephen Van Cortlandt. In turn, they collaborated with English rule and grew wealthier. The governor's new economic regulations (unlike Stuyvesant's old ones) promoted trade—in which, not by chance, the duke also had an interest.

Enforcement of Andros's iron will came from his handpicked courts of assize, seven for New York, and three apiece for the Jerseys and the three lower counties on the eastern shore of the Delaware River (later the Delaware Colony). The courts acted as miniature legislatures, executive bodies, and true courts of law. From them, he got a portion of all fines, fees, and confiscations. Andros's administrative tribunals were a worst-case scenario of mixing the powers of government.

Immediate resistance to Andros's ham-fisted rule first came from the Puritans of Long Island. He replied with a simple message: obey or be declared outlaws. Andros then warned Governor John Winthrop Jr. of Connecticut not to interfere. The Long Island towns bowed to the inevitable and took oaths of allegiance to the duke. Next he impressed the Leni-Lenapes that they must submit to his stewardship. They conceded. Then he dealt with Connecticut farmers trespassing on lands belonging to the duke in eastern New York. They backed away from their claims.

But his critics were not done with him. No sooner did he travel to England, in 1677, to arrange family affairs, than merchants in the city left out of his circle began to petition for his removal. He returned in 1678 to find that the murmur of criticism had become a roar. His achievements in diplomacy hardly weighed in the balance against his enemies' vigor. In 1682, he was recalled to England to account for himself. But the duke did not forget his loyal servants, and in 1688, two years after he returned to America, Andros resumed his deputy governorship of New York.

Andros had little patience for domestic politics and no affection for representative legislatures, and none convened in the colony during his tenure. This situation changed with the arrival of Thomas Dongan, another royalist veteran, in 1683. Dongan, needing money to ensure the colony against the French threat, called the first assembly, and it in turn crafted a "Charter of Liberties and Privileges" to define the franchise and prevent taxation without legislative approval. Much of the text of the charter was borrowed from the Magna Carta (1215), updated. Dongan and his council approved the document, and not coincidently, the assembly voted him a generous salary. A year later, after some amendments, the duke gave his approval. So uppity did the newly called assembly become, however, that the duke reconsidered the matter in 1685 and dissolved it.

The assembly was not the only bar to New York's imperial rulers getting their way. The mixture of peoples and customs in the colony undercut the duke's lieutenant governors. Neither the duke's laws nor the duke's men could dictate religious uniformity to so diverse a people as New York's. The Catholics, Anglicans, Dutch, and Puritans worshipped in their accustomed fashion. After the colony of New York became a royal province in May 1689 and the number of professing Anglicans grew to a significant minority, Governor Benjamin Fletcher again tried to impose an Anglican establishment upon the colony but failed. In the Vestry Act of 1693, he did induce the reinstituted assembly to require each county to set up vestries and support them, but could not ensure that each vestry chose an Anglican minister. An Anglican filled the pulpit of New York City's Trinity Church, but other parishes chose dissenting ministers. No one ever succeeded in establishing any one religion in New York.

New York City

The Duke's Province initiated a new pattern in the American colonies—a colony whose focus was a city. Boston and Charleston never exerted the influence in Massachusetts and South Carolina, respectively, that New York City (and later, Philadelphia) had in their colonies, and the Chesapeake colonies had no major urban centers.

Under the Dutch, New Amsterdam was dirty and disheveled. Important men lived in their *bouwers*, or farms, on the outskirts of the city. Within the wall that became Wall Street, the city literally stank, for the canal cut to facilitate passage into the city from the tip of the island of Manhattan had become an open sewer. Soon after he arrived, Stuyvesant complained that the fort had no gates. Two years after his death, in 1672, despite his efforts, the situation differed little. Wild hogs overran the fort and rooted in its cellars. Repairs had cost so much that the city fathers did not bother with them.

Only the polyglot population kept the city pulsating with energy, for many of the Dutch, Portuguese, Jews, English, French Protestants, and men and women of multiple ancestry in the city had come to do business and brought with them ties to merchant communities in Europe and the West Indies. Leading import-export merchants bought or built ships to ply the trade routes of the Atlantic with the wheat and

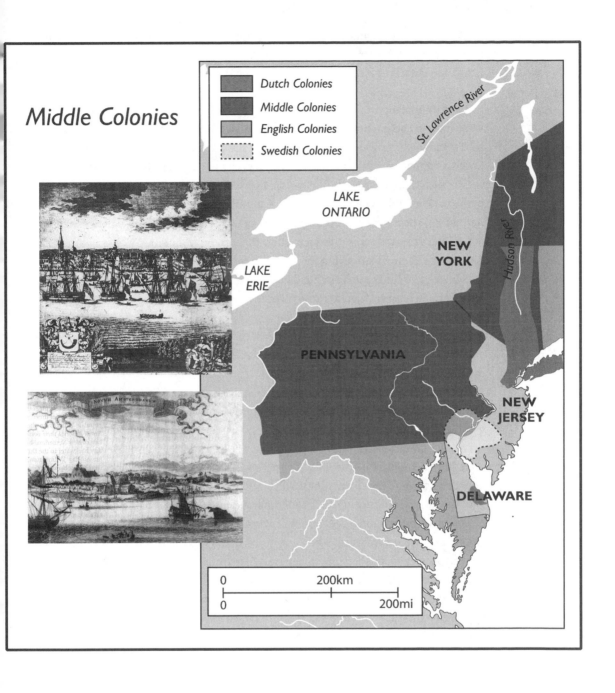

Middle Colonies

Legend:
- Dutch Colonies
- Middle Colonies
- English Colonies
- Swedish Colonies

St. Lawrence River

LAKE ONTARIO

LAKE ERIE

NEW YORK

Hudson River

PENNSYLVANIA

NEW JERSEY

DELAWARE

0   200km

0   200mi

livestock of Long Island, the furs of the upper Hudson, and the tobacco of the Delaware Valley settlements. In a way, this city was the model for the diverse population and entrepreneurial vigor that would characterize northern cities to our own time.

Most important for the improvement and growth of the city was its trade with the West Indies. The city merchants did not confine this trade to the English sugar islands, and fortunes were made trading with the French and Spanish enemies of the English crown. In addition, the leading merchants carried on a clandestine trade with French Canada, even though Canada served as base for French and Indian raids into New England. When the fur trade gave out, the merchants turned to a wide variety of substitute exports, including cheese, livestock, flaxseed, candles, tanned hides, and manufactured products such as pottery and clothing. Merchants also acted as middlemen supplying the city with foodstuffs from the countryside.

Beneath the tiny group of elite merchants labored a larger cadre of less wealthy businessmen who yearned to move up to the higher rank, battled with city and colonial governments to gain favorable rulings on prices and monopolies, and dickered with area farmers over the cost and quality of their produce. These merchants worked endless hours, diversified into the sales end of the business, and invested in ships of their own.

Like their counterparts throughout the British possessions, all the merchants preached a gospel of fiscal responsibility and on-time payment of debts, and then gambled on credit. A single shipload of cargo, delivered to the right customer at the right time, might bring windfall profits, but ships might also be lost to storms or seized by enemies as prizes. Most of these merchants left behind small estates—a house and garden, part ownership of a ship, uncollected notes and bills of exchange, and, on the other side of the ledger, shipping debts and unpaid bills.

Using the profits of trade, New York City slowly began to improve its governance and its physical appearance. Andros ordered repairs to the fort and the waterfront. Dongan gave the city a very liberal charter of incorporation in 1684. The newly fashioned wards of the city each chose an assistant and an alderman. Together with the mayor, they constituted a council with autonomous rule-making power. Under the new regime, the city ordered the canal filled (it became Broad Street) and laid out new streets, paved with stones. The city paid for carters to remove rubbish.

The city council, legally a private corporation, encouraged enterprise within the city by giving some companies monopolies and regulating others. The city's bakers were the first of the monopolists, causing an outcry from bakers in surrounding towns. The ferrymen next received the blessing of the city fathers, and riders soon complained about the fares. When the colonial legislature resumed regular meetings in the 1690s, it heard the complaints of the outlying communities that had lost business or paid higher prices because of the city monopolies and the counterarguments of the city's representatives. Disputes over regulation of the economy continued well into the next century.

New York City also witnessed battles between organized labor and business. Various groups of laborers and artisans demanded the freedom to associate and keep others from practicing their trades. The coopers (barrel makers), for example, joined together to set prices for their work in 1684. The council prosecuted the coopers for "criminal conspiracy." The carters and porters also tested the resolve of the council and lost their jobs. Like the combat between city and countryside, the struggle for control of the price and wage mechanisms within the city became a regular feature of city life.

Slavery in the City

There were slaves in New Amsterdam from its founding—one-fifth of the population—but the Dutch allowed their slaves to own property and trade, and manumitted (freed) one out of five of their slaves. Some of these men and women became landholders themselves, using "freedom dues" the Dutch West Indies Company granted. When English slave traders replaced the Dutch, the profits of the slave trade to the English West Indies flowed into the city. So did the slaves.

By 1703, one-third of the families of consequence in the city had slaves, usually working as domestics. Other slaves became porters on the docks. Slaves constituted 20 percent of the city's population in the early 1700s. Although the percentage would decline over time due to the tremendous increase in European immigration and natural increase among free families, the absolute number of slaves steadily increased.

Excavated slave graveyards in the city prove that these bondmen and women endured deprivation from the time that they were young. Slave children were undernourished. Adults suffered from broken joints and bones. The graves also reveal that slaves retained West African burial customs, suggesting that slaves found comfort in their cultural traditions. Indeed, when freed slaves built their own houses, they favored West African floor plans.

Some free persons consorted with slaves, entertaining them in their homes or sharing spirits with them at the many taverns in the city. Some slaves were able to buy or otherwise gain their freedom, and they became tradesmen and laborers. Other slaves plotted rebellion. In April 1712, a group of slaves burned down a house in the city and then murdered the people who came to put out the fire. The courts indicted forty-three slaves for the crime, convicted twenty-five, and executed eighteen of them. One, a ringleader, was burned to death.

In 1741, a larger suspected conspiracy literally and figuratively set the city ablaze. A small group of slaves boasted that they would burn the city down and ally with the Spanish, whose fleet they expected in the harbor any day. Much of the plan was braggadocio—fueled by drink. A scrofulous tavern keeper and receiver of stolen goods abetted the scheme, hoping to rob houses when their owners were out fighting the fires.

The elite of the city were frightened by the fires and even more by the rumors of revolt. Arson was a real threat, for the buildings were largely wooden and sat cheek by jowl on crowded streets. Already suspicious city officials believed that the fires were part of a slave uprising. Rumors became accusations, then grand jury indictments. Trials quickly followed, at the end of which thirteen slaves were burned at the stake for petty treason, sixteen slaves were hanged along with four free persons for arson, and more than seventy slaves were banished from the colony. The trials proved that slave owners and civil authorities in the city were as adamant about protecting the institution of slavery as their southern counterparts.

The Dutch Struggle against Assimilation

At the beginning of the eighteenth century, the city still looked Dutch, and names like Haarlem (after the Dutch city), the Bowery (after one of the Dutch *bouwers*), and Bronck's farm (later shortened to the Bronx) still marked the land. Streams that ran into the bays were still called "kills," and the English absorbed Dutch words like *stoop*, *cookie*, *waffle*, and *boss*. Wealthy Dutch families imported silverware and tableware from the Netherlands, and Dutch town homes featured elegant inlaid cabinets and chests of Dutch design. Many Dutch clung to their own language and attended the Dutch Reformed Church services. Even the poor could obtain Dutch-language Bibles and hymnals at low cost. After 1690, Dutch pietist preachers came to the city to offer an alternative to the Dutch "high church" ministry. The pietists spread out over New York and the Jerseys, bringing charismatic preaching and Puritanical moralism to outlying Dutch communities.

Up the Hudson, Dutch families laid out their farms in traditional fashion, giving roughly equal parcels to various branches of the family. Kin lived in the same neighborhoods, often on the same plats as their parents and grandparents.

The land was divided and assigned according to oral agreements. Only when the English insisted did the Dutch farmers file their claims in court. Later divisions of meadows, fields, and woods were just as egalitarian as the original grants. Property was held in common by husbands and wives and went to the survivor of the marriage.

Couples married at a younger age than in nearby English communities—as soon as the couple was ready rather than when the prospective husband could be assured of his own farmstead. Families were large, averaging over eight children per household, though mothers and fathers could expect that a third of their offspring would not reach maturity.

But the Dutch could not resist Anglicization. By 1710, the English had surged ahead of the Dutch in wealth, population, and influence in the city. Small Dutch merchants and shopkeepers had to compete with English and French merchants, using

English law, English weights and measures, and English shipping rules. Leading Dutch landholders taught their children English and arranged marriages for their children into important English families. By the middle of the 1700s, the Dutch, one contemporary observer noted, "were beginning however by degrees to change their manners and opinions, chiefly indeed in the town and in its neighborhood; for most of the young people now speak principally English, go only to the English church, and would take it amiss if they were called Dutchmen and not Englishmen."

For Dutch women, Anglicization posed special challenges. Under Dutch law as practiced in New Netherland, women had far more rights and status than they did under the English law of New York. Under Dutch law, the conjugal unit was paramount, rather than the head of the household. Husbands and wives prepared joint, or "mutual," wills. Property held in marriage was communal—both partners had a say in its use and sale, and when one partner died, the other inherited at least half of the estate. Future husbands and wives routinely made premarriage agreements to keep separate property. Finally, Dutch wives had by law and by custom an important place in the family's business affairs—far more so than in English practice.

Faced with the loss of these privileges, Dutch women tried to bend English law to Dutch purposes—for example, retaining mutual wills and prenuptial agreements. Dutch husbands, however, found the paternalistic views of their English neighbors attractive, and began to adopt English practices to pass property directly to male children.

In New York City, during the years from 1660 to 1679, twenty Dutch husbands composed wills. All but two were "mutually" prepared by husbands and wives. By the last decade of the century, twenty-nine Dutch husbands made up wills, and in twenty-seven of them wives took no part. Seventeenth-century Dutch fathers routinely postponed their children's receipt of any of their inheritance until their mother's death. By the middle of the next century, only 45 percent of fathers gave to their widows their entire estate. Although Dutch husbands were still twice as likely as English husbands to will all their property to their widows instead of dividing it up among wife and children, the shift toward English legal norms was unmistakable.

At home, in a domain that women controlled, Dutch housewives still clung to their cultural heritage. Dutch cooking, featuring beets, endive, spinach, parsley, dill, and onion-potato-carrot stew, brought the flavor of the home country to the Dutch in the city. Dutch creature comforts like bed warmers and coverlets were handed down from mother to daughter. Even their dress proclaimed their refusal to Anglicize. As Sarah Kemble Knight, a New England visitor to New York City, observed with some astonishment in 1704, "the Dutch, especially the middling sort, differ from our women, in their habit [clothing] go loose, wear French muches which are like a cap and a head band in one, leaving their ears bare, which are set out with Jewels of a large size and many in number. And their fingers hooped with rings . . . which you should see very old women wear as well as young."

THE JERSEYS

The Duke's grant included the Jerseys, for they had been part of New Netherland, but the duke transferred the land to Sir George Carteret and Lord John Berkeley in July 1664. The new owners assumed that they could treat the parcel as they had the Carolinas—that is, govern, although the duke had not conferred that power on Carteret and Berkeley. Nevertheless, in February 1665 they proclaimed the Concessions and Agreements, an attempt to attract settlers. The Concessions guaranteed a general assembly, the right to trade freely, and religious toleration (though for Protestants only). The proprietors proposed to appoint a lieutenant governor and a council, as well as all officials of the colony. The assembly could tax the settlers but not the proprietary lands.

The Concessions laid out plots that ranged in size from 2,100 to 21,000 acres (one-seventh of which were reserved to the proprietors), and permitted the creation of towns. Heads of emigrant families would get 150 acres, in addition to 150 acres for each servant. Servants who stayed the course of four years were entitled to 75 acres on which to begin their own farm. These were liberal terms, for the proprietors sought settlers. But when they came, New Jersey's settlers proved ungrateful and contentious.

Squabbles and Tumults

In 1665, Philip Carteret, cousin of the proprietor and first lieutenant governor under the Concessions, sailed into a maelstrom of conflict over land titles. The Dutch settlers in Bergen accepted his authority, but the Puritans, Quakers, and Baptists who came from Long Island, claiming their parcels under grants that Nicolls made before he knew about the duke's conveyance to Carteret and Berkeley, never bowed to the proprietary government. They set up Elizabeth, Woodbridge, Piscataway, Middletown, Shrewsbury, and Newark, but refused to pay their quitrent to the proprietors and showed no disposition to obey Carteret. In 1668, at the first assembly Carteret called, delegates from towns established under New York patents rejected other delegates' appeal for a tax to support the proprietary government.

With little to gain from the duke's largesse, Berkeley sold his interest in the colony to Quakers Edward Billing and John Fenwick in 1674. Billing, facing bankruptcy in England, sold his interest to a cartel of Quakers, including William Penn. In 1676, Carteret agreed to partition the colony, giving the Quakers West Jersey and keeping East Jersey (the northern half of the colony) for himself. West Jersey lay south of a line from the Upper Delaware River to Little Egg Harbor on the Atlantic Coast, more or less conterminous with modern "South Jersey."

William Penn

Penn, the foremost of the Quaker purchasers, was one of the most remarkable men of his age. In an era of official corruption and private venality, Penn's public-minded fairness and personal uprightness shone brightly. Born into an upper-class family—his father served as the Lord Admiral of England under Charles II—Penn was educated in England and Ireland, went to both Oxford and Cambridge, studied law, and entered the royal diplomatic corps. He was by upbringing a gentleman, and through his father's political and naval connections, met and formed a friendship with the duke. But in his early twenties, after hearing members of the Society of Friends preach, Penn had a change of heart about society and religion.

In 1667, Penn formally became a Quaker—a time when membership in the Society of Friends required not only a profession of faith but a willingness to face the anger of authorities and the ridicule of family. Penn did all of this, and more: he went to jail for his beliefs and wrote books and pamphlets defending his own faith and the right of everyone to worship as they chose. His connections at Charles II's court protected him to some extent, and James remained Penn's patron.

Penn hardly qualified for sainthood. His outward calm and strength when facing judges and princes hid a prickly rebelliousness and intemperance of speech. He could be a bitter and energetic polemicist, a negligent patron, and an indifferent friend. As a businessman, he squandered his family fortune, not for lack of energy, but because he could not be bothered with details like minding the bottom line. Above all, he was never a happy man. He restlessly traveled throughout England and its possessions, a man who comforted others but could not find comfort himself.

The End of the Proprietary Period in the Jerseys

The severing of West Jersey and East Jersey did not end the tumults in either place. In West Jersey, Fenwick established a settlement at Salem, on the Delaware, but New York authorities refused to allow him to act as governor of the colony. Arrested in 1676 and warned to desist, he persisted instead in his claims, and Andros had to depose Fenwick by force.

In 1677, Penn and the other proprietors proclaimed the Laws, Concessions, and Agreements for West Jersey, promising trial by jury, liberty of conscience, and a representative assembly of inhabitants, but this program had no more authority in law than the 1665 Concessions and Agreements that Carteret and Berkeley had announced, for Penn and his associates could not purchase what Berkeley could not sell—the right to govern the province.

Nevertheless, the proprietors named Billing governor in 1680. In 1683, the assembly that Penn and the other proprietors had created, illegally, decided that the proprietors had no right to govern the colony, and just as illegally took that right upon themselves. They selected their own governor and council.

In East Jersey, the assembly acted as though they ruled, passing laws taxing the townships, setting the price of wheat and pork, inspecting leather before it was exported, defining crimes and punishments, and establishing courts and fees for judges. The assembly also resisted paying customs duties to New York, which brought down Andros's wrath. In 1676, he began to collect the duties, and four years later he claimed the governorship of East Jersey. When Philip Carteret protested, Andros arrested him.

George Carteret, the proprietor, died in 1680, and East Jersey was sold by his estate to a group of eleven Quakers, once again led by Penn. When Andros was recalled in 1681, Philip Carteret resumed his post, but he antagonized the assembly by resorting to the same high-handed ways that had made Andros so despised. In March 1688, the duke took a direct hand in the matter, causing both colonies to forfeit their charters, but James lost his throne that June (in a "Glorious Revolution" discussed in the next chapter), and in 1692 the proprietors resumed control.

Again tumult reigned in both Jerseys. The non-Quaker inhabitants had never accepted the authority of the proprietary government, and after 1692 brayed even louder against the proprietary interest. Led by men like Lewis Morris in East Jersey, a man who had no love for the Quakers, committees of safety assembled and closed the courts. Remonstrances and petitions flew to England against the proprietors.

So diverse were the claimants that disputes over land titles and business deals were almost impossible to disentangle. North Jersey settlers could claim title through the proprietors, purchases from Indians, and royal grants. Dutch settlers had even earlier titles. Disputes over titles in Perth Amboy, for example, provided fees for three generations of colonial lawyers. Some of the suits were still going strong when the colonies declared their independence from England.

For confirmation of their land titles, a promise that the two colonies would be joined (and not subordinated to New York), and a guarantee of religious toleration for Quakers, the proprietors finally surrendered control of government. In 1702, the Jerseys were again united as a crown colony. Morris, rewarded by the crown for cutting the ground from under the proprietors, became one of the largest landholders in the new colony and was named acting governor.

A Mixed Multitude

New Jersey hosted a mixed multitude. Morris's power base was in the north of the colony, where by 1700 Scottish Presbyterians and English Congregationalists lived in the New England way. The streets of Newark, for example, featured square, two-story clapboard houses that just as easily might have lined streets of New Haven, Connecticut, from which many Newarkites had come. Dutch Reformed settlers flowed into the northern part of the colony from New York.

In the south, Quakers dominated. The Quaker meetinghouses in West Jersey were constructed of stone, with slate shingles, like an English Midlands farmer's house—solid and substantial, but plain. So, too, the Quakers practiced plain speech, with its "thees" and "thous," and plain dress. The idea was to avoid excess, whether in eating, speech, or manners.

Among the Quakers, a plain style of pleading suits predominated. In Gloucester

County, for example, the courts of common pleas allowed parties to begin with complaints and petitions framed in the simplest, nontechnical terms. In the records one occasionally finds a word in Latin or "law French," but often as not it was misused and almost always misspelled. Most often, litigants came to court and made a declaration of the facts. When both parties arrived for the sessions of the court, the case was then and there tried, compromised, or referred to arbitrators. Until the middle 1690s, the vast majority of cases were handled in a single session of the court; thereafter, most cases were continued for no more than two sessions.

Quaker litigants often asked the monthly meeting rather than the courts to resolve disputes. The meeting served the spiritual needs of the Quakers and helped to administer everyday affairs. The quieter voices of the women's meeting reminded Quakers of their commitment to loving fellowship. The women's meeting could not engage in public affairs, but it did have charge of training young women, mediating domestic troubles, and framing policy for educating the young. Quaker women of high standing in the community formed an inner circle of respected spiritual advisers at the women's meeting. They took the lead in giving or withholding certificates for women who wished to attend another meeting. In addition, they inquired into the fitness of couples who planned marriage, not so subtlely prompting young women to marry within the Society of Friends.

As in their legal disputes, the Quakers of the Delaware Valley never turned away from the hurly-burly of the material world, but within their domestic relations they created a refuge from the outside. Quaker virtues of honesty and tenderness were basic to private as well as public conduct, and the Quaker family was based on affectionate relationships. Women had higher status within Quaker marriages than in other English households. Child rearing was tender and supportive, bordering on the permissive. Little use was made of shaming, Quaker parents preferring earnest admonition and good examples. Although many parents did not have formal educations, they insisted that their children read and write. Penn himself had written on the subject: "For their learning, be liberal. Spare no cost, for by such parsimony all is lost that is saved; but let it be useful knowledge, such as is consistent with truth and godliness, not cherishing a vain conversation or idle mind."

The Quakers of New Jersey believed that time must be redeemed by hard work, but did not drive themselves to work hard just because they feared that failure signified damnation. They acted not as stewards, but as trustees of the fruits of the earth, and so condemned dishonest dealing and accumulation of wealth for its own sake. Of course, not everyone was able (or willing) to live up to these ideals, and the monthly meeting had to deal with disputes over prices and wages all the time. Other Quakers disregarded the injunction to do charitable works and share the wealth, amassing land and possessions instead. Still, the ideal was self-imposed peace and harmony, and for much of the time, many Quakers obeyed this inner dictum.

Despite the Quakers' fondness for learning, New Jersey boasted no printing presses until midcentury, no regular newspaper, no library until one was founded in Burlington in 1758, and no schools of higher learning until a group of Presbyterians, seeking to train their own ministers, arranged for the College of New Jersey to sit in Elizabethtown. Six years later, after agents for the group toured England and Scotland raising funds for the college, its operations moved to Princeton.

The Garden Colony

Rustic, isolated New Jersey farmers became the butt of jokes and the stuff of folklore. It was said that New Jersey marshland mosquitoes were so numerous and pesky that the Swedish immigrants in the 1640s named their settlement Fort "Myggenborg"—Fort Mosquito. The names of New Jersey villages had a prosaic quality absent from some of the more grandiose efforts of the colony's neighbors. Most of them reflected the geography of the area, like Sandy Hook or Barrentown. Others recalled a local memory, like Bear Swamp. Occupations such as bog iron mining gave names to Colliers Mills and Hanover Forge, just as Fishing Creek and Bivalve reminded travelers of the fishing industry.

In a tribute to ethnic diversity, English New Jerseyites often retained Dutch descriptive place names, in which a *kill* was a stream, a *cobble* was a hill, a *gat* was a passage, a *vly* was a valley, a *vlachte* was a meadow, a *wyck* was a town, a *dael* was a dale, and a *dorp* was a village. But the English speakers of New Jersey lost the Dutch meanings, so they invented stories to fit the names. For example, Kill Van Kull, the straits between New Jersey and Staten Island, should be Van Kull's River, but the English told the story of one of Henry Hudson's sailors who "killed one gull" as the *Half Moon* sailed past the site.

Not to be outdone in their old tongue, New Jersey's Dutch farmers tried to preserve their language, particularly in the worship services, but ended up borrowing words from English, Indian dialects, and Africans living in the colony. In turn, the Dutch shared their words with others. Thus the Leni-Lenapes cooked *pankok* after watching the Dutch prepare their *pannekoek*. The English called them "pancakes." The result was a rural dialect that featured "New Jerseyisms" like "pot cheese" from the Dutch *pot kees*, which English speakers elsewhere recognized as "cottage cheese."

As the frequent reference to food in the folklore suggests, New Jersey turned out to be a farmer's paradise. As one traveled west, northern New Jersey coastal marsh gave way to richly forested Piedmont and highlands of chestnut and oak. In central and southern New Jersey, a broad coastal plain was watered by streams flowing east to the Atlantic and west to the Delaware. The shore itself was an extension of the Atlantic littoral—sandy and low lying. New Jersey farmers occupied the Delaware River and Atlantic Ocean shores first, slowly moving inland.

The farmers' major crops were English wheat, peas, oats and barley, garden vegetables, and fruits, along with livestock. Some of the land on every farm was devoted to apple orchards and table crops like turnips, onions, potatoes, cabbage, beets, and carrots. As a Swedish visitor observed some years later, "Near almost every farm was a spacious orchard full of peaches and apple trees, and in some of them the fruit had fallen from the trees in such quantities as to cover nearly the whole surface of the ground." A good portion of the produce of these farms went to local markets or were exchanged as part of the household economy. But another portion was destined for distant markets, some as far away as the West Indies or the Mediterranean.

A farmer's neighbors cooperated to raise houses and barns, but hired skilled craftsmen when necessary. Most farmers turned to their own families or a few hired hands to plant and harvest. A few slaves worked in the fields, in groups of two or three alongside their masters' family members. Unlike great planters, New Jersey masters did not assume the pose of patriarchs or regard slavery as a natural part of a divinely ordained social hierarchy.

PENNSYLVANIA

After 1681, a new colony—Pennsylvania—occupied the opposite side of the Delaware River from New Jersey. Penn could have contented himself with the development of West Jersey, but his restlessness and his declining finances led him to a bolder stroke. He petitioned the crown to settle outstanding debts to his dead father by giving him the land between Virginia and New York.

His petition for a proprietary grant was perfectly timed. The Stuarts were fending off a movement in Parliament to exclude James from the succession to the throne, and Penn was a strong supporter of the duke. In November 1680, a draft of Penn's charter was sent by Charles II to his legal advisers. Unlike earlier proprietary charters, whose boundaries and terms were often vague, Penn's charter underwent strict scrutiny by the chief justice of England and other royal legal experts to ensure that Pennsylvanians (unlike the settlers of the Carolinas and the Jerseys) obeyed the laws of England. Royal fears that the inhabitants of the new colony would ignore the laws on trade initially cost Penn the right to control the military, give the laws, and settle churches, but subsequent amendments restored these powers, and the charter issued in February 1681.

The Haven

Penn quickly moved to make his colony a haven for his coreligionists, Quakers long persecuted in England, Wales, and Puritan New England. Penn and his sales agents lobbied diligently among the wealthy Quakers of the Society of Free Traders, offering special privileges for purchases of ten thousand acres or more. Although he courted the "first purchasers" who bought the largest tracts, his prospectus (once again called the Concessions) guaranteed fifty acres to every servant after their term of service. To all prospective immigrants he promised: "Those that go into a foreign plantation, their industry there is worth more than if they stay'd at home, the product of their labor being in commodities of a superior nature to those of this country. . . . More being produced and imported than we can spend here, we export it to other countries in Europe, which brings in money."

In April 1681, he sent his cousin William Markham to the Delaware Valley to inform its inhabitants of his plans and survey the land. Markham chose the site for the future capital of the colony, Philadelphia, and purchased the land from Swedes living there. In October, the first group of settlers left for the colony. Most came from London and its environs, but the original 587 purchasers included Welsh and Germans. Francis Daniel Pastorius, a Frankfurt lawyer and agent for German immigrants, obtained a grant to the north and west of the city for his countrymen and women, and "Germantown" soon filled with immigrants. Nearly half were craftspeople, but a fair number were well-to-do merchants and professional people.

In the first two years of settlement, four thousand men, women, and children sailed up the Delaware and alit on the Pennsylvania side, and by 1685 there were eight thousand people in Penn's new colony. Fully one-third were indentured servants, joined by a mass of yeomen farmers and artisans. The wealthiest purchasers did not come, sending others to farm their land and build houses in the city. Still, a good number of the lesser purchasers removed to Pennsylvania, and they became the elite in this truncated social hierarchy.

Penn's prospectus for the new colony became its Frame of Government (1682). Penn could have distributed the land in his grant and run its government as he chose, but from the start he encouraged participatory self-government among the colonists. Although he believed in government by "men of wisdom and virtue," he opened the door to far broader power sharing.

Scholars believe that Penn had read James Harrington's utopian essay, *The Commonwealth of Oceana* (1656). In this imaginary community, there were no hereditary kings or nobles, for Oceana was a republic. Offices were to be elective, rotated, and based upon the consent of "the people." Servants, women, and the poor could not vote, because, Harrington supposed, they did not exercise independent judgment. So revolutionary were Harrington's views (and so imprudent was his continued advocacy of them after the restoration of Charles II) that the king clamped Harrington in jail on a phony charge of conspiracy. He died there, insane, in 1677.

Penn no doubt knew Harrington's fate, but shared Harrington's commitment to rotation of officeholders and participation by the "democracy" in government. In both his West Jersey Concessions and his Frames of Government for Pennsylvania, Penn provided for a council composed of the leading planters and an elective assembly, the latter with the power to accept or reject his and the council's legislation.

The rights Penn guaranteed included jury trial, which had saved the Quakers from conviction in English courts, along with moderate punishment for crimes, modest fees for civil litigation, the right to counsel, and protection against arbitrary searches and seizures. Social misconduct, wantonness, abuse of officials, and violent conduct were punishable, but the penalties were far less severe than anywhere else in the king's domains or the colonies. In December 1682, Penn confirmed the assembly's act that all who declared Jesus to be the Son of God could worship as they saw fit, a grant of religious toleration that only Roger Williams's surpassed.

Pennsylvania's Indian relations followed the pattern of mutuality, trust, and fairness that Penn laid down for his colonists. Fortunately for his plan, the first Quaker arrivals in the Jerseys and Pennsylvania did not have to face the French or their Indian allies. As they had proved in their attack on Lewes, the Leni-Lenapes could be aggressive, but they lacked the numerical strength of the northern and western tribes. Perhaps romanticizing the realities of the situation, Pastorius depicted the Indians as paragons of simple virtue: "They strive after a sincere honesty, hold strictly to their promises, cheat and injure no one. They willingly give shelter to others, and are both useful and loyal to their guests." Pastorius, a Lutheran pietist himself, had conferred on the Leni-Lenapes the traits that the Quakers and other pietists valued, implying that they were nature's nobility.

Penn did not romanticize the Indians, but he recognized the need for peace, and his official policy was legalistic in a wholly different way from that of the Puritans. He did not deploy law to force Indians to give up their old ways. Instead, his object was a good-faith purchase of land from the heads of the tribe, followed by good-faith dealings. In aid of this goal, Penn required "that all Differences between the Planters and the Natives shall also be ended by Twelve Men, that is by Six Planters and Six Natives, that so wee may Live friendly Together, and as much as in us Lyeth, Prevent all Occasions of Heart Burnings and Mischiefs."

Philadelphia

Pennsylvania life was greatly influenced by Penn's "green country town," Philadelphia. Even before he came to the New World, Penn had designed the layout of the city. Probably influenced by plans that architect Christopher Wren had drafted for the rebuilding of London after the great fire of 1666, Penn planned rectangular housing blocks interspersed with open squares. The green squares were not intended as common land for grazing, but as fire breaks. Penn then exercised the skills he had honed as a religious tract writer to advertise the new town to merchants. "Your city-lot is an whole street . . . that by God's blessing . . . will naturally grow in . . . reputation and profit. I am sure I have not turned my back upon any offer that tended to its prosperity."

Once he saw Markham's choice for the location of the city, Penn expected settlement to move from the Delaware River on the eastern side of the town to the Schuylkill River on the western edge of Philadelphia, but the Delaware River, with its wide, winding course to the sea, proved too attractive a commercial venue for the founder's plan to develop exactly as he had foreseen. Soon jetties and rude ware-houses ranged up and down the Delaware shore. The Society of Free Traders grabbed the lots along Dock Creek, the best frontage on the river.

The Delaware not only connected the town to the sea, it tied the town to the coun-tryside. Creeks and streams that fed the Delaware powered mills for grinding the farmers' wheat. To the west, the Susquehanna Valley teemed with game. Its soils were rich, and soon farmers spread across it.

Penn had recruited merchants, but even he could not have predicted how attrac-tive his colony would be for them. They dominated not only the new city but the colony's politics for the next twenty-five years. Between 1682 and 1689, over fifty mer-chants set up shop in Philadelphia. Another thirty arrived by 1700. Like the first planters of Virginia, most of the first merchants were not able to pass on to sons and grandsons their businesses, and by 1720 new families dominated the Philadelphia merchant community. Disease—the Delaware swamps bred malarial mosquitoes—bankruptcy, and the rawness of the colony caused the turnover.

A Disputatious People

Penn's plans for economic development ran smack into the colony's raucous polit-ical life, though the New Jersey experience should have warned Penn that liberal laws encouraged partisanship. The immigrants resented the power of the absentee large landholders; Quaker versus non-Quaker and English versus non-English tensions erupted; wealthy Quakers battled with poorer Quakers over the assignment of real es-tate plots; settlers of the lower counties (later the independent colony of Delaware) ob-jected to rule by an upriver clique; and no one wanted to pay quitrents to Penn.

In 1683, Penn agreed to revise the Frame of Government, reducing the size of the council from seventy-two to eighteen to make the government more efficient, and during his first stay in the colony, from 1682 to 1684, he tried to retain day-to-day governance in his own hands. Penn's attempt to pack the assembly seats with his supporters failed, and he had to fight to keep his veto power over legislation, even though the charter explicitly gave him this power. By 1684, he and his council were battling a recalcitrant assembly majority. Flexing its muscles, the assembly even im-peached judge Nicholas More, a Penn supporter, for misconduct in office.

Penn left for England in 1684 and stayed there until 1699, first to answer charges against his misconduct in the colony; then, after 1688, to explain his loyalty to the ousted James II; and finally, to straighten out his personal finances. In his absence, loose and shifting factions became hard and fast parties as Penn's supporters lined up against dissident Quakers, with the settlers of the lower counties sniping at both sides. The Pennsylvania assembly (like the assembly of West Jersey in 1683) had tasted self-government and liked it. Quakers who had once distrusted the power of the English government eagerly vied to use government to hound one another.

The Quaker ideal of a "Holy Experiment" in the wilderness became a contest among those claiming to be holier than others. Free of persecution, Quakers split into religious factions, posing, for the first time, tests of doctrine for "true" believers. Religious contests became political ones and vice versa.

When George Keith, a Quaker who came to the colonies in 1685 and to Philadelphia in 1689, used the meeting to preach that well-to-do Quakers like Penn were "fools, idiots, silly souls, hypocrites, hereticks, heathens, rotten ranters, tyrants, and Popes," he threatened the political foundations of the colony as well as its religious harmony. Many of his followers were political and economic opponents of the Quaker elite, and the dispute over religious orthodoxy was for these men and women a way to challenge the hegemony of the well-to-do. The meetinghouse became a place of imprecation.

After three years of royal rule of the colony (1691–1694), Penn regained most but not all of his chartered powers. He returned to the colony in 1699 but only stayed until 1701. Even his presence could not quell the assembly's determination to usurp the chartered powers of the proprietor. His young secretary, James Logan, had become a reliable agent for the proprietary interests in colonial politics, but neither Logan nor his master could shake free of the opposition of the assembly. One telling sidelight: in these years of tumultuous politics and personal backbiting, Pennsylvania courts heard more cases of slander and defamation than New England or Chesapeake courts, despite the grim authoritarianism of officials in the former and the touchy pride of the planters in the latter.

Penn died in 1718, after a lingering illness, having tried, unsuccessfully, to sell his colony back to the crown. His "Holy Experiment" was a shambles. His sons and grandsons would succeed him as proprietor and have no better luck in curbing the factiousness of their colonists, even though they abandoned the Society of Friends for the Church of England. But in the bustle of political and religious dissent, and the hustle of business activity, Pennsylvania became something no one had foreseen—a remarkably open society.

DELAWARE

The sandy coastal shore of Delaware remained a backwater of settlement well into the eighteenth century. A part of the Duke of York's grant and later of the Penn proprietary, few Europeans stayed. The Leni-Lenapes were not forced off their lands, but disease carried off much of the Indian population before 1700. The survivors retreated across the Delaware River, then beyond the Susquehanna, and finally found a home in Canada.

Whose Colony?

Although the Dutch claimed the area as part of New Netherland, their sovereignty existed only on paper. A reconnaissance ended in disaster when the Dutch and the

Indians came to blows over a stolen tin Dutch coat of arms. The Dutch and Indians agreed to put the incident behind them, and in 1632 the Dutch obtained permission to harpoon whales along the coast in the region that the Dutch called Swanendael (Swan's dale). The settlement failed, but its brief existence prevented Leonard Calvert and his Marylanders from absorbing the land into their colony.

In 1638, the New Sweden Company sent its vessels to Delaware, and at Fort Christina, named after the queen of Sweden, established a trading post. Its leader was Peter Minuit, the former and now-disgraced governor of New Netherland. Minuit remembered what happened to the first Dutch intruders at Lewes and bought the land from the Indians according to both Indian and Dutch protocols.

The colony survived because the twenty-eight residents bought pelts and tobacco from the Indians and paid off the debt the company owed to its Dutch and Swedish investors. Swedes and Finns expanded the little colony, bringing with them their Lutheran faith, the log cabin, rye and barley, and cattle. They also built the first brewery in the region. Governor Johan Printz practiced a good-neighbor policy with the Indians, despite some provocations. But few men would come to Delaware unless they could bring their wives, and the population remained small—no more than 183 settlers in 1647.

The Dutch in New York, despite orders from Holland not to disturb the Swedes, offered provocations of their own—for example, building forts to cut off Swedish trade with the Indians. Printz begged the home country for aid, then went to Sweden to lobby for the colony. A relief force arrived in New Sweden in 1654, but the Swedish initiative only provoked Stuyvesant, and he led an invasion force that overawed the Swedes in August 1655.

New Sweden became part of New Netherland, renamed New Amstel. Still, few Dutch relocated of their own free will, and even paupers from the workhouse refused to journey to the Delaware coast. Those who came felt isolated and soon fled to Maryland. The only industry that flourished were the breweries—by 1663 the Swedish brewery had two Dutch rivals.

In 1664, the English took control of the colony. The western shore of the colony remained in Maryland's hands, despite Nicolls's attempts to pry it loose. Again, few settlers chose Delaware as their home, in part because the coast was exposed to raiding during the Anglo-Dutch wars. Andros brought the full weight of the duke's authority to the little colony in 1675 and ran it as the generous master of a personal fiefdom.

In 1682, Delaware became part of the Penn grant. The three counties (sometimes called the "lower counties") of the grant gained all the rights of Pennsylvania settlers, in addition to which they were to have their own assembly. Delaware chose to join with the larger colony in an Act of Union concluded in December 1682. Its assembly remained independent. When Penn's council lost power, and political turmoil erupted, much as it had in New Jersey, Delaware leaders pressed for self-government. From 1690 to 1693, the lower counties ruled themselves. Although Penn healed the breach for a time, in 1701 he conceded to the lower counties' desire for separation, and in 1704 Delaware became a distinct colony under the proprietorship of the Penns.

The Fruits of Labor

Political unrest did not prevent Delaware from exploiting its geographical and agricultural advantages. New Castle (formerly the Dutch port of Fort Casimir) on the Delaware River became a major port town, and New Castle County was second only to Philadelphia County in taxable wealth in the 1690s. In the 1740s, a traveler recorded its appearance: "This town stands upon stony ground just upon the water, there being from thence a large prospect eastward towards the Bay of Delaware and the province of the Jerseys. The houses are chiefly brick, built after the Dutch model."

Tobacco, early a profitable crop, drew settlers from other colonies. Marylanders brought their slaves and their tobacco know-how to the southern counties of Kent and Sussex, where slavery became a fixture of life.

Pennsylvanians filled out northern New Castle County, and turned it into a garden for the city. Their mercantile interests led to the establishment of Wilmington on the Christina River in 1739. From the first, this market town attracted Quaker merchants, and soon surpassed New Castle in wealth and population. The southern part of the colony resembled the tobacco coast, while the northern part maintained ties to the eastern Pennsylvania region.

––––––––

The middle colonies were chartered under semifeudal precepts, but men like Nicolls and Penn recognized that wise and prudent governors must accept the fact of diversity. Penn went the farthest in this direction, not only in toleration of religious differences but also in conceding that the people had a rightful place in government and that guarantees of freedom of conscience, jury trial, and representative assemblies made a polity stronger. So, too, in the realm of economics, Penn understood that people who owned land would have a stake in keeping order and participating in government. Though he did not adopt Harrington's idea of equal distribution of land (after all, Harrington had the advantage of inventing a commonwealth), Penn set aside small lots as well as extensive manors.

If personal empowerment and improvement seem exemplified in Penn's departures from seventeenth-century conventions of political and social order, some were left out of the program. Penn opposed slavery, but Quakers acquired and sold slaves. Quaker women had more status than women in other cultures, but their role was domestic, not public. The Quakers made ample provisions for the poor, but believed that poverty was the natural state for some people.

Among non-Quakers in the early middle colonies, divisions between the privileged and the subordinate were even sharper. The Dutch and the English in New York not only owned slaves, they participated in the international slave trade. Among the Dutch, women actually lost status as "Anglicization" set in. Congregating in waterfront shanties and back streets, New York City's poor had already become a problem. For the unemployed, the hungry, and the disfavored, the high promise of the middle colonies meant little.

8

The Critical Years, 1675–1700

The years between 1675 and 1700 constituted a critical period in the history of the European colonies in North America. Powerful forces threatened to undermine the still fragile colonies. Colonial farming and timbering methods had denuded the land in the first settlements. As the settlers moved inland, widespread and devastating conflict with the native peoples again erupted. Internal disturbances imperiled the colonies, as factions of the ruling party battled for power among themselves and landless laborers demanded redress from oppressive elites. In 1688, England erupted in civil war, a political upheaval that worsened existing colonial political unrest. A result of the overthrow of the English government, a new European war reached out to the edges of the empire, pitting the French against the English colonists. The violence and uncertainty unleashed fears that the end of the world was near, and that the devil and his witches had targeted God's chosen people in New England for a terrible fate.

THE END OF THE MIDDLE GROUND

When colonial and Indian presence in a region was roughly equal, and both sides needed the other, diplomacy, trade, and social intercourse created a "middle ground." On this middle ground, people from different cultures could engage in creative, sometimes even deliberate, misreadings of one another's culture and still find ways to negotiate. If neither side fully understood the other's ways, so long as both sides respected each other, some accommodation could be found when trouble arose. On the edges of the great European empires in America, in the Great Lakes region, for example, and along the Mohawk River, such middle ground provided time and space for gift giving, speech making, and amity. But in 1675, this system began to crumble.

1675

In 1675, the backwoods of the English settlements were alive with rumors and rumblings of war. The Iroquois of New York were grow-

I can remember the time, when I used to sleep quietly without workings in my thoughts, whole nights together, but now it is other wayes with me. When all are fast [asleep] about me, and no eye open, but his [God's] who ever waketh, my thoughts are upon things past, upon the awfull dispensation of the Lord towards us; upon his wonderfull power and might, in carrying of us through so many difficulties, in returning us in safety, and suffering none to hurt us.

—Mary Rowlandson's narrative of her captivity during King Philip's War, 1675–1676

ing restless, sending raiding parties into Canada, the Ohio Valley, and the Great Lakes region seeking furs and captives. The Indian peoples they met, like the Shawnees and Miamis of Ohio and the Cherokees of Carolina, either fled or huddled in makeshift multitribal camps.

The French and Spanish reached out to the refugees, offering trade goods and protection if they would join the French or the Spanish side in the imperial conflict with England. In response, the English promised better trade goods if the Indians would pledge their loyalty and war on the Indians allied to the French and Spanish. In South Carolina, unscrupulous Scots traders and land-hungry English planters induced the Indians to raid one another and sell the captives as slaves to the English. It was exactly what the English philosopher Thomas Hobbes, some years earlier, had meant when he said that the state of nature was "the war of each against all."

Garacontié's World

In New York, the Onondaga orator and statesman Garacontié was plying all his oratorical skills, mastery of native diplomatic courtesies, and indefatigable efforts to balance one European power against another and protect the Iroquois League. To placate the French after the Iroquois made war on France's Great Lakes Indian allies, Garacontié publicly converted to French Catholicism, offered up ten Onondaga youths for instruction in the faith at Montreal, and built churches for Jesuit missionaries in Onondaga villages.

But Garacontié needed help the French could not provide against the Iroquois' implacable southern enemy, the Susquehannock Indians of Maryland and Pennsylvania. With the connivance of Maryland authorities, the Susquehannocks made war on the Iroquois. To their side, the Susquehannocks called on the Iroquois' traditional enemies, the Hurons and Ottawas of Canada, and the Shawnees and Eries of Ohio.

Then, in a turnabout worthy of the greatest of diplomats, Garacontié reoriented Iroquois loyalties to save his people. In this critical year of 1675, he accepted an offer from Edmund Andros to ally the Iroquois once and for all with the English. Although the pro-French faction among the Iroquois stayed home as Garacontié ratified the covenant chain with Andros and the English, the consequences of the new pact were momentous. The Iroquois would secure the boundaries of New York from French incursions, and Andros would convince Maryland to turn its back on the Susquehannocks.

Now the dominoes began to fall. Abandoned by their English allies, the Susquehannocks became the target of Virginians eager to open the frontier. Barbarities on both sides set the Virginia and Maryland frontiers aflame. The echoes of the war reached New England and Canada, as alliances shifted and Indian war parties numbering in the thousands crowded the pathways through the forests.

Garacontié's partner in the Iroquois about-face faced a similar crisis. Garacontié's aid allowed Andros to rationalize imperial policy on the frontier, but Andros could not impose the new policy on the colonists. In fact, the colonists refused to take part in the defense of their own frontiers unless there was an immediate danger. Moreover, insofar as the new military policy was the opening scene of the duke's play for greater control of his New York colony, the colonists refused to act the role of obedient subjects.

The Iroquois-Susquehannock War dwarfed all previous intra–Native American conflicts, but the conflagration would not have fundamentally altered relations between the European settlers and the natives had it not echoed and reinforced longer standing disputes over land use and the means for resolving disputes.

By 1675, the buffer of sparsely inhabited space between natives and newcomers in the coastal colonies was just about gone. Worse from the native viewpoint, Indian population once again spiraled downward. In Virginia, by 1685, there were just twenty-nine hundred Indians living east of the mountains. The Iroquois had suffered irreparable losses from 1620 to 1675. The Algonquians of the New England coast had dwindled to a shadow of their former number.

With the disappearance of the middle ground and the decline in Indian population, native groups were less inclined to credit European goodwill and Europeans less willing to seek peaceful ways to avoid friction and resolve disputes. The Pequot War in 1637 had demonstrated the danger when natives and newcomers found themselves standing on the same piece of land unwilling to budge in their demands, and its ferocity foretold the crisis of European-Indian relations in the last quarter of the century.

CHANGES IN THE LAND

As the Indian warriors made their silent way through the woods, the colonists faced an ecological crisis. In a cruel irony, by 1675 colonial farmers in New England and the Chesapeake had discovered that the very richness of the land that had first attracted the immigrants was losing its fertility. Without realizing the consequences of their actions, the English had fundamentally altered the ecological infrastructure of the coastal area.

When the English arrived, the environment had supported a great diversity of species. Eastern woodlands Indian horticulturalists set brush fires to clear land for planting, but their fires burned the land lightly and sweetened it with a carpet of nutrients. When they finished using their fields, they moved on, allowing the fields to become parkland, and then return to forest. These edge cultures fostered the diversity of species that the first European settlers so appreciated. Indian stone axes could not dent some of the hardwoods, and thus the natives left the climax (original growth) forests alone. In fact, Indians regarded many woodland sites as sacred and would not have disturbed them even if they could.

Plows and Axes

The English had no intention of living in harmony with the original landscape. They set about transforming woods into farms and meadows by clear cutting entire forests, leaving no trees standing. English immigrants regarded the woodland differently from the way its native inhabitants saw it. Few English men and women lived in woodlands surroundings in the Old World. The great oak forests of medieval England had long since vanished by 1600. In the English imagination, forests played host to all manner of fantastic creatures. Knowing this, Shakespeare set his fantasy *A Midsummer Night's Dream* (1594) in deep woods and populated the woods with fairies and sprites.

Not all the woodland denizens were as lighthearted as Shakespeare's Puck. In 1611, English courts uncovered a supposed coven of witches in Pendle Forest, Lancashire, that made news all over the kingdom. Neighbors had long complained about secret meetings in the woods, and readily believed stories about the mischief the forest concealed. Even the witches confessed that they had chosen the forest to conceal their meetings.

Thus when the immigrants arrived in America, the forest seemed impenetrable and ominous. The Puritans called it a "howling wilderness." The night calls of wolves, cougars, and bears terrified settlers who had never encountered anything like American wildlife. The Indians' ability to move swiftly and surely through the forests also unnerved the English, for most of them regarded the Indians as one more natural predator.

In addition to their distrust of the forest, the immigrants had practical, economic reasons to cut down the trees. One of the great attractions of America was the abundance of timber for heating. Studies of tree rings tell us that winters in England and North America were especially cold in the seventeenth century—a "little ice age"— and immigrants exhausted two to three face cords of firewood every winter. Moreover, the English-style homes the settlers reproduced in America required extensive supplies of wooden boards, framing studs, and bark shingles.

English lumbermen found overseas markets for the products of the forest. Lumber mills throughout the colonies devoured whole forests for the West Indies and the British Isles. For the Royal Navy, the colonists exported pitch, tar, and masts for ships. Even the great hardwoods could not withstand the English onslaught. Impervious to the Indians' stone axes, the hardwoods fell before the so-called American axe (actually a Scandinavian design) with its long curved handle and its tempered metal head.

The destruction of the forest meant that animals that had lived in the woodlands lost their habitat. They either disappeared like the eastern buffalo or became predators within the settlements. The English had to set bounties on wolves because the wolves' natural prey, like deer, had declined in numbers, and wolf packs attacked sheep and calves instead.

If timbering denuded the land, English farming practices ravished it. At first, the settlers copied Indian hoe culture—building mounds of earth in which to plant corn, beans, squash, and other crops. Hoe culture does not seriously deplete the nutrients in the soil.

Soon, however, the English returned to more familiar plow culture. Unlike Indian gardens of corn and squash, grown in relatively small fields near the village, the English preferred to deep plow the land and plant their "English grasses" like barley, rye, and wheat in long, rectangular strips. The plow scarred the earth. The soils began to erode in rain and wind, and flowed down streams and rivers, leaving the land barren. Colonial planters tried to use fish bones and animal excrement as fertilizers, but lost fertility could not be recovered, and the land went to meadow and scrub.

Livestock Breeding and Herding

Colonial herds of cattle, sheep, and pigs further damaged the native ecology. More colonial wealth was invested in herds of cows and bulls than in any other chattel (personal property) except slaves, and European domestic animals ran riot over the land. The attractiveness of many New England town sites lay in the proximity of saltwater or marsh grasses for that purpose, and farmers cut, stacked, and dried the grasses as winter feed. English cattle also vied with deer for forage. In the Southwest, cattle competed with buffalo for water and food.

Some Indians made a living as herdsmen for colonial farmers, and a few sachems had herds of cattle of their own, but Indians grieved when cattle replaced deer in the meadows. Hunting deer proved a man's spiritual power and physical prowess. No one hunted cattle. Deer meat and skins provided the Indians with food and clothing, but cattle were the colonists' property and off limits to the Indians.

Although the colonists most prized their cattle, it was the pig that colonized the North American scrublands. Pigs are omnivorous and, allowed to run wild, made no distinction between Indian fields and crops, colonial gardens, and wild foods. Indians complained constantly to colonial authorities about the damage that scavenging pigs did to Indian gardens, but rarely received any compensation.

More solicitous of the colonists' individual property rights, colonial governments passed laws requiring owners to identify their animals. The most common identifying mark was a distinctive cropping of their ears. Clerks of courts drew pictures of the crop marks into county court record books.

Runaway servants and slaves, strolling poor laborers, and Indians sometimes made meals of wandering pigs, but had to pay fines or face prison terms when the owners were able to point to the crop marks in court. For this reason, one enterprising Pennsylvania thief cut off and hid the head of a pig he had stolen and cooked.

Horses cost too much for the average English farmer to own—New Englanders relied on oxen to pull their plows and wagons, but wild horses came into their own in the Southwest. Horses allowed Coronado's troops to travel through the vast expanse of Arizona, New Mexico, and Texas. By the beginning of the eighteenth century, one Spanish visitor to the region remarked that the land was "overrun" with wild ponies, called *mesteños* (mustangs). The mustangs competed with the buffalo for water and grazing in the Southwest, and in times of drought denied to the buffalo vital food sources.

At first the animals awed the Indians, but soon the Apaches, Navajos, and Pueblos owned and rode horses. Plains Indians like the Pawnees, Comanches, and Sioux entirely rebuilt their cultures to take advantage of horses.

The colonists left the trapping of beaver and other fur-bearing animals to the Indians, but in inducing the natives to overhunt fur-bearing animals, the colonists further disturbed the ecology of the New World. Untended beaver dams collapsed, spilling rich soils downstream. Without the dams, fast-running northern streams carried soils to the sea. Along with clear cutting of timber, deep plowing, and the explosion of domestic livestock, the extirpation of the beaver left the colonies far poorer in land, plants, and animals. The English thus left their mark in a way that millennia of native occupation had not: the land was drained, exposed, and wasted.

As the colonists discovered that their style of farming consumed land and left it infertile, they determined to bring more and more land under European-style cultivation. This led directly to confrontation with the Indians whose remaining farmland the colonists coveted. The confrontation came first in New England, and it was catastrophic for everyone concerned.

KING PHILIP'S WAR IN NEW ENGLAND

By the 1670s, New England Indians realized that their way of life faced extinction. On the one hand, their traditional hunting grounds and farmland shrank daily. On the other lay the temptations of assimilation to European ways. Indeed, the more that English missionaries promised the Indians eternal life if they would abandon old beliefs and practices, the more tension they created in Indian society.

At the same time, as British governments threw their support to the Iroquois in the war against the Susquehannocks, every Indian leader within the English sphere of interest knew that the balance of power in the Indian world had forever changed. New England Indians opposed to English policies would have to look to French Canada for support or forever concede supremacy to the English. The tinderbox of frayed New England Algonquian nerves only needed a single match to explode. An angry, humiliated, and frustrated Wampanoag sachem named Metacom lit it. King Philip's War in New England (1675–1676) was the result.

The Indian Devil

From the moment the war ended, observers disagreed about its character and significance. For the Puritans who lived through it and wrote their story, Metacom was satanic. In part, the Puritans' unwillingness to see the Indian side of the quarrel as it escalated grew from frustration with missionary efforts. They had convinced themselves that the Indians could be converted. Ministers like John Eliot told his Massachusetts Indian friends that they must "be civilized, by being brought from their scattered and wild course of life, unto civil co-habitations and government." In 1654, they consented to be "examined" to determine if they were truly ready for conversion. "What is God?" Eliot asked them, and they replied, "God is eternal, infinite, wise, holy, just."

Converts so spiritually open to preaching surely would not consider violence against those who had opened the Indians' way to salvation. The missionaries reported that converted Indians attended church, cut their hair, practiced monogamy, put up dividers between men's and women's quarters in their dwellings, and became year-round farmers. In abandoning their "naked" state and their greasy deerskin breechcloths and shawls, they had visibly renounced the savage and adopted civilized ways. By one missionary's count, in 1674 there had been eleven hundred sincere conversions.

When converts joined non-Christian Indians in war against the settlers, all of those comforting assumptions crashed to the ground. Increase Mather, the intellectual spokesman for the Boston ministerial association, concluded that the rebels were superstitious primitives easily duped by the devil. They mistook the devil, whom they take to be "a tall man, [dressed] in black cloths," for God. They forsook the "blessed design" of peace and conversion that the ministers offered. Such an opponent was hardly worth hearing out, much less an object of fair treatment.

King Philip

Metacom—"King Philip" in English records—must have understood the irony of his English name. By baptizing him as one of their own, his English neighbors denied him an Indian identity and placed him under English law. That they also styled him king demonstrated that they still did not understand that Indian sachems never ruled their fellow men and women, though some colonists regarded the title as a joke and tittered at the very idea of an Indian king. Yet Metacom had begun to act among his own people like a European potentate, demanding absolute loyalty.

Throughout the 1660s, Metacom chaffed at Plymouth Colony's increasing control over the Wampanoags. Through purchase and fraud, Rhode Island and Plymouth farmers nibbled away at Wampanoag territory, and they also stole Indian cattle. His attempts to frighten off speculators in the 1660s had failed, and in 1671 the colony disarmed his warriors (or thought it had, for the Wampanoags had been secreting away muskets and ammunition for years). Worse was to come. In 1672, he was forced to bow to the colony in a disgraceful treaty. Under it, he could not defend his people without the express consent of the Plymouth government, or sell any of his lands without its approval. Thus he was no longer able to play off Massachusetts against Plymouth—the one tried-and-true tactic of every Indian sachem.

Plymouth's insults infuriated Metacom, but Governor Josiah Winslow did not see the peril. He placed his confidence for the defense of the colony in the militia system that he had created. Each town had bodies of armed men drawn from the freeholders. They drilled each year. He did not realize that they had little knowledge of how to fight a hit-and-run war in the forests, the very skill they would need if Metacom began raiding the towns.

The murder of John Sassamon, a former Metacom ally turned informer, raised the stakes for both sides. Sassamon discovered that Metacom was making plans for war, and rushed to tell Governor Winslow. Winslow dismissed the report, saying that "one can hardly believe them even when they speak the truth," but Sassamon paid with his life for his loyalty to the English. On his return from Plymouth, three of Metacom's warriors ambushed him and dumped his corpse in a pond. Another Christian Indian claimed to have witnessed the act and informed on the murderers. On June 8, 1675, the three defendants were tried before a mixed jury of English and native converts, and condemned to death.

If Winslow did not appreciate Sassamon's sacrifice, he might have paid more attention to Benjamin Church, one of his militia captains. In early June 1675, Church attended a council at the Saconnet Indian village as the guest of the female sachem, Awashunks. Metacom and his advisers arrived to plead for her support, and Church replied on behalf of the colony. Church told all this to Winslow, but the governor did not act until Metacom struck at Swansea on June 24. Metacom burned houses and corncribs, and Plymouth called for aid from Rhode Island and Massachusetts and marshaled its troops to chase the Wampanoag chief. Metacom fled from Mount Hope, his home village, and killed ten English settlers in his path. Had the English pursued him immediately, they might have ended the uprising then and there, for his band was reduced to a few men, and he had no allies. But he slipped through their fingers and found refuge with the Narragansetts.

A General Uprising of the Indians

What had been little more than brush fire now became conflagration. All the tensions simmering beneath the surface burst into flame. One of the converted Indians, retreating from a smoldering Medfield later that year, tacked a note to a tree explaining how many Indians felt: "Thou English man hath provoked us to anger and wrath and we care not though we have war with you this 21 years for there are many of us [who] . . . have nothing but our lives to loose but thou hast many fair houses cattell and much good things." Hopelessness motivated the Indians. In response, the English arrogantly retaliated by making war on the Narragansetts, a dangerous potential foe, but until the attack a neutral in the war. Soon there were no neutrals.

Over the course of a year of brutal on-the-job training, the New England militia learned the art of war in the woods—firing from cover at targets as they appeared, setting ambushes and avoiding ambushes, and burning villages and fields to deny shelter and food to the enemy. Still, the militia could not stop small bands of Indian warriors from sacking the settlements at the edges of the colonies.

Pocumtuck, for example, was a small community of former Dedham men and women near the confluence of the winding Pocumtuck River and the "Great River" (the Connecticut), in north-central Massachusetts. Its rolling meadows, in spring a floodplain of the Pocumtuck River, had been the home of Algonquian-speaking Indians for hundreds of years, but they were victims of Iroquois expansionism in the seventeenth century, and the land seemed deserted when the settlers occupied it. Three weeks into King Philip's War, the Indians returned, drove the English off, and burned the village. (When the war was over, the English came back and renamed the site Deerfield, full well knowing that its position on the invasion route into New England from Canada would expose them to further depredations.)

Colonial unity of purpose would have shortened the war, but troops from the seaboard towns refused to march out into the western regions for fear of exposing their homes to retaliatory raids from Indians who lived on the coast. Connecticut, Plymouth, and Rhode Island cooperated with Massachusetts, but New York could not provide much help. Andros had other priorities. Fortunately, from the colonists' point of view, the Indians had no greater sense of unity than the English. Andros's Mohawk allies razed Algonquian villages in western New England. The Mohegans and their old adversary, the Pequots, both fought alongside the English against the Narragansetts, who had aided the English in the Pequot War.

Women and children on both sides felt the full fury of the war. Because the principal tactic was sudden raids on villages, there was no clear line between combatants and noncombatants, and the "honors of war" (including the decent treatment of wounded enemies and the exchange of prisoners) that uniformed European forces were just then beginning to accord one another in battle did not apply in the wilderness.

The most poignant example of this slaughter of the innocents came three days after peace. A small group of Indian women and children from a group loyal to the English left their compound to gather berries on a hill. A band of militia came upon the Indians and murdered them. Making belated amends, Massachusetts authorities tried and convicted the murderers, and executed two of them.

When the Indians took women and children captive, they ransomed them or incorporated them into their tribes. They would not tarry for the weak or the wounded, however, and killed those who could not travel. Surviving prisoners' tales of their captivity, like Mary Rowlandson's, were moving testimonials of faith, hardiness, and courage in the face of terror.

Taken from her home in 1675 after watching a number of her family and friends killed or wounded, and dragged from Indian encampment to encampment, often hungry, always tired, and denied sight of her children, Rowlandson nevertheless learned a little of the Indians' language and found protectors among their number.

Ransomed when the hostilities ended, she had little sympathy for her captors' motives or plight.

Rowlandson's agony began on February 20, 1676. Her description of the attack on her fortified house is heartrending, and more so her account of the death of loved ones. Her sister, hearing that her son was dead and Mary was wounded, cried "'and lord, let me die with them,' which was no sooner said, but she was struck with a bullet and fell down dead over the threshold." Providence with a grisly twist; surely, almost irony.

Recalling that day after her release from captivity, Rowlandson mused upon the state of her sister's soul. "I hope she is reaping the fruit of her good labors, being faithful to the service of God in her place," for in her younger years, "she lay under much trouble upon spiritual accounts." The God that Mary hoped would take her sister to his bosom was there, in that place of carnage, "and by his almighty power preserved a number of us from death." Yet Rowlandson knew that it was the Indians—not God—who had chosen whom to take as captives and whom to kill. Providence would not be so arbitrary and callous—would it?

The content of Rowlandson's account distinguished it from men's. Men viewed the hardship of captivity as a test of masculinity. They took stock of directions and distances, looked for cover, and kept powder dry. Rowlandson located herself from the first in domestic pursuits, replicating in improvised fashion the everyday concerns of New England farmwives. They always kept one eye out for dangers to children. On the trail, she continued to watch over the captive children. Farm women were weavers, sewers, and menders. In captivity, Rowlandson mastered Indian dress ways. When her captors adorned themselves for a dance welcoming Puritan emissaries, she reported that the Narragansett sachem Quinnapin, her owner, "was dressed in his holland shirt, with great laces sewed at the tail of it, [and] he had his silver buttons, his white stockings, his garters were hung round with shillings, and he had girdles of wampum upon his head and shoulders." So, too, as women were the primary food preparers in New England, Rowlandson reported on the Indian menu.

She visited briefly with Metacom, evidence of her high status among the captives. He asked her if she would smoke with him; she rejected the offer, even though she had taken "a pipe or two" regularly before the raid. He meant it to be the token of a temporary truce between them (after all, he had lived as a good neighbor to many like her from his birth, and he still thought that his grievances against the English were genuine enough for some among them to see justice in his rebellion), but she now regarded it as "a bait, the devil lays." She did comply with his request that she sew a shirt for his son. Thus the devil wore homespun in her narrative.

The Consequences of the War

By midsummer 1676, colonial troops had finally driven most of the Indian raiders away from the towns. The Wampanoags and their allies, deprived of their own food sources, were starving. Metacom himself had retreated to his old town, Mount Hope, and died in an ambush that Benjamin Church set. The shot that felled him came from one of Church's Indian scouts. His killers decapitated and hacked Metacom to pieces. Church allowed his men to take portions of the body as souvenirs and stuck the late sachem's head on a pole, a gruesome reminder of the Algonquin practice of dismemberment of enemies. The rotting head became a tourist attraction.

By the end of hostilities, half of the native population had been slain or driven from New England. Most of those who fled found refuge in French Canada. Captured Indians were sold into slavery in the West Indies, a sure sentence of death. Christian Indians who served alongside the English troops and yearned for the blessing of the Christian God and the teaching of the Christian ministers were herded into compounds or isolated on coastal islands. Far from their homes and sacred places, the praying Indians succumbed to disease and want.

Little commiseration for the suffering of the loyal Indians appeared in the books and sermons that Puritans wrote during and immediately after the war. Instead, they featured one atrocity tale after another. For authors like Boston minister Increase Mather, the uprising pit the Puritans against red devils. Given such a racial interpretation of the meaning of the conflict, one could hardly expect sympathy for the Christian Indians.

Mather's hardness of heart reflected the New Englanders' losses: 5 percent of the male English population of New England died as a consequence of the war. The financial cost to the New England colonies far exceeded that of any subsequent colonial war. English survivors agreed that the war was a form of divine judgment, another in the long line of trials that God had supposedly set for his chosen people. Puritan ministers used the lessons of the war to call their congregations back to their old faith—the faith of their fathers. In jeremiads—sermons whose inspiration came from the Hebrew prophets—the clergy inveighed against backsliding and trimming.

New England's political leaders concluded that European and Indian societies could not live together. Indians must become Anglicized and live according to New England law, or they must be driven from the land. Henceforth, eastern New England was no longer multicultural. Though Indians still lived in villages next to colonial towns, walked the old trails, and practiced traditional arts and crafts, the English were masters of the land.

BACON'S REBELLION IN VIRGINIA

In somewhat different fashion, Native Americans played a crucial role in the second great crisis of the critical period of colonial history. In January 1676, the Iroquois-Susquehannock War reached the backwoods of Virginia, and its repercussions rocked the Old Dominion. Indian raids on the Maryland-Virginia border killed dozens of settlers around Piscataway Creek, and perhaps more important, the fear of Indian raids raced through the frontier communities. Homesteaders fled to the coast, their atrocity stories growing more frightening with each retelling.

Tidewater planters joined the frontier families in demanding that the government act, but Governor William Berkeley refused to move precipitously. He knew that a punitive expedition against one group of Indians could easily become an all-out war. But Governor Berkeley had little chance to weigh his options coolly or to persuade Virginians to exercise patience. In complex but compelling ways, the raids and the rumors exacerbated deeper tensions within Virginia politics and society, tensions for which he, in large measure, was responsible.

The Green Spring Faction and Nathaniel Bacon

In 1676, Virginia wore two faces. Yeoman farmers, many of them former servants, still struggled to make ends meet. Those men and women who were still indentured servants knew that their chance to break the cycle of poverty was growing slimmer. The price of tobacco had fallen, crushing the hopes of the smaller farmers.

For a lucky few, Virginia offered a different prospect. For well-to-do planters, the rude cabins of the first generation were giving way to two-story manors, houses that were large enough to hold eight rooms with parlors to greet visitors, like Green Spring, the home of Governor Berkeley. The new houses marked an emerging elite. Byrd, Bland, Burwell, and Carter would soon become household names in Virginia politics and society. The younger sons of southern and western English gentry, they understood instinctively the mechanics of patronage. Though they had only recently come to the colony, they soon formed a circle of wealth and power around Berkeley.

By the 1670s, Berkeley was an old man, but he retained his power with an iron grip. At his side was a young wife, Lady Frances Culpepper Stephens Berkeley, who knew and loved wealth and pomp and had important family connections in the colony and in England. The Green Spring faction accumulated the offices of country sheriffs, justices of the peace, and seats in the House of Burgesses. They and their cronies pillaged the public treasury and corrupted the government. The poll taxes they imposed fell upon everyone but them. At their height, the taxes amounted to one-fourth to one-half of the average planter's income.

But there were those who had no love for Berkeley, even among the elite. A younger generation of ambitious planters, some newly arrived from England, others the sons of yeomen farmers, believed the door had closed to their advancement. They found a leader in a recent immigrant, Nathaniel Bacon.

Bacon was a well-born Englishman distantly related to Berkeley and shown great favor by the older man. At age twenty-nine, Bacon joined the governor's council at Berkeley's invitation. But Bacon would not work within the system of patronage that the governor manipulated. With characteristic bluntness, he dismissed the Green Spring faction as a "powerful cabal" and demanded: "Let us see what sponges have sucked up the Public Treasure and whether it hath not been privately contrived away

THE CRITICAL YEARS, 1675–1700 **231**

by unworthy Favourites and juggling parasites whose tottering fortunes have been repaired and supported at the public charge."

In the spring of 1676, Bacon's frustration with the ruling clique found a focus: Berkeley's unwillingness to engage in all-out war with the Indians. In April, Bacon raised a small company of planters and their servants and carried on his own campaign against the Indians. When Bacon came to Jamestown to take his seat in the government, in late May, Berkeley arrested him as a traitor.

Although Bacon privately despised the "giddy multitude" of servants, laborers, and yeomen, crowds spilling out of the taverns started chanting his name and urging him to speak for them. Among the servants and yeoman planters who surged to Bacon's aid were veterans of the parliamentary side in the English civil wars. They had no love lost for a royalist stalwart like Berkeley or his circle of aristocratic friends.

Perhaps inadvertently, Bacon had hit upon a brilliant stroke to forge a political alliance among members of his own class, anxious about their falling status under Berkeley's rule, and the "giddy multitude" whose future prospects Berkeley's greed had stymied. Indians became scapegoats for the discontent of the upper classes and the anger of the lower-class whites. Bacon's movement turned economic and political frustration into race hate.

The Civil War Erupts

In custody, Bacon offered to drive all the Indians from the colony, but Berkeley demurred. The governor, who unlike Bacon had a military background, knew that friendly Indians made the best scouts. What was more, Berkeley could tell the difference between Indian friends, whose lives he was honor bound to protect, and Indian enemies. Berkeley's opponents snickered that he refused to act because he had a share of the profits from trade with the Indians. Finally, who would trust a young hothead like Bacon with a military commission?

On June 5, 1676, Bacon confessed his errors, and Berkeley, recognizing the danger that Bacon's allies posed to the peace of the colony (and the Green Spring faction's pillaging of the treasury), but unwilling to force a trial of Bacon—think what such a trial might reveal about the governor's own conduct—pardoned Bacon and restored him to the council. When Bacon, apparently humbled, went home, Berkeley tried to cut the yeoman support away from Bacon's movement by broadening the franchise.

Bacon neither knuckled under to the governor's show of force nor accepted the gesture of reconciliation. On June 23, Bacon returned to Jamestown, this time at the head of five hundred armed men. All he wanted, he said to the incensed governor, was a commission to kill Indians. Berkeley relented and issued the commission, and Bacon led his rabble on a tour through the colony, commandeering horses, guns, and wagons from outraged farmers and killing every Indian he could catch. Berkeley changed his mind once again, but when he tried to raise troops to arrest Bacon, they refused to serve. On August 3, Bacon began a military campaign against the governor, driving him from Jamestown on September 18. The next day Bacon burned the town.

Bacon rewarded his followers by allowing them to gorge upon the property of Berkeley's friends. As one of the victims wailed, "thus is that country by the rashness of a perverse man exposed to ruin, and is in a most calamitous and confused condition." Worse, as far as Berkeley's aristocratic clique could see, Bacon had let loose "an insulting rabble . . . who account the law their manacles, and like swine turn all into disorder and become insolent, abuse all in authority." The plundering continued through the fall.

Bacon also offered immediate freedom to the servants and slaves of those loyal to the governor and ridiculed the genteel affectations of the wives of Berkeley's aristocratic followers. He had become, without intending to and without realizing it, a genuine social rebel, flouting the conventions of rank and hierarchy that Berkeley and his circle had so recently constructed. But Bacon had no program of lasting reform, no vision of a society without ranks and privileges. For example, women supported his movement, but he had denigrated the women of the planter classes and in the sack of Jamestown, even used captured planters' wives and servants as a human shield. Bacon never doubted that women should serve men.

Bacon dreamed of genuine independence from England. At a council held at Berkeley's mansion after the sack of Jamestown, Bacon urged delegates from Maryland and Virginia to throw off their allegiance to the crown. Had he not died in October 1676 of dysentery, the movement might have spread still further. But the crown had at last taken notice. Urged to repressive measures by Lady Berkeley, who returned to England in May to lobby for her husband, the king had already sent a small squadron to clear the rebels from the York and the James rivers. With the support of the squadron, Berkeley drove the rebels back into the interior, and his troops began their own looting. On the spot, they executed captured rebel leaders.

The End of Virginia's Autonomy

By January 1677, the civil war sputtered to a close, and formal trials of Baconians began. Berkeley held courts martial to try his former enemies and condemned four of Bacon's lieutenants. Only the arrival of a full regiment of regular troops stemmed the course of Berkeley's revenge. The king's commissioners offered a royal pardon to all who would swear their loyalty to him, and hundreds of former Bacon supporters who still roamed the countryside armed and angry agreed to lay down their arms and submit to the mercy of the crown. For his high-handed ways and his misuse of the martial law, Berkeley was to answer in England. There was peace at last, but on royal terms.

Bacon had left behind no structural changes in Virginia society for the royal commission to dismantle. Indeed, the lesson of Bacon's rebellion was just the opposite of actual social reform: Berkeley and his loyalists had learned that poor whites and rich whites could make common cause, or at least find common cause, in racial animosity.

Bacon's target had been the Indians, but Berkeley and the great planters feared not the Indians but an alliance between poor whites and poorer blacks based on common economic needs. Bacon had shown them the way to avert it. Henceforth, by offering the poorer whites the chance to see themselves as part of the master class, a union based not on common economic interests but on racial fears and animosities, the elite could ensure that the poorer farmers would willingly bow to the hegemony of the large planters. Such racial solidarity was a cultural construction—a conscious device that the planter elite could manipulate to ensure the support of the white servant and yeoman populations.

THE SLAVE UPRISING OF 1675 IN BARBADOS

Race stood at the center of the next crisis of the critical years. Barbadian planters did not have to manufacture a concept of racial solidarity. Conditions of slave life on Barbados had been deteriorating steadily from the 1650s to the 1670s. The planters had made the strategic economic decision that the sugar crop was worth more than the lives of the slave laborers.

There had been no real uprisings before 1675, but sensible that the system could not be changed and that their lot was not improving, a group of slaves from the Gold Coast set in motion a plot to kill all the whites. Word went from plantation to plantation at night, for the slave laws of Barbados forbade slaves going from one plantation to another without a pass, and "patrols" of whites enforced the law harshly. A house slave named Fortuna warned her master, a leading planter, who informed the governor. He wasted no time calling out the militia—all free white males were members of the militia—which captured and examined the ringleaders using torture to gain the names of all the conspirators.

One of the slave plotters refused to reveal anything about his cohorts. "If you roast me today," he told his inquisitors, "you cannot roast me tomorrow." For him, execution was a kind of assisted suicide—so terrible was the prospect of one more day of slavery. Unimpressed by his courage, a court convened for the purpose sentenced him to death, along with thirty-five others.

The brutality of the punishment seems out of proportion to the crime—for the slaves had actually done nothing but plot. In their quarters, out of earshot of masters and overseers, slaves must have discussed the possibility of revolt or escape innumerable times. Of course, by 1675 the slaves outnumbered free people five to one, and the conspirators did not aim at their freedom, but at the extermination of the whites. Technically, the crime was "petty treason," for servants and slaves who plotted against their masters were likened in law to subjects plotting against their sovereign. Petty treason did not have to result in the death of the master for it to be a capital offense. In reality, the punishments were meant as a highly visible proof that insurrection could only end in agonizing death for the rebels. The planters assumed that the more grisly the punishment, the more effective the message. The sanguinary display did not prevent other uprisings, however, and in 1692 the colony's slaves actually raised armed rebellion.

THE PUEBLO REVOLT OF 1680 IN NEW MEXICO

In the Spanish colony of New Mexico, native-European tensions also erupted in rebellion—but this time the Indians gained the upper hand, at least for a time. The first Spanish *entrada* into New Mexico had ended abruptly and badly for the newcomers in 1542. But the lust for riches and the quest for souls did not die out in Spanish Mexico, and it brought a second thrust north in the 1590s.

In 1598, under a commission from the crown, Juan de Oñate led settlers up the Rio Grande valley to the base of the Chamas Mountains, and set the capital of his new colony in what is now the San Juan Pueblo. The trek, in summer, must have been hellish, across dried riverbeds and over the sand hills, the altitude steadily rising to the seven-thousand-foot-high Española plateau.

After the processions and mock battles that the Spanish always staged to impress and intimidate the natives, after the first church was laid out with geometric precision and the first drainage/irrigation ditch was dug, the trouble began. Indian towns were taken by leading Spanish colonists as *encomiendas*. Once again the Spanish exacted tribute, including food from the Indians' drought-depleted supplies. The Indians responded by abandoning their occupied villages to the Spanish. One of these, in nearby Santa Fe, became the capital in 1610.

The New Mexico Colony

Imperial Spanish law forbade such treatment of natives, but Oñate and his men were far from the Spanish court. The Franciscans among them pled for the starving Indians, but even the Franciscans grew hot when the Indians resisted Christian teachings. A Spanish offer of protection from marauding Apaches and Navajos convinced some of the Pueblos to return to their towns, but the Spanish continued to demonstrate their condescension in a thousand ways.

For example, the Spanish rebuilt the Indian towns to new specifications, opening plazas on which forced Indian labor constructed churches. Indifferent to patterns of Indian communal farming, the Spanish granted land outside of the town to individual Spanish farmers, whose plots became haciendas (ranches). For hundreds of years, the Indians had built their dwellings by "puddling" clay into balls of varying sizes and piling the balls up into walls. The Spanish insisted on precisely shaped adobe bricks, measuring rods, and architectural plans. Indians wondered why the

Spanish buildings had to be so massive and strong-walled when everyone knew that the most important activities in daily life took place outside the walls. The Spanish insisted that only inside the church, hacienda, and presidio (government complex) could a person be civilized.

The Pueblos accommodated themselves to the outward trappings of Spanish rule and worship and practiced their own religious rites in secret. This is not to say that Indian conversions to Christianity were disingenuous, but that they added Christianity rather than abandoned Indian traditions. The missionaries knew this, and belittled and shamed native priests to root out the old ways. In one recorded encounter, a priest berated an Indian father who taught his son the old ways, "Is it not sufficient that you yourself want to go to hell without desiring to take your son also?" As one Indian later reported to a Spanish captain, "The resentment which all Indians have in their hearts has been so strong, from the time this kingdom was discovered, because the religious [orders] and the Spaniards took away their idols and forbade their sorceries and idolatries . . . and that he has heard this resentment spoken of since he was of an age to understand."

The Rebellion

To the Pueblos' policy of open accommodation and secret resistance, the Spanish responded with harsh measures. In 1675, all kachina dances were banned, and shamans were whipped and publicly humiliated. The Spanish martyred four recalcitrant Indian priests. Only when the Indians threatened to rise in rebellion did the Spanish relent and free the rest of the shamans. But when another wave of disease swept through the pueblos, carrying off a new generation of young people, Indian resolve to resist hardened.

For the Spanish, the situation could hardly have been more perilous. Spanish settlers from the South were unwilling to make the long and dangerous trip up the Rio Grande from Mexico. As late as 1680, there were but two thousand Spanish and Mexican settlers in the river valleys of New Mexico, half of whom were Indians from the South who had come with their Spanish masters into the Pueblos' country. By the 1670s, the only military levies the governor could get were convicts.

In 1680, at the urging of Popay, a Santa Clara Pueblo priest who suffered the humiliations of 1675, native leaders determined that they must drive every Spanish settler from their midst. For some reason, the southern Pueblo peoples did not join the conspiracy. Their loyalty to the Spanish may have been greater, or the northern Pueblos may not have trusted their southern brothers and sisters.

Early in August 1680, soldiers rushed to Governor Antonio de Otermín's presidio in Santa Fe to report atrocities in nearby pueblos. Missionaries had been beaten to death by their parishioners; settlers had been ambushed; even the soldiers had to flee for their lives. Friendly Pueblos warned that a rising was at hand. On August 10, an Indian army was at the gates of Santa Fe.

In an inversion of the rituals at festival days, when Spanish missionaries paraded with crosses, the Indians offered Otermín a choice of two crosses—white for surrender, red for war. The governor, who had already barricaded himself and the settlers within the fortified government block, refused to choose. The Spanish sallied out to do battle, but Indian reinforcements arrived in time to drive the Spanish back. The struggle then focused on the water supply, without which the Spanish could not survive. After ten days of the siege, with the water cut off and the governor wounded twice in the battle, the Spanish realized that they could not hold out.

For the next two months, the retreating Spanish column of nearly two thousand men, women, and children marched back down the Rio Grande valley, toward Mexico. In a reversal of Oñate's proud procession, Otermín's bedraggled force dispiritedly recrossed the desolate piñon- and juniper-strewn plain. The settlers nearly starved, for the Spanish had abandoned their southern settlements, and the Indians had removed all food stores. But with the Spanish in flight, the Pueblos held back their main force, contenting themselves with harrying the Spanish flanks. The Indians had no desire to exterminate the Spanish, only to drive them away.

THE IMPOSITIONS OF EMPIRE

In the 1680s, with the colonies still reeling from their internal convulsions, a second round of crises burst upon them. This originated in an old controversy—English Protestant nobles' fear of Catholicism. In 1678, Titus Oates, an adventurer of somewhat questionable veracity, denounced an alleged Catholic plot to overturn the religious settlement of the Restoration. James was a practicing and committed Catholic, so tensions over religion had never relaxed during the Restoration, but Oates's claim that the Catholics intended to kill the king in order to bring his brother to the throne was ludicrous. Nevertheless, this "Popish Plot" set off reverberations throughout England exceeding the suspicions aroused in the United States by the "Red Scare" in the early 1950s. Several Catholics were executed, although it later appeared that they were innocent.

The First "Whigs"

Lord Shaftesbury and other Protestant leaders organized a political party in Parliament, calling themselves the Whigs, to exclude James from the succession. The Whigs wanted to offer the crown to James Scott, the Duke of Monmouth (and Charles II's bastard son), or to James's Protestant daughter, Mary, married to a Protestant Dutch leader, William, Prince of Orange—anyone rather than James.

In aid of their project, the Whigs produced political propaganda, held rallies, and lobbied for support in Parliament. Locke had prepared two treatises on government to justify the exclusion. In these treatises, he argued that life, liberty, and property were natural rights of subjects, and if those rights were abridged by a king (or might be abridged by a king in waiting), the people had the right to remove officers of government. Government was a trust, and erring trustees could be ousted.

The king dissolved the Parliament, and new elections ensued. But the "exclusion crisis" continued, as the House of Commons in the newly elected Parliament contained a majority that favored exclusion. Charles II dissolved it in 1681 and decided, like his father, to rule without Parliament until the electoral districts could be rigged to ensure a majority for his brother's succession to the crown. In 1683, Shaftesbury and Locke prudently decided to relocate to the Netherlands.

To ensure a favorable vote on the succession in Parliament, Charles's attorney general began quo warranto (literally, "show cause") proceedings in the king's courts against two-thirds of all the chartered boroughs in the country. These charters conferred the voters' privilege to send a representative to the House of Commons. The legal writ of quo warranto was usually employed to abrogate town or corporation charters when the town council or corporation board of directors violated the terms of the charter. Employing these writs against Whig-dominated boroughs allowed the king's judges to dissolve the charters.

The king then reissued charters that guaranteed a Tory Party (the Tories were the friends of the king) returnee from the rechartered borough, in effect gerrymandering the electoral districts in Parliament. As soon as the project was complete, the crown planned to authorize a new election in which James's succession would be secure. When some of the judges refused to act as pawns in this political chess game, the king purged the judiciary (who served during the king's "pleasure" and could be removed at his whim) and filled it with loyal supporters.

In 1685, Monmouth returned from exile and raised a rebellion in the southwest of England that was almost immediately crushed. Monmouth's supporters were quickly tried, and the wholesale executions that followed (called by many the "bloody assizes") reminded the Whigs of the power of the crown. That same year, Charles died, and James succeeded him.

The Abrogation of the New England Colonial Charters

The writ of quo warranto could also be used against colonies that posed difficulties to the crown—for example, by offering refuge to enemies of the crown or disobeying the laws of Parliament. The New England colonies were prime candidates for the writ under both of these categories. Despite the fact that Massachusetts, Connecticut, and Rhode Island had belatedly proclaimed Charles their rightful king in 1661, all the New England colonies were irritants. The anti-Catholic sentiments of the Puritans in New England verged on hysteria.

But the most obvious excuse for rescinding the New England colonial charters was the colonies' disregard of the customs duties. These were part of the so-called Navigation Acts (a fuller explanation of which appears in the next chapter). Edward Randolph, named commissioner of customs for New England in 1673 and later made commissioner for the North American colonies, documented the tactics of the New England smugglers in convincing fashion. New England officials obstructed him and his helpers, but he obtained hard evidence that New England merchants routinely engaged in illegal trade with non-English ports. Other scams were equally blatant. Ships fulfilled the letter of the law in the first port of call, then secretly unloaded and loaded at nearby streams and inlets. Small boats ferried goods illegally to and from shore. Ship captains carried false sets of papers to fool the searchers.

When all else failed, the owners appealed confiscation orders in royal courts, alleging all manner of defenses. Prosecutors had to pierce the veil of phony ownership arrangements that English front men worked out with foreign investors. English attorneys general offered contradictory rulings, but in the end the courts and royal legal officers almost always decided cases in favor of the prosecution. After all, the customs service not only policed the trade, it provided revenue for the crown.

Randolph suggested making Massachusetts the first target of quo warranto, and King Charles warned the colony that continued resistance to the law would cost it its charter. The colonial leadership then divided into hard-liners who argued for defiance and compromisers who wanted compliance with the laws, but the latter could not persuade the former to give in to the king.

In the spring of 1684, the mill that had ground so slowly (recall that the first legal attack on the Massachusetts Bay charter began in 1635) at last produced a decree of quo warranto that the colony must produce and defend its charter. When the colonial government refused to comply with the order, the Court of King's Bench in Westminster entered a judgment against the colony, and the old charter was annulled. Joseph Dudley, one of the compromisers, became the acting royal governor of the colony, though he was not to rule for long.

Within three years of James II's taking the throne, he brought all the New England colonies under one administrative roof. By 1688, the chartered colonies of Connecticut, Plymouth, Rhode Island, and New Hampshire, as well as the settlements on the Maine coast joined Massachusetts in the Dominion of New England. James expected the new creation to toe the royal line. Andros, still in the king's confidence, became the governor, with a council of leading New England men who saw their best interest in cooperation with the new order.

Councilors like Dudley had tacitly conceded that Massachusetts could no longer regard itself as a covenanted commonwealth of saints. The monopoly of the Puritan established church was gone, although Puritanism would continue to influence politics, and Congregational and Presbyterian churches would continue to receive support from the towns' treasuries. Andros himself was an adherent of the Church of England and openly favored its interests.

In response, hard-liners in the former New England colonies redoubled their resistance. Some, like father and son Boston ministers Increase and Cotton Mather, called upon their fellow colonists to return to the covenant ideal of the founders of

Massachusetts. Increase Mather went to England to lobby against the Dominion and Andros, while Cotton Mather remained in Boston, where he so agitated Andros that Andros decided to throw him in jail.

Other hard-liners began to raise a new kind of argument, not based upon carrying out God's mission, but upon a conception of political liberty born during the 1650s in England. There, Harrington and Algernon Sydney, among others, had argued that freemen were not subjects but citizens whose right to hold and use property, to be free of arbitrary and novel legal burdens, and to express their political opinions and take part in the political process was founded not in royal favor or grants of privileges, but in fundamental law. Harrington's *Oceana*, which had so moved Penn, told these Massachusetts leaders that men of property and probity—men like themselves—should run the state without royal interference.

New Englanders who shared some of Harrington's views were protected from his fate by distance from England and by Andros's need for colonial assistance in protecting the frontiers. Indeed, because Andros's official duties took him to Rhode Island, New Hampshire, Maine, Connecticut, and, after 1688, New York and New Jersey, he was not around to hear all the muttering in Massachusetts against his royal master.

The Glorious Revolution in the Colonies

James's Catholicism, his unpopularity, and his abrupt, abusive manner had disenchanted all but the most loyal supporters of the Stuart family, and he still faced the problem of gaining acceptance from Protestant England for a Roman Catholic monarchy. In June 1688, his wife bore him a son, James, who was christened in the Roman Catholic rite, and the nation faced the likelihood that a Catholic king (instead of James's Protestant daughter, Mary) would follow James to the throne. A convention of his enemies met in that month and decreed that they were the Parliament and offered the crown to Mary and her husband, William of Orange, a Dutch nobleman. William crossed the channel with an army, and James, though his forces were as numerous as William's, fled the realm.

William marched to London, where at his insistence, he and Mary were jointly crowned. It was a "Glorious Revolution," at least compared to events in the 1640s. In 1689, as part of the settlement, William and Mary accepted Parliament's Declaration of Rights. Henceforth, Parliament would have control of the finances of the realm. Religious toleration of all Protestants was guaranteed. Catholics and Jews might worship in private, but they could hold no offices and could not vote.

James invaded Ireland, hoping to use it as a base for his return to power, but his forces were beaten at the Battle of the Boyne in 1691. The Stuarts would continue to lurk in the shadows, and in 1745 a pro-Stuart rebellion was launched in Scotland, but like the Irish campaign fifty-four years earlier, it failed.

Locke, who returned to England from his Dutch exile when the coast was clear, took the *Two Treatises* he wrote during the Exclusion Crisis out of his trunk and, ever cautious (for he had gained high office under William and Mary), printed them anonymously. Read in their new context, they seemed to be an exultation of the power of Parliament and became the apology for the Glorious Revolution. Although Locke had actually argued that all the branches of government were the trustees of the people and could be removed or punished for violating their trust, in the context of the parliamentary triumph of 1688–1689 he was understood to praise a mixed government in which Parliament was supreme.

In the American colonies, the news of the Glorious Revolution set off reverberations of unexpected proportions. In Massachusetts, on the morning of April 18, 1689, a crowd chased Andros down and forced him to surrender the reins of government, then imprisoned him, along with the much despised Edward Randolph. Only the intervention of Cotton Mather and other "gentlemen," according to one witness, "regulated the unheaded people . . . to hinder the peoples proceeding any further than to reserve the criminals [Andros and Randolph] for the justice of the English Parliament." The Boston town meeting immediately prepared a Declaration of Grievances, arguing that Andros and the Dominion were part of a "horrid Popish plot . . . to crush and break a country so entirely and signally made up of Reformed churches."

Receiving regular reports from his son Cotton and others while visiting in England, Increase Mather, the leader of the Massachusetts ministerial association, petitioned William and Mary to recall Andros, which the monarchs did, but they refused to return the old charter to Massachusetts. Instead, listening to advice from longtime imperial administrators about how Massachusetts evaded the Navigation Acts, they offered in 1691 to prepare a new charter for the colony with a royal governor and judges picked by the crown.

In Massachusetts, a provisional government held the reins of power, and its members looked much like the old charter government. A mixture of hard-liners and compromisers resumed power, with old William Bradstreet as the caretaker governor. In Rhode Island and Connecticut, there was neither rebellion nor resistance—the mantle of the Dominion had always been worn lightly, and now it was shed.

There is another plot twist to the story about the Glorious Revolution in New England that needs exploration, though we can only glimpse its outlines. So long as Massachusetts had its old charter, the General Court could control immigration. That is, the government could deny entry to religious sectaries like the Quakers and exile dissenters like Roger Williams. Paupers could be "warned out" and Indians enslaved and sold to the West Indies. There was no need for statutes to define the unwanted.

After 1689, the colonial government could not bar entry to Anglicans, Quakers, Baptists, and a host of others, including slaveholders who brought their bondmen and women with them to the colony. There had been a handful of slaves in Massachusetts before 1692, but nothing like the number brought thereafter. In addition, after 1692 the assembly suddenly noticed race as a legal category, and began passing legislation designed to regulate the conduct of "Negroes."

In Maryland, the Glorious Revolution brought down the proprietary government. Already infected with the indisputable connection between Roman Catholicism and the French enemy, the proprietary was fatally damaged when James II was ousted. The lieutenant governor, William Joseph, himself a Catholic, had to prorogue the assembly (in effect adjourn it without dissolving it or calling for new elections) to forestall it from proclaiming the end of the proprietor's right to rule.

When news of William of Orange's advance on London reached the colony, a "Protestant Association" sprung up and seized the government. Its leaders were men of means hitherto excluded from the inner circle of proprietary favorites, but they had a broad popular following. From July 27 to August 1, 1689, they snuffed out the last sparks of resistance from the proprietor's appointees in a bloodless revolution, proclaimed William and Mary the legitimate sovereigns of England and its colonies, and filled all local government posts with their allies. A new assembly, elected under their supervision, ratified their actions and repealed the proprietary acts on toleration.

The new monarchs, William and Mary, put their seal of approval upon the end of Maryland proprietary rule in 1690. A year after the Maryland rebels had announced their success, Colonel Francis Nicholson, an old soldier who had served James II but switched sides in 1689, was named royal governor. The Calvert family was not done with the colony, however. Not only did they retain their extensive land holdings in Maryland, in 1715 they would persuade the first Hanoverian king of England, George I, that they ought never to have been ousted from political power. The heir to the family title and fortune, Benedict Leonard Calvert, Lord Baltimore, changed his religion to the Anglican faith and was restored to power in Maryland in 1715. The proprietary government (albeit with a greater role for the assembly) lasted until the Revolution, with Catholics still barred from offices within the control of the assembly, but not from those in the gift of the proprietor.

Leisler's Rebellion in New York

Unlike Maryland and New England, in New York violence greeted the news of the Glorious Revolution. In 1689, Andros rushed to Boston and left behind in New York City three councilors and one bewildered lieutenant governor, Francis Nicholson. The councilors happened to be three Dutch businessmen, none with any influence over the factious Long Islanders, who again decided that they wanted to be part of Connecticut. Genuine grievances (principally about the short-lived assembly, taxes, and the apparent monopoly of the colony's trade by a few well-connected merchants) fed into continuing Dutch-English animosity.

Nicholson called a meeting of his advisers and militia captains, among whom was Jacob Leisler, a German-born city merchant. After some days of confrontation between loyal regular troops and militia levies, Leisler took charge. His allies arranged for a "committee of safety" (precedent for which lay in both New England and the home country) and the committee duly elected Leisler commander in chief of the colony. The office had no legal standing but sounded a lot like a governor-general.

Leisler's following had an ethnic tinge: strong among the Dutch, weaker among the English in the colony, for the Dutch still resented the English. What brought Englishmen into the alliance was their mistrust of the Anglo-Catholic supporters of the deposed king. The Leislerians tagged Andros's remaining supporters as the "Roman Catholic party," and drove them from office.

The Leislerians also relied for support on a broad range of New York City's inhabitants. Some were middle-class men who had little experience at the top of society or in high offices of government. Others were working-class people frustrated with the imposition of English imperial rule. Leisler's enemies would later call this popular support group a "mob," a harsh pejorative, for in those days "mob" was synonymous with a dangerous and illegal gathering of unprincipled and violent men. No one, including Leisler, advocated mob rule.

The committee pledged its allegiance to William and Mary and set about preparing for the defense of the colony against France—for when William and Mary assumed the throne, their first order of diplomatic business had been to renounce the Anglo-French alliance James had forged and to reestablish ties with France's enemy, the Netherlands. The English-Dutch alliance brought England into a European war against Louis XIV and France. War in America soon followed—King William's War as it was called in the colonies.

In New York, the Leislerians imprisoned all suspected opponents, citing military necessity as a justification, with some truth. Count Frontenac, governor-general of French Canada, was at that very moment leading a force of Huron and Canadian troops against Schenectady and Albany. Leisler sent a relief party that chased the invaders all the way back to the gates of Montreal, but could not bring the French to battle. Leisler contemplated a full-fledged attack on the French, and called a conference of the other colonies at Albany to organize the campaign. Only a few New Englanders attended, so enraging Leisler that he threw the New England commander, Fitz-wait Winthrop of Connecticut, in jail.

Leisler's opponents were not impressed by his martial ardor and busied themselves denouncing him to William and Mary's advisers in England. There, Colonial Henry Sloughter accepted a commission as governor of New York with instructions to end the violence in the colony. Though it took him nearly a year to get to New York (he arrived in winter 1691), when he presented his credentials he made plain that Leisler was to surrender power. Leisler delayed, refused, and finally conceded with ill grace.

Sloughter brought criminal charges against the upstart merchant. A rump court Sloughter created held an abbreviated trial at which Leisler refused to plead. A handpicked jury of anti-Leislerians convicted Leisler of the charge of treason. Sloughter did not refer the conviction to the courts in England or to the Privy Council, the new monarchs' inner circle of advisers. Knowing that he was fated to die, Leisler protested to the end that he had never sought personal power, but only acted "to maintaine against popery or any Schism or heresy whatever the interest of our sovereign Lord and Lady that now is [William and Mary] and the reformed Protestant Churches in those parts." In short, he saw himself a martyr to the Protestant cause. He perished on the gibbet on May 16, 1691.

King William's War

Sloughter's rush to judgment must be understood in the light of his situation. He was a soldier with a war to fight, but no idea how to do it. He had extensive experience in Europe, where regular armies fought sieges and maneuvered over open ground using rules of engagement that had evolved since the fifteenth century. In America, the combatants in King William's War obeyed no such rules of engagement. The French and their Indian allies moved swiftly and silently through the forests, hitting and running. The English and their Indian allies followed suit. Gaining territory was less important than causing havoc.

New York and New England bore the brunt of the fighting. Brave and arrogant, loved by many in Canada, but pitiless to his enemies, Frontenac displayed an energy and administrative capacity that sustained Canada's military efforts. The French governor commanded the twelve hundred men of La Marine Regiment, in addition to the male settlers of the colony, organized in militias, and numerous northern Indian bands, whose interests he cultivated and whose distrust for one another he allayed. With lightning swiftness, he raided Albany, New York, and Salmon Falls, New Hampshire, in the spring of 1690.

Far away and absorbed in conflict on the continent of Europe, England was no help to its northern colonies, so the colonists retaliated on their own. In March 1690, William Phips, a Maine-born ship carpenter turned adventurer, convinced the acting government in Massachusetts to sponsor an assault on the French coastal possessions. With seven hundred men and fourteen ships, he took and burned the French fortress of Port Royal, and made its French inhabitants take an oath of allegiance to Britain, then returned to Boston and acclaim. His expedition had little lasting effect, but it buoyed public morale and ultimately won him nomination as the first royal governor of Massachusetts two years later.

Frontenac replied by ousting the English from Hudson's Bay and besieging Fort Loyal (later Portland), Maine, a year later. Assured that they would be protected by the French under the laws of war, the garrison of Fort Loyal, including women and children, filed out of the gates and were immediately assaulted by the French Indian allies, the Abenakis. The French belatedly apologized for the slaughter, which, in any case, they were probably powerless to prevent, but it was an ominous precedent.

The New York forces Leisler had assembled mounted their own raid. In the summer of 1690, some forty New Yorkers, including Iroquois, paddled the length of Lake Champlain and up the Richelieu River to La Prairie, across the Saint Lawrence from Montreal. They killed six Indians, took nineteen prisoners (to trade for prisoners the French had taken), and shot 150 head of cattle. In the meantime, flushed with his success against Port Royal, Phips led a larger contingent of colonists against Quebec itself. The besieged city held out as disease reduced the strength of the besiegers. They withdrew after an exchange of prisoners.

Sloughter had instructions to bring the Iroquois into the fray. He gave presents, exchanged gifts, and polished the covenant chain, and the battle for the Lake Champlain region was begun in earnest. When Sloughter died suddenly, his replacement, Benjamin Fletcher, carried on a vigorous war program. In 1692, Frontenac could only muster a small force to burn and pillage homesteads in central New York. The New York commander, Peter Schuyler, answered by chasing the raiders back to Canada. Many Iroquois, tired of what appeared to be an endless round of thrusts and parries that left Indian warriors on both sides dead to no purpose, began to listen to Frontenac's offer of neutrality and let the covenant chain with England rust.

Throughout the war, the colonies refused to coordinate their efforts. New York looked due north. Massachusetts looked to Maine and the sea. No help came from the Quakers of the Delaware Valley. The planters and yeomen of the Chesapeake had their own concerns, and Carolina was busy countering Indian and Spanish forces on its frontiers.

The lack of cooperation did not cool the blood of William Phips. Back from England with his commission as governor of Massachusetts in the late spring of 1692, he immediately set out for Maine and renewed war with the Abenakis. He drove them from their villages and claimed a triumph, leaving behind garrisons. Two years later, the French and Abenakis struck at Oyster Bay (later Durham), New Hampshire, and into New York. Living in constant fear, frontier settlers built farmsteads that looked like the blockhouses of forts, with overhanging upper stories and gun ports. England sent a few companies of regular troops, who were almost worthless in the woods, but did a fair job of eating and drinking their way through commissary stores.

Stung by Phips's success and encouraged by the Abenakis, in 1694 the French massed a full-scale attack on the coast of Maine, dislodging the Massachusetts garrisons. Massachusetts called on the redoubtable Benjamin Church, who led a force of five hundred men and captured the French general. Henceforth, the French contented themselves with sinking English fishing boats off Newfoundland—a violation of the truce that had existed for one hundred years off "the banks." Conflicts between large forces of militia and regular troops dwindled, though the raiding continued, marked by incidents of casual brutality and remarkable courage. The Peace of Ryswick (1697) closed this phase of the border warfare, but not before every settler on both sides of the line had lost loved ones or at least heard rumors of atrocities.

THE SALEM WITCHCRAFT CASES

The legacy of this decade of war on the northern frontier was a kind of free-floating anxiety that occasionally crested in panic. In 1691, Indian raids on the Maine border sent a flood of refugees into the comparative safety of established coastal towns like Salem, Massachusetts. The refugees carried with them firsthand experience of the horrors of the war and spread rumors of Indian atrocities, inflaming the hatred of Indians, Catholics, French Canadians, and strangers that already existed in New England's northern settlements.

Salem, like the other older towns nearby, had troubles enough of its own. Long settled, there was too little land left in the town for some of its young people to start families. Even the more prosperous clans felt the pinch. Long-standing quarrels over timber and farm fields and more recent suspicions of newcomers fueled gossip about strange and incurable illnesses and mysterious conduct of neighbors.

By the end of 1691, with the war going badly, the rumors of impending catastrophe and gossip about misfortunes began to coalesce around a single theme: the devil had singled out New England. The refugees told stories of Indian witchcraft. With witchcraft accusations in the air, old suspicions of outcasts, beggars, braggarts, and miscreants took on a new solidity. Had the political situation in the colony been more settled, the magistrates could have quieted the people's fears, but the magistrates were themselves unsure of their power. With only a provisional government and no charter, they failed to act.

The Shapes of the Devil

From January 1692 to May 1693, the men and women of Salem, Massachusetts, and the neighboring towns engaged in a manic witch hunt. Hundreds were accused, many of whom languished in jail for months. Neighbor turned against neighbor, children informed on parents, and congregations expelled members. Between June 2 and September 21, 1692, nineteen women and men were tried and executed for the crime of using their spectral powers to assault a group of girls. Four other suspects died in jail. One man who refused to cooperate with the court was pressed to death with stones.

Such witch hunts, ordinarily aimed at older, poor women, had torn apart European communities since the thirteenth century, and condemned hundreds of thousands of defendants, most of them innocent of all wrongdoing, to death. But by the 1690s, the witch-hunt craze had all but disappeared, especially in England. True, the vast majority of English people, including those in the colonies, still believed that witches had the power to hurt people by making pacts with the devil. And although ministers inveighed against the practice, people from all walks of life and all ranks in society engaged in countermagic and indulged their fantasies with lurid tales of evil in the "invisible world" of specters and demons. But the outbreak of witchcraft fears in Salem and its environs did not grow out of the larger context of European beliefs or result from the prevalence of countermagic. Instead, the Salem crisis had its roots in the critical-period brew of rumor, panic, local animosity, and inequality.

In the midst of the war, long-smoldering quarrels in the western, Salem Village section of the town of Salem flashed into flame. For two years, from 1689 to 1691, people in the village had argued about whether to retain the services of minister Samuel Parris. Quarrels over the retention of ministers were common in New England towns, but this one was carried on with great venom because it overlay a struggle between the two most powerful families in Salem Village, the Putnams and the Porters. The Putnams were a close-knit clan of farmers, whose political fortunes and influence waned. The Porters, with ties to the commercial elite of the seaport, waxed more powerful each day. The Putnams supported Parris vocally. The Porters worked silently to oust him.

To all of these local tumults were added, in the winter of 1692 (one of the coldest winters of the age), the inexplicable illness of Parris's daughter and his niece, eleven-year-old Abigail Williams. Parris, whose own fortunes had fallen on hard times (his father had been a wealthy planter in Barbados), and who was reduced to pleading with his own vestrymen for firewood, saw his daughter's illness as an inexplicable judgment on him. But other girls in the village soon complained of the same symptoms. Adults were baffled until the girls accused three local women, one of them the Parris's slave, Tituba, of bewitching the girls.

The prodding of parents and ministers had undoubtedly played a role in changing free-floating anxiety into accusations of crime. For example, when well-meaning Puritan ministers and other authority figures tried to help the girls, the ministers themselves raised the possibility of witchcraft. Frightened by the hideous shapes of their own imaginings, parents and preachers may have actually fed the girls the accusatory lines they spoke.

Official Action

At the end of February, the Putnams summoned the Salem magistrates to examine the accusers and the suspects. Under relentless questioning, Tituba declared that a man in black had accosted her and demanded she sign his book in her blood. Helplessly, she related, she had acceded. She also claimed there were seven other witches in the village.

Accused by the girls and Tituba, old Sarah Good, sick and deaf, could not understand what was happening, but conceded that others might be witches. Sarah Osborne, another elderly woman fingered by the girls, fought back, but her anger proved to her examiners that she might be a secret witch. Over the course of the next few months, the girls and their families widened the circle of accusation. Caught in the net were men and women of sterling reputation as well as men and women of ill repute. No one was safe, for no one could deny what the girls said they saw—the specters of witches.

Although there were men among the accused, women defendants predominated. In the language that the magistrates, judges, ministers, and grand jurors (all men) used to condemn the suspects—for example, associating certain portions of women's bodies with "devil's marks"—one can see evidence of antifeminism in the prosecutions.

Witchcraft had always been a "women's crime," associated with women's sexual congress with the devil. Although English and colonial prosecutors had to prove that the accused witch had actually harmed someone, the accusations always involved sexually tinged language. On a more practical level, some accusations were clearly motivated by spite against women who held property or women who challenged male authority.

But antifemale attitudes among male authorities do not explain all of the gendered features of the Salem witchcraft crisis. Young women and girls predominated among the accusers, and older women were more likely to be accused than younger ones, patterns that force scholars to look at the pressures young women faced in these troubled days. The accusers were in a way victims themselves—of abusive masters, demanding parents, and a society that offered few opportunities to women. Perhaps the witchcraft accusations empowered young people and gave them a place in the limelight, at least as long as the hearings and trials continued.

On the other side of the dock, women confessed to being witches when they plainly were nothing of the kind. Their confessions (and their later recantations) illuminate the unique way that the notion of sin fit into women's lives. Magistrates browbeat both men and women into confessing, but men grudgingly admitted the bare minimum necessary to cooperate with the authorities. Women opened their hearts in their confessions and searched for signs of their own sinfulness.

In May 1692, with the weather turning warm and nearly 150 people crowding the jails, the danger of an outbreak of disease added urgency to the crisis. Governor Phips arrived from England with the new charter and realized something must be done. The assembly had the power to create regular courts under the new charter, but it was not yet in session. Faced with the crisis, he used his discretion to fashion a special court. To its bench he named former assistants like the merchant Samuel Sewall; Nathaniel Saltonstall, a prosperous farmer; William Stoughton, the lieutenant governor who coveted Phips's post; and local justices like Hathorne and Jonathan Corwin. All believed that there was a devil and that he contracted secretly with men and women to do his evil work in the colony. Witches thus had, at least in theory, power from the devil to leave their bodies and in spectral form assault their victims.

Asked for his advice on spectral evidence, minister Cotton Mather, whose Boston congregation included Stoughton and other judges, hedged, but he had no doubt that the devil was in league with the Catholic forces threatening England and New England. Jesuit participation in Indian attacks confirmed his fears. Thus he told the judges to prosecute the cases with vigor. With Mather's admonition before them, the judges allowed into evidence every assertion of confessed witches (including their supposed flights through the air on poles to midnight masses in open fields) and every one of the girls' complaints of punches and pinches delivered by invisible witches. Even saints like Rebecca Nurse were accused.

Nurse and five others faced the court on June 29. In two days, all were indicted by grand juries and tried. Moved by her demeanor and knowing her reputation, the trial jurors acquitted her, but Stoughton harangued them into changing their verdict. She was hanged on July 19, her last words on the gallows so moving that the onlookers would have rescued her had not Cotton Mather intervened and convinced them to let her punishment stand. By the end of the September sessions of the special court, every defendant had been convicted and executed except pregnant women. They were to be hanged after they delivered their babies.

The End of the Trials

Nathaniel Saltonstall was so appalled at the work of the court that he quietly resigned from the bench. The leading ministers (except for Cotton Mather) protested against the proceedings and convinced Increase Mather, Cotton's father, to turn their criticism into a tract on the dangers of believing spectral evidence. He agreed that spectral visitations might be the devil's instrument to fool the credulous and cast blame on the innocent. At any rate, admitting spectral evidence in court was playing the devil's game.

Increase Mather's work was widely circulated. Phips was convinced and ordered the suspension of the trials. He would reconvene them in the winter, but this time spectral evidence was not allowed. All but three women were acquitted at this new round of trials, and Phips pardoned them, as well as everyone else, by the spring of 1693. Stoughton, furious that he could not finish his work of ridding New England of witches, resigned his commission.

Five years after the trials, one week after burying his own young sons, Sewall asked forgiveness of God and his fellow congregants for the tragedy of the Salem trials: "Samuel Sewall, sensible of the reiterated stroke of God upon himself and family; and being sensible, that as to the Guilt contracted, upon the opening of the late Commission of Oyer and Terminer at Salem [the special court that tried and condemned the suspects] he is, upon many accounts, more concerned than any that he knows of, Desires to take the Blame and Shame of it, Asking Pardon of men." Sewall would later inveigh against slavery and call for fair treatment of Indians. A decade later, Cotton Mather admitted the error of his own credulity. The General Court had already begun to pay reparations to the families of the defendants. For his part, Stoughton never looked back.

The end of the Salem witchcraft trials brought to a close prosecution for witchcraft in New England. Although the ghosts and demons of the spirit world remained a staple of folk culture and folk tales, judges rejected Stoughton's precedent. If neighbors still suspected one another of misdeeds, and sometimes they complained to the magistrates that someone was a witch, the officials did not credit the story. Indeed, in the early 1700s ministers and magistrates cooperated to expose an episode of fraudulent and spiteful accusations.

Behind the changing conduct of the courts lay a more sweeping and potent shift in the way that educated elites (including judges) viewed the world. The new consensus about evidence at trial was part of the growing importance of experimental science in Western thought. In England, scientific contributions like Isaac Newton's laws of motion and energy, William Harvey's demonstrations of the operation of animals' organs, and Robert Boyle's precise measurements of the characteristics of gases reduced the importance of the invisible world. To be sure, even these avatars of the Age of Reason had not lost their fascination with the spirit world—Boyle believed in witches and Newton was a mystic—but in their work they looked for experimentally verifiable results, not phantoms and mysteries.

————

Buffeted by successive waves of internal and external violence in the critical years, the colonies had teetered on chaos. But in the maelstrom, tossed by powerful currents, floated the bits and pieces of a resolution to the fundamental causes of the crises. If the Indian and slave uprisings and civil insurrections like Bacon's or Leisler's led nowhere but to the grave, the language of protest these short-lived rebellions adopted defied old assumptions about divine providence and deference to one's betters. Traditional ways of organizing political life and making sense of public adversity were cracking under the strain.

The first recognition of the implications of the breakdown of the old paradigms of hierarchy and order came not in the colonies, however, but in the centers of empire. There, a new cadre of imperial bureaucrats worried that rebellion and consequent concessions by local governments would undermine central control of the New World empires. In Paris, Madrid, and Westminster, monarchs listened and began to take note of the crisis. They and their ministers of state ordered a thorough shake-up of the apparatus of imperial government at home, a renewed commitment to government of the colonies abroad, and a reassessment of the purposes of empire.

From Provinces of Empire
to a New Nation

The crisis times at the end of the seventeenth century ended when central imperial authorities reinvented their strategies of governance and reconceptualized the purposes of empire. Henceforth, monarchs and their ministers decided, empires would be collective enterprises of the home country and the colonists. Imperial leaders switched from delegating authority to proprietors to direct administrative supervision of the colonies.

Political stability imposed from without allowed colonial communities to exploit local resources and frame more stable institutions. In the colonies, distinct American cultures appeared. These mixed local and imperial values and goods. Economic ties to the home country grew stronger and economic regulations more voluminous and taxing. Local politics, based in part on deference and in part on negotiation and reciprocity, evolved as well. With the imperial connection strengthened and members of communities fashioning distinct lifestyles, the European footholds in America evolved into stable, mature provinces of empire.

The colonists recognized this maturity by the middle of the century. In the British colonies, the settlers had begun to refer to themselves as "British Americans" or simply "Americans" rather than as Englishmen or women or Scots living away from home. Indeed, for some observers, the mature American identity of the colonies was marked by the appearance of a new kind of person, different from denizens of the Old World. As Ronald Takaki, one of the foremost modern students of American immigration history, wrote recently, "As Americans, we originally came from many different shores, and our diversity has been at the center of the making of America." Hector St. Jean de Crèvecoeur, a French Canadian who emigrated to upper New York in 1763, celebrated the "invisible transformation" that had reformed the varied multitudes of Europe into "a new man, who acts upon new principles. . . . Here individuals of all nations are

Order is Heav'n's first law; and this confest / Some are, and must be, greater than the rest.
—Alexander Pope,
Essay on Man, IV (1744)

Friends Meeting House at Market Street Corner broke open by the American Soldiers, where they have taken up their Abode.
—Elizabeth Drinker,
diary entry, July 16, 1776

melted into a new race of men, whose labors and posterity will one day cause great changes in the world."

Both Takaki and Crèvecoeur suggest that the key to understanding American culture and economic life lies in recognition of the diversity of America's population. Modern scholars use the word *pluralism* to depict this beneficial mixing of different ethnic traditions and interest groups. The term did not exist in the eighteenth century. In fact, the word originates in the early-twentieth-century empirical philosophy of academics like the English logician Bertrand Russell. He argued that the universe had a plurality of causes. American social scientists borrowed the term to describe the variety of economic interest groups in this country vying for a voice in the legislative process.

According to the idea of pluralism that American political scientists made popular in the 1950s, competition among various groups gives rise to conflict, but also provides avenues for resolution of conflict. The more inclusive and vocal the interest groups, the closer the society comes to true democracy. Sociologists joined in, likening the social pluralism of American society to a "salad bowl." Unlike the early-twentieth-century metaphor of the "melting pot" in which ethnic differences are boiled away, a "salad bowl" society features different ethnic groups lying side by side but keeping their distinctive shape and color. And that is what happened in the eighteenth-century colonies.

Maturation, diversity, and the accompanying pride of achievement alleviated the growing pains of the critical period but brought their own tensions. These manifested themselves in matters as ordinary as how one used leisure time and how one earned a living. One can visualize these tensions as stretching across vertical and horizontal axes. On the vertical axis, one can locate a growing divergence between high, or elite, culture and folk, or popular, pastimes, as well as an increasing gulf between the well-to-do and the working classes. In other places and times, similar oppositions led to social upheavals, but not in the mid-eighteenth-century colonies. Here, religious enthusiasm, the rise of domestic sentimentality, the popularization of science, the appearance of economic opportunity, and consumerism drew the high and the low together often enough to forestall class warfare.

The horizontal axis represents the tug of war between the centers of empire and the American provinces. The very fact of maturation created this tension. As Benjamin Franklin put it, how could an island govern a continent? The answer was: not by might alone. The imperial authorities could never have governed their colonies without the consent of the colonists.

In other words, the essential ties of empire were not just political; they were cultural and economic. But as the colonies matured, they no longer depended so heavily upon the home countries, in the same way that young people's ties to their parents stretch thinner as boys and girls become men and women. In culture, this horizontal tension played out as a competition between Old World polish and New World freshness, between imported silk and homespun. In economics, the horizontal contest was more subtle, for home countries and colonies were mutually dependent, but differences of opinion over the Navigation Acts, customs and credit policies, and the flow of currency pit colonists against the imperial authorities.

Did maturation and its accompanying tensions in culture and economic life increase or reduce the distance between progress and oppression? In other words, which of the two stories do cultural developments and economic growth in the eighteenth century tell? The answer is both. On the one hand, culture and commerce helped to create a comparatively fluid, open, and egalitarian society. Crèvecoeur's "new man" had opportunities in America duplicated nowhere else at that time. On the other hand, as Howard Zinn, one of the foremost critics of the pluralist theory, writes, "A close look at this pluralism shows that it is very limited." Late colonial society continued to marginalize and mistreat certain groups, but in play and work and worship, these groups were not powerless. They exerted a profound influence upon their own and others' lives.

These groups played a part as well in the convulsive events of the American Revolution. Arguably, the American Revolution was the most important event in early American history. It welded thirteen jealous and quarrelsome British colonies into a confederation of republics whose size and potential wealth dwarfed the home country. In Gordon Wood's words, it "brought to the surface" and absorbed and transformed ideas of liberty and republicanism, giving them a form that has lasted for over two hundred years. It accelerated the egalitarian impulses in colonial society, opening the way to genuine democracy long before it was achieved anywhere else in the Western world.

Ironically, the very persuasiveness of such a reading of the impact of the Revolution poses a problem. The Revolution becomes a veritable black hole whose gravity sucks into itself all the events and ideas preceding it. One begins to think of it as though it were inevitable and unstoppable, when in fact no one in the imperial government or in the colonies could have foretold in 1763, 1770, or even 1774 that the Continental Congress would declare independence in 1776 or that hitherto uncooperative colonies could join to pursue common military and economic goals. Thus the drive to independence is the final and perhaps the most important irony in the early American story.

Before the 1770s, a handful of theoretical pieces, authored by British bureaucrats and ministerial advisers, addressed the danger of colonial separatism, but the suddenness and the comprehensiveness of the break with Britain bewildered the British and inspired the revolutionaries to believe that history was on their side. As Thomas Paine, the English émigré who became the foremost propagandist of the breach, wrote just before the Continental Congress declared independence, "I have never met with a man, either in England or America, who hath not confessed his opinion, that a separation between the countries, would take place one time or other . . . but we need not go far, the inquiry ceases at once, for, the *time hath found us*."

One way to avoid Paine's self-fulfilling and ahistorical interpretation of the events leading up to independence is to widen the time frame of the inquiry. The closing chapters of *Brave New World* fit the crisis and its consequences into the context of the collision of two great empires, beginning with the French and Indian War of 1754–1763.

One of the more common pieces of coup d'oeil is the drawing of overlapping black and white objects on the same page. When focusing on either color, the viewer sees a recurrent pattern in it (people's faces or fish, for example), and the opposite color becomes mere background. War and peace in the eighteenth-century colonies present the same puzzle for the eye: which was the dominant pattern, which the background?

Whichever of the two dominated, their juxtaposition sharply defined the contradictions inherent in the imperial system. Had the peace of 1714–1739 prevailed, the British and colonial treasuries would not have faced the financial crisis of 1763. Had war continued or the French maintained their North American empire after 1763, the colonies would have remained wedded to the British army and navy. Instead, the alternation of draining war and uncertain peace forced colonial leaders and imperial authorities to reconsider the balance sheet of benefits and liabilities of empire.

In 1763, the British colonists were proud of their contributions to the war effort, and expected to reap immediate benefits from the end of a century of war on their borders. At the same time, with peace the British government acquired expanded responsibilities, and these dictated actions displeasing to many in the older colonies.

As part of the terms of the treaty of 1763, the British tried to find an all-embracing solution to the competing aims of Native Americans, British settlers, and French Canadians. But Britain's failure to consult its own colonists when they granted legal and religious privileges to the French Canadians and confirmed the Indians' titles to the trans-Appalachian territory angered Anglo-Americans. Coupled with ministerial leader George Grenville's heavy-handed and easily misconstrued new policies for governing and taxing the British colonies, Britain's concessions to its newest American subjects induced leading colonists to protest to Parliament and the king. After repeated confrontations, the logic of opposition evolved into a rationale for resistance.

Within thirteen years of celebrating the end of the French and Indian menace on the borders of the mainland British colonies, the colonists and the British found themselves mired in deadly conflict. Even such avid promoters of empire in 1763 as Benjamin Franklin had by 1775 concluded that a closer union with Britain "will only be to corrupt and poison us also," for "here [in Britain] numberless and needless places, patronage positions, enormous salaries, pensions, perquisites, bribes, groundless quarrels, foolish expeditions, false accompts [accounts] or no accompts, contracts and jobbs devour all revenue, and produce continual necessity in the midst of natural plenty."

A year later, in 1776, thirteen of the American colonies threw off their once proud allegiance to Britain and "assumed their rightful place among the nations," as a confederation of independent republics. All around the new "United States of America" European empires still thrived, but in the new states republican political institutions and concepts triumphed.

There remain two knotty questions. First, the shadow of "might have been" and "should have done" looms over all the events in this part of the book. One cannot help but wonder whether the crisis could have been averted. Or are some events inevitable—so widespread and deeply rooted—that they cannot turn out other than they did? Even though these sorts of ruminations have no real answer, by posing counterfactual hypotheses along the way, that is, by asking what if so-and-so had acted in such and such a fashion (unlike what actually occurred), one can gain some insight into the matter of inevitability.

The second question involves causation. What forces, decisions, and acts caused the movement for independence? Causes in history are arguments that historians make from pieces of evidence. Might the loyalists be correct in their assertion that it was all a conspiracy by a few die-hard ingrates, smugglers, and mean-spirited partisans? Hardly. A more convincing argument about the origins of the Revolution entails multiple, partial causation. There was no single person, event, or development that mandated the uprising. Instead, the acts of many people and the course of many trends came together in these years to foment protest and rebellion.

Yet for the "losers" in the crisis of these years, those men and women who remained loyal to the crown and the empire, the irony of the book's thesis and antithesis could not have been more pronounced. The revolutionaries spoke of defending liberty and property as they took both from the loyalists. At the same time, the revolutionaries' ideals of representative or "republican" government based upon the sovereignty of the people, the fabrication of the idea of rights, and the incorporation in the polity of commoners held out the bright promise that, in the future, the betterment of some need not rest upon the oppression of others. Thus the coming of the Revolution actually confirms the theme that prefaced this study—the simultaneity of improvement and sacrifice.

The story of the American Revolution does not end with the Declaration of Independence, the Peace of Paris, or even the creation of the confederation of the states. Not quite returning to Locke's "state of nature" to write their fundamental laws (for example, Connecticut and Rhode Island merely restyled their old charters "constitutions"), the revolutionaries nevertheless discarded monarchy in favor of a representative form of government wherein ultimate sovereignty rested with the people—

in short, republicanism. The new constitutions featured checks and balances, bills of rights, and provision for regular rotation and removal of incumbent officials.

The revolutionaries borrowed many techniques of governance from English and Continental models, but taken as a whole revolutionary constitutionalism was something quite without precedent. American fundamental law made the people sovereign. They had to ratify the new constitutions before they went into effect, except in South Carolina, where a lowland planter aristocracy ensured its own dominance by drafting and adopting a constitution with minimal popular participation. Theoretically, the interests of the people were paramount in these new governments; henceforth, all officials and representatives would be the trustees of the people, acting in the interest of the governed and removable upon demand. Most states adopted some form of impeachment and trial by an upper house to ensure accountability within the government.

If the language of these documents exhibited great uniformity, there were marked differences in the structures of state governance. Pennsylvania and Georgia fashioned unicameral legislatures with universal white male suffrage, limited the power of courts and magistrates, and inched toward democracy. Pennsylvania mandated popular election of justices of the peace, as far from the original of that office as one could go. New York and South Carolina required that men possess substantial property to hold office and vote. The other states fell between the Pennsylvania and South Carolina extremes. Despite the pleas of able advocates of women's rights like Abigail Adams, no state save New Jersey gave women the right to vote, and New Jersey soon recanted its liberality.

The new state constitutions spoke of the liberty and equality of citizens. The reality was different. Slaves, women, aliens, non-Protestants, Indians, and the poor—the "others" in revolutionary America—were not accorded equal status to free, Protestant white men of property. Slaves stood outside this sacred circle of citizenship. Women were still legally "covered" by their fathers or spouses, and Indians remained wards of Congress, permanent strangers in their own land.

But what historian Bernard Bailyn has called a "contagion of liberty" had began the slow process of dis-establishing the churches, abolishing slavery by law in the northern states, and opening political office to those from the middle and lower ranks of society. In Virginia, Jefferson and Madison drafted and Madison (with Jefferson away on a diplomatic mission to France) would push the Virginia Act of Toleration through the House of Burgesses. Other states followed suit, until only Massachusetts and Connecticut had religious establishments.

Massachusetts ended slavery in a series of court fights; Pennsylvania, New York, and New Jersey arranged for gradual abolition; and New Hampshire and Rhode Island abolished slavery by legislative fiat. After the War of Independence brought the lands between the Ohio River and the Great Lakes into the United States, the states in 1787 agreed that this "Northwest Territory" would be free. By the 1820s, most of the states abolished property qualifications for voting and holding office, a process begun during the Revolution.

The new state constitutions diverged from the older colonial codes in another significant respect: a gradual but discernible separation of public and private law appeared. The first colonists had believed that liberty lay in fulsome elucidation of all laws, because one's liberty was determined by one's status. A settler could claim certain "liberties"—the right to follow a trade or vote in an election—by law or custom. Good law enumerated such liberties so that everyone knew where he or she stood.

In the revolutionary era, American political theorists began to assume that one of the purposes of government was to protect personal liberty and private property rather than to grant and define them. Bills of rights laid out these liberties. Beneath this change in political ideology was a deeper shift in social attitudes. Revolutionary lawgivers no longer believed that personal identity derived from membership in a community. Instead, they claimed that individuals had rights simply because they were human. Revolutionary republican law confirmed rather than conferred these rights to life, liberty, and the pursuit of happiness, though again some people had more rights than others.

The story of the war is part of the birthright of the new nation. The colonial militia did not transform itself into a regular army. Indeed, though it demonstrated great courage and some ability, it only journeyed to battlefields "in season." But George Washington and his staff were able to create a regular army and keep it in the field. Men like Washington set an example of disinterested virtue for the officer corps.

To the Continental side rushed warriors from all over Europe. France sent an army and a navy without whose aid victory might never have come. From Germany and Poland came experienced officers to whip a citizen soldiery into the equal of Britain's legions. Formations like the Maryland "line" (regular troops) set an example of their own of fortitude and suffering. There are other stories—of greed and incompetence among the "commissaries" who supplied the army; of rivalry and backbiting among the commanders; of desertion and cowardice; and even a mutiny that Washington himself had to quell.

The achievements of the revolutionary generation after 1776 speak for themselves. Many sacrificed family and business to serve in legislative, judicial, and executive capacities in the new states, under the Articles of Confederation, and in the federal government. They wrote the federal Constitution of 1787. Three became presidents of the new nation.

Jefferson's Declaration severed the ties that had bound thirteen colonies to the empire by declaring independence, but there was another declaration in the text. With the choice of phrases like "all men are created equal" and "inalienable rights," Jefferson implied, and Congress seemed to agree, that the new nation would be based upon an extended concept of citizenship. But such ringing words remain hollow without implementation. Which path would the framers follow—the road toward full realization of the rhetoric of their protests, wherein all those created equal by God would exercise equal rights, or the road to continued oppression of Africans, Indians, women, religious minorities, and the poor? Which theme would predominate in the years to come?

CHRONOLOGY — PART TWO

1636	Harvard College founded
1689	Toleration Act passes Parliament
1693	College of William and Mary founded
1696	Board of Trade established
1701	Yale College founded
1702–1713	Queen Anne's War
1708	Presbyterianism takes hold in Connecticut
1710s–1720s	German and Scots-Irish immigration to the colonies grows
1711–1714	Tuscarora War in North Carolina
1714	King George I crowned
1716	Yamasee War in South Carolina; Spanish missions founded in Texas
1718	New Orleans founded
1721–1748	Robert Walpole serves as prime minister
1724–1757	Duke of Newcastle serves as secretary of state
1727	King George II crowned; Franklin creates the Junto group
1728	John Bartram plants first American botanical garden
1732	Georgia Colony chartered; Franklin launches *Poor Richard's Almanack*
1734	Edwards's revival in New England begins
1738–1741	Whitefield preaches in the colonies
1739	War of Jenkins's Ear begins; Stono River Rebellion in South Carolina
1740s	Great Awakening spreads through America
1740–1748	King George's War
1743	American Philosophical Society created
1746	College of New Jersey (later Princeton) founded
1750s	Consumer revolution spreads through colonies; Franklin experiments with static electricity; Baptists gain in southern colonies
1754	Kings College (later Columbia) founded in New York City; French military buildup in West; Washington defeated at Fort Necessity; Albany conference

1754–1763	French and Indian War
1755	Braddock defeated at Fort Duquesne
1756	Fall of Oswego to the French; Seven Years' War begins in Europe
1757	Siege of Fort William Henry; William Pitt becomes prime minister of England
1758	British take Forts Duquesne and Louisbourg; Indian neutrality spreads
1759	Quebec falls to British; Cherokee War
1760	Montreal falls to British; King George III crowned
1761	Writs of assistance cases in Massachusetts
1762–1763	Peace negotiations end war; Pitt and Newcastle give way to Bute and Grenville
1763	Pontiac's Rebellion; Proclamation Line of 1763; Parson's cases in Virginia end
1763–1773	Surge in British immigration to America
1764	Sugar Act passed
1765	Stamp Act passed; Sons of Liberty formed; stamp riots in America; Stamp Act Congress
1766	Rockingham ministry repeals Stamp Act; Declaratory Act passed
1767	Townshend duties passed
1767–1770	Colonial boycotts; Regulator movements in Carolinas
1768	Troops land in Boston
1770	Boston Massacre; Lord North becomes prime minister; most Townshend duties repealed; Spanish move up California coast
1772	Committees of Correspondence appear
1773	Tea Act; Boston Tea Party
1774	Coercive Acts passed; First Continental Congress
1775	Battles of Lexington, Concord, and Bunker Hill; invasion of Canada; Second Continental Congress
1776	Paine's *Common Sense* published; debacle in Canada; Washington defeated in New York; Declaration of Independence; state constitutions written; *Articles of Confederation* drafted
1777	Battle of Saratoga; British occupy Philadelphia
1778	Treaty of mutual aid with France; war erupts on the frontier; British take Savannah, Georgia
1779–1781	War spreads in the South; siege of Charleston, South Carolina; British invade the Carolinas; French forces join Washington; American victory at Yorktown; *Articles of Confederation* ratified; peace negotiations begin in Paris; Lord North's ministry falls
1783	Peace treaty agreed to; Newburgh conspiracy by Continental Army officers; war ends; Washington resigns and returns home

9

The Empires Reinvented, 1660–1763

In 1710, three young Iroquois and one Mahican warrior visited London. Though their arrival caused a stir, the visit seemed to Queen Anne and her government to make eminent sense. The British had embarked upon a program of imperial consolidation and centralization, one facet of which was courting the Indians.

The four natives did not have the authority to represent their peoples, although one of them, Theyanoguin, renamed Hendrick, was a councilor among the Mohawks. Nevertheless, the English authorities called them kings and received them with formal diplomatic honors. Garbed in fancy dress they obtained in England from a theatrical tailor, with formal courtesies spoken for them by interpreters, they bowed at the queen's feet. In proper Indian fashion, they gave and received gifts. They also met with leaders of the Anglican Church eager to convert all Indians to Christianity.

Crowds gathered to watch as the "four kings" toured the mansions of the West End of London and the workhouses on the meaner streets in the old city, but not everyone was impressed. Some wags satirized the warriors and dismissed the very idea that Indians could be kings. Other writers took the Indians' part, and used their apparent natural dignity and politeness as a foil to criticize the fopperies and fads of Queen Anne's London.

In the end, the "four kings" came to be what others wanted them to be, proof of the splendor of the empire in every way. They were nature's noblemen come to bow to the superiority of English civilization; fearsome allies in England's ongoing war with France for control of North America; and, above all, symbols of the success of Britain's efforts to bring civilization to the wilderness.

Between the 1680s and 1750, Britain (after 1707 England and Scotland joined in the United Kingdom, or Great Britain) and its imperial rivals engaged in a program of reform of their overseas holdings, increasing bureaucratic oversight while liberalizing economic controls. Above all, the imperial powers began to make their empires a focus of national policy. The empires had struck back against the chaos of

Westward the course of Empire takes its way.
—George Berkeley, "On the Project of Planting Arts and Learning in America," 1752

the critical period, creatively and effectively reasserting European control of colonial territories.

But the imperial rulers could not dictate the shape or operation of colonial government. No matter how centralized the empires looked on paper, the officials in London, Paris, and Madrid could not impose policy without bargaining with ruling segments of colonial society. Instead, at any given time the governance of empire depended upon the interaction of three sets of institutions: those formally charged with governance of the empire, usually sitting in the metropolitan capital; an informal set of overlapping and sometimes competing interest groups connecting the officers of the central government to the important people of the colonies; and local administrative institutions within the colonies themselves. Through the interaction of these three sets of institutions, the internal political conflicts and border wars that roiled the colonies in the last quarter of the seventeenth century were quieted and empire made profitable.

RETHINKING THE PURPOSES OF EMPIRE

War in Europe and the extension of hostilities to the colonies left the French and Spanish empires reeling, but they survived because new ideas and a renewed commitment to imperial reform among the rulers permitted far greater latitude to the settlers. In particular, the British Empire emerged from these troubles stronger than ever, because the British recast their policy to favor commerce over proprietorship and material gain over political obedience.

The Mercantilist Theory of Empire

Historians have incorrectly attributed the theory of mercantilism to sixteenth-century empires. Empires like Philip II's were bullionist, not mercantilist, that is, designed to find and extract from the colonies gold and silver (bullion) that could be turned into coin and used to pay European armies. With the coming of the trading frontier in the beginning of the seventeenth century, the idea of empire appeared in a new light. It became a potential source of raw materials for European workers to transform into salable goods in Europe. But theory lagged behind practice. Even after commerce had replaced extraction as the motive for settlement of North American colonies, Europeans still did not have a well-defined concept of the commercial value of empire.

English and French sponsorship of royal societies for science and philosophy after 1660 may seem distant cousins—if related at all—to the project of imperial governance, but the experimental and theoretical scientists abetted the imperial administrators' attempts to recast the purpose of empire. In the second half of the seventeenth century, some of the leading intellectuals in this "Age of Reason" participated in the colonial project. For example, John Locke wrote colonial constitutions for his benefactor, Lord Shaftesbury, himself a patron of science and philosophy. In the same years, France's foremost minister of state, Jean-Baptiste Colbert, conversed with France's academic luminaries about the wealth of the colonies. The same principles that Colbert, in France, and English economists like William Petty and Charles Devenant used to survey and report the wealth of their kingdoms were put to use to assess the resources and plan the exploitation of the empires.

In treatises on the political economy of states, European intellectuals fashioned the basis for the theory of mercantilism. They argued that investment in colonies would be justifiable if the home country had a favorable balance of trade with the colonies. Colonial raw materials would supply home country industries. In turn, the settlers would become consumers of the products of the home country. Any trade with other imperial systems or the colonies of other empires would be controlled by the home country. Any competition by foreign buyers for the exports of the colonies or by foreign producers of manufactured goods for the colonial market would be channeled through the home country. Trade would be limited to the ships and crews of the home country or its colonies, aiding the growth of the nation's merchant marine and shutting out foreign competitors.

Theoretically, instead of merely adding to the wealth of a few in the imperial metropolis, the wealth the new system generated would rain down on all the subjects of the realm. The sharing of wealth would make the colonists partners in the imperial enterprise, rather than mere laborers for the crown or a handful of crown-sponsored monopolies.

Only a hundred years later—when it was under attack by advocates of free trade—would the new system actually get the name mercantilism and its full implications be understood. But even without a particular name, the new ideas spread far and wide in the private sector of the economy. Although it was a state-sponsored and state-run system of economics, mercantilism offered merchants an ideology that favored private enterprise. Insofar as it encouraged migration to the colonies and protected buying and selling within any given empire, mercantilism made that empire a more level playing field for anyone who could promise to add to the wealth of the home country. By policing the outer boundaries of the empire more closely, mercantilism allowed entrepreneurs greater freedom within the empire.

Mercantilism also denied one's European rivals a share of the spoils of one's own empire, for whenever the home country so wished, foreign manufactured exports could be frozen out of colonial markets, and foreign manufacturers denied access to the exports of one's colonies. Indeed, the moving force behind the initial adoption of mercantilist schemes in England and France was their merchants' and governments' desire to crush their Dutch trade rivals.

During the interregnum, at Cromwell's urging, Parliament passed the Navigation Act, requiring that colonial exports travel in English or colonial ships and colonial imports first pass through English ports. The act was aimed at the Dutch Atlantic carrying trade. Cromwell was not the first English leader to recognize the economic potential of the Atlantic empire, but he was the first to conceptualize an Atlantic imperial system pumping wealth into the home country.

In 1660, the first Restoration Parliament confirmed Cromwell's instincts about trade. In a second Navigation Act, the legislators restated the requirement that the carrying trade be in English or colonial bottoms, captained and owned by English or colonial subjects. The command that all foreign goods be "laid on shore" in England was temporarily eased, for Charles II's government wanted to restore good relations with France and the Netherlands. The new law merely "enumerated" certain staple goods that had to go first to England. These included some imports from Europe, but far more important for the elaboration of a colonial system, the act also named the major staple crops of the American colonies—tobacco, sugar, and dyestuffs. Money and slaves were never enumerated, allowing a free trade within the empire in these essential commodities.

In 1662, Parliament added a third Navigation Act, to prevent fraudulent evasions of the 1651 and 1660 acts, and in 1663, yet another, requiring that almost all European products meant for the English colonies must be landed in England and reloaded in English ships for the continuation of the voyage. Portuguese salt, Irish and Scottish horses and linens, wines from Madeira and the Azores, and a few other items were exempted because special interest groups interceded.

The multiplicity of statutory enactments suggests that the home government had become aware of the basic flaw in the system—sly disobedience was often more profitable than law-abiding conformity. Colonial governors were supposed to watch for violations and arrest violators, but no sooner was the latest act in place than evidence poured in from all sides that it was evaded or ignored. As one southern colonial governor reported back to his masters in Westminster, "I have endeavored to hinder illegal trade, but have met with great difficulty, especially in the courts and the assembly. I believe that it will be found, if examination be made, that the Acts of Trade and Navigation are oftener broken than kept here."

To close the loopholes and police the trade, Parliament passed additional statutes. In 1673, Parliament established a colonial arm of the customs service. Customs collectors and onboard and onshore searchers had long monitored English harbors. Now their counterparts were sent to colonial ports—though in the smaller of the ports one man usually did all the different jobs. The collectors were at first paid fees based on the number of clearances from ports and received a share of confiscated goods and fines. Later, they were given salaries. Surveyor generals watched everyone, creating a system that was foolproof on paper and fallible in practice—for there were too many places where one could unload and load along the shore and too few honest imperial officials.

In response to this problem, the collectors were required to post bonds for their own good behavior—a system of "watch and warn" that resembled the way that English justices of the peace kept order in their counties. This mimetic recycling of forms of governance was a feature of all empires—indeed, a country's style of imperial governance often derived from or mirrored its domestic political practices. Such institutional mimicry often disfavored the colonists, for it imposed on them laws that ill-suited the colonists' condition.

Mercantilistic colonial policies like the Navigation Acts went hand in hand with the new idea that government regulation of the economy could be systematically and efficiently managed. At the same time as they put into place the administrative apparatus of mercantilism, European governments began to rationalize their tax systems and their law courts. Kings and princes began to offer bounties to industries and trades, creating a prototype of the "promotional state" wherein the government fostered opportunities for private businesses.

The French and Spanish sent intendants with powers of civil administrators to watch the governors-general, whose powers were now limited to military and diplomatic matters. The result was closer supervision and incorporation of native and mixed-ancestry elites into the ruling class. In the British Empire, governors had to share power with customs collectors, searchers, controllers, and naval officers, all of whom had overlapping duties over the same matters of trade and business and reported to different officials at home. The result was a forerunner of the checks and balances system that would become basic to American revolutionary constitutionalism (an irony if there ever was one).

The French Empire Repaired

In the second half of the seventeenth century, the French enterprise in North America lay in disarray. By the 1720s, despite ruinous wars with the English colonies, the French colonies of Acadia, New France (Canada), and Louisiana enjoyed some prosperity. The restoration of the French interest was hardly an accident. Colbert set out to save it. To secure the boundaries of Acadia and Canada he sent troops "de la Marine"—regular troops recruited for service in the colonies. After their term they would be rewarded with land in America. Colbert opened up the empire to all French trading companies, the object of which was to increase the flow of naval stores like pitch, tar, and masts, as well as grain, furs, fish, and foodstuffs, to France.

Colbert also imposed a military-style organization with clear-cut lines of command. The king sat at the top, and his minister of the marine ran all colonial affairs. A governor-general, in charge of military affairs, diplomacy, and law and order, and an intendant for civil matters, including finance, holding courts, and everyday governance, were the chief on-site officers. Under the governors-general served governors of each of the provinces. The intendants had subordinate officers as well, usually living in the large towns. The settlers of Canada could voice their opinions in the Sovereign Council, meeting in Quebec, but the council acted as a court of appeals rather than an originator of legislation. The intendants formulated the law.

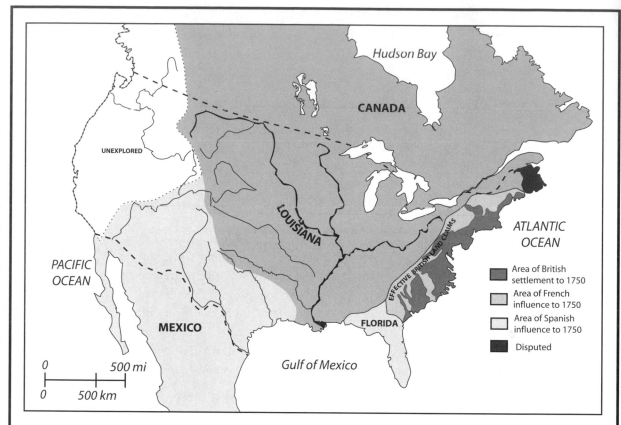

French and Spanish Occupation of North America to 1750

Militia captains spoke for the ordinary people. Crown appointees, these captains were invariably middle- or lower-class inhabitants rather than noblemen and carried the complaints of their men to the government. The captains held local assemblies on an ad hoc basis when the intendant needed to know what was happening in the localities. A bishop represented the interests of the established Roman Catholic Church, but bishops had little influence upon political affairs. Colbert, ever the rationalist, feared religious interference in politics.

When Colbert died in 1683, his replacement as secretary of the marine, Jérôme de Pontchartrain, carried on the Colbert program. Though dismissed by his detractors as a one-eyed, pox-marked, heavy-jowled incompetent, Pontchartrain was a hardworking man sympathetic to the problems of the settlers. He was opposed to military rule but not to military preparedness. Above all, he wanted peace, trade, and growth. If, during most of his tenure, France was at war with England, and hence the borders of the French American provinces were aflame, his policies contributed to the modest progress of French America.

Indeed, by all conventional measures of success, French policy had begun to succeed. The French population of Canada grew from ten thousand to fifty-five thousand in the thirty-five years from Colbert's death to the end of the 1720s. The densely populated Quebec-Montreal corridor grew from less than 10,000 to over 30,000 inhabitants by 1730. The French had spread from settlements along the banks of the Saint Lawrence well up into the Canadian Shield and west toward the northern shores of the Great Lakes. A new colony, Louisiana, stretching from the Gulf of Mexico up the Mississippi, created an arc of French posts around the English colonies.

Colbert wished to limit the expansion of France's American empire, but the ever-receding fur frontier drew France deeper and deeper into the North American continent. Its coureurs de bois (fur traders) traveled into the Great Lakes region and down the Mississippi in search of new sources of pelts. French-born priests walked in the tracks of the traders and established missions in Indian towns from the southern end of Lake Superior to the mouth of the Mississippi.

In 1673, the Jesuit Father Jacques Marquette and the trader Louis Jolliet traveled down the Mississippi at the behest of Count Frontenac, the governor of Canada. Their task was to claim the land for France and determine the course of the "Father of the Rivers." They were disappointed to learn that it flowed south, toward the Spanish provinces, but their reports paved the way for the Sieur de la Salle's military expedition in 1682.

La Salle was a French nobleman who owned land in Canada, toured the Great Lakes, and saw himself as another Cortés. La Salle's haughty and impatient personality alienated many, but his energy and boldness outweighed those character flaws—for a time. With a small band of soldiers and Indian guides and interpreters, he established the French presence on the long course of the Mississippi. But his men mutinied and on March 19, 1687, murdered him and three of his lieutenants. Many of the places La Salle visited never bore a mark of his presence, but La Salle left behind him a small fortress on the bluffs above the confluence of the Mississippi and Missouri rivers. He named the post Saint Louis in honor of Louis IX of France, one of the Crusader kings, and it became a major trading center for the French.

Pontchartrain, ever on the alert for sources of funds, viewed the trans-Mississippi West as a treasure house and ordered the occupation of the river's basin and the coast around the mouth of the river. He selected the Sieur d'Iberville to establish the French claim, and late in 1698 sent that nobleman and two ships to begin the process. Franciscans and Jesuits followed to save the souls of the natives and the soldiers of the garrison. When officials and priests continued to complain about the loose conduct of the soldiers, the French sent young orphan women of marriageable age for the European troops, but some of them never found husbands and ended up as ill-treated in the colony as they had been in the home country. In the meantime a métis (literally, "mixed") subculture emerged of French-Indian couples and their offspring that would survive long after the French colonial rule was ended. To Louisiana also came experienced Canadian trappers, farmers, and merchants, but they seemed to have, in words of d'Iberville, "a poor attitude." Many of them would eventually leave and return to their northern homes.

In the early 1700s, renewed war with the Spanish and later the English on the frontiers of the new colony had spurred the French to build a series of fortified towns, notably Mobile and New Orleans, to watch the coast and serve as ports for the French fleet. Private proposals floated in France to improve these settlements went unheeded. The French tried using the settlements as a penal colony, but the felons died or fled. Germans recruited to farm the land perished by the hundreds. The whole colony had but two hundred French inhabitants in 1710.

Return on the French investment came only when the crown and private investors realized that the colony was a perfect spot for a slave market. In 1719, the Company of the Indies, chartered for the purpose, brought 450 slaves into New Orleans. In 1721, another 1,312 arrived. In 1724, the French introduced the harsh law codes of the West Indian islands. By 1739, there were 4,000 slaves in the colony, and fully two-thirds of them were born in Louisiana. Slaves were not only used as labor in the city, they served farmers on the coast and settlers on the lower Mississippi River.

As the French had moved up the rivers that emptied into the Gulf, they came into contact with the Creek Confederation in Alabama, and the Creeks' neighbors, the Chickasaws of northern Mississippi and the Choctaws of southern Mississippi. Trade in deerskins and other forest goods, in return for French manufactured goods, held together an alliance of natives and French traders, but the natives were quick to realize that the French could be played against the English and the Spanish.

Thus necessity and prudence dictated that French policy toward the Indians in Louisiana mix admonition, conciliation, and negotiation, just as in Canada. For example, the French preferred to work through converted or friendly Indian leaders rather than try to impose the will of the French government, unlike the Spanish. If the French were afraid that Indian ways led to endless rounds of revenge and reprisal and the Indians were convinced that French ways ill suited Indians, both sides needed the other.

The Spanish Empire Revived

By the end of the seventeenth century, the Spanish American empire, though still vast in size, had fallen on even harder times than the French. Spain's domestic economy was crippled by high prices and a lack of productivity. Ironically, the same influx of New World silver and gold that had paid for Spanish adventurism in Europe in the sixteenth century caused runaway inflation in the seventeenth century, effectively pricing Spanish goods out of the market. The fruitfulness of the empire might have helped the home country recoup these losses, but without naval supremacy, lost in

1588, Spain's seventeenth-century empire brought in less revenue than Britain's or France's.

Observers like England's Sir Josiah Child blamed the decline of the Spanish Empire on its administrators' preference for conquest over commerce, but by the end of the seventeenth century the Spanish crown could not defend the frontiers of the empire, curb the abuses of its governors, or prevent the settlers from trading with Spain's rivals.

In the eighteenth century, the same enlightened imperial thinking that remade the French Empire made its way into Spain. The new Bourbon kings of Spain, cousins of the French royal line, saw promise in a rational model. Thinkers like the Benedictine monk Benito Feijóo y Montenegro argued for an empire that was efficient, educated, informed, and practical. Other reformers called for a secular mission to complement the religious missionaries' efforts. The goal would be a kind of state-sponsored capitalism—in a word, mercantilism. As secretary to the minister of the Indies José del Campillo y Cossió argued in his *A New System of Economic Government for America*, true power came not from feats of arms but the wise investment of wealth. To attain that goal, the empire needed the labor of the native population. Del Campillo y Cossió urged Spanish ranchers, farmers, and mine owners to treat the Indians with kindness and respect—an old admonition in the service of a new ideology.

Under the first Bourbon kings, the church-dominated Council of the Indies was reduced to a judicial appeals body. The crown conferred day-to-day administration on a new Ministry of the Marine and the Indies. Its staff consisted of imperial bureaucrats, and it oversaw a reduction of duties on trade goods and the expansion of free trade areas within the empire. The ministry pressed for the end of government monopolies and encouraged private investment in businesses in the Americas. It also cracked down on corruption in the local governments, and established the same division of powers between a military governor and a civil intendant as Colbert introduced fifty years earlier in the French possessions.

But the bustle of the new ministry brought little actual change. Despite petition after petition against local corruption and tyrannous government from the provinces, the central government moved slowly. New rounds of viceregal visitations led to proposals but little actual reform. For example, not until 1778 did the crown abolish the monopoly on incoming trade granted to the port of Cadiz in the sixteenth century.

Still, the bureaucrats could be excused their caution. In 1701, war had once again come to Europe, and Spain was in the middle of it, for the war was fought over the new Spanish-French Bourbon alliance. Even in the years of peace that followed the Treaty of Utrecht in 1713, the Spanish crown could not effectively govern its vast New World territory.

In addition, Spain and France remained rivals on the North American frontier for the fur and deerskin trade. Though the French aided the Spanish on the Gulf Coast against the English in Queen Anne's War (1702–1713), the French took the opportunity to expand their Louisiana colony at Spanish expense, and the Spanish closed their ports to the French. All along the lower Mississippi, French and Spanish traders vied for Indian allegiance and trade goods. The French pushed west into Spanish Texas, and the Spanish arrested the French tradesmen.

The era of good feelings, if there ever was one, between Spain and France ended in 1719 with renewed war in Europe. Now Spain fought alone, and all its imperial borders were under constant threat. Although the Spanish were correct to fear French intentions, unsubstantiated rumors caused the Spanish to exaggerate the French threat.

For example, in 1719 the governor of New Mexico convinced himself that an army of French and plains Indians would soon descend on Santa Fe and destroy it. To forestall that event, he sent Pedro de Villasur and a battalion of forty-five Spanish troops and sixty Pueblos to reconnoiter the northern approaches to New Mexico. At the confluence of the Platt and Loup rivers, in Pawnee country (modern Nebraska), the Pawnees surprised the party and killed thirty-two of the Spaniards and eleven of the Pueblos, apparently without the help of a single French soldier. Thereafter, the Spanish left the plains to its native inhabitants.

But even if the Spanish lost battles, Spain's North American territories remained intact. Upon the body of so vast an empire, it was almost impossible to land a knock-out blow.

THE ENGLISH EMPIRE REDISCOVERED

James II had tried to impose the will of the crown on the English colonies, and he might have succeeded but for his ignominious departure from the realm. A man of real administrative vision up to the arrival of William of Orange and his army, James's nerve failed him in 1688. In any case, the colonists had not taken well to his program of close supervision and meddling in local politics, and their passive resistance ruined many of his initiatives.

Had James an administrative machine to support it, his plan might have survived his abdication, but he ruled through commissions, committees, and boards of self-interested, ill-informed politicians and brusque army officers. As soon as he returned to England, Charles II chartered a Committee of Trade and Plantations within the Privy Council, the inner circle of crown advisers. This body proved inadequate to the task, for many on it had little or no knowledge of plantations. The king's chief counselor, Lord Clarendon (whose interest in the plantations was whetted by his Carolina proprietorship in 1663), commissioned a Council on Plantations. Its forty-eight members offered a bewildering variety of more or less helpful opinions, but when Clarendon fell from favor its duties reverted to a committee of the Privy Council and then to a Council of Foreign Plantations. By 1676, the empire was in the hands of the Lords of Trade, a body that reported to the Privy Council. The Stuarts' plan to make the empire in reality what it was in theory—the personal domain of the king—floundered.

William and Mary recognized the flaw in the Stuarts' imperial thinking. The empire could not be likened to a kind of giant royal hunting preserve, open to the king's friends but closed to the general public. Instead, they and their advisers wished a more efficiently administered empire through which commerce flowed smoothly. New measures were needed.

In 1696, the English government extended the vice-admiralty courts of England to the colonies. In the home country, these courts had jurisdiction over cases of smuggling, marine wrecks, disputes over seamen's contracts, and prizes taken in war. Vice-admiralty courts were to perform the same functions in the colonies. Presided over by officers of the navy trained in marine law, these courts did not have juries—a tremendous advantage for the crown in trials in local courts with local juries, which were invariably friendly to colonists accused of smuggling.

In the same year, new regulations gave customs collectors commissions to board ships and search cargoes for smuggled goods. But these search warrants, called "writs of assistance," were not commonly used in the colonies until the middle of the next century, and then only in daytime with prior consent of the courts. The system also relied on networks of informants who were to receive a portion of the fines and confiscations of cargoes and ships.

Piecemeal reform of the customs service and introduction of new courts did not reinvigorate the imperial administration, but these adjustments heralded farther-reaching changes in the way people and information were managed. A spirited and trained imperial bureaucracy assumed the everyday duties of information gathering and policy making. A revolution in transportation of people and ideas literally and figuratively brought the home country and colonies closer together and supplied these bureaucrats with a steady flow of reliable information on colonial events. The introduction of a new kind of public meeting place in London created an arena in which government officials and merchants could share ideas and plan for the future. All of these changes fostered a more sophisticated appreciation of the security needs of the empire.

Parliament supported these changes with legislation, but generally refrained from taking the lead in policy making until 1763. That belonged to the king's great ministers of state. Although from 1689 to 1714 there were ten secretaries of state for the Southern Department (the minister charged with administration of the American colonies), a rate of turnover that hampered consistent enforcement of policy, two of the ten, Daniel Finch, the Earl of Nottingham, and Henry Saint John, Viscount Bolingbroke, took pride and pains in close supervision of the colonies. After 1724,

Thomas Pelham-Holles, the Duke of Newcastle, held the job, and although they were not his highest priority, he missed little that transpired in the colonies.

The Rise of an Imperial Bureaucracy

When we think of the eighteenth-century English empire in North America, we ordinarily imagine the majesty of kings, the cunning of great ministers of state, and the conniving of special interest groups. Queen Anne had a passing interest in America, but the first two Hanoverian kings of England, George I and George II, took little direct interest in the colonies. Instead, the monarchs passed control to parliamentary party leaders and their cabinet ministers like Sir Robert Walpole and the Duke of Newcastle. If "Whigs" like Walpole and Newcastle had any principles about colonial rule, they preferred to leave the colonies alone, so long as the colonies produced an income.

Who ran the everyday business of the empire, then? Clerks and secretaries reading and writing boring documents in small, drab offices did. Trained, dedicated, a bit stuffy, men like these made a career of their jobs and developed a loyalty to their offices. They worked according to rules and regulations and tended to be jealous of their own administrative areas.

These new men and new posts did not replace the older patronage system—they overlay it. The result was a cadre of orderly, cautious, industrious civil servants. Such bureaucrats made work for other bureaucrats. The twelve hundred civil servants employed in 1660 grew to twenty-five hundred by 1688, and exploded to twelve thousand by 1720. All for the maintenance of the empire. Many of these officials were averse to the casual corruption and self-dealing that besmirched seventeenth-century part-time bureaucrats, for the new administrators were determined to spend their entire careers in government service.

The nerve center of the new colonial bureaucracy was the Board of Trade (the full title was the Lords Commissioners of Trade and Plantations) created in the same 1696 omnibus colonial administration reorganization act that sent the vice-admiralty courts to the colonies and strengthened the hands of the customs officials. The board, meeting in Whitehall, gathered and sifted information and recommend policy and personnel decisions to the Privy Council and the ministers of state. Its sixteen members included "ex-officio" appointees (men of influence and standing) and professional administrators. Some of the monarchs dropped in to hear the deliberations of the board (Queen Anne was a semiregular attendee), but in general the board was left to its own devices.

If the board had no formal powers, save its statutory power to recommend the appointment of the colonial upper houses, the skill and cunning of its members like William Blathwayt and Martin Bladen, who between them served on it for fifty years, gave the board great influence. Although accused of dawdling and occasional neglect, the board's professional staff exemplified the new breed of career official.

The prototype may well have been Blathwayt, auditor general of the plantations revenues, appointed in 1680 and retained in office through four reigns and three dynasties of English kings and queens until 1717. Foremost among Blathwayt's successors in the period between Queen Anne's War and the French and Indian War was Martin Bladen. He seemed to know everyone of importance in government, and everyone learned to confide in him. He wanted to "reform" the colonies by bringing them more directly under the control of the imperial government, a policy that many in Whitehall found appealing, though he was ahead of his time.

Coffee, Tea, Sugar, and the Business of Empire

The new bureaucracy held court in the London "coffeehouses." The first of these establishments appeared in the 1650s, and by the beginning of the eighteenth century there was a coffeehouse on every corner in the heart of London. The merchants who formed clubs to lobby Parliament and the members of Parliament who listened to the merchants met the bureaucrats in these public places. As poet Alexander Pope sneered in 1712, "Coffee makes the politicians wise."

In coffeehouses men consumed huge amounts of the ground and roasted beans of a tropical shrub, which had become the rage in England. Whether at the breakfast table or in the coffeehouse, coffee woke people up and kept them active. It was not only a stimulant; its importers and purveyors believed it to have medicinal properties. Equally important, coffee consumption reminded the English that the pleasures of empire could be widely shared, even if the wealth of empire remained in the hands of a few.

As coffeehouses proliferated, individual establishments gained reputations for their clientele and their product. Edward Lloyd's coffeehouse on Lombard Street became the gathering place for ship owners, captains, and insurance brokers. Over the years, the operation moved from the coffeehouse to an office building, and became Lloyd's of London, the world's leading marine insurance exchange. The West Indies planters gathered at the Jamaica, in the heart of the old city of London. Pennsylvania visitors to the imperial capital met at the Pennsylvania, in Birchin Lane. When Benjamin Franklin was in London, he collected his mail at the Birchin Lane shop. Other coffeehouses routinely served as post offices, with racks of pigeon holes for regular customers. Coffeehouses began to blend their own house varieties, and connoisseurs could tell the difference between different varieties of beans and styles of roasting.

Coffeehouses passed rules to ensure that all their customers behaved themselves, for London was still full of toughs and drunks. There was to be no fighting or quarreling in the coffeehouse. Patrons were asked to moderate their conversation so as not to bother the customers at the next table. Although many coffeehouses charged a penny for entrance, there was no rank or precedence in seating—customers were to take the next available seats. "Nor need any, if finer persons come, rise up to assigne to them his room." In a sea of privilege, the coffeehouse was an island of equality.

Coffeehouses offered merchants and officials access to racks of newspapers with the latest news on prices, imports, and exports. Bits of information changed hands, and deals were made. Careers might depend upon coffeehouse contacts. People who did not have a formal rostrum for their political views could share the news of the day and express personal opinions on the ministries and the officeholders. Messengers from powerful political figures conspired with aspiring "hacks" (men of letters who ghostwrote pamphlets for one political faction or another) like Daniel Defoe to produce the essays and exposés that would be read by everyone in the coffeehouse the next week.

The fermented and dried leaf of an Asian evergreen tree, tea was more expensive than coffee, but its advocates claimed that it cleansed the body and purified the blood. Between 1650 and 1700, British tea imports totaled 181,545 pounds. In the next fifty years, the total rose to 40,000,000 pounds. Neither figure includes smuggling, principally of Dutch tea, for the tea trade was formally the monopoly of the British East India Company. The coffeehouse was a male preserve, but tea shops catered to both men and women, and in the home, tea time, at which women presided, introduced tea cups, tea pots, and tea cakes.

Whether one chose coffee or tea as a stimulant, one had to have sugar. Consumption grew with each passing year. Between 1700 and 1740, British use of sugar products doubled, from four to eight pounds per person per year, on average. Sugar (along with chocolate and milk) was also pressed into candies, and these increased the caloric intake of people in all walks of life. In addition, sugar-based desserts, along with sweetened tea or coffee, became the final course in most meals, adding to the demand for the products.

Consumption of these wares of empire changed not only mealtimes, but the whole workday. People who used sweetened, caffeinated beverages could work longer and harder than those who drank wine, beer, and cider—all soporific, dehydrating liquids. What had once been luxuries, ordinary people now deemed essential. The supply of coffee, tea, and above all sugar must not be diminished. One could say that the imperial powers had become addicted to the products of their own empire. The empire was running harder on caffeine and sweets, but the demand for the stimulants and sugar required ever greater investment and management. In the end, like Alice in Lewis Carroll's nineteenth-century fable *Through the Looking-Glass*, the caffeinated masters of the empire had to run faster and faster just to stay where they were.

The Communication Revolution

Even when caffeinated and sugared drinks allowed them to work longer hours, the bureaucrats complained that there was too little time to manage the flow of information arriving from the colonies. By the beginning of the eighteenth century, the sea lanes had become highways for cargo, people, and news. Atlantic crossings took but eight weeks on some routes. Coasters linked the North American ports with one another, and New England merchants' vessels serviced the British West Indies. Port cities on both sides of the ocean grew in size.

Every ship carried vital information. Data on markets and prices, bulletins of departures and arrivals, and offers of goods for sale and job openings enabled merchants and factors to plan ahead. Political news, copies of colonial laws, and confidential assessments from insiders helped officials to make decisions and enabled interest groups to target their lobbying campaigns. To the London townhouses and country mansions of amateur geologists, botanists, entomologists, and zoologists came a flood of facts on American geology, botany, and biology, as well as specimens of all sorts of animals, plants, rocks, and seeds. British collectors' libraries and museums filled with New World objects.

The speed of transmission and the volume of information flowing from the center of the empire to its peripheries and back again grew rapidly. In 1689, communication of the news of the Glorious Revolution to the colonies was spotty, and news from the colonies was chancier still. Six months or a year might pass before fears of war could be allayed or preparations for war ordered. By the 1720s, however, the crown's regular postal service had improved tremendously, in large measure because a regular packet service now crossed the Atlantic.

The planning for the service began in 1701 when Edmund Dummer approached the government with the proposition that he run mail packets between London and the West Indies. A designer of ships, Dummer had powerful friends in the administration. Referred to the Board of Trade and the Admiralty, he gained their consent, on condition that the service was extended to all the colonies. Dummer wanted support to build four or five sloops, fast and agile two-masters. Letters and instructions would thus not have to wait long for a boat in port, nor depend upon the schedule of individual ship captains. His contracts with the government ran into snags, and the service was slow to begin, but by 1715, when his monopoly ended, others had followed his example.

By the 1720s, the posts were filled with a new kind of mail—newspapers. English newspapers could now be delivered to American readers when the news was still relatively fresh. American newspapers benefited by combining reprints of English news with advertisements and letters to the editor. To this, colonial editors added news from the colonies and political viewpoints. The newspapers in the colonies also reprinted colonial laws and important court decisions. These papers could then be sent back to England in the mails and find their way to the coffeehouses.

The Militant Empire

As far as the rulers of the empire were concerned, the most important bits of information coming from and going to the colonies involved military matters. The colonies had always been the border "marches" of the empire, but the changing scope and nature of warfare in the Americas had made the communication of information more important in the years after 1688 than it had been before. The vast areas of comparatively empty space that had separated the European rivals' settlements in the New World had filled. Where in the seventeenth century it took weeks, sometimes months, for troops from one colony to strike at the borders of its rivals and the number of troops available for raids rarely exceeded a few hundred, by King William's War, the space between the European rivals' colonies had all but disappeared, and the size of the opposing forces had grown to five figures.

King William's War also introduced a new kind of professional warfare, replacing the deadly but sporadic and localized fighting of previous years. The American focus of the war, as described in the previous chapter, was the New York—New England frontier with Canada, and militia and Indians carried on much of the combat, devastating entire tribes and frontier regions. Proprietors of colonies found that they simply could not defend their own borders without intercolonial cooperation and help from the crown.

War returned to the northern border in 1702 (Queen Anne's War) and roiled the frontier until 1713, when the Treaty of Utrecht ended the War of the Spanish Succession in Europe. During the war, Massachusetts forces thrust at France's fortified maritime possessions, notably Port Royal in Nova Scotia, finally taking it in 1710. French Acadia became a British possession, though only nominally, for almost all of its five thousand French and Indian inhabitants refused to take the oath of loyalty to the English crown.

The next war commenced in 1739 and had an even broader scope, requiring more bureaucratic coordination. It began in the Caribbean, where Spanish authorities allegedly cut off the ear of a British sea captain named Jenkins. The ear, exhibited in Parliament by an outraged member (hence the appellation War of Jenkins' Ear in England; it was called King George's War in the colonies), became an excuse for a British naval assault on Spain's Caribbean ports. Early in 1739, a British fleet captured Porto Bello on the east coast of Panama, and the next year British recruiters raised four battalions of Americans for service in an invasion of Cartagena, the Spanish port on the coast of modern Colombia.

The invasion failed, and many of the Americans died from tropical diseases complicated by malnutrition. Those who returned told harrowing stories of brutal military discipline. The navy impressed (forcibly recruited) a few of the survivors to cover its losses, a final indignity that Americans remembered when the Royal Navy called on the port of Boston in 1747. Then a press gang trying to round up sailors had to fight its way out of a mob.

Except for the period of peace between 1714 and 1739, when the size of the army was reduced for fiscal reasons, the wars of the years from 1680 to 1763 marked the transformation of a partisan, nonprofessional, relatively small and inexpensive defense force to a standing, well-trained, and expensive military establishment. Overall, the British army and navy tripled in size, and most of the expenditures, reaching by the end of the period into the hundreds of millions of pounds sterling, went not into barracks or guns for the army, but dry docks, building yards, and stores for the navy—in effect, for the defense of the empire. The scale of naval operations expanded even more rapidly than the expenditures, for large fleets had to be kept at sea for longer and longer periods of time to protect the colonies.

Take the matter of food: supplying these fleets was more complex than any task the government had attempted before 1700. In 1760, for example, the navy board purchased 481,600 pounds of hops, 3,819,200 pounds of flour, 4,636,800 pounds of biscuits, 10,830,400 pounds of beef, 3,628,800 pounds of pork, 2,486,400 pounds of cheese, and 1,064,000 pounds of butter. Given such a monotonous and ill-nourishing diet, it was no wonder that so many British sailors deserted their ships, but the victualing of the fleet was one proof that the British navy had become a huge and expensive institution. Almost all the expense went to carry on war or deter piracy in imperial waters.

To keep expenses of patrolling the land borders of the empire down (particularly in time of peace), the English government encouraged private military and quasi-military ventures. One of these, the settlement of the colony of Georgia, illustrates how military thinking influenced imperial expansion.

The story of the Georgia Colony is inseparable from that of James Oglethorpe, a country gentleman whose Jacobite (pro-Stuart) background did not disqualify him from military service under William and Mary and the first two Hanoverian kings or from holding a seat in Parliament. After a brush with bankruptcy himself, Oglethorpe became interested in the fate of debtors imprisoned for failure to pay their creditors.

With a group of twenty others, including noblemen like John Perceval, the Earl of Egmont, Oglethorpe proposed that the lands between South Carolina and the Spanish colony of Florida be set aside as a charitable trust for the "worthy poor" (debtors rather than wastrels, vagabonds, or convicts). Parliament chartered the colony on this basis in 1732, and Oglethorpe, named its first governor, rushed to gather settlers and load equipment for the journey.

Though he had a charitable purpose, the underlying task of the colony was to guard the southern frontier against the Spanish in Florida. Thus from the moment he arrived at Charleston, South Carolina, in the winter of 1733, Oglethorpe began looking for a defensible site for the capital of his colony. On bluffs above the Savannah River, he laid out squares of land for buildings and parks following the Wren plans for the rebuilding of London after the Great Fire of 1666. But unlike William Penn, who adopted a similar design for Philadelphia to prevent fires and increase street frontage for commerce, Oglethorpe's motive was to provide for the common defense. The city had easy access to the sea (in case the Georgians had to flee), and the layout of Savannah from the air resembled a Roman military camp. All this because, from the first, Oglethorpe acted the role of the governor-general.

Oglethorpe insisted that his colonists be prepared for war—and thus not imbibe rum and not purchase slaves. Drink and the debauchery that came with slavery destroyed the morale of soldiers. He also insisted on fair treatment for the Indians, for he knew that they would be valuable allies, as they proved to be. The irony of Oglethorpe in Georgia was that his aggressive military operations failed to achieve their objective; although he protected the frontier, he was not able to oust the Spanish from Florida. In time, all of his forward-looking rules were abandoned, and Georgia, when it became a royal colony in 1753, would embrace rum, slaves, and the dispossession of the Indians.

Georgia was not alone in its sentry duties. Northern New York, western New England, western Pennsylvania, and the Piedmont areas of the western Carolinas abutted the French and Spanish empires. Settlers and Indians were the sentinels against foreign encroachment. Sometimes British colonists caused trouble with Britain's Indian allies by wandering into Indian lands, but more often than not colonial governors, with the support of imperial authorities, sent colonists west to act as buffers.

For example, a succession of Virginia governors in the early eighteenth century either gave land to settlers on condition that they guard it against the Indians or planted full-scale communities, colonies of colonies, in the midst of Indian populations. Collusion between royal officials and local authorities to dump groups of unsuspecting German and Swiss immigrants into such exposed positions had unfortunate but predictable results, infuriating the Indians whose lands were appropriated.

THE FORMAL APPARATUS OF ENGLISH IMPERIAL GOVERNANCE

Supported by its bureaucrats, tied into the communications revolution, fueled by the caffeine pipeline, policing its borders with ever-increasing investment in its armed forces, the British Empire revived. Ministers of state who had once paid little attention to the far-off corners of colonial settlement now had the personnel, information, and energy to involve themselves, if they wished, in the everyday political affairs of North Americans. There was no comparable minister in England to the French and Spanish ministers of the marine, but the responsibility for the empire fell on the secretary of state for the Southern Department and the ministry of the treasury.

The principal enforcement officers of colonial policy in the colonies were the governors-general of the colonies and their deputies and lieutenants. With the exception of Rhode Island and Connecticut, whose charters allowed them to elect their own governors, and the proprietary colonies of Maryland and Pennsylvania, whose lieutenant governors were chosen by the proprietors, all other governors were nominated by the secretary of state for the Southern Department.

The Duke of Newcastle's Empire

In 1724, the Duke of Newcastle assumed his duties as the secretary of state for the Southern Department. He held that office until 1748, when he became the secretary of state for the Northern Department, responsible for Britain's European diplomacy and then, in 1754, first lord of the treasury until 1767. On his father's side, Newcastle was a country squire, on his mother's, a landed magnate. He married into a family even more wealthy than his own. His brother-in-law was Robert Walpole, the longtime prime minister.

Regarded at first as an ambitious but inept and fussy nonentity, Newcastle surprised everyone with his canny political instincts. He grabbed the patronage that the Board of Trade had hitherto exercised and reduced the board to his secretariat. He opened channels of communication to the colonies directly, through hand-picked governors. In the infighting within the administrative system, he emerged the unquestioned champion.

He was also a superb parliamentary politician, a position he solidified by buying up and controlling a number of the seats in the House of Commons. These "rotten boroughs" were in fact very old electoral districts whose population had so shrunk over time that the few qualified voters in them could be controlled by noblemen like Newcastle. The king had a number of such boroughs "in his pocket"—hence another derogatory term: "pocket boroughs."

Newcastle had no overarching plan for the colonies. He was no great mercantilist, like Colbert. Nor did he wish to "reform" the colonies (that is, administer them more stringently) like Blathwayt and Bladen. Newcastle had no idea of colonial rights or liberties—indeed, the terms meant little to him. Instead, he wished to protect only his own and his friends' interests in the colonies. When rival groups in the colonies petitioned him, he weighed how much he had to gain from supporting one or the other. When both had claims on his friendship, he delayed or finessed the solution.

Sensitive as he was to the importuning of friends and the intrigues of enemies, Newcastle early mastered a crucial lesson about governing the colonies—colonial agents and groups had a good deal of influence in the home country. Anyone who wished to manage the colonies must learn to manage these interests, and the way to do this lay through colonial patronage. The number of colonial appointive offices in the duke's grasp grew steadily, from forty-one in 1724 to sixty in 1730 (the bulk of the increase came from the Carolina proprietors' cession of their colonies to the crown). Newcastle's problem in parceling these offices out was too many candidates for too few posts, but he pulled the strings on these appointments like a master puppeteer.

Because he was primarily interested in partisan gains rather than efficient management, Newcastle imposed on the colonies a number of unscrupulous and incompetent men. The worst of them was the man he named to govern New York and New Jersey—William Cosby. Between 1732 and 1734, Cosby's grasping, shortsighted, and unscrupulous conduct brought colonial government to a standstill. Only Newcastle's support for his appointment—he had to replace two members of the Board of Trade to get the job done—prevented Cosby's ouster and his patron's embarrassment. Newcastle scarcely did better with North Carolina, appointing George Burrington as governor. Burrington refused to travel far from his home, spent much of his time figuring out ways to amass land for himself, and was so quarrelsome that he was impeached by the lower house. Newcastle had to intervene once more to protect a subordinate. Newcastle's choice for Virginia, William Anne Kemple, Lord Albemarle, a Scot, never even went to the colony, though one of his deputies, Robert Dinwiddie, was for a time an effective defender of the interests of the crown.

Watching Newcastle's moves from this side of the water, some observers mistakenly concluded that Newcastle actually had a policy of "salutary neglect," in which the colonies were allowed to lobby for their own interests in England and to prosper if they could. At the end of King George's War, Newcastle joined Lord Halifax, head of the Board of Trade, to reform what Newcastle himself had corrupted, namely the administration of the empire. But it was too late—the colonies had learned how to evade and complain so well that the "reform" went nowhere.

Colonial Governors

Newcastle's early blunders underlined the extent to which the tempo, style, and effectiveness of imperial administration in the colonies depended on the colonial governors. Royal governors had (in theory) powers in the colonies superior to those the king exercised in England. These governors advised on appointments in the colony, including the high court judges and the members of the upper house. The governors could veto legislation, dissolve the assembly and call for new elections, or prorogue the assembly, leaving it in place but denying it the right to meet. They chose the Speaker of the lower house, set the agenda for it, introduced all money bills, and partitioned and granted western lands. Governors in some of the colonies, like Virginia, presided over the highest appellate courts and sat with the upper house when it met. Thus the governors not only had executive power, they had legislative and judicial power as well.

In fact, governors needed the support of powerful patrons in England, as Cosby's and Burrington's cases proved. The outright buying and selling of offices was unseemly, but governorships were patronage plums, and governors saw their office as a license to make money. This was an age when officials made little distinction between the public good and their own.

The moment a candidate knew he had been chosen governor or lieutenant governor, he thanked the king and waited upon the leading ministers of the government. The board gave the governor his instructions and reminded him that these were not to be revealed in the colony save in emergencies. Most appointees already knew who was who in the colonial power structure, particularly in the assembly, for the colonies had various interest groups and agents in England who whispered into the governor-to-be's ear. (Knowing who was who was vital, for until 1773, the assembly paid the governor's salary.) Next, the bishop of London, the Anglican cleric charged with the interests of the Church of England in the plantations, had a few words of wisdom to impart. The vast majority of the governors were Anglicans, and the bishop expected them to further Anglican interests in the colony. The admiralty, the treasury, the customs, and other administrative offices briefed the governor or the lieutenant governor before he departed for his new post.

A wise governor continued to cultivate his English patrons after he had arrived in the colonies. Perhaps the best exemplar of this unwritten instruction was Joseph Dudley, for the first fifteen years of the eighteenth century governor of the politically factious and stubbornly independent colony of Massachusetts. He thrived in this cockpit of faction by flattering the ministers of state who appointed him, keeping the Board of Trade informed of his actions, and allaying the qualms of the bishop of London.

Dudley's survival skills (recall he served with the assistants and then as a member of Andros's Dominion of New England) were remarkable but not unique. Andros surmounted his critics' barrage. Francis Lovelace, driven from New York in disgrace, returned as its governor in the early 1700s. Andros's and Lovelace's contemporary Francis Nicholson, another former officer in the army, served as acting deputy governor of New York in 1689, became governor of Maryland in the 1690s, and then served as the first royal governor of South Carolina in 1719. In between the last two posts, he commanded the assault on Port Royal in 1710.

As the three colonels' careers in the colonies remind us, the full title of the governor was governor-general, and many had military backgrounds. In fact, a governorship in the colonies was a kind of pension plan for trustworthy officers no longer needed in the European theater of combat. One of the best of this type of military governor was Robert Hunter. He was a young Scottish officer in the army that ousted James II and welcomed William of Orange to England. For having guessed right in the royal game of chance, Hunter received a commission in one of the regiments of dragoons (mounted infantry) that scouted for more heavily armed forces. In Ireland, Hunter's troops ruthlessly suppressed civilian dissent. Evenhanded, they were just as brutal against disloyal Scottish Highlanders.

When war again erupted in Europe in 1702, Hunter returned to the Low Countries to fight the French, this time serving alongside George Hamilton, later ennobled as the Earl of Orkney, and the Duke of Marlborough. Though he served well and bravely, Hunter inadvertently alienated the duke, the most important man in England after the royal family. But the earl had not forgotten Hunter, and when Orkney was made governor of Virginia in 1705, he selected Hunter as his lieutenant governor.

Although he was unable to take the Virginia post, Hunter accepted the position vacated by the sudden death of New York's governor, Lord Lovelace, in 1710. He sailed with a small fleet and a number of German Palatines (refugees from war and oppression in their homeland who had migrated to England). They were to settle in the frontier area west of the Hudson River and protect it for the crown. Hunter assumed that as governor of New York and New Jersey, his primary job would be the defense of the colony, not realizing that the French and their Indian allies posed the least of his problems. His real difficulty would be keeping his London masters happy while convincing New York's citizens to obey the law.

The factionalism of the Leisler years had not disappeared with the hanging of Jacob Leisler, and Hunter relied on his long experience as a junior officer and his briefer stint as an office-seeker in London to make friends with influential people. He reached out to Lewis Morris and Robert Livingston, two veteran New York politicians. Livingston was a true manorial baron living on vast Hudson River estates. Morris was a clever and able speculator.

Unfortunately for Hunter, friendship with Livingston and Morris meant the enmity of their opponents, the powerful DeLancey and Van Cortlandt clans. Worse, neither Hunter's power as governor nor his friends in high places could convince the city merchants to pay their taxes and the large landholders to remit their quitrents. No one could tell the Palatines what to do, and Hunter ended up using military force against the very refugees who had seen him as their savior. The war with France in America went badly, and antiproprietor elements in New Jersey kept the pot boiling there.

Hunter was soon exhausted by the political infighting. His wife, Elizabeth, died in 1716, thirty years old, during a smallpox epidemic. Now fifty, suffering from arthritis, Hunter had five small children to raise on his own. He longed to return to England, and in 1719 he did. But in the end, like Lovelace, Hunter died far from home serving as governor of Jamaica.

Few executives matched the high standards of probity and hard work that Hunter set. But there were other ways to govern. One could, like Virginia's lieutenant governor Alexander Spotswood, gain the trust of an entrenched and united planter aristocracy by becoming one of them. Spotswood remained in office from 1710 until 1722 largely because he adopted the ways and manners of that aristocracy. He quarreled with important men on his council over the collection of quitrents and the apportionment of lands, but these were more like quarrels within the aristocracy than quarrels between it and the crown. When he was replaced, Spotswood retired to the vast lands around Fredericksburg that he had accumulated as governor, living in a fashion that impressed even native-born magnates like William Byrd of Westover.

Another way for royal governors to navigate the minefield of local politics was to act the part of the local politician. Such a man was Massachusetts governor William Shirley. He was born to a Sussex, England, gentry family, married well, became a lawyer and merchant in London, speculated heavily, lost much, and then tried his luck in the provinces. In Massachusetts, Shirley paid court to Governor Jonathan Belcher. Belcher got Shirley a job prosecuting a case before the vice-admiralty court in the colony. In it, Palatines petitioned the court for redress against a captain who starved them on their way to Plymouth. Shirley's prosecution of the ship captain gained the lawyer a popular following. In short order, Shirley became a judge of the vice-admiralty court (an appointment within the power of Governor Belcher), and then its advocate general (chief prosecutor). He traveled to vice-admiralty courts all over New England to prosecute cases, making friends and political connections at every stop.

Shirley presented himself as a harmonizer of colonial interests and crown instructions; in 1741, when Governor Belcher succumbed to the wiles of his political opponents, Shirley abandoned his former mentor and, with the help of family connections, gained appointment to the governorship. In office, Shirley courted popularity and avoided taking hard and fast stands on anything controversial.

For example, faced with a financial crisis during King George's War, he impaneled task forces to advise him on defense of the colony, better enforcement of the Navigation Acts, and the empty treasury of the colony, then waited to see what his supporters in London wanted him to do. On one issue only did he refuse to bend— his own £1,000 salary. For eight years he operated in this fashion, trying not too hard to enforce unpalatable trade laws, and promising aid to the Anglicans while doing little for them in their quest to proselytize among the Congregationalists and Presbyterians.

BACKSTAIRS CONNECTIONS

If the concern of ministers of state like Newcastle and governors-general like Hunter was, at least theoretically, the public weal, the motives of the movers and shakers on the backstairs to the offices of empire were wholly private. This was in itself something of a revolution. Under the prevailing ideology of public life at the outset of the eighteenth century, one was supposed to work for the public good rather than for private interests. Indeed, even the word *interests* had an aura of disreputability. In practice (certainly in Newcastle's practice), the public good often amounted to little more than one man's gain, but the language of public life still put public welfare over private aims. But an ideology that sanitized private interests and defended special interest groups was gaining momentum, slipstreaming behind fast-moving events in politics and commerce.

Public Life and Private Property

Until the era of the English civil wars, the nobility ran the government. Already possessed of most of the land and a good portion of the capital in the realm, they could present themselves as disinterested and incorruptible public servants. The parliamentary army that opposed the king offered to men of lower rank the chance to rise on their ability. Some of these men went on to public careers. Equally important, from 1642 to 1660 official censorship of political writings and speeches collapsed. The new freedom to argue about the ideal state resulted not in the radical reform of government that many of the new men in politics demanded, but did introduce a far richer and potentially transforming vocabulary of political ideas. Central to these was a new meaning for the word *liberty*.

The old meaning of liberty derived from privileges that the king gave to individuals or groups to pursue some activity. Thus one might have the liberty to vote or hold office, or start a colony. In effect, liberty was an emanation of royal power. Republican political theorists of the interregnum like Harrington reconceptualized liberty as an individual's natural right that checked abuse of power by the crown.

Behind the reformers' conception of personal liberty was an even more potent idea: the right of the individual to gain, hold, and dispose of property as the individual chose. Such property was an emanation of the individual, not a gift of the king. Thus personal liberty and private property stood shoulder to shoulder against illegal or unfair taxation, the taking of property without just cause or due compensation, and royal monopolies upon business enterprises. The new liberty promoted private enterprise, competition, and the accumulation of more property.

It might seem that mercantilism, based upon state regulation of the economy, clashed with these new notions of liberty and property, but the reverse proved true. Mercantilism required that the balance of trade always be favorable to the home country, but mercantilists were aware of the growing demand side of the economy. Conspicuous consumption had long been practiced; now it was praised. Spending, including spending on oneself, was no longer a sin. As Daniel Defoe wrote in 1728, "tis by [the consumers] multitude, I say, that all the wheels of trade are set on foot, the manufacture and the produce of the land and sea, finished, cur'd, and fitted for the markets abroad . . . and it is by their expensive, generous, free way of living, that the home consumption is rais'd to such a bulk, as well of our own, as of foreign production." England was becoming the greatest consumer nation in the world, and the mercantilists benefited, for the imported goods for the consumer came from the empire. Thus mercantilists advocated liberty and private property within the empire.

The great overseas trading companies like the East India Company, the Royal Africa Company, and the Hudson's Bay Company were examples of the fusion of liberty, private property, and mercantilism. The directors of these companies might claim that they were merely the corporate embodiment of the well-being of the kingdom, but in fact they were congeries of private investors. They paid lobbyists to ensure that their private interests were not subordinated to state policy. If throughout the eighteenth century political theorists and reformers continued to argue about the misuse of private property, the dangers of luxury (that is, the danger of one person or group amassing too much property), and the ideal balance or distribution of property within the realm, everyone knew that special interest groups devoted to private property were here to stay.

The rise of new kinds of private property sustained this shift in attitude. At the outset of the seventeenth century, the property that mattered most in English thinking was real estate. Thus, for example, when Charles II had wished to reward his supporters, he gave them vast tracts of land in the New World. The idea that land was the most important kind of property went hand in hand with a certain concept of public duty. To own a parcel of land of any size implied that one accepted certain public obligations. For example, only landholders could vote because only they had the requisite stake in society.

But by the end of the seventeenth century, England's wealth was less and less its land, and more and more its trade. As "negotiable paper" like bank notes, bonds, and assignable contracts grew in importance, the connection between the idea of property and the idea of public duty weakened. Speculation in negotiable paper never connoted a public interest, its object was private gain, and public figures rushed to invest in all manner of such schemes.

Special Interest Organizations

Hints of a permanent connection between interest group special pleading and the new ideology of liberty and property appeared as early as the 1650s in England. With Cromwell's tacit consent, the city of London became the refuge for hitherto persecuted religious groups like the Jews, the Baptists, and the Quakers. Quietly, some of these sectaries formed associations to lobby the government for economic benefits. Businessmen's clubs found quarters alongside the sectarians' houses of worship. The biggest of the new clubs drew from the tobacco merchants and the West Indian sugar interests. The merchants also began to agitate for their interests in Parliament.

During the Restoration, the interest groups reached out from England to find and organize allies in port cities like Boston, New York, and Philadelphia, and like-minded interests in the colonies found allies in London. Merchants in New York City sent representatives or petitions across the sea to the merchants who traded with the city. The merchants who did business with Virginia were even better organized. They met regularly and collected dues to hire lawyers to speak for them at the Board of Trade. Even Harvard College established a transatlantic support network.

The same communications revolution that allowed the ministers of state to keep track of colonial politics permitted the colonial lobbies to feed information to the ministries. The lobbyists' practice made perfect in figuring out whom to lobby for what purpose. In general, the target of the lobbyists was the Board of Trade. Speaking through their London connections, Quakers pressured for toleration; tobacco merchants nominated friends for posts in the Virginia and Maryland governments; New York City merchants petitioned for profitable import and export rates; and patrons of Palatine German immigrant groups pleaded for land grants in New York, Pennsylvania, and North Carolina. Colonial assemblies sent over or hired in England "agents" to present petitions to Parliament and confer with imperial bureaucrats.

Religious groups carried on the most relentless of these lobbying campaigns. Nonconformists, or "dissenters" as they were sometimes called (that is, Baptists, Congregationalists, and Presbyterians), in England had to fight an uphill battle against the Anglican establishment. Under Queen Anne, the Anglicans had almost succeeded in denying dissenters the right to hold office or operate schools. Under George I, this policy of overt persecution fell into disuse, but dissenters remembered how near they had come to disaster. Thus the English dissenters organized, met regularly, and solicited support from American correspondents.

The Anglican interest in the northern colonies was just as hard put to make headway against the Congregationalists and Presbyterians there as the dissenters were against the Anglicans in England. In a mirror image of the dissenters' call upon the Puritan colonies for aid, Anglican missionaries of the Society for the Propagation of the Gospel in Foreign Parts and their congregants in New England sought assistance from the Anglican hierarchy in England.

The taffy pull over toleration in both New and old England gained new urgency in the 1750s when the Anglicans in Connecticut and Massachusetts approached the bishop of London with a plan to establish an American bishop. As far as the northern Anglicans could tell, the need was obvious, for young Americans who wished to be ordained as Anglican preachers had to go to the trouble and expense of crossing the Atlantic. But to the descendants of the Puritans, the idea smacked of an attempt to establish the Anglican Church in New England. The pamphlet war over an American bishop was still raging when the American Revolution erupted.

THE COUNTRY STYLE OF GOVERNMENT

In law, all local officials in America held office at the pleasure of the monarch. Colonial charters could be revoked at will, as Massachusetts and the other New England colonies discovered from 1684 to 1687, and Penn's colonies learned in 1688. Colonial assemblies had no more rights and privileges than English city councils. Colonial supreme courts were subject to supervision of the Privy Council and the royal courts. But great distance and the passage of time had created a cushion for local discretion and autonomy against royal and parliamentary intrusion.

Distance from the center of empire permitted local political institutions to flourish. Although the Privy Council and the king had final say on all colonial laws (in theory, such laws had to contain a clause that prevented them from going into operation until they were approved in England), and the Privy Council annulled some of them, colonial legislatures often had passed new laws before the original law was even quashed. The same theoretical subordination to English rule was true with the decisions of colonial supreme courts. These could be appealed directly to crown courts in England or to the Privy Council, but appeal took time and money because of the distance.

The course of time had directly aided the development of this colonial autonomy—for the thousand kinds of passive resistance to English rule that the colonists practiced had gained a kind of legitimacy through long usage. Persistence paid dividends when the Privy Council or the Board of Trade conceded to colonial variations from English law. For example, New England assemblies provided that when a person died intestate (without a will), the real estate was to be divided among the children. English law dictated that the land pass intact to the oldest son ("primogeniture"). In two cases, *Winthrop v. Lechmere* (Connecticut, 1728) and *Phillips v. Savage* (Massachusetts, 1733), colonial high courts upheld the American version of the law and managed over time to convince the crown to allow the exception to primogeniture. Such victories could not claim the force of precedent in the same way that English high court decisions rested upon precedent, but they created an expectation in the colonies that old ways would be observed. Even when Governor Benning Wentworth of New Hampshire waved the opinions of the Privy Council in the face of recalcitrant colonial representatives, as he did in a dispute over who had the right to call for a new election to the assembly there, he could not make the assemblymen bow. It took him seven years, from 1745 to 1752, to win his point, though he had law and authority on his side.

The structure and function of colonial governance differed from English styles of rule, providing another layer of insulation from direct imperial rule. As English imperial governance became more efficient, professional, unitary, and centralized, colonial local government embraced localism, amateurism, committee governance, and partisanship. Examples of this "country style" of decision making appeared in the work of the assembly and the operation of the courts.

Colonial Assemblies

In their relations with governors, assemblies had taken for themselves the privileges of little parliaments. Had not Parliament itself, in the settlement at the end of the Glorious Revolution, won its supremacy from the king? By refusing to settle permanent incomes on royal officials and scheduling fees and fines by statute, the assemblies controlled the public purse. They wrested from colonial governors control over the choice of Speakers of the lower house, appointment of militia commanders, the right to look over the account books of the colony, and the writing of finance and tax bills. Some aimed even higher—to control the time and place of their election, the length of their sessions, and the qualifications of their membership. They could not achieve this goal, but in the effort they defined a legislative sphere that governors had to respect.

The assemblies were more successful in their campaign to name or at least approve the minor executive officers and to set the policies for the conduct of these officials. The governors (following instructions drafted in England) still named the judges, but colonial assemblies created the courts, and resisted hotly, as during Cosby's tenure in New York, executive attempts to create new courts without assembly approval.

The manner of elections and the theory of representation for the assembly further insulated the assembly from crown supervision. Property, gender, and religious qualifications for voting for the House of Commons in England limited the franchise to a small portion of men. In the colonies, only those free men with property could vote for the assembly, but in many of the colonies, just about every free white male could muster the minimum property qualifications for voting. The American assemblies were thus far more representative bodies than the House of Commons, and knew it.

The official British rejoinder to American criticism of the unrepresentativeness of the Commons was that members of Parliament represented the people of England as a whole, rather than the voters of their particular districts. This ideal of "virtual representation" was a fiction, and Americans were not fooled. Nothing of the sort could describe the conduct of the colonial legislators. They held instead to a delegate theory, wherein elections were frequent and elected assemblymen promised to take care of the needs of their voters.

As Richard Beeman has conclusively demonstrated, the proportion of the population eligible to vote (the "franchise") and the actual number of voters participating in elections varied from colony to colony. (Bear in mind that at the maximum estimate, less than one-fourth of all free white propertied Protestant adult Englishmen could vote for members of the House of Commons. The House of Lords was not an elected body, nor was any part of the executive branch, nor was any member of the judiciary in England.) In Massachusetts, by contrast, the electorate comprised over three-fourths of the male population.

This did not mean that everyone voted. In most elections, only a small portion of eligible voters actually cast ballots. In New York, perhaps as many as 80 percent of the free white males could vote, though rarely did more than 25 percent of these voters exercise their franchise. Two-thirds of Virginia's free white males held the franchise; rarely did more than one-fourth of them exercise it. The same pattern held in Pennsylvania—nearly 75 percent of the adult white males could take part in elections, but only when they were hotly contested, as in the 1760s, did more than half the voters bother to vote. While the laws of South Carolina gave to almost all free white males the right to vote, fewer than 10 percent regularly cast ballots. City folk, more easily roused by electoral contests, voted more often than country folk.

Colonial assemblies met for short periods of time. Tops were Pennsylvania, South Carolina, and Massachusetts, averaging three or four months a year. Assembly sessions were more frequent and more businesslike as the century wore on, and assemblies became centers of protest against the crown.

By the middle of the eighteenth century, colonial legislatures were active organs of law making, administration, and adjudication. Indeed, in their relations to other branches of colonial governments, as in their view of the imperial connection, colonial assemblies ignored theoretical limitations on their authority.

First, colonial legislatures had become increasingly active makers of statute law. For example, the number of laws passed in the Massachusetts General Court increased from seventeen or eighteen at the beginning of the century to thirty-eight each session at the end of the 1750s. These were not so-called private bills for the convenience of an individual petitioner but public acts similar to modern legislation. Virginia averaged over thirty bills per session, New York over twenty-five, and Maryland nearly as many. Equally important, the acts were printed and circulated in the colony and served to regulate the inhabitants' behavior far more effectively than the first assemblies' regulatory efforts. Even the language of the acts became more precise as more and more lawyers agreed to serve in the legislatures.

Second, the colonists often turned to their assemblies when they might have gone for relief or action to the governor or the courts. For example, by midcentury the New Jersey assembly was effectively handling six times as many petitions as it handled thirty years earlier, many of which might well have gone to the governor's office. Upon the petition of the leading planters, the Virginia legislature fashioned an intelligent and comprehensive system of quality control for tobacco. In New York and Massachusetts, legislative action had aided the interests of the ports of New York City and Boston and regulated wages and prices in the seagoing industries.

There were exceptions to this rule. Though the South Carolina legislature sat for many days, its work product was small compared to that of its northern neighbors— fewer than fifteen laws per session. In part this may be due to the relative paucity of the petitions for redress it received—under twenty per session compared to over two hundred for Massachusetts.

Such legislative activities prove that separation of powers among the three branches of government was a postrevolutionary conception. For example, the Pennsylvania assembly routinely carried on administrative and judicial functions. The lower house selected and oversaw commissioners to collect taxes and record legal transactions. Payment for these officials came from fees on a schedule set by the legislators. The assembly did not shrink from granting monopolies for such official functions. The Connecticut assembly functioned as a high court of appeals throughout the colonial period, as did the legislative upper houses in the southern colonies.

Third, colonial legislatures' notorious penchant for ignoring royal authority and intimidating royal governors proved that they did not see themselves as the subordinate partner in the imperial relationship. Governors and their assemblies clashed over who could choose the Speaker of the lower house and how the seats in it were to be apportioned. When the proprietor asked the Pennsylvania assembly, in 1739, to raise funds to support the war efforts, the assembly simply refused. In Massachusetts in the 1730s, the General Court tried to charter a land bank and issue paper currency on its investments over the objections of Governor Belcher. His veto of the bank in 1741 cost him his job. In these and other cases, rudimentary political party organizations radiated out from the assemblies into the electoral districts, and candidates for legislative office often campaigned against imperial policies.

Colonial Courts

Eighteenth-century colonial courts did a little better than assemblies in copying English forms and obeying crown precepts. But unlike the English system of compartmentalized and specialized tribunals, almost all of the colonies developed an overlapping hierarchy of courts of generalized jurisdiction.

Petty sessions held by the justices of the peace were the lowest level of official tribunal. Above them sat county courts on whose bench were the very same justices of the peace. Supreme or superior courts were the highest courts in the colony. Often the same men sat as justices in local courts and judges on the high courts. A case might move from a lower court to a higher court on appeal and be reheard in its entirety—from initial pleading to jury verdict (although not all colonies allowed such de novo hearings).

In almost every colony, the county court was the workhorse of justice. Meeting as a court of common pleas, it heard civil suits. Reconstituting itself as a court of "general sessions of the peace," it performed the regulatory tasks of the English quarter sessions courts and disposed of serious misdemeanors. County courts could not hear cases of life and limb (felonies) or civil business in excess of some monetary ceiling.

The justices of the peace commissioned to hold court came from the landed or commercial elite of the county but only rarely had formal legal training. The first colonial county courts often sat in taverns or private homes. Although the courts bought books of law and some justices had their own law libraries, justices used what may be called "situation sense" as much as legal precept to decide cases. More often than not, the neighbors of the parties in court played a decisive role as well—as jurors, witnesses, mediators, and arbitrators. In the end, local knowledge—the information that neighbors provided—was more potent than legal book learning.

County courts regularly heard the presentments and indictments from the grand jurors, men of some substance and standing in the county. The offenses the grand jurors presented to the court tended to run in waves determined by changing regulatory statutes, the arrival or departure of certain disreputable individuals, and deeper alterations in social values. Presentments fell on men and women who had been contemptuous of authority, failed to perform court-ordered duties like clearing the roads of brush, or committed misdemeanors. Indictments were reserved for suspects of more serious crimes. Statutes that criminalized an activity naturally increased the number of suspected violators presented to the court. So did the appearance in the town or country of rowdy or larcenous individuals.

For the historian, the most intriguing cause of surges in presentments was changing social values. For example, in the early eighteenth century the grand jurors in all of the colonies presented an unusually large number of people for premarital fornication. In later years, premarital pregnancy actually increased (demographers know this by calculating the period between the birth of a couple's first child and the date of their marriage), but the presentment rates declined. We may surmise that the justices and the community they represented no longer saw premarital pregnancy as a great danger to order and morals.

As had their predecessors in the seventeenth century, eighteenth-century justices also heard civil lawsuits. Most of these concerned the survey, sale, and inheritance of land. In the hands of these justices, colonial land law diverged from English law in the direction of simplified conveyance and recording of deeds. A significant portion of civil litigation also revolved around debt and commercial transactions. Indeed, there was a virtual explosion of this kind of litigation in the 1720s and 1730s, as colonial economies came to include more "arm's-length" transactions between buyers and sellers or lenders and borrowers who did not know one another. Suspicions that the other party was not playing the game fairly by (the old) rules of barter and exchange led people to sue when previously they would have used other means to gain satisfaction.

The county courts were also the first (and sometimes the only) administrative agencies in the colonies. Although as time passed the crown would create an administrative superstructure for the colonies, imperial administrators rarely penetrated to the interior of the colonies. The only royal bureaucrats one might find on shore were surveyors, Indian agents, and, during wartime, officers of the king's army. Instead, justices of the peace and their grand jurors made sure that the roads were clear, nuisances were repaired, the fees and fines schedules imposed by colonial legislatures were obeyed, and local taxes were paid on time.

Although colonial justices of the peace were not much different from their English counterparts, the higher court judges in America were very different from the English central court judge. English judges were full-time professional jurists, and though almost invariably advanced in their careers because of their political allegiances, they were invariably well trained and much experienced in the law. Colonial supreme court justices were men of affairs and authority in their communities who were acquainted with law but rarely trained in it. Moreover, they were never full-time jurists. After three-quarters of a century of operation, the highest courts of Massachusetts and Virginia rarely included more than one well-educated lawyer. The legal skills of the judges in Pennsylvania were no higher. Only New York, after 1694, could boast a legally literate bench. This pattern continued well into the eighteenth century in most of the colonies.

To these higher colonial courts came all serious crimes. In some colonies, such as Virginia, the high courts only met at the capital. In other colonies, such as Massachusetts, the high courts went on "circuits" and sat in the various county seats. At these sessions, grand juries sat to decide whether there was sufficient evidence to find a true bill of indictment against an accused felon. If the grand jury found the true bill, the defendant could ask for a jury trial or let the judges decide the case.

In the planter colonies, "freeholders courts" specially convened when slaves were defendants provided the only exception to the rules for felony trials. Freeholders court judges were men of property who might or might not hold commissions as justices of the peace. There were no juries in freeholders courts; slave defendants could not call witnesses in their behalf and had no right to cross-examine prosecution witnesses, although the slave's master might assert these rights.

By the middle of the eighteenth century, much of the rough edges of the early colonial legal system had been smoothed over, and lawyers had appeared to sand down what remained of local knowledge and common sense. With the veritable explosion of litigation over commercial transactions in the first half of the century, law had become a more lucrative profession and drew to its practice the sons of some of the best families. Despite criticism from some quarters, the formalization of the legal profession was a movement that seemed unstoppable. With it came more and more of the external garb—literally wigs and robes in the case of judges—of English legal practice.

———

Looking back upon this confusing pattern of overlapping and ill-fitting sources of authority, which later generations of Americans fondly misconstrued as "salutary neglect," it is easy to lose sight of the achievement of the early-eighteenth-century British imperial system. By shifting from a proprietary to a bureaucratic system of governance, the British improved efficiency. At the same time, the ministers of state and the Board of Trade retained the elements of patronage and clientage that kept the administration of empire inexpensive. By allowing colonial interest groups to climb the backstairs to their offices, the royal authorities increased the flow of information and allowed leading colonists to gain some access to power at the center of empire. Finally, by conceding to colonial elites a measure of self-government, the imperial governors co-opted key elements of the American polity and helped diffuse the internal tensions that led to the critical period.

But the reinvention of the British Empire, like the resuscitation of the French and Spanish empires, was still a concession of privileges, not a recognition of rights. The source of power remained the metropolitan centers of empire. Every colonist had to accept that ultimately the decisions of the king's ministers, his Parliament, and his courts were final, however much conciliation and negotiation went into the framing of those decisions. The colonists were still subjects, as far as the crown was concerned.

10

Provincial People and Places
in the Eighteenth Century

They live in so happy a climate, and have so fertile a soil, that nobody is poor enough to beg, or want food.
—Robert Beverley, on conditions in Tidewater Virginia, 1705

It would be a great novelty to a Londoner to see one of these congregations—the men with only a thin shirt and pair of breeches or trousers on—barelegged and barefooted—their women bareheaded, barelegged, and barefoot with only a thin shift.
—Charles Woodmason, touring the Carolina backcountry, 1766

The refashioning of imperial and local political institutions provided an immediate answer to the disorders of the critical period at the end of the seventeenth century, but imperial politics lay on the surface of colonial life, not at its root. While the imperial bureaucrats arrived to monitor trade and manage Indian relations, developments within the colonies provided a more lasting resolution of conflicts and tensions.

By 1700, over half of the colonies' free population was born in America. Even in the disease-ridden planter colonies, a native-born majority dominated local life, and its young men and women replenished their numbers through natural increase. As proud as these colonists might be of their association with empire, their identity derived from another source—the hardships and joys of everyday life in America. At the core of this localism was an enterprise as old as the archaic Indian settlements—the transformation of physical space into social place.

Native peoples solved the problem of identity by changing wilderness into a patchwork of villages, trails, and cornfields. Among groups like the Creeks, village squares were not just grounds where people gathered, they were hallowed sites that gave meaning to the gatherings. The sacred fire, burning at the center of the village, was the soul of the village. The Creeks' great rivals, the Cherokees, bounded their land by blazing trees. European colonists likewise domesticated natural landscapes with roads, homes, courthouses, and churches. By ordering the land they created social paths as well as physical ones, leading to collective worship, play, and governance. Thus they reknit what the crises at the end of the seventeenth century had unraveled.

This chapter moves down the coast of North America, from the French Canadian settlements to the British West Indies and the Spanish borderlands of the Southwest, taking the measure of these provincial societies in the first half of the eighteenth century. At each stop,

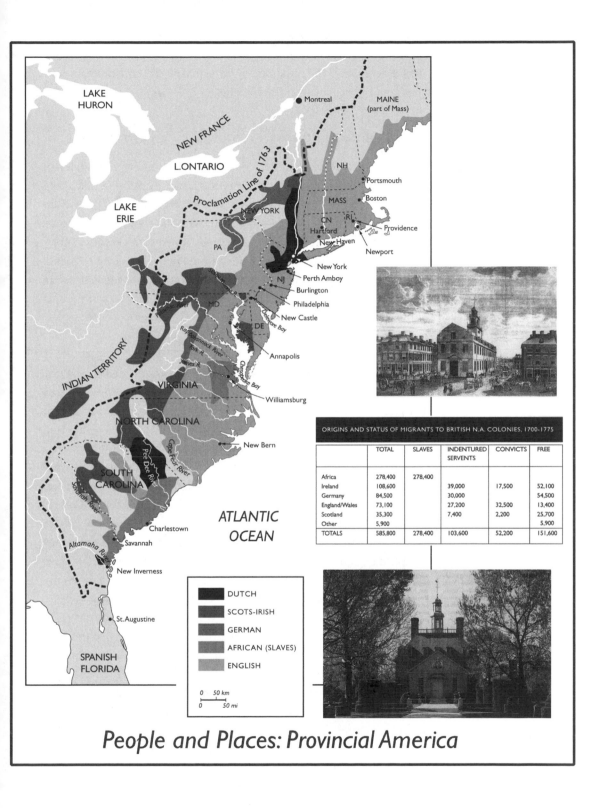

LAKE
HURON

NEW FRANCE

L.ONTARIO

LAKE
ERIE

Proclamation Line of 1763

Montreal

MAINE
(part of Mass)

NH

Portsmouth

NEW YORK

MASS

Boston

PA

CN
Hartford
New Haven

RI

Providence

Newport

NJ

New York
Perth Amboy
Burlington
Philadelphia
New Castle

MD

DE

Annapolis

INDIAN TERRITORY

Rappahannock River
York R.
James R.

Chesapeake Bay

VIRGINIA

Williamsburg

NORTH CAROLINA

Cape Fear River

New Bern

Pee Dee River

SOUTH
CAROLINA

Savannah River

Charlestown

ATLANTIC
OCEAN

Altamaha River

Savannah

New Inverness

St. Augustine

SPANISH
FLORIDA

DUTCH
SCOTS-IRISH
GERMAN
AFRICAN (SLAVES)
ENGLISH

| 0 | 50 km |
| 0 | 50 mi |

ORIGINS AND STATUS OF MIGRANTS TO BRITISH N.A. COLONIES, 1700-1775

	TOTAL	SLAVES	INDENTURED SERVANTS	CONVICTS	FREE
Africa	278,400	278,400			
Ireland	108,600		39,000	17,500	52,100
Germany	84,500		30,000		54,500
England/Wales	73,100		27,200	32,500	13,400
Scotland	35,300		7,400	2,200	25,700
Other	5,900				5,900
TOTALS	585,800	278,400	103,600	52,200	151,600

People and Places: Provincial America

one sees that the textures of ordinary life depended upon geography, climate, and natural resources as well as the values and purposes of the people. Instead of one "America" or three "empires," the settlements in North America constituted a congeries of disparate and often isolated little societies.

HABITANTS AND "BLACK ROBES" UNDER THE CANADIAN SHIELD

The northernmost of the French American possessions lay under the Canadian Shield from the Great Lakes to the coast of Nova Scotia. In the critical period at the end of the seventeenth century, these lands had been cockpits of war. But the French habitants (French-speaking settlers) and the Roman Catholic clergy, led by the Jesuits, called "Black Robes" by the Indians, persevered. Nineteenth-century historians like the Boston-bred Francis Parkman regarded the French-speaking residents of these lands as priest ridden, superstitious, and bloodthirsty, but that depiction was prejudiced. The habitant militia fought for land, country, and faith the same as did English-speaking New Englanders and Virginians.

Acadia and New Canada

By the early 1610s, Champlain's little outpost in Quebec provided a base for French expansion up and down the Saint Lawrence. Soon all of the riverine provinces contributed to the French trading network. In 1613, a new French company of traders was formed to exploit Champlain's achievement. They returned to the now deserted site of Hochelaga and founded Montreal. Champlain ferried back and forth across the Atlantic, securing the colony in battle against the Iroquois on the western shore and bargaining for the life of the colony with merchants and royal officials in France.

Diseases the French brought reduced the native population, and under Colbert the French recruited immigrants for Canada and Acadia from western France, where life was hard and prospects poor. In Canada, daily wages were four times what they were in the old country, and land was four times cheaper. If a family could survive the first generation of settlement in the New World, its chance of rising to the equivalent of the highest rank of the peasantry in the old country was excellent.

From the 1660s, when Canada became a royal province, throughout the eighteenth century, a small but steady flow of families arrived in the colony. According to the census of 1762, there were slightly fewer than eighty thousand French Canadians. Fully half of these lived in the Quebec region, most of them north of the Saint Lawrence River. By the mid-eighteenth century, women equaled men in numbers. Still, the French government had to subsidize immigration. Despite the opportunities in Canada, French farmers preferred not to emigrate. French merchants and administrators sometimes referred to service in Canada as "purgatory." Nearly two-thirds of the migrants eventually returned home.

Few habitant farmers expected or sought to rise into the seigneurial (land-owning) classes. Instead, the habitants only sought a cushion against want for themselves and their children. In the woods, the newcomers cleared small farm plots, on average about fifteen arpents (a little smaller than an acre). Their tools put a premium upon sheer physical strength. Axes, hoes, and sickles wore out backs, shoulders, and biceps. The local gentry had horses to draw their plows and servants to walk behind the horses. The poor had their own legs.

Because of the climate, farmers spent the time from June to the end of September in unceasing physical labor. All planting, harvesting, and cutting firewood had to be completed before the snow and cold returned. House repairs were essential as well—new stone for the foundation, wood siding and roofs, and straw and earth for insulation. The winter was long and often cruel, and when it came, every tool, cart, animal, and sheaf of wheat had to be sheltered.

The cycles of planting and harvesting merged into the other rhythms of life. The French Canadian farmers ate the "white" bread made from the wheat they grew (much preferred to the corn products of their native neighbors) and fished the lakes, rivers, and ocean around them. Meat comprised a far larger portion of their diet than it did in France, not because the French Canadian farmer was an especially successful herdsman, but because there was still game to hunt in the forests. Farmers doubled as carpenters and weavers, furniture repairers and toy makers.

Frequent feast days and the Sabbath provided respite from labor and opportunities for social intercourse. Visiting was a real pleasure for the hosts and the traveler, for many farmsteads were isolated. Singing and dancing were not only forms of entertainment but good sources of exercise. Church attendance in winter was difficult, but mission houses and churches dotted the landscape, where Roman Catholic rites were fundamental to all stages of life, from baptism and marriage to burial.

The French settlements on Acadia (Nova Scotia and northern Maine) suffered from hostilities from their founding at the beginning of the seventeenth century until the English rounded up the French inhabitants and deported them in the late 1750s. The name derived from an Algonquian term for a place (*coddy*), and Acadia served the French variously as a depot for the fur trade, stations for their fishing fleet, and a first line of defense against marauding English raiders. Acadia was also the home of some of France's most trustworthy Indian allies. The Micmacs and Abenakis of Acadia accompanied French troops as far afield as western Pennsylvania.

The extensive woodlands and long coast remained sparsely populated throughout the period of French dominion because of the unique manner of the French settlers' agriculture. Instead of deep plowing the land, they cut dikes into the marshy coast and planted garden crops inside the dikes. Abundant spruce and fir provided raw materials for strong, snug houses, and the population grew steadily through natural increase.

Acadians got by without much supervision from the French government, in part because the Indians and Acadians got along well. Micmacs and Abenakis were not farmers, and the French had no desire to encroach upon the Indians' hunting or fishing grounds. After 1713, a treaty between France and Britain gave the British nominal sovereignty over the five thousand French-speaking inhabitants of Acadia, but try as they might, the British could never get any sizable portion of the Acadians to shift allegiance.

The French and the Indians

As Champlain had discovered in 1610, French Canadian policy had to ensure the amity of the natives. There would never be enough French migrants to defend the French North American colonies without Indian support. For Champlain, trade was the key to that amity, but in later years the French constructed two more ties. The first was religious. The second was diplomatic.

Conversion of the natives was never a high priority for the fur-trading companies, but by the 1620s the missionary zeal of religious orders like the Jesuits and the Recollects (the "Gray Robes") made up for lost time. Catholic missionaries penetrated to the far reaches of the empire. In the seventeenth century, 115 Jesuits came to Canada, many among them the best-educated youths in Europe.

The Jesuits discovered that shame was the natives' greatest fear, and a Jesuit who could read and write, who lived celibate and simply, and who could not be shamed might convert those who admired him. The Black Robes were adepts at learning languages (they already knew French, Greek, and Latin) and were able to use local dialects to fashion analogies between native worship and Christianity.

The Jesuits became familiar figures among the northeastern tribes, adapting Indian customs like the wearing of magic amulets but replacing native charms with Christian objects. Their most powerful weapon was the inability of the Indian shamans to cure the diseases the French brought. Seemingly impervious to chickenpox, mumps, and other illnesses, the Jesuits belittled and insulted the shamans when they tried to cure the sick in traditional fashion. If the Jesuits did not root out the native religion (and indeed, some were martyred in trying), many natives adopted Catholicism because of the Jesuits' efforts.

The Recollects did not try to fit into Indian ways, nor did they travel to Indian villages. Instead, they attempted to "civilize" the Indians, insisting that they learn French, dress in European fashion, and abandon their customs. Only then could the natives fully enter into the mental state required for conversion.

The Recollects founded hospitals, schools, and churches, and arranged for reserves of farmland for the converts, but as time passed they grew less confident that they could alter what they regarded as the Indians' "stupid, gross, and rustic" habits of mind. Gradually, between the 1620s and 1670, they left Canada's Indians to the Jesuits' ministrations, but the reserves the Recollects set aside became stable and loyal Catholic Indian villages along the Saint Lawrence. From these, particularly Kahnewaka (sometimes spelled Caughnawaga) opposite Montreal, would come staunch allies in time of war.

The other key to amity between the French and the Indians was diplomacy. On the frontier, military men served as agents of the French state. They doubled as notaries, judges, and juries. The commandants relied upon negotiation rather than fiat in dealing with the Indians, for Indians refused to accept the French notion of the absolute authority of the state. To be effective, the commandant must follow Indian precepts of a good father, patiently mediating complaints. The French and the Indians thus preserved the middle ground long after the English settlers had driven the Indians away.

WOODSMEN, POOR FISHERMEN, AND PRAYING INDIANS OF COASTAL NEW ENGLAND

Most of New England's settlers were farmers, and the push inland in search of arable land is the most commonly told story of New England farm families (about whom more appears in chapter 12). Those without land moved about from town to town, finding occasional work until town officials ordered the transients to leave. Sometimes these wandering poor were young (surviving records show they were likely to be younger than town residents), and life held better things for them. Too often, they were old or infirm, and unsympathetic sheriffs chased them from poorhouse to poorhouse until they died.

But three groups of coastal New Englanders in the early eighteenth century are left out of this story. The first tried to farm the rocky soil of the Maine coast. Its three counties were provinces of Massachusetts. The second made their living as deep water fishermen, sailing out of port towns like Portland, in Maine; Portsmouth, in New Hampshire; and Bedford, Gloucester, Salem, and Marblehead in Massachusetts. It would be hard to find a greater contrast in one place than the ramshackle two- and three-story shanties of the fisherfolk and the two- and three-story mansions of the merchants in these seaports.

The third group of people often ignored were the descendants of New England Algonquians, principally Nipmucks, Wampanoags, and Narragansetts. Some of them had assimilated English ways; others retained native traditions. They lived in their old settlements on Martha's Vineyard, Cape Cod, and Nantucket, in so-called praying Indian towns like Natick, and amid the English in their towns and villages near the shore.

Proprietors and Squatters

Maine land had always attracted two very different kinds of people. The first, well connected and wealthy, saw in the vast expanse of land a field for speculation. Going back to Fernando Gorges at the start of the seventeenth century, these would-be great proprietors angled for grants of vast woodland. They were, in effect, the ancestors of the timber barons of America's nineteenth- and early-twentieth-century history. Successive waves of these entrepreneurs gained land from the crown or from the General Assembly of Massachusetts.

To cut the wood, the proprietors sent loggers and surveyors into the hinterlands. They built sawmills, forts, and small settlements. Another group of men had their eyes on the land: poor farmers who simply squatted—took possession, improved, and then claimed the land as their own—or purchased the land from Indians and others whose titles were easily contested by the proprietors. Hence the land and the people were perpetually engaged in rounds of litigation and riot. The proprietors feared that the farmers would cut timber for firewood. The farmers lived dreading the prospect that the proprietors would reduce them to tenants.

Life in these settlements was harsh. Houses were scattered along the many rivers that ran from wilderness to ocean, isolating the inhabitants. The few villages were small and uninviting. Long, cold winters required huge amounts of firewood, and theft from woodpiles was as serious an offense as horse stealing on the western frontier. Debt was an ever-present menace, and although there was only a little socioeconomic distance between the poorest renter and the squire in his mansion, debtors went to jail when they could not pay their taxes or repay their loans. Farm women supplemented bread, cheese, and fish with garden vegetables and herbs. They wove and spun, and cared for children, elderly, and the infirm. Isolated as this society was, epidemic diseases managed to find it and carry off the weak and the unlucky.

Fisherfolk

Codfish made New England fisheries profitable. In the late seventeenth century, fishermen working in small groups set out in shallops, worked long and very dangerous hours, brought their catch to market, and spent their short wages on consumables like rent, food, and alcoholic drink. The trade passed down from father to son, each generation complaining that they were the "merchants' slaves."

There was some truth in the charge. Though fish merchants did not own the boats, nor were the fishermen indentured to the merchants, the merchants underwrote the enterprise by outfitting the fishermen in return for a guaranteed number of salable fish at a fixed price. These executory contracts formed the basis of the "clientage" system. In clientage, certain merchants and certain fishermen developed ongoing relationships based on the extension of credit to the fishermen. For the merchant, clientage ensured a supply of fish.

Despite their well-rehearsed complaints about enslavement to the merchants, clientage had its advantages for the fishermen. Most fishermen had little beyond their own skill and willingness to work when they went into business, and thus could not put up collateral for a conventional loan. What was more, under clientage, fishermen did not have to pay interest on the money the merchants laid out. Finally, clientage did not stop a fisherman from negotiating with other outfitters if he could find better terms. The merchant who sued a fisherman for debt infuriated other fishermen. When Philip English, a Salem fish merchant, dragged indebted fishermen to court, a mob sacked his warehouse.

The merchants' interest in the fisheries ended at the shoreline, but fishermen's worries extended far out to sea. For those who labored on others' boats, finding steady work was not easy. Half the year fishermen went unemployed, for fishing was just as seasonal as farming. The season ran from early spring to fall. Even during the season, the cod might not be running, or the boat might not be in the right place at the right time. Crews spent the entire season off the coast of Maine or Newfoundland. Gales, high seas, and sudden squalls easily overturned the open shallops, and crew members had little chance of survival in the icy waters.

Even without mishaps, the labor was backbreaking and unrelenting. Each fisherman manned two or three heavy lines weighted with lead. A single line would be baited and thrown out hundreds of times a day if the fish were plentiful. Fishermen prepared the catch by slitting open the fishes' bellies, chopping off the heads (reserving the liver oil), removing the spine, and salting the fillets.

"Shoremen" waiting at jetties dried and weighed the catch each day, allowing the fishermen to resume their work at sea. Not every shoreman was reliable. One, Richard Bedford, "would make himself drunk . . . and would lie under the flakes or in one house or another and let the fish lie 'upon spoils.' He would also get others to drink it with him, with the bottle in the knees of his breeches." No doubt Bedford found others willing to share his bottle. Away from family for half a year, running against the clock and the tides, the fishermen found strong drink irresistible.

Like the pioneers on the frontier, the fishermen came to their work young and single. Most worked for a few seasons out of one of the fishing towns and then moved on. If they married, their spouses became part of the circle of the fishery life. Most fishermen's families had acquired little more than a few sticks of furniture and household tools. Fishermen's families were notorious for the number of their offspring and their children's rowdiness, and the wharf district was usually the roughest and most crime ridden in town.

The worst features of this system abated in the early 1700s. The number of skilled fishermen rose, and the amount of capital available for investment in the fishing industry grew large enough for merchants to pay for and shipwrights to construct a new kind of fishing vessel—the ketch, or schooner. The new ship was a two-master, thirty-five to sixty-five feet in length. Its covered decks and raised cabins rendered it seaworthy in all but the worst weather, and it could carry provisions for long voyages and sleep a decent-sized crew.

Salem, the richest of the port towns, led the way in the development of the new fishing industry. Its merchants invested in the schooner fleet, and their crews chased the cod into deeper waters. Fishermen gutted and salted the catch on the deck of the vessel. With bigger holds for the catch on board, there was no reason to run to the shore with the day's catch, and crews spent the entire voyage at sea. The take from the sea tripled. Advances in the technology of fishing led to the demise of clientage and the appearance of tighter credit and more competitive negotiations between merchants and ship captains. In the new, semifree market situation, loyalty meant little and bargained-for profits a lot.

After 1700, the life of the fishermen and their families improved. Better pay translated into a little more sugar on the shelves, and a few more shelves to accommodate the sugar. If, when they passed away, fishermen still left minuscule estates, and their families still dwelled in rented apartments, the family could stay together, children were educated, and couples accumulated more consumer durables.

Postwar Indian Life among the English

King Philip's War had devastated the villages and took the lives of many eastern Algonquian Indians who allied themselves with the English. For example, Natick's returnees made do with wigwams instead of houses. But the Indians persevered. They replanted cornfields and sold baskets and woodwork to their English neighbors. As well, they hunted and trapped (averaging about a hundred deer a year). On Cape Cod, the Indian reserve of Mashpee became a focal point for men and women scattered during the war. There Indian and English preachers built three churches for the nearly three hundred adult Indian congregants.

Residents of these towns fought to retain their land, but by the 1720s the number of separate Indian settlements had declined precipitously, and the number of Indians living in most of these enclaves had fallen to double figures. A few towns, notably Natick and Mashpee, retained their native character by incorporating families from smaller settlements, but they were the exception. As Indians left ancestral homes, English farmers moved onto the land.

In their postwar settlements, Indians merged traditional and English forms of inheritance, land, and domestic law. For example, early in the eighteenth century sachem Thomas Waban of Natick convinced his followers to adopt a hybrid system of communal and individual landholding that withstood challenges from land-hungry English neighbors. He introduced English inheritance practices to keep family holdings together. Then the Natick Indians' council assigned individual families lots from the common store. "Proprietors" managed the lands corporately to prevent foreclosures and fraudulent purchases by whites.

But nothing could prevent the swelling English population from seeking to obtain Indian farmsteads, particularly when Indian men died without heirs. Without heads of families or reserves of capital, widows and children had to sell out. They moved to larger towns to work as servants, and sometimes sought aid from the town.

Landless Indian men commonly found employment as herdsmen, gardeners, or sailors. Women labored as maids or street-corner vendors. Even those Indians who found work faced burdens of accumulated debt, and some sold themselves into servitude. Poverty and psychological depression ravaged Indian communities and families, resulting in a declining birth rate. In the eighteenth century, the average Natick Indian family saw two and a half children survive to adulthood, compared to five children reaching adulthood among their English neighbors.

THE BEST POOR MAN'S COUNTRY

In the same decade that the eastern New England Indian population visibly declined, thousands of young men and women of German, Scots and Scots-Irish, Welsh, and English extraction immigrated to the rolling hills and long valleys between the majestic Delaware River and the wide, swift-flowing Susquehanna River. Climate in this rectangle of forty-eight hundred square miles was moderated by onshore wind currents and featured, on average, two hundred growing days a year. The soil was well-drained loam, cut by a series of swift streams, and suitable for wheat farms, livestock herds, and orchards. The watercourses provided power for iron foundries and flour mills. The region soon gained the reputation as "the best poor man's country."

In Chester County, to the south of the city of Philadelphia, in Bucks County to the north, and in Lancaster County to the west, the growth of population was remarkable. As a whole, the colony of Pennsylvania grew from 8,800 souls in 1690 to 250,000 in 1770. A good portion of this growth was due to immigration, but with the exception of Philadelphia, the region was generally healthy and prosperous, and life expectancy was far better than in western Europe.

Starting Out

Most of the immigrants began their adulthood as laborers, tenants, or renters. Some, particularly in the western edge of the region, simply "squatted" on lands not already occupied by its legal owners. Tax records show that one-fourth of these settlers paid no taxes. Some in this group were incapacitated, addled, old, or otherwise unable to compete. Others were "sturdy beggars" or strolling poor who simply moved from job to job with long periods of unemployment in between. But most were young people starting out, and for them, dependency or servitude of some kind was one stage of life's course. Few had the capital to buy farmsteads of their own.

These young laborers were not content with being someone else's servant or with working another person's land. If tenants, they agitated for better lease terms. If servants or apprentices, they longed to start out on their own.

Even the sons and daughters of farmers were remarkably mobile within the region. One-third of Bucks County sons sold their inherited lands and moved from their home township within a few years of gaining possession. Sons not inheriting lands moved even more often. But they did not move from the region. They wanted land of their own, but not because they were attached to the land like their European forebears, but because buying and selling land was a way to move up the economic ladder.

To be sure, purchase of land meant taking a risk, for the new farmstead was likely to be heavily mortgaged, and like every farmer of middling means, Pennsylvanian farmers lived in the shadow of debt. But the buyers and sellers took risks, calculated risks, in part for profit, in part to ensure that there would be a decent future for their children. The extent of the risk could be reduced by diversification in production (as we will see in chapter 12), and settlers pastured herds, grew cash crops, and invested in business ventures.

Official policies abetted the settlers' program of acquisition. The proprietary government sold land rather than granting it to powerful men or allowing town leaders to divide and distribute it by lot. Land deeds and leases were negotiable, promoting speculation and development. The legislature, without the assent of the proprietor (who was worried what impression these laws would make in England), also provided bounties (fixed sum awards) for the production of certain exportable crops like hemp, created import duties to aid local producers (a kind of colonial tariff system), and printed paper currency to allow debtors more flexibility in paying what they owed. The government even lent the money at low interest rates to householders. All of these direct aids to the economy betokened a partnership between government and citizen, and an active role for government, that was at odds with more traditional models of government.

Improving and Providing

For these farm, mill, and trade families, the goal of life was self-improvement and provision for the future. One's primary allegiance to family, sect, and home dictated that some portion of present earnings be set aside for the next generation. But the enlightened self-interest of the eastern Pennsylvanians did not result in a close-minded and tight-fisted outlook on the world. Instead, these men and women were both acquisitive and inquisitive.

Hints of these optimistic priorities appeared in all manner of mundane places. For example, as families spread through the region, letter writing became a part of everyday activity. Of course, only the literate could write letters, so English-speaking Pennsylvanians began to invest in schools that emphasized reading, writing, and arithmetic for the many instead of elite classical subjects for the few. Non-English-speaking peoples like the German immigrants retained the old culture but added to it an appreciation of the language and customs of their new home. Associations of various kinds, many based on economic, intellectual, or philanthropic activities, provided another means of gathering and disseminating information.

The ideal of improvement began with the individual, but private goals merged into a larger public program of enrichment of common spaces and communal institutions. This commitment to public life expressed itself in a variety of ways in Philadelphia, from the creation of libraries, hospitals, schools, and private charities, to an interest in art, theater, and museums, to the paving of streets and the erection of street lamps.

No one more personified this ideal of improvement than Benjamin Franklin. Born in 1706 to a large Boston family of a candle maker, he early on showed signs of genius. Though his father was a full member of a Congregational church, young Franklin was never a devotee of conventional religion. Secretly he came to believe that a benevolent and rational God had left evidence of his creation everywhere in nature. This faith left a person's fate in his or her own hands—just where Franklin wanted it.

Franklin was apprenticed to his older brother, James, a printer, and they jointly published one of the first American newspapers, the *New England Courant*, a single-sheet newspaper. From it Franklin learned the importance of good management, but it was not business sense that distinguished the sixteen-year-old printer's devil. Instead, his contribution was literary. Though still a teenager, Franklin introduced a novelty to the American press. Inspired by his reading of the English magazine essays, he fabricated letters to the editor from "Mrs. Silence Dogood." As he recalled late in life, "being still a boy, and suspecting that my brother would object to printing any thing of mine in his paper if he knew it to be mine, I contrived to disguise my hand, and writing an anonymous paper I put it in at night under the door of the printing house." The fictitious Dogood was the widow of a country minister, and the fourteen essays under her name satirized everything from women's clothing to hypocrisy in religion.

When his relationship with his brother became unbearable in 1723, Franklin skipped out on his remaining years of apprenticeship and sailed first to New York City, then to Philadelphia. He worked as an assistant to Andrew Bradford, Pennsylvania's public printer, but yearned for wider horizons. With letters of introduction from his employer in hand, he traveled to London and there perfected his skills as an author and a printer, then returned to Philadelphia in 1727 to open his own printing shop.

Just as he had improved himself, he sought to upgrade the intellectual life of his colony. He was something of a gadfly, sponsoring public improvements and educational institutions, inventing and adapting practical technologies like the stove-oven (often called the Franklin stove because its shape, potbellied, resembles Franklin's). In 1727, he founded a club, the Junto, for discussion of science and philosophy, and continued with contributions to a Free Library Company (1731) for working people, a public hospital, and finally to a college for the colony (1751). No one more than he knew the value of education.

Franklin was the consummate provincial. He longed for recognition from England, and later in life, angled for an appointment to high imperial office. His lobbying for the colonies did not preclude these self-interested efforts. He had allies, but in the end foreclosed the option of royal approval by siding with the protesting colonists. Only then did he become the true patriot of later days.

CHESAPEAKE PEOPLE

In 1707, one hundred years after Christopher Newport entered the mouth of the James River, the landscape of the Tidewater scarcely resembled what he had seen. The tobacco mania of the planters had transformed the Powhatans' quilt of forest and parkland into a patchwork of irregularly shaped clear-cut fields and zigzag fences of rough-hewn logs. Dusty or muddy roads, ragged one- or two-story clapboard houses, and gardens, with their tobacco curing sheds, were ubiquitous.

The few surviving natives were lost in a sea of Europeans and Africans. In 1700, the colony contained 60,000 men and women; by 1750 it was home to 230,000. In 1700, 90 percent of the settlers were European, the rest were Indian or African. By 1750, 40 percent were African American. Indians had not required maps to know which cornfields belonged to which village. Virginians, on the contrary, devoted themselves to the legal rituals of domicile. They created counties, then subdivided them into parishes. Within the county courthouses, books of deeds platted every holding.

The Ordered Society

As the compulsion for recording land holdings demonstrated, in the eighteenth century a stable and prosperous society had replaced the seventeenth-century miscellany of orphans, widows, and single men. People now lived long enough to fashion networks of kin and clan. In one sense, its extremes defined a rank-ordered society. The mansion on the hill belonged to the great planter. As William Byrd II of Westover wrote to an English correspondent, "Like one of the patriarchs I have my flocks and my herds, my bond-men and bond-women, and every soart of trade amongst my own servants, so that I live in a kind of independence on everyone but providence. However this sort of life is without expense, yet it is attended with a great deal of trouble. I must take care to keep all of my people to their duty."

The wooden one-room cabins clustered down the hill at the rear of Westover and mansions like it were the slaves' quarters. A quiet revolution in slave housing had changed the quarters from a series of barrackslike elongated huts, in which unmarried men shared bunks, to individual dwellings. Byrd regarded the men and women in these cabins as his extended family, and spoke of them as though he were a biblical patriarch. Another planter saw the slaves as "those poor creatures who look up to their master as their father, their guardian, and protector." Privately, masters conceded that many of their slaves wanted their freedom and would never act the role of the docile child, and in counterpoise to the great planters' assumption of parental authority, the growing size of the workforce on plantations like Byrd's gave slaves more chances to fashion families of their own and to live close to parents and relatives.

Most Virginians were neither planters nor slaves. Their homes signaled their intermediate status in the ordered society. The poorest free farmers dwelt in two-to-four-room single-story cabins, with no glass for their one or two windows, a floor of pounded dirt, and a weatherboard roof. The better-off had glass windows, a raised wooden floor, and a shingled roof over an attic room. The wealthiest of the farmers were still not planters, but they had a two-story house whose upstairs and downstairs rooms were divided by interior walls.

Visible clues to status abounded. The gentleman rode; the yeoman walked and tugged his cap when the gentleman passed. Slaves stepped off the road when a free person passed, but at night slaves made their own paths to relatives on nearby plantations, or foraged in the woods to supplement the family diet. Clothing also marked class. A wig was a sign of rank, as were lace, finery, and braid. The poor farmer wore rougher fabrics. The badge of slavery was not clothing but color. African Americans exhibited a wide variety of shades from light brown to ebony, but any darkness of skin gave rise to a presumption of bondage. A few free African Americans lived and worked in every county, but these men and women took care not to provoke their free neighbors. Cases of reenslavement were not uncommon.

Like clothing and housing, one's work defined rank, but everyone had a stake in the harvest and watched the weather. Life conformed to the rhythms of the seasons of planting and harvesting. Some men of substance like Sir John Toddy, a character in John Munford's popular play *The Candidates* (1770), disdained work, preferring to "kill the time," but most others, like Byrd, rose at dawn and retired late, after a full day of labor.

Women's work was truly never done. Young gentle-born women learned to dance, say a few words in French, and look for advantageous matches with others of their class. Good marriages created networks of kinship. But gentle-born women had their duties: they tended the sick and old, watched over children, and managed the household staff. Poor white women toiled over food preparation, sewing and mending, and nursing the ailing. On occasion they helped their menfolk in the fields as well. Slave women worked from sunup to sundown six days a week on the master's tobacco and corn crops, often at the most onerous tasks of manuring or trimming the sharp-edged tobacco stalks.

The average married woman gave birth every three to five years, putting her in continual peril from the complications of pregnancy and delivery. The number of births presented the mother with an unending round of child-care duties. Wealthy women had servants to help; poorer women depended upon relatives and older children. Slave mothers, often forced to return to their household or field duties shortly after they gave birth, depended upon the assistance of other slaves and older children. There is no real evidence that slave masters saw black women as breeders rather than laborers. Few Tidewater slave owners sold young ones away from their mothers in this period, though many went off to Piedmont plantations with their masters.

Boundaries and Reputations

Visible lines bounded the land as well as the people. The fields might take a bewildering variety of shapes, but surveying the land was a matter of grave importance to owners. A man handy with surveyors' tools could always make a living, though working conditions—nights in the open, having to hunt for game, and watching out for sudden raids by disgruntled natives—were harsh.

In 1728, when the governors ordered a survey of the boundary between Virginia and North Carolina, tempers frayed. Surveyors for the two colonies, egged on by the colonies' gentlemen commissioners of the survey, accused each other of deliberately making mistakes in computation. William Byrd, one of the Virginia commissioners, regarded his North Carolina counterparts as fools and knaves. Their view of him, probably equally uncomplimentary, has not survived. To resolve the long-standing dispute over the dividing line between Pennsylvania and Maryland, the proprietors hired English surveyors Charles Mason and Jeremiah Dixon, and paid them for three years of arduous labor for calculating the so-called Mason-Dixon Line.

Less momentous contests among heirs and executors of wills over land surveys and deeds bedeviled Tidewater courts for years at a time. Ownership of real estate meant more than wealth—it meant that one could start a family, vote, and hold office. Legal documents referred to creeks whose courses had shifted over the years, trees long since cut down, and old Indian names for landmarks whose meaning or location no one remembered.

On the land itself, the ubiquitous worm fence separated cornfields from tobacco fields. Corn required weeding and planting in rows. Too much rain or too little sun could spoil the crop, as could insects, weeds, and a thousand other inflictions, but corn could be planted and harvested either before or after the planting and harvesting of the tobacco crop.

Tobacco required a year-round workforce, a keen eye for soil and weather, and skill in cutting, curing, stripping, stemming, and packing. Determining when to cut and how long to cure were individual decisions, and although there was a good deal of informal discussion among "tobacco masters," there was no sure guide to the planter. It was a great compliment to a Virginia planter to say that he grew fine tobacco. The accusation that a planter's tobacco was of poor quality might start a feud.

Under the terms of the 1730 Tobacco Act, government inspectors opened all hogsheads and threw away inferior grade tobacco. Smaller planters complained that they were being driven from the market by the act, for under it they could no longer compete with larger, better managed tobacco farms. Tobacco inspection certificates were so valued and so trusted that they circulated as currency.

Planters' competition for the best crop was typical, for planters competed over everything from horse races to public office holding. The planters' world was one of shame and public appearance. A man's honor rested on his public reputation, not, as in Puritan New England, his public testimony of private regeneration. The concept of honor percolated down from the great planters to the humblest white servants, and among the latter tavern brawls, public eye-gouging matches, and deadly serious affrays vindicated aggrieved dignity. Formal duels did not become fashionable until the end of the century, but one-on-one matches with fists, swords, and firearms were common.

Slaves had no honor—how could they, when they had no personhood? Despite (or perhaps because of) the fact that many Tidewater men and women had mixed parentage, the law drew strict lines around the "races." The "black code" of 1705 reminded Virginians of the rule: slaves were property. Of course, the irony of the law was plain and poignant, for individual slaves and individual masters knew one another's smiles, stories, and skills from childhood. Within the small world of the plantation, contact each day disproved what the law said.

Although the slaves and the free made the Tidewater together, there was distrust and fear alongside affection and comradeship. The law gave every advantage to the master, but the slaves' own cunning, wit, and boldness, and their masters' genuine affection or kindness of spirit on occasion, gave slaves some informal leverage. So, perhaps, did the fact that much of the planter's available wealth was invested in slaves. For a multitude of reasons, the master or mistress who treated slaves well and whose slaves were well behaved gained great reputation.

With that leverage, slaves created their own world in the Tidewater. They gained a sub rosa legal title to their tools, household items, clothing, and even the animals they reared. They fused Christian worship with older African and Caribbean religious beliefs to create potent religious hybrids and practiced these rites. The continuing influx of newcomers from Africa in the quarters stirred memories of traditional forms of worship. The remembered shapes of West African hearthstones and storage jars reappeared in slave cabins. Bead necklaces of glass and semiprecious stones refashioned by slave women reminded them of the adornments worn by their ancestors. Handkerchiefs, turbans, earrings, and other African dress ways persisted, as did West African food traditions.

If slaves were visible everywhere—there was no arbitrary, physical segregation of slave and master in the mid-eighteenth-century Tidewater—when it came to formal public power, the slaves became invisible. Thus, typically, although crimes including intraslave violence were endemic in the slave quarters, they went largely unrecorded in the court docket books. Planters simply administered discipline themselves. Some planter diaries are filled with masters' efforts to "correct" slaves who stole food or clothing, ran away, or misused farm implements. In such cases, the planters regarded themselves variously as merciful or wrathful parents and the slaves as heedless or willful children, but planters rarely saw slave life from the slaves' eyes and misunderstood the purpose of pilfering and vandalism. Slave "crimes" were acts of defiance and resistance, as well as expressions of frustration, anger, and just plain hunger.

Some planters dreamed of transforming the Tidewater into a bustling commercial mart. Tobias Mickleburrough was a Middlesex County planter who owned twenty slaves. He filled out his time and income by running a small store on the Rosegill Creek above its union with the Rappahannock. In the store he stocked nails, thread and cloth, buttons, glass, and shoe buckles. He kept debts and credits in a ledger. In no way was the store different from the many crossroads and dockside retail shops whose business was based on credit and trust, but around it, on land that the Robinson brothers gained from the legislature, grew a small town.

In the four years between 1704 and 1708, through delays and disputes over who was granted what parcel of land by the House of Burgesses, the Robinsons turned a marshland at the confluence of Rosegill Creek and the Rappahannock into the town of Urbanna. Down the road sat the courthouse. Across the creek sprawled the Wormeley family's Rosegill plantation. In the town site, twenty-three new lots echoed to the sounds of saw and hammer. A wooden landing for tobacco boats thrust itself out into the river as though by magic. A few merchants relocated themselves to Urbanna, and thirty houses were soon grouped about the few streets. A tobacco warehouse appeared next, a reminder of the purpose of the whole affair. New stores carried a wider variety of consumer goods than Mickleburrough's shop. Tools, dishware, eyeglasses, curtains, and French brandy were hot consumer items, and the storekeepers were full-time retailers, not part-time planters.

Williamsburg

For a small part of the year, those who could took themselves and their servants to Williamsburg, the colonial capital. Williamsburg was in many ways a unique city in the colonies, for it had the distinction, along with Philadelphia; Annapolis, Maryland; and Savannah, Georgia, of a preexisting design. Governor Francis Nicholson, who had previously designed Annapolis as Maryland's new capital, replacing Saint Mary's, laid out Williamsburg on the land of the "middle plantation" between the James and the York rivers.

The plan for Virginia's new capital incorporated baroque European design elements—broad streets and ornate facades. Under a 1699 law that Nicholson helped draft, houses on the principal street, named after the Duke of Gloucester, were to stand six feet or more back from the brick roadway and be enclosed by fences or low walls. A market square with a courthouse, a church, and open-air stalls interrupted the flow of houses and businesses on the nearly mile-long street. At the beginning of the street stood the College of William and Mary, an imposing, four-story brick building.

At right angles to the midpoint of the thoroughfare a wide, short avenue led to the governor's palace. This three-story residence, office, and conference center was roofed by 1710, occupied by 1715, and gained a park and formal gardens five years later. Its symmetrical "wings" served as meeting rooms. Formal sitting rooms flanked the central hall, and into the back of it flowed a huge, curved staircase to a formal reception room and bedrooms above. No one who entered could fail to be impressed.

A third brick and mortar edifice occupied the end of the Duke of Gloucester Street. The capitol sheltered the House of Burgesses and the council in its two wings and central portico. The meeting rooms were elegantly furnished and richly paneled, as befit the social status as well as the political authority of the delegates and appointees.

More important, the city itself was a public space in which the preexisting rules of rank and privilege could be visibly reinforced. The public buildings were red brick, expensive, and visually striking at a time when wood was the standard housing material. Placed so that the eye fell naturally upon them, their symmetry, size, and ornamentation immediately conveyed their importance. The same act that provided funds for the survey of the city mandated substantial houses on its major thoroughfares, so that the entire city, like the outbuildings leading up to the planter's big house, served to magnify the gathering of Virginia's elite when the assembly was in session.

Public functions reinforced the hierarchical arrangement of public spaces. Ceremonies at the palace and the assembly reminded people of their rank. On holidays and the anniversaries of royal births and accessions, the governor led the parade of grandees. Footmen bearing the seals of Britain and the colony preceded him. Rank determined the order of the rest of the procession. Even mealtimes at the palace and the opening and closing of sessions of the House of Burgesses and the council had set rituals that reminded onlookers and participants of the difference between high and low status. Seating in the Bruton Parish church followed this pattern. The governor and the grandees sat in the best pews in the front of church; lesser ranks sat in lesser seats. As public space mimicked private distinctions, so public functions restated private privileges.

The council, when sitting as the highest court in the colony, met on the second floor of the capitol building. The judges' bench in this room was elevated, and the walls, dark with richly polished woods, reflected beams of light from high octagonal windows behind the bench. The councilors (the upper house) doubled as the judges and presided in their high-backed, cushioned chairs, the governor sitting in the center chair. Thus justice was never abstract or distant—it was but another face of the provincial social order that everyone was expected to know and accept.

INDIANS AND SETTLERS IN THE BORDERLANDS

Although for many years American historians called the western edge of the English settlements a "frontier," implying that beyond the line of cleared farms and cabins lay a wilderness, nothing could be farther from the truth. In fact, the western edge was exactly that, a shifting and contested borderland between Indian country and colonial lands. Often those claims overlapped. In the woods of western Pennsylvania, for example, Indian villages and colonial settlements lay on both sides of the north-south divide. As settlers pushed into the Ohio Valley and the southern Appalachians, they came to live next door to the Indians.

Trading Partners

Trade was an essential part of backwoods life, and experienced traders like John Lawson in the Carolinas and George Croghan in Pennsylvania became "go-betweens," translators and negotiators between settlers and native peoples. Such men might be trusted by one side or the other, but they never really brought the two sides together.

At the fords in rivers or the crossing of trails on the frontier, villages with mixed populations became year-round marts. Indians from different groups frequented the cabins and sheds that traders erected to service their clients. Some of these meeting places were of Indian origin, like the Creek town of Okafuse, on the upper Coosa River in Alabama, and Pickawillany, on the Miami River in Ohio. Indian leaders in the Ohio Valley shifted the sites of their villages to gain better access to European trade goods. Other gathering places were set up by ambitious traders, like George Croghan's trading post at Logstown, on the Ohio River. Still others, like Quebec and New Orleans, were founded by Europeans on the ruins of older Indian settlements. Some, including the Forks of the Ohio (later Pittsburgh), Saint Louis, and Detroit, had long been convenient natural gathering sites for Indian peoples. European traders went where their native customers were.

In these multinational trading post / towns, the Indians learned pidgin French, Spanish, and English, as the occasion demanded. Living among the Indians and sometimes intermarrying, the French and Spanish tried harder and were more successful than the English at mastering the native tongues, but modern English contains thousands of North American Indian place names and object words, including *moose, caribou, hominy, skunk, chipmunk, mahogany, yucca, maize, squash, succotash, pemmican, wigwam, tepee, moccasin, wampum, tomahawk, sachem, sagamore, powwow, caucus, toboggan,* and, of course, *tobacco,* not to mention place names like Massachusetts, Connecticut, Alabama, and Mississippi.

Although the older Indians clung to their traditions of communal hunting and sharing, and wise traders learned to conform their behavior to Indian norms, traders like Lawson and Croghan profoundly changed Indian life. They particularly influenced the younger men. The traders wanted furs and deerskins for sale abroad, effecting a falling domino sequence of changes in native life. Deer had been a major source of protein, clothing, and footwear for the Indians of the eastern woodlands, but the lure of European trade goods in return for the skins caused warriors to overhunt the deer.

What was more, the new trade system undermined the communal structure of the hunt. The Catawbas, Creeks, and other eastern Indians had hunted deer the way that prehistoric-era plains Indians had hunted buffalo, as a seasonal event involving every able male. Large numbers of shouting hunters drove the deer herds to the kill site. The villagers divided the kill. But the English trader exchanged goods not with a village but with particular hunters, rewarding their prowess, rather than the group.

The firearms, mostly flintlock muskets, obtained in trade for the deerskins became the means by which warriors could transform the hunt into a source of individual gain. Armed with the gun, a hunter could kill deer in any season, without the aid of others in the village. Successful hunters were still expected to share their wealth with the village, but a vital part of the communal life of the hunters disappeared. Soon individual Indians began to hoard the trade goods their hunting brought them, violating another of the foundational values of Indian culture—the idea that high status belonged to whoever gave away the most, not whoever had the most. Older Indian leaders admitted that they could no longer control the young men who had been corrupted by the lure of trade goods.

Firearms not only helped in hunting, they provided protection against warlike neighbors. Ironically, as some traders noted with alarm, and as colonial authorities in Philadelphia, Charleston, and Williamsburg confirmed, the spread of firearms among the Indians increased the danger that they posed to settlers. Although adoption of firearms made the Indians more dependent upon their European trading partners for repair of barrels, flints, and ammunition, the English had no monopoly of these trade goods and services. Indians disgruntled at English trading practices could visit French or Spanish suppliers.

At the same time, dependence on European merchants undermined the self-esteem of formerly self-sufficient Indians. More and more, they found the sellers of powder and shot to be arrogant and insulting. The number of incidents in which Indians ambushed or assassinated their erstwhile trading partners mushroomed. In another sad irony, the alcohol that European traders supplied to lubricate the trade fed the violence, as drunken Indians and Europeans turned on one another.

The Indians' New World

Missionaries and microbes completed the process of remaking the Indians' world that European traders and trade goods began. In Great Lakes, Mississippi, and Ohio Valley villages, Catholic missionaries used wiles and warnings to convert Indians. Some priests developed genuine rapport with Indians, bringing over leaders to the

Christian camp. The Jesuits had some success among high-ranking Indian women, emphasizing the idea of sexual purity.

The Catholic missionaries used visual aids—for example, depictions of Christ and the Virgin Mary—to share the message of salvation through the sacraments with Indians, mixing teaching with gift giving to meld together European ideas and traditional Indian ceremonies. Missionaries' preaching fit into Indian appreciation of public speaking, and missionaries who could go on for hours gained the respect reserved for great Indian orators.

In western Pennsylvania, by contrast, Moravian preachers impressed Indians with their community spirit and hospitality. Whole villages of the Moravians welcomed Indians and shared goods with them in social rather than commercial exchanges. This kind of exchange was traditional among Indian societies, and distinguished the Moravians from the traders.

New outbreaks of disease remade Indian life in the Southeast. Everywhere Carolina trader and surveyor John Lawson and his Indian interpreters traveled in the Piedmont backcountry in the early 1700s, they saw evidence of catastrophe. Abandoned Indian villages, their wooden palisades falling into ruin and their unworked fields returning to brush, littered the landscape. "These Indian are a small people," he reported. "Having lost most of their former numbers . . . by the Small-pox, which hath often visited them, sweeping away whole towns."

The disease struck suddenly. Smallpox has a fairly short incubation period. A high fever was followed by the blood-filled pustules. The disease would run its course in two to three weeks, but Indians who had it were contagious, and Indian curing rituals—cold baths or sweating—were deadly for a smallpox victim. Indian social customs for dealing with the sick, involving the intervention of native shamans and the gathering of close relatives, only spread the germs more swiftly.

The plague of 1697–1701 had swept like wildfire through the Southeast. Peoples who had escaped earlier epidemics of European disease because they had then lived in widely dispersed settlements had now inadvertently brought themselves within the reach of the epidemic when they moved their towns closer to their European trading partners. Lawson admitted, "Neither do I know any savages that have traded with the English, but what have been great losers by their distemper."

In the wake of the epidemic, remnants of once-populous Piedmont peoples were forced to rethink older customs. Groups that had once been rivals began to come together in confederations, or, as the Europeans called them, "nations." Lawson visited one such nation—the Catawbas of Sugar Creek, South Carolina. Composed of the exiles of many peoples of the Piedmont and the coast, the Catawbas, like the Creeks to the west, asked their new brothers and sisters to respect local customs. The Catawbas and other Piedmont peoples remained villagers, mobile but not nomadic, and each village still had its own leaders and walked its own path. Councils and exchanges were continuous among the villages, but no one person commanded allegiance, much less obedience, from all of them.

Frontiersmen and Women

In 1893, historian Frederick Jackson Turner told his audience at the World's Columbian Exposition in Chicago that the frontier remade Europeans into Americans. It stripped them of the old ways of obedience and tradition and dressed them in the deerskin shirt of democracy and freedom. The continuing westward movement of the frontier supposedly kept that process alive, reinvigorating American ideals of self-sufficiency and rugged individualism. Few historians adhere to that thesis now, and the preponderance of evidence suggests that the frontier was not the cutting edge of a uniquely new and praiseworthy culture.

On the western fringes of the British Empire, the settlers still lived in "English wigwams" with stamped dirt floors and little furniture. The only difference between the colonists' and the Indians' living quarters was the handful of nails the colonists used to put up a permanent roof. Pioneers slept in their clothes on straw piles, were afflicted with vermin, and ate around an open fire, usually with their fingers.

Their prized possessions were everyday objects, tools, and ware—knives, plates, tubs, basins, pots, pans, needles, scissors, axes, hammers, spinning wheels, and with a little more time, perhaps, looms. Laurel Thatcher Ulrich's research reminds us that New England backcountry women gained praise for their spinning and weaving skills. Even in the rudest cottage in the smallest clearing, household production was essential. Homespun cloth for bedding, clothing, and repair supplemented store-bought materials. Women also saw to the livestock, gathered herbs and nuts, and prepared the meals. There was little furniture in the cabin—the same array of trunks, benches, and bed frames that the first settlers of the coastal communities had. The edge of settlement was harsh.

What linen and woolen production was to the womenfolk, hunting was to men. A sharp-eyed hunter became a natural leader in a society that matched manhood to prowess with weapons. Men like Daniel Boone led by example rather than formal office-holding. Indians came to respect such men among the settlers, as white hunters like Boone mastered the skills that Indians already possessed—to move silently and quickly through the woods, to read animal signs, to shoot from cover, and to accept hunger and cold on the trail. Like the Indians, the white hunters shared the bounty of the hunt with homesteaders who did not participate. But because they were trespassing on Indian hunting grounds, even the most expert white hunters had to practice extra caution. Surrounded by real and imagined enemies, they hid their fears from one another.

Hospitality was a rule among the settlers in these bare surroundings, just as it was in Indian villages, but unlike the Indians, who lived communally and farmed together, the backwoods colonial family worked its own land and had to rely on itself. The nearest neighbor was another farmer who lived acres, sometimes miles, away. Though as we have seen, many of these settler communities were the advanced guard of well-to-do land speculators, and some frontier families, like the Mathewses in the Shenandoah Valley, lived in fine houses.

Isolation on the frontier meant that children did not socialize through schooling. They learned their letters, if at all, from siblings and parents. Ministers rarely visited, so that people worshipped, married, named children, and died without the comfort of the Word, much less the sacraments.

The rudeness of manners resulting from isolation was the butt of criticism when members of the elite visited. William Byrd of Virginia derogated the backwoods people of North Carolina as lazy lubbers, and others compared the frontier people to African slaves, because both wore worn-out clothing and occasionally went barefoot. To George Washington, the frontier folk were little more than Indians. But those who were sympathetic to the poverty and isolation of the backwoods settlers saw them differently. The Reverend Charles Woodmason, traveling the same Carolina backcountry as Byrd visited, albeit some years later, recalled, "many of these people walk 10 or 12 miles with their children in the burning sun" to join him at prayer services, "so desirous of . . . becoming Good Christians, and good Subjects."

The Carolina Hills

Conflict in the backwoods during these provincial years was endemic. Only a few regions—for example, Pennsylvania—were spared. In one of the most notorious of the endless rounds of raid and ambush, the town of Deerfield, Massachusetts, figured prominently. In February 1704, a coalition of Indians allied to the French swooped down on the unsuspecting villagers (who should have kept better guard, it is true), and killed 39 of the townspeople. Another 112 were carried off to Canada to be ransomed—or not, if they converted to Roman Catholicism or otherwise were persuaded to live among their captors. The Indians' grievances included a massacre of their number at a peace conference some years earlier—but in this war of each against all, specific grievances were overlain with long-standing grudges and feuds.

In 1704, Massachusetts's existence was not imperiled by the raiding on its frontier (the dispersion of the Indians after King Philip's War saw to that), but ten years later backwoods Carolina was decimated by Indian attacks. For many years, the local authorities in Carolina, often in direct contradiction to the orders of the proprietors, had set Indians against one another to gain Indian captives as slaves. The domino effect of this crass and violent practice reached as far as the Mississippi to the west, Florida to the south, and Virginia to the north. Nothing matched the South Carolina slave traders' avarice.

No sooner did the Carolinians stake their claim to the land than they began trading in Indian slaves. They needed Indian laborers for their own farms, and they sold the surplus to West Indian planters. A 1708 census recorded fourteen hundred Indian slaves in Carolina. Creeks and other Indians aided Europeans in raids on Apalachee lands in northern Florida to capture and enslave thousands of Christian Indians nominally under the protection of the Spanish. Soon Creeks, Cherokees, and other Indians became slave traders themselves, razing villages to capture slaves for the English slave market. Fearing such a fate, a band of Yuchi Indians chose suicide over capture by the Cherokees.

South Carolina slave traders, like Eleazer Wigan and Alexander Long, who had convinced the Cherokees to raid Yuchi settlements for slaves, continued their activities, safe in the knowledge that the slave trade was profitable to the Indians as well as to the Europeans. Thus the Indians of the Southeast became fatally enmeshed in the slave traders' commerce.

Even those Indians who could protect themselves against the slave traders, like the powerful Tuscaroras of the North Carolina Piedmont, faced the insidious advance of colonial settlement. In 1711, the North Carolinians ignored Indian land rights by building towns like New Bern, on the Neuse River, in the middle of Tuscarora homelands. The Tuscaroras complained, got no satisfaction, and attacked the Palatine Germans and English in the town.

The North Carolina militia assembled and marched into the Indian towns, burning houses and crops. After two years of sieges of Indian forts that ended with both sides withdrawing, and chases through canebrake and forest, the Tuscaroras could see that they had failed. They agreed to a peace with the North Carolina government that denied them the lands they once roamed freely, then decamped to New York to seek membership in the Iroquois League. The League accepted the newcomers as "younger brothers."

A few native peoples seem to have found a way to avoid the perils of slavery and the pressure of colonial expansion. The Yamasees lived in close proximity to the South Carolina settlers and had helped the Carolinians to destroy the Tuscaroras when they rose in 1712. In return, the South Carolinians made the Yamasees the best armed of all the Indian nations. But soon after their service in that war, the Yamasees realized that their turn had come. Settlers planted their farms on Yamasee land. Fewer deer browsed nearby—driven off by the settlers' cattle herds. With the decline of the deerskin trade, the Yamasees could not pay for European goods and fell into chronic debt.

Much like the dairy farmers of rural Connecticut and the yeomen tobacco farmers of Virginia, the Yamasees had become producers in a market system they did not control. The burden of debt and dependence weighed especially heavily on the Yamasees, because they saw a way of life vanishing—along with the independence that way of life had meant. All they had left to offer for the trade goods on which they had become so dependent was the enslavement of their Indian neighbors or their own servile labor.

The South Carolina authorities, no longer needing the Yamasees as scouts, added insult to penury by refusing the Yamasees their accustomed yearly gifts of clothing, powder, shot, and other goods. The English had always seen the distribution as bribes, but the Indians had regarded the goods as a matter of diplomatic courtesy.

Offended by the conduct of their former friends and insulted by the Scots traders whom they had never liked, the Yamasees sent emissaries to the council fires of former friends and enemies throughout the Piedmont urging a common war against the English. By the spring of 1714, Yamasee diplomats had convinced many village headmen among the Creeks, Cherokees, and Catawbas that they must act in concert against the Carolinians. The resulting "Yamasee War" erupted with terrible ferocity. Nearly a hundred traders in the backcountry were killed, sometimes after torture, and well-organized and well-armed groups of Indians drove the settlers from their farms to the edge of Charleston itself.

South Carolina bore the brunt of the war. The ruins of abandoned outlying plantations and farmers' dwellings crisscrossed the Piedmont, and Indian raiders carried off those settlers who might bring ransom or be added to the tribes. Virginia and North Carolina promised aid, but little came. Every colonist was expected to bear arms, but the Indian confederacy had more warriors than the colony had militia. Only the fact that the Indians ran out of gunpowder, despite the eagerness of the Spanish to remedy the problem, prevented greater slaughter. By the end of 1715, many Indians had stopped large-scale siege operations and gone back to hit-and-run tactics.

Meanwhile, the Carolinians, with the aid of African American slaves and a few friendly Indians, relearned the lessons that Benjamin Church and his New England troops mastered during King Philip's War in 1675–1676. Under militia leaders like George Chicken, South Carolina forces began to surprise marauding Indians by adopting Indian tactics. In the meantime, the government of South Carolina, after months of dithering, finally hit upon a larger strategy that offered a chance of ending the war. Old Indian rivalries within the ranks of the enemy might be exploited to drive a wedge between the Indian allies.

With a force of three hundred militiamen, Colonel James Moore traveled to the Cherokee town of Tugaloo in January 1716 to ask the Cherokees to turn upon the Yamasees' chief supporters, the Creeks. The Cherokees were reluctant allies of the Creeks in any case, for the two peoples were longtime rivals for ascendancy in the region. Moore knew this, for he was an experienced slave trader. He now acted the part of a proper Indian diplomat, but the Cherokees did not immediately accede to Moore's proposal, for a deputation of sixteen Creek chiefs, led by the great warrior Brims, had also arrived at Tugaloo to press the case for continued resistance to the English.

With the outcome hanging by a thread, a group of Cherokees who wanted the English alliance treacherously fell upon the Creek emissaries and slaughtered them. Now there was no turning back for the Cherokees. They would need English weapons and ammunition to defend themselves against the Creeks, for the Creeks would never (and never did) forgive the Cherokees.

With the Cherokees on their side, the English triumphed. By 1717, the Yamasees, once slave traders, were sold as slaves, but South Carolina had learned how deadly a trade in Indian slaves could be. They ended it, opening the way for increased importation of African bondmen and women. The Creeks had to make their own peace with the English, but carried out a war against the Cherokees that lasted another century. The Cherokees, now firm allies of the English, suffered for their betrayal of the Creek diplomatic delegation, but closer contact with the English would lead to an assimilation movement within the Cherokee people. New leaders, many of them of mixed parentage, began to adopt English styles of farming, education, and religious worship. The Cherokees, who once traded in Indian slaves, became owners of African and African American slaves themselves. In the future, some would become large-scale planters.

The Catawbas had begun to withdraw from the war confederation before the incident at Tugaloo. A deputation of Catawbas traveled to Williamsburg to try to play the Virginia authorities against the Carolina government, but found that Carolina officials were already discussing the common defense with Alexander Spotswood, the lieutenant governor of Virginia. Evidently, the English, unlike the Indians, could not be pit against one another in time of war.

RICE NABOBS AND GULLAH SLAVES IN THE SOUTH CAROLINA LOW COUNTRY

In the first half of the eighteenth century, the South Carolina lowlands exhibited the sharpest and most unbridgeable gulf between the ideal of self-improvement and the reality of social hierarchy and economic oppression on the North American mainland. A black majority labored to make a handful of white rice nabobs (an Urdu word for a person of great wealth applied to the English in eighteenth-century India) enormously rich.

The Slaves' Fate

By the 1720s, the low country of South Carolina was a land of black people. They outnumbered whites two to one overall, and on the rice plantations the ratio was even higher. To manage the black majority, the master class deployed the harsh slave codes of the sugar islands, but some masters did not bother to consult the code. They applied more direct methods. As Charles Wesley, a visiting minister, reported, "Colonel Lynch cut off the legs of a poor negro, and he kills several of them every year by his barbarities. Mr. Hill, a dancing master in Charleston, whipped a female slave so long that she fell down at his feet, in appearance dead. . . . These horrid cruelties are less to be wondered at, because the law itself, in effect, countenances and allows them to kill their slaves by the ridiculous penalty appointed for it." The fine for causing the death of one's slave was seven pounds, colony money.

Because most slaves in the low country, unlike those in the Chesapeake, worked in settings surrounded by other slaves, and because the Carolina rice planters continued to import a large proportion of their slaves from Africa, the slaves retained far more of their African heritage than slaves to the north. This included foodways, dress, language, and religious customs. Slaves utilized the time that the task system gave them to grow market crops and to hunt and fish, however, creating more social and economic space for themselves than the slaves had in the Chesapeake. The formation of an African American society was thus delayed.

Slaves resisted the barbarities of slavery, as they had in the sugar islands, by slowing down their pace, breaking tools, hiding, stealing, and running away. Every year, barns mysteriously caught fire, some, no doubt, the work of slave arsonists. A few slaves "stole themselves" by fleeing to the swamps or to Florida.

All Africans responded to their bondage by making the slave quarters into a refuge for the spirit and the body. In their Gullah Creole tongue, they reworked song lyrics and story lines of African origin to fit their new surroundings. For example, slave storytellers adapted the African folklore "trickster" figure (an animal whose cleverness enabled it to outwit stronger adversaries) to fit tales of foolish masters and clever slaves.

As ably as some slaves coped and as strong as their commitment to their ancestral ways might be, the fact is inescapable that slave independence in the early days of the South Carolina colony was gone by the end of the colonial era. Even sadder, the unique African cultural traditions of individual slaves dimmed with the passing of the years. More and more, they became generic "Africans," or worse, were denoted only by the corruption of the Spanish word for black, *negro*, as "Nigras."

Rebellion at Stono Creek

South Carolina whites always worried that their bondmen would rebel. Their fears were justified by the most significant slave uprising in North America. On the evening of September 9, 1739, a slave drainage crew labored at a crossing on the Stono River, twenty miles west of Charleston. The law required masters on adjacent parcels of land to supply slaves for "laying out, cutting, sinking, and maintaining" drains and water passages in rivers. The work was tiring, dirty, and dangerous. In the murderously hot and humid summer, cutting drains was so debilitating that some masters refused to supply their slaves, and were fined. In addition, masters rarely sent their skilled workers to the drainage crews, and the men at the drainage ditch knew that the skilled slaves were selling their labor for food or clothing while the crew sweated. The last straw was that it was a Sunday, and the law required that slaves be given the day off, unless the work was urgent. That determination was left to the commissioners appointed by the colony to finish the work, and they were driving this crew hard to repair the drainage system.

Most of the slaves hailed from Angola, so they spoke dialects of Bantu—close enough that they understood one another. Some also knew Spanish or Portuguese, for the Portuguese ran the Angolan slave trade, and Portuguese missionaries had converted some Angolans. Some of the gang must have served in the myriad local militias that contested Angola's endless rounds of civil war. Last but not least, the work crew had heard conversations among masters about the coming of war with Spain, and guessed that they would be free if they could reach the Spanish colony of Florida.

The men decided to flee to Florida, and then, who knew, perhaps home. They swore one another to stand, march, and fight as one, a blood oath. "Courage! Look out, beyond, and see / the far horizon's beckoning span! / Faith in your God-known destiny! / We are part of some great plan."

First they must have firearms. Angolan soldiers used firearms, and at least some of these men saw themselves as soldiers and regarded their band as a military formation. They broke into a crossroads storehouse, killed the two watchmen when they resisted the robbery, and stole arms and ammunition, crimes from which there was no turning back. Their flight turned into a martial procession down country lanes, destroying farmhouses and setting upon any whites in the way. Probably the slaves chanted martial airs and fired their weapons.

A mass escape had become a rebellion, led by men who had seen such rebellions in Africa. Twenty became fifty, and fifty swelled to nearly a hundred in the band by midmorning. True, their recruiting efforts had largely failed. In a countryside swarming with slaves, they garnered relatively few enlistees. The leaders were Angolans, and slaves from other African nations, including the many Gold Coast and Slave Coast bondmen, either watched or actively aided their masters to flee the advancing troop. One slave, July, helped his master, Thomas Elliot, and his master's family to escape, while another persuaded the rebels not to look for his master, whom he had hidden. When the rebellion was over, the colonial assembly rewarded thirty-one such slaves, most of them probably native born or long in the colony.

But even without significant reinforcements from plantation slaves, the road crew turned rebel force left their mark upon the land and its owners—killing some two dozen whites and burning half a dozen plantation houses on their way. The rebels' progress was marked by the smoke of the houses they destroyed. It was easy to understand why they killed all the whites they met. African armies caused terror by leaving the land wasted. Revenge was surely another motive, for burning destroyed the masters' most valued possessions.

By late in the day, the African company had marched ten miles from the Stono River to the Edisto River, plundering along the way, and stopped to celebrate the day's events. They danced, sang, beat drums, and drank confiscated spirits. While some whites later sneered that the Stono slaves celebrated too soon, in fact the African troop was preparing for battle and waiting for the reinforcements from the countryside they expected to join them. In addition, numbers of their original band were still straggling in, arms loaded with spoils from abandoned plantation houses and barns.

At four in the afternoon the first company of mounted militia arrived in the field where the rebels reposed, and engaged them in musketry. The battle lines were drawn by color, whites killing blacks, blacks killing whites. One can find no better evidence in the whole of American colonial history of the way in which color had become the badge of slavery.

Used to the skirmish warfare that characterized the beginning of an Angolan combat, the rebels fell back to fight individually, using cover, abandoning the wounded and allowing the advancing South Carolina forces to capture those who had tried to hide themselves in the field. The militiamen left in control of the battlefield did not spare the wounded or the captured, as armies would have in an African war. They questioned the captives, then executed every rebel on the spot. In the end, no rebel escaped.

Charleston

South Carolina growth was interrupted but not derailed by the Yamasee uprising or the Stono rebellion, and was helped tremendously by the growth of the little port town of Charleston into a true city. There were few urban areas in the colonial South, for reasons that historians still debate. Charleston was certainly an exception that proved the value of urban life.

Not only was the city a port, mart, gathering place, political capital, information storehouse, and social center, it was a source of investment. Charleston merchants, tradesmen, craftspeople, and artisans invested in South Carolina agriculture by giving mortgages to planters. Though the return set by legislative enactment on these loans was but 10 percent, the mortgages continued to be a vital part of the economy itself, growing tenfold from 1710 to 1730. The planters who received the funds put up their land as collateral, but the lenders rarely foreclosed on the liens, for the planters put the borrowed money to profitable use, expanding and improving their operations, including buying more slaves.

Charleston became the largest city in the coastal South, a haven for planters in the deadly lowland summer, a gateway to the southern slave trade, and the port of exit for coastal rice, indigo dyestuffs, and naval stores. By 1750, slaves outnumbered free persons three to one in the city, and performed the heavy labor of loading and unloading the ships. Forts, batteries, and breastworks faced out to sea, waiting for the Spanish and French to attack. There was no college, but gentlemen had endowed a library, many beautiful churches lined the wide streets, and townhouses for the rich imitated the large, square faces and multiple windows of London's Augustan architecture. Pelatiah Webster of Philadelphia visited Charleston in 1765 and recalled, "I was used very genteelly and contracted much acquaintance for the time I staid here. The heats are much too severe, the water bad, the soil sandy, the timber too much evergreen, but with all these disadvantages, 'tis a flourishing place, capable of vast improvement."

THE SPANISH SOUTH

The Spanish border with South Carolina and Georgia was never settled until after the Revolutionary War. Instead, the boundary between the old colony of Spanish Florida and the newer colonies of Carolina and Georgia was the subject of a war of maps. In 1663, King Charles II gave his Carolina proprietors lands that were already claimed by the king of Spain. The Spanish did not accept that grant as a fair one. Just as this borderland between the English and the Spanish empires was contested by the two nations, so it was contested in the two nations' maps.

On the eve of the transfer of the South Carolina charter to the crown and the appointment of a royal governor for the colony, in 1729, Herman Moll, a Dutchman living in England, produced the last of his many maps of the region. His aim was to justify the English claims to the disputed lands between Florida and South Carolina, and he included both the 1663 grant line and, beneath it, the 1729 claim—well south of the Spanish city of Saint Augustine.

The Spanish surveyor Antonio de Arredondo found Moll's claims "debatable" and tried to prove it by drawing a competing map. His 1742 plan suggested that English settlers had wrongfully occupied the northern part of Spanish Florida. The upper east-west solid line on the map denoted the land supposedly belonging to Spain by right of first conquest and by law; the lower solid line (still north of Moll's upper line) showed the limits of Spain's occupation of Florida—though in fact it was the northernmost habitation of Spain's Indian allies.

In 1755, as war between the English and the Spanish again erupted, Parliament asked John Mitchell to produce a new map of the Georgia-Florida boundary. Mitchell placed the southern boundary of the royal colony of Georgia well into the country that Arredondo had asserted belonged to Spain. The Mitchell map was perhaps the most famous in colonial history, for it was used to negotiate boundaries between Georgia and Florida at the end of the French and Indian War in 1763 and at the end of the American War of Independence in 1783. Although for its time it was incredibly detailed, it had the same partisan purpose as Moll's and Arredondo's earlier efforts. It was a weapon in the ongoing debate over which nation had legal title to the borderlands. As the war of the maps hinted, the borderlands were contested regions in which native peoples and Spanish settlers marked out a unique multiracial social system under terrific economic and military stress.

Saint Augustine, Florida

After the victory in the Yamasee War ensured English hegemony over the Piedmont frontier, eastern Florida became a refuge for indigenous Indians and slaves fleeing the English provinces. Those willing to convert to Roman Catholicism were integrated into the polyglot Spanish colony. Thus a few hundred Spanish soldiers, tradesmen, and missionaries, along with a slightly larger number of settlers and a few thousand surviving Guales, Apalachees, and other natives, guarded the northeastern edge of the Spanish Empire in North America.

As was so often the case in the colonies, European survival depended upon a fortress. In coastal eastern Florida, this was the Castillo de San Marcos, at the northeastern edge of the town of Saint Augustine. Marsh, river, and land defenses made the fort safe from land attack, and the shallow approaches from the sea prevented warships from coming too close. Thus protected, the fort withstood a two-month siege by South Carolina troops under James Moore and his one thousand Creek allies in 1705 and a later bombardment by Georgia's governor-general James Oglethorpe in 1739. In times of trouble like these, the entire population of the town crowded into the fort. It functioned the way that a castle did in a medieval city, as a refuge for the people as well as a strong point and armory.

Despite the fact that the Spanish had occupied the site for over 150 years by the beginning of the 1730s, and the role of Saint Augustine as the administrative, military, and religious center of the Florida colony, the town itself remained small and bore the marks of a frontier outpost throughout the eighteenth century. The few amenities the townspeople enjoyed were imported from Havana or elsewhere in the Spanish Empire.

The crown was aware of the general desuetude of the town, and early in the century made funds available for rebuilding the governor's mansion and improving the parish church. Much labor went into keeping the fortress in good repair, and a few wealthy inhabitants had two- or three-story homes. But even these had a fortresslike appearance, for, like the fort, they were made of "tabby," a compound of seashells, lime (made from boiling down the shells), stones, and clay that is waterproof and almost impenetrable by cannon or small arms fire, but heavy and not easily worked. What is more, even the best homes on the plaza across from the church crowded together, as though they, too, were refugees.

Though the conditions of life for everyone were primitive, a class system entrenched itself. The governor and his military and civilian aides stood at the top of society. The officials of the church and the wealthy merchants were next. Indians and Africans occupied the bottom rung. Indians lived in villages on the outskirts of the town, though some worked as servants in the homes of the wealthy. Their pottery and dress influenced local fashions, but Indians had no part in Florida's governance.

Two miles to the north of the city-fortress lay the planned town of Garcia Real de Santa Teresa de Mose. Manuel de Montiano, governor of the province, ordered it built in 1738 to house and to repay the services of runaway slaves. A trickle of these men and women had found a safe haven in the colony from the end of the previous century, under King Charles III of Spain's edict (1693) that they should not be returned to their Carolina owners. Though never more than a few dozen men, the black militia of Mose fought loyally and effectively alongside the Spanish against Oglethorpe and his Georgia troops and on later occasions. The town and its polyglot people survived intact until 1763, when the British took East Florida from the Spanish.

Santa Fe, New Mexico

The Spanish that the Pueblo peoples drove from New Mexico in 1680 had abandoned their farmsteads and buried their plows and furniture (too heavy to carry with them in their flight), but they had not left the borderlands. Instead, they founded a ragged settlement at the edge of the Rio Grande they called El Paso del Norte, the North Pass. Forbidden by the viceroy of New Spain (Mexico) from moving any farther south, they passed twelve years in miserable adobe hovels, waiting for their revenge. To their aid came a proud, vain, and desperately brave new governor, Diego de Vargas, whose self-proclaimed mission was to reconquer the province. He planned a two-stage return—a reconnaissance in force to drive the Indians from Santa Fe and the other settlements, followed by the reentry of the Spanish settlers.

Three former thrusts, in 1681, 1688, and 1689, had failed miserably, but Vargas was clever. On August 12, 1692, leading a flying column of forty soldiers, fifty Mexican Indians, and two Franciscans (for the altars had to be ritually cleaned and made sacred again), Vargas reentered Santa Fe and announced to the surprised Pueblo garrison that he had come to pardon and forgive all those who had wronged the Spanish.

Surprise, Vargas's interruption of their water supply (the same tactic that had driven Governor Otermín from the city in 1680), the arrival of additional soldiers with cannons, and Vargas's continued promise of pardon swayed the defenders. They stopped shouting insults and agreed to make peace. Vargas embraced the Indian leaders and retired into the old Spanish fort (refashioned by its most recent inhabitants into a native pueblo) to change into European court dress. Reappearing in his robes and jewelry, he announced the resumption of Spanish rule and watched as the Franciscans absolved the Indians of their backsliding ways.

The Indians were not fooled by the truce, and neither was Vargas. They refused to vacate the homes of the former settlers, including those on the plaza facing the fort. Vargas knew that the bedraggled band of seventy families on its way to Santa Fe would not accept the situation and in any case had no intention of letting his former enemies occupy a position on his doorstep. Aided by southern Pueblos and the settlers, Vargas led the assault on the recalcitrant Indians on December 29, 1692. After two days of house-to-house fighting, the Spanish took by force what they could not gain through negotiation.

Over the next four years, Vargas broke the resistance of outlying pueblos, and gave Indian lands to the settlers, setting aside what he thought was owed him. The tradition of the *adelantados* lived on. Reducing stronghold after stronghold, he abandoned his pose of reconciliation and ignored the Franciscans' warning that a repressive policy would stir a new Indian revolt. Attracted by gifts of land expropriated from the Indians, the trickle of Spanish families into the province grew into a steady stream. In the winter of 1695–1696, drought and severe cold brought renewed hardship to the Indians, and in June 1696, deprived of their stores of corn by the Spanish, the Indians rose again. By November, Vargas had crushed the revolt.

Two years later, Vargas languished in jail. He had lived in a style he thought befitted a governor-general—too high a style, for his liveried coachmen, bejeweled armor, and imported shirts and suits with their gold buttons raised suspicions of corruption. Even his dishware was silver. When his successor, Pedro Cubero, a man of far lesser social rank than Vargas, arrived in 1697, he was appalled. From the account books, Cubero discovered that Vargas had extorted funds from the settlers and stolen money from the treasury.

For three years, Vargas paced a drafty and damp jail at one end of the multiblock government presidio while Cubero drafted and redrafted criminal charges at the other. In the end, Vargas had enough pull at the provincial capital of Mexico City and enough powerful friends in Spain to be exonerated for his extravagances and honored for his conquests.

In his defense, he claimed, as did many of his Spanish predecessors and not a few of those who came after him in the governor's office, that his enemies were little men who lacked his vision and energy and allowed the colony to fall into ruin. And when Cubero's replacement was on his way, Cubero proved Vargas right: he packed up all his belongings and disappeared before his successor could do to him what he had done to Vargas.

While the governors jousted with one another, the Navajos and Apaches again jeopardized the frontiers. A new governor of New Mexico, Francisco Cuerbo y Valdés, responded with the first offensive campaign against the raiders. Although there were few decently armed (and very few decently trained) militia available (he found but 194 men in his muster of 1703), Cuerbo y Valdés put together a small army of fifty regular troops, forty militia, and three hundred Pueblo allies and struck at the Gila Apaches to the south and the Navajos to the north.

The report his commander, Roque Madrid, left of the expedition against the Navajos reveals the difficulty of a campaign fought over vast stretches of mesas and mountains broken by fast-running streams. Fighting through Navajo ambushes by utilizing superior Spanish firepower, the Spanish and their allies destroyed Navajo grazing lands and campsites. Few of the governor's troops and few of the Indians were killed, for the Spanish had not waged a European campaign. Instead, Roque

Madrid had adopted the same hit-and-run tactics that the Navajos used against the Pueblos, destroying crops and bringing terror.

The Spanish settlers had learned another lesson. In the countryside, where once they had built isolated, fortresslike haciendas and forced the Indians to labor in their fields of Spanish barley and wheat, they now clustered together in small villages laid out in rectangular blocks of some thirty or forty houses. The village included a store, a church, corrals, irrigation ditches, and wells. The fields spread beyond the village, about as far as a person could walk in an hour.

In the village, rows of dried clay and straw (adobe) homes resembled miniature fortresses. The life of the home centered on the inside *placito*, or patio, to which the rooms opened. Settlers transported wood for rafters and roofs down from the mountains in wagon trains. The heavy ponderosa pine trunks became *vigas* (cross beams) to support roofs of rough-milled slats laid side to side. Over these the owner packed earth. Home repair consisted of adding mud and straw to the walls and renewing applications of soil to the roof. Cloth hangings caught the debris that fell between the cracks of the slatted ceiling. The dryness of the climate and the billowing winds out of the mountains filled the air with dust, and cleaning houses and street fronts was a never-ending battle. Temperatures in summer reached three digits, but the lack of humidity—yearly rainfall averaged no more than seven inches—made the heat bearable.

By 1750, a thousand people lived in Santa Fe, the largest of these pueblos. Spanish, Indian, and mixed-ancestry families were large. Mothers trained daughters to become wives, for Spanish mores dictated that women find husbands and bear children. Public life was closed to them, though much of the work of the colony was done by its women. Toiling in groups, women performed the myriad and endless tasks of laundering, repairing, and decorating clothing; growing, preparing, and serving food; and keeping track of household tools and possessions. In addition, women played important parts in church rituals. They might not be allowed to celebrate the mass, but without their church attendance the religious fabric of the society would have torn and unraveled.

With a semblance of peace on the frontier and steady if slow growth of their towns and villages, the Spanish no longer demanded Indians' absolute obedience. Instead, Christian rituals and Indian customs merged imperceptibly at their edges. In the churches on the town plaza, natives and newcomers mingled, their faith stirred by illuminated religious paintings and carvings. A person's *razón* (literally "reason" but more or less equivalent to race), the definition of all legal rights, became a porous category. One could buy whiteness and its privileges.

Another, less savory amalgamation was the combination of native and Spanish superstitions, particularly about witches. The Navajos and Pueblos feared witchcraft, often suspecting female neighbors and family members when misfortune or sudden illness arrived, and severely punished suspected witches. The Spanish, though some-what more lenient in their views, held regular inquisitions to sort out accusations.

ISLANDS OF SLAVES

The British sugar islands were the jewels in the crown of the old empire. By 1700, Barbados exported almost £425,000 per year in sugar products (cane, molasses, and rum), to which Jamaica added over £110,000 each year. In addition to the sugar crops, the colonies exported indigo, cotton, ginger, lime juice, cocoa, and hides. What was more, after the Treaty of Utrecht ended Queen Anne's War in 1713, the British gained the right to sell slaves to the Spanish settlements in the New World. The sugar is-lands served as way stations in the trade.

Jamaica

Although the number of English immigrants to Jamaica had fallen off from the high levels of the 1670s and 1680s, settlers from the home country continued to try their luck in Jamaica throughout the eighteenth century. Almost fifty thousand came in the years 1650 to 1780, two-thirds of whom were male. A few migrants had en-joyed high status in England. Many more were servants or transported convicts. A small number of Jews and Roman Catholics came as well. Still, the white population did not sustain itself—death and out-migration exceeded the number of emigrants, a pattern typical of European tropical colonies.

Although this was a truly Creole society, with many peoples from many lands and children of mixed ancestry living and working in close proximity, it retained a highly visible system of rank and privilege whose purpose was to benefit the colonizing power. The white elite ran the government. The colonial assembly was composed of planters and merchants, much like its counterpart in Barbados. Europeans filled the vestries, the administrative boards, the clergy, the executive, and the courts, and all the militia officers were white. Some freed slaves served in the militia, and others had positions of responsibility on the plantations and in the many "cattle pens" (ranches) on the islands, and people of mixed ancestry held minor offices, but the few privileges given these junior officials only underlined the fact that the source of all official authority was the master class.

Life was never easy in the tropics, even for the elite. Hurricanes, epidemics, and pirates plagued the islands. Rainstorms with gusts of wind of over eighty miles an hour cut a swath of wreckage through the wooden buildings of the port towns and the plantations, causing everyone to huddle in fear. Epidemics of malaria and yellow fever carried off all those not "seasoned" by acquired immunities, and some of those who were. Pirates infested the nearby islands. Some of the Welsh and Scottish pirate leaders had been privateers who turned to crime. Crews included a mix of races and national origins. Some of the crews were democratic, splitting earnings equally and electing captains. When the British navy caught a pirate, the usual punishment was death, but some pirates gained pardons from the crown.

Maroonage caused the planters the most sleepless nights. Jamaican maroons built their own villages and chose their own leaders. Sometimes these communities survived only a short time, but others lasted for many years. Most maroons were young male Africans, but by the 1720s many native born and not a few women lived as maroons. Maroons could not have survived without the covert aid of plantation slaves, often relatives or lovers. Sometimes help even came from free persons of color or white servants.

Efforts to root out the maroons were fitful and foolhardy, for, unlike Barbados, whose entire expanse was cultivated by the 1720s, the mountains of Jamaica sheltered the rebels. In 1774, Edward Long compared the maroons' hit-and-run tactics to those of the North American Indians. Thus the planters, townspeople, and retired soldiers (for a farm on Jamaica was one reward for long service in the English army) rarely traveled, much less lived, in the mountains.

The first maroon war ended in 1738, when authorities agreed to meet with the maroon leader Cudjoe and arranged a peace. Other maroon bands soon followed Cudjoe's example. The rebels gained their freedom and parcels of land, as well as the right to hunt feral hogs and jurisdiction over the crimes of their own numbers. Although isolated outbreaks of racial violence continued, the maroons did not organize resistance on a large scale for another fifty years.

Plantation and Pen

Maroonage was not typical of the sugar islands, however much it occupied the minds of the master class. Life for the planter and the slave revolved instead about the workday on the sugar plantations. Mesopotamia, a plantation of middling size in the Westmoreland Parish of western Jamaica, was typical. The plantation was laid out in 1700 and owned for a hundred years by the Barham family. On it, three hundred slaves worked in gangs to plant and harvest the cane and boil down the sugar. The records show twice as many deaths as births over the long course of the plantation's life. Women, who worked in the fields alongside the men, were more likely to be invalided at an early age, though the Barhams instructed their overseers to treat women of child-bearing age with particular care.

In addition, Jamaica offered certain slaves an alternative work site to the sugar plantation—the cattle pens. Livestock were not only a vital part of the inventory of plantations (worth more in pounds sterling than sugar), they were particularly suited to the terrain of Jamaica. The average pen had about a thousand acres, over which ranged a few hundred cattle, as well as horses, scores of goats (the source of much of the milk on the island), hundreds of chickens, some geese and ducks, and the ubiquitous pigs. Although only slightly more than one in ten slaves worked in the pens, these slaves bore more responsibility and had more freedom and time to themselves than any on the island's sugar plantations.

Labor in the pens was based on a specialization and the task system. Pen keepers were in charge of the operation, and with the stock handlers, they spent much of their time away from the pens, usually fetching and carrying between the pen and the main plantation and rounding up strays. Everyone was responsible for penning the animals each night. Skilled shepherds tended the goats. Other skilled slaves repaired fences and buildings. A small cadre of trustworthy slaves served as watchmen. Women worked as hard as the men with the stock, though half served in domestic roles. Everyone doubled as field hands when the season required additional laborers. Overseers and slave drivers might hunt together, eat together, and drink together. But the tensions of the system were never far away. A dance, a feast, or a celebration could be a festive time, or turn ugly.

The Vineyard pens were satellites of the Friendship plantation. In the pens' some 1,120 acres, Thomas Thistlewood oversaw forty-two slaves. Many of the slaves were new to the island, and most of these newcomers were Africans.

Thistlewood brought to the pens one of the worst characteristics of slavery—the systematic sexual abuse of slave women. He used his power to punish and reward to gain the sexual favors of slave women. His diary recorded one conquest after another. He also noted every coin he gave to his victims as payment for his assaults on them. It is possible that some of these liaisons were voluntary, or based upon a bargained-for exchange, but most were nothing more or less than rape. Over 10 percent of the total births on the plantation were of mixed ancestry.

———

A traveler who toured the provinces from the Canadian woods to the Jamaica cattle pens would see that a dazzling variety of distinct provincial societies had evolved in the New World. In each, men and women placed different emphases on cooperation, competition, spiritual life, and material gain. Some societies were harmonious, and others roiled with enmity.

In these "peripheries of empire," lucky and determined colonists built new and better lives for themselves and their families, but growth and development had their price. Not only did progress rest on the backs of servants and slaves, reports of economic opportunity in America lured new waves of immigrants to join the swelling numbers of native-born colonists, and resulting population pressures drove up commodity prices and exhausted natural resources. Native populations were pushed aside by the flood of newcomers. Social growth stimulated both economic progress and unrest.

11

Common Pastimes and Elite Pursuits

New World culture—the customs, habits, attitudes, expressions, and yearnings of Americans—brought people together in common pastimes at the same time as it divided different groups and classes according to their avocations and aspirations. A growing divergence between popular and elite preferences—the difference between Knight's comments and Fithian's observations at right—gave rise to highbrow and lowbrow cultures.

But one should not erect too high a wall between the folk and the elite cultures. In fact, they lay along a spectrum of activities from which individuals and groups might make selections. Any division of colonists into fixed and distinct categories of leisure and working classes fails to capture the complexity of eighteenth-century Americans' cultural attitudes. Cultural events cut across the boundaries of class, bringing together and then separating groups in shifting patterns.

COMMON PASTIMES

The market, tavern, churchyard, and city street were public spaces that all classes might frequent. Exchanges and performances in these public places did not erase all traces of rank and status, but sometimes leveled social differences. Take, for example, the day when the county court met. Men and women of lower social ranks could sue and be sued, testify, and command their betters to attend court to answer to charges or civil actions. The yeoman farmer sat next to the planter or the merchant on the jury bench.

But court day had its well-established, highly visible hierarchies. The judges or justices sat on raised benches or in high-backed chairs at the front of the chamber, sometimes wearing wigs, robes, or other marks of office. Women might visit the courthouse to watch a trial, give evidence under oath, and plead for themselves at the bar, but they never sat on the bench or in the jury box, and they could not be licensed lawyers. In court, as elsewhere, American culture at midcentury pulsed with a complex tension of elite and common.

We may observe here the great necessity and bennifitt both of Education and Conversation; for these people have as Large a portion of mother witt, and sometimes a Larger, than those who have bin brought up in Citties; but for want of emprovements, Render themselves almost Ridiculous.
—Sarah Kemble Knight, after a visit to a dirty tradesmen's shop, Connecticut, 1704

When the candles were lighted we all repaired, for the last time, into the dancing room; first each couple danced a Minuet; then all joined as before in the country Dances, these continued til half after seven . . . here I could join with them, and indeed it was carried on with sprightliness, and Decency.
—Philip Vickers Fithian, tutor in the household of planter Landon Carter, 1773

Natural Rhythms

The seasons of the year provided a backdrop for shared cultural activities. The eighteenth-century calendar was full of holidays. Puritans still refused to celebrate traditional "anniversaries" like May Day and April Fool's Day, and rejected Christmas, but fast days and days of thanksgiving brought them together for sermons, speeches, and communal activities. On election day, a minister chosen by the General Court gave the most important sermon of the year. Quakers went farther than the Puritans, abolishing the traditional calendar entirely. Instead of a Sabbath, they reckoned a "seventh day," for all days "alike are holy in the sight of God."

In contrast, backcountry Scots-Irish and Scottish border immigrants celebrated Christmas with a roaring bonfire and revelry. Christmas and Easter Monday brought together widely dispersed households to feast and drink. In the Tidewater, planters strictly observed the Anglican religious calendar, including Michaelmas, Twelfth Night, Shrovetide, Lent, Easter, Ascension, and Lady Day. At Christmas, planters held extravagant dances and parties, and exchanged gifts.

Seasonal events also brought Indians together. In "Indian Summer" (in fact, early fall), all able-bodied males joined in the communal hunt. When winter came, male children faced their first initiation, a series of harsh and demanding tests, including isolation in the woods and deprivation of sleep. Women joined in seasonal rites as well. Among the Senecas, women led the winter ceremony that thanked the maple trees for their syrup and ensured that life would be renewed in the spring. In that season, the Creek women's corn dance celebrated the importance of the coming planting. The Pueblo peoples' calendar had as many days of religious festivals on it as the Anglicans', and the Indian ceremonial dances were open to everyone in the town.

The rising and setting sun also shaped the colonists' activities. The difference between day and night was sharp. In the daytime, farm animals and insects lowed and chirruped. Neighbors and workers chatted. The noise level in the streets of the towns and cities deafened passersby. Peddlers hawked their wares at the top of their lungs, and cart drivers barked obscenities at each other and luckless pedestrians.

At night, the lanes and streets of the towns stilled, and in the country the screeches and howls of predators broke the silence. Only the wealthy could afford to pay for candles, so after dark most colonists' homes were lit only by the embers in the fireplaces. Good people did not go about their business at night. Massachusetts even made "nightwalking" a crime.

Play

There were no organized athletic leagues or teams in the colonies, but colonists and Indians avidly sought diversions from everyday toil. For example, Indians divided up into teams of dozens of men to play a forerunner of lacrosse. Colonists enjoyed their own game of football, a mixture of modern soccer and rugby.

On the sidelines, spectators and players bet on the outcomes. Gambling was an all-American pastime. The Indians wagered on dice and cards, vices the colonists had brought from Europe. The colonists bet on horse races, pig races, dog fights, cockfights, and wrestling contests. True sportsmen demonstrated their masculinity by stoically accepting the outcome of their gambling, but every gambler believed that winning was not just "luck." Success at cards, dice, or wagers on races and contests was a sign that the winner had a special kind of power to predict the future.

Playing music, singing, and dancing were common amusements. The upper crust listened to the music of Handel and other European baroque composers. Well-to-do Americans imported flutes, cellos, organs, and other instruments, along with sheet music published abroad, and held recitals at home and concerts in public. The elite also danced at evening gatherings, often imitating the latest steps and music from Europe.

Such balls had their own miniature hierarchy. At the top were state balls, held in the governor's mansion or the statehouse. Less gaudy but still elegant were private balls, sometimes sponsored by private societies, but more often the production of a family celebrating an important life-cycle event. Men organized these events and led the dances. Women decorated the dance with their presence and contested in dress, demeanor, and grace. As one Philadelphia gentleman named Joseph Shippen wrote of the ladies at the ball: "'Tis far beyond the painter's skill / To set their charms to view; / As far beyond the poet's quill / To give the praise that's due." But Shippen's poetry was hardly off the cuff. His verse, like the grace and lightness of the dancers' steps, fit the expectations of polite society. One might say that gentlemen and women saw themselves as performers constantly on stage.

A formal ball would have been out of place on the frontier, but young folks fiddled and strummed tunes recalling hundred-year-old English and Scottish ballads. The floor of the tavern served as the ballroom, and the dancers watched one another and compared notes just as the elegantly garbed dancers did on the Atlantic seaboard. Native Americans sang and danced to rhythms hundreds of years old. For them, dance was not only entertainment, it brought entire communities together.

The love of music made its way from the tavern and the ballroom to the church. Ministers were among the first to import musical instruments. Many Germans had brought with them a love for music and a rich vocal tradition. Martin Luther had written hymns, and the German Lutherans used organs in their churches. The Moravians added flutes and oboes, sang in many languages, and kept in touch with the latest trends in choral music. John Adams was so impressed with the sweetness of the Gregorian chants of Roman Catholic priests in Philadelphia's Saint Joseph Church that he "wondered [how] the Reformation ever succeeded."

Puritan congregants objected to bringing instruments into the holy service, but the Psalms of David were reprinted in New England hymnals like the Bay Psalm Book (1640), and congregants raised their voices in discordant song. By the end of the seventeenth century, singing in New England churches was so bad that ministers complained "our tunes are left to the mercy of every unskillful throat to chop and alter, to twist and change." A ninth edition of the *Bay Psalm Book* (1698) added musical notation, but some congregations still resisted the change (in particular, the requirement that they sing in harmony), and churchgoers walked out the door when they heard the first notes.

In meetings of evangelicals and enthusiasts, music rang out loud and clear. Baptist preachers turned to Isaac Watts's hymnbook for words of inspiration, but they rejected musical notation in favor of "limning out," in which the leader sang out the melody and was echoed by the congregation. In contrast, Methodists put a high premium on harmony.

Drink

The Baptists inveighed against alcoholic drink, but the singers in the tavern and the dancers in the ballroom were often inebriated. Seventeenth-century medical authorities believed that wines, beer, and brandy aided digestion and could cure colds and relieve depression. Plantation masters like William Byrd offered their slaves liquor as an inducement to finish an onerous task or work on the Sabbath. At militia musters over which he and other planter-officers presided, the men consumed spiked "punch," beer, and cider. On election day, candidates treated voters to gallons of spirits, and every official dinner began with numerous toasts.

As prices of rum and other distilled beverages fell and the number of distilleries and breweries mounted in the eighteenth century, public drunkenness became a problem. Sermons and official decrees condemned open displays of alcoholism. Baptists railed against excesses of drinking. In Boston, Congregationalist minister Charles Chauncy warned the poor against squandering their paltry wages on strong liquors. Critics called the proliferation of drinking establishments "a pest to society."

But owners of distilleries and breweries lobbied against any restrictions on the sale or consumption of their products. Western farmers who turned excess produce into spirits agreed. In literature and song, the tipsy drinker remained a comic figure rather than a dangerous deviant, and drinking clubs like the Tuesday Club of Baltimore flourished. In Newport, Rhode Island, there were twenty taverns by 1725, one for every twenty inhabitants of the city. The number of licensed taverns in Boston and Philadelphia doubled from 1700 to the middle of the century.

Adult per capita consumption of alcohol in the colonies by 1770 exceeded seven gallons per year. Assuming that women drank far less than men (an assumption based on overwhelmingly male tavern attendance and the fact that much drinking took place in taverns) leaves us with nearly fourteen gallons a year for the average adult male. The colonists drank everything from punch (usually rum based) and cordials (fortified wines) to beer, fermented cider, and "strong water" (whiskey). Every meal at the best tables in the land included alcoholic beverages, and serious drinking always accompanied a night at the tavern.

All taverns (also called public houses or "ordinaries") had to be licensed. Indians, servants without their masters, and children without their parents were not supposed to frequent taverns, but the tavern keepers looked the other way so often that violations of the rules comprised one of the largest categories of misdemeanors in the county court record books. In addition, householders opened unlicensed "tippling houses." In New England, town magistrates tried to control public drunkenness by canceling the permits of offending taverns, fining drunks for disturbing the peace, and requiring neighbors to put up bonds for alcoholics' future good behavior.

In 1681, the General Court of Massachusetts tried a different tack. It ordered the reduction of licensed taverns in Boston from forty-five to twenty-four, cut the number in the seaport towns like Salem, and allowed no more than one per town elsewhere. The order had the opposite effect, as drinking continued in unlicensed tippling houses. Faced with a veritable crime wave, the General Court reversed course and allowed exceptions to its own statute. As the number of taverns returned to its former figure, the assembly tried yet another device to prevent drunkenness. In 1712, it forbade the sale of cheap, potent rum in taverns.

By the pricing of their wares and by catering to a particular clientele, taverns, like London coffeehouses, developed local followings. In the years between 1710 and 1720, a number of Boston tavern owners spruced up their establishments to lure a better class of drinker. At its prime location on the Long Wharf, the Crown offered patrons a coffee room and a bar room, and set diners' tables with linen tablecloths and forks. The Indian King in Philadelphia offered its patrons "the regular ordinary [daily special] every day of . . . the very best provisions and well dressed, at 12d. A head." For those who came mounted or in carriages, "the very best use [is] taken of horses."

Other taverns had a less reputable clientele. At the Sign of the White Horse, in Newport, Rhode Island, one patron recorded that he "was almost eat up alive with bugs." Rebecca Fowle's tavern in Boston was a notorious haunt for the disorderly poor, but the selectmen of the town reluctantly allowed her to keep her license. Without it, she would need poor relief herself.

Inside the tavern, ranks were leveled and hierarchies dissolved in alcohol. In Nathaniel Ingersoll's Salem tavern, next to the meetinghouse, Indians and Europeans, servants and masters, and women drank and played games of chance. Other taverns were homes to social clubs and benevolent societies. People not only drank, they ate, read newspapers, played board games, and talked. Taverns doubled as hotels, putting up travelers, sometimes two and three to a bed. Male tavern owners regularly served as town selectmen, for politics was a preoccupation of tavern sociability. Often, voters gathered at the tavern before going to cast their ballots, or retired there after the election results were announced. Tavern keeping was also one of the few professions in which women played an important role, many succeeding their deceased or absent husbands as owners.

Tavern patrons had to be careful what they said to one another, especially in the South. Insults sometimes led to brawls and duels. On Thursday, September 13, 1711, after the Middlesex County, Virginia, militia had mustered and trained, and the militiamen engaged in impromptu horse races, a down-on-his-luck farmer and minor officeholder, Benjamin Davis, and his neighbor, George Wortham, a successful planter and captain of the militia company, lifted a jug together at the nearby tavern. The conversation drifted to the subject of one of the leading men of the county, a man whose reputation Davis defended and Wortham demeaned. Within a few minutes, Davis had called Wortham, his social better, a "rogue and knave," and members of the company had to intervene. A sword fight followed, less a duel than a drunken scuffle, but Davis died from his wounds.

Talk

The allure of the tavern was only partly the inebriants it served. The real point of going was to talk. Of all the diversions in early America, talking was the most important. Among common folk, a good storyteller was always in demand. People chatted before and after church, and sometimes during services when the sermon dragged. Polite discourse had to be elevated, but not abstruse or arrogant; flirtatious, but not offensive; intimate, but not familiar. Benjamin Franklin humorously proposed accurate rules for "making oneself a disagreeable companion" in polite conversation: "When other matter fails, talk much of yourself, your education, your knowledge, your circumstances, your successes in business, [and] your victories in disputes."

The same topics that dominated conversation at the planter's table and in the merchant's sitting room concerned the common people—health and disease, war and peace, prices, and the foibles of neighbors and relatives—but the damage to one's reputation from slipping into coarse or abusive speech was far greater in elite society than among commoners. The genteel conversationalist constantly had to weigh how others might hear him or her.

A person with an astute ear could tell the station of others from conversation, for elegant conversation was the mark of rank. At planter Robert Carter's table after dinner, everyone was expected to engage in polite conversation. As Christmas 1773 approached, the young man Carter hired to tutor his children, Philip Fithian, was not impressed by the topics. "Nothing is now to be heard of in conversation, but the balls, the fox-hunts, the fine entertainments, and the good fellowship" of the coming holidays, but he had learned how conversation marked the station and breeding of men and women.

As Dr. Alexander Hamilton of Annapolis, Maryland, traveled about the colonies for his health in 1743, he took careful and often caustic note of the speech of his traveling companions. At the outset of his journey, one Hart took Hamilton to Hart's abode, and there they "drank some punch and conversed like a couple of virtuosos." On the road a Mr. Dean, a minister, only offered "rambling conversation." Hamilton's landlord's contribution was "so very lumpish and heavy that it disposed me mightily to sleep." Fortunately for the doctor, not all the innkeepers droned on. In Newtown, Maryland, "a deal of comical discourse passed in which the landlord, a man of particular talent at telling comic stories, bore the chief part." Hamilton's exchange with a New Light zealot named, inappropriately, Thomas Quiet, ended in an argument. "He told me flatly that I was damned without redemption."

From their manner of speech Hamilton could tell (or thought he could) his traveling companions' learning, background, and refinement, though some fooled him. William Morrison, whose speech proclaimed him a "plain, homely fellow" had "good linen in his bags, [with] a pair of silver buckles, silver clasps, and gold sleeve buttons." Hamilton's assumption that speech made the man was shared by many who could tell "a person of more than ordinary rank" by their "polite conversation."

Extemporaneous conversation was not the only form of talk Americans enjoyed. Colonists and Indians esteemed oratory and gathered to hear speeches, addresses, and sermons. Indians honored those who could discourse with power and dramatic effect, and the rhetorical force of Indian leaders' speeches at councils and diplomatic gatherings amazed even English and French diplomats accustomed to flowery orations.

Among the colonists, a galvanizing preacher could bring scores of listeners to the church, or thousands if he preached in the open. The "plain style" of seventeenth-century New England sermons, featuring learned two- or three-hour explications and applications of the Bible, moved over to make space for colorful and literary sermons. Some ministers adopted dramatic inflections of voice and histrionic gestures to keep their congregations' attention. Whether a dry-as-dust exegesis of a biblical text or a withering depiction of depravity and grace, ministers' speech exuded authority, particularly in rural areas, where it had little competition.

Common people and elites shared another form of talk—gossip. Gossip was a social leveler, allowing people to talk about and listen to curiosities, moral lessons, and bits of news. Gossip embroidered by good storytellers became an informal popular entertainment, anticipating the modern radio and television talk shows.

Gossipmongering could descend into slander. Ministers, citing the Bible as authority, condemned gossip as a nuisance. Planters like William Byrd, touchy about any slight to their reputation, regarded unflattering gossip as a serious breach of social etiquette, and guarded their tongues, lest they inadvertently give offense. Colonial court dockets in the eighteenth century still overflowed with cases of defamation.

Even worse than gossip but just as common, rumors could turn harmless conversation into occasions for panic. Unlike gossip, rumor has a narrative structure. Often, that structure rests on stereotypes and fear of others. Colonial courts tried to control rumors by fining or whipping people who spread false stories, but sometimes the authorities licensed rumormongering by giving credence to reports of impending foreign invasions, slave uprisings, and outbreaks of witchcraft. In Salem, during the witchcraft crisis of 1692, rumor influenced more people than eyewitness evidence. The testimony at the pretrial hearings became highly popular dramatic readings of rumor.

Acting and Reading

The deadly theatricals that the accusers enacted at Salem were ironic, given that Puritan authorities would not allow a regular theater company to put on plays in the colony. Indeed, all colonies except Virginia and Maryland prohibited theater companies from performing, fearing that the troupes of actors would corrupt the morals of the audience. But theater came to Annapolis, Charleston, New York City, Philadelphia, and Williamsburg. The plays included Shakespearean classics and more recently written English dramas and comedies. Americans did not always catch all the sly political digs in these English plays, but the ribaldry and the wordplay tickled American audiences.

Often, plays were merely read aloud. After dinner was over and the family and guests had reassembled in the drawing rooms of Tidewater plantations like William Byrd's Westover, everyone took turns reciting dialogue. At Westover, Byrd closed the evening by critiquing the relative skills of the performers. College students put on readings during vacation time to raise pocket money. Unemployed actors traveled about declaiming portions of plays to earn a living.

The college students' skill at reading aloud was not unique to them. Just about all New Englanders, male and female, could read. Some colonists mastered many languages and classical texts. The entrance examination for Harvard College required a reading knowledge of Greek and Latin. Though many people could not even sign their names to their wills, deeds, or legal depositions, making instead a "mark," their inability to write did not mean they were illiterate. Recent studies suggest that a majority of colonists could read but fewer could write.

Throughout the eighteenth century, literacy in the colonies gained ground. Perhaps even more important, that improvement included writing as well as reading. The introduction of "spellers," books that offered instructions on how to sound out words, in the early eighteenth century sparked a modest revolution in writing. Joining books of "forms" for secretaries, like The Young Secretary's Guide in 1713, and later, Franklin's contribution to this rapidly expanding market, The American Instructor (1748), a reprint of an earlier English speller, the speller stressed skills in forming syllables. Unlike the reading primer, whose selections were religious, the spellers combined religious and secular texts. But as in so many other areas of print culture, progress in reading and writing did not extend to slaves, Native Americans, people in isolated rural areas, and the very poor.

Literacy rates declined as one moved south and west in the English colonies, with the exception of German immigrants, French Huguenots, and Jews. They had to be multilingual. Few Indians and African Americans could read or write. But even those who could not read could be good listeners, for reading was not then a private act as it is today. In taverns, on courthouse greens, and on church steps, the literate read official notices, newspapers, and almanacs aloud for those who could not read themselves.

Colonial newspapers first appeared in Boston, with the *Boston News-Letter* in 1704, followed by the *Boston Gazette* in 1719. Initially, they reprinted British essays, featured British and foreign news items, and offered local advertisements. Newspapers were elite reading fare; they were too expensive for the average person and had little in them that would interest such a reader. Over time, growing competition for readership induced editors to add items of more general interest to their pages. Favorites included political satires and accounts of crimes. Newspapers also printed advertisements, literary essays, and notices of runaway slaves and servants. By the end of the colonial period, the number of newspapers throughout the entire colonies had grown to twenty-one, and they would play a more polemical role in colonial politics.

From their inception, American newspapers were powerful vehicles for political propaganda. Printers had to be cautious—any criticism of the government was a crime. Truth was no defense (indeed, according to English law, criticism based on truth was even more dangerous than falsehood). Nevertheless, party leaders in the cities enlisted printers to put out newspapers so that they could spread the partisans' political views.

In 1735, one printer, John Peter Zenger, had to fight to stay out of prison after criticizing New York governor William Cosby. Fortunately for Zenger, his lawyer convinced the jury that truth should be a defense against the charge, and the jury believed what Zenger said about Cosby's overweening avarice. In 1754, William Livingston and his friends William Smith Jr. and John Morin Scott launched their weekly *Independent Reflector* to blast the New York Anglican establishment for supporting a sectarian college in New York City. During a later crisis in Anglo-American relations, "patriots" sponsored Charles Crouch's Charleston *South-Carolina Gazette* to lambaste the British government.

Equally popular were almanacs. By the 1750s, there were dozens of colonial almanacs, each including calendars, poetry, stories, and scientific information of varying degrees of reliability, although most almanacs made no distinction between science and astrology. They always included astral charts. Franklin's entry in the field, *Poor Richard's Almanack*, was America's first best seller. Of it, in 1756, he remarked, "I have constantly interspersed in every little vacancy, moral hints, wise sayings, and maxims of thrift, tending to impress the benefits arising from honesty, sobriety, industry, and frugality." And he promised not to raise his prices.

The cities all had bookshops, and they advertised their stock of Bibles, how-to books, histories, romances, and the latest imports from England. Boston had dozens of bookshops, and most stores in the Massachusetts hinterlands carried a few books on their inventory. Sometimes people bought books because they wanted to demonstrate that they were members of a literary elite. Leading southern planters lined the walls of their libraries with leather-bound first editions of English novels and sets of law books.

Eighteenth-century reading habits demonstrated that buyers had a wide variety of interests. Southern planters favored confessional books and travel journals, the former little more than soap opera, and the latter filled with misinformation and fancy. New Englanders not only read the Bible and printed sermons, they enjoyed tomes on history, prophecy, heroic tales, and nature. Steady sellers at the end of the seventeenth century included Michael Wigglesworth's long and gloomy poem, *The Day of Doom*; English writer John Bunyan's allegorical *Pilgrim's Progress*; confessional stories of fallen and redeemed men and women; and tales of the occult. By 1750, New England tastes had become a little more secular and racy as tastes evolved to embrace English novels. New England bookstores could not restock works of romance and betrayal fast enough to supply the demand.

Learning

"Book learning" was only a small part of education for the colonial child, for life experiences counted more than reading, writing, and basic mathematics. The poor were educated, if at all, at home, or in "English schools" (sometimes called petty or common schools). There students struggled with reading, writing, and arithmetic. Writing meant handwriting, not creative literature. In "grammar schools," instructors added Latin and Greek to the curriculum.

In English schools and grammar schools, textbooks changed little over time. Henry Dixon's *The Youth's Instructor in the English Tongue* (1731) served long after it was published. James Hodder's *Arithmetick* (1661) was still in use a hundred years after it first appeared. The Latin and Greek primers were even more antique than the English school texts. The standard Greek textbook was William Camden's, published in 1595.

Schools had no grades, and the young and old sat together, often in a single room for the entire day. Schoolmasters ran the gamut from the Quaker Anthony Benezet of Germantown, whose advanced ideas and liberal sympathies led him to oppose slavery, to schoolmasters who resembled the fictional Ichabod Crane of Washington Irving's early-nineteenth-century mock horror story, "The Legend of Sleepy Hollow." Crane loved to eat, wooed and lost a wealthy young woman, and spent most of the day staring out the window of his schoolhouse. A handful of academies catered to the needs of the rich. Academies added an eclectic mix of courses to the curriculum, sometimes including French, dancing, and instrumental music.

Educational standards and institutions varied by region. In 1647, the Massachusetts General Court required towns to have a school and hire a teacher. Masters and parents were enjoined to ensure that their apprentices and children could read. Although many towns flouted the law, some hired schoolmasters and rented schoolhouses to deny "the old deluder, Satan," the chance to influence young minds. On southern plantations, planters employed tutors for their children. Older children might be sent to England for "finishing" and later went to colleges like the College of William and Mary in Williamsburg.

College was not the expected conclusion to a young person's education, but by midcentury, neither was a college education a rarity. The Puritans insisted that their ministers have college training. The General Court founded Harvard College in 1636 to provide ministers for the towns and also to educate future town leaders. A few colonial colleges, including Harvard in Cambridge, Massachusetts; Yale in New Haven, Connecticut; the College of New Jersey in Princeton; King's College (after the Revolution renamed Columbia for obvious reasons) in New York City; the College of Philadelphia (later the University of Pennsylvania); and the College of William and Mary provided advanced instruction to colonists, but they scarcely rivaled leading European universities. The president and the professors of the colleges oversaw classes and administration, while the colony, local communities, and private subscribers paid the bill. American colleges had boards of trustees or overseers to please from their inception.

There were women at college, washing, cooking, sewing, visiting, and selling, but women were not allowed into the ranks of ministers, magistrates, and future professors that the college trained, so their absence from classes did not seem strange to the men who ran, taught in, and paid for colleges. There is no evidence that women sought entrance either, but their presence as maids and servants and their absence as students and teachers remind us of the casual discrimination women everywhere experienced in eighteenth-century America.

The students generally came from the best families. Indeed, class "rank" at Harvard College was not based on grades but upon the wealth and standing of one's parents. Everyone took the same courses, and bored or rambunctious students abused their tutors and led food riots. Princeton suspended students who used telescopes to peer into the bedrooms of private houses.

Private Societies

The colonial college was a private society, mirroring in many ways the multitude of similarly male-dominated institutions in the eighteenth century. Within colleges, young men formed voluntary associations to improve themselves through discussion and mutual aid. To counter the incidence of student misconduct, Harvard students formed four such clubs in the years from 1719 to 1728. The Tell-Tale Club and the Philomusarian Clubs pressed for the reformation of good manners and breeding, while the Society of Young Students and the Young Men's Meeting sought to revive piety at the college.

Most men's clubs had less solemn purposes than Harvard's fraternal organizations. The Tuesday Club of Annapolis had literary aspirations, while the Bow Bell Club of Bridgetown, Barbados, provided occasions for men to eat, drink, and dance. The Saint John's Fox Hunt Club in South Carolina and the Fishing Company of the Colony in Pennsylvania offered recreational retreats. More serious than the eating and fishing clubs, Freemason lodges had a long and distinguished history in Europe. In America, Franklin and other luminaries belonged.

Excluded from the men's clubs, women fashioned their own polite private societies. These "salons" met in gardens, tearooms, and mansion drawing rooms. Without the formal charters of the men's clubs and fraternities, the salons brought together men and women for conversation and refreshments. Elizabeth Graeme's salon in Philadelphia in the 1760s was a model of its kind. With her wit, poetry, and self-tutored erudition in foreign languages and literature, she held together a coterie of English and American admirers.

FAITH

As one historian has aptly written, the American colonies were "awash in a sea of faith." Religious worship brought Americans together, though some religious practices reinforced social hierarchies. The period after 1680 was one of especially active organizing. Much of this was outside of "established" churches and in some cases challenged them and their government support.

Various branches and sects of Protestantism openly and without persecution vied for adherents, a unique phenomenon in a Western world where law established churches and penalized nonattendance. Many had, by midcentury, accustomed themselves, if not to religious liberty, at least to voluntarism and toleration. To be sure, in only three colonies was this toleration a matter of official policy. In Rhode Island, Pennsylvania, and Maryland no laws discriminated against members of any Protestant sect, and Roman Catholic and Jewish worshippers practiced their religions freely. Elsewhere in the colonies, state churches and tithing laws cracked beneath the assault of denominationalism.

Denominationalism

When a church was "established" in a country as in England—that is, when there was an official, state-sponsored religion—the law demanded conformity of worship. Lawmakers feared that toleration of religious differences would undermine allegiance to the crown. The dispersed and disorderly nature of settlement in the colonies undercut but did not undo the formal relationship between civil and religious authority. Civil authorities in the colonies, hard put to protect the settlers against Indian and European raiders, weakened by disputes over colonial autonomy with English authorities, and underfunded and understaffed from top to bottom, simply could not enforce strict conformity to any established church. The unintended but pervasive result was denominationalism—the spread of a multitude of competing churches. In turn, competition for adherents brought out the worshippers.

In New England, the settlers had adopted a congregational form of worship that placed church governance in the hands of the full members of the church. But to prevent individual ministers and their congregations from diverging too far from accepted doctrine, leading ministers like Increase Mather and Cotton Mather convened synods to prescribe doctrine to the congregations. In Connecticut, a Presbyterian system became the norm.

But no one could tell ministers like Solomon Stoddard of Northampton or John Wise of Ipswich what or how to preach. Both men, for somewhat different reasons, opened the doors of their churches widely. Stoddard refused to accept the requirement of a confession of grace for full membership, and Wise, a giant of a man whose father had come to the colony as an indentured servant, saw the church as a miniature democracy. In 1692, he protested the witchcraft trials and kept their infection from Ipswich, and for the next thirty-two years he argued that all people had fundamental rights of conscience as well as civil liberty.

After 1701, the Anglican Society for the Propagation of the Gospel in Foreign Parts, a missionary effort directed by the bishop of London to Christianize the Indians, entered the New England colonies. Then it turned to efforts to converting Puritans back to Episcopacy. If it did not win all New Englanders' allegiance, the society did at least foster a resurgence of Anglican worship in the northern colonies. On New Haven Green, for example, an Anglican church stood alongside the Presbyterian meetinghouse. In Boston, church spires dotted the skyline—as if every neighborhood had to have its own house of worship. In New York, adherents of the orthodox English faith built beautiful houses of worship and gained political preferences from colonial governors and royal officials who were also Anglicans.

The somewhat sorry state of the ministry in the southern churches, where Anglican worship was established—some ministers were able and well born, others were not so respectable or competent—inadvertently encouraged an unofficial but pervasive religious pluralism. In Virginia and South Carolina, Anglican ministers were ill paid. Vestrymen, chosen for their status in the community rather than their piety, quarreled with their ministers over salaries. Membership and attendance lagged.

The fastest-growing denomination was the Baptists. Many of its gains came in the Chesapeake hinterlands, where lay preachers exhorted flocks of poorer farmers, tenants, and even slaves. In rude wooden churches, in fields, and by ponds, worshippers gathered to sing and rejoice as ministers baptized dozens of men and women. Entire congregations would weep and "lift up their hands and faces toward heaven." The Anglican vestries were upset and harassed the lay preachers, but could not break up the new congregations.

In New England, Baptist leaders like Isaac Backus fought against the taxes the colonies levied on all churchgoers to support the Congregationalist and Presbyterian establishments. Awakened from his spiritual lethargy in 1742, he became an itinerant preacher in the middle 1740s, a "Separatist" minister in 1748, and a Baptist in the early 1750s. In 1753, as his fight against taxation of the Baptists to support the state church got under way in earnest, he warned, "My dear fellow man, be entreated no longer to take things by tradition but first examine your own standing." The established clergy dismissed Backus as an illiterate and "deluded" layman, but could not silence him. As he wrote in 1753, "the Lord was pleased to call me forth into this great work of preaching the Gospel," and neither the obstacle of formal ordination (which Backus lacked) nor the catcalls of those who were ordained but did not have a spiritual call to preach would silence him. He saw "with fresh clearness and weight to my soul." That was enough.

Denominationalism made churchgoing one of the foremost social as well as spiritual activities of Americans in the eighteenth century. Over half of the adults in the colonies belonged to a church and attended worship services more or less regularly. From the pulpit, some ministers read government announcements, and the congregation discussed current affairs before and after the service. Among congregations that observed the sacraments, a minority of the churchgoers took communion, primarily because they took the sacrament seriously and thought themselves unworthy of it (although full membership also brought more obligations). Perhaps as many as four out of five attendees did not seek full membership.

But churches were jam-packed on the Sabbath. In Boston, eighteen churches served the city's Congregationalists, Presbyterians, Anglicans, Baptists, and other creeds. The largest congregation numbered fifteen hundred souls, and ministers were upset when the church was not full. The middle colonies had more congregations per capita than New England. Philadelphians filled twenty churches. New York City had eighteen churches and more congregants than Boston. German Lutheran pastors and German Reformed ministers were too few in number to fully serve ethnic congregations in the middle colonies. Laymen had to lead services in some of the churches.

Among the most enthusiastic attendees of the eighteenth-century churches were women. Mothers took primary responsibility for the moral education of their children and found in religion spiritual refreshment and solace. At lessons, women proved that they could not only understand church doctrine and biblical lessons but that they could expound as well. Had Anne Hutchinson lived a hundred years later than she did, her assertiveness and piety would not have been held against her so strongly. Among the Baptists, women preached, and among the Quakers, women gave witness in the meeting. In German and Swedish Lutheran congregations, women outnumbered men, though women did not attain leadership roles.

Children and old folks also came to church. The young ones did not sit with their parents. In New England churches, they sat in the aisles, on stairs, or in balconies, where older monitors cuffed the young ones if they made silly faces and rude noises. Ministers formed societies for young congregants. Lutherans and German Reformed sects limited services to adults and older teens. The elderly were honored with pews near the front of the church. Ministers and vestrymen visited the aged ill who could not attend services.

The English missionary effort to convert Indians had little success. Indians in "praying towns" in New England were a notable exception. On the Pennsylvania frontier, Moravian missionaries converted some Indians and gained the trust of others. Presbyterians arrived as well, but did not make much headway. Anglican missionaries in the Carolinas had almost no success. The French and Spanish Jesuits' and Friars' labors bore far more fruit, and large communities of Roman Catholic Indians lived in Acadia, Canada, Louisiana, Florida, Texas, and the French and Spanish Caribbean possessions.

Few slaves were practicing Christians. Often, religious instruction and counseling of slaves encountered strong resistance from the slaves themselves, but some slaves sought out ministers and asked for instruction in the Christian faith. At least legal records and planter diaries mention "Christian Negro slaves." Anglican ministers in the Chesapeake baptized thousands of slaves, far more than Anglican ministers in the Carolinas. When the masters joined in the effort to convert slaves, they risked their neighbors' censure that too much Christianity was not a good thing for slaves—it might give them notions of equality and promote restiveness with their servile condition. A few slaves began to practice as ministers of the Christian faith themselves, holding impromptu worship services in the quarters. Among communities of freedmen and women, African American preachers acted as secular as well as clerical leaders.

Enthusiasm

A movement of evangelical religiosity swept through the colonies in the 1730s and 1740s. At the time it was called "a great and general awakening." Later historians term it the "Great Awakening" although it was not a single event at all, but a long-term process that moved in fits and starts.

Throughout the Western world, the early eighteenth century was an era of religious revival and renewal. Pietists from northern Europe and the British Isles entered the British colonies in the 1720s. The Moravians preferred to live among their own, but other pietists mingled with other colonists. In the same decade, Puritans like Cotton Mather called for a reformation of people's hearts to make them more open to the word of God. Dissatisfied with the conventional training of ministers, William Tennent, a Scots-Irish convert to Presbyterianism, began to train his sons for the ministry at home. In 1736, the home school became the "Log College" of Bucks County, Pennsylvania, and Tennent's sons, notably Gilbert, began to call for a religion of the feelings and expressed a contempt for the preaching of ministers who were not truly saved (Anne Hutchinson's complaint).

A revival in minister Jonathan Edwards's Northampton, Massachusetts, congregation also heralded the Awakening. Edwards had more or less inherited the congregation of his minister grandfather, Solomon Stoddard. Edwards's own father was a clergyman, and young Jonathan graduated from Yale intending to follow in his father's footsteps. He had a mystical bent, a brilliant mind, and a strong love of nature. As a youth of seventeen, he had a conversion experience, though like any good Puritan, he wondered all the time if he had merely fooled himself. He was tall, good looking, methodical in his preaching, and well aware of the apparent decline in piety throughout the region—until the revival began.

In 1732, young people in Northampton began to attend services more regularly, and a number of young women confessed to him their spiritual crises. By 1734, the behavior of the young began to change as well. They seemed more conscious of the need to act in decorous ways, and more eager for guidance. "And then, a concern about the great things of religion began," Edwards wrote to another minister in that year: "among old and young, and from the highest to the lowest; all seemed to be seized with a deep concern about their eternal salvation. . . . Persons seized with concern are brought to forsake their vices, and ill practices. . . . This town never was so full of love, nor so full of joy, nor so full of distress as it has lately been."

News of the revival in Northampton was spread through Edwards's moving *Faithful Narrative of the Surprizing Work of God* (1736). Edwards thought the conversions genuine. His congregants had learned to open their hearts and experience grace. To help them, he reminded them of their natural state, "out of Christ—that world of misery, that lake of burning brimstone, is extended abroad under you. There is the dreadful pit of the glowing flames of the wrath of God; there is hell's wide gaping mouth open; and you have nothing to stand upon. . . . It is only the power and mere pleasure of God that holds you up . . . much as one holds a spider, or some loathsome insect, over the fire."

While Edwards traveled the New England circuit with the good news, George Whitefield, an ordained English minister, was touring the colonies with his own message. Whitefield, like Edwards, had come from the middle class, but a conversion experience convinced him that he must preach to the masses. During his second visit to America, in 1739–1740, he moved rapidly from pulpit to pulpit, a whirlwind of sound and gesture. By the end of his tour, he had gone to just about every colony, beginning in the South and working his way north. Influential ministers opened their churches to him, and astute advance publicity gained him a reputation and a following.

Handsome, slender, trembling with emotion, his melodic clear voice and perfect diction could be heard throughout the hushed crowds at open-air meetings unprecedented in their size. The first of the modern evangelists, he swayed thousands. In rural Connecticut, news of Whitefield's preaching brought farmers at the gallop. As one eager auditor from Middletown reported, "I saw before me a cloud of fog rising . . . but as I came nearer the road I heard a noise of horses' feet coming down the road, and [realized] this cloud was a cloud of dust. . . . I could see men and horses slipping along in the cloud like shadows . . . a steady stream of horses and their riders, scarcely a horse more than his length behind another, all of a lather and foam. . . . Every horse seemed to go with all his might to carry his rider to hear news from heaven for the saving of souls."

Whitefield was no theorist and rarely used notes, and his doctrinal contribution was negligible. His message was simple: be born again in Christ. The rest followed naturally. Those who heard him often began conversion experiences on the spot, figuratively and literally wrestling with their sinfulness as they rolled on the ground, seeking release from doubt and shame in a renewal of faith. As different as Whitefield was from Edwards (who always preached from extensive notes and followed the traditional division of sermons into doctrine, explication, and application), both men had the same effect on their listeners—salvation lay in their hands.

Edwards, Whitefield, and the Tennents had pioneered not only a style of preaching, but a language of worship. Young ministers recast old Calvinist ideas of the Christian's utter dependency on God and predestination in an innovative lexicon. The new, emotionally rich and compelling vocabulary implied that by seeking grace one could find it. Even Benjamin Franklin, who wore religion lightly, was impressed. "From being thoughtless or indifferent about religion, it seemed as if all the world were growing religious, so that one could not walk through the town in an evening without hearing psalms sung in different families of every street."

Edwards, Whitefield, and the Tennents should have anticipated that the excitement would precipitate cleavages in congregations and arguments within the ministry, for by 1740 some revivalists regarded the new style as a test of fitness. Against this test they measured the more traditional of their colleagues and found them wanting. "Look into the congregations of unconverted ministers," Gilbert Tennent wrote in 1740, "and see what a sad security reigns there; not a soul convinced that can be heard of, for many years together, and yet the ministers are easy; for they say they do their duty."

At the same time, many ministers decided that the new revivalism was no more than a fad. They were appalled by the sight of people crying out, writhing in pain, and collapsing alongside the pews in church or by the benches at outdoor meetings.

As one Anglican Virginia minister complained in 1747, "these [evangelical] itinerants . . . make it their study to screw up people to the greatest heights of religious frenzy, and then leave them in that wild state, for perhaps ten or twelve months, till another enthusiast comes among them, to repeat the same thing."

In the hubbub of ministers' raucous accusations against one another, how could a congregant tell who were the converted ministers and who not? Who among the ministers was a counterfeit of true grace, secretly living in sin, or hypocrisy, or false hope? Edwards and others offered that one way to tell the true minister from the huckster was to see how the minister's preaching affected the congregation. Certainly Whitefield passed this test. His slightest gestures transformed the audience. In 1742, one convert recalled that in watching Whitefield preach, "I fell under a great terror . . . hell was represented to my mind, as a pit at the foot of a hill, and a great drove of people marching into it, and I along with them, and when I got very near it, I thought I looked over my shoulder, and saw a very beautiful man, who smiled on me and made a motion to me with his hand to come back." As another revivalist, Jonathan Parsons, preached, his congregation began to "weep, sigh, and sob."

James Davenport, whose pulpit was on Long Island and whose preaching included bursts of song and shouts of joy, made himself into a one-man inquisition into the state of grace of his fellow ministers. When he visited New London in March 1743, he enjoined his audience to throw their gaudy clothes and wigs into a bonfire, and to follow the raiment with ungodly books. According to one less than complimentary eyewitness account, he shouted over the blazing fire, "Thus the souls of the authors of those book, those of them that are dead, are roasting in the flames of hell." When, the next night, the bonfire was relit, Davenport called for an end to the idolatry of things—clothing in particular. That which was "worn for ornament" must be sacrificed in the cleansing flames. Davenport contributed his britches, saying "go you with the rest."

Supporters and opponents of the revival divided congregations into factions. Revivalist New Light Congregationalists and conservative Old Light Congregationalists sparred over who should retain control of the church and which ministers were regenerate. By 1741, there were open schisms in the Presbyterian synods, enthusiastic New Siders waging war against distrustful Old Siders over the place of affection and reason in the church.

Davenport's extremism and the growing schisms of the churches notwithstanding, the Great Awakening had a compelling impact on localities. In Gloucester, Massachusetts, the Great Awakening arrived in 1742. It did not split the church (local disputes had already done that), but it did intensify concern with all things religious. Gloucester, like all the Massachusetts coastal towns, had sent off its young men to fight in King George's War two years earlier. Business deteriorated during the hostilities. A generation had come of age not knowing the last of the old Puritans, and, denied their wisdom, yearned for explanations for the town's agony.

In January 1742, schoolmasters and parents in Gloucester began to notice increasing interest in religion among young people. They invited a New Light preacher, Nathaniel Rogers, to join town minister John White on the pulpit of the meeting-house. The Awakening revival worked its transforming effect on everyone from the town's most prominent citizens to their African American servants. Rich and poor, European American, African American, Native American, and peoples of mixed ethnic backgrounds might all be found at services writhing in fear of damnation and then leaping up in joy at the discovery of the sweetness of regeneration. The old uncertainties of Calvinism were still on the books and on the pages of the sermons, but a new sense of the safety of coming to the judgment day had appeared in the pews and on the benches where the worshippers gathered.

THE RISE OF AFFECTION

One could glimpse in the expressions of the husbands and wives praying together at the evangelical meeting a profound transformation of domestic values sweeping through the colonies in midcentury. Students of early modern culture have characterized this movement as a turn from the patriarchal to the affective family style, replacing male-dominated, authoritarian relationships in marriage and child rearing with reciprocity, companionship, and nurturance. In midcentury, the process had only just begun, but its outlines were becoming clear among the better-off. More and more unions rested on consent and mutuality. Parents started to regard children as innocent rather than inherently sinful. The home became a refuge of sentimentality.

Family

The changeover within the domestic circle was almost imperceptibly gradual. Everywhere the outward forms and the old patterns of family persisted. The father-dominated nuclear family remained the norm. The father or husband was still legally the head of the family; wives deferred to husbands; and children rose when their father entered a room. Social norms dictated honor and respect for the elderly, though they were only 2 percent of the population. In turn, the old "condescended" to the young, a term that meant kindly patronage. For Puritans, particularly, God was the eldest of the elders, and in the meetinghouse, all other considerations of wealth and status being equal, pious old age got one a seat in the front pews.

Wives and daughters agreed to their subordinate position in the family, a kind of hegemony that rested not only on consent but on law. The English rules of coverture gave control of the couple's property to the male partner. The children were his, not theirs, took his name, and could be punished by him without the intervention of the state. The head of the household could even legally demand the conjugal bed and "moderately" punish his wife.

Three dramatic events in midcentury sped the shift toward the new domestic culture. First, the spread of religious enthusiasm altered the role of women in the family. Traditionally, men were the dominant figures in a family's religious orientation. The wife followed the husband to church, sat beside him in the pew, and reared the children according to his religious beliefs. While not overturning this pattern, evangelical religious movements allowed women to give voice to their religious yearnings and credited women's piety.

Second, King George's War, the most disruptive of all the colonial conflicts to date, upset the basic patterns of family life, particularly in New England. More men than ever before went off to battle and did not return or came back lame or ill. Women took charge of households, reversing the traditional patriarchal roles of their husbands and fathers. They managed farms and businesses, educated children, and represented the family in the outside world.

Finally, the rise of consumerism and the new emphasis on refinement (the former a topic treated in chapter 12 and the latter a topic discussed below) added to the status of women. Women shopped, decorated homes, set standards for domestic etiquette, and otherwise contributed to the feminization of polite culture. While their public role remained circumscribed, their place as managers of the home and arbiters of good manners, and their control of the household purse strings, empowered middle-class and upper-class women.

Urged on by the changing roles of women, the new family style entrenched itself. Instead of castigation in sermon, story, and ballad for bewitching or seducing men, women were increasingly characterized as nurturing and caring, models of morality. Demographic evidence confirms the appearance of new values. In the 1720s, premarital pregnancy rates zoomed, suggesting that young people saw physical expressions of love as the normal prelude to marriage. Parents still arranged marriages with one eye on economic advantage, but prospective wives seemed to have gained more of a say in whom they would marry. More and more often, daughters married out of birth order, suggesting that parental control was giving way to the desires of children. Parents allowed their children to hunt for a suitable partner. Often, children who married moved away from parental homes, suggesting that the new household was based not on ties between the parents' families but on affection between the newly wed.

Not all wives and daughters enjoyed the revolution in sentiment. Court records document continuing wife and child abuse among all classes of men and women. Virginia's William Byrd II beat his bondwomen for being immoral, and his wife took a branding iron to an unruly servant girl. Favored house slaves like Landon Carter's body servant, Nassau, administered whippings within the quarters as well. Although masters and servants might know one another intimately, the institution of slavery rendered lasting affection a dangerous illusion.

Child Rearing

In the area of child bearing and child rearing, the shift from authoritarian to affective customs and attitudes reformatted the internal dynamics of colonial families. The outward parameters of child rearing seemed unchanged. Demographic studies show that, granting regional variations, the average size of households was about the same in 1770 as it had been in 1670, save in the Chesapeake, which had become considerably healthier for children and mothers, leading to larger families. Most mothers conceived between five and nine times during the course of marriage, with the result that families still had very young children underfoot when the parents had reached their late thirties or early forties, if they lived that long. Parents manipulated family wealth to control the conduct of children.

But the medical prospects for individual children had improved dramatically, and with the increased likelihood that children would survive to adulthood, attitudes toward children changed. In the previous century, one could expect one out of two children in the Chesapeake to die before reaching adulthood. By the 1740s, only one out of five was so destined. Better diet and sanitation improved life expectancy, but more important were officials' efforts to control epidemics of childhood diseases. Vaccination for smallpox, for example, reduced the peril for middle-class and upper-class children. Coupling the decline in child mortality with data on stable family size points to the surmise that married people practiced birth control. Abstinence and withdrawal were the favored methods, which suggests that women exercised growing control over procreation, another evidence of the shift toward mutuality in marriage.

As more children survived infancy, parents began to invest more emotion and capital in each child. By midcentury, the American family was slowly but surely becoming child centered. The trend was most pronounced among families of above-average economic and social status, but not limited to any particular region of the colonies. In New England, for example, parents no longer gave the names of deceased children to newborns, an indication that each child had his or her own identity in the parents' eyes. Parents bought books designed for children's enjoyment, like the *Mother Goose Nursery Rhymes*. In the middle colonies, portraits of families, which once had the children surrounding the adults, now featured children at the center.

Some families still beat the devil out of the child, but many others were either indulging their children or at least gently but firmly pushing them toward obedience and conformity. In these families, children were no longer regarded as miniature adults and childish anger or pranks no longer treated as sins. Behind the altered conduct of parents lay enlightened theories of psychology, like John Locke's hypothesis that infants' minds were "tabula rasas," blank palettes, on which parental guidance and education wrote lessons.

In general, the children of the poor did not share in this revolution in childhood. Poor children remained at greater risk to die young than their wealthy counterparts.

Even when healthy, poor children still slept many to a bed of straw or flax, or on unswept dirt floors, and ate inferior quality food. Magistrates ordered orphans into the care of strangers, and paupers' children were put out to service with other families or apprenticed to craftspeople. For lower-class children, there was no clear-cut demarcation between childhood and adulthood. At ages six or seven, boys left the house to work alongside older servants or laborers in fields, shops, and mills, and girls toiled by the side of older women.

THE ELITE AND THE POPULAR

As one sees in the disparate experience of children, by the middle of the eighteenth century American culture had bifurcated into two streams. The division had already taken place in elite and popular views of the natural world. At the beginning of the seventeenth century, educated and laypeople agreed about the spirit world. A few critics of the invisible world poked fun at what they called "superstition," but they constituted a small minority. Elite ministers, teachers, and scientists not only wrote and debated with one another learned disquisitions on the spirit world, they pressed civil authorities to investigate supposed cases of possession and witchcraft.

By the start of the eighteenth century, the ghosts and goblins of the invisible world remained a staple of folk culture and folk tales, and folk worship still incorporated charms, spells, and countermagic formulas, but the educated—including the educated ministry—were no longer so credulous. Instead, elite culture, based in part on science and rationalistic philosophy, and in part on a new theory of literacy that raised the sensible and the elegant above the popular and the common, questioned the utility of omens and prodigies. Although Cotton Mather had collected notices of omens and prodigies and published a book of them in 1683, by the 1710s he concluded that folk preoccupations like astrology and divination would just not do for a gentleman of letters.

Still, the boundary between the elite and the popular was no thicker than a semipermeable membrane, and people and ideas flowed between the two cultures. Highbrow culture was open to people of ordinary means. At theater performances, well born and low born mingled. Everyone in the audience participated in the show, stamping, shouting, hissing, and applauding. Anyone might demand the musicians play a different tune or threaten to chase an inept actor off the stage. The clown who aped the foppish manners of the aristocrat for the amusement of the common folk and the English actor who played the border ruffian in a mannered farce mixed the two cultures for their audiences.

Rude Ways

Today the word *rude* means impolite. In the eighteenth century, it meant rough or unrefined. Much of the colonies fit that description. In the cities, where the elite resided in mansions and worshipped in churches with high steeples and soft-cushioned pews, the streets were filled with young people of lesser means. They were servants, apprentices, or immigrants looking for work. Many of the jobs available to them in the city were dangerous, like working in the shipyards, or dirty, like carting refuse. The leading merchants regarded these laborers as "the rabble" and worried aloud that so many rough people about were an invitation to social disorder.

To some extent, this complaint had a factual foundation in crime rates and poor relief. The cities were breeding grounds for gangs of sneak thieves, cutpurses, and robbers. The crime rates of colonial cities were not excessive for the era (London had a far higher rate of crime than Philadelphia) or for the region (there was more crime in the Virginia countryside than there was in Boston), but the raw frequency of crime in urban areas was greater than rural areas because of the density of population.

The absence of formal police forces in the city encouraged perpetrators. The night watchmen and the sheriff's constables were often recruited from the same groups that violated the law. Jails were flimsy constructions, and suspects broke out regularly. One Salem, Massachusetts, prisoner, himself a multiple escapee, testified that "he saw one man pull up one of the boards overhead in the prison with his hand, going into the chamber of the prison, and others went out under the groundsill and some went out next to the watchhouse. They found not one room there that was sufficient to keep in a man who had the dexterity of an ordinary man."

Jury trials of criminals were shouting matches among victims and accused. Lawyers were rarely seen at these affairs, even when, as in over half of the colonies, counsel was permitted the accused. Penalties for most crimes were less strict than in England (where taking a wallet worth more than twelve pennies was a capital offense), but some men and women were still hanged for murder, piracy, arson, and repeated acts of robbery and burglary. Trials and executions were public spectacles. Crowds gathered to see ministers stand on the gallows next to the convict and preach final messages of redemption and warning. The prisoner was then given a chance to speak. Printers brought out broadsides and special editions of newspapers to publish the minister's sermon and the felon's last words.

Even for those poor who had legal employment, living conditions were vile. For example, in alleys behind the grid of the wide Philadelphia streets Penn had laid out for the merchants, the poor lived in rickety shanties, and fell prey to "agues" (probably malaria), typhus, and typhoid fever. An epidemic of the "black vomit" ravaged Charleston's poor in 1745, and smallpox hit Boston in 1752, killing over five hundred, infecting ten times that number, and causing thousands to flee to neighboring towns. Fully 18 percent of the young people buried in the city cemeteries were victims of periodic outbreaks of smallpox, a rate higher than London's. The introduction of vaccination to treat smallpox worsened the plight of the poor, because they could not afford vaccination, but could catch the disease in its natural, virulent form from contact with people newly vaccinated.

Refinement

For the upper classes, being part of an elite was not just a matter of having more wealth than the middling classes. Although the appurtenances of gentility like mansion houses and fine furniture cost money, the difference between the genteel classes and their emulators from the lower orders surpassed expense. The true mark of gentility was refinement of manner. Thus conspicuous consumption had a cultural purpose. The first time that the English adopted the French term *gentil*, in the sixteenth century, it was translated as "gentleman," but by the middle of the eighteenth century it had a second meaning—"genteel"—that described the cultural aspirations of the better sort.

Modern good manners were introduced to the English-speaking world in the eighteenth century, in part through the publication of popular manuals on etiquette. Written for the aspiring young man and the polite young woman, the books of manners urged self-control and grace. These were manifested in erect posture, steady eye contact, modulated voice, respectful but not fawning comportment before superiors, and easy but reserved conversation with equals.

Even the gestures of the hands mattered. As John Adams, watching Connecticut's Roger Sherman rise to speak in the Second Continental Congress, noted, "Sherman's air is the reverse of grace. There cannot be a more striking contrast to beautiful action, than the motions of his hands. Generally, he stands upright with his hands before him. The fingers of his left hand clenched into a fist, and the wrist of it, grasped with his right hand . . . when he moves a hand, in any thing like action, [the English illustrator William] Hogarth's genius could not have invented a motion more opposite to grace. It is stiffness, and awkwardness, itself. Rigid as starched linen or buckram."

Adams had no doubt read in his youth Eleazar Moody's *The School of Good Manners*. The supposed author was a Boston schoolmaster who taught children that terms and gestures of respect for elders and superiors not only garnered praise, they were essential to a well-regulated society. The young were instructed to "hold up your head; look the person you speak to in the face. Speak in a distinct and elevated tone of voice." As one midcentury broadside reminded youths, ill manners included "omitting to pay proper respect to Company, on entering or leaving a room; putting fingers in nose or ears; contempt in looks, words, or actions; surliness of all kinds; vulgarism in expression; and too much attention to the faults of others."

Refinement was a discipline that the gentleman and the lady imposed on themselves. It could be calibrated with precision. Politeness, delicacy, sensibility, and taste required the lady or the gentleman not to shout, to eliminate the overly passionate gesture, and to treat inferiors with formal courtesy. George Washington was a model for those who wanted to behave like a gentleman. He looked a visitor in the eye when he spoke, listened politely, and refused to say anything that was not "deliberate, deferential, and engaging." (Washington was too refined, in fact, for one young Harvard

College wag, who made General Washington the target of a verse of "Yankee Doodle": too gaudy by half, both proud and foppish.)

Being accepted in any polite company required being seen to have good manners. The English aristocrat Philip Stanhope, Lord Chesterfield, reminded his son in the most famous correspondence about etiquette in the eighteenth century, "One of the most important points of life is decency; which is to do what is proper, and where it is proper . . . by which you will see how necessary decency is, to gain the approbation of mankind."

The most visible physical symbol of the genteel lifestyle was the mansion. By 1750, a revolution in house construction and ornamentation had swept over the land. The solid stone house of the middle colony farmer, the heavy-timbered overhung dwelling of the New England squire, and the plain, two-story-plus clapboard abode of the planter all gave way to the Georgian mansion. Its facade was symmetrical and imposing. Its windows and doorways beckoned with fans of light.

The windows, and the decorative molding around them, could be seen from a distance—for visitors should be able to discern the quality of the house from their first glimpse of it. As Eliza Lucas Pinckney of Charleston recorded of Crowfield mansion on the Cooper River, "the house stands a mile from, but in sight of the road, and take a very handsoume appearance; as you draw nearer new beauties discover themselves." Garden walls, pathways, and gates contrived to capture the visitor's eye and expand her imagination.

Inside, the signs of refinement were even more striking. Older houses had low ceilings and small casement windows. Their central fireplaces barely heated their rooms. The mansion of 1750 had high ceilings of gleaming plaster and wainscoted walls, with large, double-hung sash windows framed by draperies. As one Newport merchant wrote approvingly, "sash windows are the newest fashion." In fact, the first sash windows appeared at Louis XIV's palace at Versailles. James Stuart, always impressed by French fashion, had them installed at Windsor Castle late in the 1680s.

Brightly lit in daytime, the walls of rooms featured floral or patterned wall papering or wood paneling. Expensive candles of spermaceti whale oil gave off a perfumed and even light (cheaper animal-fat candles burned poorly and literally stank). Chimneys at either end of the house allowed for a fireplace in every room. The fireplace itself was a thing of beauty, often framed by imported Dutch painted tiles and surmounted by a rich wooden mantle. These elegant fireplaces and mantles mattered so much to refined people that they would rather, in Franklin's words, "submit to have damaged furniture, sore eyes, and skins almost smok'd to bacon" than surrender their fireplaces.

Houses made a series of points about refinement that went beyond mere size, lightness, and expense. The entire effect was calculated to impress the senses and lift up the spirit. Walking through the doorway, visitors entered a new kind of chamber—the central hallway—rather than stepping directly into a room. Specially designed hall furniture lined the walls—softly cushioned long benches, so that visitors might wait in comfort and style for the family to greet them. On either side of the hallway were public rooms for receiving and entertaining company. The stairway, with its wide, smoothly polished hardwood risers and its ornate banisters, reminded visitors that there were elegant bedrooms above. Thus the refined home protected the privacy of the family while opening the house to guests.

The benches and straight spindle-back chairs of fifty years earlier disappeared, replaced by imported, soft, fabric-covered sofas and armchairs whose gracefully curved lines suggested elegance and ease. There were enough chairs now for the entire family, not just its head, and for guests as well. Visitors and family members sat comfortably in the new furniture, which facilitated genteel conversation.

The gentility of the mansion house attracted imitators among the middle-class merchants and tradesmen. From the streets of Philadelphia, to the crossroads of small Delaware towns, to the bluffs above the James River, middle-class families emulated their social superiors in the construction of homes. The middle-class house was now incomplete without mirrors, books, draperies, and tea and coffee services. Refined manners soon followed. The common trencher and all-purpose bowls and spoons gave way to complete table settings including individual plates, knives, and forks. One now "dressed up" to go out and washed up before meals. One taught one's children "table manners"—no talking with mouths full or eating with fingers.

Table manners were among the many virtues that made up "good taste" for an ever-widening circle of people, but they remind us that a larger gendered transformation went along with refinement. The refinement of polite society gave more scope to women to express their individuality. For genteel women, feelings—not passions, that would be going too far—could be expressed freely. English books of manners and novels like Samuel Richardson's *Clarissa*, published in its first American edition in 1772, explored the limits of freedom for genteel women. Oppressed by parents who did not understand her, seduced and abandoned by an unprincipled suitor, Clarissa maintained her refined and noble sense of virtue.

Like Clarissa, the genteel American woman trembled or glowed with delicate emotions. In conversation, she was gay, witty, and vivacious. She might display her French or musical attainments, or play party games, with modesty and decorum. And she was expected to have read the latest English novel. When she was far from company, letter writing was encouraged, and the letter itself was a kind of performance. An extension of conversation, letters were to be composed in polite and graceful tones. The handwriting was to be open and flowing, unlike the crabbed hand of the previous century.

Refinements of the sort here described were not just ways of exhibiting and measuring the distance between the upper classes and the lower orders. True refinement rested upon a kind of conspicuous consumption that both exceeded and satirized the commonness of mass consumption, but the truly refined man or woman did not go overboard. The genteel colonist avoided the garish display of personal adornment that marked the nobility of the previous century. Indeed, there were times when one could not tell the gentleman from the tradesman. When Robert Carter, one of Virginia's most wealthy planters, went to visit one of his gristmills, he took along his clerk. The clerk dressed in a bright and handsome scarlet jacket. The planter wore simpler garb and a frazzled wig. Good taste lay in self-control and studied austerity.

In this sense, refinement might seem to be an extension of the idea of "self-improvement" one saw in Benjamin Franklin's essays. But genteel self-improvement, by its very definition, was exclusive rather than inclusive. It intended to enhance visible boundary lines between the orders of society that mere material acquisition blurred. As the middle classes sought to imitate the good taste of their betters, the latter invented new signs and signals to distinguish true gentlemen and women from upstarts, pretenders, and social climbers. Finally, the upper classes introduced the language of "natural aristocrats" and "men of talent and learning" to differentiate themselves from the ambitious tradesman and artisan.

ENLIGHTENMENT

Alongside the refinement of manners in America came a refinement of thought, an affirmation of the value of science and reason. The European Age of Reason blossomed in the final years of the seventeenth century. The European Enlightenment of the eighteenth century continued the trend, becoming one of the major intellectual movements in Western history. Although the ideas of the Enlightenment spread to all classes, the burst of intellectual activity was largely confined to the elite. Among the elite, the Enlightenment promoted an empirical, materialistic view of the workings of the world.

Historians dispute the extent and the form of the reception of eighteenth-century European ideas in America. But few European conceptions escaped modification, and overall, the Enlightenment in America was a collage of borrowed, adapted, and homegrown notions. As oddly fitting as some of this collection might seem, on the whole it had a powerful liberating effect on Americans' thinking. As Thomas Jefferson, a child of the Enlightenment, testified before he died, because of the Enlightenment, "All eyes are opened, or opening, to the rights of man. The general spread of science has already laid open to every view the palpable truth, that the mass of mankind has not been born with saddles on their backs, nor a favored few booted and spurred, ready to ride them legitimately, by the grace of God. These are grounds of hope for others."

Science
American Enlightenment thinkers were a band of spirited amateurs whose curiosity about astronomy, geology, and botany flowed over into the study of politics

and society. Men like Franklin were this-worldly empiricists. They longed to know more about the world by experimenting, observing, and measuring it, and believed in the power of human intellect to reveal the secrets of physical nature, although they retained much of their skepticism about human nature.

Many of these scientists had traveled far from their seventeenth-century predecessors' intellectual roots. John Winthrop IV, Hollis professor of "natural philosophy" (a more common term than experimental science) at Harvard College from 1738 to 1779, was the scion of a clan of Puritan magistrates. He was a religious man, but his real interests were astronomical and geological. He traveled over the northern colonies taking sightings of the planets and comets and measuring the effects of earthquakes and geological movements. He dabbled in botany and animal biology as well. His crowning achievement was organizing a Harvard expedition to Newfoundland in 1769 to view the transit of Venus across the sun, an event that would occur only twice in a typical lifetime. Using this and other points of measurement, he hoped to calculate the distance between the planet and the sun precisely.

While Winthrop and his students packed their bags, the engineer David Rittenhouse of Philadelphia assembled his "orrery," a mechanical device designed to duplicate the motion of all the planets about the sun. Rittenhouse, a farmer's son, had neither Winthrop's pedigree nor his professorship, but in Franklin's Philadelphia, the intellectual climate favored clever mechanics, novel experimenters, and intellectual risk-takers. Rittenhouse gave lectures on the stars, collecting fees for spreading the gospel of science. The orrery was a popular attraction, for when its crank and gears were set in motion, not only did the planets move to the commands of men, but its dials showed audiences the position of the planets in years to come. The mysteries of the starry skies were gone. As Isaac Newton's laws proved that the world was a giant machine, Rittenhouse's device demonstrated that ordinary people could watch the machine at work.

Equally important, Rittenhouse united science with technology. If anything, Americans were more impressed with the application of science than with theory. For example, a practical interest in gardens and plants occasioned American contributions in botany. Virginia planters like John Clayton and ministers like John Bannister were more observers and catalogers than experimenters, but they made day-to-day observation of garden plants into something of a science, and the Royal Society reprinted their reports in England. If botany had nothing useful to contribute, no way to improve human life, then it would have no place in American science. Not by chance was Clayton the first president of the Virginia Society for the Advancement of Useful Knowledge.

American amateur scientists sought fame as well as progress. Philadelphia Quaker John Bartram was a case in point. Largely self-educated (like Franklin and Rittenhouse), Bartram named a number of species of plants. He also dabbled in geology and astronomy. But only recognition abroad brought him true contentment.

Cotton Mather gloried in his election to the prestigious Royal Society. James Logan, secretary to the proprietors in Pennsylvania and Bartram's patron, hungered for reputation as well, and stole time from his job to crossbreed plants and report his findings to the Royal Society.

Sometimes, like Logan, the circle of naturalists in America included government officials. Cadwallader Colden held high office for a time in New York, but in 1750 retired to his farm for a time to pursue his interests in natural history. He wrote an account of the Iroquois confederation, making him one of America's first anthropologists. His work as a botanist won him, as it had Bartram and Winthrop, membership in the Royal Society, and before he died, he began to explore the causes of gravity.

Colden's interest in medicine (the field in which he was trained in Scotland before he emigrated to America) admitted him to a circle of medical researchers that included Dr. William Douglass of Boston, another Scot who had formal medical training, and Dr. Alexander Garden of Charleston. Douglass was also an amateur historian, anthropologist, and astronomer. Garden visited Philadelphia in 1754, meeting in person some of the natural scientists who would become his correspondents. Before he was done, he had discovered many new species of plants. All of these Americans admired the Swedish naturalist Carl Linnaeus's system of classification of living things, and Garden collected specimens for Linnaeus.

Many of these naturalists complained about the lack of institutional support for scientific inquiry in the colonies. Only Harvard and Yale supported the teaching of science and mathematics. Other colleges lagged behind in these fields. The College of New Jersey and the College of Rhode Island (later renamed Brown after the chief benefactor's family) did not teach science on a regular basis until the end of the 1760s; Kings College in New York City appointed its first professor of science in 1758; the College of Philadelphia introduced regular courses in science soon after its founding in the 1750s; and the College of William and Mary hired William Small to lecture on mathematics and science in 1758.

What is more impressive, even in the midst of economic downturns, Philadelphia, Boston, and New York City merchants contributed to the creation of medical schools and societies for useful knowledge. In Philadelphia, after his second return from England, in 1743, Franklin's circle of friends revived his club and rechristened it the American Philosophical Society. The learned society sponsored research papers and practical experiments; indeed, its full title included the phrase "for Promoting Useful Knowledge." The next step was to publish its "transactions"—for useful knowledge was knowledge wisely disseminated.

Typically for the times, the line between elite science and popular ideas of nature was blurred. Even Franklin contributed to the murkiness of the distinction, for while he was interesting himself in the elite science of electrostatics, his almanacs collected and displayed all manner of astrological calculations and folk remedies. In one sense, then, the emergence of the American Philosophical Society and the publication of its official transactions were attempts to draw such a bright-line distinction, and to claim the mantle of authority for the elite experimenters. Still, the society counted among its members many men who had no formal education and whose interest in science was rooted in practical rather than theoretical concerns.

Not much of any purely scientific value was discovered by the Americans, save for Franklin's work on static electricity and electric charges, and the naming of hitherto uncataloged species of plants and animals, but the Americans' concern for scientific topics, and the avidity of American researchers, demonstrated to European scientists that the colonists could contribute to the general store of scientific knowledge. Indeed, the Americans' fascination with indigenous animals and plants was the transatlantic continuation of Europe's curiosity about American nature dating back to Columbus.

Philosophy

The eagerness with which Americans sought European recognition for their scientific contributions suggests that they would be eager consumers of European philosophy. American intellectuals' libraries included the works of leading European Enlightenment thinkers, and the ideas of the latter permeated American essays and correspondence. In particular, forward-looking Americans felt an affinity for European reformers' notions of human agency and moral responsibility.

In the Enlightenment era of the eighteenth century, a cadre of intellectuals had emerged in western Europe whose contributions to political, social, and moral philosophy overthrew older conceptions of natural and social order. Indeed, as Anglo-Irish essayist Jonathan Swift satirically noted at the beginning of the century, the "moderns" had triumphed over the "ancients."

The first and foremost of these moderns was John Locke, though the formative period of this thought lay a half century earlier. His *Essay Concerning Human Understanding* (1690) argued that human knowledge arose from everyday perception and experience. He believed as well in the natural goodness of human beings, that people seeking pleasure rationally could make common cause. Liberty furthered by individual pursuit of truth and improvement was not inconsistent with the general good. Locke's views became the foundation of an empirical search for the laws of human society. Even conventionally religious writers like the poet Alexander Pope boasted, "Know then thyself, presume not God to scan; / The proper study of mankind is man."

The same kind of rationalistic open-mindedness led philosophers to question the divine right of kings. Political theorists like the Baron de Montesquieu (Charles-Louis de Secondat) and Voltaire (the pen name of François-Marie Arouet) in France began to argue that constitutional monarchy or enlightened monarchy was better than absolute rule of kings. Only under the former would dissent, toleration, and liberty be protected. Wisely, both Montesquieu and Voltaire camouflaged their criticisms of the power of French kings by praising Locke's ideas rather than criticizing French governance, but French censors were not fooled. Voltaire's work was condemned and burned by the public hangman in Paris.

American thinkers also welcomed the political and moral philosophy of Enlightenment Scotland. The wealth that the colonial trade brought to Scotland had spurred increased investment in cities like Edinburgh and Glasgow, which in turn elevated the universities of the two cities to first-rank status. In the 1720s, thinkers there began to work out a practical, realistic, humane, and progressive view of political and economic development. Francis Hutcheson, a minister and professor, first outlined this worldview. For the nearly twenty years that he held the chair of moral philosophy at Glasgow, he taught that ethics was social. All people had reciprocal duties to one another, all people were equal in nature, and all should learn to live with one another in peace. Moral principles like these were learned, not innate; relational, not absolute.

Hutcheson's philosophical outlook echoed in William Robertson's writings. Robertson was the genial center of Scottish intellectual life in Edinburgh in the generation after Hutcheson's. As principal (president) of the University of Edinburgh and a leading figure in the Church of Scotland, he recruited and defended a wide range of intellectuals, from skeptics to orthodox believers. When the orthodox tried to excommunicate dissenters for suspected atheism, Robertson protected them. There would be no Inquisition in Scotland. Robertson's contributions to the Scottish Enlightenment took concrete form in his histories of Scotland, Europe, and the American. Throughout the lively, anecdote-filled volumes, Robertson preached that learning followed the progress of commerce. Superstition and war would soon bow to enlightened, material self-interest.

In later years, Robertson's students and supporters like philosophers Adam Ferguson and Thomas Reid would flesh out a philosophy of commonsense morality. Economist Adam Smith credited Hutcheson with opening his eyes to the importance of freedom. But the brightest star in the Scottish intellectual galaxy was David Hume. He openly discarded the idea that God ordered the world and that human perceptions were only reliable because God was a trustworthy source of innate ideas. Instead, Hume argued that human ideas came from human experience. Thus morality could not rest upon revealed religion or revelation. It had to be the product of customs and consent among people. As Hume put it in his A Treatise of Human Nature (1739), "Justice takes its rise from human conventions." Unconventional and tough-minded, he doubted the validity of all established religions, and his essays on morals, politics, and human understanding stressed the human origins of social conventions. The origin of people's religious, social, and political ideas was this-worldly, not divine.

In the writings of the Scottish philosophers, American thinkers found support for their realism and optimism, but these values were not the only intellectual exports of the Scots. In the eighteenth century, evangelical Presbyterians had gained control of the Kirk, the conference of the Scottish church. Much influenced by their reading of the New Side sermons, Scots like John Witherspoon, son of a minister and a minister himself, reached out to Presbyterians in the colonies. In 1766, he accepted the offer of the presidency of the College of New Jersey, a seat of learning founded by evangelical American Presbyterians. Witherspoon recruited other Scots to teach in Princeton, and he required students to read the works of Scottish moral and historical writers.

The real contribution of American philosophy lay in the realm of political ideas. To be sure, much came from enlightened Europe, but as both Richard Beeman and Gordon Wood remind today's students, basic political ideas of republicanism and the morality of good government were already present in the colonies by the middle of the century. The protests of the 1760s simply brought these ideas to the surface, made them central to the practical needs of government, and spurred a process of experimentation—a kind of practical philosophy that taught its students through doing.

American thinkers like Franklin, Thomas Jefferson, and John Adams were all "bricoleurs," that is, they mixed and matched philosophical ideas from many sources. Franklin put science to use in his essays on politics, demography, and commerce. Jefferson, trained as a lawyer, was an avid and able amateur botanist, astronomer, and climatologist. He felt no hesitation combining his interests in natural and moral philosophy to arrive at a liberal view of world progress and the necessity of liberty. Adams, more conservative and traditional in his religion than Franklin and Jefferson, readily combined law, history, and philosophy to argue for separation of powers in government and against slavery.

Deism

About as far away as one could get from evangelical Protestantism, deism was another important Enlightenment influence on American thinkers. Never a simple or unified platform for religious reform, English deists instead formed a loose supportive intellectual circle. Their work was closer to a persuasion than a faith. Its purpose was an attempt to make religion logical. Thus deists like John Toland took aim at miracles, inconsistencies, follies, mysteries, rites, and revelations. Other deists expressed skepticism about the existence of God and doubted that Jesus was the messiah. Most were furiously anticlerical, and all were controversialists.

The English deists' criticism of priestcraft gained a following in France. There, anticlericalism had become something of a religion itself, and intellectuals like Montesquieu and Voltaire adopted deism. By 1760, Voltaire's deism was open, and his conversations and published letters mixed the amused and sardonic condemnations of all churches. But deism in England and France lacked an affirmative object and captured neither the imagination of the ruling classes nor the hearts of the masses.

In its American form, deism struck a more gentle and optimistic note. Instead of an assault on established religion, deism in the colonies expressed a faith in a benign creator and the promise of universal salvation. In Virginia, for example, deism began to catch on among the more enlightened planters. Young men like Thomas Jefferson and James Madison, avid readers of English deism, found the doctrine of a natural religion congenial. Franklin owned a pew near the front of Christ Church in Philadelphia, and wrote, before he died, that Christian morality was the best system he had ever uncovered, but quietly embraced deism. Natural religion was the closest intellectual system to his own religion of nature.

————

Anyone in America could be a deist. Anyone might join an evangelical prayer meeting. Anyone might attend a public exhibition of Franklin's static electricity or Rittenhouse's orrery. By the 1760s, American religion and science had created a kind of cultural "middle ground" in which highbrow and lowbrow might mingle. Refinement of manners seeped down from the topmost layer of society into the homes of the middling sort, narrowing the gap between the classes. A number of intellectuals envisioned a world of liberty and equality of the mind, but the real gap between the haves and have-nots did not close. A multitude of signs—from powdered wigs and gold-embroidered waistcoats to where one sat in church—reminded people of "their place."

12

Mercantilism and Markets

I believe people increase
faster by generation in
these colonies, where all
can have full employ
and there is room and
business for millions yet
unborn.

—Benjamin Franklin,
Poor Richard's Almanack
(1750)

In the previous chapter, we discovered how colonial culture both separated and united elites and commoners. In similar fashion, mutual economic interest and shared business activities brought people from all classes together, while trends in economic development favored some and hurt others. This chapter examines these interests and activities at midcentury, beginning with the imperial economy, mercantilism, the Navigation Acts, and the patterns of transatlantic business. Next, we turn to regional economies and fit them into the larger imperial pattern. Then we examine occupations, consumerism, and poverty. We conclude with the great depression of 1763.

The economic approach to history focuses on continuities and discontinuities. Did the colonial economy move at a more or less steady pace, jump through distinct stages, or make sudden, periodic leaps? There is evidence for all three explanatory models. On the one hand, colonial productivity seems to have grown in a linear fashion. Colonial consumption of imports, on the other hand, took sudden jumps. Regional economies like tobacco planting in the South passed through recognizable stages from infant industries on the frontier, to youthful expansiveness, to stable maturity.

Economic history, like economics, prefers the quantitative and analytical mode to the narrative and assumes the rationality of economic "actors"—markets, demand, supply, costs, and prices. But one must not lose sight of individuals' and groups' motives and values. From the standpoint of the imperial authorities, the root purpose of colonization was economic gain for the home country. The colonists were to serve as producers and suppliers of staple crops and raw materials. For the colonists, economic growth was equally vital, but they looked at it in terms of their own economic prospects and buying power. Indeed, one can characterize the economics of empire in these years as a struggle between adherents of a system that channeled wealth toward the home country and promoters of a system that rewarded its producers, in other words, between mercantilism and marketism.

With the conflict outlined above in mind, one can assess the colo-

COLONIAL PRODUCTS

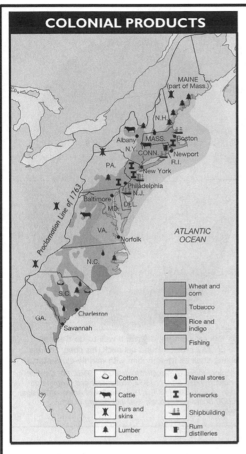

MAINE
(part of Mass.)

N.H.

Albany
N.Y.
MASS. Boston
CONN.
Newport
R.I.
PA.
New York
Philadelphia
N.J.
Baltimore
DEL.
MD.
VA.
Norfolk

N.C.

S.C.
Charleston
GA.
Savannah

Proclamation Line of 1763

ATLANTIC
OCEAN

Wheat and corn
Tobacco
Rice and indigo
Fishing

Cotton
Cattle
Furs and skins
Lumber
Naval stores
Ironworks
Shipbuilding
Rum distilleries

TRADE ROUTES

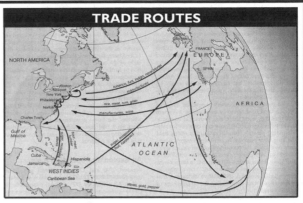

NORTH AMERICA
EUROPE
GREAT BRITAIN
FRANCE
SPAIN
PORTUGAL
AFRICA
Boston
Newport
New York
Philadelphia
Norfolk
Charles Town
Gulf of Mexico
Cuba
Jamaica
Hispaniola
WEST INDIES
Caribbean Sea
ATLANTIC OCEAN
tobacco, furs, indigo, naval stores
manufactures
rice, meat, rum, grain
manufactures, wine
slaves, gold, pepper

TOBACCO PRICES

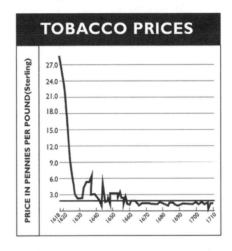

PRICE IN PENNIES PER POUND(Sterling)

27.0
24.0
21.0
18.0
15.0
12.0
9.0
6.0
3.0

1618 1620 1630 1640 1650 1660 1670 1680 1690 1700 1710

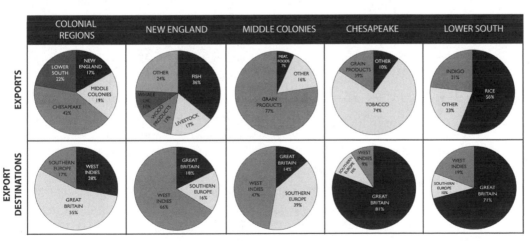

	COLONIAL REGIONS	NEW ENGLAND	MIDDLE COLONIES	CHESAPEAKE	LOWER SOUTH
EXPORTS	LOWER SOUTH 23%, NEW ENGLAND 17%, MIDDLE COLONIES 19%, CHESAPEAKE 42%	OTHER 24%, FISH 36%, WHALE OIL 6%, WOOD PRODUCTS 17%, LIVESTOCK 17%	MEAT, FOODS 7%, OTHER 16%, GRAIN PRODUCTS 77%	GRAIN PRODUCTS 39%, OTHER 10%, TOBACCO 74%	INDIGO 21%, RICE 56%, OTHER 23%
EXPORT DESTINATIONS	SOUTHERN EUROPE 17%, WEST INDIES 28%, GREAT BRITAIN 55%	GREAT BRITAIN 18%, SOUTHERN EUROPE 16%, WEST INDIES 66%	GREAT BRITAIN 14%, SOUTHERN EUROPE 39%, WEST INDIES 47%	WEST INDIES 9%, SOUTHERN EUROPE & MORE 10%, GREAT BRITAIN 81%	WEST INDIES 19%, SOUTHERN EUROPE 10%, GREAT BRITAIN 71%

Colonial Economy

nial economic system's performance on the whole. As a producer of staple goods, the colonies excelled. For a time, the shortage of labor hindered growth, but colonial planters turned to African slaves, and in the eighteenth century a veritable flood of new immigrants from Germany, northern Ireland, and Scotland pushed into the cities and the frontiers. Planters joined with merchants and shippers to develop a complex trading system reaching all over the Atlantic Rim.

Initial high prices for staples like sugar, tobacco, rice, indigo, timber and naval stores, and livestock supported the rapid deployment of large-scale staple crop production. Over time, the returns on these crops leveled off (in part because the high level of production forced down the prices), but the staple economy fueled the accumulation of wealth among planters, merchants, and professionals, and this wealth percolated down to the lower economic classes, except the slaves.

At the same time as the staple export sector prospered, increasing population put pressure on the price structure. European and African newcomers did not bring investment capital with them, but they had to have clothing, housing, food, and other consumer goods. This is what happened in sixteenth-century Europe, as we have seen in chapter 4, and it recurred in the eighteenth-century American colonies. The result was the creation of a class of desperately poor free people.

THE IMPERIAL ECONOMY

The colonies were part of an Atlantic system of trade and production. Imperial authorities imposed the fundamental structure and the rules of operation of that system. But as we have already discovered, decisions in European capitals did not mean that two thousand miles away the colonists obeyed.

Just as the politics of empire entailed negotiation between metropolitan officialdom and provincial magnates, so the economics of empire required accommodation. Sometimes this took illegal forms, as when customs officers winked at colonial smuggling. Sometimes a particular sector or region of the colonial economy benefited in fact when, theoretically, the home country should have had the upper hand. For example, under mercantilism, the balance of trade should favor the home country, particularly when the commodity traded was one of the enumerated articles, but tobacco and rice producers had a favorable balance of trade with Britain. Britain accepted this imbalance because British middlemen could resell the plantation colonies' staples to earn even more profits.

The imperial system raised British living standards, providing jobs for British workers at a time when other jobs, particularly in agriculture, were disappearing. According to T. H. Breen's research, colonial consumption of British manufactured goods rose by the end of the 1760s to nearly 26 percent of home country output, and colonial demand spurred technological and financial innovation in Britain. The profits of the colonial trade brought prosperity to import/export firms. The economic value of the North American empire to Britain far exceeded the returns on French and Spanish investments in their New World lands, for reasons that will be examined in the section on regional economies below.

The Elaboration of the Navigation Acts

The Navigation Acts introduced in the 1660s underwent elaboration over the next hundred years. The list of enumerated articles expanded, not merely to increase revenue from the duties, but to ensure that the flow of trade favored the home country. Enumeration of cotton, indigo, and ginger, along with certain rare hardwoods, ensured raw materials for English textile workers and furniture makers. Parliament added rice to the list in 1704, for somewhat obscure reasons. It could have been freely traded within the empire like other foodstuffs, but it was instead classed with sugar as a prime revenue producer. In 1765, colonial rice growers convinced Parliament to exempt rice again. Molasses permanently joined the list in 1704, for molasses was essential for the English distillery industry. Nevertheless, New Englanders smuggled in large amounts of French molasses, and bought molasses from English jobbers, and New England distilleries thrived.

Although the legislative elaboration of the Navigation Acts system seemed haphazard to the colonists, it was still going strong in the 1770s because it still served its purpose. Thus to the list of enumerated articles Parliament added statutes preventing colonies from printing their own money and statutes barring colonial entrepreneurs from competing with English manufacturers. These apparently arbitrary restrictions upon colonial economic growth in fact furthered the same goal as the much older prohibition on the direct importation of foreign manufactured goods into the colonies and on the use of foreign-flag ships in the carrying trade.

As skewed as the system seemed to be in favor of English interests, it offered substantial benefits to the colonists, including easy credit, ready shipping facilities, cheap marine insurance, and the protection of the British navy. Colonial merchants could use their contacts throughout the empire to reduce the cost of warehousing and marketing. The enforcement system was so ineffective that smuggling supplemented legal income, assuming that the smuggler was willing to risk confiscation of cargos and ships.

Economic Growth

The change from 1650 to 1770 in the estimated gross national product (GNP) per person in the colonial economy was 2,500 percent over the 120-year period. This gives a yearly growth rate of 2.7 percent for the British American empire as a whole and 3.2 percent for mainland British colonies. Two qualifications stand out. First, the base line of 1650 reflected an undeveloped or frontier economy, so the rise in the GNP is not quite so striking. Second, overall growth was not linear, nor did it affect every individual equally. There were speed bumps in the road, when the colonial economy suffered through hard times. A few families became incredibly wealthy, while the income of slaves ("in kind"—as food and clothing) did not increase much.

Average personal net worth, quite low by modern standards, suggests that the capital for reinvestment in colonial enterprises came from outside the colonies. The ordinary New Englander left but £33 in personal worth at death. The average free southerner's estate had £132, reflecting the value of slaves.

But overall growth meant that outside investors must have found the colonies attractive. The level of enterprise—that is, of starting new businesses—exceeded that anywhere in the world at the time, as did the overall standard of living of ordinary free persons. The best conjecture on the latter estimates a twofold increase in personal income from 1650 to 1774. If slaves are excluded from this estimate (for technically, slaves had no income), the rate of increase appears even higher. Given that the standard of living rose when population from natural increase and in-migration was rising just as fast, using up resources, the robustness of the colonial economy is undeniable.

The colonial growth pattern exhibited the same cycles of boom and bust that characterized the U.S. economy after independence. The periods 1645–1655, the late 1660s, the middle 1690s, 1701–1705, 1708–1710, 1714–1716, 1719–1721, 1726–1729, 1730–1731, 1734–1736, 1738–1740, 1741–1745, 1749–1750, 1752–1756, 1763–1765, and 1767–1770 were times of contraction. The years from 1773 to 1775, for somewhat more complicated reasons (discussed in chapter 14), were equally depressed. War fouled the usual mechanisms of business, as did the outbreak of epidemics of disease and political unrest. Colonial downturns also coincided with recessions in the home country, reflecting the close ties between the two. For self-sufficient farmers, the crashes were annoying. For merchants and city laborers, the dips could be devastating.

As the connection between dips in the economies of the home country and the colonies suggests, trade was the lifeblood of the empire. For the home country, trade took the form of importation of raw materials and export of finished goods. For the colonies, trade involved the reverse process—but both metropolitan center and colonial periphery benefited from intangible (sometimes called "invisible") parts of the trade. The invisibles were the services that entrepreneurs supplied. For the colonists, one of these was freight haulage. A major invisible for the home country was interest received on loans.

Adding intangibles to the ledger reveals a truer picture of the balance of trade. Colonial importation of non-British items outside of the Navigation Acts, like molasses or sugar from the French, or tea from the Dutch, has to be factored in as well. In the years 1768 to 1772, for which fairly reliable figures exist, the British North American colonies as a whole had debts of £1,120,000 per year, most of it reflecting the difference between exports of staples to Britain and the West Indies and the cost of imports from Britain and Ireland. The trade with the West Indies and the profits of shipping and other services did relatively little to defray this imbalance. British merchants' credit carried colonial clients.

The Challenge to Mercantilism

The purpose of seventeenth-century mercantilism was the enrichment of the state. As the French minister of the marine Colbert explained, "Everyone agrees that the might and greatness of a state is measured entirely by the quantity of silver it possesses." In his mind, a favorable balance of trade with the colonies and the construction of roads, canals, and bounties to manufacturing at home had the same purpose: to allow Louis XIV's France to maintain its position as the leading nation in Europe. He gave no thought to the standard of living of the ordinary subject of the king, whether at home or in the New World.

The defense of private property and special interest was already nibbling away at the intellectual foundations of mercantilism by the 1690s, however. The new theory did not place private property above the public good, but argued that the public good required the accumulation and easy transfer of private property. The wealthier the subject, the better off the state would be. The "liberty" so often mentioned and so prized in English and American essays, editorials, and pamphlets in the first half of the eighteenth century was in part the freedom to buy and sell—in short, a celebration of a freer marketplace.

In England, this transformation was already under way. England's economy had never been as centralized as France's or Spain's. No English minister of state had the powers of a Colbert. Parliament gained control of the purse strings after 1689, and was soon the target of lobbying by all manner of private economic interests. Private haulers used the coastal shipping lanes as highways. Parliament provided for improvements to rivers and harbors and passed "private bills" to enable entrepreneurs to build toll roads, called "turnpikes," connecting rural areas to urban centers. The number of turnpike miles grew from thirty-four hundred in 1750 to fifteen thousand in 1770. By the middle of the century, private companies were investing heavily in canal construction.

The same pattern of market-driven private investment fueled a series of industrial innovations, like Abraham Darby's invention of high-temperature furnaces to turn coal into hot-burning coke, which in turn could be used to turn iron into steel. Similar technological advances like James Watt's steam engine, John Kay's "flying shuttle," and Richard Arkright's spinning machine allowed British manufacturers to move production of fabrics and clothing from the cottage to the factory.

The implications of free market economic theory and practice undercut mercantilism at every turn. A truly free market was one regulated not by artificial intervention of government, but by the value of the goods and the services themselves. In fact, no such markets ever existed in commercial nations (except in the minds of economists), for the intervention of government—for example, parliamentary private bills, tariffs, or bounties, and favorable court decisions on the use of property—not only encouraged private business, it made it possible. But dyed-in-the-wool opponents of mercantilism like the French physiocrats François Quesnay and Victor de Mirabeau regarded the relationships among market variables like supply and demand as natural laws, like Newton's laws of gravitation and motion. They popularized the phrase *laissez faire* to capture the idea that all state interference was against natural law. The Scottish professor of moral economy Adam Smith, greatly influenced by the physiocrats, argued in his *Wealth of Nations* (1776) that only through free trade could the economy enjoy the full benefits of a people's productivity.

Free trade theory was not "value free." Quite the opposite: advocates of free trade based their case upon moral grounds. Free trade was good. Unnatural restrictions, regulation, and interference were bad because they denied producers the full rewards of their productivity. A little farther afield, market-based economics fit neatly into the movement for the political liberalization of the state in the eighteenth century. The logical tie between the demand for freer circulation of goods and the demand for more political participation could not be missed, and was not by critics of mercantilism like Benjamin Franklin. Franklin believed that the strength of the colonial economy lay not in its value to the British state, but in its return value to colonial workers. Only when they shared in the fruits of their labors would the empire be worthwhile. Economic oppression of the colonies by the home country thus could be made into a political issue, should colonial leaders wish to press the matter.

REGIONAL ECONOMIES

It is a misnomer of sorts to speak of "the colonial economy" as though the transatlantic trade was a single stream of commerce shaping all production and consumption in America. In fact, the colonies were not an integrated economic system at all, but a series of geographically distinct regional subsystems directly tied to the home countries. Few roads linked the colonies together, and none connected the western portions of the colonies. North-south travel was blocked by fast-moving rivers that flowed west to east. The same river systems directed trade from the hinterland to the coast within individual colonies.

Although each colony experimented with its own system of currency emission, regulation of prices and wages, and other economic policies, the proper unit of economic analysis is not the colony but the region. Regions like New England, the Middle Atlantic colonies, the tobacco colonies, the Carolinas, and the West Indies shared a common history, climate, labor use pattern, and marketing culture. Similarly, French Canada and the Spanish borderlands were internally integrated economic systems.

New England

New England's business leaders combined a strong sense of piety with a passion for enterprise. By 1750, the coastal cities of Salem, Boston, and Newport had grown and diversified, as merchants, bankers, and shipbuilders elaborated the basic economic strategy developed in the middle years of the seventeenth century.

The regional economy rested upon profits generated by the carrying trade (predominantly freight charges), shipbuilding, and exports of local produce and timber. Overall, the carrying trade, the sale of ships, and other charges to customers brought in at least £427,000 in an average year between 1768 and 1772. The returns of the coasting trade cannot be precisely determined, but they probably amounted to £300,000 per year. Were one to add earnings from smuggling between New England ports and French ports in Newfoundland to the official totals, they would nearly double.

The pattern of legal exports reveals the vitality of the New England–West Indian connection that London and Boston merchants fashioned in the 1660s and maintained for the next hundred years. Over half (£278,000 of £439,101) of the annual value of exports from New England in the years 1768 to 1772 went to the West Indies. New England shippers sold to French and other buyers in the islands as well as to British consumers. The largest item on the planters' shopping list was dried fish (£94,754 annual average), followed by livestock (£89,118), wood products (£57,769), whale products like candles and oils (£20,416), and cereal grains (£15,764). Indeed, almost all livestock, wood products, and grain exported from New England went to the West Indian market. West Indian demand kept New England's export trade afloat.

To a lesser extent, city merchants and craftspeople gained from consumer purchases in the city and the surrounding countryside. Population growth in the rural areas around leading New England towns had declined from seventeenth-century highs, but consumer demand for durables like tableware, furniture, and clothing in rural areas steadily increased. For farmers, income from market produce could not offset indebtedness, so they bartered their goods and services. Local tradesmen kept track of credit and debt in books. Although most of the shopkeepers were men, women often kept the books, and one of the exceptions to the general rule that women had little to do with courts of law were book debt cases. Courts gave full credence to women's testimony against recalcitrant debtors in such suits.

But as consumer goods from all over the Atlantic Rim flowed into New England, the arrangements for payment became more impersonal, distant, and formalized. Instead of owing a neighbor an afternoon or two in the apple orchard, one owed a fixed amount of money to a shop in Boston, or New Haven, which in turn owed money for its purchases to a firm in London, Bristol, or Glasgow. Such transactions involved forms of commercial paper that businesspeople understood but farmers found foreign. In the end, both sides needed lawyers to sort out disputes.

New England farmers responded to growing indebtedness by bringing more land under cultivation. More land meant larger farms and more produce, the latter allowing the family farmer, with good management and luck, to pay debts and put aside a little reserve. Developers looked west, along the upper reaches of the Connecticut River, to Deerfield and Northfield. They also moved north, into the coastal areas past Portsmouth, New Hampshire, and Portland, Maine. Kittery, Wells, and Bath, Maine, founded in the early seventeenth century, expanded to accommodate the internal migration. In Connecticut, settlers filled in the shore of Long Island Sound, moved west toward the Hudson River, and carved out farming communities amid the forests in the northwest of the colony.

But land expansion had its limits in New England, and they were soon felt. By midcentury, populations within long-settled towns had grown so dense that parents were no longer able to provide farms large enough for their children to support families. Thus New Englanders coming of age in the 1750s had the choice of migrating or finding work as laborers on others' lands. Working for someone else, which had once been a part of most young New Englanders' life cycle, became a permanent way of life for an agricultural underclass. In the meantime, New England land speculators cast longing eyes on the Wyoming Valley of Pennsylvania and the Ohio country.

Rhode Island's unique solution to the debt problem came after half a century of economic stagnation and political atrophy. At the end of the seventeenth century, under Governor Samuel Cranston, Rhode Islanders decided that all roads, literally, must lead to Newport. Deploying a system of farm subsidies and trade bounties, the colonial government subsidized the Newport merchants. The merchants became infamous for the risks they took investing in privateers and the avidity with which they entered into the business of slave trading.

Middle Atlantic Region

If overseas trade saved New England's economy, New York City and Philadelphia merchants so mastered the arts of commerce that British firms complained to Parliament about the competition. The region as a whole benefited from the entrepreneurship of the merchants, because they channeled the productivity of Long Island, the Hudson Valley, New Jersey, eastern Pennsylvania, and Delaware farmers into the Atlantic trading system. By the close of the colonial era, New York City and Philadelphia businessmen dominated a corridor of enterprise that extended from Baltimore in the South to the Saint Lawrence River in the North.

The Dutch and the Quakers laid the foundations for this pattern in the seventeenth century. Men like Peter Stuyvesant and William Penn understood the importance of trade and encouraged it. Immigrants to the region brought capital, which they invested in the cities and the surrounding agricultural areas. City merchants established a carrying trade, and coasters cleared both New York and Philadelphia for Hudson and Delaware River anchorages. More than half of the region's trade was with the West Indies or other American ports. Grain products (£379,380 per year from 1768 to 1772) exceeded twice the total of all other exports combined. The latter included flaxseed (for linens), wood products, iron, livestock, and potash.

Overall population grew so fast that Benjamin Franklin called the region the "American multiplication table." From 1700 to 1760, New York's population rose from 19,000 to 117,100; Pennsylvania's grew from 18,000 to 183,700; New Jersey's went from 14,000 to 93,800; and Delaware's expanded from 2,500 to 33,200. The slave portion of this increase in population from 3,700 to 29,000, was noticeable but not as significant as in the planter colonies. With rising population, the number of towns grew apace—in Pennsylvania, for example, three new towns appeared in the 1730s, eleven in the 1740s, sixteen in the 1750s, and twenty-two in the 1760s.

Economic opportunity in the cities and the surrounding countryside attracted immigrants. In 1710, the first of the Palatine Germans began arriving in New York City. Rhineland Germans filled Philadelphia after 1720. George I, himself a German from Hanover, and his successor, George II, opened the colonies to the émigrés. The Germans were soon joined by an influx of Scots-Irish migrants from Northern Ireland. Discriminated against by Anglicans (most of the Scots-Irish were members of dissenting sects) and oppressed by economic conditions at home, more than one hundred thousand of them would cross the ocean in the years 1713 to 1770.

Middle Atlantic cities of a few thousand in 1710 after 1720 bulged with thousands of new inhabitants, most of whom were young men looking for work. Slaves and indentured servants came as well, slaves predominating in New York City and indentured servants in Philadelphia. The latter's city leaders, watching with concern the growth of slavery in New York City, legislated a stiff importation fee on slaves.

The only break in the growth of the two cities came when the shipyards fell idle. So dependent were the two port cities on the shipping trade that downturns in that trade had a domino effect on the rest of the urban economy. The cities flourished when the farmers of the surrounding countryside had good harvests. So long as demand for grain and livestock overseas remained high, New Yorkers and Philadelphians reaped in the profits of foreign sales. When foreign markets could not absorb farm products and shipping sales faltered, however, the city economy staggered, as it did in New York in the later 1720s and early 1730s. Then the city's newspapers wailed, "our shipping are sunk." The ripple effect was frightening: "the baker, the brewer, the smith, the carpenter, the boat-man, the farmer, and the shop-keeper" went unemployed. But the cities always recovered. Philadelphia population rose from 13,000 people in 1743 to 23,750 in 1760. Over the same period, New York City went from 11,000 to 18,000, surging past Boston.

The rising population strained the functioning capacity of government and the physical infrastructure of the city to the limit. New York City and Philadelphia had borrowed the English model of a chartered private corporation. In the "closed" version of these corporations, the city council, the aldermen, the mayor, and the "recorder" (a part administrative, part legal officer) governed without elections. In 1731, New York City revised its charter to open elections of the alderman and councilors. The Pennsylvania assembly permitted substantial Philadelphia property holders (the minimum was a £50 taxable estate) to vote for "assessors" to join the council in setting tax rates. Even after opening their governments, the authorities in both cities had trouble collecting rents on city property, taxes, and fees.

As difficult as financing government proved for city councils, providing adequate public services raised even more problems. There were no zoning restrictions to control building. Rickety warehouses and elegant townhouses shared the same streets. Some of the former were literally thrown together and fell apart without warning.

Much of the new construction also posed fire hazards for which the cities were unprepared. Bucket brigades could not cope with the danger of sprawling expansion, particularly when warehouses contained gunpowder and other explosives. Worried city governments introduced regular fire companies, with eight men to a heavy iron pumper engine. Philadelphia put four new engines into service, but still depended upon volunteer "fire societies" to man the pumpers.

In part because of its open geometric design, with whole blocks set aside for greenery, Philadelphia had no major fires, inducing investors to organize a fire insurance company in February 1752. It was the first in the colonies. Naturally, Benjamin Franklin was a charter subscriber. New York deployed a fire company for each of its six wards, and the fire company captain had the authority to order private citizens to assist in time of emergency. Despite the companies' efforts, New York's densely packed, narrow streets suffered a series of major fires in the colonial era.

As the fire hazard reminded all concerned, the cities depended upon water reserves. The quality of drinking water presented more problems than the quantity of water for fire fighting. Private wells in New York City were brackish and germ ridden. Public water supply did not improve until 1753, when a new tax underwrote repairs and increased the number of city water pumps. Philadelphia, by contrast, had an excellent city water system.

In both cities, underground sewers drained the water, but the smell and the overspill from the sewers made certain street corners noxious. William Livingston, a New York City lawyer, cited one such nuisance at "Rotten Row," where "the putrid stink arising from that sink of corruption" rose into the neighborhood shops. In Philadelphia, the open sewer at Arch and Vine streets was an eyesore as well as an assault on the nostrils.

Porters, often slaves, carried human waste out of the city in tubs. It could not be trusted to the cities' leaky sewers. People dumped other refuse, including food slops, into the streets and alleys. Pigs roamed New York City and Philadelphia, consuming waste food, but hogs were as much a nuisance as an aid. New York City's sheriff had to notify homeowners and businesspeople that they were responsible for cleaning their own stoops and the leavings of their horses. City governments hired carters to sweep and remove trash, but the streets remained filthy.

Urban traffic was a nightmare. Runaway horses and wagons trampled the unwary pedestrian. Cartmen were notorious for their foul mouths and sometimes raced one another up and down crowded thoroughfares. In winter, there were sleigh accidents. Parking rules did not exist. The noise level kept residents awake well into the night, for the wagons bringing farmers' goods to market were iron-tired and howled like banshees.

Despite the noisy roads, merchants kept late hours in their street-front town-houses. Although the elegant furnishings and bright spaciousness of their dwellings impressed visitors and clients, the merchants' eyes were focused on their ledgers. The good merchant sought the outward appearance of caution, reliability, and pru-dence—in short, trustworthiness. The last quality was essential, for every merchant had debts, and creditors looked to the reputation of prospective borrowers. Bank-ruptcy was not only financially damaging, it was psychologically mortifying. Mer-chants were also lenders—creating a network of reciprocal credit and debt. A few merchants came from families with extensive land holdings, but the vast majority were the sons and siblings of other merchants, including Welsh, Scottish, French Huguenot, and Jewish immigrants. Such merchants manipulated marriage and family to further their interests.

King George's War and the French and Indian War brought mixed blessings to the New York City and Philadelphia merchants and the people who depended upon trade for their livelihoods. Unlike Boston, whose sacrifices to the war effort included thousands of dead from dysentery, burdensome taxes, a collapsing currency, and runaway inflation, New York City and Philadelphia prospered from the wars of em-pire.

New York City emerged as the privateer capital of North America—the point of origin for attacks on French shipping and the point of return for captured ("prize of war") ships. During King George's War, the value of these prizes exceeded £600,000. Jostling with the "legal" privateers in the harbor were scores of ships engaged in il-licit trade with the enemy. Philadelphia did not get rich on King George's War, for Quaker merchants refused to participate in the privateering business, but the in-creased demand for bread and meat in the British West Indies brought extravagant profits to suppliers.

As in New England, the regions around the middle colony cities played a vital role in their growth, for the presence of the cities gave farmers an outlet for their sur-pluses. In eastern Pennsylvania, yearly profits from the average family farm (with five people) averaged £40 on an investment of £60. From 1717 to 1751, overall personal estates rose in value by 23 percent.

Satellite market centers, for example, Bristol in Bucks County, grew out of these investments. There, local merchants and tradesmen doubled as brokers and bankers, and innkeepers and tavern keepers provided their own specialized services. Ironmongers and gristmill operators utilized the fast-flowing streams of the area to power their mills, in turn making it cheaper for farmers to buy nails and have their wheat ground. In this way, the investment in land and crops had a "multiplier" effect, spawning small pockets of industry and creating more jobs.

The Upper South

The upper South's economy still depended on tobacco. The price of tobacco had fallen sharply in the years 1622 to 1680, and planters had responded by bringing more and more land under cultivation. In time, improved techniques allowed planters to cut their costs, raising the profit margin as the price of the crop fell, but the mounting expense of labor and the exhaustion of Tidewater lands caused the tobacco industry to stall from the 1680s through the 1710s.

By the middle of the eighteenth century, the return on tobacco once again fully justified the planters' reliance on it as their staple crop. Prices stabilized and rose slightly by 1760 to two pence per pound. More important, from 1710 to 1770 planters quadrupled their tobacco exports to Great Britain, an increase in gross weight from twenty-five million pounds to one hundred million pounds. In 1733, tobacco exports from Virginia were worth £121,078. By 1773, this figure had grown to £337,391.

Some planters had assayed a different solution to the problems of single-crop agriculture. Chesapeake farmers had always grown corn to feed themselves and their livestock, but in the middle of the 1700s planters began to grow wheat and corn for export. The new export crops spurred ancillary businesses, like gristmilling, and put farmhands to work at times of the year when tobacco cultivation was slack. The value of exported wheat and grain products like bread rose even more spectacularly than tobacco in the years 1713 to 1770, from £9,447 to £145,360.

Variations in prices and demand over which they had no control taught planters that they needed help from government. At first, leading planters sitting in the legislature urged limitation of production. Later statutes inaugurated inspection systems, grading, and bonuses for first quality tobacco, which eased some problems but exacerbated others. Attempts to use legislative action to lessen debts to foreign merchants failed—the Privy Council protected the English and Scottish merchants who lent money to Chesapeake planters. And in fact such loans were essential— without them the planters lacked the capital for expansion of their operations. But what the merchants reckoned as easy credit the planters regarded as loathsome and unmanly debt.

Planters invested so much of their capital in their labor force and land acquisition that little was left for city building. With the exceptions of Norfolk and Baltimore, each having about six thousand inhabitants in 1770, there were no upper South cities. Williamsburg had but two thousand people and Annapolis, the capital of

Maryland, but thirty-two hundred. Geography also conspired against the growth of port cities in the upper South, for planters relied on the extensive river system that fed the Chesapeake to get their goods to market.

Despite the absence of cities and the reliance on bound labor, the tobacco colonies experienced striking population growth in the eighteenth century. For example, in 1704 Maryland's population numbered 30,673. In 1755, it was 107,209. Much of this increase can be attributed to the importation of slaves; but free farmers and their families increased even faster than the number of slaves. From 1700 to 1760, Chesapeake's slave population rose from 12,900 to 189,600. Its free population rose over the same years from 85,200 to 312,400.

The Lower South

The Carolina coastal planters were even more aggressively capitalistic and innovative than the tobacco-colony planters, adapting semitropical crops like rice and indigo, turning marshy coastal land into profitable agricultural enterprises, and building a city, Charleston, that rivaled northern ports in business volume and population.

Unlike tobacco prices, rice prices rose steadily throughout the eighteenth century. In the years 1768 to 1772, rice exports led all other low-country staples in value, amounting to £305,533. Of this total, £198,590 worth went to Great Britain, while southern Europe and the West Indies split the remainder. By another measure, pounds of rice produced per inhabitant, the colony exported 69 pounds per capita in 1700, 380 pounds per capita in 1720, and 900 pounds per capita in 1740. The average field hand harvested over 2,000 pounds of rice a year.

Enumerated exports like indigo (£111,864 annual value per year from 1768 to 1772), deerskins (£37,093), and naval stores (£31,709) had to be delivered to Great Britain. Indigo dye from Jamaica and the French sugar islands had a ready market in England, but King George's War cut off the supplies. Carolina indigo growers received a parliamentary bounty of six pence per pound. After the war, the bounty was lowered, but Carolina continued to produce the crop profitably. The deerskin trade had no external rivals, but the supply of deerskins declined as Indians reduced the herds to near extinction. Naval stores (pitch, tar, resin, hemp, masts, yardarms, and planking) had once been a mainstay of the infant colony. In the mid-1720s, Charleston exported over 60,000 barrels of pitch and tar a year. The export declined in value after 1724 because Carolina workers could not satisfy the admiralty's standard of quality.

The prosperity of the export trade caused a substantial rise in the free population, but free persons found themselves in a sea of imported African slaves. By 1730, South Carolina imported over 2,000 slaves per year. By 1740, the colony's population ratio was 2.6 slaves to one free person.

The similarity between the southern Carolina coast and the sugar islands is striking, even though Carolina planters were not absentee landlords like their Caribbean counterparts and in Carolina small family farms dominated the uplands. A last difference favored South Carolina's economic fortunes. The sugar islands were graveyards for slaves, absorbing as many as the slave trade could bring. Although it was unhealthy for slaves, South Carolina slaves lived long enough to produce children who could be put to work or sold.

The experience of the French Huguenots, a group of immigrants initially excluded from Carolina political life, was the opposite of the Africans'. Fleeing to the colony to escape persecution for their Protestant religious beliefs in the 1680s and 1690s, the Huguenots encountered fierce discrimination in their adopted home. They tried to raise silk and grow wine grapes, and failed miserably. Although they became naturalized citizens after 1697, the Huguenots still faced ridicule. In response, the Huguenots followed the same path as the Dutch in New York. They intermarried with the dominant English families, carried on their business and social life in English, and gradually abandoned French-language worship services.

Equally important for their assimilation into the Anglican culture, Huguenots became avid slaveholders and rice growers. Daniel Huger's plantation in Saint John's Parish had one of the largest concentrations of slave laborers in North America. Numbers of Huguenots invested in the slave trade. John Gerard, for example, became one of Charleston's leading slave merchants, and other wealthy Huguenots like Gabriel and Peter Manigault, Solomon Légaré Jr., and the brothers David and John Deas prospered in the slave trade. Not every Huguenot family achieved economic prominence, but those who did modeled themselves upon the English.

The Sugar Islands

However harshly one judges the conditions of bound labor on the sugar islands of the West Indies, contemporaries regarded the British possessions of Jamaica and Barbados, along with the smaller islands, as the most valuable colonies in the empire. The islands' markets for timber, livestock, and grain from the mainland colonies sustained the colonies' export economies, and sugar, rum, and molasses from the islands made a fortune for importers and manufacturers.

The price of sugar remained stable in the eighteenth century, but sugar exports to London rose from thirty million pounds in 1700 to over one hundred million pounds by 1760. In the years 1768 to 1772, the islands annually exported £3,002,750 worth of sugar and £350,700 worth of rum to the British Isles and £183,700 worth of sugar and £333,337 of rum to the mainland colonies.

In the early part of the century, the rising cost of slave labor and the stability of sugar prices caught the planters in a bind, but they increased production and found new customers by 1750. They had help—the "sugar interest" in London, composed of absentee sugar planters, lobbied Parliament to keep customs duties low. In fact, they rose 600 percent from 1660 to 1770, but the British Caribbean growers' monopoly on the British market, enforced by the Molasses Act of 1733 (one of the Navigation Acts), more than compensated for the rise in customs duties. Although the planters' efforts to snuff out the trade between the mainland colonies and the French sugar islands failed, there is no evidence that the importation of French molasses reduced demand for the English product.

The Backcountry

The backcountry was the most amorphous region of the colonial economy. It stretched in a huge arc from the Canadian Shield into western New York, Pennsylvania, and Virginia; over the Piedmont country of the Carolinas; down the river systems that drained the Creek lands in Georgia and Alabama; to the Gulf of Mexico. On the European side lay dispersed settlements of subsistence farmers, trappers, and traders. On the native side lived the new tribal configurations of Indians thrown together in the wake of the European onslaught. The Europeans, thus far, were few; the Indians were many, having recovered some of their numbers from the epidemic years.

Although the farmers on the European side of the frontier consumed almost all that they grew, their very presence on the land made them a vital part of the commercial world. True, some farmers were "squatters," having no title or claim to their farmsteads, but most came west under arrangements with land developers and land speculators.

Land speculation—buying or obtaining through government grants large tracts of undeveloped land and selling it to would-be cultivators—was a passion among merchants, government officials, planters, and just about everyone who had money or credit. Land speculation entailed risks—for speculators borrowed to purchase the tracts, attract the farmers, and outfit the expeditions. In addition, there was no cushion of reputation to soften the fall for frontier land speculators facing bankruptcy as there was for the coastal merchants, for land speculation in the West was a cutthroat business. Debtors who could not hold off their creditors went to prison, a fate that overtook some of the most prominent Americans.

But by opening up western farmlands, frontier farmers and land speculators generated an investment opportunity for eastern and European businessmen. The capital pumped into the economy by these investments, redistributed to other economic activities, had a multiplier effect.

Beyond the farmsteads, the frontier exchange system recapitulated the culture of the seventeenth-century fur trade, but the seepage of European hunters and farmers into the fertile valleys west of the Appalachians hastened the demise of the game and pushed the deer and beaver hunt farther west. In the Ohio Valley, trade was still the name of the game—the Indians playing off the European traders against one another the way that buyers at a mall visit different shops looking for bargains and retailers watch their competitors like hawks.

Tribes like the Ojibwas and Sioux in the North, who had sporadic contact with

Europeans, were pulled into the orbit of the trade, while long-established trading partners of the Europeans like the Cherokees of the Piedmont and the Senecas of western New York faced chronic shortages of commodities of the hunt to swap for European goods. If trade with the imperial powers lagged in some regions, an exchange economy continued to link Indian peoples with one another. In the Southwest, for example, barter of skins and meat for garden produce and pottery continued much as it had for a thousand years.

European traders bound for the frontier packed their horses and mules with red and purple blankets and shirts, tools for cooking and gardening like pots and hoes, and sewing ware like needles, thread, scissors, lace, calico, linen, and buttons. The demand for domestic goods strongly suggests that women's preferences comprised a significant motive for trade on the Indian side. European wearing apparel gained in trade or as a gift adorned Indians going to war, celebrating marriage, and solemnizing funerals, taking the place of more traditional Indian gift goods during these ceremonies.

The traders knew this firsthand, for many of them had taken Indian wives and lived for part of the year among the Indians. The male offspring of the unions of Europeans and Indians became important figures in the trade, and later in the politics of the frontier, though they faced the enmity of Indians who clung to traditional ways and the distrust of Europeans.

The Canadian Riddle

The French Canadian economy at midcentury presents a riddle. Rich in resources, the region stagnated relative to its Anglo-American neighbors. It may be that sparse settlement, harsh climate, and short growing seasons reduced the yield of Canadian farms and that some of the region's trade was drained off by illegal trafficking with New York and New England. France invested less in its Atlantic Canadian provinces than England did in its own colonies. The devastation of the colonial wars slowed the Canadian economy, particularly when the English stormed Louisbourg in 1745. But all of these problems, including the dislocations of the war, affected Britain's northern colonies as well, without derailing their productivity.

Governors-general in Quebec complained to the crown about the cost of gifts and food and supplies to the Indians, but the Indian alliance system that protected the Canadian interior was spectacularly cost effective. Indian-related expenditures accounted for only one-fourth of the total bill of the province's defense, and equivalent numbers of regular French troops would have cost four times more.

Looking more closely at a single Canadian industry, one can see that competition for furs with the Hudson's Bay Company to the north may have reduced the value of the French fur trade, as did the progressive decline of the beaver population. As the fur frontier moved west, the cost to bring each pelt to the market increased, reducing profit margins. In fact, the fur trade not only dragged down the overall economy, it had a negative growth rate for long stretches of time in the first half of the eighteenth century. But the fur trade was only 13.5 percent of the output of the colony, so problems in the fur trade cannot explain the slow development of the Canadian economy as a whole.

Historians have suggested another explanation which rests on cultural rather than economic considerations. It may be that the habitants and their Indian trading partners lacked the quasi-religious attachment to material success and profit that animated their English counterparts. As one visitor to Canada wrote early in the century, "you meet with no rich men in this country." Even the nobility, whose wardrobes included imported lace and jewelry, did not care for business. For example, land speculation, so vital a part of economic growth in the English colonies, did not play a role in French Canadian development because the aristocratic owners did not trade, sell, or, in short, "commodify" their land grants. Roman Catholicism, with its strong sense of moral order, curbed exploitation of Indian and peasant workers; no one could use them as the English planter colonists employed their slaves.

There are other possible cultural explanations for the sluggish commercial growth of French Canada. Literacy remained comparatively rare among the French habitants, which prevented them from entering into complex market transactions. The same tendencies that blunted the land market and pervaded religious life tended to dampen general intellectual activity. At any rate, "high end" economic activities like banking, large-scale manufacturing, and overseas trade remained in the hands of French, rather than French Canadian, entrepreneurs.

The Spanish Borderlands

If the economy of French Canada seemed stagnant, business on the Spanish borderlands was treacherous. As the king's military adviser in the region wrote in 1768, after touring the frontier, "the tremendous damage His Majesty's subjects suffer daily from the barbarians," meaning the Apaches, Comanches, and other native raiders, often brought commerce to a standstill. Presidios and garrisons of soldiers had replaced missions and Franciscans as the advance agents of Spanish civilization. The crown expected these troops to dress, parade, and comport themselves in European fashion, almost impossible in the circumstances the garrisons faced. Even the weapons—long lances and slow-firing muskets—were inappropriate for fending off mounted Indian raiders. A new book of regulations in 1772, more extensive fortifications, more troops, and periodic inspections did not prevent the raids.

Still, for a people whose predecessors brought the motto *más allá* (onward) to the American West, the raids were an obstacle, not an insuperable barrier to economic progress. Though isolated from the rest of the empire (supplies sometimes took four years to reach Santa Fe), the Spanish of New Mexico exploited established Indian trading patterns to obtain buffalo hides. More important, expanding their grip of the Southwest to include Texas in the early eighteenth century, the Spanish, along with converts from Cuba and Mexico, created a cattle frontier.

Although Columbus brought cattle to Hispaniola in 1494, and they roamed on all the Spanish Caribbean islands, the cattle herds of the Southwest dwarfed all others. It was simply a matter of space and pasturage. The plan for cattle rancheros originated in the plains of central Spain and evolved in the semiarid wilderness of the Southwest. The Spanish adapted Moorish techniques of horsemanship—for example, shifting from the heavy cavalry saddle to the lighter Moorish *jineta*. The vaqueros (cowboys) of the Southwest learned to ride in the brush and up and down the banks of the arroyos as well as on the grasslands, literally living on their horses.

On the llanos, they bred the "longhorn," tough, rangy cattle able to survive the long, hot summers of the Southwest. The ranchers exported some of the animals, but like rural Connecticut and western Virginia farmers, consumed most of what they produced. Although the Indians poached cattle and harried the rancheros in southern Arizona, they allowed the ranches to expand along the San Antonio River valley in Texas. The Apaches even agreed to a peace ceremony of sorts, literally burying a lance, six arrows, and a live horse in the plaza at San Antonio de Bejár in 1749.

Clandestine Economies

Some economic activities produce income illegally, through black markets or smuggling. One might say that the latter activity had become a way of life in the eighteenth-century colonies. In 1725, nearly fifty years after Edward Randolph revealed the secrets of New England smugglers to the customs officials in England, the surveyor general of customs in Boston was still pleading with authorities in England for help. New Englanders made small fortunes sneaking Dutch linens and French brandies ashore. Worse than the occasional surreptitious landing, New Englanders blatantly ignored the customs duties the Navigation Acts mandated.

Two figures are revealing. Between 1738 and 1750, legal importers of foreign molasses paid £5,603 in duties, while smugglers lost £7,616 in confiscated ships and cargoes. After 1763, when the duties on imports of molasses from non-English ports were set equal to the duty on molasses from Jamaica and Barbados, and there was no longer any advantage to the latter, the amount of foreign molasses mainland importers declared rose from 2,824,060 gallons to 4,878,794 gallons. The numbers speak for themselves: before the equalization of duties, British colonial importers must have brought 2,000,000 gallons of illegal molasses into colonial ports.

Customs officials begged for additional manpower, but Parliament dragged its feet. No effort was made to increase the customs service appropriation, though additional searchers were added in the new colony of Georgia, and resident collectors were sent to ports in Maryland, North Carolina, and New Jersey. Collectors' salaries still ran between £40 and £80 a year, plus a portion of condemned ships and cargoes.

The temptation to accept a bribe and look the other way induced many collectors to fail in their duties.

Smuggling may have been the most lucrative clandestine business, but it was not the only one. Ordinary crimes against property flourished in all the colonial cities. In addition to pilfering, picking pockets, and petty theft, colonial criminals counterfeited paper money, "clipped" coins, and forged commercial bills of exchange and promissory notes. Warehouses and piers in port cities presented attractive targets for gangs of thieves. Criminal court records suggest that most convicts were not professionals and that there was no criminal underclass, although some offenders seem to have been well known to the courts. Over 90 percent of the accused were young, poor white males. Women rarely were "principals" in serious crimes against property but participated in crime rings as lookouts, and as harborers of thieves and their booty. Without organized police forces, merchants had to hire guards. Crime rates fell only during wartime, when many young men were away.

WORK

One's job was a source of identity among free colonists. The vast majority worked on farms, but the typical colonist had more than one occupation. Farmers and planters opened retail stores. Field hands doubled as skilled workers in carpentry and smithing. Schoolteachers did odd jobs. Midwives were also herbalists, nurses, and counselors. Farmwives and daughters doubled as seamstresses, weavers, spinners, and horticulturalists. Lawyers, doctors, and job printers rarely depended solely upon their practices to pay their bills. Ministers taught school, ran farms, and sold books to make ends meet. Only a few occupations required the exclusive attention of their practitioners, though merchants, surveyors, and mariners, when fully employed, had to devote all their time to their work.

Over the years 1660 to 1760, the pace of work in the colonies accelerated and intensified. Throughout the British colonies, families abandoned the traditional English five-hour workday in favor of an eight- to ten-hour day. As planters diversified their crops, older seasonal cycles of labor and rest gave way to year-round enterprise. The increasing availability of attractive consumer items (a subject of the next section of this chapter) provided an incentive for the extended workday, and the signs of the new commitment to work were everywhere. One telling example: in New England, farmers shifted from slow but cheap teams of oxen to more expensive but faster horses to pull plows and wagons.

Gendered Workplaces

By and large, women and men worked apart and in different sectors of the economy. For example, women rarely went to sea and never practiced law, though they might be "attorneys" representing another layperson in court. Free women rarely worked in the tobacco fields, even in the poorest of families. Men worked alone more than women, or in groups of fathers and sons, servants, and apprentices. Women generally worked in or near the home, often with their daughters or mothers and other women. A much smaller number of women worked in the marketplace, running businesses like taverns and shops, most often under licenses originally granted to their husbands. When husbands or fathers were away, women acted as surrogates.

The interaction of men and women both supported the separation of their spheres and allowed the domestic economy to flourish. Without the contribution of the women, farms would fail. In rural New England, for example, women weeded the flax that the men planted and harvested. In the home, groups of women combed, spun, wove, bleached, and sewed flax into linens. Men cut and stacked the firewood; women drew the water and kept the pot boiling over the hearth fire. Men butchered the livestock, but women dressed, salted, and cooked the meat. Although more clothing was bought than made at home, women altered and repaired store-bought goods and made shifts and petticoats, aprons and jackets, from rags and discards.

The products of the domestic economy not only supplemented family income, they comprised a microeconomy. In this local exchange system, a woman's skills and experience profited her. An able midwife or seamstress had greater purchasing power than a house servant or washerwoman. But the limitations of the domestic economy still applied—even the woman who ran a tavern or a farm on her own earned less than a comparably situated man. As a result, men owned 90 percent of the wealth.

An examination of women's wills and estates reaffirms this imbalance of wealth. (Only those better-off had estates to leave, so the following data reflect the upper half of colonial society.) In Essex County, Massachusetts, from 1660 to 1673, women were 9 percent of those who left wills to be probated by the courts, but their property only amounted to 4.3 percent of the total left by testators (people who wrote wills). In Tidewater Virginia, from 1660 to 1676, women were 3 percent of the testators, but their property amounted to 1.4 percent of the total. In the same region, from 1724 to 1729, women were 9.4 percent of those who left wills, but they held only 6.1 percent of the property. In early-eighteenth-century Bucks County, Pennsylvania, women left 9.5 percent of the wills but had only 5.3 percent of the property to distribute.

Crafts and Trades

Most householders had to engage in a wide variety of chores, but colonists hired master craftsmen for finished or fine work. Rural villages could usually boast at least one carpenter, sawyer, joiner, cooper, weaver, tailor, tanner or shoemaker, and blacksmith. A first-rate craftsman could always find a job.

Rural artisans opened shop early and closed early, relying upon natural light for their work. Although "bespoke" (preordered) goods were the rule, and specialized artisans like gunsmiths might take months to finish a single item, most craftsmen used shortcuts to manufacture as much as they could as fast as possible. Nails and glue sufficed where joints were hidden from view, and paint concealed defects in wood.

In the cities, craftsmen of a particular type often lived in the same neighborhood. Germantown, Pennsylvania, just north and west of Philadelphia, became known for its stockings, and turned out seventy thousand pair a year. Lynn, Massachusetts, shoemakers were almost as prolific. In Norwich, Connecticut, candy makers cooked up five thousand pounds of chocolate each year.

The most respected and wealthy craftsmen, including silversmiths, goldsmiths, and printers, mingled with the elite of provincial society, while at the lower end of the scale, tailors, weavers, and sailors were members of the proletariat. Women who worked in the clothing trades as spinners, seamstresses, and milliners always had lower status than men in comparable jobs. Apprentices got small wages and "found" (room and board) and if they had a family had to struggle to make ends meet. The craftsman who got lucky or was exceptionally skilled might become a businessman. While his apprentices did the rough work, he finished jobs, visited customers, and solicited new business.

A few people had to travel far from home to earn a living. Sailors, fishermen, land surveyors, woodcutters, and rural peddlers had to leave home to work. Men of the sea always stood out in a crowd of "lubbers." The mariner's trade was the most dangerous in the colonies, and sailors ashore looked wrinkled and leathery, whatever their age. Many were tattooed or wore jewelry. Like fishermen, ocean sailors never made much money and spent much of their pay in the first few days in port.

The Professions

If the sailors' dress and manners worried townspeople, popular response to lawyers was even sourer. As a group, lawyers were vilified, though particular lawyers might be much in demand, for increasing numbers of disputatious Americans were asking lawyers for counsel. Consumer demand raised the prominence of the legal profession. Increased litigation in the 1720s and 1730s surrounding the introduction of commercial paper and more complicated economic transactions made lawyering lucrative and attracted able young men. Women were not accepted as apprentices in lawyers' offices, nor were they licensed to practice law for fees.

Once engaged by parties to a suit, the lawyers introduced more formal language, including the arcane formulas of English common law pleading, to American courts. Lawyers manipulated technical pleading not only to further their clients' interests but also to establish the indispensability of the legal profession. Lawyers' pay was based on legislated fee schedules—a certain sum for each writ prepared and submitted to the courts. The result was the prolongation of litigation, as lawyers opposing one another filed more and more paper with the courts.

American lawyers trained themselves by "reading" law as clerks and juniors in established lawyers' chambers or offices. Some lawyers—for example, Joseph Hawley in Massachusetts, William Smith Sr. in New York, James Alexander in New Jersey, John Dickinson in Pennsylvania, Samuel Chase in Maryland, and George Wythe in Virginia—were sought-after law teachers. Many law students found their apprenticeship intellectually deadening, however. John Adams, who slogged through years of apprenticeship before being admitted to practice himself, filled his diary with complaints about the silly pedantry of the one- and two-hundred-year-old English law books he had to memorize.

Adams deplored mindless legal education, but young lawyers like Adams were very professional and had no use for unprofessional conduct or inferior ability. William Livingston attacked the governors of New York for acting as chancellors of the court of chancery because "very few instances can be assigned of their having been bred to the Profession, or Study of the Law; without a considerable Knowledge of which, it is impossible any man can be qualified for the important Office of a Chancellor." As we have seen, the colonial high court judge was often less educated than the men who practiced in his court.

Unlike the lawyers, whose professional expertise and personal status rose together, colonial doctors came from all social classes. There were no medical schools in the colonies, but some physicians had training in Edinburgh, London, or on the Continent. Doctors doubled as bonesetters, bleeders (they used leeches), and prescribers of all sorts of home remedies. Some leading physicians advocated "heroic" treatment of ailments, giving their unwary patients toxic purgatives and emetics like the jalap root and the poisonous mercury derivative calomel.

Manuals of good health were popular reading, offering advice on exercise, diet, and "female problems." Women still birthed most children without the help of doctors, and midwives doubled as nurses, herbalists, and health counselors (though doctors began to displace midwives in the mid-eighteenth century). Tobacco was a favorite folk cure-all, and when all else failed people turned to the opiate derivative laudanum.

Clergymen were always in short supply in the colonies, even in the well-established Anglican, Congregationalist, Presbyterian, and Dutch Reformed faiths. The amazing flowering of Baptist churches after the middle of the eighteenth century, added to the growth of Lutheran and German Reformed congregations, increased the demand but not the supply of ministers. Congregations divided over whom to choose to lead them, and, after a minister was selected, fussed and fumed over his personality, or his sermons, or his approach to church discipline, causing endless headaches for the pastors. In addition, charlatans, prophets, and fly-by-nights obtained pulpits and brought disrepute on the profession.

Stabilizing elements like synods and clerical societies restored some order. So did powerful individuals like James Blair, the Anglican commissary of Virginia. Blair worked assiduously to gain job security for Anglican pastors in the colony. With his help, the status of Virginia's ministers rose, and by 1726 over half of the clergymen had gone to college. Maryland Anglicans earned nearly £200 a year, an inducement that raised the quality of ministerial applicant. Colonial colleges like Harvard and Yale, and later the College of New Jersey and Kings College, trained generations of ministers, many of whom not only found preaching a respected calling, but became leading figures in their communities.

Even with the assurance of a pulpit and the aid of a college education, many ministers faltered when confronted with the exhausting daily rounds of riding circuit, holding services at chapels of ease in rural areas and in private homes as well as in churches. Southern itinerant preachers traveled hundreds of miles and slept in rude log cabins ministering to their scattered flocks. Even in settled congregations, churches were drafty, rectories needed repairs, and congregations proved stingy.

Pastors of German Lutheran and Reformed churches faced a special set of problems. Not only did they have the usual internal difficulties like contentious congregants and backbiting among the ministers, they had to adjust to the surrounding English culture, in many ways more tolerant and liberal than the traditions they left behind in Germany. Ministers like Henry Muhlenberg adapted well to the American pulpit only to find themselves criticized for their Anglicized ways by more recently arrived colleagues.

Bound Labor

At the opposite end of the spectrum from the professions, bound labor comprised more than half of the American workforce. In the eighteenth century, indentured servants still came to the colonies in large numbers, many from Scotland and Northern Ireland. Hungry or in debt, whole families and villages agreed to sell their labor for a term to pay for the cost of transshipment to America. Immigration agents who recruited these bound laborers promised them a land of milk and honey. When the new immigrants arrived, they found only marginally better conditions than those they had left. Finished with their contractual duties, they removed themselves to the frontiers of the colonies.

Attempts by colonial employers to enforce on indentured servants the fourteenth-century English Statutes of Artificers failed. These English laws empowered magistrates to imprison workers who left their jobs before their contract period had expired. But the statutes were based upon a conception of labor as a personal, not a contractual or market, relationship, and the market/contract system had taken hold very early on in America. Thus workers who left their jobs here faced suits for nonperformance rather than jail time.

From 1718 until 1775, over fifty thousand convicts came to the colonies as indentured servants under the Transportation Act of 1718. Felons had to agree to be "transported" to the colonies, but the alternative, imprisonment in one of England's filthy jails or on the prison hulks in the Thames, was unattractive. Fully 70 percent of London's felons agreed to chance the voyage. Penal servitude imposed terms of seven or fourteen years, depending upon the severity of the crimes. At debarkation, agents for colonial planters or independent labor jobbers purchased the convicts' labor and sold it to bidders at auction when the convicts arrived in the colonies.

The biggest markets for convict laborers were in the plantation colonies, where 80 percent of the transportees became field hands. Many of the convicts were felons or gang members, but others were Irish and English agricultural workers who violently protested against the horrific conditions of their class. Even though few transported convicts committed crimes in the colonies, planters constantly complained about the bad influence convicts might have on other servants and slaves. After they served their term, most returned to England. Running away to England before completion of the term of service could bring the death penalty.

By far the largest class of bound laborers were chattel slaves. As indentured servants never hesitated to point out to their masters, Anglo-American servitude differed completely from slavery. Quakers like Anthony Benezet and Puritans like Samuel Sewall, along with a handful of ministers, lobbied for an end to slavery, but in the main the Protestant denominations countenanced the owning and trading of slaves. By 1770, slaves constituted fully one-third of the population of the British American colonies. What was more, both the internal and the external (overseas) slave trades contributed profits to the home country's economy.

Slave labor cost less than free labor, but not because every slave was ill fed, poorly housed, or denied clothing. Most slaves ate, wore clothing, and lived in housing about as good as that of the poorest segment of the free society. Slaves cost less because the master got more work out of them than the employer could have gotten from free labor, despite the long chain of complaints masters made about their lazy and unreliable slaves. Equally important, unlike free labor, slaves could not bargain for higher wages in planting and harvesting seasons. Nor did slaves compete with the master—for example, in bringing new land into cultivation or producing crops for the market. Finally, the slaves themselves added to the value of slavery by having children who became slave laborers.

From the West Indies to the colonies of Virginia and Maryland, slave women worked primarily in the fields, often performing the most onerous and mind-numbing tasks. A few served as house servants. Slave men not only worked the fields, they became blacksmiths, carpenters, herdsmen, stablemen, stevedores, haulers, loggers, and "pioneers." As one advertisement for a runaway slave in Virginia proclaimed, "the Negro fellow name Bob" was "an extraordinary sawyer, a tolerable carpenter and currier, pretends to make shoes, and is a very good sailor." On the plantation, slave men could rise to the rank of "drivers," supervising other slaves in the performance of their tasks. In sum, the work experience of slave men was far more varied and interesting than that of slave women.

Slaves labored under different conditions in the northern colonies. Although there were many slaves in northern port cities like Philadelphia, New York City, and Newport (indeed, nearly 10 percent of the population), few worked on northern farms. The growing season in the North was too short for farmers to invest in the year-round expense of slaves. Slave women worked in the home, cleaning, cooking, nursing, and caring for children, far less onerous tasks than their sisters performed in the plantation colonies. Slave men worked alongside free men in shops, on the docks, and as garbage haulers and baggage carriers. A number of slaves served as mariners. Slaves were not a vital part of the northern workforce, although they were highly visible, and their presence caused free laborers to resent the competition.

A CONSUMING RAGE

Slaves were consumers but had no buying power—that is, their remuneration was in kind. Had they been paid wages and been free to purchase goods and services in the market, they would have taken part in a veritable revolution in consumption that swept over the colonies in the middle of the eighteenth century. As important as productivity might be to the colonists' place in their empires, consumption enabled Americans to enjoy the benefits of their own labor. Indeed, one may say that colonial consumption of imported goods gave the eighteenth-century empires their distinctive materialistic character.

A fever of consumption roared through the English colonies in midcentury. From 1750 to 1773, importation of English consumer goods—perishables (groceries) and durables (everything from massive mahogany tables to delicate teacups)—increased over 120 percent. Everyone up and down the social ladder engaged in the rage to buy, use, and display the widening array of consumer goods. Colonists spent about 20 percent more of their yearly income on the purchase of imports from Great Britain in the years 1750 to 1770 than their grandparents had fifty years earlier. Newspapers, featuring advertisements for an increasingly varied array of imports, boosted their own sales on the same swelling tide of consumerism. The number of newspapers in the colonies skyrocketed from three to twenty-one between 1720 and 1760. The new imports had to be displayed in the home—and that meant sales of cabinets and chests with glass doors. Everyone who was anyone had to have gloves, and every well-to-do home flaunted its new carpets and curtains. Peddlers carried a smaller selection to backcountry stores—but even the pioneers loved their buckles, buttons, and brass ornaments. New terms like *conveniences* and *fashion* became the watchwords of buyers and sellers.

Buying

The upper tiers of colonial society carried on the vast bulk of the buying. But the demand to own and display durables was itself so compelling that a new category of society was created—the consumer class. These men and women had the credit and the cash to shop, and their "fancy" caused shopkeepers to press their suppliers for seasonal inventories. Winter goods had to be in stock by late summer, and summer goods by early spring. Pattern books and pattern cards to facilitate selection became standard items.

Eighteenth-century English essayists, ministers, and political leaders condemned conspicuous consumption, the purchase of goods simply to display them. Critics linked the craving for personal luxury to public misconduct and private mischief. Yet at the same time, observers glorified production, for manufacturing and selling goods to the colonies ensured that mercantilism turned a profit. Thus the irony: no one doubted that consumer purchases of woolens, lead, glass, beer, furniture, tableware, and other durables, along with comestibles like sugar, coffee, and tea, pumped up the English economy, but moralists sniffed at any untoward display of wealth. It may be that there was some social class–based snobbery in this, for increasing lower-middle-class consumption of groceries and acquisition of household goods was a kind of social leveler. If anyone could afford to enjoy sugar candies and serve tea from a porcelain pot, what distinguished the better sort from the rabble?

Americans seem to have had fewer compunctions about consumption than the English. Contemporary observers remarked on the avidity of American buying habits and the increasing variety of household goods displayed in American homes. Indeed, novelty itself motivated American purchasing habits, as retailers urged customers to try on the latest fashions, browse latest books, and subscribe to the most recently arrived newspapers and magazines.

The number one item on the shopping list was clothing. Most colonists wore simple dress during the working day—woolens, leather, linens, and some cottons—but these garments were not usually homespun. Americans imported more woolens and linens than they produced or purchased domestically. All silk and lace came from abroad. Ten percent of the per capita yearly budget of the average American went for imported apparel.

Although almost all the colonies could feed themselves, groceries comprised the second largest import. In some regions of the colonies, notably the West Indies, cereal products and meat had to be imported. The mainland colonists depended upon foreign suppliers for tea, coffee, condiments like salt and sugar, and most spices. Although the colonists distilled spirits and brewed beer, most fermented drinks, including wines and fortified wines, came in the holds of ships. Colonists drank more homemade cider and milk than hard liquors and wines, but imported inebriants graced every well-laid table by the 1750s.

All told, colonists devoted perhaps as much as 30 percent of their yearly income to imported consumer items by 1770. Measured as a proportion of estate inventories, consumer durables constituted about 21 percent of decedents' property in Massachusetts and 11 percent in Maryland and Virginia. The regional difference is explained by the fact that, in the tobacco colonies, slaves comprised a large percentage of wealthy people's estates, but slaves were never counted as imports.

One important byproduct of consumerism in the colonies was that women gained control over a larger share of the family's expense budget, for women bought the fabrics, selected the meal plans, and arranged the furniture in the home. Nor was this empowerment limited to the wives and daughters of the rich. As the cost of many imported items declined over time, poorer people could join in the buying spree. Indeed, by midcentury the poor spent a larger proportion of their income on consumer items than the rich.

Not all consumer goods were imported. Many were the products of American forges and farms. In general, domestic producers catered to the lower end of the market. The most common local industries were distilleries and breweries. By 1770, there were in the colonies 140 distilleries converting West Indian molasses into rum—this compared to a mere twenty-six refineries changing raw sugar into the finer variety colonists preferred for tea and coffee. American producers also excelled at manufacturing barrels, casks, and ships to transport consumer goods. Although colonists preferred English iron and iron products (notably nails), colonial entrepreneurs built forges wherever the water ran fast enough to turn mill wheels, bog iron was plentiful, and wood supplies could be converted to charcoal for the furnaces. Gristmills and timber mills dotted the streams, keeping pace with colonists' need for milled flour and lumber. Finally, colonial craftsmen built wagons, assembled guns, made paper products, and blew glass.

The most important of the domestically produced goods were foodstuffs. Even in areas that produced staple exports, like the tobacco country of the Chesapeake, much time and energy were devoted to food production for local sale. Plantation workers raised cattle for meat and dairy products, and herded goats, sheep, and hogs. Animals were slaughtered and the meat pickled or salted and smoked for shipment abroad. In addition, Chesapeake men fished and hunted. Wild fowl, mussels, oysters, and clams were not only consumed in homes, they were sold to local businesses. Piles of shellfish reached hill-sized proportions behind Williamsburg's taverns.

The rage for material things aided local economies. In the 1750s, Massachusetts farmers hauled or paid carters to transport loads of food and fuel to markets on average twenty miles away. This was not production for exchange or use, but for sale to strangers. When prices of groceries rose, as they did in the 1750s, market farmers did well. With their profits, they became purchasers. Thus consumption of food in cities and market towns begat consumption of consumer durables on the farms.

Selling

The rise in consumption of imported and domestically produced goods spurred the growth of the retail industry. On the frontier, peddlers hawked candles and Bibles, among other items. Some backwoods landowners tried their hand as shopkeepers. In the Shenandoah Valley of western Virginia, George and Sampson Mathews took time off from land speculation to start a small chain of dry goods stores. In Staunton and elsewhere in the countryside, they sold beef, bacon, tobacco, seed, saddles and bridles, soap, blankets, and fancy ivory combs. They gave liberal credit terms, for the customers were also voters, and the Mathews brothers sought public office as well as private gain.

On the bluffs above the Mohawk River in New York, trader and Indian commissioner William Johnson sold tobacco, sundries, groceries, pots and pans, and teacups to Dutch, German, Scottish, and Indian customers. These settlers and natives rarely had cash, so he took in barter furs, skins, and bushels and barrels of food crops. He, too, saw his role as more than a merchant. He was the only government these settlers knew, the representative of the far-off imperial "father," and he would need the loyalty of his customers if and when the French swooped down Lake Champlain from their Canadian fortresses.

From eastern Pennsylvania to Aquidneck, Rhode Island, and beyond, dry goods merchants supplied retail outlets with a great variety of imported goods. Although these merchants kept better books on their customers than did the Mathewses and Johnson, and were sometimes paid in cash, the shopkeepers still offered credit to regular customers. The closer the store was to the city or older settlements, the more likely the sale would be on a cash and carry basis. There was in general little cooperation (or collusion—for example, price fixing) by rival shopkeepers. A few mercantile associations existed, but the only regulation of prices came from city councils or colonial legislatures. These regulations were often flouted.

If there was no internal network among the storekeepers, the distribution of the shops over the land formed a kind of grid. Wherever farms were productive, stores appeared. Thus in eastern Massachusetts, 82 percent of towns had stores. To the west, in poorer regions, only 42 percent had stores. Farmers' purchasing power drew the shopkeepers to the hinterlands, although many of the shopkeepers were themselves part-time farmers.

In the port cities, stores abounded. In 1771, Boston tax collectors counted 519 stores. Salem had 172, and Newburyport, Massachusetts, had 96. Fashionable shops were fewer in number and kept to the cities. The best shops advertised, as did the higher-volume trades. Their advertisements in the colonial newspapers called upon "gentlemen and ladies" as well as the "general publick" to patronize the store. Satisfaction was, of course, guaranteed.

Together, buying and selling, shopping and advertising, served to unify the colonies in a way that politics could not. In law and public life, the colonies were distinct and sometimes competing entities, with closer ties to Britain than to one another. The consumer revolution changed all that—for goods crossed colonial lines and moved up and down colonial coasts. People in both Massachusetts and South

Carolina could share in the "baubles of Britain," could appreciate the relationship with British merchants that importation gave to Americans, and would soon recognize that buying power could translate into political power in times of crisis.

POVERTY

Although witness to an explosion of consumerism, the colonies in 1750 faced the growing problem of the permanent impoverishment of a large segment of their population. Servants, laborers, and slaves were poor, and the increasing importation of slave labor during the eighteenth century further eroded the informal bargaining power that skilled slaves possessed. Whatever strategies of self-improvement servants and laborers assayed, and whatever tactics of resistance and accommodation slaves adopted, their personal wealth remained slight.

City Poor

In the cities and towns, government and private charities as well as churches attempted to alleviate the travails of the "honest poor" who could not work because of age or infirmity. By midcentury, the city had to augment the traditional method of "out relief," wherein overseers of the poor brought firewood, food, and clothing to the house of the widow or the poor family, with large-scale institutional arrangements. Orphans were bound over as apprentices, and poor people seeking aid had to work in institutions like Boston's Manufactory House, spinning and weaving. The society that established the house found that it neither taught industry to the poor nor made a profit. Five years after opening its doors, it closed, in 1753.

Every city had its poorhouse or workhouse, supervised by overseers, but these were soon overwhelmed with the number of poor. Keepers of the almshouses denied charity to strangers and "sturdy beggars" who could work but had no job. There was no effective provision for the temporarily insane or the chronically ill. In general, Indian and African poor received no aid unless they were very young or very old, and women received aid only when they proved that they were morally fit.

War worsened the problem of poverty. Many of those going on the poor rolls had lost breadwinners to war wounds or camp fevers. In Boston alone, the war effort of 1745–1746 left twelve hundred widows. Soldiers and sailors returning from the wars found their jobs were gone. What was more, the huge tax burden that war imposed upon the cities meant that there was less public and private money available for the poor.

The money printed to pay the taxes inflated the economy and made workers' fixed wages worth less in real terms. Recession followed every colonial war, mild in New York City and Philadelphia, severe in Boston, which meant even fewer jobs to be had overall. After the French and Indian War, recession hit every city.

The Crash of 1763

Although the desire to consume was an established way of life by the 1760s, a severe depression beginning in 1763 crippled the buying power of ordinary shoppers. The sudden reversal of fortune stunned the seaboard cities, for much of the boom had rested upon wartime building contracts, selling stores to the British navy, and preying upon French ships at sea. After the war, a flood of new immigrants from Ireland and Scotland arrived, further burdening the cities' ability to care for their needy. Merchants' credit, already stretched to the limit by wartime borrowing, snapped, and many small merchants had to close their doors. The ripple effect was immediate— unemployment spread out and down from the merchant's brick townhouse to the day laborer's rickety walk-up.

Shopkeepers, tradespeople, and craftspeople who had slowly but steadily climbed into the middle classes now suddenly slipped back into the ranks of the urban poor. Unemployed men and women had to spend far more of their incomes on necessities of life. In 1752, Philadelphia workers had to disburse 34 percent of their household income on food; by 1762, the cost of food had risen to 55 percent of the workers' available funds. The cost of firewood for heating and other basics grew apace.

Such sharp downturns in business, with the inevitable layoffs and bankruptcies, were not unusual in the eighteenth century. There had been serious depressions before 1763, but never had a depression been coupled with such frustration—for the good times and high employment that had fed the rise of consumerism left people unprepared for the downturn. Some blamed the merchants for charging too much, others blamed foreigners for unfair practices. Some denounced local government for doing too little, while others accused the imperial government for strangling the colonies with regulations.

––––––––

The desire for material comfort and the goad of material needs led to the most extreme contradictions in the colonies. The growth of the colonial economy by midcentury offered hope for general improvement of living standards, but the class of permanent poor grew disturbingly large. Philadelphia merchants had built city townhouses and country mansions, but as one visitor to Philadelphia in 1750 recalled, "Att my entering the city, I observed the regularity of the streets, but att the same time the majority of the houses were mean and low and much decayed, the streets in general not paved, very dirty, and obstructed with rubbish." Behind Virginia's Tidewater mansions lay rows of rude slave cabins and dormitories with packed-earth floors and leaky roofs. Economic progress divided communities into the rich and the poor. The crash of 1763 served notice that the schism was there to stay.

13

The Last War and the Lost Peace, 1754–1763

In the waning days of June 1754, two bodies of men moved swiftly toward each other in the Allegheny Mountains of western Pennsylvania. From the east, a band of poorly armed and hastily trained Virginia and South Carolinian militiamen marched toward the headwaters of the Ohio River. Most were farmers, and had little experience with the muskets provided them by their colonies. They wore a ragtag collection of uniforms and homespun, proceeded in gaggley disorder, and made enough noise to announce their presence for miles around.

From the north came an entirely different kind of fighting force. French *troupes de la marine*, Canadian militiamen, and their Indian allies were a trained, highly experienced force. Ethnically diverse, unlike the Anglo-American column, the French units nevertheless understood their respective roles. Discipline had welded the *troupes de la marine* into superb shock troops. Skilled in woodlands combat, the French colonial militiamen doubled as foragers and sappers. The Indians served the column as scouts. They went to war as to the hunt.

When the two bodies of men collided at the forks of the Ohio, where the Allegheny and Monongahela rivers meet (adjacent to modern Pittsburgh), the French and Indian War began. The imperial rivalries and local animosities that had brought terror three times before in the century propelled the two columns of men toward one another, but this war would be different from its predecessors. This time the English and French committed to the American conflict masses of regular troops and larger navies than had ever before been seen in the Atlantic world. The size and the expense of the effort made defeat not just unpalatable, but unthinkable.

In a complex fashion, the war years hinted at a resolution of the bifurcation of Americans into haves and have-nots, elites and also-rans. Common fears, shared sacrifices, and the sense, at the end of the war, of achievement, united Anglo-Americans. A growing sense of unease, bordering on animosity, at Britain's conduct after the fighting had

We found the French colors hoisted at a house from which they had driven Mr. John Frazier, an English Subject. . . . There were three officers, one of whom, Captain Joncaire, informed me that he had the command of the Ohio. . . . They told me, that it was their absolute design to take possession of the Ohio, and by G—— they would do it.
—George Washington, journal of a tour over the Allegheny Mountains, 1753–1754

subsided spread throughout North America. The most devastating of all the colonial wars laid the foundations for the construction of a revolutionary consciousness.

A WAR TO END ALL WARS

The peace treaty of 1748 that ended King George's War laid the seeds for the French and Indian War. The pact confirmed the French presence in the upper Northwest and the English claims to the cis-Appalachian East, but neither power gained control of the Ohio River valley. Indians who lived there divided their loyalties and their trade. The French, recognizing that the loss of their Ohio Indian allies would mean the doom of their program to encircle the English settlements on the continent, decided upon a bold move—they would extend to the south the chain of forts they had built along the Great Lakes to manage Indian affairs and service their allies.

Forts Frontenac (on the north shore of Lake Ontario), Niagara (between Lake Ontario and Lake Erie), Presqu'lle (on Lake Erie), Le Boeuf, and Machault (on the Allegheny River) reached down toward the forks of the Ohio. There the French intended to set the linchpin of their new system, Fort Duquesne. With the French again flexing their muscles, the Shawnees and the Miamis cleaved to the French side.

A Different Kind of War

As we have seen, early modern Europe owed its shape to warfare. But in the eighteenth century, warfare entered a new and, on the surface at least, more civilized stage. The moving force behind the makeover were the kings of Prussia. Seeking to expand their power and faced with a limited territory upon which to draw for men and matériel, the Prussian kings developed a new kind of army. It was so successful that England, France, and Austria began to follow suit. The keys to Prussian victory were a superbly trained and highly motivated officer corps, sternly disciplined and well-armed soldiers recruited from the provinces of the state, and a new concept of year-round availability of ordnance.

But these new tactics, so fitted to European warfare with its sieges of fortresses and set-piece battles in open spaces over well-mapped terrain, ill-suited combat in America, where combatants often could not see one another, much less form ordered lines of infantry. On the frontier, no roads existed. One had to clear a road or drag one's artillery pieces into position by hand. Here the Indians had taught Europeans to fight from cover, firing their weapons at targets rather than loosing off massed volleys, the hit-and-run tactics that fitted the frontier. No Indian corps would stand and take the kind of casualties that European troops in set-piece battles sustained, and neither would colonial levies.

Indian and European customs of ransoming captives differed as well. Indians took captives with one of three thoughts in mind: ransom, adding the captive to the tribe, or torturing the captive. Europeans took prisoners according to an entirely dif-

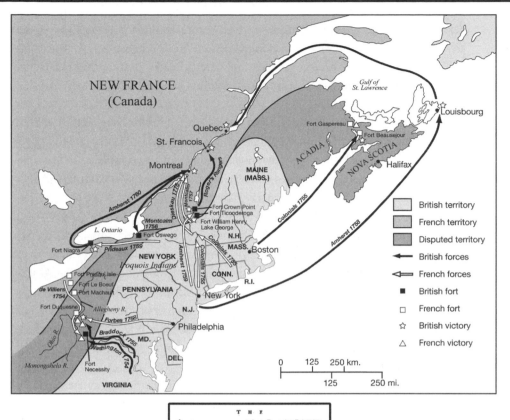

NEW FRANCE
(Canada)

Gulf of
St. Lawrence

Quebec

St. Francois

Montreal

Fort Gaspereau

Fort Beausejour

Louisbourg

ACADIA

NOVA SCOTIA

Halifax

MAINE
(MASS.)

Roger's Rangers

Amherst 1760

L. Ontario

Montcalm
1756

Fort Oswego

Fort Niagra

Prideaux 1759

Iroquois Indians

NEW YORK

Fort Crown Point
Fort Ticonderoga

Fort William Henry
Lake George

Johnson 1757

Dieskau 1757

Amherst 1759

N.H.

MASS.

Boston

Colonials 1755

Amherst 1756

Fort Presqu' Isle

Fort Le Boeuf

Fort Machault

de Villiers
1754

Fort Duquesne

Allegheny R.

PENNSYLVANIA

Colonials 1755

CONN.

R.I.

New York

Forbes 1758

N.J.

Philadelphia

Ohio R.

Braddock 1755

Washington 1754

MD.

DEL.

Monongahela R.

Fort
Necessity

VIRGINIA

	British territory
	French territory
	Disputed territory
←	British forces
⇐	French forces
■	British fort
□	French fort
☆	British victory
△	French victory

0   125   250 km.

125   250 mi.

THE
AMERICAN MAGAZINE,

PRÆVALEBIT ÆQUIOR.

AND

MONTHLY CHRONICLE for the BRITISH Colonies.

Vol. I. Nº. VI. For MARCH 1758.

CONTAINING.

I. DEBATES in MARYLAND.
II. PHILOSOPHICAL MISCELLANY.
III. MONTHLY ESSAYS.
IV. POETICAL ESSAYS.

V. HISTORY of the WAR in NORTH AMERICA.
VI. MONTHLY CHRONICLE.

To be continued (Price One Shilling Pennsylvania Currency each Month)

By a SOCIETY of Gentlemen.

Veritatis cultures, fraudis inimici.

PHILADELPHIA.

Printed and Sold by WILLIAM BRADFORD, at the Corner-House in Front and Market-Streets.

French and Indian War in the Colonies

ferent set of rules. Victorious forces "paroled" captured officers who promised not to fight for a period of time and exchanged prisoners of "other ranks" for their own soldiers. Unlike the Ottawas, Mohawks, and others, European troops never ate their dead enemies to prevent their spirits from finding peace or to gain their enemies' strength.

The unique character of American warfare conferred importance on the qualities of individual combatants. Instead of disciplined but faceless ranks of interchangeable infantry, colonial levies were outspoken individualists. Persuaded of the righteousness of their cause or the danger the enemy posed to family and homeland, they could be turned into ferocious fighters. Without motivation, they fought indifferently, ran from battle, and deserted when they wished.

Here, commanders personally recruited men for individual campaigns. French officers like de Beaujeu at Fort Duquesne gained the trust of bands of Indians by speaking their language and walking into battle alongside them. The Anglo-American colonists often elected their officers, and kinfolk joined units to serve together. Sheer size and personal magnetism, or "charisma," raised some colonial officers to command rank. Serenity of mind and self-discipline aided the officer; courage in battle and an unflinching sense of duty communicated one's inner virtues to one's troops.

Leadership was highly visual, for the body was the mirror of the spirit. In effect, only a man with a certain kind of body could lead a body of men. Virginia's George Washington and New York's William Johnson, to name two men of imposing physical presence and reputation in their communities, commanded colonial units even though the two had no prior military experience or formal training.

Washington, in particular, was fit for command of a body of men not just because he was a gentleman or had political connections, but because he was a young "man of parts," tall, broad, and strong-featured. Barely twenty-one in 1753 when commissioned a captain in the Virginia militia and sent by his governor, Robert Dinwiddie, to determine French intentions at the forks of the Ohio River, Washington exemplified the virtues and values of the Virginia gentry and survived the diseases that carried off his beloved older half-brother, Lawrence; his father; and two other siblings.

Honor was the prime virtue in which Washington schooled himself. Though his formal education ended when he reached the age of fourteen, he learned by heart the written rules for gentlemen—to consider others' feelings, act in appropriate ways—and the most important (albeit unwritten) rule: find a powerful patron.

Fortunately, his neighbor was the last of the Fairfaxes, heir to the millions of acres between the Rappahannock and the Potomac. The last in the family line had come to the colonies in the late 1740s to manage his estate, hunt, drink, and play the lord of the manor. Washington caught the nobleman's eye, kept himself in it, and profited thereby. For Fairfax, young Washington mastered the surveyor's art, traveled widely in Virginia's backwoods, and learned to live off the land—as events would prove, a valuable skill.

Washington at the Forks of the Ohio

In 1753, the forks of the Ohio were technically in Pennsylvania, but Virginia's governor Dinwiddie, anxious to protect Virginia land speculation schemes in the area (to which he was a party), obtained the Duke of Newcastle's permission to warn off the French. Newcastle, facing a huge debt from the previous war, wanted peace. In fact, neither Britain nor France officially declared war until 1756, when the Seven Years' War in Europe pit Britain and its ally Prussia against France.

Thus Dinwiddie had to rely on the militia of his own colony and whatever support his neighbors were willing to render. In 1753, the governor sent Washington to Fort Le Beouf to tell the French to leave, and the French commander, Joncaire, politely rebuffed the young planter. Dinwiddie, himself a former officer, decided to oust the French from the Ohio, but in the winter of 1753–1754 his impolitic posturing put off Governor James Glen of South Carolina, who then actively undermined Dinwiddie's attempts to bring Creek and Cherokee warriors north to the aid of Virginia. Only one company of South Carolina troops joined Dinwiddie's forces.

In early March, Washington, now a lieutenant colonel, and his column of men marched into the forest without the operational intelligence that Indian scouts ordinarily provided. Within a few days march of the Monongahela, Washington encountered the Leni-Lenape sachem Half-King and a handful of his warriors. They reported that a thousand French and Indians had debarked at the confluence of the rivers. As Washington knew from his previous year's mission, Half-King was fickle and vain, but for now he pledged his support to the British.

Half-King brought more news: a party of thirty-two French regulars, including a senior officer named Joseph Colon, the Sieur de Jumonville, was camped just ahead of Washington's column. What Half-King did not say (and perhaps did not know) was that the French were on a diplomatic mission to the Virginia government. Washington, unaware of the French party's purpose—he should have given them a safe conduct to Williamsburg—ambushed it. When the French asked for quarter, Half-King and his men began killing and scalping the prisoners, including Jumonville. Washington stopped the slaughter and saved the remaining twenty-two prisoners, which offended Half-King and his warriors. They decamped, leaving Washington dishonored by his error and without scouts.

Still, Washington's surveyor's eye chose the right place for a fortification, Fort Necessity, a little distance away from the forks. Shortly after Washington laid out defensive positions, the French and their Indian allies opened fire. To stay and fight was ludicrous, and flight was impossible. He surrendered the next day, and the

French granted him and his men the full "honors of war" on July 4, 1754, preventing their Indian allies from celebrating victory as Half-King had but a few days earlier.

The Albany Plan of Union

On June 15, 1754, with evidence pouring in that the French were gathering their strength on the frontier, delegates from the New England colonies, Pennsylvania, and Maryland met the Iroquois at Albany for a conference. New York's governor, James DeLancey, a merchant who had political ambitions of his own and owed his place to Newcastle, hosted the meeting. The point of the congress was to arrange for intercolonial cooperation and to conclude a treaty with the Iroquois. The League listened, but only the Mohawks agreed to join in the war and took the wampum belt given them back to their council.

Next, the delegates turned to Benjamin Franklin's Plan of Union (later called the "Albany Plan"). Franklin, though not a military expert, recalled the lack of cooperation in previous conflicts and in 1751 had discussed a union for the common defense of the colonies. As detailed in some "Short Hints" he drafted on his way from Philadelphia to Albany, the crown would appoint a governor-general to prosecute the war, and the colonial assemblies would choose members of a grand council. The number of delegates from each colony (ranging from two to seven) would depend upon their contributions to the imperial treasury. On July 10, after much debate, the delegates at the congress adopted Franklin's plan. DeLancey objected that the plan denied the colonial governors (who were, after all, themselves governors-general) and the upper houses of the colonies any role in the new union. Franklin countered that the colonial governors were the agents of the crown and need not fear any loss of power.

When the delegates carried the plan back to their assemblies, not one approved the idea. Some, like Connecticut, feared that the proposed governor-general would have too much power. In Rhode Island, the assembly argued that the plan deprived the colony of its chartered rights. Massachusetts, after initial enthusiasm (Governor Shirley strongly supported the plan—perhaps hoping to be the first of the new governors-general), rejected the plan. Word had reached the assembly that a plot was afoot in England to use the union to tax the colonies. In fact, Newcastle opposed the idea of union, for who knew where a union of colonies would lead?

Indeed, the British government, with its eyes firmly focused on a worsening European situation (Prussia, Britain's newest ally in its attempt to check French interests, had invaded Austria, France's ally), was trying its best to ignore the war gaining momentum in America. The last one was ruinously expensive for both Britain and France. But both countries knew the advantages of their North American empires and could not ignore the other's provocations.

Thus the French sent a fleet of nineteen ships filled with six regiments of regular soldiers to Canada in 1755. The British failed to intercept the fleet but dispatched two regiments of regulars to Virginia in 1755, hardly a force to sweep the French from the North American continent, but perhaps just enough to oust the French from Fort Duquesne.

Braddock's Campaign

General Edward Braddock arrived in Virginia in February with one thousand infantry and a reputation for bold and brutal conduct on the field of battle. He had certainly seen enough of it, having served in every major European war since he entered the army in 1710. Unfortunately, he did not understand the nature of forest warfare and scoffed at the fighting abilities of the French and Indians.

In April, with Dinwiddie as host, Braddock met Governor Shirley of Massachusetts, now charged with command of the northern theater of combat, Governor De-Lancey, and Governor Robert Morris of Pennsylvania, a merchant whose colony had yet to play any role in the hostilities save play unwitting host to the French invaders. Maryland and North Carolina were represented, but South Carolina's governor— still miffed at Dinwiddie—stayed away. The general and the governors-general plotted a joint attack on all four French forts in the Lake Ontario–Ohio River picket line. Braddock's two regiments, augmented by American levies, would assault Fort Duquesne.

Dinwiddie, whose lack of political skills matched Braddock's lack of woodland fighting experience, again bungled the job of providing a substantial number of Indian scouts. Failure to use Indians as scouts and skirmishers invited disaster. Worse, Braddock had to hack his way through western Virginia, Maryland, and Pennsylvania to reach his objectives. Braddock was incensed: "Nothing can well be worse than the road I have already passed and I have an hundred and ten miles to march thro' an uninhabited wilderness over steep rocky mountains and almost impassible morasses."

Pride marched before Braddock's fall—for he knew nothing of the French and Indian dispositions, but they followed his road-clearing operation closely. The British marched four abreast. At first, skirmishers to the sides and front of the column provided security, and scouts ranged ahead. Within eight miles of the fort, twelve hundred men, of the nearly twenty-five hundred in Braddock's array, formed an advance corps, taking with them a few cannons and thirty wagons.

Fort Duquesne, built of logs and clapboard, with no bastions and only a few pieces of artillery, could not withstand an assault from Braddock's forces, and some of the French prepared for retreat, but others argued that Braddock could be slowed or stopped by an ambush. Accompanied by thirty-six French officers and other ranks, about 630 Indians sallied out to contest the British advance at the ford of the Monongahela.

Lieutenant Colonel Thomas Gage commanded the leading troops, but he had grown lax and had pulled his men into a slow-moving, snakelike column, following a track through the woods to the fort. Had he led his three hundred men in a fan ahead of the long columns of Braddock's main body, he would have fallen in with the enemy. Braddock would then have had breathing room to organize an attack or defense. As it was, the Indians and French were able to attack the flanks of the strung-out British from both sides of the road.

The British formed ranks, shot aimlessly into the woods, and then broke and ran headlong into Braddock's advancing forces. The Virginians went to cover and began to return the Indians' fire, but Braddock ordered his entire force into line, and tried to fight in the European manner. In the confusion of battle, British detachments began to fire into each other. Braddock tried to restore order, but after two hours ordered a retreat. Before he could ensure that his men withdrew in good order, he was shot. His men now panicked and fled, abandoning the dead and wounded. The British had left 814 "other ranks" out of 1,373 soldiers and sixty-three of eighty-six officers dead or dying in the woods and on the banks of the Monongahela. The Indians swept in on the dead and wounded, and took booty and scalps. French and Indian casualties were under fifty.

Washington, ill throughout the campaign, defended the conduct of the Virginians and worried that the British would use the defeat as an excuse to abandon the frontier settlements. The surviving officers and their commanders spent the rest of the summer and well into the next year accusing each other of mistakes that were made by all. Braddock could not defend himself. He had died in agony three days after the battle.

THE NORTHERN FRONTIER

The defeat of Braddock's forces and the general withdrawal from the frontier that followed in 1755 was only the end of a campaign. War in these years was never continuous. Instead, it consisted of a series of discrete operations, usually fought after careful buildup, in mid or late summer. Winter conditions barred full-scale attacks, because armies could not be supplied with food and fuel, and snowfall disrupted maneuver. Mud in spring prevented the assembly of troops. Late fall was the time for the hunt, and large groups of Indians could not be brought together for battle.

Even before Braddock's defeat, French and British attention focused on the New York–Canadian theater. From the time that Andros made New York the fulcrum of the British counterattack on Montreal and Quebec, the frontier between French Canada and New York pulsed with military activity. During King George's War, northern New York and Laurentian Canada became a no-man's land. In 1745, the French, Hurons, and Abenakis attacked Saratoga and Albany, and the British and Mohawks raided along the Saint Lawrence. Even after 1748, France's Indian allies continued to take and bring captives to Montreal for ransom.

The Killing Ground

Geography dictated that the New York–Canadian boundary would worry military planners on both sides. A water highway connected Montreal to Albany. The Richelieu River slithered south from the Saint Lawrence into the deep blue glacial waters of Lake Champlain. Wood Creek connected Champlain to Lake George. A few miles south of Lake George flowed the upper reaches of the Hudson River. Heavily wooded on its flanks, the region around the lakes was home to prowling bands of Mohawks who were allies of the French and Mohawks who had cast their lot with the English.

At the southernmost tip of Lake Champlain, the French had built Fort Saint Frederéc and armed it with forty cannons. The stout stone walls and a bomb-proof, four-story tower were visible for miles, a stark contrast to the hasty wooden palisades of the British forts of the day. The British called the spot Crown Point. Ten miles farther south, where Wood Creek emptied into the northern end of Lake George, the French built the even more imposing stone citadel of Fort Carillon. The British would call it Fort Ticonderoga. In the summer of 1755, Canada's governor-general, the Marquis de Vaudreuil, marched three thousand regular troops of the French army into these bastions.

French gifts, diplomacy, and religious conversions to Roman Catholicism had created a coalition of Indian allies. The parties included Abenakis, Hurons, and Ottawas from Canada, and Miami and other tribes from as far away as the Great Lakes, as well as the Kahnewaka Mohawks. Many of these natives were ancestral enemies, and tensions among them floated in the air like mist on a winter morning. Only the constant intervention of French native-speaking captains and the segregation of peoples in different camps kept the Indian allies from attacking one another. Fierce fighters but undisciplined and liable to leave the field when they had booty or captives to trade back or ransom, the Indians were invaluable but not reliable.

Arrayed against these French bastions, Fort Edward stood at the northernmost navigable point on the Hudson River. Other British strongpoints, like Number Four in Charleston, New Hampshire, on the Connecticut River, and Fort Nicholson, at the southern end of Lake George, were makeshift camps of upright pine logs driven into the ground, not much different from the Iroquois fortifications of two hundred years earlier.

"Chief Much Business" Goes to War

William Johnson's trading post and mansion lay at the edge of this killing ground, north of the Mohawk River. No one could miss or mistake him. He was well over six feet tall and in middle age had considerable girth. Born in Scotland, through the patronage of a cousin he had become an important land speculator and merchant in the region. Like Washington, he was a man whom others would follow. The Iroquois among whom he lived and whose debts he forgave regarded him as a brother. So he was, for he had an Iroquois wife. The English, Scottish, and German settlers in the region of New York between the Finger Lakes and the Hudson trusted him as well. Newcastle named Johnson superintendent of Indian Affairs for the northern colonies in 1754, a post that fit his unique dual position in British and Indian life.

Though the Indians had adopted him as one of their own ("Chief Much Business" was the English translation of his Mohawk name), he had little experience with war. Thus he listened with mounting apprehension when he learned of Washington's defeat in 1754, for he knew that his unique position of trust among the Mohawks would lead the British to call on him. The call came in the fall of 1754. First, Governor DeLancey, whose treatment of the Iroquois had angered them and infuriated Johnson, asked him to take command of the Indians and prepare them for war. He refused. Then Governor Shirley pleaded with Johnson. He reluctantly accepted.

Braddock gave Johnson his formal orders at the April 1755 conference in Virginia. His assignment, to take Fort Frederéc with a motley collection of his own Iroquois brothers and colonial militia, was lunacy. Still, Johnson assembled his Mohawks, regulars, and militia in Albany. There he discovered that New Englanders regarded the New York troops as lewd and immoral and that the New York troops resented the New Englanders' arrogance. Hendrick, over seventy years old, wearing his favorite western-style waistcoat and hat, arrived with a detachment of Mohawks, and Johnson marched to the relief of Fort Edward on the morning of September 8, 1755.

A French and Indian force, under the Baron Dieskau, waited in ambush. One of Johnson's columns, with Hendrick and his men in the van, came under withering fire. The Americans rushed to the aid of the desperately outnumbered Mohawks, but arrived too late to save Hendrick. He died a loyal servant of the monarchy he had visited some forty-five years earlier.

The colonial militia fell back on Johnson's camp, pursued by the French. Johnson had ringed his camp with timbers and mounted cannons. Dieskau pressed on nonetheless, trusting in the éclat of his two infantry regiments until he was wounded and his men scattered. With the dead and wounded lying everywhere, the Indians on both sides scavenged the bodies and then went home. The regular soldiers lay down their muskets and picked up axes and trenching tools. Unlike the Indians, who preferred the forests, the European soldiers loved stout walls.

The Siege of Fort William Henry

After the humiliation of the ambush of Johnson's troops put the security of the region in peril, the British government awoke to the need for stronger fortification of the frontier. At the southern end of Lake George, in the winter of 1756–1757, the British built Fort William Henry. John Campbell, Lord Loudoun, the new commander in chief, selected Captain William Eyre of the royal engineers to construct a fort comparable to Carillon. The stronghold would sit above the lake, protected on its flanks by a marsh and a bluff. The dirt from a thirty-foot-wide ditch became thirty-foot-wide walls—a gigantic sandbox braced by pine logs driven into the ground inside and outside the enclosure. Completed, Fort William Henry was connected by a wide road to Fort Edward, ten miles to the south; surely reinforcements from the latter could aid the former were it besieged, just as Fort Frederéc could support Fort Carillon.

While Eyre pushed his labor battalions to finish the walls, plans for a British thrust north in 1756 stalled. The colonial militia went home, leading to the ouster of the commander, Governor Shirley, and his replacement by General Daniel Webb, a regular British officer. Webb passed command on to a senior officer, James Abercrombie, who bowed to his newly arrived superior, Lord Loudoun. While the Anglo-American command played musical chairs, the French seized the initiative. In August 1756, Oswego fell to the French. Like dominoes, the western outposts of the British Empire were crashing down, one onto another. Loudoun's twelve thousand men sat where they were.

With the Mohawks departed and winter approaching, Johnson recruited scouts from among the frontiersmen of New Hampshire. Robert Rogers led these men, training them on the job, and they claimed a few startling successes in the winter of 1756–1757. Rogers's company of "rangers" irritated the French, patrolled the no-man's land, and took prisoners. On January 21, 1757, the rangers staged a full-fledged assault on French encampments at the edge of Champlain, but the French regulars repulsed the attack.

Thousands of Indian allies still aided the French, but in winter the Indians seemed more determined to eat and drink their way through the French stores than to harass the British. In the spring of 1757, the French promised the Indians a decisive battle under a new commander, Count Louis de Montcalm. The Indians, knowing that no battle was ever really decisive, preferred to think of the campaign as the occasion for settling scores. Still, over three hundred joined a French force of twelve hundred in a preliminary sortie against Fort William Henry.

Montcalm, the French field commander, had arrived in Canada in May 1756. A career officer and a slight, short figure of poise, grace, gentility, and quick wit, he seemed as out of place in the forest as Braddock. But unlike the brusque and direct Briton, Montcalm was a romantic. As brave as any officer, with wounds all over his body to prove it, he had an almost mystical sense of the grandeur of France and a self-depreciating sense of humor. As he wrote to his family, "I see that I shall have plenty of work. Our campaign will soon begin. Everything is in motion. Don't expect details about our operations; generals never speak of movements till they are over."

For the second assault on Fort William Henry, Montcalm assembled one thousand Indians from the Great Lakes region. Hundreds more came from Canada and New England. By the middle of July, he could also call on six battalions of regular infantry, some 2,570 men. The *troupes de la marine* contributed over 600 men, and the Canadian militia on hand numbered 2,546 men. Two hundred and fifty open boats brought the troops and cannons (some of the guns captured from Braddock) to the southern foot of Lake George, from which the attackers could clearly see the walls of the fort. On August 3, the siege began.

Colonel Henry Monro had at his disposal some fifteen hundred men, most of them colonists serving in newly established regiments, to hold the fortress. Webb, who was with Monro, left in a hurry, saying that he was off to raise reinforcements. Instead, he locked himself in Fort Edward and stayed there for the rest of the battle.

Montcalm arrived, ordered the encirclement of the British position, then offered to parley with Monro. Montcalm's representative politely asked if the British would surrender, and Monro politely declined. The French then carried out a textbook eighteenth-century siege, digging zigzag trenches to inch their cannons and even more deadly mortars closer and closer to the walls. On August 9, Monro agreed to surrender. Montcalm's terms were generous, for the British had fought well and deserved, according to the customs of war, honorable treatment. The British were allowed to march out of the fort with their arms and one cannon, so long as they promised not to fight against the French or their allies for the next eighteen months.

The Indian allies of the French were astounded and felt betrayed. Where were the spoils of war? Where the prisoners to be ransomed? Montcalm explained the terms to the chiefs who assembled at his behest, but not all came, and those who came could not guarantee to control their warriors. No sooner had the British opened the gates and allowed the French to enter, than individual Indians rushed into the fort to scavenge the officers' closets full of gaudy uniforms. Montcalm had to appear to quiet disputes. Fearing more serious mischief, the French and British agreed that the garrison, including women and children, would leave under escort.

The Indians quickly tumbled to this subterfuge, and by the morning, as the British troops began their march south, thousands of Indians gathered around the rear of the column and fell on the wounded. As many as sixty or seventy Anglo-Americans died in the few minutes before the French gained control of the situation. French priests and officers rushed into the melee at considerable risk to themselves to save the lives of the British and colonials. French officers persuaded the Indians to take prisoners rather than kill and scalp their enemies. The French attempted to ransom the prisoners on the spot, reunite families, and aid the wounded.

Seeking the safety of Fort Edward, the troops in the van began to run. When the fastest reached Fort Edward, they told tales of terrible carnage. For obvious reasons, those who had fled the scene of the massacre exaggerated its duration and severity— else their flight would seem cowardly. Webb, still paralyzed with fear, refused to budge. Four days later, on August 14, the French returned some five hundred of their prisoners, including Colonel Monro, in perfect health. (Only the barest outlines of the story of the "massacre" in James Fenimore Cooper's *The Last of the Mohicans* are true.)

During the siege, William Johnson was raising Mohawk troops to rescue the garrison. One of Montcalm's aides heard that Johnson visited Webb during the siege.

As it happened, Johnson was wearing native dress and accompanied by Mohawk warriors. When Webb refused Johnson's plea to rush to Monro's aid, "Chief Much Business" and his friends began to strip off their clothing and throw it to the floor in disgust—a Mohawk insult.

Johnson would later take part in the 1758 and 1759 campaigns in New York, and in July 1759 besieged and took Fort Niagara from the French. Johnson prevented his Mohawk brothers from any repetition of the events at Fort William Henry. He caused his regular troops to line both sides of the road over which the French evacuated the fort from the gates all the way to the water, where boats awaited the departing French. The days of Indian-style warfare were coming to a close. Regular armies decided the outcome of battles.

In the meantime, the news of the "massacre" at William Henry had spread far and wide throughout the British colonies. With each telling it became more gruesome. Even counting the losses in the massacre, the British casualties, some three hundred men, were lower than the French losses. But despite the facts, the massacre became an excuse for later British commanders, notably Major General James Abercrombie, in 1758, and Lord Jeffrey Amherst, a year later, to give no quarter to France's Indian allies. In his Lake George–Lake Champlain campaign of 1759, Amherst implemented the policy that the only good Indian was a dead Indian.

Provincial Levies

Although some Americans joined regular army formations—by 1758 eleven thousand British colonists had left the militia and joined regular formations like the Royal American Regiment—most American soldiers served in their own units, under their own officers. They enlisted for a campaign (usually a single season) and then returned to civilian ranks. Most of the soldiers had been manual laborers on farms or worked in craft occupations. The average age of the New England recruits was twenty-three years. Few of these had traveled or had lived away from home. Most found the £15 colonial money recruiters paid for enlistment an important inducement, but others joined to be with kin or for the adventure.

Unlike the abusive features of British army recruitment and discipline, provincial regiments reflected the voluntarism of colonial life. The governors selected the regimental colonels, but the lower-ranking officers were either elected by their men or persuaded others to join the company. Fully assembled, companies averaged fifty men and regiments five hundred, but the numbers varied because a regiment's existence was only temporary. Unlike the British career soldiers who remained in camp the year round, colonial units vanished at harvest time.

Life and service in the provincial army differed from regulars' experience. Colonial units never suffered the same rate of casualties as the regulars, though Americans complained about the conditions in camp and witnessed the carnage of battle. One could tell a colonial battalion's camp from a regular regiment at a glance—so disorderly was the former compared to the latter. Unlike the regulars, colonial troops despised close-order drill and performed it poorly. Thus colonial troops had none of the discipline in combat that the regulars demonstrated and were likely to run in the face of concerted enemy fire.

The British commanders noted with disgust the fighting qualities of the American soldier and assigned provincial troops noncombat tasks like digging ditches and building roads. Colonial officers and men understood the insult and returned it in kind. They regarded the "lobsters," or "lobsterbacks," as brutal and immoral, and the regulars' officers as condescending and haughty.

The New England provincial troops saw their participation as one-part contract and one-part divine mission. When the terms of their enlistment were not fulfilled— for example, supplies of food were inadequate—the soldiers gathered to protest, went on strike, or openly deserted (all of which would have been immediately punished in a regular unit). Colonial junior officers sometimes joined with their men in these demonstrations. Senior colonial officers responded by naming committees to hear grievances and sometimes giving in to the complainants.

In camp, army chaplains, drawn from the country New England ministry, held services. The sermons reminded New Englanders that they were God's chosen people, carrying out his work. Ministers in the camps also used the attendance of the troops at services to urge them to greater personal morality. The reward would be God's intervention in battle on the side of the New England forces.

Women and the War

Women are conspicuous by their absence from traditional accounts of the war, yet the conflict deeply affected their interests and in some cases imperiled their lives. In western New England, northern New York, and on the Ohio River, British and German women and their children fell prey to Indian raids. The lucky ones were taken captive and either ransomed back or incorporated in Indian tribes. The French did their best to prevent atrocities and facilitate the return of these prisoners, but could not curb their native allies. After the war, the British demanded the return of all captives as a price of peace, but some of the women and children refused to leave their adoptive homes. They had become attached to their Indian families, or feared the contumely of former neighbors and relations.

Women followed their kinfolk to the military camps to be with and take care of loved ones. Regular army troops, particularly officers, recruited women as nurses, washerwomen, and prostitutes. Women in military camps were subject to military regulations and discipline, including corporal punishment. Worse, they fell ill with camp fevers.

Farm women who remained home suffered from the war as well. Army commissaries requisitioned farmers' draft animals, wagons, and foodstuffs for the war effort. The wagons, vital to haul wheat and corn to mills or flour to markets, rarely returned from the camps. For families that had invested much of their capital in draft horses and oxen, the loss was catastrophic. The absence of husbands, sons, and fathers for a season could be borne, but their deaths or dismemberment was devastating. One in ten of the colonial recruits never came back. When the survivors were mustered out, they reentered civilian life bearing the psychological scars of combat. Wives, mothers, and daughters were unprepared for these changes.

THE TURN OF THE TIDE

Wars are rarely won by a decisive battle, and the French and Indian War was no exception, but one great campaign and its decisive battle marked the beginning of the last phase of the war. Under the new ministry of William Pitt, commencing in June 1757, the British prosecuted the war with great vigor. Pitt, acting as secretary of state for the Southern Department, sent additional troops to America and committed the wealth of the realm to successful prosecution of the war. More important, he ordered that the war be carried to the heartland of the French colonies.

The British Campaigns of 1758 and 1759

In the summer of 1758, the British were ready to strike again in western Pennsylvania. John Forbes, like Braddock a career officer, received from Loudoun an independent command in Pennsylvania. With a Highland Scottish regiment of a thousand men, four companies of the Royal Americans, over two thousand provincial troops, and the support of almost five hundred Cherokee warriors, he marched against Fort Duquesne. Recognizing that the siege could only have one outcome, the French fled. Thus when Forbes finally pushed through the woods to view the fort, he found it destroyed and abandoned.

Forbes's victory underlined the fundamental weakness of the French hold on the West. Without a substantial habitant population in the Ohio Valley, the French had to rely on regular troops and Indian allies. The British navy's blockade of both French and Canadian ports restricted the ability of the French to land large formations of their army on American soil. France's Indian allies had no intention of getting involved in pitched battles with massed formations of British regulars and British colonial levies. Braddock's defeat had been a fluke. Forbes's triumph was not.

In July, James Abercrombie hurled twelve thousand men against Fort Carillon. Montcalm, with three thousand men, not only held out, his command inflicted over fifteen hundred casualties on the attackers. A colonial diarist named Caleb Rea recorded the slaughter: "It is said the regulars who gave the first attack were almost all swept off by grape shot from the cannon as well as by small arms." Rea could not understand Abercrombie's sacrifice of his best infantry, but when Abercrombie returned to England at the end of the year, he was promoted to lieutenant general for his gallantry. Others had paid the price for his advancement. Montcalm withdrew later that year.

The British struck directly at Canada as well. The door was the Saint Lawrence River, and its hinge was the French fortress of Louisbourg. The colonists had taken it once, but it was returned to the French in the peace treaty of 1748. The British assembled a fleet of thirty-eight warships, including twenty ships of the line, the biggest in the British navy, and a hundred transports carrying twelve thousand soldiers, to join forces with a smaller fleet at Halifax, Nova Scotia. The French surrendered on July 17, after a month of bombardment.

Brigadier General James Wolfe had led the troops ashore. In his late thirties, Wolfe was an awkward, ungainly man and something of a hypochondriac, but he was a professional officer from a military family and had plenty of experience in combat. On the eve of the Canadian campaign, he wrote to a fellow officer, "I have this day signified to Mr. Pitt that he may dispose of my slight carcass as he pleases, and that I am ready for any undertaking within the compass of my skill and cunning. I am in a very bad condition both with the gravel [kidney stones] and rheumatism; but I had rather die than decline any kind of service that offers." Pitt made the offer in the winter of 1758–1759: crush the seemingly impregnable French fortified city of Quebec.

Quebec's position on the bluffs above the north side of the Saint Lawrence, as Cartier and Champlain had seen long before, menaced all river traffic. The watercourse below the fortress was shifting, and shoals awaited the unwary navigator. The French garrison, under Vaudreuil and Montcalm, outnumbered the British regulars under Wolfe's command by fifteen thousand to twelve thousand, though Wolfe had some of the finest battalions of infantry in British uniform and Montcalm's men, though able, included a number of local levies. Nevertheless, Montcalm had only to hold off Wolfe and the supporting naval forces until winter made the campaign untenable.

Late in June 1759, Wolfe was able to place batteries on islands opposite the fortress and batter its buildings into rubble. Admiral Sir Charles Saunders then pushed two of his forty-gun frigates and another nine ships up the river past the guns of Quebec. Wolfe's troops now controlled the river, and he spent days dressed as a common soldier examining every foot of the steep cliffs opposite his encampment, patrolled by over three thousand French troops.

Close observation and the willingness to take a gamble convinced him that he could land a body of Highlanders at the foot of a narrow natural stairway to the top of the cliffs, 180 feet below the Plains of Abraham. From there, it was a two-mile hike to the city walls. He set the plan in motion for the early morning of September 13, 1759, himself leading the force of forty-eight hundred men. By six o'clock in the morning, the whole of Wolfe's army was drawn up on the plains.

Montcalm now made the mistake that doomed the French in Canada. He sallied out with his regulars (Governor Vaudreuil refused to commit his marines and militia to the battle) instead of waiting out a siege. Perhaps Montcalm feared that Quebec would become another Fort William Henry. In fact, Montcalm's regulars could have withstood stronger forces than Wolfe's.

The two lines of infantry drew up opposite each other—one in bright red, the other pure white. Wolfe's line charged. The French fired their first volley too soon. The British held their fire until they were twenty yards from the reloading French, then discharged all their weapons simultaneously. The French broke and ran. Wolfe was wounded twice in front of a battalion of his infantry, the second and fatal time preparing to lead them in a charge. Montcalm was killed by British fire while trying to stem the headlong retreat of his men.

Four days later, the French surrendered the city to the British. The British fleet destroyed the French fleet sent to reinforce the colony. The next year a three-pronged attack, two from the south and one up the Saint Lawrence, trapped the French in Montreal. The French capitulated on September 7, 1760, nearly a year after Montcalm's men had fled from Wolfe's troops. Britain lionized Wolfe. Montcalm remains a hero to the French Canadians.

A World War

The French and Indian War may have commenced in a small corner of the American forest, but by 1761 it had become a true world war, spreading to the Caribbean, India, and West Africa. The wealth of the French sugar islands of Guadeloupe and Martinique had long tempted the British. During the war, a French fleet watched over the islands, but French merchant ships leaving the West Indies loaded with sugar and vessels attempting to supply the islands fell prey to swarms of privateers sailing out of Anglo-American ports. So lucrative were the pickings that British sailors deserted Royal Navy ships in colonial harbors to join the privateer crews.

The Dutch, Danes, and the Spanish—neutral in the war—sought to supply the French, but the British announced that neutrals could only trade with the French if they had been allowed to carry on the trade before the war erupted. None fit this description, and the Royal Navy began to seize the interlopers. Anglo-American smugglers tried their hand at the game. Their excuse, if caught, was that they were carrying on "flag of truce" exchanges of prisoners. Some smugglers even hired Frenchmen to act as prisoners to give verisimilitude to the ruse. British authorities saw through these thinly veiled alibis, but could not police all the approaches to the French islands.

In late 1758, Pitt decided that the British must conquer the French islands. The first target was Martinique, nerve center of French Caribbean armed forces and civil administration. The British assembled a huge force for this expedition under the command of Thomas Hopson. Hopson had seen combat in Canada and knew his business. The fleet sailed in October 1758 and arrived at Barbados on January 3, 1759, then set out for Martinique.

Hopson landed his infantry some distance from the French fort and found tough going through the underbrush. The French held the high ground, and the British had trouble landing their artillery. Hopson made the best of a bad bargain by pulling back to his ships. Ironically, on the same day that Hopson decided to withdraw, the French commandant, the Marquis de Beauharnais, planned to blow up the outworks if the British continued their assault, but Hopson had already turned his sights on Guadeloupe.

Guadeloupe's population, nearly ten thousand Europeans and forty-one thousand Africans and Indians, the vast majority slaves, far exceeded that of Martinique, and the sugar plantations of the island made it a more enticing economic target than a strategic military one. Hopson had also learned from the Martinique fiasco. Instead of a direct assault on Fort Royal, whose position made it impregnable, he attacked the town and then besieged the fortress.

Meanwhile, the deadliest enemy of the British was already at work. Nearly fifteen hundred of Hopson's six thousand men lay shivering and burning up in their hammocks with parasitical diseases, food poisoning, and diarrhea, but the British persisted. French counterattacks failed, as the superior numbers of the British allowed them to flank the defenders, driving them from the countryside toward the town. The planters, watching their fields and homes go up in smoke, begged the French governor to surrender, and he did on May 1, 1759.

Two years before the British took the French Caribbean islands, England's United East India Company routed the French Compagnie Des Indes in India. Robert Clive, using native Indian troops (sepoys) and British regulars, defeated both French and native armies. Two more years of war destroyed the French Indian enterprise. Pondicherry, the last bastion of the French, fell on January 14, 1761. England was now free to polish the newest "jewel" of its empire. Clive made out like a bandit, plundering the colony for himself as well as the East India Company.

In 1760, British army and navy forces ousted the French from coastal enclaves in Senegal and Gambia in West Africa. Pitt ordered a renewal of the campaign against Martinique. The island's defenders, disheartened, surrendered on February 3, 1762. Pitt's plan to drive the French from all their overseas possessions verged on total triumph.

The War Ends

But Pitt's exertions had exhausted his country and its colonies. The British treasury was all but empty. Most of the colonial assemblies had at last roused themselves to contribute to the war effort, and in dead and wounded, expenditures and diminished tax base, loss of wagons and horses, not to mention the destructiveness of a war fought in their backyards, some of the colonists had suffered proportionally

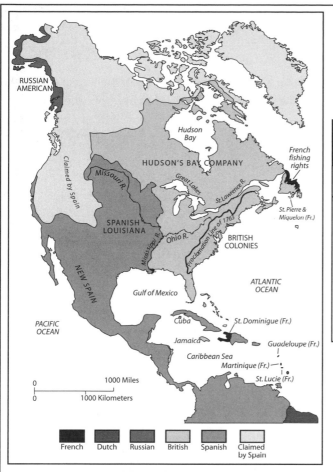

SLAVE POPULATION AND PERCENTAGE OF TOTAL POPULATION OF ORIGINAL THIRTEEN COLONIES, 1770

COLONY	SLAVE POPULATION	PERCENTAGE
New Hampshire	654	1%
Massachusetts	4,754	2
Connecticut	5,698	3
Rhode Island	3,761	6
New York	19,062	12
New Jersey	8,220	7
Pennsylvania	5,561	2
Delaware	1,836	5
Maryland	63,818	32
Virginia	187,600	42
North Carolina	69,600	35
South Carolina	75,168	61
Georgia	15,000	45

French Dutch Russian British Spanish Claimed by Spain

THE THIRTEEN ORIGINAL COLONIES

	Name	Founded by	Year	Charter	Made Royal	1775 Status
1.)	Virginia	London Co.	1607	1606 1609 1612	1624	Royal (under the Crown)
2.)	New Hampshire	John Mason (and others)	1623	1679	1679	Royal (absorbed by MA., 1641-1679)
3.)	Massachusetts Plymouth Maine	Puritans Separatists F.Gorges	c.1628 1620 1623	1629 None 1639	1691	Royal (merged with MA, 1694) (Bought by MA ,1677)
4.)	Maryland	Lord Baltimore	1634	1632		Proprietary (controlled by proprietor)
5.)	Connecticut	MA emigrants	1635	1662		Self-governing (under local control)
	New Haven	MA emigrants	1638	None		(Merged with CN,1662)
6.)	Rhode Island	R.Williams	6136	1644,1663		Self-governing
7.)	Delaware	Swedes	1638	None		Proprietary (merged with PA, 1682; same governor, but separate assembly granted 1703)
8.)	N. Carolina	Virginians	1653	1663	1729	Royal (separated informally from SC in 1691)
9.)	New York	Dutch Duke of York	c.1613 1664	1664	1685	Royal
10.)	New Jersey	Berkeley & Carteret	1664	None	1702	Royal
11.)	Carolina	Eight Nobles	1670	1663	1729	Royal (separated formally from NC in 1712)
12.)	Pennsylvania	William Penn	1681	1681		Proprietary
13.)	Georgia	Oglethorpe & others	1733	1732	1752	Royal

The Thirteen Original Colonies

greater privations than the British. In an act of goodwill, the British government sporadically reimbursed colonies for their expenditures, further prostrating public finances at home.

With the capitulation of French Canada and the success of the British navy in the West Indies, the American phase of the war was all but over, but the burden for Britain had not eased. The war in Europe dragged on. England's ally, Frederick of Prussia, who had started the European phase of the war without British consultation, much less consent, had cost Britain millions in subsidy. Spain, furious at the mistreatment of its ships by the Royal Navy, and courted by the French, entered the war on the French side in 1760. Although Spain posed little threat to Britain's forces, the prospect of adding the Spanish Empire to their own induced the British to overextend themselves. They sent armies to seize Havana, Cuba, and Manila, in the Philippines. War in the tropics decimated British troops and sailors.

It could not go on. George II, Pitt's patron, died in 1760, and the new king, George III, favored peace. The war in central Europe was winding to a close as the diplomats gathered in Paris for peace negotiations. There was some thought on the British side of retaining Martinique and Guadeloupe, the French sugar islands, but wiser heads (Newcastle's and Pitt's) prevailed, and the British kept Canada and the trans-Appalachian west instead. In return for Hesse and Hanover, conquered by the French during the war, the French retained Louisiana west of the Mississippi and regained Martinique and Guadeloupe. Various other islands, forts, and bastions were exchanged, like prisoners of war. The French were again allowed to share the cod fisheries off Newfoundland, and the habitants in Canada gained from Parliament the right to worship as they chose and the titles to their lands.

But some Franco-Americans were never to enjoy their prewar lives. The French settlers of Acadia had long been a thorn in the British side. After one last demand that they take the oath and another mass refusal, Governor Charles Lawrence ordered their removal. It began on October 8, 1755, and over six thousand people were exiled. The British claimed military necessity for their acts, but the cruelty of removal remained a blot on the British reputation. Eighty-two years later, Henry Wadsworth Longfellow recaptured the poignancy of the events in *Evangeline, A Tale of Acadie*. Many of the evacuees, like one of the lovers in *Evangeline*, ended up in Louisiana. There "Acadian" became "Cajun."

THE LOST PEACE

News of the peace brought celebration throughout the British colonies, but Britain still faced a myriad of problems. To sort these out, George III turned to his longtime tutor, the Scottish Earl of Bute. Bute was an intellectual, and had an intellectual's disdain for the compromises and corruptions of English politics. The king named Bute secretary of state for the Northern Department, and to him fell the burden of negotiating the peace when Pitt, stung by criticism and unstrung by intrigue, resigned as chief negotiator. In March 1762, Newcastle had retired, and the field was clear for Bute to elevate a younger protégé, George Grenville, to a place of leadership.

Grenville had waited a long time to rise to the top of English politics. He was a product of the "squirearchy"—that is, the local lower nobility. He went to Oxford, then studied law at Lincoln's Inn and practiced at the bar. Involved in politics from his youth, he opposed Walpole and waited patiently for advancement in office. Though he held positions of responsibility on various boards, his brittle personality and disdainful manner cost him each of those posts. In 1762, he was fifty years old, a quarter century younger than Newcastle, but to Grenville, laboring away in bureaucratic posts in semiobscurity, the Newcastle years must have seemed interminable and Newcastle's self-interested trimming insufferable.

The "Reform" of the Empire

Bute and Grenville committed themselves to austerity and reform, a central theme of which was forcing the colonists to bear some of the groaning financial burden of the war. The "reform" of the empire project was old, but the debt crisis lent new urgency to the plan. First, Bute and Grenville presided over the dismantling of the army and navy. The only exception was a doubling of the size of the American garrison to a standing force of seventy-five hundred regular troops. The colonists were to pay for this enlarged posting.

Even before Bute and Grenville began their economizing, the Board of Trade and the Privy Council tried to rein in the colonial governments. First, the board advised the Privy Council to set aside Virginia's Two Penny Act (1758). The House of Burgesses had artificially set the price of tobacco at two pence per pound, after a drought had driven up the price to four and a half pence. The legislature had to act, because tobacco was the currency of Virginia, and most debts and many public contracts allowed payment in tobacco certificates. One of those contracts set the salary for Anglican clergymen. Although others hurt by the artificially low price did not complain, the Anglican ministry sent one of their number to England to lobby for the disallowance of the act as prejudicial to the Anglican Church in the colony. The board heard the petition favorably in May 1759. In August, the Privy Council concurred.

In Virginia, the ministers were elated at the news and sued their respective vestries for back pay. Unfortunately for the clergymen, the same men who served as vestrymen filled the jury box, and the ministers lost their cases. Governor Dinwiddie, though instructed to aid the clergy, could do little, and one case became a cause célèbre, not the least because it introduced to American politics a young lawyer named Patrick Henry.

The son of a prosperous immigrant planter and local officeholder, Henry's disastrous stints as a shopkeeper and bartender convinced him that his gifts lay elsewhere. He decided to read law. In 1760, after six weeks of haphazard study, Henry managed to convince his examiners that his "abysmal ignorance of the law" was offset by his natural genius for disputation. Fortunately for Henry, local law practice did not depend upon book learning, and his energy, oratorical skills, and willingness to represent anyone in any matter, added to his local status, brought him business and prosperity.

For two hours on December 1, 1762, in the case of the *Reverend James Maury v. Fredericksville Parish*, known as the "Parson's Cause," Henry harangued the jury, arguing, among other things, that if the king took away from the colonial assembly the right to legislate, he must be a tyrant. The jury found for the vestry.

If the Privy Council's disallowance of the Two Penny Act had been an isolated event, it would have been ignored or overlooked in the colonies, as the most onerous provisions of the Navigation Acts had long been ignored or overlooked. But in 1760, the Board of Trade turned its attention to the Massachusetts General Court. The General Court had passed an act setting fees for officials, unexceptionable in itself, but missing the "clause of suspension" that held the new schedule in abeyance until the Privy Council gave its approval.

If the board got its way, every act of the Massachusetts assembly would have to wait for Privy Council approval to go into effect. This was, in fact, long established in imperial law, but no legislature will voluntarily concede to delay, and the General Court instructed its agent in England to protest against the board's action. A joint resolution of the lower house added an additional instruction: "the liberty of all men in society is to be under no other legislative power but that established by consent"— to wit, the General Court that Massachusetts voters elected. The implication of the additional instruction was that imperial boards, royal councils, and even Parliament had no rightful power to order the General Court to do anything, for Massachusetts voters elected none of these British bodies. The joint resolution even could be interpreted as a declaration of legislative independence, although the General Court had no legal authority to make such a declaration.

Massachusetts generated its own legal crisis in the same year as the Board of Trade precipitated the conflict over the fees act. The origin was the Massachusetts attachment to smuggling that had so enraged Edward Randolph and brought down the Massachusetts charter in 1684. Massachusetts merchants regularly smuggled French molasses, Dutch tea, and other illegal goods into local ports. The only way to make charges against smugglers stick was to obtain evidence of goods brought into the colony illegally. The customs collectors based their right to search and seize such evidence on both English and colonial statutes and practice.

Almost all of the colonies allowed customs officials and magistrates to search and seize evidence in criminal cases under a search warrant. Edmund Trowbridge, a Massachusetts lawyer, drafted the colony's forms for such "writs of assistance" from a model he found in a book of English writs. Unfortunately, he chose a writ for inspection of customs at the English port of Dover that was already out of date in England, and worse, Trowbridge did not fully adapt the Dover writ to the Massachusetts situation. It was this writ that was in use in the 1750s, however, without much protest from anyone.

In December 1760, Charles Paxton and the other collectors of customs had to obtain new writs of assistance because the old ones, issued under the authority of the late George II, were no longer valid. Stephen Sewall, the much-loved chief justice of the Superior Court of Judicature, but no lawyer, had refused to issue the new writs until the full court could assemble for a hearing on the question of whether the court had jurisdiction to issue such writs. The underlying, vexatious question was which courts should hear disputed customs cases—common law courts like the Superior Court of Judicature that impaneled juries or vice admiralty courts that did not.

Before the court could meet, Sewall died, and Governor Francis Bernard named a new chief justice, merchant Thomas Hutchinson. Hutchinson came from one of the wealthiest and best-connected families in the colony but was hotly opposed by James Otis of Barnstable. Otis had been promised the post by Bernard's predecessors, Governors William Shirley and Thomas Pownall. Bernard did not feel bound by others' promises and deemed Hutchinson, though not a lawyer, a safer choice to protect the interests of the crown. The factional forces released by Bernard's decision exploded when Hutchinson convened the Superior Court of Judicature in February 1761 to hear the customs officers' request.

Attorney General Jeremiah Gridley argued for the writs, citing English precedent and statutory authority that customs officials had the right to obtain the writs to search suspected violators' premises. Oxenbridge Thacher replied for the merchants, insisting that the writs were overbroad. He had before him evidence that the Massachusetts writs were too general by English standards, perhaps a result of Trowbridge's inept effort to copy the Dover writs.

The dispute had political as well as legal implications because Thacher did not have the last word in the case. James Otis Jr., agitated by the slight to his father as well as by love of colonial rights, had volunteered to join Thacher. When Otis's turn came to address the court, he drove directly to the political question of Parliament's authority over the colonies. Otis insisted that the writs violated fundamental law, the law that controlled the actions of Parliament when that body passed statutes. The fundamental law of England made a man's house his castle, safe from illegal searches and seizures. He conceded that Parliament was supreme yet proclaimed that even Parliament could not transgress the fundamental rights of Britons. It was an inconsistent thesis but a galvanizing performance, at least according to a young lawyer named John Adams, who recorded the events in his diary.

Hutchinson backed away from the confrontation, ruling that the customs collectors would have to wait until the English procedure was more fully reported. But who could mistake the lesson of Otis's challenge to the authority of the imperial law? The six judges of the supreme court, bewigged and richly robed in red, representing the majesty of the common law, hesitated to render a judgment against an argument resting not on settled points of law but on a constitutional theory of dubious provenance and insidious implication. The Massachusetts Superior Court of Judicature later ruled that the writs were legal, but the writs were never effective again in the Bay Colony.

Discontent with British legal impositions and British imperial scrutiny was not confined to Virginia and Massachusetts. In May 1761, the Board of Trade noticed that a South Carolina act omitted the "clause of suspension." The Privy Council disallowed the act. Governor Thomas Boone, newly arrived and unfamiliar with the get-along go-along strategy that his predecessors had mastered, asked the South Carolina legislature to rewrite the law in conformity with the Privy Council's wishes. The lower house ignored his request; elections under the disallowed act ensued; and, among others, Christopher Gadsden of Saint Paul's Parish was chosen by a large majority of the voters. The governor flatly refused to let Gadsden take his seat. After an exchange of shrill messages, the legislators resolved to have no more to do with Boone. When he left the colony, in May 1763, the issue remained unresolved.

In New York and New Jersey, the Privy Council tried to reassert royal control of colonial courts. In the colonies, as in England after 1701, supreme court judges held their posts "during good behavior." Beginning in 1754, the Board of Trade recommended and the Privy Council issued instructions to governors changing the terms under which colonial judges sat from good behavior to "at pleasure." In effect, this gave to the imperial government the authority to remove summarily a judge whose rulings displeased Westminster.

Nothing came of this shift in language until New York's acting lieutenant governor Cadwallader Colden, in 1758, asked the opinion of the Board of Trade on the matter. The Board of Trade took the occasion to recommend to the Privy Council a stronger statement of the new view of judicial office-holding. In November 1761, the Privy Council acceded to the board's initiative. Watching from Massachusetts, John Adams thought the change "would come naturally enough from the mouth of a tyrant, or of a king or ministry about [to] introduce an arbitrary power."

In New Jersey, popular governor Josiah Hardy renewed his colony's judges' tenure under the old standard, and the board recommended that he be dismissed from office for catering to local interests. Benjamin Franklin interceded, not for Hardy, but in support of the candidacy of his son, William Franklin, for the governorship. The younger Franklin replaced Hardy. In 1762, Benjamin Franklin and his son were still fervent supporters of the concept of an expansive, aggressive empire, and Franklin was lobbying in London for a royal charter for Pennsylvania.

Controversies over Bishops, Land Grants, and Indian Policy

While Grenville pondered the fiscal crisis and the Board of Trade and the Privy Council pursued evasive colonial legislators, Henry Caner, rector of the Anglican

King's Chapel in Boston and an activist in the Anglican Society for the Propagation of the Gospel in Foreign Parts, addressed a query to his superior, the archbishop of Canterbury, Thomas Secker. Caner's concern was twofold. First, he worried that Anglicans had become too lax when it came to tolerating other Protestant sects in the colonies. Second, he feared that the Puritans still despised the Anglican rite and conspired against it. Secker listened attentively, for he had built a career around hard-line orthodoxy. They agreed to place a new church in the Puritan heartland: Cambridge, Massachusetts, where Harvard College trained future Puritan ministers. Christ Church rose up across the street from Harvard Yard.

The next year, 1762, Caner and Secker collaborated on a second project—getting the Privy Council to disallow Massachusetts legislation that hurt the society's missionary work with the Indians. The General Court had arranged for a rival to the society. The two Anglican clergymen succeeded—the legislative act was disallowed in 1763. An anonymous contributor to the *Boston Gazette* struck back by ridiculing the society. Caner's colleague, East Apthorp, publicly defended the work of the society, provoking an intemperate reply from Jonathan Mayhew, a Boston Congregationalist minister who was convinced that the Anglicans intended to jam a bishop down the New England nonconformists' throats.

Mayhew was right—Secker would have loved to appoint a bishop for the colonies. But as he told one Connecticut Anglican correspondent in 1760, it was best to move cautiously. Still, he sought support for the project from allies in Parliament and the Grenville ministry. Word reached Mayhew and left him apoplectic: "Will they never let us rest in peace?" he moaned. Soon congregants on both sides took up the cudgels. Leading Anglican and Congregationalist laymen, in 1750 at peace with one another, became grim-faced and tight-lipped with suspicion when the issue arose, even though nothing came of Secker's plan. Throughout the 1760s and the first half of the 1770s, the issue roiled religion and politics in the New England colonies.

While the clerics argued about an American bishop, land speculators and military planners in London began to work out a policy for development of French and Spanish territories taken in the war. During the conflict, attempts to regulate the Indian trade met with sporadic success, for no policy enunciated in Whitehall could control traders or their customers along nine hundred miles of thinly populated frontier. The Treaty of Easton (1758) had mollified Britain's Indian allies, but subsequent events proved that Britain could not control its own settlers, and the Indian chiefs could not curb their warriors.

The new secretary of state for the Southern Department, Lord Egremont, asked the new president of the Board of Trade, Lord Shelburne, for advice on May 5, 1763. A month later, the Board of Trade offered an omnibus solution: incorporate Canada whole into the empire, divide the former Spanish and French portions of Florida into two colonies, East and West, and create an Indian country west of the mountains. No one was to settle beyond the spine of the Appalachians, though anyone might trade with the natives—a limitation that would pacify the Indians and protect the interests of British manufacturers.

By early October 1763, the board had readied a formal proclamation that, with some amendments, reflected its initial proposal. Army veterans gained first claim on settlement of Nova Scotia and the Floridas. A new colony called Quebec (now the province of the same name) was also opened to the former soldiers. George III announced the policy on October 7, 1763.

The Proclamation Line of 1763, seen from Whitehall as a magnanimous gesture to the Indians and a prudent method to ensure peace on the frontier, looked different to colonial land speculators. They assumed that the trans-Appalachian West would be their bonanza when peace came. Instead, it was closed. Darkly, they muttered about a conspiracy among British speculators and imperial officials, the latter corrupted by the former.

Virginia land speculators, including planters like George Washington, Patrick Henry, and Richard Henry Lee, hoped against hope that the British government would lift the barrier. Colonial leaders in Britain, like Benjamin Franklin, himself an investor in colonial western land speculation, lobbied hard for a reversal or an exception to the policy. Lord Shelburne, elevated to Egremont's post for the Southern Department, called for a yearlong study of the problem, even as his Indian superintendents were gathering chiefs and assuring them that the line would remain forever.

The Indians of the Ohio Valley were not fooled. They could see that the colonists violated the new policy with impunity. Virginia settlers were slipping into Kentucky. Families from Pennsylvania were heading for the Ohio Valley. The only bar to an all-out Indian rebellion was the Indians' internal division.

But the powwows the British and French held with representatives of many tribes during the conflict had the inadvertent consequence of bringing together Indian groups that had long eyed each other suspiciously. Some rivals, like the Cherokees and the Creeks, would never make common cause, but others, like the Shawnees of the Ohio Valley, the Ottawas of Canada, and the Senecas of western New York, found that they had similar interests. These Indians decided on a policy of neutrality in the later stages of the French and Indian War. Behind the new era of cooperation grew the fear that if the British won, as seemed increasingly likely, Indian lands west of the Appalachians would become Anglo-American farmsteads, just as settlers had swallowed up Algonquin lands on the coast and Cherokee and Creek lands in the Southeast.

In fact, the settlers' voracious appetite for Indian land, abetted by Virginia and South Carolina refusals to supply the usual gifts to Indians and British commander Jeffrey Amherst's merciless raids on peaceful Indian villages, had already motivated factions of hitherto friendly tribes like the Cherokees to rebel against British control. From 1759 to 1761, the "Cherokee War" ravaged the southeastern countryside. Although the British, with Catawba and Mohawk aid, razed Cherokee villages and destroyed Cherokee crops, the Cherokees had the better of the fighting, proving that isolated Anglo-American garrisons were never safe in Indian country.

This information fell on receptive ears in 1763. In that year, when the French laid down their arms, Leni-Lenape and Shawnee religious leaders forecast the end of the Indian world as it was known. One Pennsylvania prophetess challenged the authority of the men who led the Six Nations, and other medicine makers urged unity among the Ohio Indians. Neolin, an Ohio Leni-Lenape, inspired a wide coalition of Ohio Valley and Great Lakes Indians to drive the British into the sea.

Pontiac, an Ottawa leader, found Neolin's prophecy convincing. In a brilliant oration to the Great Lakes peoples, he brought together all the prophetic themes. Manitou (the Indian Great Spirit), speaking through Pontiac, told the gathering: "I love you, you must do what I say. . . . I do not like that you drink until you lose your reason, as you do, that you fight with each other. . . . This land, where you live, I have made for you and not for others. How comes it that you suffer the whites on your lands? Can't you do without them? . . . You might live wholly as you did before you knew them. . . . You had no need of gun nor powder nor the rest of their things. . . . When I saw that you went to the bad, I called back the animals into the depths of the woods. . . . You have only to become good and do what I want, and I shall send back to you the animals to live on . . . but as regards those who have come to trouble your country, drive them out, make war on them!"

On May 9, 1763, just as George III's government was drafting the Proclamation of 1763, Pontiac and his allies struck, besieging the British garrison in the old French post of Detroit. Within a month, seven weakly garrisoned British forts fell, some to ruses, some to simple assault. The bigger forts like Detroit, Fort Pitt, and Fort Niagara held out.

The Indians and their French allies did not have cannons, and could only ambush supply convoys. The British rushed reinforcements of regular troops and colonial levies west, ensuring the survival of the three forts. When Pontiac lifted the fruitless siege of Detroit in October (it was time for the autumn hunt), large-scale warfare abated. For the Anglo-American settlers in the valleys west of the mountains, the war was terrible. Thousands died in their homes or fleeing Indian raids. The Ohio River, whose name came from the Wyandot word for beautiful water, now led into what many called "a dark and bloody land."

In 1764, Amherst mounted punitive missions against the Indians, rarely catching them but destroying their villages and food supply. His olive branch was the Proclamation line of 1763, and his big stick was a force of regulars in the thousands. When Amherst left America in 1765, General Thomas Gage, his replacement, and William Johnson, the Indian superintendent, waved the olive branch and the stick in turn, and Pontiac's allies, short of powder and recognizing the fragility of their unity, arrived at Fort Pitt in May 1765, beating drums and singing their peace song.

It was during this period of uneasy peace that the English participated in the one documented anti-Indian atrocity. Colonel Henry Bosquet consciously included blankets infected with smallpox in a "gift" to the Indians. The result was the devastation of a number of Ohio Valley Indian villages by the disease.

Seeking a more permanent end to hostilities, the British turned to Pontiac, who acceded to their request to call a council of peace in July 1767. At Oswego, New York, he addressed the British as "father," and asked them to treat the Indians as the French had, with respect. The British tried, with William Johnson doing his best to balance the claims of his own clients, the Iroquois, with his official duties as Indian superintendent. When the colonists again burst through the line of 1763 and spread into Ohio and Kentucky, Johnson managed to gain further land cessions from the Leni-Lenapes at the Treaty of Fort Stanwix, in 1768. But the situation remained volatile.

————

Pontiac's rebellion began as a statement that the Indians would not allow the British authorities to treat the Indians as junior partners or dependents in the making of policy relating to Indian lands. The British listened, but a solution fair on its face came apart because the British could not control colonial settlers, land speculators, and hunters. As John Killbuck, a Leni-Lenape chief, reminded the British in 1771, "Therefore, brethren, unless you can fall back upon some method of governing your people who live between the great mountains and the Ohio River and who are now very numerous, it will be out of the Indians' power to govern their young men, for we assure you the black clouds begin to gather fast in this country."

Killbuck and the British officials to whom he addressed his petition had evidence that the "numerous" settlers of the old British mainland colonies could be as disrespectful to the crown as Pontiac had been, when colonial interests clashed with British policy. By 1763, the scope of the coming clash was already visible on the horizon. The growing consensus among British American elites that the purpose of empire was their own advancement made them restive at British postwar policy. Grenville's next moves would turn colonial anxiety into anger.

14

A Nation in the Womb of Time, 1764–1775

John Adams was a lawyer, and he left the dirty work of protest against British impositions like the tax on tea to others, but he admired the courage of the men who dumped the tea chests into the sea in December 1773. As a patriot, he gloried in defiance to distant and uncaring imperial authority. As a lawyer, he knew that such acts of vandalism would bring a swift and painful response from the British government. But neither the patriot nor the lawyer knew what would happen next.

Momentous events like the American Revolution are defined by the scope of the change they leave in their wake. Such changes, including a civil war, independence from Britain, and a new political and legal order, must flow out of deep-seated, long-term causes. These may be material—for example, irresolvable or festering conflicts over natural resources—or nonmaterial—for example, widening cultural gaps or religious differences.

As we have seen in chapter 13, the French and Indian War and the Treaty of Paris forced the colonists and the home country to face basic differences in perspective. Yet no one in 1763 expected the sporadic and diffuse quarrels over colonial legislative autonomy to escalate into widespread violence and the end of the old empire. Indeed, a substantial portion of the British Empire in America, including newly acquired French Canada and Spanish Florida, did not join in the protest movement, and Anglo-Caribbean planters joined in the protest but not the Revolution.

Pursuing these lines of inquiry reveals that the crisis forced the British and the Americans to choose sides. But the alignment of protestors versus loyalists (or to borrow the pejorative terminology of the former, "patriots" versus "Tories") cut across colonial class, ethnic, and gender lines.

Some people of wealth and standing supported the protest all the way through separation from England. Other well-to-do families wa-

Last night 3 cargoes of Bohea Tea were emptied into the sea. . . . This is the most magnificent movement of all. There is a dignity, a majesty, a sublimity, in this last effort of the patriots, that I greatly admire. . . . What measures will the ministry take, in consequence of this? Will they dare to resent it? Will they punish us? How?
—John Adams's diary, 1773

vered, then ultimately chose the British side. The Irish and French in the colonies (saving the French Canadians) strongly supported independence, while Highland Scots and newly arrived Germans favored the crown, but other ethnic groups divided in their preferences. Fragments of Native American tribes stood by the British; other groups joined the colonists or remained neutral. Women adhered to both sides. Some slaves ran away from their owners to help the British, but other slaves elected to remain with their rebelling masters. Religious affiliations predicted some of these decisions, but did not dictate them. Most Congregationalists and Presbyterians attached themselves to the patriot cause, but not all, no more than all Anglicans adhered to Britain. In the backcountry, neighbor fought neighbor. In the cities, the revolutionaries controlled the mobs, but mobs did not sway everyone.

At the same time, the crisis gave to people who had not had power or held office the chance to exercise the former and enjoy the latter. In contrary fashion, some groups that had long held power found themselves packing their belongings and fleeing for their lives. In complex ways, the Revolution altered the structure of have and have-not, ruler and ruled.

THE INHERENT PROBLEMS OF EMPIRE

Whatever the miscalculations of the heads of state in Britain and the provocations of colonial leaders after the French and Indian War, the American Revolution would not have occurred without deep-seated economic contradictions, profound social and cultural tensions, and multiple, overlapping political asymmetries in the imperial system. In the years between 1764 and 1775, the inherent contradictions of an island ruling a distant continent worked their way to the surface of colonial life.

Economic Contradictions

Before 1764, the imperial economic system had functioned well. Although a few colonial entrepreneurs feared that Britain would ultimately stand in the path of American economic growth, in fact the benefits of empire outweighed the costs to American producers and consumers. Neglectful enforcement of the letter of the laws proved salutary, and partnership in the empire profited colonial overseas traders and land developers. The Navigation Acts placed restrictions on colonial paper money, but there was enough currency, coin, and commercial paper circulating in the colonies to sustain economic growth. The customs duties were not onerous either, although the rapaciousness of the customs collectors was a constant irritant.

The productivity of American agriculture and the many markets within the empire for agricultural products allowed both growers and merchants to prosper. The balance of trade with Britain was negative only for the New England colonies, and its merchants found ways to make a profit in the interstices of the empire as well as outside of its boundaries. Overall, there was a modest rise in income levels in the colonies, and enough wealth had been accumulated to allow some reinvestment in the economy.

But the combination of Grenville's policy of strict scrutiny and rigorous enforcement of the Navigation Acts and the depression of 1763 exposed the inherent defects of mercantilism. With the French rivalry over, the wartime booms that had boosted the economy would be gone. Colonial producers and consumers correctly assumed that they would pay the price for a thoroughgoing reform of the system. More important, they were reminded that they were the junior partners in the empire and could not control their economic situation. The depression of 1763 highlighted the problem of debt and hinted that it might become a debilitating fixture of the economy. The end of the war opened the western gate of the empire to thousands of impoverished immigrants from Britain, who in turn would absorb surpluses of food crops, further depress wages, and keep up prices.

Despondency over unpaid and unpayable bills turned merchants' despair into suspicion that success did not depend upon hard work, sound practices, and good character, but on illicit deals and corrupt payments. For southern planters, indebtedness was a personal affront. As William Nelson confessed, "to remain in debt I could never bear but with the greatest pain." Gentleman slaveholders regarded debt as a species of slavery—for the debtor was figuratively "enslaved" to the merchants who encumbered next year's crop to pay for this year's purchases. In 1764, with his creditors closing in, Robert Beverley moaned, "I dread very much from the appearances of this day that [the whole colony] will be condemned forever to a state of vassalage and dependence." Slaveholders used this language without a trace of irony or self-reproach.

Farmers in Pennsylvania and New York faced a different problem. Up to 1763, they had been able to sell much of their produce to the French sugar islands. In time of war, this was treason; in peace, it violated the Navigation Acts; and after 1763, it became impossible. During the depression, farmers could not get credit locally, fueling the fear of foreclosure on their mortgages. On top of everything else, in the years 1755 to 1765 killing early frosts had ruined barley and wheat crops in the North, causing farmers who could not shift to earlier-maturing crops great hardship.

Even the largest landholders like the Van Rensselaers, Phillipses, and Van Cortlandts on the east side of the Hudson River felt the pinch. They attempted to convert their tenants' long-term leases and rental agreements into higher-paying, short-term contracts. Threatened with eviction, the tenants responded with mass meetings, rent strikes, and finally violence, in which Connecticut and Massachusetts squatters on New York lands joined. The ringleaders were arrested, but discontent sizzled under the surface. Only the intervention of regular British troops—an ominous foretaste of future events—prevented wholesale civil war.

Social and Cultural Tensions

The Hudson River rent wars proved that America's manor lords could not dominate their tenants like English squires or French and Spanish grandees. German Palatines contested the authority of the New York aristocrats. Irish immigrants hated Anglo-American landlords. New Jersey and eastern Pennsylvania Scots-Irish tenants and day laborers refused to bow to the local gentry, regarding themselves instead as "lords of our own little but sufficient estates." This spirit of independence undermined the claims of the wealthy or the wellborn to deference.

At the top of colonial society, royal officials had nothing like the social prestige that the landed squire claimed in England. Some imperial placemen had titles of nobility, but by 1763 such titles meant little in America. Even the Fairfaxes on the "Northern Neck" in Virginia had to fight off rivals in court. Royal governors lived in an elegant manner far beyond their means to prove a point that the colonists never conceded—that political office must rest on social prominence. The great exception to this leveling of colonial society was the master's power over the slave—an enormous exception to be sure. Indeed, white small freeholders were more likely to defer to the great slaveholder than to the royal official because of the authority that owning slaves conferred.

Colonial churches once reinforced social rank and order, but after the Great Awakening, pietism flattened social hierarchies. Revival meetings were inherently democratic and antiauthoritarian. Not that the preachers encouraged disorder—some of the sectarians preached social conservatism—but the way in which the revivalists challenged the authority of "unregenerate" ministers and the volatile language of the revival meetings cut across social ranks. Long after the Awakening had quieted, the revival style's egalitarian message still echoed.

For example, Boston minister Jonathan Mayhew welcomed the attendance of the "vulgar and middle sorts," preached the heresies of Jacob Arminius that salvation could be found by everyone who sought it, and assaulted the "corruption and venality" of governments. A popular hero by the early 1760s, he used his pulpit to celebrate resistance to tyranny the same way that Patrick Henry had used the courtroom in the Parson's Cause. Mayhew claimed that "religious obligation" dictated his actions. His condemnation of "luxury, debauchery, venality, intestine quarrels, or other vices" from the pulpit applied to politics as well as personal life.

Political Asymmetries

In politics, men like Patrick Henry and Jonathan Mayhew labeled themselves "Whigs," harking back to Lord Shaftesbury's campaign against James's succession and the aims of the leaders of the Glorious Revolution of 1688. In this context, the word implied that the colonists opposed tyranny. They labeled and libeled their opponents as "Tories," suggesting that they desired tyranny.

In adopting these appellations, the American Whigs followed the precedent of three generations of English "commonwealthmen" like John Trenchard and Thomas Gordon, authors of *The Independent Whig* and later *Cato's Letters*; the essays of the clergyman Benjamin Hoadley; Thomas and Thomas Brand Hollis's letters; and the historical disquisitions of later writers like James Burgh and Catherine Macaulay. These radical critics of British government demanded that it live up to the highest ideals of the English constitution.

In fact, the English constitution was nothing more or less at any given time than a collection of parliamentary statutes, high court decisions, and royal pronouncements. Under the terms of the settlement of 1689, it could be altered at Parliament's whim. But the radical Whigs saw the constitution as the embodiment of a series of fundamental precepts. These controlled (or should control) what Parliament could and could not do, and protected liberty against arbitrary power. Thus, while they had relatively little impact on British politics, the commonwealthmen gained fame in America after 1763.

A correspondence between Thomas Brand Hollis and Mayhew creating the conduit for the English commonwealthmen's ideas here and in the early 1760s, Mayhew's sermons drew sustenance from these radical Whigs' writings. Then their ideas and his works became part of a veritable explosion of political pamphleteering in America. By the end of the crisis, the American Whigs had produced and disseminated reams of these publications, running the gamut from one-page handbills to long tracts and heavily annotated treatises.

The pamphlet authors ran the gamut as well, from ministers like the even-tempered Charles Chauncy to the fiery Mayhew, from prudent southern jurists like Daniel Dulany of Maryland to street politicians like New York City tradesman Alexander McDougall. Some of the pamphlets, like James Otis Jr.'s and John Dickinson's, were masterful works of legal learning. Others, like Paine's essays, were cunning exercises in propaganda.

As colonial writers cataloged what they took to be the signs of deteriorating liberty in England, they concluded that liberty had found its true home in the colonies. Indeed, they argued that immigration to the colonies swelled when liberty faced the greatest peril in England. The colonies represented the best of England, the asylum of the oppressed, according to this version of the history of liberty. As William Livingston wrote in 1768, "Liberty, religion, and science are on the wing to these shores: the finger of God points out a mighty empire to your sons."

Whatever the truth or falsity of the historical picture these men painted, American representative bodies had already removed themselves some distance from strict imperial scrutiny. Leading the charge for still greater legislative autonomy were men whose names would reappear on lists of revolutionaries. The Virginia House of Burgesses, for example, boasted Richard Henry Lee, Patrick Henry, and, later, Thomas Jefferson. They did not speak for a united planter elite, but they gained the upper hand in the assembly, and it became a vehicle for petitions, protests, and resolutions against the Grenville program and its successors. The low-country elite in South Carolina, led by planter nabobs like Peter Manigault, Charles Pinckney, and Christopher Gadsden, not only controlled the lower house, they cowed the royal lieutenant governor, William Bull. Charleston's merchants, led by Henry Laurens, belatedly joined the cause.

In Massachusetts, Whig leaders John Adams and his cousin Samuel Adams, along with John Hancock and James Otis Jr., sat in the General Court. They could not dislodge royalist leaders like Lieutenant Governor Thomas Hutchinson and his kinsmen Andrew and Peter Oliver, but they could use agitation against the crown to cement alliances and gain anti-imperial majorities.

New York's Robert R. Livingston, along with cousins William and Philip, led the clan into the fray. More cautious lawyers like James Duane and John Jay provided legal arguments for the protest. They all fought against James DeLancey and his kinsmen for control of the assembly, using the DeLanceys' close ties with the royal government to embarrass them. The Livingstons and their clients were no more democratic than the DeLanceys, but opposition to imperial authority enabled the Livingstons to forge an alliance with middle-class and lower-class voters.

In Pennsylvania, still a proprietary colony, politics were a little more complex and somewhat less raucous. Benjamin Franklin led the old Quaker party against the Penns to seek a royal charter for the colony. Franklin was naturally reluctant to attack the Grenville ministry at the same time as he importuned it for revocation of the old proprietary charter. But some of his allies, notably Dickinson, merchant Robert Morris, and Irish immigrant Charles Thomson, pushed the protests against both crown and proprietor. In 1764, they would abandon the Quaker party's moderation and begin to organize a thoroughgoing opposition.

Despite the growing power of the colonial legislatures, neither the commonwealthmen nor their American acolytes ever committed themselves to government by democratic means. They eschewed democracy because they feared the whims of the "rabble" and the wiles of demagogues as much as they dreaded the venality of aristocrats and the ambition of princes. Instead, the goal was a balanced government, within which each branch of government limited the others' power.

But the logical implications and the political necessities of protest would open the door to popular politics. The spread of newspapers and the explosion of pamphlet literature created a novel force called "public opinion" and allowed those who dissented from British policies to propagandize their views freely.

In Rhode Island, for example, the competition between the Hopkins clan of Providence and the Wards of Newport stirred mass partisanship. Although there were class and regional dimensions to the struggle, it resulted in both heightened public awareness of political issues and increased voter turnout. Even in the Tidewater, where gentlemen candidates still thanked voters in person, younger politicians now openly campaigned for election. One loser, Maryland's elite planter Charles Carroll of Carrollton, lamented in 1765 that "a mean, low, dirty envy . . . creeps through all ranks and cannot suffer a man of superiority, of fortune, of merit, or of understanding."

By calling upon city working people to aid in protests, elite Whig political managers further popularized politics. Street mobs were long a part of colonial and British life. At set times in the calendar—like "Pope's day," in early November, commemorating the uncovering of the Roman Catholic plot to blow up Parliament in England in 1605—Boston gangs traditionally met to trash the city. On other occasions, mobs shut down bawdy houses, rioted against smallpox vaccination, and otherwise acted as the conservators of a rowdy folk morality. With local civil authorities choosing to ignore what was occurring, mobs turned their anger on naval press gangs in anti-impressment riots. By encouraging the crowd to reinvent itself as the Sons of Liberty, the Whig leadership co-opted the ablest among them and held out to the masses the prospect of participation in a new kind of populist governance.

The rural riot was another matter entirely. The Hudson River rioters had long-standing grievances against their landlords, maintained their organization over a course of years, and threatened the "security of property" that was the elite complaint against the British. In 1768–1772, rural rioters in South Carolina protested the lack of government action against criminals in their midst. This "Regulator" movement included smaller planters, local tradespeople, and landless laborers. When regular governments ignored their protests, the Regulators took matters into their own hands.

South Carolina governor Charles Montagu temporarily defused the protest with threats of militia action. In North Carolina, matters went farther. Men like Herman Husband began to formulate a democratic plan to relieve the "aggrievances" of the western farmers. Other North Carolina Regulators formed vigilante companies to cleanse the land of brigands. When supporters of the Regulators began to decry the royal government as "so corrupt, so void of humanity, and every Christian virtue," North Carolina governor William Tryon acted. At a battle in May 1771 in Alamance, North Carolina, the Regulators were dispersed, but the rural multitude in arms evidenced the asymmetries of colonial politics in the 1760s.

Taken together, systemic economic dysfunctions, social tensions, and political asymmetries energized colonial protest, but none of them mandated independence from Great Britain or the creation of representative republican forms of government. Instead, these long-term problems were like powder kegs in storage, potentially explosive but safe enough for the present.

THE PIVOTAL YEARS, 1764 – 1765

In 1776, Thomas Jefferson called the acts of the British government after the French and Indian War a "long train of abuses and usurpations." Boston minister Andrew

Eliot hesitated to subscribe to this view. As much a patriot as Jefferson, he conceded, "It is possible we may be mistaken; things may appear very differently to others as upright as ourselves."

George III wanted his hand on the tiller on imperial governance, but he did not know in which direction to steer. Along with Bute, George resented the patronizing attitude and casual corruption of the veterans of Whig politics, but how were the king and his mentor to find a ministerial team that would be free of the old corruption yet able to manage a Parliament whose every action was oiled by patronage and party interest? The result was a succession of ministries, eight of them in the ten years from 1760 to 1770, in contrast to the long tenures of Robert Walpole and Newcastle.

In the confusion of ministerial shifts, American interest groups did not know whom to approach. Pitt, now seen as the friend of the colonists (though in fact he favored far stricter rule), stepped down, and Newcastle, the old intriguer and partisan who had also been somewhat imaginatively recast by the colonists as a friend, followed. Grenville listened to the agents' pleas, but did not hear them.

Had senior British officials traveled in the colonies or better attended the warnings of the former colonial officials, agents, visitors, and lobbyists, they might have seen the dangers in the reform course of action. Had colonial leaders taken a broader and more empathetic view of Britain's expanded geographic responsibilities and crushing economic burdens, the colonists might have given Grenville greater leeway.

With their eyes focused upon English politics and trapped in authoritarian ways of reading political situations, the Grenvillians overlooked or ignored the perils in their path. And the colonists, equally narrow in their outlook, disregarded or disparaged all but their own interests. Thus, although the controversies of the pivotal years of 1764 and 1765 look from a distance like a series of botched opportunities and nearsighted miscalculations, that is an unfair verdict. Instead, the misunderstandings were mutual, natural, and in some sense inevitable.

At the same time, as Eliga Gould has written, there was considerable support among Britain's ordinary people for the Grenville idea of reform and for later acts to regulate colonial commerce, bring the colonists into compliance with the Navigation Acts, and fill the British treasury with colonial taxes. English patriotism included the notion that the colonies were dependencies, however the colonists might choose to view or question that status. If not exactly a plot against colonial liberty, the British government and the British people agreed that something must be done.

The Sugar Act of 1764

From Grenville's point of view at the start of 1764, the British government's fiscal crisis had worsened. His attempts to handle the Indian question and reassert the authority of king and Parliament over colonial legislatures had led to bitter controversies that remained unresolved. The English national debt had doubled, in large measure to support the war effort in the North American colonies. Smuggling cost the customs service as much as £700,000 a year, and the Navigation Acts were overdue for a thorough overhaul.

A revision of the Molasses Act of 1733, scheduled to expire in 1764, seemed the obvious place to raise revenue and remind the colonists of their obligations. The Molasses Act placed a tariff on legal importation of molasses, rum, and raw sugar from non-British colonies. Rather than pay the six pence per gallon duty under the law, importers on the mainland colonies smuggled in molasses.

As early as the fall of 1763, Grenville proposed to lower the duty on foreign molasses to three pence per gallon, while enforcing its collection. On March 9, 1764, he formally presented the Sugar Act to Parliament. The act increased the duties on coffee, indigo, and wines imported directly into the colonies, doubled the duty on foreign goods reshipped to the colonies through England; added iron, hides, silk, potash, pearl ash, and whale fins to the list of enumerated articles; and banned the colonial importation of foreign rums and French wines (in effect requiring colonists to buy these from British exporters). The act passed on April 5.

To colonial waters Grenville ordered eight warships and twelve armed sloops "to seize and proceed to condemnation of all such ships and vessels as you shall find offending against the said laws." Grenville caused the customs board in England to remind all its American collectors that failure to do their duty would result in instant dismissal. Finally, at his urging, Parliament provided that "libels" (the legal term for suits by the crown against suspected smugglers) be tried in vice admiralty courts. Ship captains and owners had to fill out all sorts of documents and post a bond for their compliance with the act.

Vice admiralty courts were nothing new—they had come to the colonies in 1696, but they had made little impression. Common law courts stole cases from them. In Rhode Island, the legislature set the admiralty judges' fees so low that the judges complained to England. Admiralty court prosecutors like William Shirley pandered to colonial maritime interests. But when the Sugar Act directed the vice admiralty courts to hear and determine cases of customs violations, and created a new vice admiralty "supercourt" at Halifax, Nova Scotia, colonial importers cried foul. The prospect of dragging their cases to Halifax gave colonial shippers nightmares.

The Salem and Boston merchants ordered Massachusetts's agent in England, Jasper Mauduit, the handpicked crony of the Otis-Adams faction in the General Court, to plead for a mitigation of the rigor of the act, but Mauduit got no satisfaction from the Grenville ministry. In the meantime, Massachusetts merchants sought support from other New England colonies. Newport's merchants complied immediately. Rhode Island's thirty distilleries depended upon foreign molasses and exported rum in trade for West African slaves. New Haven merchants joined the protest, and it soon spread to New York City and Philadelphia. The merchants and the colonial legislatures sent petitions to Parliament, but Grenville continued in his course.

A Crisis over Stamps

Grenville next laid the groundwork for an extension to the colonies of the English stamp tax. On March 9, 1764, he told Parliament that he "hoped that the power and sovereignty of Parliament, over every part of the British dominions, for the purpose of raising or collecting any tax, would never be disputed." Had not the English borne such taxes for years? Moreover, the taxes were earmarked for colonial expenses, principally to supply troops stationed in America. While he held out the possibility that the colonists could find some way to tax themselves, he must have known full well that such an event was unlikely.

On February 6, 1765, Grenville brought the Stamp Tax Act to the House of Commons. Colonel Isaac Barré, who had served in the colonies, objected. The colonists had little help from England in the past, he opined, and they ought not be burdened with England's debt. Richard Jackson, another member of Parliament and an agent for Connecticut and Massachusetts (Mauduit's replacement in that thankless role), tried to introduce petitions from the colonies against a stamp tax but was declared out of order. General Henry Conway, a veteran of the French and Indian War, asked that the colonies have the chance to formulate their own subsidy bills, to no avail. The act passed on March 22, 1765.

According to the act, the tax would fall on "every skin, or piece of vellum or parchment, or sheet or piece of paper" used for certain documents. Legal documents were hardest hit, because these had to be filed in courts, and the judges could easily monitor compliance with the act. Bail papers would cost two shillings (twenty-four pence). Similar fees applied to pleadings, deeds, and "libels" in chancery, superior, vice admiralty, and church courts. Attorneys' licenses were similarly assessed, a mistake in light of the influence lawyers exercised in colonial political councils. Tavern keepers' licenses were burdened, angering the men and women who dominated local politics in many towns and cities. College degrees would cost two pounds sterling. Every newspaper, pamphlet, and broadside publication was to be printed on stamped paper.

The act was to go into effect on November 1, 1765, but in the best of circumstances, administering and enforcing the act would be a nightmare without the voluntary compliance of the colonists, and men and women who had systematically evaded the customs laws so well for so many years would surely find ways to undermine the new impositions. Worse, it offended colonial leaders who had heretofore been cautious and private in their criticism of the Sugar Act.

Given the financial burden the new act laid on legal practice, lawyers naturally opposed it. Even conservatives like Daniel Dulany of Maryland prepared objections. Scion of a leading planter family, Dulany had studied law at the Middle Temple in London and from 1746 built a lucrative practice in the colony. In politics, he was a leader of the proprietary party, but Dulany thought the new tax an unconstitutional innovation and said so in his *Considerations on the Propriety of Imposing Taxes* (1765). Parliament, he wrote, did not have the right to tax the colonists without their consent.

His argument had three parts, all of which became orthodoxy in the colonial Whig canon. First, Dulany assumed that the colonists had absolute "rights" rather than "privileges" the king or Parliament could revoke. He derived this claim from John Locke's *Two Treatises*, the most widely circulated and closely read tract on political philosophy in the colonies. Dulany relied on Locke's idea that government began in and rested on a social compact. Under this agreement, governments must act as the trustees for the benefit of their subjects and their subjects' property. Legislation like the Stamp Act that took property without consent violated the foundational agreement.

Next, Dulany argued that Parliament was supposed to be a representative body. This was a complex issue, and had long concerned English reformers. Dulany insisted that representation must rest upon the actual consent of the governed. Consent could not be inferred from long acquiescence or silence. Nor could Parliament claim to represent the colonies "virtually," because its members "represented the whole" of the people rather than their own constituencies. Here, Dulany reused some of the language of the republicans of the English civil war era.

Finally, Dulany objected to the stamp tax because it was a threat to American property rights. Property was as slippery a concept as consent and representation, and the concept of private property still had its detractors in eighteenth-century Anglo-American culture. But to men of means like the Maryland planters for whom Dulany spoke, the colonists gained absolute property rights through their improvement of a wilderness into profitable farms and towns. The "security" of this property was uppermost in his mind when Dulany insisted that Parliament could not tax Americans without their consent, for taxation was a "taking." Dulany counseled modest remonstrance, but his was a voice of reason compared to the words of men who vaulted into the leadership of the colonial protest in the spring of 1765.

The Colonial Remonstrants

The conventional wisdom is that the American revolutionary protest against the Stamp Act was brilliantly conceived. Certainly, compared to rabble-rousers like the English politician John Wilkes, whose *North Briton* essays slandered Bute and Grenville, the American Whigs' virtues shone brightly. But men like Samuel Adams and Patrick Henry had little concern for the genuine problems that the home country faced after the war. Able incendiaries and organizers of protest, their personal attributes turned a protest into a near rebellion.

Samuel Adams, the son of a brewer, attended Harvard, but classical education did not enhance his business skills, and he squandered his inheritance. Before 1765, he was a major figure in the Boston town meeting but a minor figure in colonial politics. Only as an agitator did he stand out. He led the protest against the Stamp Act of 1765 and the Townshend Duties in 1767, organized the nonimportation program in 1768, and ordered the Boston Tea Party in 1773. He founded the Boston committee of correspondence in 1772 and served in the First and Second Continental congresses.

Austere, rigid, and opinionated in politics, but highly flexible and prudent when these means served his ends, he was a master of press releases and public meetings. A moralist, verging on bigotry in his adherence to Puritan principles and views of the weakness of human nature, he was not ambitious for office or fame in the conventional sense, and believed that "no man has a claim on his country, upon the score of his having rendered public service." A true believer who willingly sacrificed himself for the cause, there was no way that Adams would compromise with his opponents.

If Adams was terse to the point of monotone, Henry was a gushing fountain of words. Henry's defense of the vestry in the Parson's Cause brought a first taste of celebrity and a seat in the House of Burgesses from Hanover County. He entered the House of Burgesses in 1765, reflecting, if not quite representing, the views of the lesser planters and the yeoman farmers. Acquisitive, he pressed his clients for his fees and amassed western lands and slaves. As his initial promise as an orator blossomed, it carried him to the front rank of the planter-politicians. Thomas Jefferson recalled somewhat ruefully that Henry's oratory was so dramatic that no one could resist it, and so devoid of intellectual depth that no one could remember what Henry had said two hours later.

But Henry fused evangelical-style preaching with the oratorical skills of a country lawyer. He turned Virginia propertied classes' love of personal honor and autonomy into a patriotic program. His famous 1775 outburst, "give me liberty or give me death," translated the planters' demand for control of property into an ideal of republican liberty.

In the course of his career, he would speak often and earnestly in the lower house, and he was among the first of the burgesses officially outlawed by Governor John Murray, Lord Dunmore, in 1775. But Henry rarely traveled outside the colony, and mired in this narrow course, defending the interests of his class and kin, he had neither knowledge of nor concern for the larger problems of the empire.

Out of narrowness of vision, as in Adams's case, or narrowness of interests, as in Henry's, the American Whigs stumbled toward a confrontation with the British over the stamp tax whose outcome neither side planned or anticipated. Led by Henry and Samuel Adams, colonial assemblies expressed outrage at the new law. In Virginia, the news arrived in May 1765, and the few burgesses still in town were furious. Patrick Henry, speaking to an almost empty chamber (most of his colleagues had left for their plantations), introduced resolutions against the act.

A French traveler recorded the scene. Henry "stood up and said that he had read that in former times, Tarquin and Julius had their Brutus, Charles had his Cromwell, and he did not doubt but some good American would stand up, in favour of his country, but (says he) in a more moderate manner, and was going to continue, when the speaker of the house said, he, the last that stood up spoke treason . . . upon which the same member stood up again . . . and said that if he had affronted the speaker, or the house, he was ready to ask pardon, and he would show his loyalty to this majesty . . . at the expense of the last drop of his blood, but what he had said must be attributed to the interest of his country's dying liberty . . . on which that affair was dropped." He never said, "if this be treason, make the most of it."

Henry's proposals, like Dulany's arguments, combined legal, philosophical, and practical political messages. He resolved, with the support of the majority of the remaining burgesses, that English migrants to Virginia had brought with them and passed on to their children all the rights of Englishmen; that the charters guaranteed these rights; that taxes could only be levied by the "people" or representatives chosen by the people, for only actual representative government protected the people's rights; that historically the colonial government had exercised control of internal taxes; and in a fifth resolution, that "every attempt to vest such power in any other person or persons whatsoever other than the General Assembly aforesaid has a manifest tendency to destroy British as well as American freedom."

Observers, including young Jefferson, recorded that the debate on the fifth resolution was "most bloody," for the members could see that it cast the die against parliamentary legislative supremacy. It passed with the slenderest of majorities. The next day, a somewhat larger number of burgesses, less Henry (he had ridden home the night of the original vote), rescinded the vote on the fifth resolution. They were not rebels yet.

But if the vote was expunged from the official journal, the five resolves appeared in the *Williamsburg Virginia Gazette* and soon echoed throughout the colonies. A Newport newspaper was the first to reprint the fifth resolution, followed by the *Maryland Gazette*. Almost by accident, Patrick Henry and the Virginia colony had assumed leadership of the battle for colonial rights.

The Rhode Island and Maryland newspapers printed two highly incendiary resolves that Henry may have drafted and the burgesses debated that did not come to a vote. The first claimed that "his majesty's liege people, are not bound to yield obedience to any law . . . designed to impose any taxation upon them, other than the laws or ordinance of the General Assembly as aforesaid." The second, equally violent, announced that anyone who defended such laws "shall be deemed, an enemy to this his majesty's colony." Rhode Island's assembly told its officers not to use the new stamps. New York, Pennsylvania, Delaware, and Connecticut followed suit.

The Massachusetts General Court, led by the Otis-Adams faction, went farther, in part inspired by the forthrightness of the Virginia assembly's actions and ashamed of their earlier timidity in the Sugar Act debates, in part because the Stamp Act broil could be used to embarrass Hutchinson and his friends. When Governor Francis Bernard reported the new act in late September, the lower house fulminated: "Your excellency will acknowledge that there are certain original inherent rights belonging to the people, which the Parliament itself cannot divest them of, consistent with their own constitution; among these is the right of representation in the same body which exercises the power of taxation." Hutchinson had privately questioned the wisdom of the new taxes, but as lieutenant governor of the colony and chief justice of the Superior Court of Judicature, he could not publicly oppose what he privately decried. "I acquiesce," he wrote, for it would be "imprudent to oppose it, and therefore [I] am silent, but it is for this reason only."

Colonial politicians who had incautiously agreed to serve as the stamp distributors found that the legislative protest was the least of their worries. Mobs took to the streets in Boston, New York City, and Charleston to prevent stamp collectors from doing their job. Village greens served as marshaling grounds of protest against the obnoxious statute.

Andrew Oliver, Boston's stamp distributor (he got the job because he was Thomas Hutchinson's brother-in-law), was the first victim of the mob. The "Loyal Nine," a secret group of Boston artisans, tradesmen, and merchants working with Samuel Adams, turned to Ebenezer MacIntosh, the leader of the South End mob and a cobbler when he wasn't throwing brickbats, to organize the protest. On the morning of August 14, MacIntosh's crew hanged Oliver in effigy and put out the word that worse would befall anyone who took the effigy down. Even the sheriff was cowed.

That evening, MacIntosh's men, newly anointed "Sons of Liberty," carried the effigy past the government house, where Bernard, Hutchinson, and the council cowered, to Oliver's dock in Boston harbor. Bernard reported to his masters in Whitehall that "we had no force to oppose to [the mob] and making an opposition to it, without a power to support the Opposition, would only inflame the people."

The mob tore down a building that Oliver intended to use as a stamp distribution center, then marched to Oliver's house, which they demolished. The next day, conceding the inability of anyone in power to succor or protect him, Oliver relinquished his post. That night a triumphant mob lit a bonfire on Fort Hill. Eleven days later, Oliver's brother-in-law, Lieutenant Governor Hutchinson, felt the fury of the mob. As he and his eldest daughter scurried off through a back alley, the mob arrived at his house, stole everything of value, then pulled down the lovely three-story mansion.

Word of the Boston mob's actions—and the weakness of official response—flew from colony to colony. In Newport, rioters persuaded the distributor of stamps, Augustus Johnston, that he had pressing business aboard one of His Majesty's ships in the harbor. The mob then took charge of the town. Johnson publicly resigned. Governor Ward, elected by the people rather than appointed by the crown, openly condemned the act and supported the rioters.

In New York, James McEvers resigned his post before anyone asked him. He was a storekeeper, and his stock and customers meant more to him than the rewards of the new post. George Meserve, New Hampshire distributor, had accepted the job in England and resigned it before setting foot in Portsmouth. Jared Ingersoll of Connecticut stepped down when accosted by a mob on his way to an assembly session. The mob's threat to hang him swayed his decision. George Mercer of Virginia, a member of the ruling elite, braved the mob for one day, and then, with the grudging acquiescence of Governor Francis Fauquier, quit. The appointees for South Carolina fled for their lives to the fort in the harbor, and there abdicated their duties. The North Carolina appointee did not know he was appointed until the mob read him the letter. He agreed with them that he should not serve. George Angus, the Georgia distributor, was still in England when the storm broke. Not a native of the colony, he arrived secretly, distributed the stamps, then disappeared.

John Hughes, a close friend of Benjamin Franklin, and by Franklin nominated for the lucrative post of distributor for Pennsylvania, never quite understood that his unwillingness to resign with dispatch and humility would end his political career in the colony. His friends protected his house and his person when the mayor and the sheriff vanished. But Hughes could not hold out forever. When he finally conceded, he made a public statement laying the blame on Charles Thomson, Robert Morris, and others in a roll call of what would become the revolutionary party. His dignity intact but his business affairs in shambles, he spent the next eight years of his life boasting of his loyalty to the crown, and he died before the tie to it was cut.

Meanwhile, in Massachusetts, Governor Bernard was sufficiently frightened to announce that he would not attempt to land the stamps when they arrived from England, then under cover of darkness deposited them at Castle William in the harbor and waited uneasily for November 1. With the colony poised on the edge of chaos, Bernard asked his solicitor general what to do. The solicitor general referred the matter to the attorney general, who sent it back to the solicitor general, who left the mess on Bernard's desk with the sorrowful confession, "I do not look upon myself as the proper person by whose advise you (in an affair of such importance and which seems to be at present a matter rather of prudence than of law) are to govern yourselves."

The Sons of Liberty had no such qualms, and no sooner had they driven the friends of Britain to cover, than the mob reopened the port and the courts. Shippers and justices sighed with relief and resumed their activities without the hated stamped paper. The reasoning of the General Court in support of the mob was simplicity itself. There were no stamps, and there was no stamp distributor, so people could not use stamps. Thus business could legally proceed without stamps.

The mainland colonies led in the protests, but it spread as far north as Nova Scotia and as far south as the Leeward Islands of Nevis and Saint Kitts. In the West Indies, planters joined the antistamp movement, for the burden that the stamp tax placed on them was three times greater than in Massachusetts (the islands cost more to defend). They instructed their agents to oppose its passage, but they obeyed the new law. In the end, the islands' dependence upon Britain, Britain's navy, and British mercantile support for the sugar market outweighed the cost of the stamps.

In the weeks between the end of active mob violence and the date the act was due to go into effect, delegates to a Stamp Act Congress from Massachusetts, Rhode Island, Connecticut, New Jersey, Maryland, and South Carolina gathered in New York City, the guests of Robert R. Livingston and his cousin Philip. The Massachusetts General Court had issued a "circular letter" calling for the Congress in June, long before the mob had begun its work.

Thus, in one sense, the violence had interrupted a far more measured, elite-dominated process of remonstration. Indeed, among the delegates in New York were men strongly loyal to the crown, like Timothy Ruggles of Massachusetts and William Samuel Johnson of Connecticut. Emissaries from other colonial assemblies would have come but for the Massachusetts letter arriving during their recess. Royal governors like Thomas Wentworth of New Hampshire, Cadwallader Colden of New York, William Tryon of North Carolina, and Francis Fauquier of Virginia simply refused to call their legislatures back into special session to consider Massachusetts's appeal.

From October 3 to October 25, the delegates met, and over the few dissents, drafted and dispatched a Declaration of Rights to the other legislatures and three petitions to the crown and Parliament. Lawyers like Johnson and James Otis looked for precedent against the absolute authority of Parliament. Hard-chargers like Thomas McKean of Delaware and Christopher Gadsden of South Carolina pushed for colonial unity and preferred "the broad common ground of those natural and inherent rights we all feel and know" to arguments based on the colonial charters. The result was a temperate, politely couched, but uncompromising manifesto that Parliament had no power to levy taxes outside of the realm of Britain.

By this time the Grenville ministry had fallen (for reasons having nothing to do with the crisis in America—Grenville had merely offended the king once too often), and its makeshift replacement, led first by the Duke of Cumberland, and then by Lord Rockingham, one of Newcastle's old cronies, showed little stomach for enforcement of the Stamp Act. Charles Watson-Wentworth, Second Marquis of Rockingham, ordered a moratorium on discussion of the Stamp Act until he knew whether the stamps had been distributed. On December 10, the bad news arrived—no stamps had been bought or used. Rockingham conceded the obvious, adding to it his own belief that the stamps would injure British trade in the colonies. Conway appended his opinion that the rioting in America was not worth the expense to put it down. Pitt rose in the Commons to announce his opinion, somewhat belatedly, that the Stamp Act was unconstitutional from its inception and should be rescinded.

Rockingham's cabinet found a way to save face, drafting the Declaratory Act, which reasserted Parliament's authority to legislate for the colonies, to accompany

the repeal of the Stamp Act. Parliamentary speakers chimed in that the colonial rioters must be condemned, the victims of the riots recompensed for their losses, and
the governors reminded of their duty, after which Rockingham deluged the house
with reports and accounts of the deleterious impact the stamps had on the commerce
of the nation, already depressed. Rockingham avoided constitutional questions—
they were too sticky, and they made the government look like it was surrendering its
sovereignty to colonial mobs.

The Declaratory Act of 1766 restored in theory what the repeal of the Stamp Act
erased in practice—the authority of Parliament over the colonies. But the real lesson
of the pivotal years could not be so easily finessed. A relative handful of colonists had
demonstrated that they could thwart the will of Parliament so long as that will was
not backed by armed force.

FROM RESISTANCE TO REVOLUTION

Thus far, colonial protests fit a model of local resistance familiar to both English and
colonial authorities. Petitions against abuses of power in England were as old as the
Magna Carta, and remonstrances, popular gatherings, vigilantes, and mobs were
common in colonial life. In the period from 1767 to 1774, however, the momentum
of the protest and the organization of standing committees and provisional conventions and congresses indicated that the colonists wanted more than the repeal of individual statutes. Both the leaders and the supporters of the resistance groped toward a fundamental restructuring of governance.

Townshend's Duties, 1767–1768

In 1766, the Rockingham ministry fell as quietly as it had risen, and in its place
the aging and gout-ridden William Pitt, raised to the peerage as Lord Chatham, returned to power. He learned with dismay that the repeal of the Stamp Act had not
brought peace to the colonies. Massachusetts denied recompense to the victims of
the mob without a general pardon for the rioters. New York politicians refused to
bow to the acts that mandated raising funds to pay for candles and other sundries
for the troops stationed in the colony.

While the Chatham ministry fumed, Charles Townshend assumed the role of
chancellor of the exchequer, England's leading financial post under the first lord of
the treasury, and hatched an alternative plan to raise revenue. Townshend, like
Grenville, was another career administrator, having sat on the Board of Trade and
in the secretary of state's office. The third son of an aristocrat, he had found government congenial, but party politics bewildered and frustrated him.

Townshend reasoned that if the colonists would not pay an "internal" tax, England could raise revenue through external taxes or tariffs on a number of imports—
notably tea, lead, paint, glass, and paper. As in the Sugar Act, the duties would be re-

duced, but revised means for their collection—an American customs board and additional collectors—would ensure compliance. In the same round of policy meetings within the cabinet, Townshend even proposed removing all troops from the colonies and shifting the burden of paying royal governors from the shoulders of the colonial legislatures. Revenues from the new duties should suffice for that purpose.

America's friends in Parliament agreed to the new duties without a fuss, and in the colonies, even those like James Otis Jr., who lambasted the Stamp Act, conceded that the Townshend duties must be legal if Parliament could claim any right at all to regulate colonial trade. The one flaw in the new duties was the dispatch of additional collectors to the colonies. To American Whigs like Scottish-born James Wilson of Philadelphia, the collectors appeared to be "a set of idle drones . . . pensioners and placemen" ready to nourish their appetites at the colonists' expense.

In 1767, John Dickinson, a respected and wealthy Delaware lawyer, prepared a series of letters from a "Pennsylvania Farmer" (the law against criticism of the government remained in place, so opponents of the Townshend duties had to use pseudonyms) to reveal the "system of oppression" behind the new duties. They were "additional evidence of tyrannical designs," more evidence that a conspiracy thrived in England against American liberty. As the "Pennsylvania Farmer" warned his readers, "you ought to be upon your guard . . . against men who . . . serve as decoys for drawing the innocent and unwary into snares."

The Stamp Act protests had surprised the British; the nonimportation agreement against the Townshend duties confounded them. Early in 1767, newspapers in Boston introduced a proposal to boycott British goods, and in their regular meetings, Massachusetts towns began to press for nonconsumption of the items Townshend enumerated. Until 1765, the instructions the towns issued to their delegates to the General Court were infrequent and usually concerned matters of purely local importance; after 1765, the instructions became stridently anti-imperial.

Reading the town meetings' instructions, Sam Adams sensed the trend toward a broader, more systemic protest, a shift from resistance to rebellion, and asked the General Court to circularize the other colonies with a request for a common policy. No doubt Adams's real intent was to spread his own views. New Jersey and Connecticut agreed to Adams's circular letter proposal. The Virginia House of Burgesses, meeting without a royal governor (Fauquier had just died), took advantage of its momentary independence of action and concocted its own circular letter, advocating strong measures of some (unnamed) kind.

The other colonies were indifferent to Adams's effort until the Privy Council unwisely directed Lord Hillsborough, graduated from the Board of Trade to the newly created office of Secretary of State for the Colonies, to order Massachusetts to retract its original letter and colonial governors to dissolve assemblies that endorsed the circular. The tactic backfired. Massachusetts refused to budge. Indeed, in August 1767 the merchants signed a nonimportation agreement, and the idea spread to other colonies. Reluctant merchants were bullied into signing by the Sons of Liberty.

Angry at Adams, Governor Bernard refused to convene the General Court, and the towns sent representatives to a convention instead—a "mock assembly," Lieutenant Governor Hutchinson sneered. But the delegates to the convention addressed the governor as if the convention were a sovereign body—an omen of more permanent extralegal colonial bodies to come. Bernard, like Samuel Adams, sensing the change in the wind, took his pension and arranged for Hutchinson to replace him as governor. Hutchinson, thinner and more dyspeptic than usual, longed for the job but knew it was too much for him. A breakdown in 1767 had already overburdened his nerves—understandable after his house was almost pulled down around his ears. He clung to the doctrine that a supreme Parliament could not be curbed by fractious provincials, but hoped that he could mediate the dispute between his beloved colony and his imperial masters.

Nonimportation was a powerful and novel weapon in the protestors' arsenal. It drew upon the increasing dependence of the British economy on colonial purchases. But its impact upon the colonists' mentality may have been even more important than its impact of the British exporters. As T. H. Breen has argued, nonimportation, followed after 1770 by nonconsumption, that is, by boycotts, enabled ordinary colonists to take part in the protest. Those without formal power—women, for example—could become patriots by refusing to buy English goods. By visibly and audibly putting aside private pleasures, they could make themselves into model republicans. By not consuming, they rejected luxury, corruption, and all the other defects that undermined liberty in the home country.

Nonimportation and boycott also fostered the creation of protesting associations and demonstrations. These need not be violent or expose the protestors to arrest, like mob action in the streets. Instead, they made the simplest of all private, personal actions, like buying and using—or not buying—goods, into political acts. What was more, because these acts could be shared by all purchasers in the colonies, they became a material counterpart to the work of the committees of correspondence unifying the protest across the face of the colonies. Thus a movement begun in the market town of Boston reverberated up and down the entire coastline and into the interior of the colonies.

Meeting together at spinning bees to protest, women wove new roles for themselves. The more than a thousand women who joined these demonstrations combined the spiritual force of the Great Awakening with the language of disinterested civic virtue to produce garments for "daughters of liberty." In 1774, fifty-one gentleborn women in Edenton, North Carolina, signed a pledge not to consume British imports, "as a duty we owe . . . our near and dear relations." Hanna Griffiths of Philadelphia set the self-imposed ban to rhyme: "For the sake of Freedom's name /

(Since British Wisdom scorns repealing) / Come, sacrifice to Patriot fame / And give up tea, by way of healing."

Mercy Otis Warren of Boston enrolled in protest planning sessions led by her cousins, Samuel Adams and John Adams, and her brother, James Otis Jr. Her husband, James Warren, hosted these meetings. For the cause, she wrote pointed political satires like *The Adulateur, A Tragedy* (1773), in which a poorly disguised Hutchinson appeared as "Rapatio." Rapatio delighted in all the vices of corrupt power: "O'er fields of death, with hasting step I'll speed, / And smile at length to see my country bleed; / From my tame heart the pang of virtue fling, / And 'mid the general flame, like Nero Sing."

Massachusetts's Agony, 1768–1773

In October 1768, at the request of Governor Bernard, almost two thousand regular British troops landed in Boston. The commander of the garrison, Major General Thomas Gage, had served in the French and Indian War and knew that the colonists would be displeased. Attempts to keep the dispatch of troops secret failed, however. Throughout September 1768, rumor and fustian kept the pot boiling. Radicals in the town vowed, "We will destroy every soldier that dares put his foot on shore."

The Fourteenth and Twenty-ninth infantry regiments landed on October 1, led by the drummers in their yellow jackets and by grenadiers, distinctive in their bearskin hats. The officers, gleaming in silver-laced caps and crimson sashes, looked every inch the Praetorian guard of empire. The regiments marched not to the safety of the Castle William in the harbor, but directly to the Commons, where they camped. Within a few days, the officers had found private lodgings, and shortly thereafter the governor leased quarters for the troops in warehouses and stores around the customhouse. The British army was in Boston to stay.

Although the much-boasted destruction of "every soldier" failed to materialize, the troops and their officers faced a continuing stream of insults and abuses from the men who had followed Ebenezer MacIntosh and erected liberty poles on Fort Hill. Only the discipline and sheer stature of the troops dissuaded the mob from precipitate action.

Then the navy saved the day. Commodore Samuel Hood brought a small fleet into Boston harbor at the end of 1768 and reestablished old friendships with Whig leaders. Hood convinced the king's officers to join in church services, and an uneasy truce (peace would be too strong a term) arose between the town and the garrison. Hood and Gage allowed the Boston justices of the peace to arrest rowdy soldiers and sailors, and troops aided the fire brigades. Hood even curbed the navy's impressment gangs.

Within a year, the soldiers were regarded as an unwelcome but tolerable force of riot police rather than an occupying army. Only the British practice of allowing sentries to challenge passersby at key points reminded the casual observer of the friction—though that practice produced enough mischief to keep the pot simmering.

One post the British could not abandon was the customhouse—the focus of so much colonial resentment. On the cold and cloudy night of March 5, 1770, after a week of fistfights between off-duty soldiers and young townsmen, a mob congregated in front of the customhouse sentry box and started hurling frozen snowballs at the sentry on duty, Private Hugh White. He was well known about the docks—a brawler himself—but he called out for assistance, and Captain Thomas Preston led six other soldiers to the rescue. Confronted by an angry mob literally no more than a bayonet away, Preston tried to reason his way out of trouble. Unfortunately, one of his relief party was knocked down and rose up firing his musket. A ragged volley followed. Perhaps the soldiers heard the mob leaders cry out "fire" (they used it to assemble their followers) and, confused, discharged their muskets. When the smoke cleared, the mob fled, leaving three men dead, a fourth dying, and a fifth, a boy who had come to see the hubbub, fatally wounded.

The Boston grand jury indicted Captain Preston and his command for murder. Wishing to avoid reprisals and sure that a conviction was inevitable, resistance leaders prevailed upon two of their number, John Adams and Josiah Quincy Jr., to represent the British soldiers. At the trial, Adams insisted that the protests must rest upon law or fail: "Whatever effect they may have on politics; they are rules of common law, the law of the land." Although Adams much later claimed that the trial proved the integrity of the revolutionary movement, in fact the royal sheriff packed the jury for the defense. Adams and Quincy could have sat on their hands and still won.

Still, a lawyer's job was zealous advocacy, and Adams and Quincy cleverly insisted that Preston should be tried first, separate from his men. In defending him, they argued that he did not give the order to fire; the soldiers acted on their own. Witnesses' testimony was conflicting; they could not even agree on what Preston wore, where he stood, or what he said. There was some evidence that Preston remained in front of his troops, surely a dangerous place to be if he intended them to fire their muskets. Preston was acquitted.

The trial of the soldiers turned on a second defense tactic. Adams and Quincy conceded that the soldiers had fired willfully and their fire had killed the five men, but they added that the soldiers feared for their lives, had no place to run, and acted wholly in self-defense. The jury agreed.

The acquittal of the soldiers notwithstanding, the resistance movement had its first true martyrs. Boston radicals like the silversmith Paul Revere subtly altered the facts to produce graphic pictures of unprovoked British brutality. His widely viewed depiction of the "massacre" showed not its confusion and nothing of the fear the troops felt. Instead, he made the night clear and the soldiers appear larger than life. As propaganda, his engraving was superb.

In the summer of 1772, the newly established Boston committee of correspondence began to distribute such propaganda throughout the colonies, linking the plans of the not-so-secret Loyal Nine to other groups of patriots throughout North America. The idea was not new—assemblies sometimes named temporary committees to correspond with other assemblies and with their English agents—but Samuel Adams's brainchild was a permanent, extraofficial institution.

The new committee became the first of a series of committees of correspondence reaching out into the colony, in effect a shadow government alongside the regular assembly, council, and governor's offices. Should the royal government falter, the committees could step in to ensure public order.

As yet, none of the Whigs had any idea what to do with the growing sense of alienation. The committees of correspondence throughout the colonies could encourage one another to keep up the political activity—but to what end?

A new ministry, led by Frederick, Lord North, had come to power in 1770 and had repealed all the duties but that on tea. North thought that the gradual weakening of the nonimportation movement signaled an end to the troubles. At thirty-seven an energetic and well-educated (Eton and Oxford) aristocrat, Lord North was as much a supporter of parliamentary supremacy as Hutchinson, but he urged a mixture of firmness and conciliation until the crisis subsided. Lord North did not understand that Massachusetts was merely a step ahead of the rest of the colonies. The same restiveness with distant British instructions and impenetrable British parliamentary politics stirred in New York, Virginia, and the other colonies.

Misunderstanding the depth and force of colonial unrest, Lord North's ministry made two critical mistakes. The first was a plan to put the entire civil list (all the royal officials) on English salaries. The charter provisions that gave to assemblies the task of paying royal officials was a privilege the crown extended to the settlers. Legally, it could be altered at will. But if the charter could be changed in this way, might it not also be changed in others?

Again, Massachusetts led the protest. When the Superior Court of Judicature's justices were added to the civil list in early 1773, the committee of correspondence, the Whig leadership of the assembly, and the local grand juries rose as one in protest. The assembly threatened to impeach any superior court judge who substituted a salary from England for his colonial paycheck. The grand juries on the superior court circuit refused to sit if such a justice held court. Hutchinson and the council blocked the impeachment idea, but the recalcitrance of the jurors in the rural counties shut down the courts.

The opposition to the new civil list could have been anticipated, but the violent response to the Tea Act of 1773, Lord North's second error, genuinely shocked the English government. In 1773, the East India Company, the source of English tea imports, tottered on the verge of bankruptcy. English warehouses bulged with unsold tea. To increase sales in America, Parliament allowed the company to export its tea to the colonies directly, at a substantial cut in cost to American consumers. But the act retained the three-penny impost and gave the company a monopoly, a not so subtle message Parliament still dictated the terms of colonial commerce.

As in the Stamp Act crisis, the Sons of Liberty forced merchants to retract their commissions to import and market the tea, except in Boston. Furious, the mob threatened the merchants. Samuel Adams then called a mass meeting for November 29 to demand that the tea waiting on ships in the harbor be returned to England, but on December 16, 1773, three ships, the *Dartmouth*, *Eleanor*, and *Beaver*, still remained in port with their cargoes. That night, Adams led a mob, some fifty of whom were disguised as Indians, to the wharfs and boarded the ships, broke into their holds, smashed the casks of tea, and tossed the bundled leaves overboard.

More moderate Whigs feared that Adams had gone overboard with the tea, but the overreaction of the North ministry saved Adams and made the "Mohawks" at the "tea party" into Whig heroes. On January 27, 1774, Hutchinson's report of the Boston Tea Party reached Lord North. The government's reaction was immediate. Solicitor General Alexander Wedderburn summoned Benjamin Franklin, agent for the colony, and blistered him for over an hour. In Parliament, even Isaac Barré turned his face away from the Bostonians.

After a month of discussion, the ministry decided not to search out the ringleaders of the Boston Tea Party, but to shut the port of Boston and revise the charter of the colony. Over the next three months, Lord North's government added four more punitive acts—the Massachusetts Government Act giving the royal governor expanded appointment and removal powers, and sheriffs (instead of town selectmen) the job of naming jurors; the Impartial Administration of Justice Act, providing for trial in England of colonial officials accused of serious crimes; a new Quartering Act, requiring private families to provide rooms for soldiers; and the Quebec Act, confirming Roman Catholic French Canadians in the rights of self-government, which the crown had just taken from the people of Massachusetts. General Gage returned on May 13, 1774, to replace Hutchinson as governor. Together, the four acts and the dispatch of a serving general officer of the army as governor imposed the full weight of imperial authority on Massachusetts.

Samuel Adams fulminated that the acts were "coercive." Others worried that the influence of Roman Catholicism, so greatly feared by Puritans in Massachusetts, had once again crept into the palace at Windsor. The committee of correspondence spread these fears throughout the colonies. Men as cautious as Philadelphia's James Wilson expressed outrage at the "Coercive Acts." On August 17, 1774, Wilson told the Pennsylvania Assembly that there had been "a great compact between the king and his people," creating a trust, which the king violated when he "altered the charter" of Massachusetts. The king was just as bound by the law—not the imperial law, but the immutable principles of trusteeship—as the colonists. With his breach of the trust, the tie of allegiance of colonists to king was also broken. "All attempts to

alter the charter or constitution of [a] colony, unless by the authority of its own legislature, are violations of its rights, and illegal." The Massachusetts charter, a privilege the king granted to the settlers, Wilson transmuted into a "constitution" that
limited the power of its royal grantor.

A New Generation of Leaders

Men like Samuel Adams and Patrick Henry had come to public life by traditional
pre-1765 pathways—local politics, service in the assembly, and royal patronage. The
widening crisis provided an alternative route to office. A generation of American
politicians rode the protests to power in the decade 1765–1775. Two of these politicians, John Adams and Thomas Jefferson, played vital roles in explaining the colonists' quarrel with Britain to the world.

In later life, John Adams insisted that the Revolution took place in the hearts and
minds of the people before the war for independence began. If so, he was one of the
foremost advocates of that transformation. The son of a farmer-tradesman and cobbler whose family arrived in Massachusetts in 1638, Adams came from the middle
class, not the elite. He attended Harvard College but did not train for the pulpit as
his father expected. Instead, he studied for the bar and began practice in 1758.

A student of languages, politics, history, and other academic subjects along with
law, Adams had a romantic streak, a love of bold ideas and distant horizons. He as-
pired to be great, somehow, and in him this pride warred with the humility of a true
Puritan. He never resolved the contradiction, and the struggle within sometimes
made him censorious, jealous, and obsessively self-critical.

By 1763, his law practice allowed him to consider marriage and a family of his
own. The daughter of a wealthy clergyman, Abigail Smith was serious, modest, and
intellectually able. She encouraged her husband in his political aspirations but moderated his fiery ambition. With Abigail's support, he threw himself into the defense
of the resistance.

Adams's *Dissertation on the Canon and Feudal Law* (1765) argued that Britain must
not send an Anglican bishop to the colonies. He entered the General Court in 1770
as a staunch Whig and James Otis Jr.'s disciple. Although Adams withdrew from politics from 1771 to 1773, the Coercive Acts brought him back, and Massachusetts sent
him to the First Continental Congress to convene in Philadelphia in September 1774.
There he attacked North's ministry and lauded the protestors as "a set of men . . .
who have sacrificed their private interest to their nation's honor and the public
good."

Virginia's House of Burgesses was in the process of selecting its delegates to the
first meeting of the Continental Congress in 1774 when Lord Dunmore summarily
dissolved the assembly. The members reassembled at Raleigh Tavern and chose delegates anyhow. Among the absent burgesses chosen was a diffident, hulking, handsome thirty-one-year-old planter, Thomas Jefferson. Illness had overtaken him on

the way to Williamsburg, but he sent ahead an essay that magnificently summarized the case for rebellion.

Jefferson's *Summary View of the Rights of British Americans* denied all parliamentary authority over the colonies. With a single stroke, Jefferson had thus found a way to solve the problem that so bedeviled Samuel Adams and the other Massachusetts Whigs. The colonies were never part of the realm, Jefferson reasoned, hence never subject to the lawful supremacy of Parliament. The colonies were the king's domain, and to his sense of justice Jefferson appealed. Yet even the power of the king was circumscribed, Jefferson argued, for the settlers of America possessed inalienable rights. It was thus to an ideal Lockean ruler that Jefferson turned, not George III.

A son of the country planter elite, Jefferson was a practicing lawyer with a growing clientele in the 1760s. In private, he demonstrated a bold and far-reaching grasp of human, as opposed to mere legal, rights. He loved liberty, yearned for a world in which men were truly equal, but pulled back from radical reforms like freeing the slaves and according equal rights to women. He feared cities, commerce, and corruption—as any planter might—but loved ancient history, the ideal of republican government, and religious liberty. In the end, the freedom he sought was a liberation of human minds from superstition and false privileges—not a leveling of social or economic ranks.

In Congress Assembled, 1774

The delegates to the First Continental Congress in September 1774 included colonial politicians of every ideological stripe. Some were elitist, and others gloried in the protest movement. Thus the Congress's function was as much social as it was intellectual or political. Men who had written to one another or knew one another only by reputation met and took one another's measure. The very fact that civil war loomed sobered the delegates. There were no mass town meetings or mobs to drown out the voices of moderates and compromisers. According to Charles Carroll, whose personal conservatism tempered his political opinions, even the "New England delegates are as moderate as any—nay the most so."

To Philadelphia not only came the delegates, but a flood of instructions and suggestions from meetings and committees of colonists. These clones of the Massachusetts town meetings and committees of correspondence proved that Samuel Adams's shadow government idea had borne fruit. The Whig collectives promised their support for Congress's resolutions.

In response to the Coercive Acts, Congress endorsed Massachusetts's "Suffolk Resolves" in favor of peaceful resistance. Congress forbore telling Massachusetts to constitute government on its own or to call out its militia. When word arrived that Gage had begun to fortify Boston, Congress remonstrated respectfully. If the overworked Gage missed the fact that Congress was taking control of individual colonies' policies, the Massachusetts delegation must have quietly celebrated their achievement—at last they had convinced a pancolonial body to act as though it were a true confederation government.

But wary lawyers like New York's James Duane and John Jay urged Congress to pay for the tea the mob threw in the harbor, and other moderate delegates wanted a permanent union of the colonies under the umbrella of the British Empire. On September 28, Joseph Galloway of Pennsylvania suggested a "grand council" of the colonies to run domestic affairs and draft "bills for granting aid to the crown." Parliament would not be able to legislate for the colonies without the consent of this colonial council. The delegates to Congress, voting by colony, delayed (indefinitely as it turned out) consideration of the Galloway plan.

Galloway intended his proposal to forestall a vote on a renewal of nonimportation, but in a series of resolutions early in October, Congress reimposed economic sanctions against the British. In a detailed fourteen-point "Association" to enforce nonimportation and nonexportation, Congress again asserted its control over the resistance movement. Congress did "cheerfully consent to the operation of such acts of the British Parliament, as are bona fide, restrained to the regulation of our external commerce," a grant of privilege to Parliament that consciously reversed the legal relationship between Parliament and the colonies.

Moderates like Galloway, Duane, and Jay could not persuade Congress to retreat, but they could keep the debate open, candid, and free of rancor and vitriol. No one conceded parliamentary supremacy. No one spoke of independence. John Dickinson pleaded for some sort of formal concession, and in the coming months would lobby for a direct petition to the crown to end the conflict. His "Olive Branch" petition was actually adopted in July 1775, long after it might have had any effect on the king or the crisis.

Choosing Sides

In the meantime, the two sides' views had hardened in the colonies. In 1763, there were no "loyalists," or rather, everyone professed loyalty to crown and empire. By 1774, "loyalists" were a distinct and formidable political cadre. John Adams estimated their number at one-third of the population. Later counts put the active loyalist contingent at 20 percent of the adult colonists.

In socioeconomic status, education, and experience, the loyalists were a cross section of the colonial population. Recent immigrants from the British Isles, longtime Quaker residents, Anglican ministers, Dutch and German culture groups, most of the Native Americans, and many of the slaves adhered to the crown in the contest. So, obviously, did retired British soldiers and mariners. Wealthy merchants with English ties, like the Hutchinson clan and the DeLanceys of New York, and poor backcountry farmers of Scots Highland descent remained faithful to the old allegiance. Imperial officeholders like William Johnson of New York and his son, John, and John Wentworth and his family in New Hampshire clove to the British cause. So did men and women who needed order and authority in their lives, and feared radical change and an uncertain future. Convenience sometimes was more important than ethnic background or political affiliation, however. As one loyalist wrote, somewhat sardonically, "We are at present all Whigs until the arrival of the king's troops."

Loyalist intellectuals carried on a campaign against Congress as openly as they dared. They had law, long usage, and more than a little right on their side. The "rebels," as the loyalists called the revolutionaries, violated solemn oaths and took up arms against their rightful king. These loyalist writers had little affection for the new populist politics and decried the mob. Such arguments were not "Tory," however they might be mischaracterized by the Whigs. They demonstrated instead "an affectionate regard for Great Britain, in veneration for her constitution and laws."

Indeed, although many loyalists were conservatives like Hutchinson, others were moderate in their views like Galloway, had opposed the parliamentary acts, and wished the colonies returned to salutary neglect. Some, like William Smith Jr. of New York's "Whig Triumvirate," led protests but balked at the idea of independence. As Governor William Franklin of New Jersey told his legislature in 1775, "You now have pointed out to you, Gentlemen, two roads—one evidently leading to peace, happiness, and a restoration of public tranquillity—the other inevitably conducting you to anarchy, misery, and all the horrors of a civil war." William Franklin had seen the future, although his view of it was highly partisan.

The Resort to Arms, 1775

In March 1775, Virginia's Whig leaders again met in what they called a "provincial convention," the shadow government introduced by the committees of correspondence taking corporeal shape. There Henry urged and Jefferson supported a resolve to set the colony in a state of defense. Dunmore fled to a British warship at the mouth of the James. When moderates cooled Henry off, Dunmore tried to reconvene the assembly to hear Lord North's proposal for requisitions from the colonies instead of taxes. Jefferson based the burgesses' reply on his own *Summary View*: Parliament had no right "to institute government here." The governor returned to his man-of-war, and shortly thereafter offered freedom to slaves who left their masters, raising the specter of rebellion within the rebels' ranks.

Before Congress could reassemble in May 1775, the British raised the stakes of the conflict in Massachusetts. Gage was a gentleman, and cautious to a fault. He would not be the first to make war on the rebels, if he could help it. But his attempts to seize local munitions supplies in Portsmouth, New Hampshire, and Salem, Massachusetts, had met with ignominious failure, in part because a spy network made up of Paul Revere's men kept the militia informed of Gage's plans.

In the meantime, the extraordinarily cold winter of 1774–1775 and the muddy, late-thawing spring of 1775 brought considerable hardship to the troops garrisoned in Boston. Desertion daily reduced Gage's strength, as Whigs ran an underground

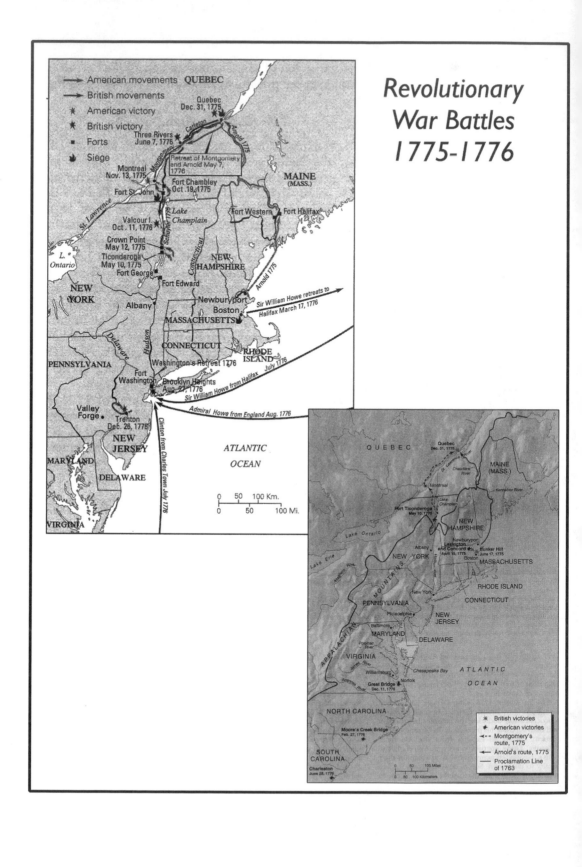

Revolutionary War Battles 1775-1776

railroad to help the deserters escape. His soldiers sold their equipment to peddlers and tavern keepers for rum. The General Court, recasting itself as a provincial Congress, met just outside Gage's reach, in Cambridge, and plotted resistance.

Gage's patience exhausted itself as his situation deteriorated. He begged Lord North for more than the three thousand troops already allotted, and North sent him four hundred marines and instructions to enforce the Coercive Acts. So Gage gambled on a single throw of the dice—a raid in force to catch the ringleaders of the resistance and destroy the colonial arsenal supposedly in Concord. Gage faced two problems: first, finding the leaders of the rebellion, Samuel Adams and John Hancock; and second, not firing the first shot. The first task required good operational intelligence, which Gage had; the second depended upon the ability of his officers and the discipline of his troops.

Gage's spies reported back that the Lexington road was the fastest way to Concord. Gage hardened his troops for the expedition with forced marches and maneuvers, keeping Revere and his informants guessing about British intentions. But Gage could not hide his final preparations. On the night of April 18, Revere's riders rushed from their beds and barns to warn the countryside that "the regulars are coming." The two lantern lights Revere displayed in the North Church steeple indicated that the British were crossing the water to Cambridge, and Revere then crossed to the Charleston side and, mounted, spurred toward Lexington.

The regulars were indeed coming. Over the course of the next day, nearly nine hundred British light infantry marched to Lexington, there engaged through error a small body of minutemen and routed them, turned back to the road (the officers having prevented the bloody accident from becoming a massacre), marched on to Concord, and spread out, futilely, to find the expected caches of powder and shot. Samuel Adams and John Hancock, forewarned, had long since fled.

While the main body of regulars searched the town, the advance guard at the town's North Bridge looked up to see two regiments of colonial militia bearing down on the bridge. As in Lexington, the British fired first, and when the colonists and British were fifty yards from each other, both let off volleys. Cut off and in danger of encirclement, the regulars ran back to the main force in the town center, leaving behind as casualties four of their eight officers. The colonists might have continued the carnage against scattered parties of regulars, but they held their fire until the main body began its long and bloody retreat.

Exhausted, hungry, and wildly outnumbered, the regulars marched back down the road to Boston while the militia fired from cover. Only the timely arrival of Brigadier General Lord Percy with a relief force on the same Lexington Green where the fighting began prevented the retreat from becoming a catastrophe. Even then, Percy's men came under merciless fire. Had he not had nineteen hundred men to add to the survivors of the original party, he might not have effected his purpose of rescue. Percy's skirmishers and flanking parties kept the road to Boston reasonably clear, and a last counterattack by the Royal Marines allowed Percy's command to reach safety under the Royal Navy's cannons in the harbor. On a piece of high ground called Bunker Hill, the troops laid down their weapons and slept.

Lord Percy, whose deployment of troops, resolve, and quick reactions made him the hero of one of His Majesty's army's sorriest days, warned that the militia was a formidable foe, and the rebels were resolved to "go through with it." Over the next months, the militia proved him correct. On June 17, 1775, Gage would again call upon his troops to fight their way out of the encircling militia, but wasted his men to no purpose at the battle of Bunker Hill (actually fought on the slightly lower elevation of Breeds Hill). In their assault upon the colonists' fortifications, the British lost over one thousand of their finest troops to 411 American dead and wounded. That the British won the field made little difference. Another such victory, General Henry Clinton commented, might well exterminate the British expeditionary force.

The colonists credited their defense of their homes to the virtue of their cause, the aid of Providence, and their natural, innate courage. They assumed that these better prepared them to fight than the close-order drill the regulars practiced, and further that elected officers could better lead troops than younger sons of English nobility who had to pay for their commissions. They concluded that their victories over Gage's expeditionary force presaged the ultimate triumph of their cause.

The Second Continental Congress gathered shortly after the battles of Lexington and Concord. News of more fighting soon arrived. Congress ordered Connecticut militia commander (and peacetime merchant) Benedict Arnold to oust the British from Fort Ticonderoga at the southern terminus of New York's Lake Champlain. Arriving in the area, he found that Ethan Allen, a feisty and popular leader of the "Green Mountain Boys" in Vermont (the "boys" spent most of their time contesting land grants in western Vermont with equally violent New York claimants), was readying to pull off the feat on his own.

On May 10, 1775, the two men, with a band of three hundred militiamen, entered the fort and caught the British literally napping. They took the fort without firing a shot. Crown Point fell shortly thereafter. With Canada pacified and the Abenakis and Kahnewaka Mohawks made subjects of the crown, the British had neglected to guard the Lake Champlain route from Montreal to Albany, New York. An impregnable fortress with thick walls a hundred feet high, surrounded on three sides by water, Ticonderoga should never have fallen to Allen, Arnold, and their hastily assembled farmers.

Congress, delighted with Allen's success, gave him the laurels for it, and Arnold resigned his commission—the first of many resentments he would harbor against Congress. But neither the victory at Concord nor the triumphs of Allen's decidedly irregular troops fooled Congress into believing that a war could be won without a regular army.

In July, with news of the carnage at Bunker Hill on their desks, Congress put aside for a time its ingrained fear of a standing army, and provided for just such an in-strument to save the cause. Everyone agreed that regular armies were engines of op-pression. The British regulars' conduct in Boston had underlined the point. Every-one preferred citizen soldiers, virtuous and courageous amateurs defending their homes. The American militia tradition was built on just such an ideal. Every colony had such a militia, but it was designed for defense of the locality, not for waging a war far from home against the might of the British Empire.

Indeed, the colonial forces that had so gathered during eighteenth-century wars for empire—for example, the American soldiers and sailors who fought alongside the British in Canada, on the frontier, and in the Caribbean during King George's War and the French and Indian War—were not the militia at all but were enlisted troops.

Unlike the militia, these American levies came from the lowest rungs of society and displayed little discipline and less inclination to stand and fight. The British mis-understood this difference, and regarded the American soldier as a despicable ally and an unworthy opponent. Gage was thus astounded that the American minutemen had done so well during the retreat of his forces from Concord and the battle for Breeds Hill—confusing those militiamen with the colonial hireling soldiers of ear-lier wars.

To explain why Congress had turned to arming the people, Thomas Jefferson pre-pared a "Declaration of the Causes of Taking Up Arms," which John Dickinson re-vised. "We fight not for glory or for conquest," the draft insisted, rejecting the tra-ditional reasons for raising an army. Instead, Congress saw the Continental army as a gathering of volunteer citizen-soldiers, an "inspired yeomanry, all sinew and soul" rushing from their plows and hearths to rout the British. Congress chose George Washington as commander, not just because he was an experienced officer, but also because his moral character seemed to embody the republican virtues. It named thir-teen other generals, none of them career soldiers.

BRITAIN'S OTHER COLONIES

Not all of Britain's colonies joined in the revolutionary movement. Britain's posses-sions in India, Africa, and the Pacific did not share the basic pattern of the North American colonies—heavily populated with Britons, semi-self-governing, and righ-teous in their indignation. Closer to the maelstrom, Canada, the West Indies, and Florida might have joined in the protest, but did not.

Canada

One of Congress's first moves, when it reassembled in June 1775, was to rescind its earlier policy on Canada. In 1774, Congress had entreated the Canadians to join in the protest. They remained aloof. The Quebec Act may have reassured some

French Canadians of the good intentions of the British, but more important was the Canadians' suspicion that the New England ministry (squarely in the revolutionaries' corner) still harbored a fierce animosity toward Roman Catholicism. French Canadian landlords were equally wary of the revolutionaries' radicalism.

Receiving no encouragement from the Canadians, Congress determined to cow their northern neighbors with the threat of force. From Ticonderoga, a motley but sizable force of New York and New England recruits pressed up Lake Champlain into the Richelieu River, took Montreal, and then besieged Quebec. Winter, disease, a lack of supply, the desertion of the short timers, the lack of ammunition, the untimely death of seasoned commander James Montgomery, the wounding of his second in command (the ubiquitous Benedict Arnold), and the refusal of the British in Quebec to repeat Montcalm's mistake at the Plains of Abraham (this time they stayed inside the walled fortress) brought the effort to a halt in the winter of 1775–1776.

The invading army of over eight thousand men had melted away to five thousand by the time that Major General John Burgoyne arrived from England with twelve thousand troops on June 1, 1776, to reinforce Governor Guy Carleton's regiments of infantry and Indians. The Canadians welcomed the arrival of the Burgoyne's troops—a marvelous boost to the sagging economy of Nova Scotia and Quebec—and joined the regulars to drive the congressional forces from the province.

The new congressional commander, James Sullivan of New Hampshire, skillfully extricated what remained of the Continental forces from the British advance, but by the end of June, when the Americans finally broke contact with the British, no one could disguise the extent of the debacle. Troops and commanders from different colonies blamed one another, Congress saw the lost opportunity as a great setback, and Washington rightly feared that the British would use the upper portion of New York as a staging ground for an invasion.

The West Indies and Florida

The British West Indies islands had shown sympathy with Congress's demand for domestic legislative autonomy. In 1774, the Jamaica assembly even declared that the island should not be subject to parliamentary taxation. But the islands never considered independence.

West and East Florida, obtained from Spain as part of the peace treaty of 1763, were too thinly populated to take any part in the protests. New England, New York, Virginia, and English land speculators and veterans groups had gained title to large tracts of land, but the only real British presence consisted of trading posts at Natchez, on the Mississippi, and New Richmond (later Baton Rouge).

A few Continental raiders sailed out of New Orleans (still Spanish) to harry the British in Florida, but the Continental army was not the real threat. The Spanish were rightfully wary that their colonies might follow the American example, but the opportunity to defeat their old British enemy outweighed all other considerations. Under the energetic leadership of Jóse de Gálvez, secretary of the Indies, the Spanish regained East and West Florida, took Mobile and Pensacola by storm, and reestablished ties with the Creeks and Choctaws. In 1779, King Charles III of Spain followed his Bourbon cousin King Louis XVI of France in concluding a mutual defense pact with the new United States of America.

————

The movement from resistance to revolution brought together groups of people from different backgrounds, social strata, and geographical regions. It did not overturn existing political or social hierarchies, but opened those structures up to men who before the crisis had little chance of occupying posts of public trust and leadership. It created new structures that incorporated elements of direct democracy, including the Sons of Liberty and the committees of safety. These small and semisecret bodies transformed urban cadres into mass political parties. Working together, the leadership and their support groups policed the colonies and coordinated action. In the latter stages of the protest, revolutionary members of the colonial governments reconfigured themselves as provincial congresses. Sitting in these, the revolutionaries rejected hereditary nobility and royal authority in favor of representative republicanism.

But the cause did not take the next step, to imbue a broader segment of the population with the rights and the obligations of full citizenship. As George Mason, one of the leading Virginia revolutionaries and a man of liberal sentiments told the Virginia constitutional convention in early 1776, one must be "in a state of society" to merit the blessings of civil rights. For Mason and his colleagues, many of their neighbors—African, Indian, female, Catholic—had not yet achieved that distinction.

15

Independence, War, and Republicanism, 1776–1783

We hold these truths to be self evident: that all men are created equal; that they are endowed by their creator with certain unalienable rights; that among these are life, liberty, and the pursuit of happiness.
—Declaration of Independence,
July 4, 1776

We hear that the inmy is kill'd and taken great numbers of our people.
—Jeremiah Greenman's diary, September 1776

A short decade after the celebration of the triumph of the British Empire in the New World, the American colonists and the British government were slip-sliding toward war. Even such avid promoters of empire in 1763 as Benjamin Franklin had by 1775 concluded that a closer union with Britain "will only be to corrupt and poison us also."

A year later, thirteen of the British colonies in the New World threw off their once-proud allegiance to Britain and "assumed their rightful place among the nations" as a confederation of independent republics. In the laws these new states passed to govern themselves and in the war they waged against Great Britain, the United States of America tested the strength and the limitations of revolutionary idealism. The conflict between the two powers lasted more than seven years and profoundly changed the course of history.

THE IMMEDIATE PROBLEMS OF INDEPENDENCE

In May 1775, John Rutledge, a leading South Carolina rice planter, asked his fellow delegates to Congress: "Do we aim at independency?" Despite the onset of hostilities, for a time it seemed as if only Samuel Adams and a handful of other delegates were ready to cut the ties that bound the colonies to the home country.

It was George III, furious that the colonists had thumbed their noses at his authority, who forced the issue. Stubborn if otherwise personable, he was a man of simple tastes who gloried in the role of patriot king. In July, he issued a proclamation that the Americans had "proceeded to open and avowed rebellion." He rejected the petition that John Dickinson had drafted seeking a compromise. In December, the king unleashed the Royal Navy to prey on rebel American shipping and blockade American ports.

In January 1776, an English immigrant to Philadelphia named Thomas Paine published a series of newspaper essays titled "Common Sense" that captured what many Americans were already thinking: "The king is not to be trusted," Paine warned, and "the authority of Great Britain over this continent, is a form of government, which sooner or later must have an end." Paine's articles were everywhere read and quoted in the colonies.

But could the united colonies survive without a king? Who had ever heard of a republic upon so grand a scale as the North American colonies? Would not factions destroy it from within? In British and American political thinking, factions were self-interested groups that conspired against the public interest. John Adams had an answer—Congress must tell each colony to refashion itself into a small republic. The confederation of these republics, supervised by the Continental Congress, would prevent anarchy and preserve liberty. His plan gained the approval of Congress after a bitter debate on May 15, 1776. In the process, Congress openly assumed responsibility for directing the rebellion.

The Great Declaration

On June 7, 1776, Richard Henry Lee, a Virginia delegate to Congress, returned from his home with instructions from the burgesses to introduce a resolution: "that these united colonies are, and of right ought to be, free and independent states." A vote on the question was not yet possible, for New York, Maryland, Pennsylvania, Delaware, and New Jersey had not instructed their delegates on the matter of final separation. So Congress marked time by selecting a committee to draft a declaration justifying independence. Jefferson, John Adams, Franklin, Roger Sherman of Connecticut, and Robert R. Livingston of New York agreed to serve.

The committee reported a first draft to Congress on June 28, and Congress began its deliberations three days later. On July 2, 1776, when it voted on the Declaration of Independence, approval of the committee's handiwork was unanimous. The words could not win battles against the might Britain was massing to suppress the rebellion, but the words could and did galvanize the American people in common cause.

Historians have decided that Jefferson played the most important role in the drafting process of the Declaration, but he had help. First, even before Congress voted on Lee's resolution, a number of the colonial assemblies had drafted their own declarations of independence. The purposes of these declarations varied. Some announced that a former colony was now an independent state. Others attempted to rally public support for the break with Britain. All of these declarations charged the imperial government with misconduct.

Second, the committee the Continental Congress created to draft the Declaration included four lawyers—Adams, Jefferson, Livingston, and Sherman (only Franklin had never practiced law). This was not surprising in light of the number of lawyers in Congress, nearly two-thirds of the delegates. Together they laid out the principal sections of the proposed document in outline during a series of meetings, as though they were preparing a legal brief to argue in a court of law—with public opinion to judge the rightness of their causes.

Jefferson accepted the charge of writing a first draft. He had not taken the leading role in demanding separation that Adams and others had. In fact, a poor public speaker, he had remained silent during much of the debate. But he was a superb writer. In later years, many Americans would honor him by praising the originality of his ideas in the Declaration, but Jefferson himself said, with truth, that he had merely assembled the common beliefs of the revolutionaries. Although the draft seemed to combine many scholarly, legal, and philosophical sources, he later recalled that he had used neither "book nor pamphlet while writing it."

Jefferson knew that the document would be read throughout the land and in foreign countries. Thus it needed a dramatic and powerful preamble to catch the ear and touch the heart of listeners. The preamble that he wrote, the only part of the document Congress did little to change, offered a ringing statement of principles that had little reality, as yet. For example, he called Americans "one people," portraying a unity of sentiment and interests that hardly existed at the time. He appealed to history ("when in the course of human events"), when history offered little precedent for the revolutionary cause. He made a rebellion in a part of the globe far from the capitals of Europe into the focal point for the "opinions of mankind." His invocation of "life, liberty, and the pursuit of happiness" hardly applied to the Africans and Indians, nor did his claim that "all men are created equal" admit to the mistreatment of slaves and the inequality of women in his own Virginia, though to be fair such contradictions were commonplace in revolutionary rhetoric.

The rest of his draft of the Declaration of Independence was a history of a political and parental relationship gone bad: "The history of the present king of Great Britain is a history of repeated injuries and usurpations, all having in direct object the establishment of an absolute tyranny over these states." The litany of injuries, infringements, and usurpations that followed proved that George III violated his own laws as well as the settled usages of the colonies. When harassment failed to produce subservience, the king dispatched armed forces to the colonies; quartered them upon private citizens; cut off trade; imposed taxes; denied trial by jury; and curtailed chartered privileges, all without the consent of the colonists. Finally, he had "abdicated government" by declaring war on his own subjects, exciting domestic insurrection among the colonists and their servants and slaves, and raising armies of foreign mercenaries to bring the people under his heel.

Third, Congress spent July 2 on the committee draft, sharpening the language and making a number of major substantive changes. We will never know precisely who in Congress suggested which of the changes, but the most striking of them, the deletion of Jefferson's scathing condemnation of the external slave trade, probably came at the insistence of South Carolina and Georgia. Both were deeply engaged in the importation of slaves from Africa and the Caribbean.

Although Congress refused to condemn the slave trade, in a very short time the Declaration would become a model for slaves and their spokesmen to petition governments for the abolition of slavery. One of these slaves' petitions for freedom, from Massachusetts, reused the language of the Declaration to make its case.

Slavery and Independence

During and after the war, efforts to end slavery bore fruit in the New England and Middle Atlantic states. The existence of slavery in the British colonies rested upon a unity of purpose among the slaveholders as well as on the aid of the colonial governments. But the Revolution pitted patriot slaveholders against loyalist slaveholders and disrupted the police powers of government over large areas. When opposing forces clashed or British troops were near, some slaves walked away from revolutionary masters and either lost themselves in the confusion or offered their services to the British in return for their freedom. Within revolutionary strongholds, slave masters found it hard to accuse the British of enslaving Americans and still keep slaves. Finally, slaves' labor became vital to the Revolutionary War effort, giving slaves more bargaining power than they had in peacetime. With this leverage, some slaves negotiated for their freedom.

By the end of the 1780s, New England slaves gained freedom through suits in courts and by acts of legislatures. In New York, New Jersey, and Pennsylvania, where slave owners were more numerous than in New England, legislators made manumission of slaves by their owners easier, but did not abolish slavery. As late as 1810, there were still twenty-seven thousand slaves in these states. Full emancipation did not come in Pennsylvania until 1847, and New Jersey still had slaves until the Thirteenth Amendment, in 1865.

In the first year of hostilities in the Chesapeake region, about eight hundred slaves found freedom by accepting Lord Dunmore's offer. Thereafter, whenever the British raided the coast, slaves flocked to the British side. When Lord Cornwallis's invasion force arrived in 1781, some five thousand Virginia slaves joined him. Other slaves took advantage of British attacks to hide in refuges like the Great Dismal Swamp on the border of southeastern Virginia and northeastern North Carolina.

Although Dunmore's call for slaves to turn on their masters caused Chesapeake planters to quake in fear, some conceded that slavery was inconsistent with the ideal of liberty. In 1782, Virginia laws made it possible for masters to free their slaves. The number of freedmen and women grew from two thousand to twelve thousand by 1790. Maryland masters freed even more of their slaves, and by 1810 nearly thirty-four thousand people of color in the state were free. Generally, masters who followed this course attached some sort of condition to the freedom, deferring it or turning it into an extended apprenticeship. Most masters simply worked their remaining slaves harder or moved their slaves west, out of the war zone.

The war had almost no effect on the long-term course of slavery in the lower

South. Charleston and Savannah were occupied for a time by the British army, and many slaves ran off to join the British army, but the British sent runaway slaves to work on loyalists' plantations. Among the revolutionary planters, the flight of the slaves raised (as it turned out unfounded) rumors of imminent slave revolt, and during and after the war, the master class fixed the institution even more tightly on the backs of the remaining slaves.

A Continental Confederation

At the same moment as the delegates from the colonies were voting on the Declaration, and slaves sought independence by fleeing their masters, John Dickinson finished preparation of another document, this one laying out a plan for a confederation of the new states. The job of getting the new states to work together troubled Congress. The colonies had little precedent for a union of any kind. (Recall the fiasco of the Albany Plan of 1754.) Any confederation plan faced two problems: first, how to divide power between the confederation government and the states, and second, how was the confederation government itself to operate?

Dickinson's "Articles of Confederation" went to Congress on July 22, 1776. The states were understandably wary of giving to Congress the sort of power that they were trying to wrestle away from Britain. Some of this fear was allayed by the plan's provisions. Under it, all states would have one vote in the Confederation, preventing the larger states from dominating the smaller ones. Second, all acts of the Confederation had to have a two-thirds majority of states' approval. Third, all changes to the Articles had to have unanimous consent of the states. Fourth, the Confederation had no independent source of income. It would have to rely on the states for voluntary contributions. Finally, all the states had to agree to the Articles for them to go into effect.

The delegates to Congress debated the draft for a year, adding to it a guarantee of state sovereignty and deleting from it Dickinson's plan to give the Confederation sole control of negotiating with the Indians for western lands. Sovereignty, the ultimate source of legitimate authority of governments, supposedly belonged to the people. That was one of the great contributions of the Declaration of Independence to political ideas. In republics, the people gave to their elected representatives the authority to rule. When states said that they feared they would lose their sovereignty, they were saying that they feared other states' voters would have more power than their own voters.

The delegates decided that the Confederation would have no executive or judicial branches. It would operate through committees, like the Continental Congress it was to replace. The Articles were finally adopted in 1781, and the new nation was to be known as the United States of America. The Articles of Confederation did not create a strong national government, but did gain Congress initiative and authority—in particular, in war-making and treaty-making. The Confederation was an unwieldy compromise between advocates of a stronger national government and supporters of state autonomy.

From its inception, the Confederation was divided into factions. The New England states were concerned about overseas trade and their right to fish off the banks of Newfoundland. The southern states wanted to protect the slave trade and to expand into western lands. States that had, as colonies, claims to large areas in the West wanted Britain to give up those areas when the war was over. States with commercial interests wanted the Confederation to shore up the currency, so that debts would be repaid in full. States with many debtors wanted relief for them. States with large populations wanted voting in Congress changed to represent population. States with small populations wanted to retain the one-state, one-vote system of the Continental Congress.

The delegates to Congress endlessly debated the problem of financing the war. Congress had early done what the colonies could not under parliamentary rules— print money. Continental paper money soon lost value, however. Attempts to replace worthless issues of money with new printings, to get aid from the states, and to obtain foreign loans eased but did not end the fiscal crisis. The delegates debated a duty on imports, but this smacked of the very methods that Britain had assayed to raise funds, and ran into opposition.

Congress then turned to the Pennsylvania land speculator and businessman Robert Morris to take charge of its finances. Morris never separated his own interests and dealings from those of Congress (he would end up in jail for fraud), but he convinced Congress to give him powers over the treasury equal to those Washington had over the conduct of the war. From 1781 to 1782, he formulated proposals for a national bank that would circulate paper money and for the solicitation of loans from Europe. Payment of interest on the bank notes and the loans would become a kind of national debt similar to the one that England was running up to pay for its exertions in the war. In addition, he wanted Congress to raise revenue on its own to pay off the national debt. The program would have enriched his friends among the creditor classes, but it also would have put the new nation on a far sounder economic footing.

A second essential function of Congress, one embedded in the very idea of a confederation, was to resolve disputes among the various independent states. These arose over a variety of issues. Some states had enacted tariffs on the importation of goods from other states. More troublesome, states argued over what to do with western lands. Many of the states based extensive land claims on colonial grants. Ignoring these grants, settlers from some states, claiming title under purchases made by land speculators in those states, occupied lands other states claimed.

One of the great achievements of the Confederation was persuading states to concede all their colonial land claims to Congress, allowing Congress to create a national domain. The national domain was not only the land belonging to the Confederation (and later the federal) government, it was the idea of a common territory open to settlement by all Americans. This domain was not an empire but a set of territories that would, in time, become states equal to the original thirteen. Thus the idea and the reality of the national domain ensured that the United States of America would remain a republic. In the coming years, the Confederation Congress and later the federal Congress would have the power to make laws for these lands, with the eventual goal of turning them into states.

Independence and the States

The manner in which Congress conceived the transformation of western lands into new states suggested that the revolutionaries had a vision of a nation composed of sovereign and equal republics. But the process of state-making, begun even before the debates over the Confederation were done, was complex and controversial. Political and economic interest groups within these states contested the shape of their governments. In addition, there were ideological disputes—for example, over how much power to give to the various branches of government in the state and whether the propertyless classes would be allowed to participate in the new governments.

There was no shortage of theory to guide the revolutionary state makers. They drew upon colonial experience, American and British political philosophy, law, history, and even the classics of ancient Greece and Rome. In the end, despite similarities between the new state governments and their colonial predecessors (notably Rhode Island and Connecticut, which merely turned their colonial charters into state constitutions), the revolutionaries broke sharply with colonial and British precedent. The revolutionary state governments were based on written constitutions that preceded, empowered, and limited government unlike any in Britain. These constitutions were regarded as a higher or "fundamental" law than mere statutes of the state legislatures and the rulings of state supreme courts.

Although the framers of the state constitutions were making important innovations, the terminology the state constitutional framers used resembled the language that the revolutionaries used before 1776. For example, John Adams's *Thoughts on Government* (1776) warned of the corruption that had undermined the English monarchy. Instead of the multiple office-holding and overlapping executive, legislative, and judicial functions that England's ministers of state, members of Parliament, and colonial governors had, Adams proposed a system of checks and balances. In the latter, three distinct branches of government—a bicameral (two-house) legislature, an executive, and a judiciary—would have the means to prevent one another from gaining too much power. He sent these suggestions to Virginia, where revolutionaries had assembled in the first state constitutional convention. The Virginia drafters adopted some of his ideas. By the end of the 1780s, Adams's ideas of checks and balances became a feature of almost all of the state constitutions.

Adams was a conservative in many ways. In particular, he did not trust the lower classes to make good laws. In some of the states, more egalitarian drafters than he took control of the process, and they produced a different kind of constitution from Massachusetts's. In Pennsylvania, radicals called for a popularly elected constitutional convention, and winning control of it, created a unicameral legislature, an executive committee instead of a governor, and elected instead of appointed justices of the peace. Georgia opted for a unicameral legislature, as did Vermont, at this time a separate republic negotiating its future with both the British and the Continental authorities.

In all these constitutions, the legislative branch was the strongest of the three, but the formula for representation varied from state to state. The revolutionaries debated the basis for drawing electoral districts—too large and no one was represented, too small and local prejudices outweighed the common good. In general, states opted for small districts, sometimes no larger than a single township or county. In most of the states, the preference for small districts gave people in the wealthier, better-established eastern regions more seats in the legislature than poorer, more dispersed western people. The struggle between eastern and western groups would become a feature of state politics for the next half century.

There were differences of opinion as well whether the colonial practice of requiring property for voting should be continued or whether all free, adult, white Protestant males should have the right to vote. Pennsylvania gave the vote to all males who paid taxes. During a controversy over the same proposal in Maryland, one proponent of universal voting insisted that "it would be unjust and oppressive in the extreme to shut out the poor in having a share in declaring who shall be the lawgivers of their country, and yet [they] bear a very heavy share in the support of government." Yet property qualifications for voting and holding office prevailed in Maryland, as in almost all of the other new states.

Only a few radical thinkers advocated more democratic ideas. Most revolutionaries thought these dangerous, for they might open the way to rule by a demagogue (mob leader) and give to the poor too much power. Elite leaders complained that "everyone who has the least pretensions to be a gentleman is suspected and borne down by . . . a set of men without reading, experience, or principle to govern them." To prevent politicians from becoming demagogues, constitutions provided for rotation in office. Maryland limited its governors to serving no more than three years in any seven; Massachusetts held annual elections for its assemblymen.

Massachusetts in 1778 introduced yet another novelty, with profound consequences. The constitution the delegates to its convention drafted had to be "ratified" by the voters of the towns before the constitution went into effect, ensuring that it rested upon the consent of the governed. Thus the ultimate source of authority rested with the people, not the government. Massachusetts's idea of ratification of constitutions became the rule for all the states and is standard practice today.

The constitutions themselves guaranteed as rights what had been mere privileges in the colonies. The latter included the array of rights embodied in "bills of rights." These included the right to due process of law, jury trial, and freedom of speech and petition. Although not all states abandoned religious establishment, most agreed with Massachusetts that "no subject shall be hurt, molested, or restrained, in his person, liberty, or estate, for worshipping God in the manner and season most agreeable to the dictates of his own conscience; or for his religious profession or sentiments; provided he doth not disturb the public peace, or obstruct others in their religious worship."

Although the new state constitutions and governments included many legal reforms compared to the colonial charters, few rights were extended to women, people of color, non-Protestants, and other minority groups. They were neither included in the drafting process nor given full civil liberties under law. Women were aware that their exclusion from the newly enlarged arena of public life mirrored their continuing subordination in the home. As Abigail Adams, John Adams's wife, wrote to him in May 1776, "I can not say that I think you very generous to the Ladies, for whilst you are proclaiming peace and good will to men, emancipating all nations, you insist upon retaining an absolute power over wives."

THE WAR AGAINST GREAT BRITAIN

Two months after the signing of the Declaration of Independence, George Washington's forces on Long Island and in the city of New York were routed by the British. The war against Great Britain had begun in earnest. John Adams wrote to a friend in Massachusetts, "we now have a nation to protect and defend . . . and I can easily see the propriety of the observation that . . . the prosperity of a state depends upon the discipline of its army."

Washington had predicted that the ill-trained, -clothed, -armed, and -disciplined troops he had in New York could not stand against the British, and events proved him right. In the course of his subsequent flight from British forces, he stopped to tell Congress that "this contest is not likely to be the work of a day" and could only be won by a "permanent establishment," in short, a standing army enrolled for the duration of the war. In truth, many of the militia who fought at Breeds Hill and in the Canadian campaign had simply gone home. In December 1776, Thomas Paine, the unofficial publicist for the cause of independence, warned, "These are the times that try men's souls. The summer soldier and the sunshine patriot will, in this crisis, shrink from the service of their country, but he that stands it now, deserves the love and thanks of man and woman."

The First Modern War

The Revolutionary War was not only the birthing time of the American nation, it would be the first truly modern war in recruitment, ideology, and scope. Everyone in the new nation would be touched by it in some way—the combatants, those who wished to be neutral, Native Americans, and women. Its battles would rage on land and sea over thousands of miles. It would draw in France as America's ally. It would reveal the heights of courage and the depths of selfishness and brutality. And it would end with a peace treaty remarkable for its generosity.

As the new nation entered the first year of its war for independence, patriotic ministers recast the sacrifice and the violence in religious terms. Although the Declaration of Independence's reference to the deity was more a reflex than an expression of genuine piety, everyone in Congress hoped that Providence would smile on Continental arms. Loyalists like Massachusetts's Peter Oliver blamed the "black legion" of Puritan ministers for bringing on the Revolution. His charge was unfair—the ministers were never in the forefront of the agitation. But evangelical voices quieted by the end of the Great Awakening now roared that the revolutionary cause was a test of God's favor. Their conservative opponents on the pulpit agreed that the war would test the morality and virtue of God's chosen people. As the impositions of a corrupt distant king were a judgment on the colonists' own sloth and extravagance, so victory would prove that God upheld "all the just rights and liberties of America."

Unlike the wars for empire fought by relatively small European troops stationed in America and militia formations recruited for a series of unconnected campaigns, the Revolutionary War would be a total war, involving hundreds of thousands of men serving for years, with campaigns lasting for many months. Unlike earlier colonial wars whose object was control of a key river or locality or borderland that had some kind of strategic value to one or the other of the imperial powers, the Revolutionary War was a contest of ideologies between an empire with a king at its head and a confederation of republican states.

The sheer size of the forces engaged from 1776 to 1783 dwarfed all previous colonial wars. Between them, the regular troops of the Continental line enrolled for the duration of the war and the state militias drew upon the entire manpower pool of the colonies. Nearly half of all adult males among the revolutionaries at some time served in the regular army or in one of the state militias. In some New England towns, the rate approached 100 percent.

In the revolutionary armies, the rich and the poor mingled. Although the typical soldier was still a poor man, and the rich could buy substitutes, the officer corps represented all walks of colonial life. What was more, a brave and able man from the lower classes could move up from the ranks into the officer corps—a fluidity unheard of in European armies until the French Revolution. Although the American revolutionary combatant would always think of himself as an individual first and a soldier second, over time he became almost as adept at drill, maneuver, and obeying orders as his European opponent.

Still, rank had its privileges. The officers ate, slept, and lived better than the ordinary soldiers. Sick or wounded, their care was better. Soldiers who committed breaches of discipline were whipped. Officers were reduced in rank or sent home. Officers who died during their term of service could expect to be buried with the honors due a person of importance. Common soldiers who died were not memorialized and often were interred without a marker.

In part, the differences in treatment derived from the simple fact that officers could pay for themselves out of their own pockets. Soldiers depended on the often late and always paltry pay Congress provided. But the acceptance of asymmetry in treatment did not lead to the same sort of arrogance and subordination one found in the British army. Continental soldiers expected to be treated fairly and with respect by their officers, and officers generally accorded their men such respect.

Other Americans served at sea. These "sons of Neptune" and "Jack Tars" not only joined anti-British protests before the war, turning the waterfront into a patriot stronghold, they served on the fifty ships of the Continental navy and some three thousand privateers commissioned by the states or the Continental Congress. Privateering (private ships whose officers and crews sailed with licenses from their governments to prey on enemy vessels and take as prizes enemy cargoes) were a common feature of war in the Atlantic and Caribbean waters as far back as the sixteenth century.

The Revolutionary War sailors included whites and blacks, new immigrants, British sailors who had jumped ship, and Europeans. Some were patriots, others were sailing for the prize money. Some had lost their livelihoods as fishermen or commercial ship crewmen and simply joined up to support themselves and their families. John Paul Jones, whose squadron raided British ports in the Caribbean and the Home Islands, became the first of a long line of famous American naval officers, even though he was little more than a mercenary.

Despite the varied motives of the officers, soldiers, and sailors, from the first battles of the war, ideology played an important role for the patriot forces. From 1775 through 1776, an intensely moral fervor motivated the American troops. They saw themselves as God's chosen instruments to establish the reign of republican virtue. Chaplains traveling with the army preached a mixture of patriotic and ecclesiastical themes. Victory would come, so long as the troops did not forget that they carried on a Christian mission. As one minister thundered: "Our fathers trusted and the Lord did deliver them . . . even so may it be with us . . . let us still under the banners of liberty, and with a Washington for our head, go on from conquering to conquer." The officers saw their participation in the war as a proof of their personal honor, and believed that their cause was the vindication of American liberty against British tyranny. The common soldiers would never lose their faith that God was on their side and saw themselves as patriots.

The Revolutionary War required the utmost exertions from the British people. Once relatively small and marginal institutions in British life, the British army and navy found themselves almost as transformed by the war as did the American militias. From a standing army of no more than forty thousand or so in 1775, in the course of the war the number of regular troops tripled.

The Royal Navy expanded its numbers from under 20,000 to over 180,000 men in the course of the war, distributed over 350 vessels. Many of these seamen were impressed into service against their will, and life on a ship of the line in the Royal Navy was only a step away from prison for some of the sailors. The officers and crews could amass small fortunes from capturing prizes, sometimes an incentive to go looking for private gain when public duty dictated otherwise.

By the end of the war, perhaps more than 450,000 British and Irish subjects had borne arms as home guards (the British militia), in the navy, or in the regular army. Not all served in North America, but together they reflect a total commitment to the struggle akin to that of the revolutionaries.

Ideology motivated the British troops, for they served the greatest empire in early modern history and were proud of it. Indeed, the rapid mobilization of the British army and navy could not have taken place without a truly national commitment to the war. The British taxed themselves unmercifully to put these forces in the field, but Britons willingly loaned the nation even more—the national debt rising from £127 million in 1775 to £232 million in 1783.

No Safe Haven

Other participants and witnesses to the combat found their lives changed almost as profoundly as the lives of the men in the armies and navies. There were no safe havens from the fighting, as Indians, women, and loyalists discovered. Most Indians would have preferred to remain neutral in the war. It was a quarrel, as one Iroquois leader termed it, "between two brothers of one [white] blood." The Oneida Iroquois petitioned Connecticut governor John Trumbull, "Take no umbrage that we Indians refuse joining in the contest. We are for peace."

But many northern Indians were still dependent on British traders or resented colonial settlers' forcible occupation of Indian lands and joined the British in the war. The Iroquois split their allegiance—the Oneidas supporting the revolutionary forces, and the Mohawks allying with the British. Mohawk war parties raided New York farmsteads, and Shawnee warriors attacked revolutionary settlers along the Ohio River. Militiamen called to protect the settlers could not tell neutral Indians from hostile ones, and by indiscriminately attacking the former drove them into the arms of the British. Farther south, older Cherokee leaders urged neutrality, but the younger war chiefs fought for the crown. Creeks and Choctaws served with the British.

Thus a war of state militias against pro-British Indians raged alongside the war of Continentals with British regulars. There were no massed armies and few uniforms in frontier war. Instead, it pitted Indian villages against small and isolated settlements of revolutionary farmers. In this sense, it was a continuation of the kind of frontier conflict that had raged on and off from the inception of European settlement of the North American continent.

Women and children suffered alongside their menfolk. Mary Jemison, a Seneca wife and mother taken as a teenager from her white family but living happily with her Indian captors, recalled the carnage of one of the revolutionary army's forays through Indian country: "They destroyed every article of the food kind that they could lay their hands on. A part of our corn they burnt, and threw the remainder into the river. They burnt our houses, killed what few cattle and horses they could find, destroyed our fruit trees, and left nothing but the bare soil and timber. . . . There was not a mouthful of any kind of sustenance left, not even enough to keep a child one day from perishing with hunger." Revolutionary accounts of Indian attacks—for example, in the Cherry Valley of New York—were equally gruesome.

Whatever choice they made, Indian life in the revolutionary era changed profoundly. Even Indians who had remained on the sidelines or supported the Revolution found that they had lost their ancestral lands to the new United States. Those who supported the English did not understand why England abandoned their interests in the peace negotiations. The destruction of Indian towns and the dislocation of Indian life through the loss of so many warriors drove many survivors to alcoholism and despair. Some Indian groups responded as Indians had after the arrival of the first Europeans—by moving west and joining with other Indian groups. Within Indian societies, reformers like the Seneca Handsome Lake and the Miami Prophet called for a return to old ways and a purification of the Indian spirit.

With the exception of a few heroic women who dressed as men and served in the army, women did not join in battle, but as Jemison's story proves, women were as affected by the war as men. Some especially unfortunate women, like the patriot women held captive in a British encampment in Hopewell, New Jersey, were "ravish'd" by enemy soldiers. Uniformed soldiers were not the only "banditti" who caused trouble for women. Although few cases of rape were documented, the fear of rape by marauding enemy soldiers was always present. Guerrilla operations in a locality posed particularly dangerous choices for women. When the British regulars invaded backwoods Carolina in 1779, women who sympathized with the Revolution "abandoned their habitations" and hid in the mountains. A similar fear drove the women from their farms in western New York during the 1779–1780 campaign there. The British commander wrote that women decamped "precipitately in the night."

Although revolutionary women had no formal public role in the new nation, many were patriots in their sentiments. They sacrificed for the war effort. As a prewar ditty phrased their determination: "for the sake of freedom's name . . . come, sacrifice to Patriot fame." Women's patriotic styles of dress included simple and homespun fabrics and designs. Patriotic women's groups raised money to support the war effort and contributed material goods to it as well. In 1780, the women of Philadelphia collected hundreds of thousands of dollars for the war effort. The women of Trenton, a much smaller city, forwarded $15,500 to Washington's army.

As in the earlier wars for empire, the absence of husbands, fathers, and sons made revolutionary women into managers of farms, businesses, and families. One Pennsylvania farm woman's efforts illustrated the range of duties that women had to perform: "all the cloth and linen were spun at home . . . most by her own hands. . . . All the business of every kind she attended to, farm, iron works, domestic matters." A few women ran boardinghouses and taverns, some of which were homes away from home for revolutionary officers and politicians, while others' homes doubled as hospitals and barracks. One boardinghouse in Philadelphia was used as a jail for suspected loyalists.

If few women saw combat, wives of officers sometimes lived in the same camps as their husbands, and a few women served as nurses to the wounded and sick. Slave women who ran away from their masters found themselves working in these camps as well. Women had to lodge troops, some of whom were arrogant, foulmouthed, and sticky fingered.

Loneliness was a common complaint among women. Women refugees from war-torn areas wrote longingly of family ties and missing loved ones, but some unmarried young women living near the army camps found the presence of so many young men an invitation to flirt. As one wrote, in the winter of 1777–1778, "here was a fine field open for a romantic girl to exhibit in." A young Massachusetts officer serving in Virginia in 1781 agreed, "The Ladies here are exceeding amorous. . . . Amorous intrigues and gallantry are everywhere approved of in this state." More than one of these flirtations resulted in marriage either during or immediately after the war.

Women also carried on a private version of the patriotic speeches and sermons men made during the war, by exchanging letters on public-spirited subjects, keeping one another's spirits high, and exchanging local news. The level of interest in the issues and events of the day in these letters is quite striking, indicating that revolutionary women understood what was happening in the wider world and believed that their exertions made a significant contribution to the war effort. As one woman urged her readers in 1780, "[We must] aspire to render ourselves more really useful. . . . Shall we hesitate to wear clothing more simple, hair dressed less elegant. . . . Who, amongst us, will not renounce with the highest pleasure, those vain ornaments, when she shall consider that the valiant defenders of America will be able to draw some advantage from the money which she may have laid out in these."

Neither the sacrifices nor the hopes of revolutionary women that independence would lead to greater equality for women were fulfilled. Wives of active political figures like Sarah Jay and Abigail Adams discussed public affairs in their private correspondence and no doubt influenced their spouses' and kinfolk's views of politics, but did not hold any office.

Indeed, women in the new nation may have lost ground politically. Under the empire, both women and men were "subjects" of the king. In the new republic, every free white man was a kind of king, but women still were subjects. They did not gain the right to vote (except for a brief time in New Jersey) or hold political office. Their property in marriage remained their husbands'.

At the same time, a more subtle, private revolution had changed the status of women in their own homes. Attitudes of men and women gradually but strikingly changed to make women into symbols of republican virtue. The personification of liberty came to be a woman. Newly worshipped as the angel of the home, women gained in moral authority as mothers and wives.

Both well-known and suspected loyalists found their lives completely changed by the war. As the crisis worsened, some tried to keep a low profile and hoped that they could avoid choosing sides, while others expected to serve in the British armed forces. When war came, and revolutionary committees of safety and state officials began seizing loyalists' property, many flocked to the British lines.

Despite the mistrust shown them by the British army and the hostility of nearby revolutionary adherents, loyalist bands carried on effective guerrilla warfare in the Carolinas, Georgia, New Jersey, and New York. Unfortunately, while loyalist men were serving with the British, British regular troops, unable to tell the difference between friend and foe among the former colonists, sometimes destroyed loyalists' property and abused loyalist families.

As doctor David Ramsay of South Carolina recalled after the war, both loyalists and patriots in the backwoods of the Carolinas resorted "to plunder and to murder," leaving in their wake "scenes of distress which were shocking to humanity." Entire regions contested by loyalist and patriot troops were left to "widows and orphans." Loyalists driven from their homes turned to Parliament, professing "the purest principles of duty and allegiance to his majesty." Many received pensions or other financial aid.

Even when they sought to lead peaceful, obscure lives, loyalists were suspected of a multitude of antirevolutionary activities, such as spying, convincing soldiers not to reenlist, and harboring deserters. George Washington suspected some female loyalists of carrying goods and information across the battle lines. One revolutionary newspaper editor wrote in 1779, "And is it possible that we should suffer men, who have been guilty of all these and a thousand other calamities which this country has experienced, to live among us?" Revolutionaries responded to fears of loyalist activity by insisting all adults sign loyalty oaths, paying informers to ferret out secret loyalists, confiscating and auctioning off loyalists' property, detaining suspected loyalists without hearings, and outlawing suspected loyalist military leaders without holding trials.

The loyalist women left behind when men went to war or were detained by revolutionaries faced particular problems. The threat of imprisonment and the likelihood of poverty, illness, and hunger were added to their anxiety about absent loved ones. Even the wealthy Philadelphia Quaker Elizabeth Drinker recorded in her diary insults and confiscations. For example, on June 10, 1780, she wrote: "James Pickering a Captain and 6 or 8 others with bayonets fixed came and demanded our horses. After some talk they went and broke open the stable and took a fine Horse bought some time ago of William Smith and a mare. They took horses from many others." Such conduct was not only condoned by revolutionary councils, it was deemed necessary for the security of the state.

The Course of Battle, 1776–1779

In the spring of 1776, General Thomas Gage passed command of the British troops in Boston to General William Howe. The British evacuated Boston and turned their attention to New York City. The British minister responsible for waging the war, Lord George Germain, told Howe to practice total warfare—destroy crops and burn cities—showing no pity. It was a policy that Lord Jeffrey Amherst had introduced against the French Indian allies in the French and Indian War. Howe, by contrast, wanted conciliation. He had served with distinction in America and saw the colonists as kinsmen and women. At every turn, whenever possible, he pressed Washington to give up the fight and accept the authority of the crown.

Howe obeyed Germain's order to oust the Continentals from New York City and use it as a base for operations. In New York, the British could expect far more support from loyal colonists than they could in Boston. New York City, held by Washington with under twenty thousand poorly trained militiamen, faced Howe's twenty thousand regular British and thirteen thousand German mercenaries.

Times were hard in the German states, and princes sometimes recruited their subjects for service in foreign wars. Britain's ties to individual German states like Hanover and Hesse enabled Britain to enroll such mercenaries. So many came from Hesse that all the German mercenaries were called "Hessians" by the revolutionaries. In addition, ten thousand seamen and a convoy of more than 150 ships under Howe's brother, Admiral Richard Howe, supported the assault.

General Howe paused to offer peace terms, first to a delegation from Congress led by Franklin, then to Washington himself. All the Americans politely refused to renounce the Declaration of Independence. Then, in a series of battles in the late summer of 1776, the Howe brothers drove Washington from Long Island and Manhattan. Washington was able to withdraw, keeping intact the semblance of an army, but as he retreated across the Hudson to New Jersey, thousands of his men were wounded or killed, or were taken prisoner. It remains a mystery to historians, as it did then to Washington, why the British did not attempt to destroy his army by close pursuit or a sweeping flanking movement. Washington had commandeered all boats

Revolutionary War Battles 1776-1783

Cornwallis's route

Chesapeake Bay

Charlottesville
VIRGINIA
James R.
Jamestown
Yorktown
(Cornwallis's surrender, Oct. 19, 1781)

NORTH CAROLINA

King's Mountain
(U.S. victory, Oct. 7, 1780)

Cowpens
(U.S. victory, Jan. 17, 1780)

SOUTH CAROLINA

Wilmington

Savannah R.

GEORGIA

Charleston
(U.S. surrender, May 12, 1780)

Savannah
(U.S. surrender, Oct. 9, 1779)

War in the South

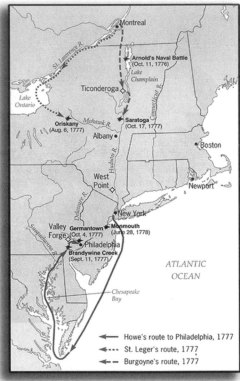

Montreal

St. Lawrence R.

Arnold's Naval Battle
(Oct. 11, 1776)

Lake Champlain

Lake Ontario

Ticonderoga

Oriskany
(Aug. 6, 1777)

Mohawk R.

Saratoga
(Oct. 17, 1777)

Albany

Hudson R.

Connecticut R.

Boston

West Point

Newport

Delaware R.

New York

Valley Forge

Germantown
(Oct. 4, 1777)

Monmouth
(June 28, 1778)

Susquehanna R.

Philadelphia

Brandywine Creek
(Sept. 11, 1777)

ATLANTIC OCEAN

Chesapeake Bay

Howe's route to Philadelphia, 1777
St. Leger's route, 1777
Burgoyne's route, 1777

War in the North

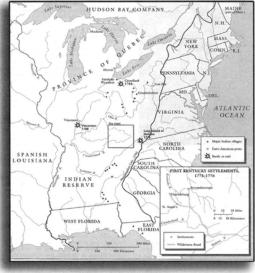

HUDSON BAY COMPANY

Lake Superior

Lake Michigan

Lake Huron

MAINE (part of Mass.)

N.H.

PROVINCE OF QUEBEC

Lake Erie

Lake Ontario

NEW YORK

MASS.

CONN. R.I.

Sandusky Wyandots

Crawford 1783

PENNSYLVANIA

N.J.

MD.

DEL.

Vincennes 1779

VIRGINIA

ATLANTIC OCEAN

Missouri R.

SPANISH LOUISIANA

NORTH CAROLINA

INDIAN RESERVE

SOUTH CAROLINA

GEORGIA

Major Indian villages
Euro-American posts
Battle or raid

FIRST KENTUCKY SETTLEMENTS, 1775-1776

Boonesborough

Harrodsburg

St. Asaph's

Cumberland R.

0   15   30 Miles
0   15   30 Kilometers

WEST FLORIDA

EAST FLORIDA

Settlements
Wilderness Road

0   150   300 Miles
0   150   300 Kilometers

War in the West

in the area, but the shipwrights with Howe could have made up the lack of boats in a week. Perhaps Howe feared a repetition of Breeds Hill on the far side of the Hudson? In any case, Howe's forces merely nipped at Washington's tail.

Howe's failure to bring massive force against Washington was a problem that British commanders faced throughout the war. As long as Washington had room to maneuver and was willing to surrender space in exchange for time to regroup, there was little that Howe could do to force a decisive battle. The miles the British forces had to cover to engage the Continental army and the distance between major British forces so engaged were so great that sustained, coordinated operations were almost impossible.

The same problem applied to supplying the army with food and ammunition. British supply lines stretched over three thousand miles of ocean, and even when they occupied major colonial ports, British commanders rarely had more than a few months of food and ammunition on hand. When the British army marched inland, it could no longer count on the support of the Royal Navy, and revolutionary militia cut the British supply lines.

For these reasons, a British thrust from Montreal down Lake Champlain into New York in the summer of 1776 was able to drive the revolutionaries from the field, but the British simply could not move far or fast enough to dislodge the revolutionaries from the whole of northeastern New York before the winter of 1776–1777 came. When the British retired to Canada for the winter, they effectually surrendered upstate New York back to the revolutionaries for another year. The same problems of distance and uncertainty ended a British invasion of the Carolinas in the late spring and early summer of 1776.

One more example of the dilemma of space and supply the British army faced occurred when Washington and the remnants of his army surprised the Hessian garrison at Trenton, on December 25, 1776. The British main force in New York City needed three days to react. Washington's crossing over the Delaware from Pennsylvania was a feat that no one expected, and before the British relief force arrived, Washington was able to slip away and strike at the British rear guard in Princeton. It was the only real victory for the Continental army that year, but it showed that the British army, regarded by many as the best in the world at that time, could not suppress the revolt.

The first truly disastrous British defeat in the war, at the battle of Saratoga, was again the result of great distances and lack of British coordination. In the summer of 1777, the British hatched a grand plan to sever the New England states from the Middle Atlantic states. General John Burgoyne, victor over the Americans in Canada in the winter of 1776, marched down the old invasion route into New York from Montreal intending to join British forces moving east from Lake Ontario and north from New York City. But the Ontario force was turned back at the battle of Oriskany; General Howe decided he could force Washington to battle by attacking Philadelphia instead of going up the Hudson; and Burgoyne, at Saratoga, found himself surrounded by Continental regulars under General Horatio Gates and Benedict Arnold and militia units from all over New England. After three days of battle, Burgoyne surrendered on October 17.

Burgoyne and his surviving troops were interned for the duration of the war. Though they were prisoners, their treatment was far better than the prisoners the British took. Some of these were dumped into the holds of ships in New York City harbor, where disease and despair killed thousands. Conditions were little better than on the slave ships in the middle passage. Some prisoners, to save themselves, switched sides. Others were treated as pirates, criminals, or servants and shipped off to British colonies in the Caribbean or Canada. A few were impressed into the British navy or army. Washington would become so furious at the mistreatment of revolutionary prisoners of war that he threatened to begin executions of the British prisoners he held.

In his movement toward Philadelphia, Howe defeated Washington's troops in a series of battles, but could not inflict a knockout blow because Washington would not commit himself to a do-or-die battle to defend Philadelphia. The British occupied Philadelphia as the delegates to the Continental Congress fled. Washington tried to surprise Howe on October 10, 1777, but his attack on the British encampment at Germantown failed when the Americans did not press their advantage. Washington then fortified the hills of Valley Forge, to the northwest of the city, and his army, poorly clothed and nearly starving, waited out the winter there. The British were more comfortable in Philadelphia, but Continental troops cut the supply line to New York, and Howe's men had to pay exorbitant prices for fuel and food. Worse, his army had put themselves out of touch with other British units.

When news of Burgoyne's defeat and Howe's inaction reached France in December 1777, the French abandoned their policy of secret aid to the United States and entered into a formal treaty of mutual defense. The key to the treaty was its second article, signed on February 6, 1778. This committed the French to "maintain effectually the liberty, sovereignty, and independence absolute of the said united States, as in matters of government as of commerce."

The French treaty was a triumph for the American diplomatic mission led by Benjamin Franklin and John Adams, and so great a disaster for Britain that the British commenced secret negotiations with the Americans in France. The treaty anticipated that step and required that neither France nor the United States would conclude peace with Britain "without the formal consent of the other first obtained; and they mutually engage not to lay down their arms until the independence of the United States shall have been formally, or tacitly, assured by the treaty or treaties, that shall terminate the war." The Spanish, under French prodding, joined in the war against Britain, as did other European powers.

Except for a few men, notably the eighteen-year-old Count de Lafayette, who embraced the principles of the Revolution, the French wanted revenge against Britain rather than American independence. Although its regular army numbered over 150,000 men, France never committed more than 20,000 men to the North American struggle. Fortunately for the Americans, the army France sent to aid the revolutionaries was highly professional, and its commander, the Count de Rochambeau, was an able officer. Unfortunately for the Americans, the French army was filled with easily offended aristocratic officers and slowed by their extensive baggage trains. (They even brought furniture.) The French expeditionary force insisted on operating as an independent command and poorly coordinated their plans with their American allies.

The war in the North dragged on from 1778 through 1780, with neither side gaining a decisive advantage. The French navy and a small expeditionary force joined in the Continentals' attempt to drive the British out of Newport, Rhode Island, but failed. Howe retreated from Philadelphia in 1778, but Washington's attempt to engage the British rear guard at the battle of Monmouth Court House ended inconclusively.

Howe's timidity and miscalculation cost him his command, but his successor in New York, Henry Clinton, did little better. Clinton was able but indecisive, fidgeting when boldness might have won the day. While the fighting around New York City continued sporadically, Clinton sent three thousand men to take Georgia in the winter of 1778–1779. The idea behind the resumption of British military activity in the South was to rouse the southern loyalists. The British occupied Savannah, Augusta, and the surrounding countryside, but again the vast distances they had to traverse and the great space they had to defend slowed further penetration of the interior.

In similar fashion, a British raid up the Chesapeake in May 1779 caused consternation in Virginia and destroyed shipping, supplies, and much of the town of Portsmouth, but had no lasting effect on the war. The raid did demonstrate that the ravaging of civilian property, rare in the first years of the war, had become commonplace. In the same year Washington ordered punitive raids against the Iroquois who supported the British in the Mohawk Valley of New York. Clinton retaliated with hit-and-run attacks on southern New England towns, whose inhabitants, burned out of their homes, bellowed in protest against "waging War against innocent women and children."

Behind the Lines

The drudgery of drill, the duration of their service, and the distance from home of their campaigns, added to the brutality in camp life, hardened the revolutionary soldiers. The lack of sanitation in the camps killed more men than enemy action. Unaccustomed to living in such close quarters with other men, some recruits acted out their frustration by picking fights. Desertion became an epidemic, and deserters' neighbors sometimes rescued the deserter from the soldiers sent to capture him.

Plundering and pilfering from civilians and other troops occurred with such regularity that Washington asked Congress to raise the punishment of offenders from one hundred to five hundred lashes. Congress, far from the scenes of the crimes and still wedded to the idea of the virtuous citizen army, refused. Still, the records show that courts-martial were always busy with deserters, thieves, thugs, and malingerers. Some were acquitted; most were punished with whipping. Upward of fifty men were executed after courts-martial for mutiny, deserting to the enemy, or committing a capital offense while in the service.

By the middle years of the war, most Americans had tired of the conflict. Farmers who had pledged allegiance to one side routinely traded with the other. For example, as the Continental army starved at Valley Forge, Pennsylvania farmers carted their harvest past Valley Forge and sold their food to the British in Philadelphia. The British had hard currency to pay for the goods, while the Continental army only had the paper money that Congress printed, and its value sunk daily. As James Thacher, a doctor serving with Washington's troops at Morristown, wrote in the fourth winter of the war, "Besides the evils above mentioned, we experience another, in the rapid depreciation of the continental money, which we receive for our pay; it is now estimated at about thirty for one."

Congress printed tens of millions of dollars to pay its troops and suppliers. In 1779 alone, the quartermaster and the commissary for the army spent $109,169,000. People who had money rushed to spend it before it became worthless. Ironically, among the biggest consumer items were tea and tobacco, still necessities despite their scarcity. As one member of Congress lamented, Americans "longed for the fineries and follies" that had corrupted England. New York City importers did a better business during the war than before the war started, feeding the appetites of the British and loyalists within the city and, when the British were not looking, the wants of revolutionaries who traded across the battle lines.

Within the army, graft and corruption spread. Quartermasters and other army officials put army wagons and horses to private use, kept public moneys for themselves, and carried on commercial businesses with their ill-gotten gains. Some army commanders took bribes to send their men home or kept pay from their men. Soldiers sold their rations and their arms. An entire vocabulary describing these misdemeanors appeared, including terms like *horse-beef* for food soldiers pilfered from farmers, whom the soldiers (often rightly) suspected of gouging the army.

In these years of doldrums, even the heroes of the battle of Saratoga were brought low. After failing to defend Camden, South Carolina, Gates lost his command. Benedict Arnold, for a £20,000 bribe, agreed to betray the fort at West Point to the British. Passed over for promotion and bankrupted by the war, his pride and greed opened him to the lure of British promises. In that, he was not very different from many Americans on both sides. Still, his treason raised fears of disunity, of the corrupting power of avarice, and of the fragile nature of virtue in republics. If a hero like Arnold defected, who would be next? Even Washington became the target of widespread criticism. Some said that he was too slow and too indecisive. Others feared that he would become a tyrant.

On the heels of Arnold's defection came even more worrisome events: wholesale mutinies by regiments of the Continental army. In 1780 and again in early 1781, unpaid and hungry troops in Pennsylvania and New Jersey demanded better treatment. The first mutinies were overcome without violence, and all but the ringleaders were pardoned. Congress came up with back pay, as did the state governments. The last of the mutinies, in 1781, resulted in the death and wounding of officers and raised the same problems as trading across the lines—what kind of peacetime citizens would corrupt officers and disobedient soldiers make? How could republics survive such widespread personal vices?

The Final Struggles and the Peace, 1780–1783

Unable to bring Washington to battle, in 1780 Clinton committed himself to a new strategy. He decided to move with the bulk of his forces to the Carolinas, occupy them, and work north. Clinton led the invasion of the South himself, in the middle of February 1780, landing seventy-five hundred men at Savannah. Marching north, he assaulted Charleston, and two months later Benjamin Lincoln's defending garrison surrendered. The British assumed that the hinterlands were filled with loyalists who would soon march with the British, and Clinton took most of his men back with him to New York.

In January 1781, Lord Charles Cornwallis, left behind by Clinton to continue the campaign, grew tired of fighting what his opponent, American commander Nathaniel Greene, called a "fugitive war" of feints, raids, and forays. A man of immense self-importance, given to quarreling with superiors and backbiting, Cornwallis often ignored larger strategic plans and acted impulsively. He decided that the time had come to march through North Carolina, crush Greene's forces, and bring all the loyalists to the king's side.

Aided by reinforcements from New York City, Cornwallis inched north, shrugging off a defeat at Cowpens, in South Carolina, and a Pyrrhic victory (the British won the ground but lost many of their best men) at Guilford Court House on March 15, 1781. Greene's army fell apart, but Cornwallis could not move quickly enough over the vast distances involved to destroy Greene's ragged remnant. As Cornwallis turned north again toward Virginia, Greene simply went south, back into South Carolina. The "fugitive war" was ending, and the final stages of the conflict were about to begin.

By May 1781, Cornwallis, ignoring Clinton's explicit orders, had reached Virginia and marched to the peninsula of Yorktown, waiting to be relieved by Clinton and the British navy. He was shocked to discover that for the first and only time in the war the French navy had beaten the British to the punch and controlled the mouth of the Chesapeake. Cornwallis was trapped, and facing him were the onrushing forces of

Washington and Rochambeau. With great magnanimity, Rochambeau had put himself and his seven thousand French troops, more than Washington's Continentals, under Washington's command.

At Rochambeau's suggestion, Washington abandoned a plan to assault New York City, and with the French moved swiftly from the New York–New Jersey theater of the war to the Chesapeake—a remarkable traverse of over 450 miles. Clinton did not follow. For the better part of September and the first two weeks of October, the combined American and French forces besieged the outnumbered and outgunned Cornwallis. On October 20, Cornwallis surrendered. A week later, British navy forces and troops arrived to rescue him.

Among Washington's aides, a young artillery commander named Alexander Hamilton distinguished himself by leading the attack on the British trenches. Another New York officer, Aaron Burr, also took part in the siege. In later years they would become major political figures, great rivals, and fight the most notorious duel in American history.

When word of Cornwallis's defeat reached England, the North ministry was staggered. On March 20, 1782, thirteen years after coming to power, Lord North resigned, and a propeace ministry took the reins. Negotiations with the diplomats Congress had sent to Europe, led by John Adams and Benjamin Franklin, swung into full gear.

At first the British were reluctant to concede American independence. They knew that the war aims of the allies—the United States, France, and Spain—differed sharply, and relations among them were not always forthright or cordial. Richard Oswald, the British delegate to the talks, tried but could not break apart the alliance. By November 1782, peace articles were ready, and on November 30 the United States and British delegates signed.

The Treaty of Paris gave to the new nation fishing rights off the banks of Newfoundland, and all the land to the Mississippi River in the West, to the Great Lakes in the North, and the Florida border in the South. The United States guaranteed that British subjects owed money would face "no lawful impediment" in collecting "of the full value in sterling money," and that Congress would urge the states to return to British subjects all confiscated property. Both sides had to know that the last two provisions were dicey—there was not enough sterling (English hard currency) in the United States to pay the debts owed to friendly French and Dutch bankers, much less to British merchants. The British, for their part, promised to remove troops from the Northwest "with all convenient speed," a promise they did not keep—for they had Indian allies to mollify, and the presence of the troops put pressure on Congress to fulfill its pledge to British creditors.

According to the treaty of 1778 between the United States and France, neither side was to make peace without the concurrence of the other, but the French did not sign a peace pact with the British until January 20, 1783. The Spanish joined in that pact.

The New Nation

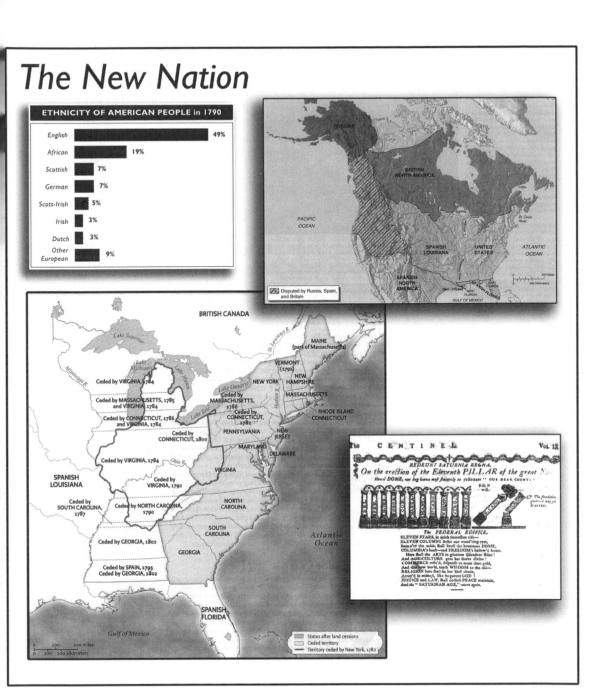

ETHNICITY OF AMERICAN PEOPLE in 1790

English	49%
African	19%
Scottish	7%
German	7%
Scots-Irish	5%
Irish	3%
Dutch	3%
Other European	9%

Disputed by Russia, Spain, and Britain

RUSSIAN

BRITISH NORTH AMERICA

PACIFIC OCEAN

SPANISH LOUISIANA

UNITED STATES

ATLANTIC OCEAN

St. Croix River

SPANISH NORTH AMERICA

New Orleans

EAST FLORIDA

WEST FLORIDA

GULF OF MEXICO

BRITISH CANADA

Lake Superior

Lake Michigan

Lake Huron

Mississippi R.

Ceded by VIRGINIA, 1784

Ceded by MASSACHUSETTS, 1785 and VIRGINIA 1784

Ceded by CONNECTICUT, 1786 and VIRGINIA, 1784

Ceded by CONNECTICUT, 1800

Lake Ontario

Lake Erie

Ceded by MASSACHUSETTS, 1786

Ceded by CONNECTICUT, 1782

MAINE (part of Massachusetts)

VERMONT (1791)

NEW YORK

NEW HAMPSHIRE

MASSACHUSETTS

St. Lawrence R.

Hudson R.

RHODE ISLAND

CONNECTICUT

PENNSYLVANIA

NEW JERSEY

MARYLAND

DELAWARE

Ceded by VIRGINIA, 1784

Ohio R.

SPANISH LOUISIANA

Ceded by VIRGINIA, 1792

VIRGINIA

Ceded by SOUTH CAROLINA, 1787

Ceded by NORTH CAROLINA, 1790

NORTH CAROLINA

Ceded by GEORGIA, 1802

SOUTH CAROLINA

Ceded by SPAIN, 1795
Ceded by GEORGIA, 1802

GEORGIA

Atlantic Ocean

SPANISH FLORIDA

Gulf of Mexico

0   100   200 miles
0   100   200 kilometers

States after land cessions
Ceded territory
Territory ceded by New York, 1782

The CENTINEL   Vol. IX

REDEUNT SATURNIA REGNA.
On the erection of the Eleventh PILLAR of the great N
Head DOME, we beg leave most sincerely to felicitate "OUR DEAR COUNT."

Rise it will.

The foundation good—it may yet be saved.

The FEDERAL EDIFICE.
ELEVEN STARS, in quick succession rise—
ELEVEN COLUMNS strike our wond'ring eyes,
Soon o'er the whole, shall swell the beauteous DOME,
COLUMBIA's boast—and FREEDOM's hallow'd home.
Here shall the ARTS in glorious splendour shine!
And AGRICULTURE give her stores divine!
COMMERCE refin'd, dispense us more than gold,
And this new world, teach WISDOM to the old—
RELIGION here shall fix her blest abode,
Array'd in mildness, like its parent GOD!
JUSTICE and LAW, shall endless PEACE maintain,
And the "SATURNIAN AGE," return again.

The British left Savannah in July, New York City in November, and Charleston in December. The king had quietly acceded to the dismemberment of a large portion of his empire. As he would write to John Adams in 1785, when Adams was the U.S. ambassador to Britain, "I have done nothing in the late contest but what I thought myself indispensably bound to do, by the duty I owed my people. . . . I was the last to consent to the separation, but the separation having been made. . . . I say now, that I would be the first to meet the friendship of the United States as an independent power."

———

When Washington ceremoniously resigned his commission to Congress, two days before Christmas, 1783, he restated the basic tenet of the revolutionary republicanism for which he had fought—government must rest upon the people's will. At the end of a speech that brought tears to many eyes, he commended "the Interests of our dearest country to the protection of Almighty God" and to the elected representatives of the states.

In so doing, he set two invaluable precedents that exist to this day. First, he established that American military forces would always be subordinate to elected political officials. Second, he disbanded his military staff and sent it home, showing that, for him, being a private citizen meant more than ruling a mighty army. Anticipating the importance of both of these precedents, Congress told Washington, "You have conducted the great military contest with wisdom and fortitude invariably regarding the rights of the civil power." The revolutionary republic had survived its birth pangs with its ideals intact. The people were sovereign. But could the United States survive the factions and special interests that had already emerged in the states and in the Confederation?

Epilogue The Way Ahead

The story of the American Revolution does not end with the Declaration of Independence, the Treaty of Paris, or the creation of a confederation of the states. The revolutionary nation held out to the world the dream of an empire of freedom. But not for everyone, and not to everyone's benefit. As in the war, there were winners and losers.

The loyalists' story was always unhappy and sometimes tragic. In New Jersey, New York, and Georgia, prosperous farm country had become graveyards. Loyalists removed to New York City, Savannah, and other enclaves under the protection of the British army and the Royal Navy. Some, like Thomas Hutchinson, abandoned careers and estates to return to the homeland from which their ancestors journeyed.

Parliament created a commission to hear loyalists' claims of losses incurred in the struggle to thwart the independence movement. Including compensation for the loyalists' claims and the costs of setting them up in other colonies, Britain spent over £30,000,000 on its exiles, even though most of the claims were settled for far less than the loyalists asked. Some exiles gained high office in the empire. William Smith Jr. of New York became Chief Justice Smith of Canada.

Of the eighty thousand to one hundred thousand loyalists who fled, a small number remained in the British Isles; most sailed to new homes in the peripheries of empire—primarily the Atlantic coast, the interior of Canada, Bermuda, and the Caribbean. For refugees from the southern colonies, a homestead in Nova Scotia or a business in Halifax was not only a step down in status. The hardship, cold, and isolation were a shock.

The majority of loyalists quietly put aside their preference for the crown and submitted to the new state governments by signing oaths of allegiance or trying to reduce their visibility in the community. Loyal Quakers in Pennsylvania, for example, simply removed themselves from public office. But even these silent loyalists suffered social ostracism, political debilities, and confiscation of property.

The stay-at-homes were joined, after the war, by loyalists returning from exile and loyalists who never left areas under the control of the British army. Most of the new states allowed these men and women to resume their old status but refused to hear their suits and petitions for the restoration of confiscated property.

The army was both winner and loser. On the one hand, the Continental army had defeated the greatest military power of its time. Washington kept military power under civilian control, even when Congress failed to provide him and his troops with basic necessities. The new republic would not have a military dictator, despite the allure of the great man on horseback to some of his officers. After becoming president, Washington avoided war. As Fred Anderson and Andrew Cayton have written, "he knew war too intimately to welcome it." At the same time, the army experience fostered a sense of national unity and an awareness of the need for a stronger national government among veterans. In the coming years, the achievement of revolutionary arms would become a source of patriotic pride.

On the other hand, the Continental soldier was never truly compensated for his personal sacrifice. In the spring of 1783, the troops were "furloughed," free to return home—empty-handed. The men got three-month "final settlement certificates" worth the paper they were printed on, and some veterans marched to Philadelphia to express their anger to the members of Congress. The congressmen, fearing for their safety, asked the governor to call out the militia. He refused. The Confederation government fled to Princeton, New Jersey. The veterans finally got pensions in 1818.

Ironically, just as the troops were muttering their dismay, the ideals of the Revolutionary War were sparking conversations among European reformers. Across the Atlantic, the American Revolution opened what historian R. R. Palmer has called "the age of democratic revolution." The ideas behind the Revolution reverberated in the Netherlands, France, Ireland, and Germany. Even in England, radicals took heart from the Americans' victory. Gatherings, societies, and salons shared in the excitement. To be sure, exportation of American constitutional concepts was not easy, but intellectuals had no trouble grasping general notions of the rights of men and the limits of government. The very idea that states could be fashioned on the basis of reason, equality, liberty, and humanity awakened European reformers' hopes for their own movements.

American revolutionaries were eager to help. John Adams, Franklin, Jefferson, and Paine were busy pamphleteers for the Revolution, and English, French, and German editions of their works were widely distributed in Europe. French soldiers returning to their homeland after the war spread revolutionary sentiments. It helped that prorevolutionary ideas could be coupled with anti-English feeling.

Even if European reformers had little factual information about the new American nation, they understood that the American revolutionaries had put rights in the place of privileges and the sovereign people in the place of kings and aristocrats. When the French began their own revolution, they looked to the United States as a model, and both Paine and Jefferson, on hand in Paris, advised the leaders of the uprising.

In later years, the beacon of the American Revolution would shine for peoples trying to throw off the yoke of imperial or foreign rule. In Latin America, early-nineteenth-century revolutionaries cited their debt to the American uprising. Greek and Hungarian rebels in the mid-nineteenth century asked for American aid on precisely that basis. German liberal reformers in 1848 claimed the American Revolution as their inspiration, and when their efforts failed, many came to the United States.

But as expansive as this vision of rights might have been, and as eager as American leaders were to expound upon the lessons of the American Revolution, the nation rarely followed its idealistic words with deeds. When, in 1793, beleaguered by external enemies (including Britain), revolutionary France asked for American help under the terms of the 1778 treaty, President Washington's administration unilaterally renounced the treaty and declared U.S. neutrality. Requests for U.S. aid from most other revolutionary movements went unheeded. Only when economic or geopolitical interests and goals made intervention valuable to the United States did it send troops or financial aid.

The reverberations of the Revolution went west and south as well as across the Atlantic. American land speculators already eyed Florida and the trans-Appalachian West. In a reprise of the land schemes of 1763, these entrepreneurs set up companies to sell off the new national domain, in particular the Ohio country, Kentucky, Tennessee, and the "Yazoo" (Alabama and Mississippi), even before the lands were surveyed. Merchants put pressure on American diplomats to open up the mouth of the Mississippi (and thus New Orleans) to American goods.

In short course, the less scrupulous among these schemers contemplated creating their own miniature empires in the Southwest and along the Gulf of Mexico coast. In the meantime, expeditions into the Ohio Indian country ended in bloody combat and the dispossession of the natives. The same pattern would unfold throughout the lands that Britain had ceded to the new nation under the Treaty of Paris. The land gained was occupied by squatters, sold by speculators, and finally possessed by farmers.

The Spanish Empire in America bordered the southern edge of these territories. Always suspicious of the Americans' motives, the Spanish had only reluctantly joined in the war effort alongside the French. John Jay, the U.S. diplomat in Madrid, correctly reported that the Spanish feared the new nation as much as it did the British Empire. Farther to the west, Spanish missionaries were creeping up the coast of California to lay claim to it before the Russians or the British arrived. At San Diego in 1769, Los Angeles in 1776, and up the coast to San Francisco by 1790, the missions, presidios, and rancheros appeared, islands of Spanish troops, settlers, and friars surrounded by a sea of Indians.

Indian hostility was allayed by the promise of salvation, and within a generation European diseases so diminished native numbers that effective opposition to the newcomers became impossible. Spanish cattle did for the native grasses what Spanish microbes did for the native peoples—colonized and conquered.

But the Spanish effort to preempt the expansion of the United States only delayed the inevitable. In 1846, the Americans fomented a rebellion against Mexico, successor to Spanish dominion. In 1850, California became a state in the Union. Its constitution bore remarkable similarities to the first states' fundamental laws.

In the revolutionary era, American political theorists announced that the purpose of government was to protect personal liberty and private property. Bills of rights laid out these liberties. Beneath this political ideology was a revolution in social attitudes. Revolutionary lawgivers no longer believed that personal identity derived from membership in a community. Instead, they claimed that individuals had rights simply because they were human. Revolutionary republican law confirmed rather than conferred these rights to life, liberty, and the pursuit of happiness.

The message of the Revolution was immediately translated into a demand for public education. The citizen of the new republic, according to the nation's first schoolmaster, Noah Webster, "should know and love the laws. This knowledge should be diffused by means of school and newspapers." Public schooling would enlighten, discipline, and energize children, fostering a new generation of republican leaders. Such men would never allow corruption, aristocratic privilege, or accumulated wealth to subvert the Revolution's achievement.

But the public schools were not for women. Their place, as angels of the home, required that they remain at home. For women, whatever gains the Revolution brought were curbed or rescinded in the years after the war.

The brightest promise of the revolutionary age—the abolition of slavery—shimmered in the mist and then evaporated. Gary Nash believes that "of all the missed opportunities in American history, it was the most tragic." Gordon Wood, as if anticipating Nash's somber judgment, agreed that the failure to free all the slaves "makes [the revolutionary leaders] seem inconsistent and hypocritical in our eyes. Yet it is important to realize that the Revolution suddenly and effectively ended" the near universal acceptance of bondage.

The way ahead for the slaves would be hard, but the promise of democracy, equality, and universal human dignity was still there. The great struggle between opportunity and oppression, dignity and degradation, freedom and servitude begun in the first settlements and carried on through the creation of a new nation would continue, and it does in our own time.

Bibliographic Essay

This bibliographic essay can only include a sample of the vast literature on early American history. However, I cite all works used in preparing the text and the captions and, in this second edition, bring the bibliography up to date.

My inspiration for the long-duration, extended-space approach is the work of Herbert Eugene Bolton. Bolton's *The Colonization of North America, 1492–1783*, written with Thomas Marshall and first published in 1921, regarded Canada, the Caribbean, and the Southwest as integral parts of the tale. A more recent version of this continental schema is Alan Taylor, *American Colonies: The Settlement of North America* (New York, 2001), a work of breadth and elegance.

The continentalist (my term, for want of a better) approach to early American history is the subject of a classic exchange between James Hijiya and other scholars in the pages of the *William and Mary Quarterly*. See Hijiya, "Why the West Is Lost," *William and Mary Quarterly* 3rd ser. 51 (1994): 276–292, with "Comments" and his response on the piece in ibid., 717–754. The *Quarterly*, published four times a year by the Omohundro Institute for Early American History and Culture in Williamsburg, Virginia, is a leading venue for scholarly research on early America.

An alternative approach much in vogue is the "Atlantic Rim" perspective. It treats the Atlantic as a great highway of commerce, peoples, and ideas connecting the Americas with Europe and Africa. There is no question that this is so, both in fact and as useful metaphor. Ongoing seminars on the Atlantic world in the age of the colonies at Harvard University and the University of Pennsylvania have produced many short pieces of considerable merit. These go far beyond the explorers-and-colonizers narratives of an earlier period of colonial historiography. A fuller synthesis of these will come in time, but model studies like Herbert S. Klein, *The Atlantic Slave Trade* (Cambridge, 1999), and John Thornton, *Africa and Africans in the Making of the Atlantic World, 1400–1800*, 2nd ed. (Cambridge, 1998), demonstrate that an Atlantic Rim synthesis is not only possible but will be highly fruitful.

In addition, the emerging field of "sensory history" has provided me with a number of insights for this edition. Some of them (word for word or very close paraphrase) have been imported from my own *Sensory Worlds in Early America* (Baltimore, 2003).

There are two collections of essays that I found to be essential bibliographic tools. The first is the three-volume *Encyclopedia of the North American Colonies* (New York, 1993), edited by Jacob E. Cooke. The second is *The Cambridge History of the Native Peoples of the Americas* (Cambridge, 1996), edited by Bruce Trigger and the late Wilcolm Washburn.

In addition, I have profited throughout my work from Carol Berkin, *First Generations: Women in Colonial America* (New York, 1996), Colin G. Calloway, *New Worlds for All: Indians, Europeans, and the Remaking of Early America* (Baltimore, 1997), and the collections of original documents and scholarly essays in Richard D. Brown, ed., *Major Problems in the Era of the American Revolution, 1760–1791* (Lexington, Mass., 1992), and Karen Ordahl Kupperman, ed., *Major Problems in American Colonial History* (Lexington, Mass., 1993). D. W. Meinig, *Atlantic America, 1492–1800*, vol. 1 of *The Shaping of America* (New Haven, Conn., 1986), is an indispensable guide to the geographical movement of people from place to place in the Atlantic world. The essays in Nicholas P. Canny, ed., *The Origins of Empire* (Oxford, 1998), vol. 1 of the *Oxford History of the British Empire*, and J. P. Marshall, ed., *The Eighteenth Century* (Oxford, 1998), vol. 2 in the same series (under the general editorship of William Roger Louis), offer excellent short surveys of the most recent scholarship on the British Empire.

PREFACE AND INTRODUCTION TO PART I. WORLDS IN MOTION

The discussion and the quotations on the *National History Standards* are taken from Peter Charles Hoffer, *Past Imperfect: Facts, Fictions, and Fraud in American History from Bancroft and Parkman to Ambrose, Bellesiles, Ellis and Goodwin* (New York, 2004).

Ronald Takaki's provocative *A Different Mirror: A History of Multicultural America* (Boston, 1993) uses *The Tempest* to make a different point about inherent conflict in the European investiture of America. Bernard Bailyn's *The Peopling of British North America: An Introduction* (New York, 1985) reminds us of the scope of scholarship on early America. Alden Vaughan's *Roots of American Racism: Essays on the Colonial Experience* (New York, 1995) explores the arrogance of the English treatment of other peoples. Two recent essays enrich our understanding of the first shipment of Africans to the Virginia colony. See Engel Sluiter, "New Light on the '20. and Odd Negroes' Arriving in Virginia, August 1619," *William and Mary Quarterly* 3rd ser. 54 (1997): 396–398, and John Thornton, "The African Experience of the '20. and Odd Negroes' Arriving in Virginia in 1619," *William and Mary Quarterly* 3rd ser. 55 (1998): 421–434.

Jack P. Greene, *Pursuits of Happiness: The Social Development of Early Modern British Colonies and the Formation of American Culture* (Chapel Hill, N.C., 1988), and Richard D. Brown, *Modernization: The Transformation of American Life, 1600–1865* (New York, 1976), argue that things got better. Jon Butler, *Becoming America: The Revolution before 1776* (Cambridge, Mass., 2000), makes the case in even stronger terms. But Richard White, *The Middle Ground: Indians, Empires, and Republics in the Great Lakes Region, 1650–1815* (Cambridge, 1991), Peter Kolchin, *American Slavery, 1619–1877* (New York, 1993), and Cornelia Hughes Dayton, *Women before the Bar: Gender, Law, and Society in Connecticut, 1636–1789* (Chapel Hill, N.C., 1995), among others, warn that not everyone shared in this progress. Indeed, as Michael Kammen, *People of Paradox: An Inquiry Concerning the Origins of American Civilization* (New York, 1973), has suggested, we cannot overlook the contradictions (what he calls "bi-formities") inherent in early American history.

Surely all these themes are relevant to the present, but Gary Nash, *Red, White, and Black: The Peoples of Early America*, 3rd ed. (Englewood Cliffs, N.J., 1992), warns against mining historical sources in search of relevant role models for today's politics. History is full of lessons but does not provide instruction on when to apply those lessons.

The notion that we might see the world of 1492 from a photo reconnaissance satellite I borrow with gratitude from the opening of Bailyn's *Peopling of British North America*. Arthur Versluis, *Sacred Earth: The Spiritual Landscape of Native America* (Rochester, Vt., 1992), connects the Indian religions to the landscape. Richard F. Townshend, *The Aztecs* (London, 1992), reconstructs the pilgrimage to the temple atop Mount Tlaloc. J. R. Hale, *Renaissance Europe: Individual and Society, 1480–1520* (Berkeley, Calif., 1977), offers a focused summary of European Catholicism on the eve of contact. On Islam in West Africa, see Mervyn Hiskett, *The Development of Islam in West Africa* (London, 1984), and J. Spencer Trimingham, *Islam in West Africa* (Oxford, 1959).

On mind and culture, see Leslie Brothers, *Friday's Footprint: How Society Shapes the Human Mind* (New York, 1997), and Howard Gardiner, *The Mind's New Science: A History of the Cognitive Revolution* (New York, 1987).

Indian views of the Europeans are traced in James Axtell, *Beyond 1492: Encounters in Colonial North America* (New York, 1992), Colin G. Calloway, *The World Turned Upside Down: Indian Voices from Early America* (Boston, 1994), and James Lockhart and Stuart Schwartz, *Early Latin America* (Cambridge, 1983).

European views of Indians in this formative period are traced in Anthony Pagden, *The Fall of Natural Man* (Cambridge, 1982), Pagden, *Encounters with Columbus* (New Haven, Conn., 1992), the essays in Karen Ordahl Kupperman, ed., *America in European Consciousness, 1493–1750* (Chapel Hill, N.C., 1995), Jack P. Greene, *The Intellectual Construction of America: Exceptionalism and Identity from 1492 to 1800* (Chapel Hill, N.C., 1992), and John F. Moffitt and Santiago Sebastián, *O Brave New People: The European Invention of the American Indian* (Albuquerque, N.M., 1996).

Roy Porter, *The Greatest Benefit to Mankind: A Medical History of Humanity* (New York, 1997), surveys the damage that European diseases wrought in the Americas. On the "Columbian exchange," see Alfred Crosby, *Germs, Seeds, and Animals* (London, 1994).

CHAPTER ONE. THE FIRST AMERICANS

The notion that Indians were natural ecologists informs popular literature like Peter Matthiessen, *Indian Country* (New York, 1992). The best recent accounts of Native Americans before and during the contact period are Daniel K. Richter, *Facing East from Indian Country: A Native History of Early America* (Cambridge, Mass., 2001), Calloway, *New Worlds for All*, and Gregory H. Nobles, *American Frontiers: Cultural Encounters and Continental Conquest* (New York, 1997). Nobles, like Calloway, in *One Vast Winter Count: The Native American West before Lewis and Clark* (Lincoln, Neb., 2003), carries the story onto the prairies and into the nineteenth century.

The First Woman story comes from Daniel K. Richter, *The Ordeal of the Long House: The Peoples of the Iroquois League in the Era of European Colonization* (Chapel Hill, N.C., 1992), and the tale of Thought Woman and the twin sisters from Ramón Gutiérrez, *When Jesus Came, the Corn Mothers Went Away: Marriage, Sexuality, and Power in New Mexico, 1500–1846* (Stanford, Calif., 1991). A convenient collection of Native American tales of origin is Frederick W. Turner III, ed., *The Portable North American Indian Reader* (New York, 1973). Quotations from Indian peoples are featured in Alvin M. Josephy Jr., *500 Nations: An Illustrated History of North American Indians* (New York, 1994).

The copiously illustrated *Smithsonian Timelines of the Ancient World: A Visual Chronology from the Origins of Life to AD 1500* (London, 1993) by Chris Scarre compares early America with Europe, Asia, the Near East, and Africa. Brian M. Fagan, *The Great Journey: The Peopling of Ancient America* (London, 1987), and Fagan, *Ancient North America: The Archeology of a Continent* (London, 1991), retell the archaeological detective story of the brave new world, but may already be out of date as new discoveries are announced.

Authoritative and technically sophisticated, E. C. Pielou's *After the Ice Age: The Return of Life to Glaciated North America* (Chicago, 1991) explains climate, geology, and paleobiology. "Nine months of darkness and three months of mosquitos" comes from Peter C. Newman's engaging story of the Hudson's Bay Company, *Company of Adventurers* (Toronto, 1985).

The literature on ecology is vast and grows daily. A readable survey of the treatment of forest is Jonathan Perlin, *A Forest Journey* (Cambridge, Mass., 1989). Kenneth A. Brown, *Four Corners: History, Land, and People of the Desert Southwest* (New York, 1995), does the same for the Southwest. William Cronon, *Changes in the Land: Indians, Colonists, and the Ecology of New England* (New York, 1983), tells the story of the treatment of forest by the first English settlers of New England, and how it differed from Indian use. Timothy Silver, *A New Face on the Countryside: Indians, Colonists, and Slaves in South Atlantic Forests, 1500–1800* (Cambridge, 1990), and Alan Gallay, *The Indian Slave Trade: The Rise of the English Empire in the American South, 1670–1717* (New Haven, Conn., 2002), trace changes in the Southeast. They are also invaluable sources for the southern colonies discussed in chapter 5.

On the Paleolithic period, Dean R. Snow, "The First Americans and the Differentiation of Hunter-Gatherer Cultures," and Linda S. Cordell and Bruce D. Smith, "Indigenous Farmers," both in Trigger and Washburn, eds., *Native Peoples of the Americas* 1: part 1, 125–200, are readable and offer bibliographies. On knapping and chipping stone, the best work is Noel D. Justice, *Stone Age Spear and Arrow Points of the Midcontinental and Eastern United States: A Modern Survey and Reference* (Bloomington, Ind., 1987).

On Indian dress, see Josephine Paterek, *Encyclopedia of American Indian Costume* (New York, 1994). Bruce D. Smith, *Rivers of Change: Essays on Early Agriculture in Eastern North America* (Washington, D.C., 1992), surveys food sources.

Joseph H. Greenberg has published many studies of ancient American language. See, for example, *Language in the Americas* (Stanford, Calif., 1987). More recent are the fine essays in Edward G. Gray and Norman Fiering, eds., *The Language Encounter in the Americas, 1492–1800* (New York, 2000), as well as Gray's own *New World Babel: Languages and Nations in Early America* (Princeton, N.J., 1999). A fine discussion of disease and domesticated animals appears in Jared Diamond, *Guns, Germs, and Steel: The Fates of Human Societies* (New York, 1997). Allan Hayes and John Blom, *Southwestern Pottery: Anasazi to Zuni* (Flagstaff, Ariz., 1996), illustrate the pottery of the Southwest.

Popular accounts on the landscape of the Southwest include Michael S. Durham, *The Smithsonian Guide to Historic America: The Desert States* (New York, 1990), Peggy Larson, *A Sierra Club Naturalist's Guide to the Deserts of the Southwest* (San Francisco, 1977), and Buddy Mays, *Ancient Cities of the Southwest* (San Francisco, 1990). The Havasupai corn dishes come from A. F. Whiting, *Havasupai Habitat*, ed. Steven A. Weber and P. David Seaman (Tucson, Ariz., 1985). The Apalachee diet is one subject in John H. Hann, *Apalachee: The Land between the Rivers* (Gainesville, Fla., 1988). On the plains Indians, the best recent collection is Karl H. Schlesie, ed., *Plains Indians, A.D. 500–1500: The Archeological Past of Historic Groups* (Norman, Okla., 1994). For more on eastern woodlands Indians, see James Axtell's *The Indians' New South: Cultural Change in the Colonial Southeast* (Baton Rouge, La.: 1997).

The many estimates of Indian population in North America on the eve of contact are ably dissected in John D. Daniels, "The Indian Population of North America in 1492," *William and Mary Quarterly* 3rd ser. 49 (1992): 298–320. A more recent work, with an estimate of eighteen million, is Charles C. Mann, *1491: New Revelations of the Americas before Columbus* (New York, 2005). The concept of the Indian's "old world" belongs to Neal Salisbury, "The Indians' Old World: Native Americans and the Coming of Europeans," *William and Mary Quarterly* 3rd ser. 53 (1996): 435–458. The notion of "the woods" comes from James Merrell, *Into the American Woods: Negotiators on the Pennsylvania Frontier* (New York, 1999), essential reading on this and the later role of go-betweens in eighteenth-century colonial Pennsylvania.

CHAPTER TWO. EUROPE IN THE AGE OF DISCOVERY, 1400 – 1500

The staying power of the old categories of European thought, even when deluged by contrary data, is one of the themes in Anthony Grafton, *New Worlds, Ancient Texts: The Power of Tradition and the Shock of Discovery* (Cambridge, Mass., 1992), the source of the Dati quote.

A readable summary of early modern European economies is Rondo Cameron, *A Concise Economic History of the World*, 2nd ed. (New York, 1993). Peter J. Hugill, *World*

Trade since 1431: Geography, Technology, and Capitalism (Baltimore, 1993), takes a more complex and theoretical approach.

The revolution in taste is discussed in Jean-Louis Flandrin, "Distinction through Taste," in Roger Chartier, ed., *Passions of the Renaissance*, vol. 3 of *A History of Private Life* (Cambridge, Mass., 1989), 265–307, T. Sarah Peterson, *Acquired Taste: The French Origins of Modern Cooking* (Princeton, N.J., 1994), Wolfgang Schivelbusch, *Tastes of Paradise: A Social History of Spices, Stimulants, and Intoxicants* (New York, 1992), and Barbara Wheaton, *Savoring the Past: The French Kitchen and Table from 1300 to 1789* (Philadelphia, 1983). Caroline Walker Bynum, *Holy Feast and Holy Fast: The Religious Significance of Food to Medieval Women* (Berkeley, Calif., 1987), offers a wealth of analogies women made between fasting and piety. The concept of the inversion of male and female roles in food production and worship is hers.

Fernand Braudel's three-volume set, *Civilization and Capitalism: 15th to 18th Century*, trans. Siân Reynolds (New York, 1979), provides much information on cities, manners, bankers, and princes.

The revolution in time is covered in David S. Landes, *Revolution in Time: Clocks and the Making of the Modern World* (Cambridge, Mass., 1983). Alfred W. Crosby's *The Measure of Reality: Quantification and Western Society* (Cambridge, 1997) is a literate study of how bookkeeping, music, and mathematics were all part of the same "tempest" of calculation that swept over Europe in the age of discovery. Chartier counts books and the readers in "The Practical Impact of Writing" in Chartier, ed., *Passions of the Renaissance*, 111–159.

Short introductions to the Renaissance are Myron P. Gilmore, *The World of Humanism, 1453–1517* (New York, 1952), and Hale, *Renaissance Europe*. John Martin, "Inventing Sincerity, Refashioning Prudence: The Discovery of the Individual in Renaissance Europe," *American Historical Review* 102 (December 1997): 1309–1342 revises our ideas of art. A fine collection of primary and secondary sources is Benjamin G. Kohl and Alison Andrews Smith, eds., *Major Problems in the History of the Italian Renaissance* (Lexington, Mass., 1995). Anthony Grafton and Lisa Jardine, *From Humanism to the Humanities: Education and the Liberal Arts in Fifteenth and Sixteenth-Century Europe* (Cambridge, Mass., 1986), debunks the "mind opening" claims of humanism, but Kenneth Gouwens, "Renaissance Humanism after the 'Cognitive Turn,'" *American Historical Review* 103 (1998): 55–82, defends the humanists' originality.

Daniel Boorstin, *The Discoverers* (New York, 1983), and Joel Mokyr, *The Lever of Riches: Technological Creativity and Economic Progress* (New York, 1990), discuss technology.

Warfare is the subject of William O'Neill, *The Pursuit of Power: Technology, Armed Force, and Society since A.D. 1000* (Chicago, 1982). I took the argument that Europe was undergoing a military revolution in the age of discovery from Charles Tilly, *European Revolutions* (Oxford, 1993). Paul Kennedy, *The Rise and Fall of the Great Powers: Economic Change and Military Conflict from 1500 to 2000* (New York, 1987), tracks the way that internal taxation reflected the demands of external wars. Michael Prestwick, "The English Medieval Army to 1485," in David Chandler, ed., *The Oxford History of the British Army* (Oxford, 1996), 1–23, details the wages of the English forces and their equipment.

Quentin Skinner's two-volume treatise *The Foundations of Modern Political Thought* (New York, 1978) is still the standard work on the subject.

W. Gordon East, *The Geography behind History*, rev. ed. (New York, 1965), explains geographical advantages and disadvantages in history. David Landes, *The Wealth and Poverty of Nations: Why Some Are So Rich and Some So Poor* (New York, 1998), links geographical advantages to invention and adventurousness. On Portugal in the age of discovery, see Bailey W. Diffie and George D. Winius, *Foundations of the Portuguese Empire, 1415–1580* (Minneapolis, 1977), and P. E. Russell, *Portugal, Spain, and the African Atlantic, 1343–1490* (Brookfield, Vt., 1995). On Spain, the single best book is J. H. Elliott, *Imperial Spain, 1469–1716* (London, 1963).

A classic overview of the European voyages of discovery is Samuel Eliot Morison, *The European Discovery of America: The Southern Voyages A.D. 1492–1616* (New York, 1972), and *The Northern Voyages, A.D. 500–1600* (New York, 1974). A readable account of the cartography of the age is John Noble Wilford, *The Mapmakers* (New York, 1981). Alfred W. Crosby coined the term "portmanteau biota" and made it common currency in *Ecological Imperialism: The Biological Expansion of Europe, 900–1900* (Cambridge, 1986).

Gwyn Jones, *The History of the Vikings* (New York, 1968), is good reading. On the end of the Reconquista, see Elliott, *Imperial Spain*. Robert S. Gottfried, *The Black Death: Natural and Human Disaster in Medieval Europe* (New York, 1983), follows the track of the plague.

On the history of Africa in the age of European discovery see Basil Davidson, *Africa in History*, rev. ed. (New York, 1991), the essays in Philip S. Curtin et al., *African History: From Earliest Times to Independence*, rev. ed. (London, 1995), and Ronald Oliver, *The African Experience* (New York, 1991). Elizabeth Donnan, ed., *Documents Illustrative of the History of the Slave Trade to America* (Washington, D.C., 1930–35), 4 vols., is the source of the Brandoan quotation.

CHAPTER THREE. THE SPANISH CENTURY, 1492–1588

For more on Queen Isabel of Spain, see Peggy K. Liss, *Isabel the Queen: Life and Times* (New York, 1992). Columbus's life story is told in the two volumes of Samuel Eliot Morison's *Admiral of the Ocean Sea: A Life of Christopher Columbus* (Boston, 1942). On the perils of piloting, see John R. Stilgoe, *Alongshore* (New Haven, Conn., 1994).

For an account of the Taíno and their world, Irving Rouse, *The Taínos: The Rise and Decline of the People Who Greeted Columbus* (New Haven, Conn., 1992), is indispensable. On the warfare that reduced the Taíno to a fraction of their former numbers, see Carl Ortwin Sauer, *The Early Spanish Main* (Berkeley, Calif., 1966). The power of naming is one subject in Jack D. Forbes, *Africans and Native Americans: The Language of Race and the Evolution of Red-Black Peoples*, 2nd ed. (Urbana, Ill., 1993).

The standard work on the Spanish *entradas* is David J. Weber, *The Spanish Frontier in North America* (New Haven, Conn., 1992). Ian K. Steele, *Warpaths: Invasions of North America* (New York, 1994), covers a broader subject. Inga Clendinnen, *Aztecs: An Interpretation* (Cambridge, 1991), probes Moctezuma's thinking. Anthony Pagden, *European Encounters with the New World* (New Haven, Conn., 1993), traces out the problems that Europeans had explaining (or explaining away) the novelty of the New World. Tzvetan Todorov, *The Conquest of America: The Question of the Other*, trans. Richard Howard (New York, 1984), re-reads the Spanish literature of conquest. Doña Isabel's story is told in Donald Chipman, "Isabel Moctezuma: Pioneer of Mestizaje," in David G. Sweet and Gary B. Nash, eds., *Struggle and Survival in Colonial America* (Berkeley, Calif., 1974), 214–227.

Charles Hudson traces de Soto's path in "The Hernando De Soto Expedition," in Hudson and Carmen Chavez Tesser, eds., *The Forgotten Centuries: Indians and Europeans in the American South, 1521–1704* (Athens, Ga., 1993), 74–103. David Ewing Duncan, *Hernando de Soto: A Savage Quest in the Americas* (New York, 1995), dramatizes de Soto's *entrada*. Douglas Preston, *Cities of Gold: A Journey across the American Southwest in Pursuit of Coronado* (New York, 1992), follows Coronado's trail. Slaving in the Southwest is the subject of James F. Brooks, *Captives and Cousins: Slavery, Kinship, and Community in the Southwest Borderlands* (Chapel Hill, N.C., 2002).

On the Pueblo peoples' sexuality and the missionaries, see Gutiérrez, *When Jesus Came*. The missionaries' systematic attack on the "harlots" of New Spain is revealed in Rebecca Overmyer-Velázquez, "Christian Morality Revealed in New Spain: The Inimical Nahua Woman in Book Ten of the *Florentine Codex*," *Journal of Women's History* 10 (1998): 9–37. On the *encomiendas*, see Lewis Hanke, *The Spanish Struggle for Justice in the Conquest of America* (Boston, 1965). Charles Gibson, *Spain in America* (New York, 1966), lays out the Spanish administrative system.

Ralph Davis, *The Rise of the Atlantic Economies* (Ithaca, N.Y., 1973), discusses the slave trade and the Spanish economy. The literature on slavery and the European New World venture is vast. Classic works include David Brion Davis, *The Problem of Slavery in Western Culture* (New York, 1966), and Orlando Patterson, *Slavery* (Cambridge, Mass., 1985). On the flow of the trade, the starting point is still Philip D. Curtin, *The Atlantic Slave Trade: A Census* (Madison, Wis., 1969), and his shorter *The Tropical Atlantic in the Age of the Slave Trade* (Washington, D.C., 1991). The roots of the African slave trade are traced in Paul Lovejoy, *Transformations in Slavery: A History of Slavery in Africa* (Cambridge, 1983), and John Thornton, *Africa and Africans in the Making of the Atlantic World, 1400–1680* (Cambridge, 1992). More recent surveys include David Eltis, *The Rise of African Slavery in the Americas* (Cambridge, 2000), and Herbert S. Klein, *The Atlantic Slave Trade* (Cambridge, 1999).

On slavery in the Spanish Americas, see Colin A. Palmer, *Slaves of the White God:*

Blacks in Mexico, 1570–1650 (Cambridge, Mass., 1976), and Gwendolyn Midlo Hall, *Slavery and African Ethnicities in the Americas: Restoring the Links* (Chapel Hill, N.C., 2005). The essays in "Constructing Race: Differentiating Peoples in the Early Modern World" in the January 1997 issue of the *William and Mary Quarterly* 3rd ser. 54 (1997) cover a broader spectrum.

The distinction between "slave societies" and "slave-holding societies" is one of the many useful points in James Walvin, *Questioning Slavery* (London, 1996), and Philip D. Morgan, *Slave Counterpoint: Black Culture in the Eighteenth-Century Chesapeake and Low Country* (Chapel Hill, N.C., 1998). On the Creole culture-brokers of the Atlantic slave enclaves, see Ira Berlin, *Many Thousands Gone: The First Two Centuries of Slavery in North America* (Cambridge, Mass., 1998), the essays in Ira Berlin and Philip D. Morgan, eds., *Cultivation and Culture: Labor and the Shaping of Slave Life in the Americas* (Charlottesville, Va., 1993), and William Frederick Sharp, *Slavery on the Spanish Frontier: The Colombian Chocó, 1680–1810* (Norman, Okla., 1976).

The resistance of slaves to slavery is discussed in Palmer, *Slaves of the White God*, Michael Craton, *Testing the Chains: Resistance to Slavery in the British West Indies* (Ithaca, N.Y., 1982), and Franklin W. Knight, *The Caribbean*, 2nd ed. (New York, 1990).

Garrett Mattingly, *The Armada*, sentry ed. (Boston, 1959), is a wonderful story.

CHAPTER FOUR. RIVALS FOR THE NORTHLAND

The French venture in the New World is covered in W. J. Eccles, *The French in America*, rev. ed. (East Lansing, Mich., 1990), and Marc Egnal, *Divergent Paths* (New York, 1996). The voyages of Verrazzano and Cartier are retraced in Morison, *Northern Voyages*. On the French backgrounds of exploration, see J.H.M. Salmon, *Society in Crisis: France in the Sixteenth Century* (London, 1975), and Mark Greengrass, *France in the Age of Henry IV: The Struggle for Equality*, rev. ed. (London, 1995).

On the native peoples of the far North, see Bruce Trigger, *The Huron: Farmers of the Far North*, 2nd ed. (Fort Worth, Tex., 1990), and Neal Salisbury, *Manitou and Providence: Indians, Europeans, and the Making of New England, 1500–1643* (New York, 1982). Trigger, with James F. Prendergast, explores the controversial ethnic origins of the people of Hochelaga in *Cartier's Hochelaga and the Dawson Site* (Montreal, 1972). Colin Calloway has collected the Indian voices from these northern regions in *Dawnland Encounters: Indians and Europeans in Northern New England* (Hanover, N.H., 1991).

A brief introduction to the Reformation and Counterreformation is François Lebrun, "The Two Reformations: Communal Devotion and Personal Piety," in Chartier, ed., *Passions of the Renaissance*, 62–109. On women in the Reformation era, see Elisja Schulte van Kessel, "Virgins and Mothers between Heaven and Earth," in Natalie Zemon Davis and Arlette Farge, eds., *A History of Women in the West: III, Renaissance and Enlightenment Paradoxes* (Cambridge, Mass., 1993), 132–183.

Henry VII is the subject of S. B. Chrimes's *Henry VII* (Berkeley, Calif., 1972) and

Jasper Ridley's *Henry VIII* (New York, 1985), voluminously detailed. Norman Jones, *The Birth of the Elizabethan Age: England in the 1560s* (Oxford, 1993), and D. M. Palliser, *The Age of Elizabeth: England under the Later Tudors, 1547–1603*, 2nd ed. (London, 1992), are comprehensive. The importance of the merchants is traced in Kenneth R. Andrews, *Trade, Plunder, and Settlement: Maritime Enterprise and the Genesis of the British Empire, 1480–1630* (Cambridge, 1984).

Reliable reference works that include essays on these subjects as well as later periods of English, Scottish, and Irish history are Kenneth O. Morgan, ed., *The Oxford History of Britain* (Oxford, 1993), and Christopher Haigh, ed., *The Cambridge Historical Encyclopedia of Great Britain and Ireland* (Cambridge, 1985).

Frobisher and Drake are followed in Morison's *Northern Voyages* and *Southern Voyages*, respectively. A readable popular biography of Ralegh (the spelling Raleigh is a later invention) is Stephen Coote, *A Play of Passion: The Life of Sir Walter Ralegh* (London, 1993). I have taken my account of the Irish uprising of 1579 from Nicholas P. Canny, "Identity Formation in Ireland: The Emergence of the Anglo-Irish" in Canny and Anthony Pagden, eds., *Colonial Identity in the Atlantic World, 1500–1800* (Princeton, N.J., 1987), 159–212, and John McGurk, *The Elizabethan Conquest of Ireland* (Manchester, Eng., 1997). The Irish settlement models are laid out in Nicholas P. Canny, "The Marginal Kingdom: Ireland as a Problem in the First English Empire," in Bernard Bailyn and Philip D. Morgan, eds., *Strangers within the Realm: Cultural Margins of the First British Empire* (Chapel Hill, N.C., 1991), 35–66.

On the ecology of the Roanoke area, see Silver, *New Face on the Countryside*. The Indian life of the region is traced in Robert S. Grumet, *Historic Contact: Indian Peoples and Colonists in Today's Northeastern United States in the Sixteenth and Seventeenth Centuries* (Norman, Okla., 1996), and Karen Ordahl Kupperman, *Settling with the Indians: The Meeting of English and Indian Cultures in America, 1580–1640* (Totowa, N.J., 1980). On the English in Roanoke, see David Beers Quinn, *Set Fair for Roanoke: Voyages and Colonies, 1584–1606* (Chapel Hill, N.C., 1985).

Excerpts from Hakluyt's *Voyages* appear in Erwin Blacker, ed., *The Portable Hakluyt's Voyages* (New York, 1965).

Did the English see the Indians as inferior from the outset of their encounter? Or did the later commitment to empire induce the English to lower their estimation of the Indians' abilities and achievements? Arguing for the position that the English, at first, treated the Indians with respect and some admiration are Joyce Chaplin, *Subject Matter: Technology, the Body, and Science on the Anglo-American Frontier, 1500–1676* (Cambridge, Mass., 2001), Karen Ordahl Kupperman, *Indians and English Facing Off in Early America* (Ithaca, N.Y., 2000), and Michael Leroy Oberg, *Dominion and Civility: English Imperialism and Native America, 1585–1685* (Ithaca, N.Y., 2001). Arguing the contrary, an extermination-from-the-outset thesis, are Richard Drinnon, *Facing West: The Metaphysics of Indian Hating and Empire Building* (Minneapolis, 1980), and Francis Jennings, *The Invasion of America: Indians, Colonialism, and the Cant of Conquest* (New York, 1975).

Hoffer, *Sensory Worlds in Early America*, takes a middle position. There was a time of genuine wonder at sensory novelties, followed, tragically, by a narrowing of vision and expanding animosity.

The price trends of the sixteenth and seventeenth centuries are reviewed in David Hackett Fischer, *The Great Wave: Price Revolutions and the Rhythm of History* (New York, 1996).

On the Indians' view of the fur trade, see Calvin Martin, *Keepers of the Game: Indian-Animal Relationships and the Fur Trade* (Berkeley, Calif., 1978), and Shephard Kretch III, ed., *Indians, Animals, and the Fur Trade: A Critique of Keepers of the Game* (Athens, Ga., 1981).

Elizabeth Ewing, *Fur in Dress* (London, 1981), and R. Turner Wilcox, *The Mode in Furs: The History of Furred Costume of the World from the Earliest Times to the Present* (New York, 1951), depict European fur fashions. On alcohol among the Indians, see Peter C. Mancall, *Deadly Medicine: Indians and Alcohol in Early America* (Ithaca, N.Y., 1995).

The first English settlements in the North are the subject of the essays in Emerson W. Baker et al., *American Beginnings: Exploration, Culture, and Cartography in the Land of Norumbega* (Lincoln, Neb., 1994), Peter A. Lenz, ed., *Voyages to Norumbega* (Norway, Me., 1994), and David Beers Quinn, ed., *English Plans for North America. The Roanoke Voyages. New England Ventures*, vol. 3 of *New American World: A Documentary History of North America to 1612* (New York, 1979).

The essays in Ida Altman and James Horn, eds., *"To Make America": European Emigration in the Early Modern Period* (Berkeley, Calif., 1991), Nicholas P. Canny, ed., *Europeans on the Move: Studies on European Migration, 1500–1800* (Oxford, 1994), and Alison Games, *Migration and the Origins of the English Atlantic World* (Cambridge, Mass., 1999), follow the great migration. For sex ratios and family sizes in different colonies, see Robert V. Wells, *The Population of the British Colonies in America before 1776* (Princeton, N.J., 1975).

The motivations for British migration are treated in James Horn, *Adapting to a New World: English Society in the Seventeenth Century Chesapeake* (Chapel Hill, N.C., 1994), and Carl Bridenbaugh, *Vexed and Troubled Englishmen, 1590–1642* (London, 1967), as well as Games, *Migration*.

On Champlain in Canada, see Samuel Eliot Morison, *Samuel de Champlain: Father of New France* (Boston, 1972). Another accessible work on Champlain is Morris Bishop, *Champlain: The Life of Fortitude* (New York, 1948). On the dire situation in France during Champlain's forays into Canada, see Robin Briggs, *Early Modern France, 1560–1715* (Oxford, 1977). The trade between the fishermen and the Indians in the late sixteenth century is traced in Laurier Turgeon, "French Fishers, Fur Traders, and Amerindians during the Sixteenth Century: History and Archeology," *William and Mary Quarterly* 3rd. Ser. 50 (1998): 585–610.

CHAPTER FIVE. THE PLANTER COLONIES

The world of the Algonquians of the Chesapeake in explored in Helen C. Rountree, *Pocahontas's People: The Powhatan Indians of Virginia through Four Centuries* (Norman, Okla., 1999), Grumet, *Historic Contact*, and in Stephen R. Potter, "Early English Effects on Virginia Algonquian Exchange and Tribute," in Peter H. Wood, Gregory A. Waselkov, and M. Thomas Hatley, eds., *Powhatan's Mantle: Indians in the Colonial Southeast* (Lincoln, Neb., 1989), 151–172.

A traditional institutional, political, and economic history of the first English colonies is Charles McLean Andrews's four-volume *The Colonial Period of American History* (New Haven, Conn., 1934–1938).

On John Smith and Jamestown, see Philip L. Barbour, *The Three Worlds of Captain John Smith* (Boston, 1964), Alden T. Vaughan, *American Genesis: Captain John Smith and the Founding of Virginia* (Boston, 1975), and Ivor Noel Hume, *The Virginia Adventure: Roanoke to James Towne: An Archeological and Historical Odyssey* (New York, 1994).

On Anthony Johnson, see Berlin, *Many Thousands Gone*, and T. H. Breen and Stephen Innes, *"Myne Own Ground": Race and Freedom on Virginia's Eastern Shore, 1640–1676* (New York, 1980). Martha W. McCartney recovers the story of Cockacoeske in "Cockacoeske, Queen of Pamunkey: Diplomat and Suzereine," in Wood et al., eds., *Powhatan's Mantle.*

Broader pictures of aspects of life in the tobacco colonies appear in Virginia DeJohn Anderson, *Creatures of Empire: How Domesticated Animals Transformed Early America* (New York, 2004), Lois Green Carr, Russell R. Menard, and Lorena S. Walsh, *Robert Cole's World: Agriculture and Society in Early Maryland* (Chapel Hill, N.C., 1991), Horn, *Adapting to a New World*, Darrett B. Rutman and Anita H. Rutman, *A Place in Time: Middlesex County, Virginia, 1650–1750* (New York, 1984), the essays by Menard, Carr, the Rutmans, and Walsh in Thad W. Tate and David L. Ammerman, eds., *The Chesapeake in the Seventeenth Century: Essays on Anglo-American Society* (Chapel Hill, N.C., 1979), and Gloria L. Main, *Tobacco Colony: Life in Early Maryland* (Princeton, N.J., 1982). Lois Green Carr looks at inheritance patterns in "Inheritance in the Colonial Chesapeake," in Ronald Hoffman and Peter J. Albert, eds., *Women in the Age of the American Revolution* (Charlottesville, Va., 1989), 155–210. Mary Beth Norton's provocative *Founding Mothers and Fathers: Gendered Power and the Forming of American Society* (New York, 1996) examines private misconduct in the tobacco colonies.

Aubrey C. Land's *Colonial Maryland: A History* (Millwood, N.Y., 1981) traces the course of early Maryland politics. Jon Butler's *Awash in a Sea of Faith: Christianizing the American People* (Cambridge. Mass., 1990) explores religion in early Maryland and Virginia.

On the Carolinas, see Richard Ekirch Jr., *Poor Carolina* (Chapel Hill, N.C., 1981), Hugh T. Leffler and William S. Powell, *Colonial North Carolina: A History* (New York, 1973), Robert Weir, *Colonial South Carolina: A History* (Millwood, N.Y., 1983), and Peter H. Wood, *Black Majority: Negroes in Colonial South Carolina from 1670 through the Stono Rebellion* (New York, 1974).

Ira Berlin, "From Creole to African: Atlantic Creoles and the Origins of African-American Society in Mainland North America," *William and Mary Quarterly* 3rd ser. 53 (1996): 251–288, Berlin, *Many Thousands Gone*, and Morgan, *Slave Counterpoint*, examine the rise of the slave culture in the low country. A good summary of the literature on the rice trade is Kenneth Morgan, "The Organization of the Colonial American Rice Trade," *William and Mary Quarterly* 3rd ser. 52 (1995): 433–452.

The English sugar islands get their due in Carl Bridenbaugh and Roberta Bridenbaugh, *No Peace beyond the Line: The English in the Caribbean, 1624–1690* (New York, 1972), Richard Dunn, *Sugar and Slaves: The Rise of the Planter Class in the English West Indies, 1624–1713* (New York, 1972), Gary Puckrein, *Little England: Plantation Society and Anglo-Barbadian Politics, 1627–1700* (New York, 1984), and Richard B. Sheridan, *Sugar and Slavery: An Economic History of the British West Indies, 1620–1775* (New York, 1972). Eric Williams's *From Columbus to Castro: The History of the Caribbean* (New York, 1970) is vivid and spirited. The (mis)conduct of the servants of Barbados is the subject of Hilary McD. Beckles, "A 'Riotous and Unruly Lot': Irish Indentured Servants and Freemen in the English West Indies, 1644–1713," *William and Mary Quarterly* 3rd ser. 47 (1990): 503–522.

Women in the Chesapeake is one of the subjects of Norton's *Founding Mothers and Fathers* and lies at the center of Kathleen M. Brown, *Good Wives, Nasty Wenches, and Anxious Patriarchs: Gender, Race, and Power in Colonial Virginia* (Chapel Hill, N.C., 1996).

CHAPTER SIX. A NEW ENGLAND

Good recent summaries of English Puritanism are Patrick Collinson, *English Puritanism* (London, 1983), and Stephen Foster, *The Long Argument: English Puritanism and the Shaping of New England Culture, 1570–1700* (Chapel Hill, N.C., 1991), but the best of the lot is Michael P. Winship, *Making Heretics: Militant Protestantism and Free Grace in Massachusetts, 1636–1641* (Princeton, N.J., 2002). Theodore Dwight Bozeman, *To Live Ancient Lives: The Primitivist Dimension in Puritanism* (Chapel Hill, N.C., 1988), identifies the yearning Puritans had for an earlier biblical world, while Philip F. Gura, *A Glimpse of Sion's Glory: Puritan Radicalism in New England, 1620–1660* (Middletown, Conn., 1984), traces the utopian highlights in Puritan thought. Perry Miller, *The New England Mind: The Seventeenth Century* (New York, 1939), remains a classic, if now regarded as somewhat skewed by excessive reliance on the ideas of Massachusetts minister Thomas Shepard. Ola Elizabeth Winslow, *Meetinghouse Hill, 1630–1783* (New York, 1952), offers a loving portrait of the Puritan churches.

The Pilgrims' chronicle is recounted in George D. Langdon Jr., *Pilgrim Colony: A History of New Plymouth, 1620–1691* (New Haven, Conn., 1966). John P. Demos, *A Little Commonwealth: Family Life in Plymouth Colony* (New York, 1970), George Francis

Dow, *Every Day Life in the Massachusetts Bay Colony* (Boston, 1935), and David Freeman Hawke, *Everyday Life in Early America* (New York, 1988), provide notes on clothing, furnishings, and housing. Menus for the first New England settlers are included in Hyla O'Connor, *The Early American Cookbook* (New York, 1974). Changes in family and household life—including a comparison of English and Indian ways—are covered in Gloria L. Main, *Peoples of a Spacious Land: Families and Cultures in Colonial New England* (Cambridge, Mass., 2001). A wonderfully suggestive analysis on the shift in the treatment of children in this era is Holly Brewer, *By Birth or Consent: Children, Law, and the Anglo-American Revolution in Authority* (Chapel Hill, N.C., 2005).

On the founding of the Massachusetts Bay Colony, see David Grayson Allen, *In English Ways: The Movement of Societies and the Transferal of English Local Law and Custom to Massachusetts Bay in the Seventeenth Century* (Chapel Hill, N.C., 1981), Andrews, *Colonial Period*, vol. 1, Virginia DeJohn Anderson, *New England's Generation: The First Migration and the Formation of Society and Culture in the Seventeenth Century* (New York, 1991), the first section of David Hackett Fischer's delightful and sprawling *Albion's Seed: Four British Folkways in America* (New York, 1989), and David Cressy, *Coming Over: Migration and Communication between England and New England in the Seventeenth Century* (New York, 1987). For more than anyone would want to know about the first iron works in New England, E. N. Hartley, *Ironworks on the Saugus* (Norman, Okla., 1957), is just the ticket.

Kenneth A. Lockridge, *A New England Town: The First Hundred Years. Dedham, Massachusetts, 1636–1736*, rev. ed. (New York, 1985), and Michael Zuckerman, *Peaceable Kingdoms* (New York, 1970), following the classic study by Sumner Chilton Powell, *Puritan Village: The Formation of a New England Town* (Middletown, Conn., 1963), suggest that towns were homogenous. Philip Greven, *Four Generations: Population, Land, and Family in Colonial Andover, Massachusetts* (Ithaca, N.Y., 1970), charts a middle course on the issue, while Allen, *In English Ways*, Stephen Innes, *Labor in a New Land: Economy and Society in Seventeenth-Century Springfield* (Princeton, N.J., 1983), Darrett B. Rutman, *Winthrop's Boston: A Portrait of a Puritan Town, 1630–1649* (Chapel Hill, N.C., 1965), and Christine Heyrman, *Commerce and Culture: The Maritime Communities of Colonial Massachusetts, 1690–1750* (New York, 1984), stress the differences among towns. On the "praying towns," see Daniel R. Mandell, *Behind the Frontier: Indians in Eighteenth Century Massachusetts* (Lincoln, Neb., 1996).

The Pequots' story is told in the essays in Laurence M. Huptman and James D. Wherry, ed., *The Pequots in Southern New England: The Rise and Fall of An American Indian Nation* (Norman, Okla., 1993), and Alfred A. Cave, *The Pequot War* (Amherst, Mass., 1996).

Daniel Vickers, *Farmers and Fishermen: Two Centuries of Work in Essex County, Massachusetts, 1630–1850* (Chapel Hill, N.C., 1994), examines early New England work. The rise of the merchants and the land speculators is traced in Bernard Bailyn, *The New England Merchants in the Seventeenth Century* (Cambridge, Mass., 1955), Stephen Innes,

Creating the Commonwealth: The Economic Culture of Puritan New England (New York, 1995), and John Frederick Martin, *Profits in the Wilderness: Entrepreneurs and the Founding of New England Towns in the Seventeenth Century* (Chapel Hill, N.C., 1991).

Religious dissent occupies E. Brooks Holifield, *Era of Persuasion: American Thought and Culture, 1521–1680* (Boston, 1989), Edmund S. Morgan, *The Puritan Dilemma: The Story of John Winthrop* (Boston, 1956), Perry Miller, *Roger Williams* (New York, 1962), and Norton, *Founding Mothers and Fathers*. Edmund S. Morgan, *Visible Saints: The History of a Puritan Idea* (Ithaca, N.Y., 1963), explains the narration of grace.

Convenient and balanced summaries of Connecticut and Rhode Island colonial history are, respectively, Robert J. Taylor, *Colonial Connecticut: A History* (Millwood, N.Y., 1979), and Sidney V. James, *Colonial Rhode Island: A History* (New York, 1975). Richard Bushman's prize-winning *From Puritan to Yankee: Character and the Social Order in Connecticut, 1690–1765* (Cambridge, Mass., 1967) carries the story into the next century. On women in the early New Haven courts, see Dayton, *Women before the Bar*.

CHAPTER SEVEN. THE MIDDLE COLONIES

On the founding of the middle colony proprietaries, the starting point is still Andrews, *Colonial Period*, vol. 3.

The Dutch overseas trading companies concern C. R. Boxer in *The Dutch Seaborne Empire, 1600–1800* (London, 1965), and Simon Schama covers Dutch economic life and culture in his sparkling *The Embarrassment of Riches: An Interpretation of Dutch Culture in the Golden Age* (New York, 1987). An entertaining biography of Henry Hudson is Philip Vail, *The Magnificent Adventures of Henry Hudson* (New York, 1965). Early New Amsterdam is graphically portrayed in Eric Homberger, *The Historical Atlas of New York City* (New York, 1994), and Russell Shorto, *The Island at the Center of the World: The Epic Story of Dutch Manhattan and the Forgotten Colony that Shaped America* (New York, 2004). Benjamin Schmidt, "Mapping an Empire: Cartographic and Colonial Rivalry in Seventeenth-Century Dutch and English North America," *William and Mary Quarterly* 3rd ser. 54 (1997): 549–578, lays out "battle of the maps," and Gregory H. Nobles, "Straight Lines and Stability: Mapping the Political Order of the Anglo-American Frontier," *Journal of American History* 80 (1993): 9–35, muses on the meaning of maps.

Dutch ways are chronicled in Firth Haring Fabend, *A Dutch Family in the Middle Colonies, 1660–1800* (New Brunswick, N.J., 1991), and Oliver A. Rink, *Holland on the Hudson: An Economic and Social History of Dutch New York* (Ithaca, N.Y., 1986). The career of Adriaen Janse, a notary, is the focal point of Donna Merwick's remarkable microhistory, *Death of a Notary: Conquest and Change in Colonial New York* (Ithaca, N.Y., 1999).

Michael Kammen, *Colonial New York: A History* (New York, 1975), offers a history of the colony, while the origins of the province are explained in Robert Ritchie, *The Duke's Province: A Study of New York Politics and Society, 1664–1691* (Chapel Hill, N.C., 1977). Religion in New York and the other proprietaries is discussed in Patricia U.

Bonomi's engaging *Under the Cope of Heaven: Religion, Society, and Politics in Colonial America* (New York, 1986). On the early city of New York, see Carl Bridenbaugh, *Cities in the Wilderness: The First Century of Urban Life in America, 1625–1742*, rev. ed. (New York, 1953), and Thomas Archdeacon, *New York City, 1664–1710: Conquest and Change* (Ithaca, N.Y., 1976). The lot of the "lesser merchants" concerns Cathy Matson in *Merchants and Empire: Trading in Colonial New York* (Baltimore, 1998). Dutch and English inheritance practices are compared in David Narrett, *Inheritance and Family Life in Colonial New York City* (Cooperstown, N.Y., 1992). Douglas Greenberg, *Crime and Law Enforcement in the Colony of New York* (Ithaca, N.Y., 1974), chronicles crime. On the supposed conspiracy of 1741, see Peter Charles Hoffer, *The Great New York Conspiracy of 1741: Slavery, Crime, and Colonial Law* (Lawrence, Kans., 2003), and Jill Lepore, *New York Burning: Liberty, Slavery, and Conspiracy in Eighteenth-Century Manhattan* (New York, 2005).

On the Iroquois dilemma in the seventeenth century, see Richter, *Ordeal of the Longhouse*, and Stephen Saunders Webb, *1676: The End of American Independence* (New York, 1984).

Colonial New Jersey is the subject of John E. Pomfret, *Colonial New Jersey: A History* (New York, 1973). On land use, the essays in Peter O. Wacker and Paul G. E. Clemens, *Land Use in Early New Jersey: A Historical Geography* (Newark, N.J., 1993), and on New Jersey folklore, David Steven Cohen, *The Folklore and Folklife of New Jersey* (New Brunswick, N.J., 1983), are indispensable.

Joseph E. Illick, *Colonial Pennsylvania: A History* (New York, 1976), is an able survey. William M. Offutt Jr., *Of Good Laws and Good Men: Law and Society in the Delaware Valley, 1680–1710* (Urbana, Ill., 1995), does considerably more than trace crime. Penn's world is fully articulated in Richard S. Dunn and Mary Maples Dunn, eds., *The World of William Penn* (Philadelphia, 1986), and Mary Maples Dunn, *William Penn: Politics and Conscience* (Princeton, N.J., 1967). On the early politics of the colony, see Gary Nash, *Quakers and Politics: Pennsylvania, 1681–1726* (Princeton, N.J., 1968). A critical book on the acquisitive habits of the Quaker merchants is Frederick B. Tolles's *Meeting House and Counting House* (Chapel Hill, N.C., 1948). A more favorable account on a later period is Thomas M. Doerflinger, *A Vigorous Spirit of Enterprise: Merchants and Economic Development in Revolutionary Philadelphia* (Chapel Hill, N.C., 1986).

John A. Munroe, *Colonial Delaware: A History* (Millwood, N.Y., 1978), recounts the history of the "lower counties."

CHAPTER EIGHT. THE CRITICAL YEARS, 1675–1700

The concept of "critical years" is, of course, a useful fiction, for in fact crises and challenges can be found in every period of colonial history. I have adapted the term from John Fiske's classic *The Critical Period of American History, 1783–1789* (Boston, 1888).

I have taken my account of Garacontié from Webb, 1676. Langdon, *Plymouth*, regards King Philip's War as a series of misunderstandings. Russell Bourne, *The Red King's Rebellion: Racial Politics in New England 1675–1678* (New York, 1990), is highly critical of New England authorities' role. Jill Lepore, *The Name of War: King Philip's War and the Origins of American Identity* (New York, 1998), places the war in the context of an identity crisis among the Indians and the New Englanders. Patrick M. Malone, *The Skulking Way of War: Technology and Tactics among the New England Indians* (Baltimore, 1993), explains how colonists taught Indians how to use firearms, and how Indians taught the colonists how to fight in the forests. On the long agony of colonial Deerfield, see John P. Demos, *The Unredeemed Captive: A Family Story from Early America* (New York, 1994).

Bacon's rebellion is treated as an event in class and race history in Edmund S. Morgan, *American Slavery, American Freedom: The Ordeal of Colonial Virginia* (New York, 1975), as a part of gender history in Brown, *Good Wives*, and as an episode in the evolution of a planter aristocracy in Bernard Bailyn, "Politics and Social Structure in Virginia," in James Morton Smith, ed., *Seventeenth-Century America* (Chapel Hill, N.C., 1959), 90–115. The idea of a southern English culture transported intact to the Tidewater comes from Fischer, *Albion's Seed*.

On slave rebellions in the English sugar islands, see Craton, *Testing the Chains*, and Dunn, *Sugar and Slaves*.

Andrew L. Knaut, *The Pueblo Revolt of 1680* (Norman, Okla., 1995), and Gutiérrez, *When Jesus Came*, explore the events in New Mexico. The Spanish use of land and bricks in explained in John Brinckerhoff Jackson, *A Sense of Place, a Sense of Time* (New Haven, Conn., 1994), and Marc Simmons, "Settlement Patterns and Village Plans in Colonial New Mexico," in David J. Weber, ed., *New Spain's Far Northern Frontier* (Albuquerque, N.M., 1979), 99–115.

The Glorious Revolution in America is traced in David S. Lovejoy, *The Glorious Revolution in America* (New York, 1972), and Leisler's rebellion gets careful treatment in Ritchie's *Duke's Province*. Land's *Colonial Maryland* follows the Glorious Revolution on its bloodless course through Maryland. Michael G. Hall, Lawrence H. Leder, and Michael G. Kammen, eds., *The Glorious Revolution in America* (New York, 1972), is a fine collection of original documents on the crisis.

Howard M. Peckham gives a concise account of King William's War in *The Colonial Wars, 1689–1762* (Chicago, 1964). Douglas E. Leach's *Arms for Empire: A Military History of the British Colonies in North America, 1607–1763* (New York, 1973) is more detailed.

The literature on the Salem witchcraft trials is voluminous. It includes Elaine Breslaw, *Tituba, Reluctant Witch of Salem* (New York, 1996), Paul Boyer and Stephen Nissenbaum, *Salem Possessed* (Cambridge, Mass., 1974), Larry Gragg, *The Salem Witchcraft Crisis* (New York, 1992), Peter Charles Hoffer, *The Salem Witchcraft Trials: A Legal History* (Lawrence, Kans., 1998), Hoffer, *The Devil's Disciples: Makers of the Salem Witch-*

craft Trials (Baltimore, 1996), Mary Beth Norton, In the Devil's Snare (New York, 2002), and Bernard Rosenthal, Salem Story: Reading the Witch Trials of 1692 (Cambridge, 1993). Carol Karlsen explores questions of possession and antifeminism in The Devil in the Shape of a Women: Witchcraft in Colonial New England (New York, 1987), while John Demos, Entertaining Satan: Witchcraft and the Culture of Early New England (New York, 1982), finds that witchcraft accusations grew out of long histories of quarreling, social anxiety and distrust, the breakdown of families, and acute psychological stress. Richard Godbeer, The Devil's Dominion: Magic and Religion in Early New England (Cambridge, 1984), suggests that magic and countermagic were part of everyday life in New England in the seventeenth century.

The shift in the evidentiary requirements of English criminal courts is one subject in Barbara J. Shapiro's "Beyond Reasonable Doubt" and "Probable Cause": Historical Perspectives on the Anglo-American Law of Evidence (Berkeley, Calif., 1991). Brian Levack's The Witch-Hunt in Early Modern Europe (London, 1995) documents the growing resistance to conviction among the English judges. Peter Burke's Popular Culture in Early Modern Europe (London, 1978) places the split between high and low cultures at the end of the seventeenth century. Michael Winship, Seers of God: Puritan Providentialism in the Restoration and Early Enlightenment (Baltimore, 1996), teases out Cotton Mather's problems with modernity and science. Douglas L. Winiarski, "'Pale Blewish Lights' and a Dead Man's Groan: Tales of the Supernatural from Eighteenth-Century Plymouth, Massachusetts," William and Mary Quarterly 3rd Ser. (1998): 497–530, reminds us that the invisible world continued to agitate New Englanders well into the eighteenth century. A handy summary of the contributions of late-seventeenth-century science is Frederick L. Nussbaum, The Triumph of Science and Reason, 1660–1685 (New York, 1953).

PART II. FROM PROVINCES OF EMPIRE TO A NEW NATION

Elaine Forman Crane, The Diary of Elizabeth Drinker: Life Cycle of an Eighteenth-Century Woman (Boston, 1994), 58, is the source of the Drinker diary entry.

The classic exposition of American exceptionalism in political science literature is Louis Hartz, The Liberal Tradition in America (New York, 1955). A more recent sociological version of the thesis is Seymour Martin Lipset, American Exceptionalism: A Double-Edged Sword (New York, 1996). The rise of the term American is traced in Richard L. Merritt, Symbols of American Community, 1735–1775 (New Haven, Conn., 1966). The family analogy concerns Melvin Yazawa in From Colonies to Commonwealth: Familial Ideology and the Beginnings of the American Republic (Baltimore, 1985). Takaki's views appear in Different Mirror, while Howard Zinn's caution against too self-congratulatory a view of early American society fills his Declarations of Independence: Cross-Examining American Ideology (New York, 1990).

Gordon Wood's The Radicalism of the American Revolution (New York, 1991) is the starting point of debates on the causes and consequences of the Revolution. But Edward Countryman's *The American Revolution* (New York, 1985) remains an alternative view, arguing for a radicalism that caused rather than resulted from the separation movement. Gary B. Nash, *The Unknown American Revolution: The Unruly Birth of Democracy and the Struggle to Create America* (New York, 2005), combines his own and Countryman's view of the importance of radicalism with Merrill Jensen's *The New Nation: A History of the United States during the Confederation, 1781–1789* (New York, 1950), arguing that the federal Constitution was a conservative counterrevolution. Robert Middlekauf's *The Glorious Cause: The American Revolution, 1763–1789* (New York, 2005) is a fast-paced and entertaining survey of the entire revolutionary era.

CHAPTER NINE. THE EMPIRES REINVENTED, 1660–1763

The visit of the four Indian "kings" is revisited in Eric Hinderaker, "The 'Four Indian Kings' and the Imaginative Construction of the First British Empire," *William and Mary Quarterly* 3rd ser. 53 (1996): 487–522.

The starting place for any study of the administration of empire once was Andrews, *Colonial Period*, vol. 4, and Leonard Woods Labaree, *Royal Government in America: A Study of the British Colonial System before 1783* (New Haven, Conn., 1930). The new standard is the essays in the first two volumes of the *Oxford History of the British Empire*. For a survey of mercantilism, see Michael Kammen, *Empire and Interest: The American Colonies and the Politics of Mercantilism* (Philadelphia, 1970). On English, French, and Spanish ideas of empire, see Anthony Pagden, *Lords of All the World: Ideologies of Empire in Spain, Britain and France, c. 1500–c. 1800* (New Haven, Conn., 1995). The close ties between empire and intellectual life are neatly summarized in Richard Drayton, "Knowledge and Empire," in Marshall, ed., *The Eighteenth Century*, 231–252.

On Colbert's and Pontchartrain's ideas of mercantilism, see Eccles, *France in America*, and Dale Miquelon, *New France, 1701–1744* (Toronto, 1987). On French Louisiana's origins, see Marcel Giraud, *The Reign of Louis XIV, 1698–1715*, trans. Joseph C. Lambert, vol. 1 of *A History of French Louisiana* (Baton Rouge, La., 1974), Daniel H. Usner Jr., *Indians, Settlers, and Slaves in a Frontier Exchange Economy: The Lower Mississippi Valley before 1783* (Chapel Hill, N.C., 1992), and Eccles, *France in America*. John Bartlett Brebner, *The Explorers of North America, 1492–1806* (New York, 1933), follows the French explorations.

The Spanish version of reform, embedded in the Bourbon reform, is covered in Gibson, *Spain in America*, Pagden, *Lords of All the World*, and Weber, *Spanish Frontier in North America*.

For more specific information on the later Navigation Acts, see Lawrence A. Harper, *The English Navigation Laws: A Study in Social Engineering* (New York, 1939). Thomas C. Barrow, *Trade and Empire: The British Customs Service in Colonial America, 1660–1775* (Cambridge, Mass., 1967), does the same for the customs service.

On the importance of coffee and coffeehouses, sugar, tea, and chocolate in the creation of a public sphere, see Jürgen Habermas, *The Structural Transformation of the Public Sphere* (Cambridge, Mass., 1989), Sidney W. Mintz, *Sweetness and Power: The Place of Sugar in History* (New York, 1985), and Schivelbusch, *Tastes of Paradise.* The communications revolution is my term; for details, see Ian K. Steele, *The English Atlantic, 1675–1740: An Exploration of Communication and Community* (New York, 1986). The professionalization of English government—with emphasis on the military—is brilliantly and forcefully argued in John Brewer, *The Sinews of Power: War, Money, and the English State, 1688–1783* (London, 1989). A history of the British army that covers the eighteenth century is Tony Hayter, "The Army and the First British Empire, 1714–1783," in Chandler, ed. *The Oxford History of the British Army,* 112–131. On Oglethorpe in Georgia, see Kenneth Coleman, *Colonial Georgia: A History* (New York, 1976), and B. Phinizy Spalding, *Oglethorpe in America* (Chicago, 1977). Warren R. Hofstra's "'The Extension of His Majesties' Dominions': The Virginia Backcountry and the Reconfiguration of Imperial Frontiers," *Journal of American History* 84 (1998): 1281–1312, links frontier development to imperial military planning. His *The Planting of New Virginia: Settlement and Landscape in the Shenandoah Valley* (Baltimore, 2004) is more comprehensive but just as readable.

On the imperial politics of the transitional era of 1688–1725, J. M. Sosin's *English America and the Revolution of 1688* (Lincoln, Neb., 1982) and *English America and Imperial Inconstancy, The Rise of Provincial Autonomy, 1696–1715* (Lincoln, Neb., 1985) are good summaries, as is J. H. Plumb's short and immensely readable *The Growth of Political Stability in England, 1675–1725* (London, 1967). James A. Henretta's *"Salutary Neglect": Colonial Administration under the Duke of Newcastle* (Princeton, N.J., 1972) traces the duke's machinations with verve.

Richard R. Johnson explains Joseph Dudley's strengths as governor in *Adjustment to Empire: The New England Colonies, 1675–1715* (New Brunswick, N.J., 1981). Mary Lou Lustig, *Robert Hunter, 1666–1734, New York's Augustan Statesman* (Syracuse, N.Y., 1983), and John A. Schutz, *William Shirley, King's Governor of Massachusetts* (Chapel Hill, N.C., 1961), are informative. Governor Spotswood's career is outlined in Walter Havighurst, *Alexander Spotswood: Portrait of a Governor* (Williamsburg, Va., 1967).

The rise of the ideology of private property is explored in Paul Langford, *Public Life and the Propertied Englishman, 1689–1798* (Oxford, 1991), and analyzed in C. B. Macpherson, *The Theory of Possessive Individualism* (Oxford, 1961). Joyce Appleby, "Political and Economic Liberalism in Seventeenth-Century England," in Appleby, *Liberalism and Republicanism in the Historical Imagination* (Cambridge, Mass., 1992), 34–57, elucidates the same issues.

On the backstairs of government and the lobbyists, see Alison Gilbert Olson, *Making the Empire Work: London and American Interest Groups, 1690–1790* (Cambridge, Mass., 1992), and Olson, *Anglo-American Politics, 1660–1775: The Relationship between Parties in England and Colonial America* (Oxford, 1973). Carl M. Bridenbaugh, *Mitre and Sceptre:*

Transatlantic Faiths, Ideas, Personalities, and Politics, 1689–1775 (New York, 1962), pays attention to the religious lobbies.

The contours of the country bureaucracy appear in Bruce C. Daniels, ed., *Power and Status: Officeholding in Colonial America* (Middletown, Conn., 1986), though the term "country bureaucracy" is mine. Differences between the idea and the actual practice of governance in the colonial scheme are explored in Bernard Bailyn, *The Origins of American Government* (New York, 1968). The rise of the colonial assemblies is chronicled in Michael Kammen, *Deputyes and Libertys: The Origins of Representative Government in Colonial America* (New York, 1969), and Jack P. Greene, *The Quest for Power: The Lower Houses of Assembly in the Southern Royal Colonies, 1689–1776* (Chapel Hill, N.C., 1963). Peter Charles Hoffer, *Law and People in Colonial America*, 2nd ed. (Baltimore, 1998), summarizes the function of the various kinds of courts and the lawyers who practiced therein.

A recent thorough summary of colonial politics, election laws, and representation colony by colony is Richard R. Beeman, *The Varieties of Political Experience in Eighteenth-Century America* (Philadelphia, 2004).

CHAPTER TEN. PROVINCIAL PEOPLE AND PLACES IN THE EIGHTEENTH CENTURY

The importance and uniqueness of little places in America is movingly portrayed in Darrett B. Rutman and Anita H. Rutman, *Small Worlds, Large Questions: Explorations in Early American Social History, 1600–1850* (Charlottesville, Va., 1994). A source for Cherokee bounding of the land is Nathaniel J. Sheidley, "Hunting and the Problem of Masculinity in Cherokee Treaty Making, 1763–1775," in R. Halpern and M. Daunton, eds., *Empire and Others* (London, 1998), 167–185.

On the French farmer in New France, see R. Cole Harris, "The Extension of France into Rural Canada," in James R. Gibson, ed., *European Settlement and Development in North America: Essays on Geographical Change in Honor and Memory of Andrew Hill Clark* (Toronto, 1978), 27–45, Raymond Douville and Jacques Casanova, *Daily Life in Early Canada*, trans. Carola Congreve (New York, 1968), and Peter N. Moogk, "Reluctant Exiles: Emigrants from France in Canada before 1760," *William and Mary Quarterly* 3rd ser. 46 (1989): 463–505. Gilles Paquet and Jean-Pierre Wallot assess French Canadian identity formation in "Nouvelle-France/Québec/Canada: A World of Limited Identities," in Canny and Pagden, eds., *Colonial Identity*, 95–114. The achievements of the missionary orders among the Indians have found a superb chronicler in James Axtell, *The Invasion Within: The Contest of Cultures in Colonial North America* (New York, 1985). White, *Middle Ground*, is the source for a study of French Great Lakes diplomacy. Usner's *Indians, Settlers, and Slaves* supplies examples of French diplomatic efforts in the lower Mississippi.

Alan Taylor, *Liberty Men and Great Proprietors: The Revolutionary Settlement on the Maine*

Frontier (Chapel Hill, N.C., 1990), and Laurel Thatcher Ulrich, *Good Wives: Image and Reality in the Lives of Women in Northern New England, 1650–1750* (New York, 1982), take readers to the Maine frontier. The poor transients of New England—actually Providence, Rhode Island—tell their tale in Ruth Wallis Herndon, *Unwelcome Americans: Living on the Margin in Early New England* (Philadelphia, 2001). The fishermen of the Massachusetts coast towns are described in Vickers, *Farmers and Fishermen*. The plight of the "praying Indians" in the eighteenth century is the subject of Mandell's *Behind the Frontier*.

On the settlers of eastern Pennsylvania, see James T. Lemon, *The Best Poor Man's Country: A Geographical Study of Early Southeastern Pennsylvania* (Baltimore, 1972), and Michael R. Yogg, *"The Best Place for Health and Wealth": A Demographical and Economic Analysis of the Quakers of Bucks County, Pennsylvania* (New York, 1988). On the backcountry of Lancaster, see George W. Frantz, *Paxton: A Study of Community Structure in the Colonial Pennsylvania Backcountry* (New York, 1988). A strongly worded critique of Lemon is James Henretta, "Families and Farms: Mentalité in Pre-Industrial America," *William and Mary Quarterly* 3rd. Ser. 35 (1978): 3–38. Richard Lyman Bushman, "Markets and Composite Farms in Early America," *William and Mary Quarterly* 3rd. Ser. 55 (1998): 351–374, tried to reconcile the two positions. Mary M. Schweitzer, *Custom and Contract: Household, Government, and the Economy in Colonial Pennsylvania* (New York, 1987), explores the tie between the economy and the state. Sally Schwartz, *"A Mixed Multitude": The Struggle for Toleration in Colonial Pennsylvania* (New York, 1987), treats religious toleration.

At rough count, there are now over 150 biographies of Benjamin Franklin. Readable older entries in this category include Verner W. Crane, *Benjamin Franklin and a Rising People* (Boston, 1954), and Esmond Wright, *Franklin of Philadelphia* (Cambridge, Mass., 1986). The most admiring of the moderns are H. W. Brands, *The First American: The Life and Times of Benjamin Franklin* (New York, 2000), Walter Isaacson, *Benjamin Franklin: An American Life* (New York, 2003), and Stacy Shiff, *A Great Improvisation: Franklin, France, and the Birth of America* (New York, 2005). Edmund S. Morgan, *Benjamin Franklin* (New Haven, Conn., 2002), is a little more reserved, while David Waldstreicher, *Runaway America: Benjamin Franklin, Slavery, and the American Revolution* (New York, 2004), and Gordon Wood, *The Americanization of Benjamin Franklin* (New York, 2004), find cracks in the facade of Franklin's nobility.

On the landscape of mid-eighteenth-century Virginia, Rhys Isaac, *The Transformation of Virginia, 1740–1790* (Chapel Hill, N.C., 1982), is superb. Town planning, including that of Williamsburg, is the subject of John W. Reps, *Town Planning in Frontier America* (Princeton, N.J., 1965), and Graham Hood, *The Governor's Palace in Williamsburg: A Cultural History* (Williamsburg, Va., 1991). The creation of free and slave communities is depicted in Allan Kulikoff, *Tobacco and Slaves: The Development of Southern Cultures in the Chesapeake, 1680–1800* (Chapel Hill, N.C., 1986), as well as Berlin, *Many Thousand Gone*, and Morgan, *Slave Counterpoint*. My portrait of Middlesex

BIBLIOGRAPHIC ESSAY **507**

comes from Rutman and Rutman, *Place in Time*. Rivalry among the tobacco planters is explored in T. H. Breen, *Tobacco Culture: The Mentality of the Great Tidewater Planters on the Eve of Revolution* (Princeton, N.J., 1985). For a display of the artifacts that slave and free peoples left behind, see Anne Elizabeth Yentsch, *A Chesapeake Family and Their Slaves: A Study in Historical Archeology* (Cambridge, 1994). The pettiness of the Virginia–North Carolina border survey is recorded in Percy G. Adams, ed., *William Byrd's Histories of the Dividing Line betwixt Virginia and North Carolina* (New York, 1967). A fine recent work on the lesser planters and their part in the coming of the Revolution is Woody Holton, *Forced Founders: Indians, Debtors, Slaves, and the Making of the American Revolution in Virginia* (Chapel Hill, N.C., 1999).

On "frontier" and boundaries, see Jeremy Adelman and Stephen Aron, "From Borderlands to Borders: Empires, Nation-States and the People In-Between in North American History," *American Historical Review* 104 (1999): 814–841. On the culture of the backwoods, see Allan Kulikoff, *The Agrarian Origins of American Capitalism* (Charlottesville, Va., 1992), Gregory H. Nobles, "Breaking into the Backcountry: New Approaches to the Early American Frontier," *William and Mary Quarterly* 3rd ser. 46 (1989): 641–670, and Stephanie Grauman Wolf, *As Various as Their Land: The Everyday Lives of Eighteenth Century Americans* (New York, 1993). Portraits of frontier hunters appear in Stephen Aron, *How the West Was Lost: The Transformation of Kentucky from Daniel Boone to Henry Clay* (Baltimore, 1996). On spinning and weaving, see Laurel Thatcher Ulrich, *The Age of Homespun: Objects and Stories in the Creation of an American Myth* (Cambridge, Mass., 2001).

Joel Martin, *Sacred Revolt: The Muskogees' Struggle for a New World* (Boston, 1991), Joshua Piker, *Okafuse: A Creek Indian Town in Colonial America* (Cambridge, Mass., 2004), and J. Leitch Wright, *Creeks and Seminoles: The Destruction and Regeneration of the Muscogulge People* (Lincoln, Neb., 1986), explain Creek customs. Eric Hinderaker, *Elusive Empires: Constructing Colonialism in the Ohio Valley, 1673–1800* (Cambridge, 1997), examines the Ohio Valley Indians. White, *Middle Ground*, tells the Great Lakes story. Jane T. Merritt, *At The Crossroads: Indians and Empires on a Mid-Atlantic Frontier, 1700–1763* (Chapel Hill, N.C., 2003), explains how "race" became part of the story of the frontier.

Demos, *Unredeemed Captive*, recounts the Deerfield massacre and subsequent efforts to recover the captives. The formation of the Indian "South," along with the contest for slaves that drove it and the devastation wars that resulted, is studied in Gallay, *Indian Slave Trade*. He has extended the account in Verner W. Crane, *The Southern Frontier, 1670–1732* (New York, 1956), to include Indian viewpoints. James H. Merrell, *The Indians' New World: Catawbas and Their Neighbors from European Contact through the Era of Removal* (Chapel Hill, N.C., 1989), explores the reformation of tribal groups after the Yamasee War.

On the low country in the eighteenth century, see Joyce E. Chaplin, *An Anxious Pursuit: Agricultural Innovation and Modernity in the Lower South, 1730–1815* (Chapel Hill,

N.C., 1993), Robert Olwell, *Masters, Slaves and Subjects: The Culture of Power in the South Carolina Low Country, 1740–1790* (Ithaca, N.Y., 1998), and Wood, *Black Majority*. Russell Menard has charted the rise of mortgages in his "Financing the Low Country Export Boom: Capital and Growth in Early Carolina," *William and Mary Quarterly* 3rd ser. 51 (1994): 659–676.

Life in Saint Augustine is described in Kathleen Deagan, "St. Augustine and the Mission Frontier," in Bonnie G. McEwan, ed., *The Spanish Missions of La Florida* (Gainesville, Fla., 1993), 87–110, and Jean Parker Waterbury, ed., *The Oldest City: St. Augustine, Saga of Survival* (Saint Augustine, Fla., 1983). Tabby construction is one subject in Albert Manucy, *Sixteenth-Century St. Augustine: The People and Their Homes* (Gainesville, Fla., 1997). On the village of Mose, see Jane Landers, "Garcia Real de Santa Teresa de Mose: A Free Black Town in Spanish Colonial Florida," *American Historical Review* 95 (1990): 9–30.

The single best work on the Southwest is James Brooks, *Captives and Cousins* (Chapel Hill, 2002). The Spanish reoccupation and the role of women in Santa Fe are imaginatively re-created by Paul Horgan, *The Centuries of Santa Fe* (New York, 1956). The short essays in David Grant Noble, ed., *Santa Fe: History of an Ancient City* (Santa Fe, 1989), are easy reading for students. Rick Hendricks and John P. Wilson edited the Roque Madrid report in *The Navajos in 1705: Roque Madrid's Campaign Journal* (Albuquerque, 1996). Village life then and now is discussed in Nancy Hunter Warren, *Villages of Hispanic New Mexico* (Santa Fe, 1987). The landscape of the eighteenth-century village is envisioned in John R. Stilgoe, *Common Landscape of America, 1580 to 1845* (New Haven, Conn., 1982). Marc Simmons recounts the witchcraft tales in *Witchcraft in the Southwest: Spanish and Indian Supernaturalism on the Rio Grande* (Lincoln, Neb., 1974).

On eighteenth-century Jamaica, see Clinton V. Black, *The Story of Jamaica* (London, 1965), and Edward Braithwaite, *The Development of Creole Society in Jamaica, 1770–1820* (Oxford, 1971). European migration to the island is the subject of Trevor Burnard, "European Migration to Jamaica," *William and Mary Quarterly* 3rd ser. 53 (1996): 769–796. On the cattle pens, see Douglas Hall, *In Miserable Slavery: Thomas Thistlewood in Jamaica, 1750–1786* (London, 1989), and Philip D. Morgan, "Slaves and Livestock in Eighteenth-Century Jamaica: Vineyard Pen, 1750–1751," *William and Mary Quarterly* 3rd ser. 52 (1995): 47–76. Michael Craton's *Searching for the Invisible Man* (Cambridge, Mass., 1978) is a full-length study of slavery in eighteenth-century Jamaica. On Mesopotamia plantation, see Richard S. Dunn, "Sugar Production and Slave Women in Jamaica," in Berlin and Morgan, eds., *Cultivation and Culture*, 73–100, and Dunn, "Servants and Slaves: The Recruitment and Employment of Labor," in Jack P. Greene and J. R. Pole, eds., *Colonial British America: Essays in the New History of the Early Modern Era* (Baltimore, 1984), 157–196.

CHAPTER ELEVEN. COMMON PASTIMES AND ELITE PURSUITS

The notion that American life and thought in the eighteenth century were riven with inconsistencies is one major theme of Kammen's *People of Paradox*. The idea of highbrow and lowbrow in American culture is engagingly treated in Lawrence W. Levine, *Highbrow Lowbrow: The Emergence of Cultural Hierarchy in America* (Cambridge, Mass., 1988). The notion that the middle class was a late-coming institution is assumed in David S. Shields, *Civil Tongues and Polite Letters in British America* (Chapel Hill, N.C., 1997). Holidays and other rhythms of life are treated in Fischer, *Albion's Seed*.

Tavern life is one subject in Carl Bridenbaugh's *Cities in Revolt: Urban Life in America, 1743–1776*, rev. ed. (New York, 1970), and W. J. Rorabaugh, *The Alcoholic Republic: An American Tradition* (New York, 1979). The relation between taverns and politics in colonial New England is the focus of David W. Conroy, *In Public Houses: Drink and the Revolution of Authority in Colonial Massachusetts* (Chapel Hill, N.C., 1995). A survey is Sharon V. Salinger, *Taverns and Drinking in Early America* (Baltimore, 2002).

John Brewer, *The Pleasures of the Imagination: English Culture in the Eighteenth Century* (New York, 1997), and Shields, *Civil Tongues*, explore conversation. Christopher Grasso, *A Speaking Aristocracy: Transforming Public Discourse in Eighteenth-Century Connecticut* (Chapel Hill, N.C., 1999), ties the sensory impact of words to their social settings. On music and dance, see Max Savelle, *Seeds of Liberty: The Genesis of the American Mind* (Seattle, 1965), and Shields, *Civil Tongues*, from which I have taken Joseph Shippen's poetry. The organ in the Lutheran church is mentioned in A. G. Roeber, *Palatines, Liberty, and Property: German Lutherans in Colonial British America* (Baltimore, 1993). Franklin's recollections of Silence Dogood appear in Leonard W. Labaree et al., eds., *The Autobiography of Benjamin Franklin* (New Haven, Conn., 1964). Additional material on printers abounds in Bernard Bailyn and John B. Hench, eds., *The Press and the American Revolution* (Boston, 1981).

The travail of the street people in the cities finds its way into Bridenbaugh, *Cities in Revolt*, Gary B. Nash, *Urban Crucible: Social Change, Political Consciousness, and the Origins of the American Revolution* (Cambridge, Mass., 1979), and Billy G. Smith, *The "Lower Sort": Philadelphia's Laboring People, 1750–1800* (Ithaca, N.Y., 1990).

On crime in the colonies, see Greenberg, *Crime and Law Enforcement in the Colony of New York*, N.E.H. Hull, *Female Felons: Women and Serious Crime in Colonial Massachusetts* (Urbana, Ill., 1987), and Donna Spindel, *Crime and Society in North Carolina, 1673–1776* (Baton Rouge, La., 1989).

Richard D. Brown focuses on communications networks in *Knowledge Is Power: The Diffusion of Information in Early America, 1700–1865* (New York, 1989), while refinement is the subject of Richard Bushman, *The Refinement of America: Persons, Houses, Cities* (New York, 1992), and Kevin M. Sweeney, "High-Style Vernacular: Lifestyles of the Colonial Elite," in Cary Carson, Ronald Hoffman, and Peter J. Albert, eds., *Of Consuming Interests: The Style of Life in the Eighteenth Century* (Charlottesville, Va., 1994), 1–

66. Jack Crowley's *The Invention of Comfort* (Baltimore, 2001) is a superb study of early modern heating, lighting, and living spaces.

Religious thinking at the outset of the eighteenth century in New England can be found in the final chapters of Foster, *The Long Argument*, David D. Hall, *Worlds of Wonder, Days of Judgment: Popular Religious Belief in Early New England* (Cambridge, Mass., 1990), Perry Miller, *The New England Mind: From Colony to Province* (Cambridge, Mass., 1953), and Winship, *Seers of God.* Isaac, *Transformation of Virginia*, traces the spread of the Baptists through the colony. The definitive account of Backus's fight is William G. McLoughlin, ed., *Isaac Backus on Church, State, and Calvinism* (Cambridge, Mass., 1968).

On the general outlines of the Great Awakening, see J. M. Bumsted and John E. Van de Wetering, *What Must I Do to Be Saved? The Great Awakening in Colonial America* (Hinsdale, Ill., 1976), Cedric B. Cowing, *The Great Awakening and the American Revolution* (Chicago, 1971), Michael J. Crawford, *Seasons of Grace: Colonial New England's Revival Tradition in Its British Context* (New York, 1991), C. C. Goen, *Revivalism and Separatism in New England, 1740–1800* (New Haven, Conn., 1962), Timothy D. Hall, *Contested Boundaries: Itinerancy and the Reshaping of the Colonial American Religious World* (Durham, N.C., 1994), Keith J. Hardman, *Seasons of Refreshing: Evangelism and Revivals in America* (Grand Rapids, Mich., 1994), Alan Heimert and Perry Miller, eds., *The Great Awakening* (Indianapolis, Ind., 1967), Frank Lambert, *Inventing the "Great Awakening"* (Princeton, N.J., 1999), and David S. Lovejoy, *Religious Enthusiasm in the New World: Heresy to Revolution* (Cambridge, Mass., 1985). Gregory H. Nobles, *Divisions throughout the Whole: Politics and Society in Hampshire County, Massachusetts, 1740–1775* (Cambridge, 1983), and Heyrman, *Commerce and Culture*, apply the lessons to localities. The eyewitness account of Davenport's eccentric style of preaching is taken from Brown, *Knowledge Is Power.*

On Whitefield, see Harry S. Stout, *The Divine Dramatist: George Whitefield and the Rise of Modern Evangelism* (Grand Rapids, Mich., 1991), and Frank Lambert, *"Pedlar in Divinity": George Whitefield and the Transatlantic Revivals, 1737–1770* (Princeton, N.J., 1994). A new and much-honored biography of Edwards is George M. Marsden, *Jonathan Edwards: A Life* (New Haven, Conn., 2003). Backus's writings appear in McLoughlin, *Isaac Backus on Church, State, and Calvinism.*

On life cycle, see Philip Greven, *The Protestant Temperament: Patterns of Child Rearing, Religious Experience, and the Self In Early America* (New York, 1977), Wolf, *As Various as Their Land*, and David Hackett Fischer, *Growing Old in America* (New York, 1978).

The notion of a revolution in sexual manners is traced in Daniel Scott Smith and Michael Hindus, "Premarital Pregnancy in America, 1640–1971: An Overview," *Journal of Interdisciplinary History* 5 (1975): 537–553, Edward Shorter, *The Making of the Modern Family* (New York, 1975), and Jay Fliegelman, *Prodigals and Pilgrims: The American Revolution against Patriarchal Authority, 1750–1800* (Cambridge, 1982). Carole Shammas has written about household government in "Anglo-American Household

Government in Comparative Perspective," *William and Mary Quarterly* 3rd. Ser 52 (1995): 104–144. Wells, *Population of the British Colonies*, provides figures for family size and age composition.

Education in the colonies is traced in Lawrence A. Cremin, *American Education: The Colonial Experience* (New York, 1970). The foremost study of reading in the colonies, a work of many decades, is E. Jennifer Monaghan, *Learning to Read and Write in Colonial America* (Amherst, Mass., 2005). Literacy figures are estimated in Kenneth A. Lockridge, *Colonial Literary* (New York, 1974).

On the Enlightenment, Daniel Boorstin, *America and the Image of Europe* (New York, 1960), and Boorstin, *The Americans: The Colonial Experience* (New York, 1958), argue that the European Enlightenment was very selectively received in America. A more positive view is Brooke Hindle, *The Pursuit of Science in Revolutionary America, 1735–1789* (Chapel Hill, N.C., 1956). Thomas Slaughter's biography of the Bartrams, *The Natures of John and William Bartram* (New York, 1996), sees father and son in transatlantic context. A classic book on the Enlightenment in Europe is Peter Gay, *The Enlightenment: An Interpretation*, 2 vols. (New York, 1969).

The men and ideas of the Scottish Enlightenment are treated in W. L. Taylor, *Francis Hutcheson and David Hume as Predecessors of Adam Smith* (Durham, N.C., 1965), Stewart J. Brown, ed., *William Robertson and the Expansion of Empire* (Cambridge, 1997), and Richard B. Sher and Jeffrey R. Smitten, eds., *Scotland and America in the Age of the Enlightenment* (Princeton, N.J., 1990). The impact of the Scots in America is traced in Eric Richards, "Scotland and the Uses of the Atlantic Empire," in Bailyn and Morgan, eds., *Strangers within the Realm*, 67–114, and Garry Wills, *Inventing America: Thomas Jefferson's Declaration of Independence* (Garden City, N.Y., 1978).

Gay's *The Enlightenment* criticizes the deists. Henry F. May, *The American Enlightenment* (New York, 1976), is more gentle. Robert A. Ferguson, *The American Enlightenment, 1750–1820* (Cambridge, Mass., 1997), connects the Enlightenment to the Revolution. The faith in science was one such tie. See I. Bernard Cohen, *Science and the Founding Fathers* (New York, 1995).

CHAPTER TWELVE. MERCANTILISM AND MARKETS

Throughout this chapter, I rely on T. H. Breen, *The Marketplace of Revolution* (New York, 2004), John J. McCusker and Russell R. Menard, *The Economy of British America, 1607–1789*, rev. ed. (Chapel Hill, N.C., 1991), Stephen Innes, ed., *Work and Labor in Early America* (Chapel Hill, N.C., 1988), and Marc Egnal, *A Mighty Empire: The Origins of the American Revolution* (Ithaca, N.Y., 1988).

On the colonial cities, see Bridenbaugh, *Cities in Revolt*, and Nash, *Urban Crucible*. The depopulation crisis in Britain and the migration to the colonies in the 1760s and 1770s are considered in Bernard Bailyn, *Voyagers to the West: A Passage in the Peopling of America on the Eve of the Revolution* (New York, 1986). South Carolina's failure of nerve is discussed in Chaplin, *Anxious Pursuit*. Jon Butler's prize-winning *The Huguenots in America: A Refugee People in a New World Society* (Cambridge, Mass., 1983) follows the Huguenots in South Carolina.

On the frontier, speculation, and Indian trade, see Calloway, *New Worlds for All*, Crane, *Southern Frontier*, Usner, *Frontier Exchange Economy*, and Aron, *How the West Was Lost*.

Innes's "Introduction," in Innes, ed., *Work and Labor*, and Wolf's section on craftsmen in *As Various as Their Land* explore work. Hoffer, *Law and People*, follows the lawyers. Doerflinger's *Vigorous Spirit of Enterprise* covers far more turf than the title admits. On women's property, see Carole Shammas, "Early American Women and Control over Capital," in Hoffman and Albert, eds., *Women in the Age of the American Revolution*, 134–154.

A. Roger Ekirch, *Bound for America: The Transportation of British Convicts to the Colonies, 1718–1775* (Oxford, 1987), David Galenson, *White Servitude in Colonial America: An Economic Analysis* (Cambridge, 1981), and Robert J. Steinberg, *The Invention of Free Labor: The Employment Relation in English and American Law and Culture, 1350–1850* (Chapel Hill, N.C., 1991), cover labor issues.

The Canadian puzzle is discussed in Egnal, *Divergent Paths*, Morris Altman, "Economic Growth in Canada, 1695–1739: Estimates and Analysis," *William and Mary Quarterly* 3rd ser. 45 (1988): 684–711, and Catherine M. Desbarats, "The Cost of Early Canada's Native Alliances: Reality and Scarcity's Rhetoric," *William and Mary Quarterly* 3rd ser. 52 (1995): 609–630.

On smuggling and other criminal activities, see Barrow, *Trade and Empire*, and Lawrence Friedman, *Crime and Punishment in American History* (New York, 1993).

Consumption figures are available in McCusker and Menard, *Economy of British America*, T. H. Breen, "'Baubles of Britain': The American and Consumer Revolutions of the Eighteenth Century," in Carson, Hoffman, and Albert, eds., *Consuming Interests*, 444–482, Breen, *Marketplace*, and Carole Shammas, *The Pre-Industrial Consumer in England and America* (Oxford, 1990). Joyce Appleby has traced the idea of consumption in "Consumption in Early Modern Thought," in John Brewer and Ray Porter, eds., *Consumption and the World of Goods* (London, 1993), 162–176. On the consequences of the consumer revolution, see T. H. Breen, "The Meanings of Things: Interpreting the Consumer Economy in the Eighteenth Century," in Brewer and Porter, eds., *Consumption*, 249–261. On the market activities of Massachusetts farmers, see Winifred Barr Rothenberg, *From Market Places to a Market Economy: The Transformation of Rural Massachusetts, 1750–1850* (Chicago, 1992).

The foods of the mid-eighteenth-century planter are lovingly described in Audrey Noël Hume, *Food* (Williamsburg, Va., 1978), and dress is covered in Karen Calvert, "The Function of Fashion in Eighteenth-Century America," in Carson, Hoffman, and Albert, eds., *Consuming Interests*, 252–283. Advertising is the subject of Richard L. Bushman, "Shopping and Advertising in Colonial America," in Carson, Hoffman, and Albert, eds., *Consuming Interests*, 233–251. The activities of the Mathews brothers are chronicled in Carol Sue Ebel, "First Men: Changing Patterns of Leadership on the Virginia and Georgia Frontiers, 1642–1815" (Ph.D. diss., University of Georgia, 1996).

The depression of the 1760s is treated in Nash, *Urban Crucible*, and McCusker and Menard, *Economy of British America*.

CHAPTER THIRTEEN. THE LAST WAR AND THE LOST PEACE, 1754–1763

On bodies at war and at rest in the eighteenth century, see George L. Mosse, *The Image of Man: The Creation of Modern Masculinity* (New York, 1996), Garry Wills, *Cincinnatus: George Washington and the Enlightenment* (New York, 1984), and Richard Sennett, *Authority* (New York, 1980). The Virginia militia muster is discussed in Isaac, *Transformation of Virginia*. A readable account of young Washington is James Thomas Flexner, *Young Washington* (New York, 1978).

The standard account of the French and Indian War fills volumes 6, 7, and 8 of Lawrence Henry Gipson's *The British Empire before the American Revolution* (New York, 1942, 1949, 1953). Collectively, the three volumes were subtitled *The Great War for Empire*. The classic account of Braddock's defeat nevertheless remains Francis Parkman, *Montcalm and Wolfe: The French and Indian War* (1884) with a new foreword by C. Vann Woodward (New York, 1984). A more reliable and equally compelling version appears in Fred Anderson, *Crucible of War: The Seven Years' War and the Fate of Empire in British North America, 1754–1766* (New York, 2001). On William Johnson, see James Thomas Flexner, *Mohawk Baronet: The Biography of Sir William Johnson* (New York, 1959). A fine re-creation of the siege of Fort William Henry and its aftermath is Ian Steele, *Betrayals: Fort William Henry and the "Massacre"* (New York, 1990). Alan Rogers, *Empire and Liberty: American Resistance to British Authority, 1755–1763* (Berkeley, Calif., 1974), traces the colonies' political responses to the war. Fred Anderson, *A People's Army: Massachusetts Soldiers and Society in the Seven Years' War* (Chapel Hill, N.C., 1984), examines the composition and experiences of the New England troops.

The most graphic recent account of the battle for Quebec is John Keegan, *Fields of Battle: The Wars for North America* (New York, 1996). White, *Middle Ground*, reminds us that Pontiac was not the bloodthirsty frontier raider of legend. Pontiac's speech is one of the documents in Calloway's *World Turned Upside Down*.

Bernhard Knollenberg, *Origin of the American Revolution, 1759–1766*, rev. ed. (New York, 1965), traces the misjudgments of the English government in the years 1759 to 1763. Jack M. Sosin, *Whitehall and the Wilderness: The Middle West in British Colonial Policy, 1760–1775* (Lincoln, Neb., 1961), follows the debate over land speculation west of the mountains. On William Franklin, see Sheila J. Skemp, *William Franklin* (New York, 1990).

The details of the war on the Ohio River are reported in Allan W. Eckert, *That Dark and Bloody River: Chronicles of the Ohio River Valley* (New York, 1995).

CHAPTER FOURTEEN. A NATION IN THE WOMB OF TIME, 1764 – 1775

For the connection between long-term economic causes and deep-seated political divisions in the revolutionary crisis, see Egnal, *Mighty Empire*. Other summaries are Lawrence Henry Gipson, *The Coming of the Revolution, 1763–1775* (New York, 1954), Middlekauf, *Glorious Cause*, and Edmund S. Morgan, *The Birth of the Republic, 1763–1789* (Chicago, 1956). A number of popular histories of the Revolution, such as Benson Bobrick's *Angel in the Whirlwind: The Triumph of the American Revolution* (New York, 1997) and Philip McFarland's *The Brave Bostonians: Hutchinson, Quincy, Franklin and the Coming of the American Revolution* (Boulder, Colo., 1998), have recently joined the older syntheses above. Noteworthy microhistories and thematic studies of the era include Robert Gross, *The Minutemen and their World* (New York, 1976), and Alan Taylor, *William Cooper's Town* (New York, 1995). Linda Kerber, *Women of the Republic: Intellect and Ideology in Early America* (Chapel Hill, N.C., 1980), and Mary Beth Norton, *Liberty's Daughters: The Revolutionary Experience of American Women, 1750–1800* (Glencoe, Ill., 1980), focus on women and the Revolution.

On the indebtedness of the planters, see Breen, *Tobacco Culture*, Alan Karras, *Sojourners in the Sun: Scottish Migrants in Jamaica and the Chesapeake, 1740–1800* (Ithaca, N.Y., 1992), and Holton, *Forced Founders*. Bonomi, *Under the Cope of Heaven*, and Alan Heimert, *Religion and the American Mind, from the Great Awakening to the Revolution* (Cambridge, Mass., 1966), treat the connection between the Great Awakening and the Revolution. The pen-portrait of Mayhew appears in Bernard Bailyn, *Faces of Revolution: Personalities and Themes in the Struggle for American Independence* (New York, 1992).

The ideological side of the story is fully discussed in Bernard Bailyn, *Ideological Origins of the American Revolution* (Cambridge, Mass., 1967), Gordon Wood, *The Creation of the American Republic, 1776–1787* (Chapel Hill, N.C., 1969), and Wood, *Radicalism of the American Revolution*. Philip Davidson, *Propaganda and the American Revolution* (Chapel Hill, N.C., 1941), regards the pamphlets as propaganda. The English foundation for the radical Whig critique appears in Caroline Robbins, *The Eighteenth-Century Commonwealthman* (Cambridge, Mass., 1961).

Jack P. Greene argues that the colonial legislatures had achieved substantial autonomy by 1763 in his *Quest for Power*. The competition of elites is the focus of Egnal's concluding chapters in *Mighty Empire*. Richard R. Beeman traces the signs of popular government in "Deference, Republicanism, and the Emergence of Popular Politics in Eighteenth-Century America," *William and Mary Quarterly* 3rd ser. 49 (1992): 401–430. Gipson, in *Coming of the Revolution*, argued that the Revolution was inevitable because of the maturation of the colonies.

The breakdown of party and intergroup connections that had formed the shadow government is traced in Olson, *Anglo-American Politics* and *Making the Empire Work*. The collapse of the agent system is treated in Michael Kammen, *A Rope of Sand: The Colonial Agents, British Politics, and the American Revolution* (Ithaca, N.Y., 1968).

The concept of mutual misperception is fully developed in Edmund S. Morgan and Helen M. Morgan, *The Stamp Act Crisis: Prologue to Revolution*, rev. ed. (New York, 1966). On the chronology of dissent and protest seen from the English side, see John L. Bullion, "British Ministers and American Resistance to the Stamp Act, October–December 1765," *William and Mary Quarterly* 3rd ser. 49 (1992): 89–107, J. R. Pole, *Foundations of American Independence, 1763–1815* (Indianapolis, Ind., 1972), J. Steven Watson, *The Reign of George III, 1760–1815* (Oxford, 1960), and Robert W. Tucker and David C. Hendrickson, *The Fall of the First British Empire: Origins of the War for American Independence* (Baltimore, 1982).

J. M. Bumsted, "'Things in the Womb of Time': Ideas of American Independence, 1633 to 1763," *William and Mary Quarterly* 3rd ser. 31 (1974): 533–564, explores ideas of independence that antedated the Revolution (and suggested the title for this chapter). David S. Lovejoy, "Rights Imply Equality: The Case against Admiralty Jurisdiction in America, 1764–1776," *William and Mary Quarterly* 3rd ser. 16 (1959): 459–484, and Carl Ubbelohde, *The Vice Admiralty Courts and the American Revolution* (Chapel Hill, N.C., 1960), trace the last stages of colonial response to the vice admiralty courts. Andrew J. O'Shaughnessy, "The Stamp Act Crisis in the British Caribbean," *William and Mary Quarterly* 3rd ser. 51 (1994): 203–226, extends the story to the British sugar islands; a fuller treatment appears in his *An Empire Divided: The American Revolution and the British Caribbean* (Philadelphia, 2000).

Pauline Maier stresses the momentum of protest and the power of radical ideas in *From Resistance to Revolution: Colonial Radicals and the Development of American Opposition to Britain, 1765–1776* (New York, 1972). Edward Countryman finds that radical resistance could have a conservative purpose—the restoration of old rights—in *A People in Revolution: The American Revolution and Political Society in New York, 1760–1790* (Baltimore, 1981).

For superb biographical treatments of the revolutionaries, see Pauline Maier, *The Old Revolutionaries: Political Lives in the Age of Samuel Adams* (New York, 1980), Richard R. Beeman, *Patrick Henry: A Biography* (New York, 1974), Peter Shaw, *The Character of John Adams* (Chapel Hill, N.C., 1976), and Merrill Peterson, *Thomas Jefferson and the New Nation: A Biography* (New York, 1970). On women in the movement, see, in addition to Kerber, *Women of the Republic*, Norton, *Liberty's Daughters*, and Berkin, *First Generations*, Laurel Thatcher Ulrich, "'Daughters of Liberty': Religious Women in Revolutionary New England," in Hoffman and Albert, eds., *Women in the Age of the American Revolution*, 211–243.

The road from resistance to Revolution is well traveled by scholars. On the Stamp Act Congress, see C. A. Weslager, *The Stamp Act Congress* (Newark, Del., 1976). The response of the Parliament is explored in Tucker and Henrickson, *Fall of the First British Empire*. Hutchinson's travails are traced in Bernard Bailyn, *The Ordeal of Thomas Hutchinson* (Cambridge, Mass., 1974). Hiller Zobel, *The Boston Massacre* (New York, 1970), does more than justice to all parties in that case. Richard D. Brown, *Revolutionary Politics in Massachusetts: The Boston Committee of Correspondence and the Towns, 1772–1774* (Cambridge, Mass., 1970), explains all the twists and turns of Samuel Adams and his allies. Jack Rakove, *The Beginnings of National Politics: An Interpretive History of the Continental Congress* (Baltimore, 1979), treats the Congress as a legislative body. Jerrilyn Greene Marston, *King and Congress: The Transfer of Political Legitimacy, 1774–1776* (Princeton, N.J., 1987), argues that the Congress acted more as a collective executive, replacing the king, than as a legislative body.

Charles Royster, *A Revolutionary People at War: The Continental Army and American Character, 1775–1783* (Chapel Hill, N.C., 1979), traces the moral underpinnings and religious outpourings of the first congressional forces. David Hackett Fischer's engaging *Paul Revere's Ride* (New York, 1994) and Michael A. Bellesiles's engrossing *Revolutionary Outlaws: Ethan Allen and the Struggle for Independence on the Early American Frontier* (Charlottesville, Va., 1993) recount the battles of Lexington, Concord, and Ticonderoga.

The Canadian campaign is the subject of Robert McConnell Hatch, *Thrust for Canada: The American Attempt on Quebec in 1775–1776* (Boston, 1979). On Natchez and West Florida, see Weber, *Spanish Frontier*, Robert V. Haynes, *The Natchez District and the American Revolution* (Jackson, Miss., 1976), and Martha Condray Searcy, *The Georgia-Florida Contest in the American Revolution, 1776–1778* (University, Ala., 1985). Williams, *From Columbus to Castro*, devotes a chapter to the Revolution in the West Indies.

CHAPTER FIFTEEN. INDEPENDENCE, WAR, AND REPUBLICANISM, 1776 – 1783

Modern thinking about the Declaration begins with Carl Becker's *The Declaration of Independence: A Study in the History of Political Ideas* (New York, 1922). Becker's concept of the "climate of ideas" tied Jefferson's work to the Enlightenment. In later years, Wills, *Inventing America*, asserted that Jefferson was reading the Scottish realists. Peter Charles Hoffer, *The Law's Conscience: Equitable Constitutionalism in America* (Chapel Hill, N.C., 1990), reminds readers that Jefferson was a working lawyer and the Declaration had the form of certain types of legal documents with which he was familiar. Jay Fliegelman, *Declaring Independence: Jefferson, Natural Language, and the Culture of Performance* (Stanford, Calif., 1993), hears the musical notes behind the words and pauses in Jefferson's text. Pauline Maier, *American Scripture: Making the Declaration of Independence* (New York, 1997), proves that Jefferson had help.

A solid and reliable account of the loyalists is Wallace Brown, *The Good Americans: The Loyalists in the American Revolution* (New York, 1969). Mary Beth Norton's *The British

Americans: The Loyalist Exiles in England (Boston, 1972) is the final word on the exiles' fate. Janice Potter, *The Liberty We Seek: Loyalist Ideology in Colonial New York and Massachusetts* (Cambridge, Mass., 1983), argues that the loyalist tracts had a common ideological message.

A brief review of the first years of the war appears in Willard M. Wallace, *Appeal to Arms: A Military History of the American Revolution* (Chicago, 1951). A more recent account is John Shy, *A People Numerous and Armed: Reflections on the Military Struggle for American Independence* (Ann Arbor, Mich., 1990). James Kirby Martin and Mark Edward Lender, *A Respectable Army: The Military Origins of the Republic, 1763–1789* (Wheeling, Ill., 2006), summarize the modern literature on the war. The classic account of the growing professionalism of the army during the fighting is Royster, *Revolutionary People at War*. Important insights also appear in Caroline Cox, *A Proper Sense of Honor: Service and Sacrifice in George Washington's Army* (Chapel Hill, N.C., 2004). On the navy, see Paul A. Gilje, *Liberty on the Waterfront: American Maritime Culture in the Age of Revolution* (Philadelphia, 2004), and William M. Fowler Jr., *Rebels under Sail: The American Navy during the Revolution* (New York, 1976). A wonderful source of the everyday life of the Continental soldier is Robert Bray and Paul Bushnell, eds., *Diary of a Common Soldier in the American Revolution, 1775–1783* (De Kalb, Ill., 1978). Fischer's *Washington's Crossing* (New York, 2004) is a gem.

From the British point of view, see Stephen Conway, *The War of American Independence, 1775–1783* (New York, 1995). Eliga H. Gould, *The Persistence of Empire: British Political Culture in the Age of the American Revolution* (Chapel Hill, N.C., 2000), explores the thinking of the English as they faced the rebellious colonists.

Though not confined to the Revolutionary War period, Allan Kulikoff's *From British Peasants to Colonial American Farmers* (Chapel Hill, N.C., 2000) is graphic in its depictions of the way the war harmed American farmers and argues effectively that the war itself was a conflict of farmers.

The radicalism of the revolutionaries is the thesis of Alfred Young, *The Shoemaker and the Tea Party* (Boston, 1999), and the essays in William Pencak, Matthew Dennis, and Simon P. Newman, eds., *Riot and Revelry in Early America* (University Park, Pa., 2002), as well as Nash, *Unknown American Revolution*, and Countryman, *American Revolution*.

Rakove, *Beginnings of National Politics*, Peter S. Onuf, *The Origins of the Federal Republic: Jurisdictional Controversies in the United States, 1775–1787* (Philadelphia, 1983), and Merrill Jensen, *The American Revolution within America* (New York, 1974), explore the beginning of the new nation. The classic work is Allan Nevins, *The American States during and after the Revolution, 1775–1789* (New York, 1924). Richard B. Morris, *The Peacemakers: The Great Powers and American Independence* (New York, 1965), is a readable work on the peace treaty.

EPILOGUE

On Washington and the army, see Fred Anderson and Andrew Cayton, *The Dominion of War: Empire and Liberty in North America, 1500–2000* (New York, 2005). R. R. Palmer, *The Age of Democratic Revolution, A Political History of Europe and America, 1760–1800: The Challenge* (Princeton, N.J., 1959), and Richard B. Morris, *The Emerging Nations and the American Revolution* (New York, 1970), explore the exportation and continuing vigor of the ideals of the American Revolution. Appleby, *Liberalism and Revolution*, solves the puzzles of revolutionary promise and limitation. On the Far West in the revolutionary age, see Taylor, *American Colonies*. On education, see Brewer, *By Birth or Consent*. Wood, *Radicalism*, sees a glass half full of democracy and equality. Nash, *Unknown American Revolution*, sees a glass half empty.

Index